Life and Morals

An Introduction to Ethics

A. K. Bierman
San Francisco State University

Harcourt Brace Jovanovich, Inc.

New York / San Diego / Chicago / San Francisco / Atlanta / London / Sydney / Toronto

I dedicate this book to the memories of
Frank Brann
and
George Moscone
two friends who died because they tried to
make morals and politics one

COVER PHOTO by Reginald Wickham.

Copyrights and Acknowledgments begin on page 577, which constitutes a continuation of the copyright page.

ISBN: 0-15-550725-7
Library of Congress Catalog Card Number: 79-93080

Printed in the United States of America

095291

Preface

Why another introductory ethics book? Why indeed, unless there is something different and useful about it. This book differs from others in three ways that I think will be valuable for students and instructors—in structure, practicality, and method.

First, its basic structure is quite simple. It is built around the opposition between the two major, contending Western views of human beings and their conduct. One view holds that morals has its source and base in human nature and our feelings, our "heart"; the other that it has its source and base in reason, our "mind."

Second, the book's method is that of dialectical development. It starts with the simple and familiar opposing claims made by advocates of "heart" and "mind." These two views then become progressively more adequate, mature, and sophisticated, as each is criticized by the other and defended and elaborated by its proponents. The development culminates in David Hume's ethical theory, the high point and classical statement of what I call moral psychology, and in Immanuel Kant's ethical theory, the high point and classical statement of what I call rational will ethics. The method of development provides a true introduction to ethics and allows students to go on to the level that is suitable for them.

Third, the book stresses the connection between moral theory and practical life. It is not confined to an exposition of major ethical philosophers and positions; it provides that, too, but it is always tied to moral and political problems of our life—hence the title *Life and Morals*. The chapter texts contain numerous illustrations, historical and contemporary, of the theoretical points. Just as important, however, are the "Reflections" at the end of each chapter on which students may test their knowledge and their ability to apply what they have learned; these Reflections provide abundant material for class discussions and written essays.

I have intentionally supplied more Reflections than can be used so that their wide range will offer ample choices suitable to a variety of students. Further, these Reflections are divided into two sets, one for application of the theory learned and the other for more sophisticated theoretical inquiry; this provides another option for students and instructors, and makes the book adaptable to various levels of courses in ethics. Students rightfully expect an ethics class to be "practical"; that is a condition of its meaningfulness and

IV value to them. I have tried to make this book especially practical by a liberal use, in both the body of the text and the Reflections, of issues, problems, dilemmas, grotesqueries, clashes, puzzles, disasters, and judgments—vain, wise, ridiculous, plausible and implausible—drawn from newspapers, magazines, and novels.

This book is not organized around the isolated exposition of major ethical thinkers, nor around a number of isolated main issues and standard positions on them. Rather, it weaves these into the developing discussion as they become pertinent. Included among major ethical thinkers are Socrates, Plato, Aristotle, Marcus Aurelius, Hobbes, Rousseau, Hume, Kant, Bentham, Nietzsche, Hegel, Marx, J. S. Mill, Dewey, Heidegger, G. E. Moore, R. B. Perry, and many interesting contemporary philosophers. There are substantial quotations from the classic texts of most of these thinkers. Included among the issues are egoism, relativism, the relation between the good and duty, hedonism, cognitive and non-cognitive bases for morality, happiness and other goods, theories of duty and obligation, human nature, human dignity and worthiness, freedom, free will, punishment, alienation, individualism, worthy ideals, authenticity, justice, objectivity or subjectivity of moral judgments, historical materialism, and death and survival. Included among the major schools of moral theory are Utilitarianism, Kantianism, sociobiology, teleology, deontology, self-realization ethics, Existentialism, Marxism, situationism, and naturalism.

There is more on Kant here than in most ethics texts, for four reasons. First, there is a growing contemporary interest in Kant as a viable alternative to Utilitarianism. Second, for students to really understand Kant—who can plausibly be seen as the world's most important ethical thinker—they must go beyond the short, respectful expositions of him common in textbooks. Third, to show plausibly that Kant's theory is practical, detailed applications of it to moral issues and a clear statement of his devices for doing this are necessary; I have made a special effort to present these applications and devices. Fourth, Kant gave to rational will ethics its first, and what is still its best, presentation, deserving an emphasis equal to that given moral psychology. Thus, it isn't just Kant who receives a careful and amply illustrated account, but rational will ethics as well.

There is more material in this book than some classes may need or be able to cover. A complete course in ethics can be given even if less than the whole book is used. This would include Chapters 1–7, 11, and the last chapter. For those who wish to cover more material but still less than the whole, I would recommend reading Chapter 8, Kant on the will and moral laws, and selecting from the following sections, which can be read independently: 9.1 and 9.2 on duties and human rights; 10.5, on lying and the Golden Rule; 10.6, on a morally perfect world; 12.5, on humans as moral thermometers; 13.3 and 13.4, on free will in a causally deterministic world; and, finally, 13.5, on punishment. Those who wish to emphasize Kant should read Chapters 7–9; and those who want to go on in Hume should read Chapter 12.

The author is grateful to the following persons who helped him to improve the various drafts of this book: the late Jane English; Robert Fogelin, the philosophy consultant for Harcourt Brace Jovanovich, Inc.; one of my ethics students, E. W. Hogg, for his stylistic editing; Louise Kanter, for keeping me anchored to reality and clarity; Frank C. C. Young, for using an early draft of this book in a community college class; Elizabeth Beardsley; an anonymous reader; L. S. Grable; K. Sundaram; and Clifford Browder for his thoughtful and painstaking editing. The author is grateful also to William Pullin for initiating the book and to Bill McLane for smoothing the way to its completion.

A. K. B.

Contents

Romantic versus Existential Authenticity, 6 and Trouble for Sociobiology

Kant's Cosmos: Nature and Humanity 7

Kant's Theories of the Will and Moral Laws 8

9   Human Rights, Obligation, and Personal Policies

10   From Maxims to a Morally Perfect World

11   Human Goods and the Basic Moral Concept

Hume and the Moral Thermometer   12

Moral Validity, Free Will, and Punishment   13

XII

14 From Hume and Kant to Marx

Figures

1
Practical Life,
Social Practices,
and Moral Philosophy

Scene: A college cafeteria.

Ez: Hey, what's happening?

Todd: Enrolling again.

Ez: You don't look happy about it.

Todd: It's not that. My ex-girlfriend is pregnant.

Ez: By you?

Todd: I think so.

Ez: Too bad for you, friend. Got carried away?

Todd: She thought she was in a safe period.

Emily: Ez, you're terrible! You feel sorry for Todd and don't even think about his girlfriend. It's the woman I feel sorry for, not Todd. Men have their pleasure and run, but it's the women who are left to have the babies. They're the ones who pay.

Todd: I feel sorry for Diana, Emily. And I've offered to pay for an abortion.

Emily: Does she want one? Or is this your idea, too?

Todd: No, she doesn't want one.

Ez: Catholic?

Todd: Yes, but mainly she likes kids. She thinks she'd like to have it.

Ez: She's crazy. I can't believe she's thought it through. How's she going to take care of a kid while she's working? And our laws aren't exactly favorable to illegitimate children, you know. And you're surely not going to marry an *ex*-girlfriend or support a child you aren't even sure is yours.

Todd: Maybe I should marry her. Maybe it's my duty.

Ez: Now *you're* crazy, too. Think, man, think. She's your ex, so you don't love her. After about a year you'll be tired of supporting the child, even if you don't marry her. And if you want to marry somebody else, your wife-to-be isn't exactly going to be jumping for joy. Won't she love your writing out support checks, especially when your own rent's due? Disaster! In fact, I think you have a duty *not* to marry her or to promise support payments. If you do either, it'll only lead to misery, hate, blame, backbiting. Anything with those results has got to be bad, bad, bad.

Emily: I think you ought to let Diana decide what she wants. If she doesn't want the baby, then paying for her abortion is fine. If she does want the child, I wouldn't try to talk her out of it. Ez makes you sound a lot more selfish than I know you are; he's still living in the fifties. If Diana wants the child, it's up to her to decide what she wants from you. She may want you to help support the child or maybe she wants to go it alone. It's up to her. If our society were saner, it would be easier for her not to have to depend on you for anything. All we've got now are a few groups helping one-parent families, and some places with child-care centers. Darn few guys will move in with her, because she's got a kid. Too many have hang-ups like Ez's. But if Diana likes kids and wants the baby, that's it. It's up to her.

Ez: That's easy for you to say, Emily. You're not the one having the baby. *Want, want, want*—is that all you can think of? Well, that cuts no ice. There are lots of other things Diana wants or will want, and won't be able to get because she decided to have the baby. The same goes for Todd. She'd better think of that—and so should you, before you start being so free with your advice.

Todd: He's got a point, Emily. Anyway, Diana can have a child later if she wants.

Emily: Your thinking doesn't impress me, not at all—neither of you. Some minds! You're just using them to figure out a way to get out of something *you* don't want.

1.1 Heart versus Mind

The controversy about whether the "heart" is superior to the "mind" has a long history. Each has had its advocates. Advocates of the heart give first place to persons with fine feelings, noble sentiments, and infinite love; on these rests human goodness. Partisans of the heart believe that putting mind first makes us too intellectual, sterile, cold, or indifferent. The French writer Antoine de Saint-Exupéry even credits the heart with superior knowledge in *The Little Prince*: "It is only with the heart that one can see rightly; what is essential is invisible to the eye."

On the other hand, those who give mind first place speak admiringly of the reflective person; such a person is logical, organized, thoughtful, checks his or her passions and impulses, and is not dominated by the mischievous appetites of the body. Those who favor the mind abhor living without taking forethought, without figuring out what is the best thing to do or to have. For them, to put the heart before the mind is to advocate mindless irrationality; love is blind, and besides, the heart pulses with blood-and-guts hate just as much as it does with noble sentiments. When the heart is in control, goodness becomes accidental and random—the hostage of fate. Whatever control humans may achieve over their destinies can come only from reason.

Advocating the supremacy of either the heart or the mind assumes that humans can choose between them; it assumes that we can decide which kind of person we want to be. Some people, however, don't think we have a choice; they think that, at bottom, human nature is simply dominated by the heart or the mind. The novelist John Gardner has Grendel, the opponent of Beowulf, vividly express this view.

The mind lays out the world in blocks, and the hushed blood waits for revenge. All order, I've come to understand, is theoretical, unreal—a harmless, sensible, smiling mask men slide between the two great, dark realities, the self and the world—two snake-pits. The watchful mind lies,

3

4

cunning and swift, about the dark blood's lust, lies and lies and lies until, weary of talk, the watchman sleeps. Then sudden and swift the enemy strikes from nowhere, the cavernous heart. Violence is truth, as the crazy old peasant told Hrothulf.[1]

In this view, the minded man may have his pride in cunning reason, but in the end blood and heart have their way, as with Todd and Ez. The mind can erect only temporary dams to check the flood of reality; in the dark, these dams will give way and violent reality will engulf and destroy the theoretical.

The German philosopher G. W. F. Hegel was as utterly and passionately convinced that reality is at bottom rational and that the rational is real as Gardner's Grendel is convinced of the opposite. For Hegel the irrational is unreal, not real or actual. In his *Encyclopaedia of the Philosophical Sciences,* he says:

> In common life, any freak of fancy, any error, evil and everything of the nature of evil, as well as every degenerate and transitory existence whatever, gets in a casual way the name of actuality. . . . The actuality of the rational stands opposed by the popular fancy that Ideas and ideals are nothing but chimeras, and philosophy a mere system of such phantasms.[2]

> Actuality and thought (or Idea) are often absurdly opposed. . . . The Idea is rather the absolutely active as well as actual. . . . So far is actuality . . . from being in contrariety with [opposed to] reason, that it is rather thoroughly reasonable, and everything which is not reasonable must on that very ground cease to be held actual. [3]

The familiar opposition between heart and mind is lodged alike in common sense, in literature, and in the most remote philosophy. One view of this dualism leads us to believe we might choose one of these over the other. Another view—Grendel's and Hegel's—leads us to believe that we have no more choice about either than we have about the nature of reality. If the real is irrational, it is ridiculous to try to govern our heart with our mind; or if the real is rational, it is absurd to try to put sentiment in charge of thought.

1.2 Feeling versus Thought

The common-sense distinction between heart and mind mirrors the distinction between feeling and thought. Just as heart and mind supposedly not only differ from but also oppose each other, so feeling and thought supposedly oppose each other, too.

This opposition between feeling and thought has generated two schools of morality. One school believes that our moral choices are or should be based on feelings, whereas the other believes that they are or should be based on thought. Since our subject is morality, we must clearly understand why common opinion holds that feeling and thought should be distinguished from and are opposed to each other.

I am using "feeling" inclusively. Feeling includes passions and emotions such as love, anger, sympathy, and jealousy; desires such as hunger, lust, and thirst; wants, appetites, cravings, and wishes; responses such as satisfaction, gratification, pleasure, and pain; attitudes such as approval, liking, and commendation; moods such as pensiveness, gloom, and contentedness; outlooks such as the pessimistic, the anxious, and the hopeful; and interests such as our own self-preservation, happiness, and freedom.

I am using "thought" inclusively also. Thought includes reasoning, which may be either deductive (drawing conclusions from premises or axioms) or inductive (generalizing from past experience or finding analogies). We predict, anticipate, and expect events in the future; we remember, recognize, and remind ourselves of events, things, and persons from the past. We doubt, affirm, theorize, speculate, meditate, cogitate, ponder, and reflect. The desired product of thought is knowledge.

The classic argument for distinguishing between feeling and thought was made by the ancient Greek philosopher Plato in his dialogue *The Republic,* Book IV. Plato thought it necessary and important to distinguish between them precisely because they are sometimes opposed. In this part of the dialogue, Socrates is talking with Glaucon. Socrates was the man most admired by Plato. He is the persistent questioner of other Athenians in Plato's dialogues, just as he was in life. Socrates haunted the marketplace, looking for conversation and argument. Finally he was put to death by opponents who thought him "dangerous to the youth of Athens." Here now is Plato's argument.

Socrates: Then the soul of the thirsty one, in so far as he is thirsty, desires only drink; for this he yearns and tries to obtain it?

Glaucon: That is plain.

And if you suppose something which pulls a thirsty soul away from drink, that must be different from the thirsty principle which draws him like a beast to drink; for, as we were saying, the same thing cannot at the same time with the same part of itself act in contrary ways about the same.

Impossible . . . .

And might a man be thirsty, and yet unwilling to drink? Because, for example, he knows the water to be poisoned.

Yes, it constantly happens.

And the forbidding principle is derived from reason, and that which bids and attracts proceeds from passion and disease?

Clearly.

Then we may fairly assume that they are two, and that they differ from one another; the one with which a man reasons, we may call the rational principle of the soul, the other, with which he loves and hungers and

6

thirsts and feels the flutterings of any other desire, may be termed the irrational or appetitive, the ally of sundry pleasures and satisfactions?

Yes, we may fairly assume them to be different. [4]

Plato bases the distinction between feeling and thought (reason) on the familiar fact that we are often torn between them. Being torn between them, we must consider them to be opposites. That this is a familiar fact can be confirmed by noting some examples of it. For instance, I want one more beer before driving home, but I know that it would be stupid to drink it. Or maybe years of anger and resentment have built up in me; I have a tremendous desire to tell my parents off and move out, but I remind myself that they might cut off the money, so I keep my mouth shut. Or I feel resentful toward a teacher because I got a low grade on an exam, but I admit to myself that I didn't study for it, so I don't go to the teacher's office to complain. Or I feel tense when I'm at a party where almost everyone is of another race, but I cover it up because it will reveal my racism, which I know to be wrong.

When torn between opposites, we have two things competing in us, one of them pushing us toward something and the other one pulling us away from it. Wanting another beer clearly falls under "feeling"; while realizing that another beer will make me an unsafe driver just as clearly falls under "thought"; they conflict, therefore they differ from each other. If the heart does the feeling and the mind does the thinking, and if feeling and thought sometimes push against each other, then the heart and mind are opposed.

Assuming we have a choice, should we let our heart or our mind govern our decisions and acts when they enter into conflict? Should we allow our feelings or our thought to dominate?

But we may not have a choice. While we may believe that we can choose either to yield to our feelings and have another drink "for the road," or to heed our reflections and forgo it, we can also doubt whether we have such a controlling choice. Consider an example just cited: long years of abuse by my parents may fester in me, heightening my anger and resentment, until I realize that I had better get out and find a job because, despite the restraint I've shown up to now, I know that someday I'll say "To hell with the consequences!" and tell them off.

Also, shouldn't we have some doubts about the outcome of our thoughtful resolve not to be racists? Won't some residue of prejudice always haunt our actions? Aren't we likely, for example, when we are with persons of our own race, to put down people of other races, even though we wouldn't do it to their face? How else can we account for this, except to admit that years of conditioning have given us racist feelings that we cannot control, no matter how wrong we think them?

On the other hand, it seems that there are times when, without even making a conscious choice, thought appears to have control over feeling. We were to meet a friend at ten o'clock; the friend is late; time passes and our annoyance heats to anger. We return home to learn that the friend has been in a car accident; our anger melts immediately and is replaced with worry and fear.

1.3 Two Ultimate Bases for Morality 7

This struggle between heart and mind, feeling and thought, that we familiarly experience in our daily life has found its way into philosophers' reflections on morality. The Danish philosopher Edward Westermarck believed that our moral judgments, decisions, and actions are based on feeling, while the English philosopher W. D. Ross believes that they are based on the mind's apprehension of moral principles.

Westermarck selects the feelings of indignation and approval as bases for morality.

> That the moral concepts are ultimately based on emotions either of indignation or approval, is a fact which a certain school of thinkers have in vain attempted to deny. . . . Men pronounced certain acts to be good or bad on account of the emotions those acts aroused in their minds, just as they called sunshine warm and ice cold on account of certain sensations which they experienced, and as they named a thing pleasant or painful because they felt pleasure or pain.[5]

But Ross holds that there are "general principles of duty" that we apprehend by reason. Such principles include fulfilling our promises, effecting a just distribution of goods, returning services rendered, promoting the good of others, and promoting the virtue of moral agents. These principles are

> self-evident; not in the sense that it is evident from the beginning of our lives, or as soon as we attend to the proposition for the first time, but in the sense that when we have reached sufficient mental maturity and have given sufficient attention to the proposition it is evident without any need of proof, or of evidence beyond itself. It is self-evident just as a mathematical axiom, or the validity of a form of inference, is evident. The moral order expressed in these propositions [principles] is just as much part of the fundamental nature of the universe (and, we may add, of any possible universe in which there were moral agents at all) as is the spatial or numerical structure expressed in the axioms of geometry or arithmetic.[6]

Ross thinks that when a person judges an act, he or she does so in accord with one of these principles, and not in expectation of certain feelings, or as a result of certain feelings experienced before or at the moment of acting.

> What makes him think it right to act in a certain way is the fact that he has promised to do so — that and, usually, nothing more. That his act will produce the best possible consequences is not his reason for calling it right.[7]

A mature person cannot turn off his or her mind, cannot stop from considering moral principles; and once having considered them, our reason, Ross avers, will affirm them as the basis for acting despite the feelings we may have had, have now, or expect to have.

8   1.4 The Theoretical and the Practical

It is important to overcome a false view about the dualism of the theoretical and the practical. The false view is that they are opposed to each other. It is important to overcome this because it has often falsely led people to believe that moral theory (moral philosophy or ethics) is impractical. Furthermore, to anticipate a central claim I make in this book, one cannot live well if one doesn't think about, theorize about, philosophize about morals. Or as Plato reports Socrates saying, "The unexamined life is not worth living." Surely, if moral theory does help us to live well, philosophy must be counted among the most practical things in the world.

People who mistakenly believe that the theoretical and the practical are opposed to each other, who think that the theoretical cannot be practical, may arrive at this conclusion by thinking as follows:

(1) The theoretical is impractical. ("Theoretically that's great, but in practice it's bunk!")
(2) Impractical is the opposite of practical.
(3) Therefore, the theoretical is the opposite of the practical.

But this is a bad argument. Its main failure lies in the first premiss, (1), which hides at least two different statements:

(1a) All theory is impractical.
(2a) Theoretically capable persons are impractical.

If we take a theory to be a relatively abstract, comprehensive system of thought about some subject matter, the following examples show that (1a) is obviously false, which means that the conclusion, (3), doesn't have to be accepted as true. Newton's physics is a theoretical system of thought—even more theoretical in Newton's time than in ours—but it is obviously practical; without it, space travel would not have been achieved. Also, Einstein's relativity physics is theoretical, yet the existence of the atom bomb testifies to its practicality. Furthermore, all the mathematics needed to state and apply their theories is theoretical, but obviously it is also practical. And Marx's work in philosophy and economics is theoretical, but considering the number of people all over the world who conduct their lives as Marxists, it has to be considered practical. In sum, because we know examples of theories that are practical, it would be false to say that theories are impractical.

The reason why the theories of Newton, Einstein, and Marx are practical is that they can be *applied* successfully to the world to get solutions to problems we want to solve, and to achieve ends we want to reach. This tie between theory, application, and success also explains why we can say some theories aren't practical. A *false* theory may not lead to successful application; in that case, since it doesn't help us solve problems or reach desired ends, it isn't practical. So the truth of the matter is that theories may or may not be practical; but we can't condemn the whole of them as impractical. False economic theories, indeed, can be very impractical: by leading us to false predictions, they lead us into unwise decisions and foolish actions. However, while bad economic theory may fail, good economic theory may succeed. Unfortunately, people remember the failures and jump to the conclusion that all theories are impractical.

And what shall we say about a theory when it has no known applications? Is it impractical? The nineteenth-century mathematician Georg F. Riemann formulated a type of non-Euclidean geometry that had no known applications to space until Einstein used it for his physics. Was Riemannian geometry impractical in the nineteenth century and practical in the twentieth? Or was it always practical, although at first no one knew it to be so?

Probably one should say that when it has a *known* application the theoretical is practical, and that when there is no known application one should call it neither practical nor impractical, but just theoretical. This should be enough to curb ignorant scoffing at ivory-tower thinkers and their theoretical productions. Today's visionary may be tomorrow's savior.

Our conclusion: Moral theory can be practical, but not unless someone applies it. So we should enter into our philosophical investigations of moral theory with an open mind about its practical use, and with a willingness to try to apply it to moral, social, economic, and political problems.

If we follow this advice, statement (1b)—"Theoretically capable persons are impractical"—is false. Consequently the conclusion, (3), won't be true under the (1b) interpretation of premiss (1). Theoretically oriented persons may also be practical people. The great American Pragmatic philosophers—Charles Peirce, William James, and John Dewey—stressed the unbreakable connection between thought and action, between theory and practice. They believed that there is no doing without thinking, and conversely no thinking without doing. Difficult and complicated doing requires thinking to match it. Sending rockets into outer space is difficult doing; it requires sophisticated theory. Dewey thought there was no mystery about the connection between doing and thinking.

> For ideas belong to human beings who have bodies, and there is no separation between the structures and processes of the part of the body that entertains the ideas and the part that performs the acts. Brain and muscles work together.[8]

1.5 Theory and the Problematic

We can now look back instructively on sections 1.1–1.4.

Human experience is not one homogenized, undifferentiated whole. We distinguish between thought and feeling experiences. This familiar distinction

10   is part of your thinking about experience; it belongs to thought, not to feeling.

You have noticed that sometimes your feelings incline you to one action, your thoughts to another. Plato's argument that feeling and thought are opposed is simply a reflective expression of this familiar experience. This theory is implicit in the very way you think about your practical life.

Feelings and thoughts are not free-floating; they belong to persons. If in a single person feelings and thoughts compete with one another, the feelings must attach to one "part" of a person and the thoughts to another "part." These two parts must be struggling with each other. We familiarly say that feelings belong to the heart and thoughts to the brain or mind; hence the heart and the brain struggle in us for dominance. This too is theory, but embedded in your practical life—it is a distinction that you already knew.

In one kind of life the heart dominates; in another, the mind. The distinctions between feeling and thought, heart and mind, and their two modes of life maintain themselves in the most theoretical moral systems; we saw this in the remarks of Westermarck and Ross in section 1.3. These opposed views about the ultimate bases for morality follow directly from the view that feeling opposes thought. This theoretical opposition you already knew because, throughout your whole childhood and youth, adults encouraged and/or forced you to curb your desires and impulses, to think of the future, and to conform with social norms and customs. You constantly resisted and rebelled against these "unnatural" confinements of what seemed to be the source of all good—your *own* desires, satisfactions, hopes. This too is theory—your own theory, embedded in your practical life.

From our reflections on sections 1.1–1.4 we can conclude that your practical life is shot through and through with theory; the practical is inseparable from the theoretical. The theoretical is not an alien, occasional, unbidden academic visitor to your life, nor should it be unwelcome. It is as much a part of you as your feelings; as well deny that you have a heart as that you have a brain. You have been theorizing all your life, which is why you count yourself a member of the human species (*homo sapiens—sapiens* being the Latin word for "wise").

The uniquely useful property of thought is that it can have as its subject matter thought itself. There can be thought about thought, and thought about the thought that was about the thought. Thought is reflexive, meaning that it can turn back on itself. At one time I have Thought 1; at a later time I have Thought 2 *about* Thought 1; Thought 1 $\longrightarrow$ Thought 2. And of course I can have Thought 3 about Thought 2, which was about Thought 1. Given the reflexive character of thought, it would appear that, once started on itself, its inner character could impel it to continue its self-reflection without stop. We do know, however, that thought about thought stops; at some point it rests content and finds no need to turn on itself forever. What contents it? One answer is: the truth.

If thought stops when it arrives at truth, then it must be motivated to go on as long as it perceives itself infected with falsity (assuming it isn't lazy or tired). It recognizes falsity within itself when we have two or more thoughts that are contradictory or contrary. That is, thought finds opposition within itself; one of the contradictory or contrary thoughts must be false. By self-reflection, thought attempts to discern which of its thoughts is false, so that it can purge itself of the false and eliminate its internal opposition. Self-reflection acquires increased urgency when it initially finds that two or more opposing thoughts are plausible—that is to say, believable. This is what we call a "problematic" state.

When we are conscious of being torn between a feeling and an opposing thought, and also realize that each of them is supported by a plausible moral theory, such as Ross's and Westermarck's, then we are in a problematic situation. In such a situation thought must go on, think about itself further, and purge itself of one of the two opposing thought systems. This was our situation at the end of Section 1.3. Ross and Westermarck were opposing each other; we needed further thought.

One moral theory asserts Thought 1: Persons follow, or should follow, the lead of feeling. The other moral theory asserts Thought 2: Persons follow, or should follow, the lead of thought.

Suppose a situation in which feeling and thought are at odds; feeling would move us to one action (to have another beer for the road), while thought would move us to a contrary action (not to have another beer for the road). This situation is problematic because, in trying to decide whether or not to have another beer, (a) I entertain two thoughts, Thought 1 and Thought 2; further, (b) I find each thought plausible because each is supported by arguments of moral theories; and (c) I find the two thoughts contrary because they justify contrary actions.

The mind must now self-reflect on Thoughts 1 and 2, since the problematic situation needs solving. A solution may occur because our subsequent thought about these two thoughts and the theories backing them may modify them. Our thought about Thoughts 1 and 2, and about the thoughts in the two supporting theoretical thought systems, may lead us (a) to give up Thought 1, (b) to give up Thought 2, or (c) to give up both and replace them with a different Thought 3 and the thoughts that make Thought 3 plausible.

This subsequent thought about Thoughts 1 and 2 is theoretical work, but it is also practical work. It is practical because thought, by modifying previous thought, may also modify future action. For example, if my subsequent thought leads me to give up Thought 1, then the action that Thought 1 justifies may not occur. I may not drink that last beer I want.

In the course of this chapter we have come to understand that theory is deeply embedded in our practical life, and to see why thought about this theory is not only theoretical but practical. Reflection may modify our practice, because it may modify the elements of thought ever-present in practice.

We have learned now that theorizing and philosophizing about morals is something that we do all the time. In this book we will undertake, although at a gradually rising level of sophistication, the same kind of thing that all of us do whenever we carefully consider a moral course of action. This book will be useful if it helps you to think better about living a good life.

12   1.6 Summary: Sections 1.1-1.5

In the previous sections I argued against a form of anti-intellectualism: the view that thought and theory are or should be divorced from human action. I tried to make clear that our everyday practical lives are laced with theory (for example, implicit theories about the opposition of feeling and thought, heart and mind). Because of this, moral philosophizing, or theorizing, is but an extension of our practical life. This means that moral philosophizing and practical moral thought are continuous and one; each is both theoretical and practical.

Philosophers who disagree with this view point out that moral philosophy is a reflection *about* our moral actions and *about* the thoughts and theories embedded in our moral action. If A is *about* B, they argue, then A is not identical to B; therefore moral philosophy, or A, is not identical to the thought, or B, that occurs *in* practical moral action.

In reply, I again point out that philosophical reflection is part of morals; although it is *about* moral thought and action, it may change, replace, and so become the new practical thoughts that we use in our practical lives.

This is most obviously true when we encounter problematic situations, situations in which our own thoughts clash; because we can't act at one time on both of two clashing thoughts, we have to select one of them over the other, or develop still another one. Whichever we do, our later thoughts replace the earlier clashing thoughts that made up the problematic situation. This follows from the reflexive and self-corrective nature of thought; our later thought *about* our earlier thought may correct and *replace* our earlier thought, and so may lead to different moral actions. In short, theoretical reflection may change our practical life and so be part of it.

Problematic situations generate further thought and theory. The kind of problematic situation on which I have concentrated thus far arises from conflict within the individual person—for example, between a feeling and an opposing thought. In the following sections I will concentrate on opposition between the thoughts of two or more persons. I will explore the practicality of moral philosophizing from a social standpoint rather than from an individualistic one.

1.7 Individual and Group Practices

The first step in this exploration is to reflect on practices. Some of the acts that we perform may be typical or characteristic. They may be characteristic of us either as individuals or as members of a group, whether the group be a family, a fraternal organization, a political party, an ethnic group, a nation, or whatever. Such typical or characteristic acts—performed regularly or uniformly in certain situations—we ordinarily call a practice or practices. At first, a practice may be consciously learned or adopted, but **13** repetition can turn it into unconscious habit.

A person may typically pull on the left earlobe before delivering the punch line of a joke, or hitch up his pants at every fifth step, or write out two and only two checks for charitable organizations on the first of every month except December, or smile at funerals. These are practices. Each of us has a set of practices, some combination of typical acts that characterize us. Such unique sets of practices distinguish us from others, give us our individual character.

Groups, too, have their distinctive character, because their members share certain practices that members of other groups do not share. The tribes of Asmat, a region in Irian Java in Indonesia, are headhunters. They raid one another's villages, bring heads home, hammer a hole in the temples, then shake out the brains and eat them. In Saudi Arabia women wear veils; religious police are empowered to spray a woman's legs with black paint if they find her in public without a veil. The Asmat and Saudi Arabian practices are typical acts of some members of each of those respective societies; they differ from characteristic group acts in the United States and Europe.

Anthropologists have several terms roughly synonymous with group practices, such as "customs," "folkways," and "conventions." They call consciously approved practices "mores," and consciously disapproved practices "taboos." All this implies that a person has both individual and group practices. However, it is more difficult to say what distinguishes them than to say that there is a difference between them. Take the Saudi practice of wearing veils. What makes it a group practice? Just the fact that all or most women wear them? Not necessarily. Some individual practices we may or may not share with others. For example, most of us might put our left shoe on before the right one. But extensive uniformity does not make this habit a custom in the way that wearing veils in Saudi Arabia is. Evidently the fact that most people perform a similar act does not by itself justify calling it a group practice.

One obvious difference between donning right shoes first and not wearing veils is that the first isn't disapproved of, whereas the second is. Religious police wouldn't punish women for not wearing veils if it weren't disapproved of, but no one cares if you put your right shoe on before your left one. Approval and disapproval by other members of a group provide one criterion for distinguishing between a group and an individual practice. Another criterion is the circumstance in which the uniformity of behavior arose. Everybody could don their left shoes first just by chance; everybody could eat with forks rather than chopsticks by training, even though chopsticks are not disapproved of; and everybody could wear clothes by training because public nakedness is disapproved of.

In this connection John Dewey remarks:

> For practical purposes morals mean customs, folkways, established collective habits. This is a commonplace of the anthropologist, though the moral theorist generally suffers from an illusion that his own place and day

is, or ought to be, an exception. But always and everywhere customs supply the standards for personal activities. They are the patterns into which individual activity must weave itself. [9]

Here Dewey makes an explicit connection between group practices and morals. I have suggested that a group practice is individuals' shared practice that is subject to approval or disapproval, or that arose by training. Dewey thinks of group practices as morals because he relates disapproval and approval to standards of conduct, with the implicit assumption that where we have such standards we have morals. He adds: "Customs in any case constitute moral standards. For they are active demands for certain ways of acting." [10]

1.8 Habitual and Reflective Practices

Dewey connects practices, habits, and morals. That practices are habitual, as Dewey emphasizes, seems correct when we think about our own activity. Normally we don't think about whether or not to put on our clothes before we go out in the morning, nor do we deliberate about depriving ourselves of human flesh for dinner. We don't contemplate disobeying the traffic laws today, or ponder the rightness of paying for the groceries at the checkout stand, nor do we examine the morality of owning our own house. We just put on our clothes, eat our fish and beef, drive prudently, pay for the groceries, and buy the house, without giving much thought about approval or disapproval. Similarly, a Saudi woman habitually puts on her veil when she goes to market; she gives no more thought to that than you do to putting on your slacks. And the Asmat eats the brains of his enemy just as habitually and ritually as Christians eat the communion bread.

Dewey traces the habitual nature of our moral activity to our weaving our behavior into social patterns. However, in the main, we don't agonizingly go through a process, individually and separately, of inventing our own morality from the start.

We often fancy that institutions, social custom, collective habit, have been formed by the consolidation of individual habit. In the main this supposition is false to fact. . . . But to a larger extent customs persist because individuals form their personal habits under conditions set by prior customs. An individual usually acquires the morality as he inherits the speech of his social group. The activities of the group are already there, and some assimilation of his own acts to their pattern is a prerequisite of a share therein, and hence of having any part in what is going on. [11]

Acquiring social practices is similar to acquiring our native tongue; learning a language may strain us at times, but once learned, it becomes second nature.

Still, there must be more to group practices than habit and thoughtless imitative learning. If there weren't, how could we explain shifts in social practices except by mindless fashion changes or by slippage, because a new generation doesn't quite "get the hang of" the older generation's practices, doesn't imitate them as well as it might. What accounts for the change? The French historian Fustel de Coulanges calls our attention to one cause: changing thought. **15**

> If the laws of association are no longer the same as in antiquity, it is because there has been a change in man. There is, in fact, a part of our being which is modified from age to age; this is our intelligence. It is always in movement; almost always progressing; and on this account our institutions and our laws are subject to change. Man has not, in our day, the way of thinking that he had twenty-five centuries ago; and this is why he is no longer governed as he was governed then. [12]

According to de Coulanges, a change in institutions, laws, customs, and social practices is due to a change in our thinking. But what prompts a change in our thinking? What prompts us to reflect on earlier thoughts and to replace them with later ones, to replace habitual with reflective practices? One answer is that we encounter challenge situations.

1.9 Challenge Situations

Philip McCombs reported in an article in the *Washington Post* that out of 3,359 Vietnamese students who went abroad to study from 1971 to 1975, only 67 returned to Vietnam. Explaining why she probably wouldn't return, one student said that the Vietnamese people (she meant the South Vietnamese) were "no longer interested in building spiritual relationships, or talking about important things, or doing good deeds, or caring for each other. Everyone is running around to find a way to feed himself, and people have lost all their goodness. Good will has disappeared in the turmoil of our society, and I blame it all on the war."

Her remarks did not, however, mean that she wanted to go back to a repetition of all the old ways. She went on: "I'm sick of formality and tradition where young people can't debate or express themselves to an older person for fear of being disrespectful or insolent. My grandfather isn't like that, though, I can talk with him. We have discussed whether the traditional virtues are still suitable in the modern world. He told me no, they're not. For example, if a woman's husband dies, she shouldn't be forbidden to remarry. It's not fair." [13]

The young Vietnamese student was lamenting a change in Vietnamese group practices: Vietnamese are "no longer interested in building spiritual relationships, or talking about important things, or doing good deeds, or car-

16   ing for each other." The traditional practices had been replaced with new ones: "Everyone is running around to find a way to feed himself, and people have lost all their goodness."

Why did this change occur? A change in circumstances—the war, with its disruptions—challenged the old group practices. People could no longer habitually perform the old practices; forced to find new ways to feed themselves, they had to think of new ways of behaving. Because many Vietnamese faced the challenge, many had to reflect, had to change their practices; and so they, the many, became a group with new practices.

Change in the practices that people perform in order to feed themselves leads to a change in other practices. The student and her grandfather agreed that a widow shouldn't be forbidden to remarry. Perhaps the old society with established, stable practices would have maintained the widow and her children, but the war and the new circumstances had dissolved the old practices. Thus the widow might need to remarry in order to survive. New arrangements were approved.

"Hopeless Case," in a letter to newspaper columnists Helen and Sue Bottel, found occasion to reflect and replace her earlier practice with another.

> Dear Rap:
>   I am 12 and I am pregnant, and a hopeless case. Don't know who is the father.
>   I don't have anyone to turn to because my mother is the neighborhood you-know-what and my father hits the bars every night. No one cares.
>   I ran around because everybody else did and mainly because I didn't want to stay home alone and think. But I have thought a lot this month and I want to reform. I'm scared. I want to start over. I don't have money for an abortion or know how to ask for one, even. Who can help me?—Hopeless case.[14]

Hopeless Case "ran around because everybody else did." She acquired a group practice. But her pregnancy changed her condition into an unwanted one, and this changed condition challenged her group practice. Faced with a problem, she "thought a lot this month" and decided to "reform"; she decided to change her practice.

While the Saudi women continue to follow, or are forced to follow, the practice of wearing veils, the women—at least the rich women—of Kuwait have abandoned it. Princess Hussa Al-Sabah, daughter of the ruling emir of Kuwait, is still close enough to the conflict of practices in the Moslem world to be reflective rather than habitual about her new ones.

> We too [like the women of neighboring Saudi Arabia] obey the laws of the Koran. My husband, for instance, is a very religious man. He prays five times a day, but he still lets me wear a swim suit on the Riviera. And now I am learning to fly a plane.[15]

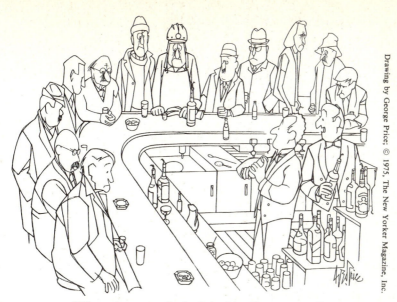

"These days, everybody *is looking for answers."*

Recalling that the Kuwaiti women once wore veils, those women and their husbands, now challenged by Western customs, had to reflect about their old practices in general. The challenge of alternative practices stimulated reflective thought. If those old practices were rationalized by religious sanctions, then those religious grounds too had to be scrutinized and perhaps reinterpreted. Once reflection starts, it may spread like water poured on silk.

Things aren't so rosy for the headhunters, either. Headhunting is banned by the Indonesian government. Although the tribesmen claim that they are born to hunt heads, the "local officials say they are striving hard to convince the Asmat tribes that headhunting is no longer acceptable in the modern world."[16] This challenge to their outmoded practice has to stimulate reflection in the Asmat tribesmen.

Habitual practices become reflective when challenged; challenge comes from conflict, often from conflict with other people's practices. The occasions for challenge are enormous in number and multiple in kind. War, American soldiers, and economic disruption challenged Vietnamese group practices. The Kuwaiti women's husbands became wealthy from oil, which brought them into contact with Western society and its challenges to their traditional practices; if these women wish to become as free as Western women, they have to change their habitual practices. The Asmat tribesmen are subject to the superior power of the Indonesian government, which actively forces reflection on them, although the remoteness of their swamplands enables them to evade a great deal of the "persuasion." Hopeless Case had to confront an unforeseen consequence of her and her crowd's practice; in this case, a challenging consequence rather than another practice forced her to reflect.

18   1.10 The Practical Syllogism

My aim in the remainder of this chapter is to demonstrate that moral theory is embedded in our practical social life. We have already seen that much social life consists of group practices and that many of these are habitual. However, because of challenge situations, these habitual practices may be replaced by reflective ones. Challenge situations are a feature of our social life; reflection too, then, is a feature of that social life. Once started and pursued persistently, reflection ripens into moral philosophy.

But for you to understand this ripening process and for me to supply a convincing demonstration of my claim, we will need a better grasp of reflection. We can get this by examining the "practical syllogism," into which we often cast our practical reflections on life. Reflecting is thinking, thinking may take the form of reasoning, and reasoning may take the form of inference. The syllogism, first treated formally by Aristotle, exhibits one form of inference. Here is an example:

> All men are mortal.
> Caius is a man.
> _____
> Therefore, Caius is mortal.

A practical syllogism differs from this example by having its conclusion express an action, as in the following:

> Happiness is an end for all men.
> Friendship produces happiness.
> _____
> Therefore, we ought to make friends.

Let's follow Aristotle's discussion of practical reflecting and thinking, and see how he relates this to the nature of a practical syllogism.

ARISTOTLE ON PRACTICAL WISDOM.   Aristotle thought the good life included the exercise of intellectual virtues, so he was interested in the relation between deliberation, or reflection, and morals. In Book VI of his *Nicomachean Ethics* he discusses "practical wisdom," which "is concerned with action."[17] "Practical wisdom, then, must be a reasoned and true state of capacity to act with regard to human goods."[18]

Practical wisdom deals with (1) the particular as well as the universal; (2) the probable rather than the necessary; and (3) the variable rather than the invariable. Let's consider what Aristotle means by these one at a time.

(1) The "particular as well as the universal" is illustrated by Aristotle with an example about healthy food. The universal knowledge that all light

meats are "digestible and wholesome" has to be supplemented with particular **19** knowledge of which meats are light; if one didn't know, for example, that chicken is a light meat, one wouldn't have the practical wisdom needed to produce health.

(2) Aristotle thought that practical wisdom is *probable* only, in contrast to mathematics; consequently, we shouldn't expect too much from writers on practical wisdom.

> Our discussion will be adequate if it has as much clearness as the subject matter admits of. . . . We must be content, then, in speaking of such subjects [virtues and ethics] and with such premisses to indicate the truth roughly and in outline, and in speaking about things which are only for the most part true and with premisses of the same kind to reach conclusions that are no better . . . it is evidently equally foolish to accept probable reasoning from a mathematician and to demand from a rhetorician scientific proofs.[19]

Finally, (3) practical wisdom deals with the *variable* rather than the invariable, because it deals with things to be done in a world of changing circumstances. Ours isn't a timeless, static world; one thing needs to be done at one time, and another thing at another time. What needs to be done, then, varies—a notion that leads straight to our next step in connecting moral theory, practical life, and the practical syllogism.

ARISTOTLE ON CHOICE AND DELIBERATION. Human action, Aristotle says, is purposive; it is done to attain an end. Jane desires to climb a mountain in the Alps; this is her end. She has to select equipment, choose a route, coordinate her effort with climbing companions and a guide, all of which are acts chosen as means to accomplish her end.

Which ends we have depends upon our desires; means, however, aren't desired but are deliberately chosen, says Aristotle, and choice "involves a rational principle and thought."[20] This thought Aristotle calls "deliberation."

> We deliberate not about ends but about means. For a doctor does not deliberate whether he shall heal, nor an orator whether he shall persuade, nor a statesman whether he shall produce law and order, nor does anyone deliberate about his end. They assume the end and consider how and by what means it is to be attained.[21]

Practical wisdom deals with acts; acts are chosen; and what is chosen depends on (a) desire for an end and (b) deliberation about the means.[22] For Aristotle moral action is, in part, action in accord with "rational desire"; deliberation and rationality about means, and the desire for ends, become linked in rational desire. Desire for the ends provides the motive power for action because "intellect itself moves nothing, but only the intellect which aims at an end and is practical moves us."[23]

20   ARISTOTLE ON THE PRACTICAL SYLLOGISM.   Because Aristotle thought action is chosen after deliberation, he cast this order of events into the practical syllogism. The premisses express our deliberation, and the conclusion our choice of action. To see how this works and how it relates to practical wisdom, let's use the example of a practical syllogism that I gave before:

> Happiness is an end for all men.
> Friendship produces happiness.
> _____
> Therefore, we ought to make friends.

The practical syllogism fits Aristotle's analysis of practical wisdom and theory of rational choice as follows: the first premiss states the *universal* end, which is what all of us *desire*; the second premiss states a *particular* circumstance upon which we *deliberate,* that friendship with some particular person will make us happy; and the conclusion states the *act deliberately to be chosen,* which is a reasoned choice of *means* to attain our desired end, namely, happiness; so this conclusion is the joint product of desire and rationality.

Our knowledge of the premisses, and so of the conclusion, is *probable* only, not certain.   And because our particular circumstances vary—sometimes I am in need of friendship, sometimes not—the action must *vary* if it is to be rational; the acts called for when I am lonely are different from when I am not lonely.

To sum up this discussion, the practical syllogism consists of the following:

Premiss 1: A sentence expressing the end we desire.   (Universal but not necessary.) Happiness is an end for all men.

Premiss 2: A sentence stating a matter of fact, or the situation in which we find ourselves. (Particular.) Friendship produces happiness.

Conclusion: What ought to be done or not done. (Variable action.) Therefore, we ought to make friends.

We can call the first premiss the "value" premiss, because Aristotle connects ends—what we aim at—with good.   Consider the first sentence of his *Nicomachean Ethics*: "Every art and every inquiry, and similarly every action and pursuit, is thought to aim at some good; and for this reason the good has rightly been declared to be that at which all things aim."   Happiness, he thinks, is the good at which all persons aim.   Then let us call the second premiss the "fact" premiss, and the conclusion the "action" statement.

Aristotle's practical syllogism is central to the remainder of this chapter. However, I make two departures from Aristotle's views. First, I believe that we *do* deliberate about ends; they are not mere objects of wishes, as if wishes were independent of reasoning.   In fact, challenge situations force us to rethink our ends.   Second, I will use value premisses more inclusively than

Aristotle, for I do not limit them to the expression of a wished-for end. The **21** value premiss may include imperatives of the kind found in moonshot instructions, sergeants' orders, and the Ten Commandments; regulations, as for instance concerning smoking, business mergers, and school conduct; laws, statutes, ordinances, and codes; rules about chess, personal conduct ("Never accept charity"), and grammar; standards such as those determining the number of fibers per square inch in percale sheeting, or the nature of personal honesty and forthrightness; and norms like those of responsible parenthood, courtesy, and punctuality for work.

Given this wide range of value premisses, you can appreciate how many particular situations in our practical life (fact premisses) and how many of our actions (conclusions) are rationalized within the framework of the practical syllogism. When asked why we are doing so-and-so or when asked for a reason, we typically answer by citing an imperative ("Sarge told me to"); a regulation ("The sign says 'No smoking'"); a law ("The death penalty is mandatory for killing a peace officer"); a rule ("*Men* not *mans,* is the English plural"); a standard ("Any person who would lie to his own mother is no damn good"); or a norm ("Eating peas with your knife is not acceptable in polite society, my dear").

Of course some value premisses may not be moral premisses, as for example the standard for a cut of beef labeled "Choice." At this point in our discussion, we need not try to formulate the difference between moral and non-moral value premisses.

1.11 Challenge Situations, Reflection, and Practical Syllogisms

Now we can describe habitual practices in terms of the practical syllogism. A practice is habitual if we are conscious only of the fact premiss and the intended act. Thus the Saudi woman knows she is going out to market and she automatically reaches for her veil. The Asmat tribesman discovers that some of his pigs have been stolen by a neighboring tribe, and he naturally readies himself for a headhunting raid. In habitual practices we do not explicitly consider the value premiss, we do not consciously think of the "value" reason for performing the action stated in the conclusion.

However, a challenge to the action makes us aware of the value premiss in the practical syllogism that rationalizes our action. The challenge forces us to reflect and to set forth explicitly the whole of the practical syllogism that concludes with the challenged act. Thus "I ought to wear my veil" (Saudi woman) and "I need not wear my veil" (Kuwaiti woman) are different action conclusions; given that each of these conclusions follows validly from the premisses of a practical syllogism, at least one of the premisses in the two syllogisms must differ. Further, because the Saudi and the Kuwaiti women

22 share the fact premiss of going to market, it must be the value premisses that differ. Thus, reasoning backward from opposing action conclusions, we are led to opposing value premisses, as shown in the first premisses of Saudi 1 and Kuwaiti 1.

Saudi 1	**Kuwaiti 1**
It is wrong for women to show their faces to men who are not relatives.	It is not wrong for women to show their faces to men who are not relatives.
I am going to market, where I will be with such men.	I am going to market, where I will be with such men.
Therefore, I ought to wear my veil so they won't see my face.	Therefore, I need not wear my veil.

Forced to make their value premisses explicit, the women would state them as above. To justify their opposite value premisses, the women would have to formulate deeper arguments in which the challenged premisses follow as conclusions. This means that these opposite value premisses will become opposite conclusions of other, deeper practical syllogisms as in Saudi 2 and Kuwaiti 2 below.

Because these other, deeper syllogisms will have these opposite conclusions, they must have opposite value or fact premisses. Saudi 2 and Kuwaiti 2 contain opposite fact premisses, whereas Saudi 3 and Kuwaiti 3 contain opposite value premisses.

Saudi 2	**Kuwaiti 2**
It is right for women to follow the laws of the Islamic faith.	She may agree with this premiss: "We too obey the laws of the Koran."
The Koran (or an interpretation of it) says that it is wrong for a woman to show her face to a man to whom she is not related.	The Koran (or an interpretation of it) does *not* say that it is wrong for a woman to show her face to a man to whom she is not related.
Therefore, it is wrong for women to show their faces to men who are not relatives.	Therefore, on the basis of Islamic laws, it is *not* wrong for women to show their faces to men who are not relatives.

Here the fact premisses are opposed; there is disagreement about what the Koran, or an interpretation of it, says about women showing their faces. Thus disagreement about what actions to perform (to wear or not wear a veil) may reveal or prompt religious differences. Disagreement about what we should or should not do, when reflectively followed through, obviously may lead to disagreement in other areas of life, as in this instance to disagreement in religion.

23

The next pair of arguments shows us that action disagreement may reveal a clash between religion and social values.

Kuwaiti 3	Saudi 3
It is right for women to play roles in an industrial society, rather than the traditional ones defined by the Islamic faith, if it will help Kuwaiti people escape from poverty.	Islamic laws take precedence over other value considerations, including economic well-being.
Changing women's roles will help Kuwaiti people escape from poverty.	Agreed: Changing women's roles may indeed help us escape from poverty.
Therefore, it is not wrong for women to abandon Islamic laws (including the wearing of veils).	Nevertheless, it is wrong for women to abandon Islamic laws (including the wearing of veils).

In Kuwaiti 3 and Saudi 3 we have a sharp value challenge, one that apparently stimulated Kuwait to free its women several years ago. Because it suffered from lack of manpower, Kuwait granted women the right to enter the civil service.

Thanks to its oil, Kuwait had the possibility of becoming a richer nation, of lifting its people out of centuries of poverty. This is a good. However, accomplishing this good called for new jobs, new roles, and a new social structure to accommodate them; further, it required that women fill some of these jobs and roles, and to do this the women had to abandon their traditional roles. Since these traditions and habitual practices were sanctioned by the Islamic religion, a conflict arose between the goods promised by industrialization, with its attendant social reconstruction, and the goods defined by Islam. Kuwait chose the goods of industrialization.

I have illustrated the application of practical syllogisms with the group practice of wearing veils rather than with one of our own practices, so that no personal involvement would distract us. But we should be aware of the passion and courage required for the Kuwaiti women to alter this group practice. Just as some women in the United States have publicly burned their bras to demonstrate their determination to liberate themselves, so the Kuwaiti women organized a public demonstration and together defiantly dropped their veils. Their act was much more daring than that of burning bras; a closer equivalent in the West would be taking bras off in public and actually baring the breasts.

We have come now to the crux of my claim in this chapter: the social action of group practices and moral theorizing are locked together, not separate. Kuwait faced practical economic and social problems whose solu-

24   tions conflicted with traditional and habitual practices. This challenge situation forced the people to reflect, to reason, and to bring the premisses of their acts to the surface. Through a series of arguments, I have shown how reflection on this practical situation brought them face-to-face with one of the most basic problems in moral philosophy: What is the ultimate basis for the rightness of our actions? Further, it brought them face-to-face with a traditional answer to that question: the ultimate basis is the word of God as revealed by prophets and/or interpreted by legitimate priests, a revelation contained in sacred scripture.

Reflection on whether or not to continue the practice of women's wearing veils in public may lead, by a series of connected practical syllogisms, to a consideration of whether to choose the goods prescribed by the Islamic religion or those of industrial society. Picking the goods of industrial society means that the Kuwaiti have concluded that religion is not the ultimate sanction for conduct. Of course they do not put the matter as baldly as this; they could not abandon the whole of their traditional society in a single stroke. They do not repudiate Islam; they modify it ("We too obey the laws of the Koran"—Kuwaiti 2). The Koran, or its interpretation, is re-interpreted. Similar issues have arisen in Christianity; once it was a sin to charge interest on loans; if this practice had continued, it would have hampered the rise of capitalism.[24] Large stakes depend on the outcome of these contests over the ultimate basis of social practices. Even today the Saudi Arabians call interest on loans a "commission," because the Moslem religion forbids interest.

The thoughts that sustained earlier social practices in Kuwait—the same as those in Saudi 1—are replaced by the thoughts in Kuwaiti 3, as softened by the modifications of Kuwaiti 2. This shows that moral philosophizing is not isolated from practical life; it becomes part of it and rationalizes new, reflective practices.

Perhaps we can heighten our appreciation of the practicality of moral theory by examining a few details of what typically occurs when a group practice changes.

Recall that a group practice is one in which the members of a group participate; a change in a group practice means that the members abandon one typical act and take up another. This does not usually occur at the stroke of midnight, with everyone shifting practice all of a sudden and simultaneously, either by happenstance or mutual resolve. Instead, the process extends over a period of time. Consider the attempt to change our racist or sexist practices; civil rights and liberation movements have been in existence for years and will surely continue.

Dropping the practice of wearing veils was also a lengthy process. A few women, particularly those wealthy ones of high social position, led the way. Certain members of a group, rather than all of them, initiate a change in practice, probably because they have been the only ones in challenge situations. Only the wealthy Kuwaiti women could travel, so at first only they wanted to participate in Western life, which set up the challenge situation for them alone. This sub-group reflected, pondering the reflections cast by me in the form of the practical syllogisms Saudi 1-3 and Kuwaiti 1-3.

Saudi 1–3 are also a part of the Kuwaiti reflections because the two **25** groups shared practices. Given that initially only a Kuwaiti sub-group broke away, we have to remind ourselves of the resistance in Kuwait to a change in practice, which is one reason why changing group practices takes time. This resistance became reflective on being challenged by the militant sub-group; Saudi 1–3 are the reflections by the traditionalists on what was formerly a habitual practice in Kuwait, and still is in Saudi Arabia.

Alert traditionalists fully realized the powerful desire to participate in the goods promised by industrialization. To defend the old practice, they had to oppose the value premises of the new practice with the value premises of the old practice; they couldn't invent these old value premisses, because they had to be faithful to the orientation of the old society, which in this case embraced the Islamic faith.

Appeal to the Islamic faith was once sufficient to hold people to the old practices, but new circumstances weakened the power of that faith. Thus challenge to it became not only thinkable, but speakable; fundamentals—the idea that religion is the basis of morality—were questioned openly. At such a point most members of society, and not just the initial sub-group, face the challenge: they feel the ground shake; a profound process envelops them; they enter a struggle that threatens the very nature of their group life. Once the Koran or an interpretation of it fails to stop women from abandoning the veil-wearing practice, other practices too may fall. Women may want to have higher education, to arrange their own marriages, to travel, to spend the family income, to get jobs, and so forth.

Thus fundamentals crumble. And these fundamentals are the precise subject matter of moral philosophy. While during some periods they may be mere academic subjects confined to the classroom, at other times they confront *everyone* in a group. At such times none may avoid reflecting on them, because a group practice, not an individual practice, is at stake. These fundamentals can then no longer hide under the cloak of habit; rather, they are exposed to searching thought.

A caution: although in this chapter I have emphasized reflective thought, this should not blind us to the fact that changing factual circumstances—such economic ones as the discovery of and demand for oil, for example—play powerful roles. These changing circumstances produce the challenge situations that provoke reflection; pure thought, isolated from social and political reality, does not often, by itself, cause group practices to change.

1.12 Religion and Morality

In the preceding section I showed how practical challenges force us to thought; how, by casting our thought into the form of the practical syllogism, we are driven into deeper thought about our conventional, habitual morality;

26   and further, how we are driven to reflections on religion. My illustration of this process was drawn from a challenge to a Moslem society. But this process can occur in any society, regardless of its predominant religion, if its members believe that their religion provides a foundation for morality.

The Judeo-Christian religion, which predominates in the Western nations, probably does not have as strong, detailed, or thorough a hold on us as the Moslem religion has on most Middle Eastern people. Yet in many, perhaps most, Westerners there is some residue of belief that morality has its ultimate basis in the divine. While you probably don't assess the morality of most of your actions by seeking guidance in scriptural texts or their interpretations, when it comes to some current issues you may. Such issues might include premarital intercourse, adultery, abortion, euthanasia, use of contraceptives, and racism.

To illustrate the connection between morality and the Christian religion, I will quote from George D. Kelsey's *Racism and the Christian Understanding of Man.*

> Men are equal because God has created them in His own image and called them to sonship. The Christian doctrine of equality does not draw at all upon measurements of talent and merit. It is a doctrine concerning the creative gift of God. . . .
>
> When Christian faith speaks of equality, it refers to the action and purpose of God. God has created all men in His own image and called all men to the same destiny. The decision as to whether or not men are equal cannot be made by looking at men; he who would decide must look at God. God alone is the source of human dignity. All men are equal because God has bestowed upon all the very same dignity. He has created them in His own image and herein lies their dignity. Human dignity is not an achievement, nor is it an intrinsic quality; it is a gift, a bestowal.[25]

To commit racist acts and to hold racist attitudes are immoral, according to Kelsey's interpretation of the Christian account of human creation. If we all are equal in God's eyes, we should treat each other alike; to do otherwise is a sin—the sin of idolatry, according to Kelsey.

While there are interesting specific moral issues whose relation to religion we could discuss, my intent in this section is to address a more fundamental issue, namely, whether religion can provide any foundation at all for morality.

This is a traditional, even ancient, issue. Ever since Socrates, there has been a quarrel between philosophy and religion. Most, though not all, philosophers are secular (or nonreligious), relying exclusively on their reasoning and observation powers when philosophizing in contrast to theologians and religiously minded philosophers, who claim to start from received doctrine or revealed truths of God. Also, secular philosophers tend to be humanists in the Renaissance sense of espousing human self-reliance and capacity for creating culture. Theologians, on the other hand, typically place us lower than the angels. They often regard the philosophers' espousal of

total human self-reliance as either sinful vanity or impudent overconfidence; **27**
humility is their watchword.   However, if religion doesn't provide a basis for
morality, we have nothing but the secular philosophers' way of thinking about
morality.   This book is written from the perspective of the secular philosopher, not the theologian.   It assumes no religious doctrine, nor the truth of
any scripture.   Rather, it examines the places where philosophers' reasoning
has taken them.

Some thinkers have stirringly deplored the human condition, should it
turn out that religion fails to provide a moral foundation. They reason
gloomily, as follows:

(1) If God is dead, everything is permitted.
(2) God is dead.
(3) Therefore, everything is permitted.

The first premiss is that of the Russian novelist Fyodor Dostoevski; the
second was advanced by the German philosopher Friedrich Nietzsche.   If they
are true, we get the skeptical conclusion that everything is permitted.   If
everything is permitted, then nothing is forbidden and nothing obligatory;
morally, all choices and acts are on a par.   If God is dead, then the fountainhead of morality, its ultimate foundation, is gone, and there is no final
moral authority.   We are thrown on our own inadequate resources; our
reason is unable to provide a foundation for morality.   The tides of feeling,
we are warned, will sweep over civilization unchecked.   The new order of the
day will be: Do as you choose.   Pure will, purged of divine guidance and
restraint, and shorn of human reason and wisdom, will be loosed to lunge for
power or to choose without guilt any chance course of action.   If God is dead,
these thinkers say, the dark perimeter closes in.

Here is how this viewpoint is expressed by the French existentialist
philosopher Jean-Paul Sartre, who announces that "man is forlorn."

> The existentialist . . . thinks it very distressing that God does not exist, be-
> cause all possibility of finding values in a heaven of ideas disappears along
> with Him; there can be no longer an *a priori* [prior to human experience]
> Good, since there is no infinite and perfect consciousness to think it.   No-
> where is it written that the Good exists, that we must be honest, that we
> must not lie; because the fact is we are on a plane where there are only
> men.   Dostoevsky said, "If God didn't exist, everything would be possi-
> ble."   That is the very starting point of existentialism.   Indeed, everything
> is permissible if God does not exist, and as a result man is forlorn, because
> neither within him nor without does he find anything to cling to.   He can't
> start making excuses for himself.[26]

The only escape from this pessimistic view is to find either that God is
not dead but still provides a foundation for morality, or that human reason is

28   adequate to the task of providing us with morality. As you will see, the challenge to a religious foundation is formidable, making optimism about the powers of human reason look like an attractive option.

To be clear about the challenge to religion as a foundation of morality, we should distinguish between God as a source of morality and God as a source of motivation to be moral. Because our topic in this section is God as the source rather than the motivation of morality, I will only briefly describe the motivation issue so as to distinguish it. One form of moral skepticism is Christian, because many Christian fundamentalists take the view that humans need divine motivation—the promise of heaven and the threat of hell—in order to be moral. Such skeptics assume that we are by nature irretrievably evil and given over to sin. Of course the most ardent Christian may recognize, and even insist, that this momentous divine motivation is insufficient to make us good; we have all sinned and deserve eternal damnation, and consequently stand in dire need of Grace, God's unrequired but benevolent forgiveness. But if God is dead, even this motivation evaporates.

The claim challenged in this section can be stated this way: An act is right if *and only if* it accords with God's will, and it is wrong if *and only if* if does not.

I emphasize "and only if" because its presence in the claim makes right and wrong depend exclusively on God's will. Were the claim stated with just the "if," we would leave open the possibility that right and wrong could be in accord with something other than God's will, such as a moral law of human reason. So the claim we are questioning is whether God's will is the *sole* source of moral law.

There are two serious challenges to this claim, both of which are on target but neither of which is my chief concern in this section. The first asserts that God doesn't exist and the second states that there is no way of determining what God's will is.

If God doesn't exist but is "dead," we can't base morality on a religion that mistakenly affirms his existence. This serious challenge has occupied theologians and religious philosophers throughout the history of thought; however, so as to get at the issue in this section, let us grant God's existence.

Equally serious is the challenge to the belief that any mortal has "received" the Word of God and truly knows what God's will is. How God communicates with humans and how conflicting human reports of God's will (those of Lutherans, Catholics, Calvinists, Baptists, Moslems, and so on) can be sorted out are indeed difficult problems. But again, so as to isolate the issue in this section, let us grant that someone truly knows God's will.

A third challenge, known as "the Problem of Evil" because it makes God responsible for evil as well as good, I defer until Chapter 7, section 7.5.

Assume, then, that God exists and that someone truly knows what God wills. The challenge to religion's claim is contained in a question that Socrates asks of Euthyphro, who is on his way to prosecute his father for killing a servant. Euthyphro justifies his action by saying that it is the holy or pious thing to do because it is pleasing to the gods.

Euthyphro: Yes, I would indeed affirm that holiness is what the
gods all love, and its opposite is what the gods all hate, unholiness.
Socrates: Are we to examine this position also, Euthyphro, to see if
it is sound? . . .
Euthyphro: We must. And yet, for my part, I regard the present
statement as correct.
Socrates: We shall soon know better about that, my friend. Now
think of this. Is what is holy holy because the gods approve it, or do they
approve it because it is holy?[27]

Putting the question another way, Socrates asks: (a) Is an act right
because God says so (the divine will makes it right), or (b) does God say it is
right (does He or She will to say it) because it is right?

If the answer is "yes" to (a) and "no" to (b), it is difficult to understand
why anyone would think that only religion stands between morality and
chaos, or why anyone would cling to religion as a sure foundation and guide
to morality. If pure willing by God makes something right, then right and
wrong seem wholly arbitrary. If God doesn't approve benevolence because it
is right, then God has no more reason to approve benevolence than to disapprove it. If God's will were that benevolence is evil, then it would be evil, according to this answer to Socrates' question. God's will puts morality in no
better position than a bandit's will would.

Surely, then, the answer to Socrates' question must be an affirmation of
(b): God says something is right *because* it is right. But this implies that the
grounds for an act's being right exist independently of God's will, in which
case God is not the fountainhead of morality. God—like the rest of us, if we
are moral—approves what is right and disapproves what is wrong. And like
the rest of us, He or She has to use intellect to find out what the grounds of
morality are, so as to know what to approve and disapprove. But if this is so,
morality exists independently of religion and is as open to discovery by us as
by God.

The upshot is that either way one answers Socrates' question, religion is
not a moral foundation—according to the first answer, because arbitrary willing doesn't provide a justifiable foundation; and according to the second,
because humans as well as God can discover morality, since we share rationality.

In defense of a religiously based morality, it might be said that the
preceding challenge is devastating only if religion takes a "legalistic" approach to morality. Joseph Fletcher makes this defense in his book, *Situation Ethics,* in which he rejects a legalistic approach to God's will. Fletcher
distinguishes between three approaches to morality: legalistic, situational,
and antinomian. He thinks Judaism, Catholicism, and Protestantism have
been predominantly legalistic. Legalism approaches moral decision-making
with codified, "prefabricated rules and regulations . . . they are *directives* to
be followed. Solutions are preset" [28] Fletcher criticizes legalism because it
fails to accommodate the concrete differences in situations. By rigidly
following the rules, legal and religious officials actually become immoral.

30   When we fail to temper the laws and rules with love, we become what "Mark Twain called 'a good man in the worst sense of the word.'"[29]

To illustrate how his own view, situationism, with its "care-ful," loving attention to differences in circumstances, differs from legalism, Fletcher cites the following case.   A woman who tried to teach her thirteen-year-old daughter chastity finally told the daughter, after her third unwanted child, "If you persist in acting this way, at least be sure the boy wears something."

> On this evidence [the mother] was convicted and sentenced.   The combined forces of "secular" law and legalistic puritanism had tried to prevent loving help to the girl, her bastard victims, and the social agencies trying to help her.   Situation ethics would have praised that woman; it would not have pilloried her. [30]

Antinomianism is the opposite extreme of legalism.   It denies that there are any moral precepts, rules, or guidelines.   "Making moral decisions is a matter of spontaneity; it is literally unprincipled, purely . . . casual"—such is the view Fletcher attributes to Christian and Existentialist antinomians. [31]   He thinks situationism is the correct approach between these two extremes.

> The situationist enters into every decision-making situation fully armed with the ethical maxims of his community and its heritage, and he treats them with respect as illuminators of his problems.   Just the same, he is prepared in any situation to compromise them or set them aside *in the situation* if love seems better served by doing so. [32]

Fletcher here puts concrete moral decisions in the hands of humans; in his ethics we do not look for some scriptural rule or interpreted principle that God supposedly revealed.   Still, it is religious because, unlike the antinomians, he thinks God does command one law and, unlike the legalists, he thinks there is only this one religious command that humans ought to apply.

> *Christian* situation ethics has only one norm or principle or law (call it what you will) that is binding and unexceptional, always good and right regardless of the circumstances.   That is love—the *agapē* of the summary commandment to love God and the neighbor. [33]

Agapē is love without desire, nonreciprocal and neighbor-regarding.   He distinguishes it from two other kinds of love: *philia* or friendship love, and *eros* or romantic, erotic love.   "Christian love is *will,* disposition; it is an *attitude,* not a feeling." [34]   In a reply to critics of his book, Fletcher concludes that "we cannot absolutize both love and law, and the New Testament makes it perfectly clear which one to choose." [35]

Theologians construct religious theories that are supposed to relate to practical life.   But are they like the system builder described by Karl Jaspers, the German Existentialist?

The system is for them [Friedrich Nietzsche and the nineteenth-century Danish philosopher Søren Kierkegaard] a detour from reality and is, therefore lies and deception. . . . The philosopher of systems is, as a man, like someone who builds a castle, but lives next door in a shanty. Such a fantastical being does not himself live within what he thinks; but the thought of a man must be the house in which he lives or it will become perverted.[36]

31

STUDY QUESTIONS

There are study questions at the end of each chapter. They have two purposes. The first is to help you identify and review your understanding of the main issues and distinctions in the chapter. The second is to help you prepare for the instructor's examinations on the material covered.

1 Why can theory be practical? Relate your answer to the reflexive and self-correcting nature of thought.
2 Explain what a "problematic situation" is and relate it to the preceding question.
3 How would you compare and contrast problematic and challenge situations? Illustrate each kind. Explain why both lead to reflection.
4 Explain what a practical syllogism is. How can practical syllogisms be related to each other? Give an example of two linked syllogisms whose premises and conclusion you believe. For example, they might be about sexual or racial equality, atomic energy, the free enterprise system, or abortion.
5 Why does Socrates' question challenge a religious foundation for morality? And how does situationism, by challenging legalism, try to rescue religion from the critical answers to Socrates' question?

Reflections on Applications

1 List the places in the cafeteria conversation between Todd, Ez, and Emily where you think the opposition between feeling and thought occurs.
2 Todd wonders whether it is his duty to marry or to help support Diana. W.D. Ross claims that a mature person who thoughtfully contemplates a moral principle can know that it is self-evidently true, just as a mature person can know that a mathematical axiom ($A = A$) is self-evidently true. Consider this principle:

A man who through his neglect impregnates a woman ought to help support the child (if the woman decides to have and keep it).

32   Is it self-evident to you that this principle is true? That it is false?
If neither, do you conclude that you (and Todd) are not one of Ross's
"mature persons"? Or do you conclude that Ross is wrong about the
self-evidence of moral principles? Or that this is not a moral principle?
Or that there is another moral principle, self-evident to you, from which
this principle can (or cannot) be deduced?

3 Suppose we changed the principle to read as follows:

> A man who, through his own and the woman's neglect, impregnates a
> woman ought to help support the child (if the woman decides to have
> and keep it).

Is there any difference between this principle's self-evident truth
(or falsity) and that of the principle in Reflection 2?

4 Do you think that the principle "Thou shalt not kill" is self-evidently
true? Is there any difference between this principle's self-evident truth
(or falsity) and the ones in Reflections 2 and 3? If you think there is a difference, what is it?

5 State one moral principle that you think is self-evidently true.

6 What would you conclude about the relationship between the heart and
the mind, if the following were the case?

There is no such thing as a feeling that has not been preceded by
a thought; every feeling is what it is because of the beliefs and knowledge
that a person has at the time he or she experiences the feeling. (See the
last paragraph in section 1.2.) During a low period in her life, the jazz
singer Bessie Smith composed a song called "Nobody Loves You When
You're Down and Out." The title of this song shows how people's feelings and behavior toward you change when they notice a change in your
fortunes; their feelings are altered by their thoughts. Once you are no
longer a source of money and good times, the song says, these "sunshine"
friends who loved you and called you "honey" walk on the other side of
the street.

7 Chris and Susie are nine-year-old gorillas in the Sacramento City Zoo.
Not having been around other gorillas, they haven't learned how to breed.
To solve this problem, the zoo director began showing them a twenty-five-
minute "educational film." Bill Meeker, the zoo director, said that the
film features the group activities of a bunch of gorillas leading up to
mating, and then the actual mating. Showing it to Chris and Susie might
"stimulate" them, he added. "We hope that through observation they
will learn there is something they have to do and have the urge to do it." [37]

Does this account support the suggestion in Reflection 6? Are you
more inclined to believe that feelings are mediated by thought, now that
you see this may even be true for gorillas, who presumably don't live as
rich a thought life as humans?

8 Arguments are central to philosophy. I'm not using "argument" as synonymous with "disputes"; rather, I'm referring to a set of sentences some
of which are premises and at least one of which is a conclusion. You can

usually tell when someone intends a set of sentences to be an argument, because there are tell-tale words used. Words such as "because," "since," and "for" are among the words that precede sentences intended as premises; words such as "hence," "therefore," and "consequently" are among the words that precede sentences intended as conclusions.

The best way to get a feel for philosophy is to construct some arguments. Here are some premises with which you can start; by adding to them and drawing conclusions, you construct an argument. The first two premises below give you the start of an argument against the adequacy of feeling as a guide to action:

> Feelings are a product of conditioning.
> Many important situations in life are unique.

The next two premises give you the start of an argument against the adequacy of thought as a guide to action:

> If nothing in the world ever felt anything, nothing would matter one way or the other.
> The mind cannot feel.

9 List five of your or a friend's individual practices.

10 List the groups to which you belong. Identify a group practice for each of them.

In identifying the groups to which you belong, you have to use various criteria. For example, you may belong to a family by birth, to a race by gene patterns, to a church by confirmation vows, to a country by naturalized citizenship, to a social class by the amount of your own or your parents' income, to a city by residence, and so forth.

11 Here is an interesting kind of challenge situation. A person may belong to two groups whose practices oppose each other. If each set of practices seems reasonable, then that person's own practices generate a challenge and a problematic situation. How should one deal with this?

For example, you might belong to a church group that advocates treating everyone equally: "All are equal in the eyes of God." On the other hand, your family group might like to imitate, tell jokes about, and make fun of homosexuals, which is not treating people equally. Here we have an instance of two groups with contrary practices. How would you as a member of both groups manage this contradiction—pretend, lie to yourself, not practice what you preach? Members of a church group may preach one thing but practice another. Do you think this is a satisfactory way of dealing with the contrary practices of two groups to which you belong? Try formulating one or more practical syllogisms supporting or undercutting this preach/practice solution.

12 Here is a particularly troublesome problematic situation, one that apparently can't be solved by the son, although you may try your hand at solving it.

34   A father has a seventeen-year-old son who is about to leave home; soon he'll be a citizen out in the world on his own, obliged to perform unaccustomed practices. Dad is worried, though: Son has been passive, unassertive, dominated. Dad figures he'd better try to shape him up, so he'll be ready to be an independent citizen. Dad talks to Son about it several times, but doesn't get any results. In exasperation he slams his fist into his palm and shouts, "Damn it, boy, stop obeying me!"

What is Son to do? If he obeys this last command, as he is inclined to do, he'll just be obeying again, doing precisely what Dad doesn't want him to do. On the other hand, if he doesn't obey him, he won't be doing what Dad wants him to do—namely, disobeying him. Son is in a dilemma: no matter what he does, he can't satisfy Dad. He can't do anything that he ought to do.

This is a problematic situation because there are two practical syllogisms that make contradictory conclusions reasonable: You ought and ought not to obey me.

Children ought to obey their parents.
You are a son (says Dad).

Therefore, you ought to obey me.

Citizens in a democracy ought not to obey authority,
but make up their own minds.
You are, or are about to become, a citizen (says Dad).

Therefore, you ought not to obey me.

Both of these syllogisms apply to Son because he belongs to two groups, the family and the state. As a son in a family he is supposed to have one group practice and as a citizen, another. [38]

Son can't stop being a son, can he? Nor can he stop being a citizen. Nor can Son take the preach/practice escape route: he can't preach one thing and practice something else, because no matter what he practices—whether to obey or not obey his father, which are the only two choices possible—he ends up doing something that doesn't satisfy his father. His actions have the same result, regardless of which he preaches. He can't even pretend to practice what he preaches.

13 There is another way to solve the problematic situation arising from our membership in two groups that advocate contrary practices. This is illustrated in the next example.

In 1975 Saudi Arabia contracted with a United States corporation to hire ex-servicemen to train troops to protect their oil fields. One of the men hired said, "My brother was furious when he heard. He thought I had turned against Israel." I do not know that this man was a Jew, but for purposes of illustration let us suppose that he was. Let us also suppose that he was the head of a family, so that he belonged to two groups.

The man hired said in response to his brother's remark, "But we have **35** skills, with no market available other than this one."

As a member of a group that identified itself as Jewish, the man was expected by his brother to perform actions that aided Israel; but helping Saudi Arabia, which was hostile to Israel at the time, might harm Israel. On the other hand, as a member and the head of a family, he had to work at what he was trained for so as to support his family and himself.

When we face contrary practices advocated by two groups to which we belong, one choice we have is to give priority to one group and its practices over the other; we may place them in a hierarchy. By giving them ratings on a scale of higher and lower priority, we introduce an element that eliminates the conflict. Clearly, the man hired to train Saudi troops gave a higher priority to the practices of his family group than to his racial or religious group, although not without qualification ("But we have skills, with no market available other than this one"). [39]

Formulate the two practical syllogisms that have for their conclusions (1) You ought not to train troops in Saudi Arabia, and (2) You ought to train troops in Saudi Arabia.

Did we have a comparable situation in the United States when Blacks and Chicanos thought it wrong for members of their respective groups to join the Nixon administration? Or today, when some people with a radical analysis of our society argue that anyone interested in real change in the United States ought not to serve in the government, regardless of the person's race? Or when unionized construction workers refuse to support an ecology conservation group because it will cost them jobs?

14 Labor unions have the practice of trying to raise their members' wages. Businesses have the practice of trying to increase their profits. Often an increase in wages decreases the profit, and an increase in profit is made at the expense of wages. In collective bargaining, the two engaged groups have contrary practices. The usual solution to this situation is for each to compromise. Is this solution open to a person who belongs to two groups with opposing practices?

Remember that a bargaining situation is not similar to a personal problematic situation, since in a bargaining situation a person does not belong to both groups: a member of the labor union is not also a member of management, or vice versa. Thus in bargaining, a person apparently does not have a conflict between two of his own group practices; instead, *two* persons have a conflict because of the practices of the respective groups to which they belong.

15 Some false-fact premises may be held by people who are resisting a change in a current group practice. For example, some persons are resisting the changes advocated by the women's liberation movement, or changes advocated by socialists; they might be resisting because they hold erroneous or superstitious beliefs about women or capitalism.

The deposed Shah of Iran once said, "What do these feminists want? Equality, you say? Indeed! I don't want to seem rude but . . . you may

36

be equal in the eyes of the law, but not, I beg your pardon for saying so, in ability.'' [40]

Identify (1) a current group practice, (2) some who resist a change in it, and (3) the erroneous belief(s) that the resisters think justifies their resistance.

16 I have said that reflection may have the form of a practical syllogism. In fact, reasoned reflection may grow into a connected set of syllogisms. This happens when part of one syllogism is made a part of another, and that in turn a part of another, and so on. How are Saudi 1 and 2 connected? How are Kuwaiti 1 and 2 connected?

17 Comment on the following remarks:

> The Cuban population itself is a young one—a 25-year-old was only ten when Castro rode in victory into Havana. And I found the minds of the young welded to the rigid postulates of Marxism-Leninism—accepted by them as articles of faith beyond rational analysis and critical judgment. These young people—in a few short years they will be the decision-makers in Cuba—are bright, trained and competent. But it's a pity their minds are closed, and doubtful they can ever be opened. [41]

18 The Fifth Commandment—given to Moses by God, according to some Christian sects—is "Thou shalt not kill." A little reflection shows that some Christians have a problematic situation.

This commandment makes no exceptions: you shouldn't kill—period. If it is true that religion and only religion, through its holy scriptures, provides a foundation for morality, and that scripture is literally the word of God, then not to obey God's commands is immoral. A great many Christians are immoral because they think it is right to kill in self-defense, to kill during wartime, and to execute murderers. This killing violates God's unexceptional command. So either they must give up their belief that the Christian religion is a foundation for morality, or they must become complete pacifists and oppose capital punishment. There is no other way out of this problematic situation.

Do you agree with this? If not, supply a counterargument.

 ## Reflections on Theory

In the main, this second set of reflections introduces arguments and considerations that could be, or have been, advanced by persons on issues dealt within the chapter. They extend the theoretical horizons beyond my representation of them in the foregoing account.

19 *Against the truth or falsity of moral principles.* Do you agree with the following argument?

So-called moral principles can't be self-evidently true or false as **37** Ross claims, because they aren't true or false to begin with. They aren't statements about what Ross calls "the moral order" of the "nature of the universe." Instead, they're really expressions of feelings or of blind custom. If they were self-evident truths, then all mature persons would agree on them. But we find no such universal agreement, so they can't be self-evident truths. That they are expressions of feeling or custom rather than truth accounts for the variation we find in the acceptance and rejection of them. This explanation is sound because we find, first, that feelings vary among persons—for example, between what Diana wants and what Todd wants; and second, that customs vary among groups of persons: in Sicily, Todd would have to marry Diana for certain, but not in the United States.

20 *Against feeling as a basis for morality.* Do you think the following argument refutes the view that feeling is the ultimate basis of morality? If you don't think it does, is it because you disagree with one or more premisses? If so, which one(s) and why?

If feelings were the ultimate basis for morality, then to cite a feeling as the basis for action would be final. But it is not final because we often find that we have feelings that are opposed to one another. Todd doesn't want Diana to have the baby because he doesn't want to make support payments; but he also wants Diana to have the baby because he wants Diana to have what she wants. If feelings were the last word on which to base our moral judgments, decisions, and actions, then Todd would decide both that Diana should have the baby and that Diana should not have the baby. He can't effectively act in accord with both these decisions because they are contradictory; therefore feelings can't be the final basis for moral action. Some minimum thought is required, because one has to think about which feeling on which to base an action; the feelings can't select themselves.

21 *Defense of feeling.* Do you think the following argument refutes the argument in Reflection 20?

Of course feelings are often opposed, but they are not of the same strength. Having feelings in opposition doesn't make it impossible to act; we act in accord with whatever feeling is stronger. This shows that we do not require thought to help us determine how to act; the difference in strength of feelings makes it possible for feelings alone to determine how we will act.

22 *Feelings dependent on thought.* The argument in Reflection 21 is a declaration of the independence of feelings from thought. Do you think that the following remarks, taken from a United Nations World Health Organization report, show that feelings depend on thought?

> Members of the health profession . . . are often ill-equipped for counseling in human sexuality, sexual behavior, family planning, etc. and may be reticent about giving such advice or unwilling to do so.

Although the health practitioner may have been exposed to the same general cultural environment as his patient, he often comes from a different social and educational milieu and rarely shares the same inhibitions and methods of expression.

To overcome the differences in response—embarrassment, discomfort, or unwillingness to speak openly and frankly with patients about sexual matters, the Report suggests that showing "films portraying sexual behavior with unusual candor" is a good training device for health profession students. The Report talks about one such tryout. "A number of these films are shown, one after the other, to a group of medical students. Immediately afterward the students are involved in group discussion in which they share their emotional reactions to the films. These usually include some degree of sexual arousal, shock, and sometimes embarrassment, disgust, or hostility. By talking over these reactions together, the group soon becomes relaxed and discovers that apprehension and discomfort have vanished. Sometimes the students are given a second opportunity to see the films and to discover how much their anxiety levels have been lowered."[42]

23 *Thought should dominate feeling.* If you agree with the following argument, then you have concluded that thought rather than feeling should guide your action. If you disagree with it, you must have an argument that leads you to the opposite conclusion. In that event, you have created a potential problematic situation for yourself from which you must escape.

Thought has an object; when we think, we think about something. Feeling too has an object; when we are angry, we are angry about or at something. When we desire, we desire something. Thought and feeling are alike in that they both have objects, but they also differ. While thought can have thought as its object, feeling cannot have feeling as its object; it is not reflexive. This is an important difference. It means that, because thought is reflexive, it can correct itself. Since, however, there cannot be feeling about feeling, feeling cannot correct itself. Since feeling can't correct itself, there is no way, on the basis of feeling alone, to evaluate a feeling as a basis of action, no way of distinguishing foolish from wise, decent from vicious, or good from bad feelings. It would be foolish to be guided by feelings that, for all we know, are foolish. Therefore we should put our future and our happiness in the hands of thought, because it alone is self-correcting and will reduce the number of foolish actions during our life.

24 *Factual and moral progress.* The headhunting tribes of Asmat believe that the skulls of their victims ward off the spirits of the dead, so they arrange them as decorations inside and outside their huts and use them as pillows. Their (perhaps superstitious) belief could serve as a fact premiss in a practical syllogism with the conclusion "It is right to hunt for enemies' heads." If the fact premiss is false, then of course the conclusion has not been justified by the syllogism. Relate this to the quotation

from de Coulanges in section 1.8, where he says of our intelligence that it is "almost always progressing." Does progress in factual knowledge— necessarily, possibly, always, seldom—lead to moral progress?

25 *In God's defense.* Do you think the following argument is a good defense against the criticism of religion as a foundation of morality that was made in section 1.12?

God approves what is right and disapproves what is wrong because they are right and wrong respectively. True, this implies that the basis for morality does not lie in God's will, and that the foundation is independent of God. We should not conclude, however, that the foundations of morality are as available to humans as they are to God. After all, God is omniscient, has infinite intelligence and wisdom, whereas human intelligence is finite. Thus the foundations may be discerned by His/Her intelligence, but not by ours. This being so, we ought to obey God's commands even if we can't find the reasons for them.

To counter this defense, are the other kinds of challenges to religion mentioned in section 1.12 pertinent? Which ones and how?

26 *Theologians and love.* Do the following observations, if true, undercut Fletcher's situation ethic with its acceptance of the kind of love called *agapē* as the one moral commandment from God (see p. 30)? Does it dissolve the last hope of defending the Christian religion as a foundation for morality? Whatever your answer, explain why you answer as you do.

> If . . . theologians cannot speak perceptively about the mystery of love, how can they hope to communicate the meaning of divine love as an existential [pure will] power? Much theological analysis has centered upon the meanings of ancient words, which hardly represents an open encounter with contemporary existential facts. An alternative approach has been grandly represented by Paul Tillich. Using an ontological [reality-oriented] approach to love, he affirmed: "Life is being in actuality and love is the moving power of life. . . . Love is the drive towards the unity of the separated . . . as the reunion of the estranged." Few theologians have been more influential for our era in recovering the importance of love for theology as well as for life than Tillich; yet his extremely broad definitions have not done much to clarify the full scope of love's meanings. . . . Theology must learn to honor the invitation offered by other disciplines to share in the pursuit for concrete and reliable insight into and understanding of man's greatness and misery within the context of the lived world. The need for religion to test its convictional [assured] language through a disciplined attention to experience is as relevant to its mission as it is to the development of theology. [43]

2
On Being Ordinary
and the Death
of Ivan Ilyich

2.1 The Three Themes of This Book

In the preceding chapter we traced the connection between ethics (moral theory) and morality (moral practice). With this chapter we begin our investigation of moral theory.

Drake Koka is an exiled black South African labor leader who helped create the Black Consciousness Movement in that country. Some remarks made by him to United States trade unionists and university audiences in 1978 express the three themes of this book. Koka said:

> Blacks know what is good for us. We are mature enough and competent enough to decide our own political and socio-economic destiny. No more having our future decided for us by people other than ourselves. We want self-realization. We believe in self-determination. [1]

The three themes are: (1) self-realization, (2) self-determination, and (3) the relation between doing and being.

I think that all of us want to realize ourselves, want to determine for ourselves what we think is right to do and worthwhile to be and become, that all of us want to understand the relation between doing right and being worthy.

These three themes prompt the three theme questions to which I address myself in a progressively more sophisticated and mature manner through the course of this book. The answers come from some of the more interesting and imporant Western thinkers. The three theme questions are:

(1) What kind of a person must I be or become, to be a worthy person?
(2) To what extent am I free to determine what I ought to do and become?
(3) What kinds of acts does a worthy person do?

Since the whole of this book explores the answers to these questions—answers that are not simplistic enough to be stated briefly and casually here at the beginning—I will briefly indicate here only their scope.

In the first question, when I ask what a worthy person is, I could be asking three possible things. I might be asking what kind of personality is good—but I am not. I am not asking whether it is better to be cheerful, sparkling, or witty than gloomy, dull, or boring. I might also be asking what social status is best, or what job or social role is most worthwhile, or which career will best use your talents—but I am not. What I *am* asking is what kind of *character* is worthy, which is a question about the moral nature we ought to attain. What are we aiming at when we attempt the self-realization of a good moral character?

In the second question, when I ask to what extent we are free to determine what we ought to do and become, I am asking to what extent we can be **43** our own master. This has two sides. I am not my own master when someone else tells me what to do or puts limits on my self-realization activities. This is what Koka was talking about. Others can achieve mastery over us either directly or indirectly. Direct mastery is demonstrated by a slaveowner selling a person, by an army sergeant ordering a recruit, or by an employer telling an employee what to do.

When others have indirect mastery over us, it is more subtle; we may not even know that it exists. When others influence our actions, values, and self-image, we may come to do, value, and become what they desire, because we have consciously or unconsciously accepted their rules, judgments, and ideals. In fact, we may even "internalize" those rules, judgments, and ideals—that is, take them for our own, so they become our second nature. The slave may come to believe that he was made for slavery, and the woman that she was made to be a wife. You need only think of the enormous internalization potential television can create in its viewers to appreciate the possible extent of indirect mastery. Tolstoy's story of Ivan Ilyich, summarized in section 2.2, illustrates the awful consequences of internalized mastery.

Let's call freedom from direct and indirect mastery by others over us "political self-determination."

In this book we will also deal with "personal self-determination." To what extent can we be masters of our own nature and capacities? This discussion involves the contrast between feeling and thought discussed in Chapter 1. The extent to which we can be masters of ourselves and control our self-realization depends on the extent to which we can control our feelings and thoughts.

Those who believe that morality is based on feeling place two kinds of limits on our ability to freely self-realize the moral character that we would like to attain. These two kinds of limits come out of what can be called the "nature/nurture" debate. Some claim that as animals who have evolved by the process of natural selection (section 5.6) we have inherited a nature equipped with instincts for certain kinds of behavior, and with built-in emotional responses to certain kinds of objects and situations. Since we aren't "free" to alter these, our self-mastery over morality is limited by an inherited, fixed human nature. (I will discuss this in Chapters 5 and 13.)

Others claim that human feelings, emotional responses, and needs are nurtured by our culture, which includes all social institutions ranging from the family to the nation-state. Nurture theorists believe that our emotions and appetites are not fixed from the start, but are shaped and molded by influences. If this molding comes from culture, we are dealing with indirect mastery by internalization. But suppose that to some extent culture is consciously created; in that event, culture and its internalized forms, and consequently our feelings and needs, are products of thought.

This leads us to inquire to what extent we are masters of our own thought. To what extent is our thought self-determined? Pretty obviously, an immense spectrum of our thought is the product of nurture. To the extent that we uncritically accept the thoughts of others, we don't have self-mastery

44 over our own thought. Do we have original powers of thought at all? The philosopher who most impressively examined the question of our personal self-determination was the eighteenth-century German thinker Immanuel Kant. He maintained that we can self-legislate our morality, and that we are free to self-realize our moral selves. My development of this theme will come in my discussion of Kant's ethics.

You can see from the foregoing that theories of human nature and capacity are intimately connected with the first two theme questions announced on page 42. This illustrates that theory and practice go together, as I argued in Chapter 1.

As for the third theme question—"What kinds of acts does a worthy person do?"—the obvious answer is "Morally right ones." But this only leads the self-determining person to ask, "But which acts are morally right?" It can't be answered simply by listing them, because you have to know what to include on the list and what to leave off. To self-determine which kind of act should be on the list and which not, you have to have a criterion or standard that allows you to explain—to yourself, at least—*why* one should be there and the other not. Later we will consider the two main kinds of standards that have been proposed: a utilitarian standard and Kant's Categorical Imperative.

2.2 The Death of Ivan Ilyich

Tolstoy's story of the death of Ivan Ilyich, a middle bureaucrat in the Russian law courts, dramatically introduces us to the first two themes of this book—a person's worthiness and self-determination.

The story of Ivan Ilyich's life was of the simplest, most ordinary and therefore most terrible. . . .

As a student he was already just what he was to remain for the rest of his life: a capable, cheerful, good-natured and sociable fellow, though strict in the performance of what he considered to be his duty; and he considered as his duty whatever was so considered by those in authority over him. Neither as a boy nor as a man had he been one to curry favor, yet there was that about him that from his very earliest years he was attracted, as a fly to the light, by people of high station. He adopted their ways and views on life, and established friendly relations with them. . . .

As a law student he had done things which had before that seemed vile and at the same time had made him feel disgusted with himself; but later on when he saw that such conduct was practiced by people of high standing and not considered wrong by them, he came not exactly to regard those actions of his as all right, but simply to forget them entirely or not be at all troubled by their recollection. . . .

But on the whole Ivan Ilyich's life ran its course as he believed life should: easily, agreeably and decorously. He got up at nine, drank his coffee, read the newspapers, then donned his undress uniform and went to the Law Courts. There he fell instantly into his well-worn harness and prepared to deal with petitions, inquiries in the office, the office itself, and the sessions—public and administrative. . . . And Ivan Ilyich did it all not only smoothly, pleasantly and correctly but even artistically. . . .

The whole family was in good health. Ivan Ilyich sometimes complained of a queer taste in his mouth and a sort of uncomfortable feeling on the left side of the stomach, but one could hardly call that illness.

But this uncomfortable feeling got worse and, though not exactly painful, grew into a sense of pressure in his side accompanied by low spirits and irritability. . . .

Suddenly he felt the old familiar, dull, gnawing pain, the same obstinate, steady, serious pain. In his mouth there was the same familiar loathsome taste. His heart sank, his brain felt dazed. . . . A cold chill came over him, his breathing ceased, and he heard only the throbbing of his heart.

"I shall be no more, then what will there be? There will be nothing. Then where shall I be when I am no more? Can this be dying? No. I will not have it!" . . .

Ivan Ilyich saw that he was dying, and he was in continual despair.

In the depths of his heart he knew he was dying but, so far from growing used to the idea, he simply did not and could not grasp it.

The example of a syllogism which he had learned in Kiezewetter's *Logic:* "Caius is a man, men are mortal, therefore Caius is mortal," had seemed to him all his life to be true as applied to Caius but certainly not as regards himself. . . .

And Caius was certainly mortal, and it was right for him to die; but for me, little Vanya, Ivan Ilyich, with all my thoughts and emotions—it's a different matter altogether. It cannot be that I ought to die. That would be too terrible.

That was the way he felt inside himself. . . .

It was true, as the doctor said, that Ivan Ilyich's physical sufferings were terrible, but worse than his physical sufferings were his mental sufferings, which were his chief torture.

His mental sufferings were due to the fact that in the night as he looked at [his servant] Gerassim's sleepy, good-natured face with prominent cheek-bones, the thought had suddenly come into his head: "What if in reality my whole life has been wrong?"

It occurred to him that what had appeared utterly impossible before—that he had not lived his life as he should have done—might after all be true. It struck him that those scarcely detected inclinations of his to fight against what the most highly placed people regarded as good, those scarcely noticeable impulses which he had immediately suppressed, might have been the real thing and all the rest false. And his professional duties, and his ordering of his life, and his family, and all his social and official interests might all have been false. He tried to defend it all to himself. And suddenly he realized the weakness of what he was defending. There was nothing to defend.

"But if that is so," he said to himself, "and I am leaving this life with the consciousness that I have lost all that was given me and there's no putting it right—what then?" [2]

We have little if any personality or character at birth. Growing up means acquiring them, either from others or by our own efforts. Self-realization philosophers think that right up until death we have the chance to "grow up" in character. Unfortunately, Ivan Ilyich stopped growing up. Upon facing death, he realized that he had not been his own master. Using Martin Heidegger's phrase, we can say that Ilyich had very little of his "own most"; Ilyich wasn't "authentic." Heidegger's German word is *eigentlich*, which is usually translated as "authentic" or "genuine," but literally translates as "own most."

Robert Coles summarizes Heidegger's view about the opportunity death offers us for confronting our *eigentlich*. Of course we can take advantage of it only if we think about death before we are dying, which Ilyich did not do.

> For Heidegger, death presents the great opportunity to the willing seeker, the confused man who wants to know before he draws his last breath what at rock bottom he can consider his "own most," because it has been rescued from the everydayness of his life—the pressures, the boredom, the appalling ingratiation, the surrender of more and more personal territory in the interests of "success" or "adjustment" or practicality, or simply out of exhaustion, if not despair. [3]

And what about *you*? Suppose you live for another fifty years. How can you make sure that at the end of that time you won't have the ultimate regret: "My whole life has been a mistake; I didn't make myself worthy."

2.3 Mistakes, Regrets, and Death

As Tolstoy's story illustrates, the realization of impending death may sweep away our pretenses and usual complacency about the value of our life. Ilyich comes face to face with the possibility that he has made a horrendous mistake. The effect of these two realizations on him is devastating.

Some mistakes bring regret, others do not. For example, taking a wrong turn, balancing a checkbook inaccurately, or buying the wrong size shirt for Uncle Charlie doesn't usually cause regret, just annoyance. Regret occurs when we recognize that our mistake has seriously harmed either ourselves or someone else.

The approach of Ivan Ilyich's death took him beyond regret into despair, because it deprived him of the opportunity for correction. By understanding his mistake, we may avoid or correct it in ourselves. We who are not yet close to death may still experience an Ivan Ilyich regret without suffering his despair—on the condition that we understand its cause.

Basically, Ivan Ilyich erred by becoming the wrong person. He saw this upon recognizing two things: first, that his mistake involved his whole life, and second, that he was ordinary. Ruminating further, he saw that his "whole life has been wrong," that it had been a mistake. But how can a **47** life—a *whole* life—be wrong, be a mistake?

To help answer this, let's contrast this mistake with several less all-inclusive ones.

We may not foresee the consequences of our acts. Certainly Philo Mentor didn't: when he started drinking, after being laid off his job as a philosophy teacher, he never dreamed he'd become an alcoholic. In his defense we can say that he is not a totally wasted human; at least his philosophy has made him a better human and a better drunk. Becoming an alcoholic need not be a mistake that embraces one's whole life.

We may misvalue. We may have overvalued a high salary, the approval of our parents, good-looking clothes or children, or fame, but we may not have misvalued other things. Thus misvaluing needn't make a whole life a mistake, since some valuations were not mistaken.

We may misjudge someone's character. For example, we may have helped someone accomplish something whereby, unknown to us, that person intended harm to another. But this kind of mistake is not the mistake of a whole life either, when it is balanced off by other character judgments that were accurate.

These kinds of mistakes differ from Ivan Ilyich's in that they are partial; they are mistaken parts of a life, not a mistaken life as a whole. Of course such partial mistakes may adversely affect our life—even the entire remainder of our life—but they are not a mistake about a life as a whole.

In discussing the goodness of life, the American philosopher C. I. Lewis said that it is "no sum of immediate goods minus the sum of transitory bads. . . . Life is a temporal Gestalt, and has its final value as a composition, not as a bank balance." [4] What does this mean?

A Gestalt (the German word for "shape" or "form") is a single whole with a character that does not derive solely from a summation of the characters of its parts. For instance, a wooden chair may have the Gestalt property of being comfortable, although this is not a feature of any of its parts, either taken separately or simply added together. Further, the Gestalt whole may determine the character of its parts rather than the other way around; in the duck/rabbit figure below, the very same parts may be seen either as rabbit ears or as a duck bill, depending on whether you see the whole figure as a rabbit or a duck.

Lewis properly speaks of life as having a "temporal" Gestalt—that is, a Gestalt expressed in time—whereas the duck/rabbit figure has a spatial

48   Gestalt. But as Gestalts they both have an organization, a relationship of parts that characterizes the whole. Lewis uses the term "composition," suggesting a comparison to a work of art such as a piece of music, a painting, or a poem, all of which also have organization. His term suggests that, just as the artist composes a work of art, so each of us composes his or her life. In each case the organization—the composition—determines the character, including the value character, of the whole. Thus we may speak of "a life"—someone's life as a whole—and say something about the value of that life as a whole. By using Lewis's suggestion of the Gestalt, then, we can understand how a life can be a mistake.

The second thing Ivan Ilyich realized was that his life was ordinary: "The story of Ivan Ilyich's life was of the . . . most ordinary and therefore most terrible," writes Tolstoy. The Gestalt property of his life was ordinariness. Ivan's awareness of this destroyed his self-esteem. He came to see himself as a person less distinguished than he had hitherto supposed.

Using Lewis's idea that our life has value as a composition, we can understand how Ivan Ilyich could link the ordinariness of his life as a whole to his loss of self-esteem. Just as from the ordinariness of a painter's output we infer his ordinariness as a painter, so from the ordinariness of a person's "life-composition" we infer that person's ordinariness as a person. Ivan Ilyich became the wrong person because his whole life, his output, was wrong—that is to say, ordinary. His loss of self-esteem depended, of course, upon his believing that ordinariness does not justify much self-esteem.

One reason for the impact of Tolstoy's story is that most of us resemble Ivan. Furthermore, our own end, if a lingering one, might be like his—racked with despair, soured by the revelation that our life has been ordinary. At the very moment when we most need the balm of self-esteem, we may lose it. The Ilyich regret is unrelenting. We realize also that the esteem of others was an illusion. What we formerly took for their esteem was merely relief that we ran our life conventionally enough not to disturb the tranquillity of their own. "Please," we can imagine them thinking, "don't disturb us now with an unconventional dying."

Imminent death may change the appearance of a life, just as a new perspective changes the appearance of the duck/rabbit figure. We may come to recognize that the organizational pattern of our life has been conventional, producing a conventional person. "As a student [Ivan Ilyich] was already just what he was to remain for the rest of his life." From the perspective of death,

it struck him that those scarcely detected inclinations of his to fight against what the most highly placed people regarded as good, those scarcely noticeable impulses which he had immediately suppressed, might have been the real thing and all the rest false. And his professional duties, and his ordering of his life, and his family, and all his social and official interests might all have been false.

2.4 Self-Realization   49

We have been trying to understand Ivan Ilyich's mistake, and for a very practical purpose; should we live another fifty years, this understanding may help us avoid living them out mistakenly, as he did. Ivan's mistake was that he became the wrong person. Lewis's ideas of a life as a Gestalt and as a composition have helped us to probe that mistake.

We have seen also how a Gestalt character of a life, such as ordinariness, leads us to characterize a person as being, in this case, ordinary. Because this is central in our growing understanding of Ivan Ilyich's mistake, we should probe the connection between the character of a life and the character of a person more extensively. We can get help by considering some moral thinkers who give self-realization a central role in their theories.

The nature of our self, the kind of person we are, would probably not obsess us if we believed that it is given and unchangeable. As persons we are creatures that live in time. We have a career. Some of this career is still to be; it lies in the future. Given that what we think and decide, and how we act, will influence that future, and given that we can think about our self, we may decide to act in such a way as to change our self. Unlike pencils, rocks, ants, and apple trees, say self-realization theorists, we can change ourselves. We are subjects, not merely objects. As subjects, we can act on ourselves as objects, just as we can act on a pencil as an object. This reflexive capacity of humans makes *self*-realization possible.

T. H. Green, the nineteenth-century English philosopher, emphasized that self-realization is a making of our own selves.

> There is a principle of self-development in man. . . . In virtue of this principle he anticipates experience. In a certain sense he makes it, instead of merely waiting to be made by it. He is capable of being moved by an idea of himself, as becoming that which he has it in him to be—an idea which does not represent previous experience, but gradually brings an experience into being, gradually creates a filling for itself, in the shape of arts, laws, institutions and habits of living, which, so far as they go, exhibit the capabilities of man, define the idea of his end, afford a positive answer to the otherwise unanswerable question, what in particular it is that man has it in him to become. [5]

The notion of self-realization is central to existentialism as well. Jean-Paul Sartre points out that a person's existence precedes his essence—he *is,* he exists, before he is *this* or *that*; man does not have an essential nature given him that he is powerless to change. Existentialism puts existence first.

> What is meant here by saying that existence precedes essence? It means that, first of all, man exists, turns up, appears on the scene, and, only afterwards, defines himself. If man, as the existentialist conceives him, is

50 indefinable, it is because at first he is nothing. Only afterward will he be something, and he himself will have made what he will be. Thus, there is no human nature, since there is no God to conceive it. Not only is man what he conceives himself to be, but he is also only what he wills himself to be after this thrust toward existence. [6]

The notion of self-realization gives point to viewing our life from the perspective of death. Recognizing that Ivan Ilyich reviewed his life too late to change it, and wishing to avoid his regret and despair, we have reason to seek out and destroy traces of our own ordinariness.

This transformation of ourselves requires, in C. I. Lewis's terms, recomposing the pattern of our lives. Further, if self-realization is not to stop before we die, as Ivan Ilyich's stopped, we have to keep changing the pattern. This is put persuasively by Wright Morris in his novel *The Field of Vision.*

In the novel, Boyd and his friends are watching a bullfight. The bull gores the bullfighter. Boyd wonders what the young boy beside him thinks of what he has seen. His wondering is shaped by his view that a person's life is not something that is already *given,* not a datum, but something that we *make.* Boyd wonders:

> What had *he* [the boy] seen? How long would it take him to puzzle it out? He was now a jigsaw loose in its box, the bullfight one of the scarlet [jigsaw] pieces, but he would not know its meaning until the pattern itself appeared. And that he would not *find.* No, not anywhere, since it did not exist. The pattern—what pattern it had—he would have to create. Make it out of something that looked for all the world like something else.
>
> Did he know that? Was there anywhere he might go to learn?
>
> First, he would have to sense that parts were missing, and then, somewhere along the way, that the curious pattern he saw emerging was himself. Everything else he had been given, in abundance, but that he lacked. It called for transformation. Out of so many given things, one thing that hadn't been given. His own life. An endless sequence of changes, a tireless shifting of the pieces, selecting some, discarding others, until the pattern—the imagined thing—began to emerge. Death would fix the outlines. Frame the picture as no man would ever see it himself.
>
> The problem? In an age of How-to-do-it, the problem was how not. . . . How to live in spite of, not because of, something called character. To keep it open, to keep the puzzle puzzling, the pattern changing and alive. [7]

Had Ivan Ilyich adopted the self-realization view embraced by Morris, Sartre, and Green, he could have reminded himself of his power to be a different kind of person than he was. Then he might not have suppressed "those scarcely detected inclinations of his to fight against what the most highly placed people regarded as good." He did not have to be ordinary. He need not have been pathetic.

2.5 The Pathetic and the Tragic   51

Ivan Ilyich's death is the "most terrible" because it is pathetic rather than tragic, and his ordinariness has made it so. Tragedy is appropriate to the misfortunes of the noble, while pathos is appropriate to the misfortunes of the base. We feel sorry about the misfortunes of both, but admire persons who deal with their misfortunes nobly.

Aristotle's theory of tragedy required that the Greek tragic hero be of noble birth; Shakespeare's Lear and Hamlet are also of noble birth and station. The decline of kings, queens, and dukes has shifted the tragic requirement from noble social rank to noble moral character; we now allow the possibility that, although a person may be of low social standing, a noble character entitles him or her to be a tragic hero. A pathetic figure has a base character. Ivan Ilyich discovered that he was base; he organized his life in such a way that, viewed as a whole or a Gestalt, it was ordinary; at his death he was only to be pitied, not admired.

It would be overconfident to think that, even with another fifty years, one's life would be happy or end happily. We do not have enough control over events to sustain that dream confidently. This is why the tragic has been a persistent theme in literature. Facing the likelihood of unhappiness, we snatch at least at nobility—or at heaven, for those who insist on happy endings. What we *are*, rather than what happens to us or what we do, becomes important. The democratic tragedian assumes that although we may not be able to control fully what we do or what happens to us, we can control who we are. We do not need to be ordinary, pathetic persons; we may make ourselves noble and therefore eligible for tragedy.

2.6 Nietzsche on Ordinariness

We have been considering Ivan Ilyich's mistake about his whole life. We have determined that a whole life can be a mistake, because a life has a Gestalt property by virtue of its organization. Knowing the Gestalt property of a person's life, we can infer the nature of the person. Being ordinary was Ivan Ilyich's mistake; if self-realization is possible, he could have changed his life and himself. Had he tried to do so, he might have been tragic rather than pathetic.

The point of these reflections on Tolstoy's story is to learn how to avoid Ivan Ilyich's mistake. To further our learning, we need to investigate ordinariness, to learn more about what we should avoid.

The nineteenth-century German thinker Friedrich Neitzsche had some interesting things to say about ordinariness in his book *Beyond Good and Evil*. He asks, "What, ultimately, is commonness?" In summary, Neitzsche

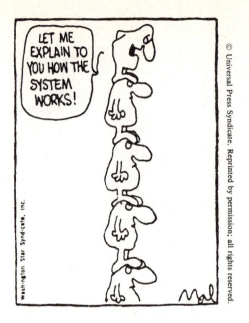

traces it to two things. First, he observes that most humans aren't self-determining; they conform like Ilyich did. Second, most humans don't self-realize a noble nature; they don't become "distinguished" but remain "despicable." Here now are some of Nietzsche's major theses that apply to the Ilyich problem.

STRUCTURE. The Gestalt property of a life depends on its pattern. How can we discover such a pattern? Nietzsche proposes that we look at a person's values. "The value-estimates of a human being reveal something of the structure of his psyche, something of the way in which the psyche sees its basic conditions for life, its essential needs." [8]

COMMUNICABILITY. One essential human need, says Nietzsche, is an easy communication of needs. He thinks commonness has such a powerful hold on us because similarity is a condition for this easy communication. Imagine how difficult it would be to communicate with intelligent beings from outer space, if they were extremely dissimilar from us.

> Assuming now [says Nietzsche] that need has always brought together only those people who could express similar needs and similar experiences with similar symbols, then we shall find, all things considered, that easy *communicability* of need, which means ultimately the experience of merely average and *common* experiences, must have been the most powerful of all the forces that have ever ruled mankind. . . . One must call upon enormous oppositional powers in order to contend against this natural, all too natural *progressus in simile,* the continuous progress of man toward similarity, ordinariness, the average, the herd-like, the *common*! [9]

Ivan Ilyich did not develop the "enormous oppositional powers" to resist his drift toward becoming common, toward being like others. He didn't develop his powers of self-determination. Having elected to move in high bureaucratic circles, he aped his superiors, wanting to be *like* them. The fact that he imitated those in high station does not save him from ordinariness; they too are ordinary because they drift toward commonness, toward being like each other. Ivan Ilyich suppressed his inclinations to fight against their values, just as we often suppress ours.

THE HERD INSTINCT. There are two meanings of "common" that Nietzsche plays upon: the first is that of "similar," the shared; the second is that of "ordinary," the mediocre. He moves from the first meaning to the second in his remarks above about communicability. He is conscious of this double meaning, this ambiguity of "common," and he thinks these two meanings are connected. He tries to justify their connectedness by showing how fear of our neighbors and superior persons drives us from needing the similar to valuing the mediocre.

> After the social structure as a whole is stabilized and secured against external dangers, it is the fear of one's neighbor that creates new perspectives of moral valuations. . . . The herd instinct draws its conclusions, step by step. How much or how little the common good is endangered—the dangers to the status quo that lie in a given opinion, or state, or passion, in a given will or talent—these now furnish the moral perspective. Here too fear is once again the mother of morality. . . . A superior, independent intellect, a will to stand alone, even a superior rationality, are felt to be dangers; everything that lifts the individual above the herd and causes fear in his neighbor is from now on called *evil*; . . . all *mediocrity* of desires comes to be called and honored by the name of morality. [10]

The moral desires of Ilyich were of course intensely mediocre—as he himself realized too late.

SLAVE MORALITY AND MASTER MORALITY. The herd instinct that propels us toward mediocrity brings a slave morality in its wake.

> Slave-morality is essentially a utility-morality. Here is the cornerstone for the origin of that famous antithesis "good vs. evil." The eye of the slave looks unfavorably upon the virtues of the powerful; he *subtly* mistrusts all the "good" that the others honor. . . . Conversely, those qualities are emphasized and illuminated which serve to make existence easier for the sufferers: here compassion, the complaisant helping hand, the warm heart, patience, diligence, humanity, and friendliness are honored, for these are the useful qualities and almost the only means for enduring the pressure of existence. [11]

In the slave morality, good versus evil is the main moral distinction. In the master morality, on the other hand, the main distinction is distinguished versus despicable. "What is despised is the coward, the timid man, and the

54 petty man, who thinks in terms of narrow utility" [12] The despised person's "good" is generated by the drive toward what is common in the shared sense; it is a morality in which conformity dominates; self-determination is forfeited. The life structure of a person who has chosen a slave morality is patterned on what is conventionally thought to be worthwhile, on what is common. Forfeiting self-determination and aping mediocre conventions doom a person to ordinariness. The death of a person who lives within the slave morality, as Ivan Ilyich did, is merely pathetic because such a person is base and despicable. Remember Ilyich's remarks: "It struck him that those scarcely detected inclinations of his to fight against what the most highly placed people regarded as good, those scarcely noticeable impulses which he had immediately suppressed, might have been the real thing and all the rest false."

NOBILITY, SELF-DETERMINATION, AND SELF-REALIZATION. Those who live within the master morality do not structure their lives by conformity, because to do so is base and despicable. "The distinguished type of human being feels *himself* as value determining; he does not need to be ratified; he judges that "which is harmful to me is harmful as such"; he knows that *he* is the something which gives honor to objects; he *creates values.*" [13] The noble person is self-determining and not imitative.

After determining and creating their own values and value pattern, "distinguished" persons create and realize their own person. They know who they are because they have made their own self; they have a sense of their person, of what is their "own most." These noble persons escape pathos and become eligible for tragedy. They distinguish themselves from ordinary persons because they do not structure their lives by the values advocated in the slave morality. They self-realize their nobility.

2.7 Egoism and Self-Realization; Egotism and Self-Determination

Ivan Ilyich faced himself and found he was ordinary. He had conformed; he had adopted the attitudes and performed the acts of his superiors; he had let them form him instead of his forming himself. By giving in to the herd instinct, he had drifted into a slave morality; this slave morality became the organizing principle of his life, and this conferred the Gestalt property of ordinariness on his life. By failing to self-determine and self-realize his being, he failed to realize a noble self.

But identifying ordinariness is different from avoiding or shedding it. We can say easily enough that self-realization and self-determination can triumph over ordinariness. But we need to know how to achieve self-realization and self-determination. To get started, let's look at Nietzsche's proposals. From my citations of his proposals, it looks as if self-determination is achieved by egotism and self-realization by egoism.

Egoism and egotism must not be confused. Egoism is the view that one does or should look after one's self-interest before or in oppositon to the interests of others. Egotism is the exaltation of oneself because one believes oneself to be superior to others.

In looking at Nietzsche's proposals, let's bear four things in mind. First, remember that we are looking for a structural principle with which to compose our lives. We want to replace the structure that yields the Gestalt property of ordinariness with a structure that yields some other Gestalt property of our lives and being.

Second, recall that Nietzsche suggested that the structure of a psyche is revealed by a persons's value estimates; ordinary persons' value estimates are dictated by a slave morality.

Third, slave morality's main value distinction is between good and evil. "Everything that lifts the individual above the herd and causes fear in his neighbor is from now on called *evil*; . . . all *mediocrity* of desires comes to be called and honored by the name of morality."

Fourth, if we want to turn away from ordinariness, we must have a rebirth of values. We must replace the slave morality with a different organizing principle of life; we must transvalue. "Where must our hopes look? We have no other choice: we must seek *new philosophers,* spirits strong or original enough to give an impulse to opposing valuations, to transvalue and turn upside down the 'eternal values'; . . . Men who will teach man that man's future is man's *will,* dependent on man's will." [14]

If we accept Neitzsche as one of his own "new philosophers," the advice we get from him for the transvaluation or rebirth of values is to replace the slave morality with the master morality. In effect, this means we should not live by the good/evil distinction but by the distinguished/despicable one. The good person in slave morality is ordinary, whereas the person who structures his or her life by the master morality is distinguished.

Were we to follow Nietzsche's advice, what would we become? What is it to be distinguished in his sense?

Negatively, the distinguished person gives up democratic and Christian values. For Nietzsche, the democratic movement is "not only a deteriorated form of political organization but a deterioration, that is to say, a depreciation of a human type, a mediocritizing and lowering of values." [15]

As to Christianity: "From the very beginning, the Christian faith is a sacrifice, sacrifice of all freedom, all pride, all self-assurance of the mind; at the same time it is servitude, self-mockery and self-mutilation. . . . It was never faith but freedom from faith, half-stoic and smiling carelessness about the serious nature of faith in their master or masters that revolted the slaves. 'Enlightenment' is what revolts, for the slave wants an absolute; he understands only tyranny, even in morality." [16]

On the positive side, to be distinguished is to take the stance of a master rather than that of a slave.

56

At the risk of displeasing innocent ears, I propose the following: Egoism [really egotism] belongs to the nature of a distinguished soul. I mean that immovable faith that other beings are by nature subordinate to a being such as "we are"; that they should sacrifice themselves to us. The distinguished soul accepts this fact of its egoism without any question mark, and also without any feeling that it is hard or oppressive or arbitrary. [17]

The distinguished type of human being feels *himself* as value-determining; he does not need to be ratified; he judges that what "is harmful to me is harmful as such"; he knows that *he* is the something which gives honor to objects; he *creates values*. This [egoistic] type honors everything he knows about himself; his morality is self-glorification. . . . Belief in oneself, pride in oneself, basic hostility and irony against "selflessness" is as sure a part of distinguished morality as an easy disdain and cautious attitude toward the fellow-feelings and "warm heart". . . . But the point at which the morality of rulers is most foreign to current taste and most painstakingly strict in principle is this: one has duties only toward one's equals; toward beings of a lower rank, toward everything foreign to one, one may act as one sees fit, "as one's heart dictates"—in any event, "beyond good and evil." [18]

Self-realization and self-determination are recommended as cures for the pathos of ordinariness. But in Nietzsche's hands, the cures seem to commit us to egoism and egotism; the "distinguished noble" gives up "compassion" and the "warm heart," and honors "self-glorification."

Are Nietzsche's cures worse than the disease? Is self-realization the facade for egoistic selfishness? And is self-determination a facade for egotistical vanity?

"Yes," you might say, "I don't want to be ordinary, but I don't want to be egotistical either." Such a response, according to Nietzsche, comes from a person trapped in a slave morality; such a person is servile, afraid to confirm his or her own worth—indeed, unable to because the person has no worth. The noble soul, says Nietzsche, does not deny its superiority. What is wrong in the noble soul's acknowledging that it is noble? To deny it is to lie. *"The Distinguished soul has reverence for itself."* [19] What is wrong with this, if the soul is truly distinguished?

Nietzsche tries to separate egotism from vanity. "Vanity belongs among the things which are hardest for a distinguished man to comprehend; . . . His problem is that he cannot imagine creatures who seek to stimulate a good opinion of themselves in others—an opinion which they do not share and hence do not 'deserve'—and who then *believe* in that good opinion." [20]

Vanity is a ruse of the undistinguished to get others to believe that they are distinguished—and then believe themselves distinguished because others believe so. The egotist, on the other hand, *knows* that he or she is distinguished, and doesn't look for confirmation of this nobility in others' opinions.

Despite these artful dodges around vanity, if self-glorification marks the egotist, you may hesitate to adopt egotism as the structural principle of your life. Of course you might be more inclined to adopt it if you thought it the only alternative to ordinariness. You might even work at becoming a noble egotist if you thought your only alternative was being a pathetic slave.

The case for choosing egotism can be made more attractive, if being ordinary is the source of the greatest evil. Philip Blair Rice remarks:

> Most of the evil in the workaday world is . . . the result . . . of the small, frightened hardening of human sympathies imposed by the pressure of convention and by gradual congealment of the spirit through prudential [self-interested] anxieties. [21]

The following observations support Rice's view. In her book *Into That Darkness* Gitta Sereny wrote about Franz Stangl, commandant of the Nazi extermination camp at Treblinka. She says in an interview: "I could see Stangl was an individual of intelligence, a man who had been intimately involved with the most evil things our age has produced." [22] At first, during their interviews, Stangl offered the usual rationalizations— he was simply obeying orders. Then he changed. "I was completely honest with him. I told him on the first day I was totally uninterested in any of the platitudes. . . . I wanted to hear about him as a man . . . and I found an ordinary, decent man." According to the article, Sereny found the Nazi was a devoted family man whose wish not to endanger his family led him to carry out his monstrous task; his "ordinary" decency toward his family made him exterminate Jews.

Stangl died of a heart attack the day after his last meeting with Sereny.

I have set forth the undesirability of ordinariness in sections 2.2–2.6, and its immorality in this one. I have cited several persons who advocate self-realization. We have seen that Nietzsche's recommended escape route from ordinariness is through self-determined self-realization. In the last few pages we have seen that, for Nietzsche, self-determination appears to be a form of egotism: we can believe in our own self-determined values because we are superior beings. Because egotism doesn't have the best moral reputation, however, we seem to be caught in a dilemma: either we are ordinary or we are egotistical, neither of which is desirable. Our only escape from the dilemma will be to find an alternative to these two modes of determining values.

Let's turn now from Nietzsche's advocacy of egotism to his argument for egoism. Perhaps we can find further cause for doubting Nietzsche's solution to ordinariness.

A heavy attack on egoism was made by Peter Marin in his article "The New Narcissism." Marin focuses on the new therapies such as Esalen, Arica, est, Scientology, the teaching of the peyote enthusiast Don Juan, and some guru cults and self-potential movements. "The trend in therapy," he says, "is toward a deification of the isolated self." That subject is "in turn a part of an even more general concern: the ways in which selfishness and moral blindness now assert themselves in a larger culture as enlightenment and psychic health. A broad-based retrenchment [revision] is going on, a pervasive and perhaps unconscious shift in value—not only on a national level but in the moral definitions and judgments we make as individuals."[23] These remarks sound as if Nietzsche's call for transvaluation has been answered.

Consider some of the moral shifts Marin has in mind. The new therapies

> become not only a way of protecting or changing the self, but of assessing the needs of others and one's responsibilities to them. . . . [They reveal] the impulse behind much of what we do these days: the desire to defend ourselves against the demands of conscience and the world through an ethic designed to defuse them both. Most of us realize at one level of consciousness or another that we inhabit an age of catastrophe—if not for ourselves then for countless others. Try as we do, we cannot ignore the routine inequities of consumption and distribution which benefit us and condemn others to misery. Each of us must feel a kind of generalized shame, an unanswerable sense of guilt. We struggle mightily to convince ourselves that our privilege is earned or deserved, rather than (as we must often feel unconsciously) a form of murder or theft. Our therapies become a way of hiding from the world, a way of easing our troubled conscience. [24]

The shift to egoism, if unchecked, finds the self so expanded that "it replaces community, relation, neighbor, chance, or God. Looming larger every moment, it obliterates everything around it that might have offered it a way out of its pain." The traditional measures of morality vanish, to be replaced solely with concern for self. Self-realization may become morally as monstrous as Stangl's ordinariness.

Marin discerns a developing opposition between idolatries, blind worship, of the state and the self.

> Our deification of the self becomes equal in effect and human cost to what Nietzsche long ago called the "idolatry of the state." Just as persons once set aside the possibilities of their own humanity and turned instead to the state for a sense of power and identity no longer theirs, so we now turn to the self, giving to it the power and importance of a god. In the worship of the state, life gives way to an abstraction, to the total submission of individual will. In the worship of the self, life also gives way to an abstraction, in this case to an exaggeration of the will. The result in both cases is the same. What is lost is the immense middle ground of human community. The web of reciprocity [mutual involvement] and relation is broken. The world diminishes. The felt presence of the other disappears, and with it a part of our own existence. [25]

Given the horns of our dilemma—ordinariness and egoism, conformity to the state and glorification of the self—the only way out is to find a third alternative. Marin points to human community, to reciprocity and relation.

Can we escape Ivan Ilyich's ordinariness through a kind of community-oriented self-realization that avoids egoism? In the next chapter, the story of the ring of Gyges supplies a tough-minded answer to this question.

59

STUDY QUESTIONS

1 State briefly in your own words the three themes to which this book is addressed.
2 Why does Tolstoy think Ivan Ilyich lived an ordinary life? Explain why this ordinariness (commonness) was a quality of his life as a *whole*. Relate this to the banality or ordinariness of evil.
3 To what does Nietzsche trace human commonness? What two meanings does "commonness" have for him, and how does he connect them? Tie his theory of commonness to his low regard for the distinction between good and evil, in such a way as to explain why he says we must go "beyond good and evil."
4 What is the difference between egoism and egotism? Relate them to Nietzsche's concepts of self-realization and self-determination.
5 Why does Marin reject egoism?

Reflections on Applications

1 Self-realization has been advocated as a way of escaping the pathos of Ivan Ilyich's ordinariness. Still, humans are complex: they have many aspects, any one or more of which a person might develop in pursuit of self-realization. For example, Charles Atlas and others have persuaded many boys and men to send away for their advertised muscle-development courses and equipment. Similar kinds of ads are found in women's magazines; here is one:

A SPIRIT EXPERIENCE The Dynamic Cheerleaders Association would like to get to know YOU at one of their many summer '75 cheerleading camps! As you work on next year's spirit programs, DCA's got what you need to be different, better, exciting. The most explosive summer camp in the country!

When you enroll for a DCA Summer Cheerleading Camp, you say YES to the challenge of being dynamic . . . and to the fun/smiles/hard work of being an outstanding cheerleader.

We've got what you need to be the best (the boogie

60 routines, the most refreshing up-to-date cheering techniques, hundreds of spirit involvement ideas . . . and MUCH MORE) besides providing you with the most unique Spirit Experience available anywhere. All you have to do is say YES. [26]

Do you think that realization of your muscular or "spirit" potentialities is a way of avoiding Ivan Ilyich's mistake? Don't highly developed muscles or an ability to cheerlead dynamically raise a person out of the ordinary? Is this the kind of unordinariness that Ivan Ilyich and Nietzsche had in mind?

2   A young Harvard student with a straight-A record recently forged letters of recommendation to medical school, to Phi Beta Kappa, and for a fellowship in England. He had been doing laboratory research in cancer studies. After the forgery became known, he said, "You have no idea of the pressure in those labs. . . . Your whole career is on the line. . . . I would approach the lab and get an anxiety attack. I would leave, sometimes wanting to cry. . . . It was a vicious cycle. I would avoid the lab, feel guilty for copping out now that the experiments weren't going well, and then avoid the lab more. . . . The letters were irrational and wrong, very wrong. I just began perceiving everything in desperate terms. Forging the letters was my way of saving myself from a desperate situation." [27]

The young man admits he made a mistake. Did he make the kind of mistake Ivan Ilyich made? Was he on his way to it? Tolstoy wrote of Ivan Ilyich, "As a student he was already just what he was to remain for the rest of his life." Is it all over for the young student? Or is there something you can say about him or to him, in the light of this chapter's discussion, that could rescue him from "desperate" despair?

3   I recently received an advertisement in the mail; it urged me to subscribe to a workbook-journal called *Synthesis*. The letter said in part: "We think that each of us wants to be more than we are. Are you becoming the person you have always wanted to be? For most of us caught up in daily life . . . there is the vague awareness of an inner person urging to be recognized, realized, and fulfilled. There are potentials to be activated. There are inner conflicts to be resolved. . . . For example, in each issue of *Synthesis* you will find a unique *Psychosynthesis Workbook,* which provides the opportunity of applying practical techniques toward fulfilling our inner needs for growth. . . . Specific exercises and methods are included—the "Who Am I" technique, the "Subpersonality Door," "The Dance of the Many Selves," and others. And full, clear explanations of how to use these methods—and the theory behind them—are provided."

A person who took the self-realization view seriously might be tempted to send off for the workbook. Do you think the following argument provides a good basis for not sending for it?

A self may be made by oneself or by others; there is self-realization and realization by others. When we are children, because we don't know enough and aren't mature enough to make good judgments, our selves have to be realized by others—by our parents, teachers, ministers, and so forth. But there comes a time when a person should cease being a child, should cease being made by others. But stopping this process isn't easy. Parents and teachers aren't the only ones who try to form our selves. Even when a person has become an adult, others still try to make you the way they think you should be made. Psychologists, for example, may try to do this; they may interfere with your *self*-realization. This *Synthesis* advertisement is one of those attempts to keep you childlike. The following part of the ad shows this: "Over the past three years, a number of leading psychologists and thinkers . . . have been developing a new vehicle to provide the specialized information, the guidance, and the practical methods so badly needed to help develop and harmonize our inner resources." *Don't* send for the workbook! It's just another attempt to keep you from *self*-realization! It's a disguised effort to keep you childlike.

4   Ivan Ilyich thinks "his professional duties, and his ordering of his life, and his family, and all his social and official interests might all have been false. He tried to defend it all to himself. And suddenly he realized the weakness of what he was defending. There was nothing to defend."

Does Nietzsche's notion of herd instinct explain why "there was nothing to defend"? Does the influence of the herd instinct imply that all our normal social order and conventions are "false?"

5   The *San Francisco Chronicle*'s "Question Man" once based a column on the question "What do you want to do before you die?" Which of the following answers do you think the dying Ivan Ilyich would approve most? Why?

> (a) "Fly a plane. I don't know how to yet, but I'm going to take flying lessons. I've always wanted to fly. Actually, that's what I'd like to be, a pilot. I don't know if I'll make it, but that's what I want."

> (b) "Just to find contentment. What I'd really like to do is live on a hill above the sea. Some place like down near Big Sur. A house on a cliff overlooking the sea."

> (c) "I would sort of like to free my spirit from all the social hang-ups that exist and evolve it to a higher awareness and break through the barrier of time and space once more."

> (d) "Talk to people about reading the Bible. I'm a preacher and I'd like to reach more people. I would like to help people get a better understanding of the Bible." [28]

6   Do you think that what Marin calls the "idolatry"—that is, the blind worship—of the State played a similar role in the ordinariness of both Ivan

62

Ilyich and Stangl?   Do the circumstances that pressure us into ordinariness show that self-realization and self-determination require sacrifice and some degree of heroism?   (As to the sacrifices involved in being ordinary, see Nietzsche on the Christian faith in section 2.7, specifically the quotation on page 55.)

7   Do these remarks by the late Nelson Rockefeller, made while he was vice-president of the United States, contain Nietzschean views?   "One of the problems in this country is that we have this Judeo-Christian heritage of wanting to help those in need.   And this, when added to some political instincts, causes people to promise more than they can deliver.   And I think this nation has over-promised, under-delivered, over-spent, and now we're in financial trouble.   This can't go on." [29]

 ## Reflections on Theory

8   *Rebirth and self-realization.*   Rebirth is theme that runs through religion, philosophy, and politics from their beginnings.   Rebirth is putting off an old self and taking on a new self.   Obviously, we hope that the new self will be better than the old one.

In this reflection part A cites some remarks about rebirth by St. Paul, Plato, and Wang Tao-ming.   Part B then provides three candidates for instances of self-realization.   Ponder the relation between rebirth (Born again!) and self-realization, and by examining the candidates for self-realization arrive at your own conception of self-realization and self-determination.   I say "candidates for self-realization," because the new self might not be better than the old self they have put away.   Also ask yourself whether these candidates escaped Ilyich's ordinariness.

(A) In Chapter 6 of Romans the Apostle Paul writes: "So we are buried with Him [Christ Jesus] in death through baptism in order that, just as Christ rose from the dead through the Father's glorious power, so we too shall conduct ourselves in a new way of living."   And in Chapter 2 of his letter to the Ephesians, Paul writes: "You too were dead in your trespasses and sins, in which you once conducted yourselves in line with the ways of this world system, controlled by the ruler of the kingdom of the air, the spirit of the one now working in disobedient people. . . . But God . . . made us who were dead in trespasses alive; with Christly grace you have been saved."   In the Christian tradition, to convert to Christianity is to be reborn; the old pagan self must die and a new Christian self be born.

Book Ten of Plato's *Republic* contains the Myth of Er: an account of souls about to go once again into the world, choosing the life they **63** would live there. First the souls drew lots to determine the order of choice. "After this the samples of lives were placed on the ground before them, far more numerous than the souls present. They were of all kinds, for the lives of animals as well as all kinds of human lives. . . . The state of the soul was not included, for this unavoidably depended upon the kind of life one chose. . . . Er said that it was a spectacle worth seeing how the souls each chose their lives. It was pitiful, ridiculous, and surprising. For the most part their choice depended upon the character of their previous life. He said that he saw the soul which had once been that of Orpheus choosing the life of a swan in his hatred of women." [30]

The Myth of Er does not have to be interpreted literally, as if Er were witnessing the transmigration of souls. We can interpret each day's end as a dying and the new day's dawning as being born again, leaving us free to choose another life than the one lived previously.

Both the Cuban revolutionary Che Guevara and the Chinese Communist leader Mao Tse-tung called for a "new man" to be brought into being; capitalist man is to be cast off and socialist man to take his place. Gaining political power is only the first step in the socialist revolution; its real success comes when the new socialist man is born. Wang Tao-ming, a young Chinese political leader, expresses this need to make himself a new person: "But it was only after Chairman Mao issued the call 'Learn from Comrade Lei Feng' that I really and truly realized the importance of ideological remoulding and began conscientiously to remould myself with Mao Tse-tung's thought. . . . In daily life, I struggle hard against any manifestation of selfishness in me and sometimes while I am eating my meal I will ask myself whether I really put others before myself. . . . It will never do to overemphasize one's own role in work and seek to win personal fame." [31]

(B) (i) *Boyd* (the character in Wright Morris's novel *The Field of Vision,* section 2.4). Boyd was determined to keep life's pattern "open, to keep the puzzle puzzling, the pattern changing and alive." How does one do this? Boyd himself and McKee, Boyd's conventional boyhood friend, dwell repeatedly on a couple of boyhood acts that were typical of Boyd's attempt to keep the pattern open and unconventional.

One involved the pants pocket of the legendary baseball player Ty Cobb. Boyd had tried to get Cobb to autograph a baseball that Cobb had fouled and Boyd caught. Boyd had run onto the field, intercepted Cobb rounding third base on a home run, chased Cobb when he veered from home plate toward the dugout, dropped the ball he wanted autographed, and instead grabbed and ripped off Cobb's pants pocket. Years later, on a visit to New York from Nebraska, McKee and his wife looked up Boyd. "They found him up there [in a loft] with his shirt off, no furniture to speak of, nobody anywhere around to look after him, and this fool ball-

64   player's pocket lying on his desk. One he'd torn off Ty Cobb's pants, way back when he was a kid." [32]

The other boyhood act was Boyd's attempt to walk on water. "Going to take a little dip?" McKee had asked, taking it for granted Boyd could swim.

"Nope," Boyd had replied, "just a walk on the water." At the creek, "Boyd had stood there at the edge of the platform taking deep breaths and then blowing them out, . . . he just stood there, his eyes straight ahead as a wooden Indian, and McKee had been so sure he could walk on water—or on the air if he cared to—that he just waited for it." [33] But Boyd sank.

Later McKee quoted a remark of the grown Boyd:

> "All Gaul's divided into three parts. . . . Juvenile, Mobile and Senile delinquents. I'm in the Mobile division. How are things with you?"
>
> Right there, in a nutshell, you had everything that was wrong with him. The way he'd keep you guessing. . . . Anything might happen with a person like that. [34]

(ii) *The Yablonski Case.* Silous Huddleston and Annette Gilly, father and daughter, confessed to killing Joseph Yablonski, his wife, and daughter for reasons related to union politics. Their testimony helped convict the United Mine Workers' president, W. A. "Tony" Boyle, whom Yablonski had run against in a union election. Huddleston and Gilly spent four and a half years in custody; for their testimony, they were released from prison. The judge's order provided for release at a secret location; they were given false names, new Social Security numbers, and fabricated life histories, "in order that no one ever know who they are again." [35]

(iii) *George Fox.* A shoemaker by trade, Fox was the first Quaker. The following is from the Scottish writer Thomas Carlyle's *Sartor Resartus,* in which Carlyle relates how such an apparently mundane act as Fox's making a "perennial suit of Leather" may signal the adoption of a new life pattern.

> That Leicester shoe-shop, had men known it, was a holier place than any Vatican or Loretto-Shrine.—"So bandaged, and hampered, and hemmed in," groaned he [Fox], "with thousand requisitions, obligations, straps, tatters, and tagrags, I can neither see nor move; not my own am I, but the World's; and Time flies fast, and Heaven is high, and Hell is deep: Man! bethink thee, if thou has power of Thought! . . . Will all the shoe-wages under the Moon ferry me across into that far Land of Light? Only Meditation can, and devout Prayer to God. I will to the woods: the hollow of a tree will lodge me, wildberries feed me; and for Clothes, cannot I stitch myself one perennial suit of Leather!"
>
> Let some living Angelo or Rosa, with seeing eye and understanding heart, picture George Fox on that morning, when he spreads out his

cutting-board for the last time, and cuts cowhides by unwonted patterns, and stitches them together into one continuous all-including Case,
the farewell service of his awl! Stitch away, thou noble Fox: every
prick of that little instrument is pricking into the heart of Slavery and
World-worship, and the Mammon-god . . . were the work done, there is
in broad Europe one Free Man, and thou art he! [36]

9 *Is rebirth willable?* A person's rebirth may be triggered by a failure to
die. A psychiatrist interviewed seven survivors of jumps from San Francisco Bay bridges. One survivor said, ''I felt like a bird flying—total
relief. In my mind I was getting away from one realm and into another.
Even now I'm still symbolically looking for the better world—I'm still
in that place between the bridge and the water.'' The survivors uniformly
experienced a sense of oneness with other humans and the universe.

Only two again attempted suicide, both unsuccessfully. The rest
said that the first attempt at suicide erased this option from their minds.
The psychiatrist David Rosen called the change in attitude a result of
''ego-death'' and ''rebirth.'' [37]

These reflections are shared by Artur Rubinstein, the renowned
concert pianist. At twenty-two he became convinced that ''my career was
absolutely dead—zero. I had to kill myself. I found an old bathrobe
with a belt, and hung up the belt and pushed the chair away. The belt
burst and I fell on the floor stupidly.'' He ''suddenly discovered a new
world. I was resurrected in a way. Everything was beautiful and exciting, and I became in love with life.'' [38]

Most reported cases of rebirth, including the ''suicide rebirths,''
appear to have occurred inadvertently. Some unplanned, unforeseen
event—for Rubinstein, the bursting of the belt—is the usual prelude to
rebirth. Do you think it is possible to deliberately set about achieving
rebirth? Or does it require unanticipated shock?

10 *Argument for intending your death.* Knowledge of impending death or
thought about death may force us to take stock of ourselves and our lives,
may strip away our illusions about ourselves. This knowledge and
thought may turn us toward self-realization. (The Japanese film *Ikuru* is
a good illustration of this.) However, such lost illusions may also lead
to suicide. The following notes from suicides express regret and despair;
death seems to be a welcome release from life, a relieved falling away from
self.

(a) ''My darling_____, I shall spend this entire day in an attempt to
explain . . . I love you,_____. This you must know. There is no connection whatsoever with my feelings for you and that which I am about to
commit to myself you are an angel of the light and I have forever been
seeking the darkness. You have been a kiss of God on my road to
death. . . . When this letter is finished (whatever time that may be) so
shall I. In the twinkling of an eye and the touch of a trigger. . . .''

66

(b) "I am sorry should I cause you unpleasantness. I do not think I did many selfish things in my life but I have to agree what I am doing is, in a way, selfish, even though it is a hard thing to do. I just can't go on, so forgive me."

(c) A mother's note pinned to her child, found after the mother drowned herself in San Francisco Bay: "To miss_____, You were born April 5, 1960. I were born Sept. 11, 1930. Good By, May God Bless. My dear baby, I hate to do this but is the only way I can. I feel sick so long. God please forgive me, your mother." [39]

These suicide notes put death in a favorable light, but usually one pities the dying because death is seen as an event to be avoided. However, the self-realization point of view suggests an argument that death, if sought, may be celebrated rather than deplored. Does the following argument convince you that the highest human achievement may be the mutual linking of death and self-realization—even though you may think yourself incapable of achieving it?

Argument: Everything a person does should be undertaken with the end of realizing a better self. This should include your own death. You should so structure or compose your life that your own death will be its culmination or verification. By planning your own death, death itself may be a self-realizing act. Two examples, Socrates and Jesus, show the soundness of this view, since both are universally recognized as exceptional human beings. Their willingness to die, and their consciously and deliberately taking the steps that led to their deaths, while not strictly constituting suicide, crowned their greatness and enabled them to escape not only pathos but tragedy as well. Socrates was convicted of corrupting the Athenian youth and of being an enemy of religion; he could easily have escaped his death sentence, but instead he chose to drink the hemlock, living up to his own admonition that proper living is learning to die. Christ, too, could have escaped; instead he waited in the Garden of Gethsemane, fully aware that the soldiers were on the way to arrest him and that Judas would betray his identity with a kiss.

11 *Criminals as Nietzsche's "distinguished" souls.* The famous photographer Brassaï has written about his fascination with "low places and shady young men." His photographs deal with people who lived "underground" in Paris—pimps, prostitutes, thieves, murderers. He connects his fascination with Dostoevsky's reflections on his prison experiences with convicts. Do you think that criminals are "distinguished" or "noble" in Nietzsche's sense? If so, does Dostoevsky's discovery about convicts' unordinariness refute Nietzsche's theory? Here are Brassaï's reflections:

"Extraordinary men," wrote Dostoevsky in *The House of the Dead*, "perhaps the most richly endowed, the strongest of all our people. . . ." And let there be no mistake. The admiration expressed by the author of *Crime and Punishment* was not for revolutionary intellectuals or for political prisoners, but for real criminals: thieves, murderers, convicts—

his own prison companions.   These criminals cast out by society became his mentors [teachers], their doctrine of life—never written, but clear nonetheless—became his ideal.   There was no pity in this.   Dostoevsky consciously adopted the convicts' code: to live life according to one's own passions, to create one's own laws!   Thus, more than a quarter of a century before Nietzsche, Raskolnikov [the main character in Dostoevsky's novel *Crime and Punishment*] had already removed himself "beyond good and evil." . . .   "How is it," he [Dostoevsky] wondered, "that they seemed then, they still seem, right to have despised me, and why is it that against my will I feel so weak, so insignificant, so—how terrible to say it—*ordinary,* compared to them?"   For me too, or rather, for that other me of forty years ago, this infatuation for low places and shady young men was doubtless necessary.   Could I otherwise have torn these few images [Brassaï's photographs] from the strange Parisian nights of the thirties before they sank into nothingness? [40]

3
The Advantages
of Being Immoral:
Plato and the Ring
of Gyges

Scene: The Goad family's rumpus room. Father, Daughter, and Son.

Daughter: Dad, why did you sell the bonds Grandma gave me?

Father: I needed the money to buy a new car.

Daughter: But they were my bonds, not yours. I know I'm only a minor and that you had a legal right to sell them, but that still wasn't right!

Father: Well, you'll get to ride in the car, and you can drive it when you get your license.

Daughter: But the bonds were to help me go to college. I'd rather use them that way than put the money into your car. You haven't the right to tell me how to spend my money, especially if I'm not going to spend it foolishly.

Father: Look. You have responsibilities to the family, too. We're in tough shape right now. We need the car. It's selfish of you to save the bonds for your own education, when we all need the money. I didn't get to go to college, and believe me I'd have liked to, but I had to go to work instead and help out when my Dad got sick. Think of others for a change.

Daughter: *I'm* selfish? *You're* the selfish one! *My* money pays for *your* car! You're just mad because you didn't get to go to college, and you're taking it out on me.

Besides, why couldn't you have bought a used car that didn't cost so much? And borrowed the money? You've got a job. You wanted a new car and you didn't want to make payments, so you could spend the money on other things. You didn't want to cut down on your martini lunches or your new clothes, so you just took my bonds and sold them! It was selfish and wrong, and you know it.

Son: Yeah, Dad. Some example you are!

Father: Listen, kids, it's time you got a little more realistic about life. The first rule is "Take care of Number One." Everybody does it—that's the way of the world. The sooner you learn it, the better off you'll be. Do you expect me to be better than anyone else? You might as well learn it at home: everybody is out for himself first. There's no room for idealism if you're going to get ahead. Believe me, I see it every day at the office. Your wanting to go to college is just another example of "me first." And I'm not going to feel guilty for thinking of myself first, just because you want yourselves to come first and want me to put *you* first and *myself* second. Nosireeee!

Son: All I say, Dad, is that you should've gone to college and taken an ethics course.

3.1 The Ring of Gyges

In Plato's *The Republic* Thrasymachus claims that Socrates is naive and knows nothing of justice and right, or of the just and the righteous.

Thrasymachus divides persons into two classes, the rulers and ruled. The rulers are stronger than the ruled. Justice or right is "nothing else than the advantage of the stronger"[1] What goes under the name of justice is not an evenhanded distribution of deserved goods and ills, but rather whatever is to the interest of the rulers, even if to the disadvantage of the ruled.

Socrates challenges this "advantage of the stronger" definition of justice. Suppose the ruler thinks that raising taxes is to his interest and orders the ruled to pay higher taxes, and they do so. Can't a ruler make a mistake? Suppose it turns out that raising taxes is not to his advantage. Then the ruler will have done something not to the advantage of the stronger—namely, himself. But this contradicts Thrasymachus' definition of justice.

Thrasymachus' definition can be saved temporarily by distinguishing between what the ruler *thinks* is to his interest and what is *really* to his interest. Since the definition says that justice is what is really to his interest, obviously the ruler shouldn't decide such matters rashly, thoughtlessly, or arbitrarily. He has to *know*, not merely think, that something is to his interest. This knowledge requirement introduces the notion of good into the ruler's deliberations. An act is not to his advantage if it doesn't actually do him some good, so he must also *know* what is good. Because Thrasymachus' egoistic definition of justice hasn't said what the good is, it can't be a satisfactory definition of justice.

In a series of arguments, Socrates leads Thrasymachus to the conclusions that justice is excellence of the soul, and that only the just man will live happily. Because this notion of justice applies equally to the ruled and the rulers, the "advantage of the stronger" notion of justice should be given up.

Thrasymachus gives up, even though he started his challenge to Socrates confidently and with bombast. However, Glaucon and Adeimantus are not satisfied with Socrates' refutation of Thrasysmachus. They point out that Socrates seems to think justice is a good in itself. But they do not think most people believe this; rather, they are inclined to Thrasymachus' position that most people prefer to be unjust than to be just, because being unjust will benefit them more. Justice in itself is no reward and is valued little; people place more value on actions that benefit them than they do on acting justly toward others.

The story is told of a shepherd—the ancestor of Gyges, the king of Lydia—who had been in the service of a previous king of Lydia. The shepherd had once found a corpse with a gold ring on its finger in a chasm opened by an earthquake. He took the ring off the corpse and put it on his own finger. As he was sitting with others planning their herding report to the king, he twisted the ring on his finger and noticed that he became invisible to the others. He marveled at this, but he also schemed. Having arranged that he would carry their report to the king, by using the ring's power he "committed adultery with the king's wife, attacked the king with her help, killed him, and took over the kingdom."[2]

Glaucon then puts a proposition to Socrates that, he says, some think a "great proof that no one is just willingly. . . . Every man believes that injustice is much more profitable to himself than justice.'' The "great proof"is as follows:

> Now, if there were two such rings, one worn by the just man, the other by the unjust, no one, as these people [such as Thrasymachus] think, would be so incorruptible that he would stay on the path of justice or bring himself to keep away from other people's property and not touch it, when he could with impunity take whatever he wanted from the market, go into houses and have sexual relations with anyone he wanted, kill anyone, free all those he wished from prison, and do the other things which would make him like a god among men.[3]

Here we have a kind of thought experiment. We conceive a situation and then imagine the results. In the Gyges thought experiment, it is assumed that both persons know what is just, and that one person has been just in the past but that the other has not. According to this "great proof," the difference in their justness will disappear if each has a Gyges ring, because the invisibility offered by the ring will eliminate the only thing that caused the just man to be just: fear of detection and punishment. With possession of the ring, injustice will now be judged more profitable than justice. Conclusion: Everyone is selfish. Even those who appear to be just to others are not just for justice's sake. They conform to the rules of justice only because they fear punishment.

If the Gyges experiment is the "great proof" it claims to be, then Marin's summons to regain human community as a way of escaping overemphasis on self and egoism is hollow. It can't be an escape route because community and reciprocity require that we be concerned with the interests of others; if we find no profitability in others' welfare, but only in our own, the attainment of community is an impossible dream. What community we have must then be forced on us. If we don't act solely in our own interest at the expense of others, it is only because others are strong enough to punish us for neglecting their interests; this punishment is designed to make it unprofitable to be unjust. However, those who have a Gyges ring can escape detection and so avoid punishment; for them injustice is profitable, because they don't have to subtract from it the unprofitableness of punishment.

It appears that the appeal "to give up your obsession with self and turn toward community and reciprocity" is foredoomed, unless we can refute the proof of the Gyges Argument.

3.2 Analyzing the Gyges Argument

By setting out the "great proof" in the form of an argument, we can distinguish the various "thoughts" in this thought experiment; and by reflecting on them, we will flush out some unstated assumptions.

G1 What is profitable to us is whatever is in our self-interest.

G2 Persons will always do those acts that they judge to be in their self-interest, regardless of the interests of others.

G3 Seizing property, having sexual relations with anyone we want, killing whom we will, and so forth, are in our self-interest, provided that we are not caught and punished so severely that such acts are made unprofitable to us.

G4 We can get more of these satisfactions mentioned in G3 by acting unjustly than we can by acting justly.

G5 Therefore, acting unjustly is more profitable to us than acting justly.

Premiss G1 limits the profitability of our actions to what is profitable *to us,* what is in *our* self-interest. What then is in our self-interest—whatever is bad? That seems quite implausible, because normally we judge something to be in our self-interest if and only if we believe it is good for us. Consequently, we should add this assumption to the explicit premisses of the Gyges Argument:

G1.1 An act is in our self-interest if and only if it has good consequences for us.

Premisses G2 and G3 are linked. G2—that persons will always do what they think is in their self-interest—is asserted to be true, but how do we know it to be true? G3 lists acts that a self-interested person would perform; G3's truth is supposed to support the truth of G2.

The thought experiment centers here on G2 and G3. We are asked to imagine what persons will do if they have a Gyges ring; what we imagine derives from what we think they will think is in their self-interest. G3 gives examples of acts that Glaucon says the Gyges ring wearers will think to be in their self-interest; they will rob, rape, mug, pillage, kill, and free all whom they wish from prisons, because they think that these unjust acts are in their self-interest, that they are more "profitable" than just ones.

It is important to the thought experiment that you seriously project situations in which all social and legal restraints are removed. We are not often in such situations, nor do we often allow ourselves to imagine them. The advocates of the Gyges Argument invite us to dare to look at the underbelly of humanity, at the side that appears boldly only in lawless situations.

To help us get into the mood of the Gyges Argument and stimulate our imagination, let's consider some contemporary situations and note how humans have acted in them.

The United States has had to curtail its use of natural resources; oil, for example, has become more expensive, and our balance of payments will be

"Was everything always crooked?"

unfavorable if we don't restrain our use of it. But will citizens restrain their use voluntarily? Will they put the interests of the United States before their own? Congressmen Henry Ruess and Mike McCormack don't think they will; compulsory conservation will be needed, they claimed in a TV appearance. Unrestrained oil consumption seems to bear out their judgment.

Garrett Hardin, in his article "The Tragedy of the Commons," advocates fewer children as the only way for the human race to survive. But, he remarks, "the social arrangements that produce responsibility are arrangements that create coercion [enforcement], of some sort." He adds: "It is a mistake to think that we can control the breeding of mankind in the long run by an appeal to conscience."[4] Without coercion, people will put their sexual desires first. The world's growing population seems to confirm this.

When the South Vietnamese were in the last stages of defeat, the breakdown of social order and authority indeed produced killings, as Glaucon suggested. A journalist reported: "Soldiers armed with M-16s stood by the roadside and sprayed the riders of passing motorcycles. Kicking aside the bodies, they mounted the Hondas—often meeting the same fate after a few miles." And on an overloaded plane: "The air force men, massed in the front of the plane, then rushed on the soldiers and hurled almost a hundred off the rear cargo ramp at an altitude of from 3000 to 4000 feet. That plane reached Bien Hoa safely."[5]

Susan Brownmiller, in her book *Against Our Will: Men, Women, and Rape,* notes that when the rules of civilization have been suspended, men have raped women *en masse;* this is a historical fact. [6]

Conflict-of-interest laws are required in order to restrain office holders from acting in their own interest. A 1938 court opinion says: "The purpose

of conflict of interest statutes is to remove all indirect influence of an in-   **75**
terested officer, so that nothing will prevent that officer from exercising absolute loyalty and undivided allegiance to the best interests of the government
which the officer serves.'' [7] Were Glaucon to comment on conflict-of-
interest laws, we can imagine him saying, ''You wouldn't need such laws, if
public officials didn't put their self-interest ahead of the public interest.''

These examples of human selfishness give credibility to the G2 and G3
premises of the Gyges Argument. That these premises were widely accepted
by Greek citizens 2,500 years ago, and that we find examples to support them
even today, prompts one to think that humans haven't changed in twenty-five
centuries—indeed, that you *can't* change human nature. Some such thought
underlies the conviction of many of us that humans pursue their self-interest
exclusively.

We can state this point about human nature as an additional assumption
underlying the Gyges Argument:

G2.1 It is human nature to pursue one's self-interest.

But suppose someone objects to this wholesale lumping of human actions under the motivation of self-interest. They might claim that from a
sampling of *some* people's behavior, we can't legitimately infer that *all* human
actions exhibit an egoistic character; these selfish examples just cited aren't
the rule, but the exception.

This objection based on exceptions to the rule can't be sustained,
however, if G2.1 is true. This human nature we have is common to all and
unchanging. We can't any more get rid of or act against this nature than we
can live without eating. Does water always run downhill? Of course it
does—because of its nature. Do humans act out of self-interest? Of course
we do—because of our nature.

Consider G3 by itself now. It lists the acts that persons can be expected
to perform if they had a Gyges ring. The contemporary examples we gave
were tied to that list. But we can ask two questions about the list: (1) Why
should those acts be on the list, and (2) are there other acts that could be
added?

To answer these related questions, we need a principle that allows us to
select instances of acts that are in our self-interest. Should giving away our
worldly goods be on the list? Or sacrificing our life so that others might live,
or denying ourselves pleasure to prevent pain in others? How can we decide
whether or not these acts are in our self-interest?

As later sections will demonstrate, this is a difficult matter. Just asking
the question arouses doubt about the Gyges Argument. But our task here is
to bring to the surface the thoughts that lend the argument its persuasiveness.
Much of its persuasiveness, I think, rests on connecting self-interest to a person's wants, needs, desires, satisfactions, and drives; ''interest'' is a general
term covering these related but different biological and psychological human

76 aspects. In G2.1 I brought in the idea of human nature. Human nature is often conceived in terms of biological instincts and psychological drives; thus wants, needs, desires, and so forth are aspects of human nature. Humans want and need sex, food, and security; they have aggressive drives and possessive instincts; they respond positively to pleasure rather than to pain; and they derive satisfactions from sex, food, power, and so forth.

Using the word "want" for the other psychological and biological terms, we can state the following additional assumption of the Gyges Argument:

> G3.1 The acts we list as in our self-interest are acts that will secure us the things (sex, property, pleasure, food, etc.) that we want.

Turning to premiss G4, we should notice that it assumes that a Gyges ring wearer knows the difference between just and unjust acts. The relativity or objectivity of justice is not at issue here, only the relative profitableness of justice and injustice. The ring wearer knows what actions he or she ought to perform. The advocate of the Gyges Argument believes that just actions may not be the same as actions motivated by wants (instincts and drives).

Premiss G4 is a straightforward empirical claim that we can get more of what we want by doing what we ought not to do than by doing what we ought to do; we can get more of what we want by not obeying moral rules and laws than by obeying them.

Collecting the additional assumptions we have brought to the surface, we can state a fuller version of the Gyges Argument.

Gyges Argument: Second Version

G1   What is profitable to us is whatever is in our self-interest.

G1.1 An act is in our self-interest if and only if it has good consequences for us.

G2   Persons will always do those acts that they judge to be in their self-interest, regardless of the interests of others.

G2.1 It is human nature to pursue one's self-interest.

G3   Seizing property, having sexual relations with anyone we want, killing whom we will, and so forth are in our self-interest.

G3.1 The acts we list as in our self-interest (as in G3) are acts that will secure us the things (sex, property, pleasure, food, etc.) that we want.

G4   We can get more of these satisfactions by acting unjustly than we can by acting justly (than by obeying moral rules and laws).

G5   Therefore, acting unjustly is more profitable to us than acting justly.

3.3 Psychological and Ethical Egoism   77

Peter Marin (section 2.7) deplores both the idolatry of the state, which produces Ivan Ilyiches who ape their superiors, and the idolatry of the self, which celebrates egoism. Neither of these idolatries is desirable, according to Marin. He suggested that we can avoid these two unacceptable alternatives by trying to recover human community. But if the Gyges Argument is sound, Marin's proposal is futile: community requires acting in one another's interest, not only in our own; but since it is human nature to act only in our own interest, community cannot be achieved.

We can sharpen the issue here by using a traditional distinction between ethical and psychological egoism. Ethical egoism can be formulated as a principle that organizes the egoist's life. There is a strong and a weak version of it.

Strong: At all times each person *ought* to perform those acts that he or she thinks are in his or her self-interest.

Weak: At all times each person has a *right* to perform those acts that he or she thinks are in his or her self-interest.

Part of Marin's proposal urging us to recover community and reciprocity can be restated as a principle that I will call ethical altruism:

Sometimes a person ought to perform an act that is not in his or her self-interest, because it is in the interest of others.

It would be inconsistent to adopt both strong ethical egoism and ethical altruism, because the latter is a denial of the former. If you are convinced that ethical altruism is the morally sound principle to adopt, then to be consistent, you have to give up strong ethical egoism.

Ethical egoism is concerned with our obligations or rights, whereas psychological egoism is concerned with how we in fact act or are impelled to act. That these are different concerns is shown by our guilty awareness that on some occasions we have in fact performed actions that we know we shouldn't have, or have failed to perform actions that we know we should have. We can state a strong and a weak version of psychological egoism.

Strong: At all times, each person is *impelled* to (cannot do otherwise than) perform those acts that he or she thinks are in his or her self-interest.

Weak: At all times, although not impelled to, each person does *in fact* perform those acts that he or she thinks are in his or her self-interest.

The latter claim is weaker than the first, because it allows the possibility that a person could deliberately act against his or her self-interest—a possibility that the strong version excludes.

Strong psychological egoism, it has been maintained, makes the attainment of Marin's ethical altruism impossible. The argument can go like this.

(1) Ought implies Can; one cannot reasonably impose an obligation to perform an action on a person unless the person can do the act. For example, we can't reasonably oblige a poor person to give two million dollars to charity.
(2) Suppose that this second premiss is the strong version of psychological egoism.
(3) Suppose that this third premiss is the principle of ethical altruism.
(4) But if strong psychological egoism is true (premiss 2), then ethical altruism (premiss 3) places an obligation on us that we cannot perform. Ethical altruism says we ought to act against what we think is our self-interest, which strong psychological egoism says we can't do.
(5) Therefore, since "Ought implies Can," it is unreasonable to place us under the obligation of ethical altruism. Marin's advocacy of community and reciprocity has to be rejected since it places an unreasonable, because impossible, obligation on us.

The Gyges Argument relies on strong psychological egoism, which must be shown to be false before we can take Marin's middle way between ordinariness and egoism.

We can appreciate psychological egoism's importance in the Gyges Argument by reminding ourselves that its G2.1 premiss states that it is human nature to pursue one's self-interest. Advocates of the Gyges Argument characterize human nature in terms of psychological drives and biological instincts; these drives and instincts are the motivations for our actions, they cause them. A cause necessitates its effect; thus our motivations—our drives and instincts—*force* us to perform the acts we do because those acts are the effects of the strongest motive operating on us at the time. The rapist raped because his hate of women was the strongest drive operating at that time; he "couldn't help himself."

3.4 Those Who Doubt Our Altruism

Before we proceed to the next sections, in which I outline Plato's refutation of the Gyges Argument, it would be useful to remind ourselves of the enormous role that psychological egoism plays in some of the world's major thought systems.

Christianity, Buddhism, and Hinduism all have emphasized what a terrible place the world is—full of misery, evil, suffering, broken promises, distress, smashed hopes, and so forth. All these misfortunes stem, these

religions claim, from human nature, primarily bodily nature: we seek to **79**
gratify our bodily needs and desires, we are psychological egoists.

Here is St. Paul in his letter to the Romans:

> For we know that the Law is spiritual: but I am fleshly, sold under sin's
> control: for I do not understand what I am doing. I do not do what I want
> to do [the good] but what I hate to do [the bad]. Now if I do what I do
> not want to do, I agree that the Law is good. However, I am no longer the
> one who does the deed, but sin which is at home in me does it. For I know
> that within me, that is, within my flesh, what is good is not at home. [8]

Here we have the source of the doctrine of original sin. We cannot help but
sin; we cannot by our own effort overcome our evil nature. Instead, our
salvation depends on the Grace of God. Only in heaven will we be freed from
sin, because there we will be free from our bodily nature; the source of our
egoism will have been destroyed with the death of our body.

The following remarks from the *Maha Yoga* show that distress due to
psychological egoism can be escaped only by transcending the transmigratory
round of normal lives.

> When the seeker has persisted long enough in the Quest, . . . the mind
> becomes reduced to the state of pure Consciousness and begins to shine
> steadily in its pure form, as the formless "I"; the Sage calls this formless
> Consciousness the "I am I," to distinguish it from the ego-sense which has
> the form of "I am this (body)"; that implies the cessation of the ego-form;
> the finite ego is swallowed up by the infinite Self; with the finite ego are
> lost all the imperfections and limitations which beset life; desire and fear
> are at an end, as well as sin and accountability. The real Self was never
> subject to these; they belong to the ego and do not survive the ego. In the
> Egoless State the Self abides in Its own glory. [9]

According to Christian and Hindu theories, we are composed of two
parts—body, and soul or spirit. Psychological egoism is true of humans with
respect to both parts, although Christianity tends to stress our preoccupation
with bodily desires. Pessimistic Christianity offers no hope that our spirit
part can curb the bodily part; we are forever sunk in sin and stand in need of
the Grace of God. Optimistic Hinduism holds out the possibility that with
sufficient discipline, however hard to achieve, our spiritual part can transcend
our bodily part and the ego consciousness that we have when the soul is
housed in a body; this may take many lives—the transmigration of our soul
into a succession of bodies—but union with egoless consciousness is eventually attainable.

Buddhism, in contrast with Christianity, denies the existence of the self;
the self is an illusion, there is no ego. Buddhists try to prove this by a series
of philosophical arguments. However, practically speaking, the self is a
powerful illusion. We may grant intellectually that the self does not exist, but
as long as we experience craving or find delight in satisfying it, as long as we

experience lust and passion, we have not put the no-self doctrine into practice. A Buddhist attempts to live selflessly, in accord with his doctrine; when he succeeds in doing so, he has reached a state of nirvana in which the normal ego-self, and with it psychological egoism, vanish.

Heinrich Zimmer examines the idea of a Bodhisattva in the Mahayan tradition of Buddhism. A Bodhisattva is one who has reached enlightenment. He is one of "those sublimely indifferent, compassionate beings who remain at the threshold of nirvana for the comfort and salvation of the world." [10] By not going over the brink into nirvana, even though they have transcended the ego and its self-interested drives and instincts, Bodhisattvas can play the role of a savior; their vow not to enter nirvana helps redeem the world; their efforts thereafter are "devoted to the universal, instead of the individual benefit." [11]

> During eons, the Bodhisattva-in-the-making progressed along a sublime path of the most especial, most highly refined psychological austerities, cancelling always every notion and emotion of the ego. And this is what brought him into possession of that inexhaustible "treasury" of virtues which, in the end, as a result of his supreme act of timeless renunciation [of nirvana], became available forever to every suffering, striving creature in the world. [12]

The lure of psychological egoism is powerful; it has always gripped the belief systems of an enormous number of people. The desire to escape its hold is almost as pervasive; it stimulated the creators of Christianity, Hinduism, and Buddhism to fashion their different escape routes. Christianity emphasizes release by the Grace of God; Hinduism, release by the transcending of the psychological self; and Buddhism, release by the intellectual and practical denial of the self's existence. As we shall see in the next sections, Plato has still a different analysis and solution.

3.5 Self-Interest and the Good

Caught between Ivan Ilyich's ordinariness and Nietzsche's egoistic cure for it, we are advised by Marin to avoid both by returning to community and reciprocity. This return is more easily advocated than accomplished, however, as Glaucon tried to show in his Gyges thought experiment. Acknowledging that the Gyges Argument has a plausibility and is widely accepted, we looked at it more carefully; we analyzed it to reveal some of its hidden assumptions, thinking that these would help us to understand its plausibility. This gave us the second version of the Argument, which we can use in interpreting Plato's attack on it. That attack removes the Argument as an obstacle to the recovery of community and reciprocity. Uncovering the shortcomings of the Gyges Argument will also help us discover that self-realization need not be egoistic, and consequently that self-realization and the recovery of community and reciprocity may go hand in hand.

Plato, in his attack on the Gyges Argument, does not reject the egoistic proposition that persons act in their self-interest. The gist of his attack is that persons do not always know what is in their self-interest; by reflecting on what is really in their self-interest, they will realize why acting justly promotes their self-interest and so profits them more than injustice. Even with a Gyges ring, a person gains more from being just than unjust; unjust persons who escape punishment because their injustice goes undetected cannot escape other consequences whose unprofitability will exceed their profitability. Plato's attack describes these "other consequences."

In the dialogue *Protagoras* Socrates says: "No man voluntarily pursues evil, or that which he thinks to be evil. To prefer evil to good is not in human nature; and when a man is compelled to choose one of two evils, no one will choose the greater when he may have the less." [13] We can deduce Socrates' claim from premises in our second version of the Gyges Argument (p. 76).

G2.1 It is human nature to pursue one's self-interest. (The egoistic proposition.)

G1.1 An act is in our self-interest if and only if it has good consequences for us.

G2.1 Therefore, it is human nature to pursue what has good consequences for us. That is, we do not voluntarily pursue what has evil consequences for us; or if we are compelled to choose between two evils, we do not voluntarily pursue the worse of the two.

Socrates also maintains in *Protagoras* that "no wise man, as I believe, will allow that any human being errs voluntarily, or voluntarily does evil and dishonorable actions; but they are very well aware that all who do evil and dishonorable things do them against their will." [14] This is a strong claim and certainly runs counter to the Gyges Argument. What would lead Socrates to make such a claim in the face of so much apparently contrary evidence? He was as acquainted as we are with the barbarism of tyrants who kill, rob, persecute, and so forth.

Such things occur even in republics such as ours, as revelations about FBI activities have shown. The late Senator Philip Hart noted that black activists, women's liberationists, antiwar leaders, and people wrongly suspected of being Communists were persecuted by the FBI. "FBI documents, Hart pointed out, indicated that such people were subjected to efforts to break up their marriages, force them out of their jobs, smear them in the eyes of parents and teachers, and, in some cases, perhaps even to kill one another." [15]

In *Gorgias,* Plato has Socrates address these kinds of facts head on. The argument cuts against G3 of the Gyges Argument, that "seizing property,

82   having sexual relations with anyone we want, killing whom we will, and so forth, are in our self-interest.'' If Socrates' argument is sound, he shows that, even if we go unpunished for these acts, they are to no one's interest; in fact, going unpunished only increases the unprofitability of doing injustice. Socrates and Polus are participants in the dialogue; Polus is an admirer of Gorgias and takes over the dialogue from him.

> Socrates: Do men appear to you to will that which they do, or to will that further end for the sake of which they do the thing? When they take medicine, for example, at the bidding of a physician, do they will the drinking of the medicine which is painful, or the health for the sake of which they drink? Polus: Clearly, the health.

> Socrates: And when we kill a man we kill him, or exile him or despoil him of his goods, because, as we think, it will conduce to our good? . . . Men who do these things do them for the sake of the good? Polus: Yes.

> Socrates: Then we do not will simply to kill a man or to exile him or to despoil him of his goods, but we will to do that which conduces to our good, and if the act is not conducive to our good we do not will it; for we will, as you say, that which is our good, but that which is neither good nor evil, or simply evil, we do not will. . . . Polus: You are right.

> Socrates: Hence we may infer, that if any one . . . kills another or exiles another or deprives him of his property, under the idea that the act is for his own interests *when really not for his own interests* [emphasis added], he may be said to do what seems best to him? Polus: Yes.

> Socrates: But does he do what he wills if he does what is evil? . . . Polus: Well, I suppose not. . . . At any rate you will allow that he who is unjustly put to death is wretched, and to be pitied?

> Socrates: Not so much, Polus, as he who kills him. . . . Polus: How can that be, Socrates?

> Socrates: That may very well be, inasmuch as doing injustice is the greatest of evils. Polus: But is it the greatest? Is not suffering injustice a greater evil? Socrates: Certainly not.

> Socrates: . . . Do we not acknowledge that the things of which we were speaking, the infliction of death, and exile, and the deprivation of property are sometimes a good and sometimes not a good? [They are not a good when one is punished for them.] Polus: Certainly.

> Socrates: Tell me, then, when do you say that they are good and when that they are evil—what principle do you lay down? Polus: I would rather, Socrates, that you should answer as well as ask that question.

> Socrates: Well, . . . I say that they are good when they are just, and evil when they are unjust. . . . Yes, indeed, Polus, that is my doctrine; the men and women who are gentle and good are also happy, as I maintain, and the unjust and evil are miserable. . . . In my opinion, Polus, the unjust or doer of unjust actions is miserable in any case—more miserable, however, if he be not punished and does not meet retribution, and less miserable if

he be punished and meets with retribution at the hands of gods and men. **83**
Polus: You are maintaining a strange doctrine, Socrates.

Socrates: For I certainly think that I and you and every man do really believe, that to do is a greater evil than to suffer injustice: and not to be punished than to be punished. Polus: And I should say neither I, nor any man: would you yourself, for example, suffer rather than do injustice?

Socrates: Yes, and you, too; I or any man would. Polus: Quite the reverse; neither you, nor I, nor any man.

Socrates: You would say that to suffer punishment is another name for being justly corrected when you do wrong? Polus: I should.

Socrates: And would you not allow that all just things are honorable in so far as they are just? Polus: Yes.

Socrates: Then the punisher does what is honorable, and the punished suffers what is honorable? Polus: True.

Socrates: And if what is honorable, then what is good, for the honorable is either pleasant or useful? Polus: Certainly.

Socrates: Then he who is punished suffers what is good? [Since the good is what is in our self-interest, we may conclude that it is in our self-interest to be punished for our injustices.] Polus: That is true.

Socrates: Then he is benefited? Polus: Yes.

Socrates: Do I understand you to mean what I mean by the term "benefited"? I mean, that if he be justly punished his soul is improved? Polus: Surely.

Socrates: Then he who is punished is delivered from the evil of his soul? Polus: Yes.

[Socrates then talks about a person's estate, body, and mind, each of which has its respective evils: poverty, disease, and injustice. The art of making money frees us from poverty; the art of medicine frees us from disease; and judges who rightly punish others free us from injustice.]

Socrates: And suppose the case of two persons who have some evil in their bodies, and that one of them is healed and delivered from evil, and another is not healed, but retains evil—which of them is the most miserable? Polus: Clearly he who is not healed.

Socrates: And was not punishment said by us to be a deliverance from the greatest of evils, which is vice? Polus: True.

Socrates: Then he lives worst, who, having been unjust, has no deliverance from injustice? Polus: Certainly.

Socrates: That is, he lives worst who commits the greatest crimes, and who, being the most unjust of men, succeeds in escaping rebuke or correction or punishment. [16]

In summary, since only the good is to our self-interest, Socrates leads Polus to consider the consequences of injustice. Those consequences include disease of the soul, which causes us to be miserable and whose only cure is punishment. Now, having a miserable soul is not profitable, nor is escaping punishment. Having a happy soul is more profitable than being miserable; only the just are happy; therefore it is more profitable to be just than unjust, and more profitable as well to be just than unjust and unpunished. We conclude that it is in our self-interest to be just.

You might be unconvinced by this argument, thinking it a bit of trickery. While the argument seems to hang together, you might think it leads to such an unbelievable conclusion that something must be wrong with it, even though you can't put your finger on it. Polus may look to you like a straight man.

Certainly Socrates makes some fast moves. He goes from punishment being a just corrective to just things being honorable, then to honorable things being a good, then to their being a good because useful. Next he goes from things being useful to their being beneficial, and from the benefit of having our soul improved to that of being delivered of an evil soul and being saved from the misery of being unjust. This series of moves seems to leave out or ignore the fact that a tyrant, for example, may want the things obtained by injustice more than he or she wants a healthy soul. By proper hardening, one grows used to being cruel, vindictive, brutish, and suspicious. These cease to bother us humans after a while, just as the sight of blood, internal organs, and a precariously beating heart no longer bother the seasoned surgeon as they once did when as a medical student he first encountered them. Guilt no longer plagues or disrupts the tyrant's soul after repeated exposure, any more than blood repulses the surgeon.

Socrates' argument may not convince you because you think he fails to deal with humans as they really are—unlike Glaucon, who is realistic. One may concede that having a healthy, serene soul, a clear conscience, and happiness uncontaminated by guilt are things that everybody wants. But they are not wanted as much as power, fame, and piles of money and what it can buy: sharp clothes, entertainment, travel, new cars, expensive presents, and so forth—none of which can be had in this competitive world without being corrupted a little or a lot. So here we are, back at the idea of human nature. Are human wants of the kind listed in the Gyges Argument more or less powerful than those Socrates talks about? The Gyges Argument still has its appeal if premisses G3, G3.1, and G4 carry the day.

3.6 Wants and Goods

Plato knew that the argument in *Gorgias* needed strengthening; in *The Republic* he expanded his analysis of human nature. To set the stage for its contribution to our topic, let us set forth again one of Socrates' distinctions in *Gorgias* that is often ignored by advocates of the Gyges Argument.

> Socrates: Hence we may infer, that if any one . . . kills another or exiles another or deprives him of his property, under the idea that the act is for his own interests *when really not for his own interests* [emphasis added], he may be said to do what seems best to him? Polus: Yes.

> Socrates: But does he do what he wills [that is, what is in his interest] if he does what is evil [that is, what is not in his interest]? Polus: Well, I suppose not. [17]

This is an important part of the *Gorgias* argument because it breaks the link between wants and goods, a link on which the power of the Gyges Argument depends.   Remember that we are using "wants" for wants, desires, likes, needs, and satisfactions.   We have the following links in the Gyges Argument:

$$
\begin{array}{ccccccc}
& \text{Link 1} & & \text{Link 2} & & \text{Link 3} & \\
\text{WANTS} & \rightarrow & \text{GOODS} & \rightarrow & \text{ENDS} & \rightarrow & \text{ACTS}
\end{array}
$$

Link 1: Between wants and goods (money, fame, power, pleasure, food, sex).

Link 2: Between these goods and the ends that are judged to be in our self-interest.

Link 3: Between our ends and the acts that we think will obtain these ends.

When we are deciding what to do, the egoist point of view advises us to go through the links: Apprehend a want; this will determine a good; a good is something in our self-interest; a self-interested good is an end for which we should figure out a means to obtain it.   Thus the rapist wants to dominate another; this want determines that exercising physical power over a woman is a self-interested good, and so the rapist's end; taking some woman against her will and (since he has no Gyges ring) having her where he is not likely to be detected will obtain the good.   The deed is done.   The monstrousness of the Gyges Argument is now pitted squarely against Socrates' "impossible dream."   The Gyges Argument's monstrousness probably is as repugnant to you as Socrates' counterargument is implausible.

The plot thickens; we want now to find out not only what Socrates' argument lacks, so that we find it implausible even while applauding it, but also what the Gyges Argument contains, so that we find it plausible even while abhorring it.

Consider the following two statements:

(1) X is what I want.
(2) X is not in my interest.

These two statements are not contradictory; they may both be true.   I

86 may want sausage before breakfast, but after breakfast, because the sausage was spoiled and made me ill, I realize that eating it was not in my interest. Two such truths make it possible to say I "made a mistake." Socrates calls Polus' attention to this when he points out that what a tyrant thinks is in his interest may not *really* be in his interest. Even tyrants can make mistakes. Appearance and reality are two different things: wants give us the appearance of goods, while further experience and reflection give us the reality of goods. This contrast justifies our talking about "making a mistake."

This opens a crack in Link 1—the link between wants and goods, upon which the Gyges Argument's persuasiveness depends. We can widen this crack into a break.

Link 1: If my wants, alone and always, determine my goods, then whatever I want is a good. (Gyges advocate)

Against Link 1: But if what I want is sometimes not in my interest (we can make mistakes), and if only a good is in my interest, then sometimes what I want is not a good. (Socrates)

These two pieces of reasoning have produced a contradiction. "Whatever I want is a good" contradicts and is contradicted by "Sometimes what I want is not a good." These statements cannot both be true; we have to choose one of them. But which one should we choose? The choice becomes clearer if we set out the arguments still more explicitly.

Argument A: (A1) X is what I want.
           (A2) Want, alone and always, determines a good. (Link 1)

           (A3) Therefore, whenever X is wanted, X is a good.

Argument B: (A1) X is what I want.
           (B1) X is sometimes not in my interest.

           (B2) What I want is sometimes not in my interest.

Argument C: (C1) Something is in my interest if and only if it is a good.
           (B2) What I want is sometimes not in my interest.

           (C2) What I want is sometimes not a good.

Socrates' refutation of the Gyges Argument, Argument A, concentrates on showing that Link 1, premiss (A2), is false. His strategy is quite simple. If he can show that this premiss validly leads to a false conclusion, then the premiss has to be false. Let's see how he does this.

First, Argument A's conclusion is contradicted by Argument C's conclusion. Arguments B and C are Socrates' connected arguments. Second, if

Socrates' conclusion is true, then, because it contradicts the Gyges conclusion, **87**
(A3), the Gyges advocate holds a false conclusion. Third, because the Gyges
Argument is valid, we have to conclude that one of its premisses—either (A1)
or (A2)—is false. Fourth, obviously Socrates doesn't think it's (A1), because
he too used it to derive a true conclusion; therefore, (A2) must be the false
premiss.

Of course Socrates' refutation isn't successful unless all the premisses in
his arguments, B and C, are true. Are they true? Let's see. If you admit
that sometimes you err about something being in your interest, as surely you
must, then you have to admit the truth of (B1). That commits you to the
truth of the conclusion of Socrates' first argument, B. Since that conclusion,
(B2), is a premiss in his next argument, C, the only premiss left to deal with is
(C1), ''Something is in my interest if and only if it is a good.'' This seems obviously true: as Socrates says, no one willingly chooses an evil for himself; we
all aim at goods, not evils.

Therefore Link 1 must be false. The truth of the matter is that wants do
not alone and always determine goods. They are not a wholly reliable guide
to what things are goods.

We have now run to ground what makes the Gyges Argument plausible
and abhorrent. Uncritical acceptance of the belief that wants, alone and
always, determine goods gives it plausibility, and this same belief also makes it
abhorrent because, if we accept it, we have no way to stop a rapist's line of
reasoning.

3.7 Goods and the Good

Now we want to account for the implausibility of Socrates' *Gorgias*
argument. To do this, I identify and make explicit a distinction that, if unnoticed (as it often is), sustains an uncritical belief in the link between wants
and goods.

You may have noticed that, in the discussion about wants, I used the
term ''goods'' or ''a good'' rather than ''the good.'' This was deliberate.
The pleasure of a good taste, the satisfaction of being appreciated for a good
deed, the achievement of getting a college degree, having a satisfying job, a re-
quited love, and so forth, may all be goods, and each of them may be a
good. We also speak of more general goods such as pleasure, satisfaction,
gratification, and fulfillment; these are more general, not being tied to particular occasions of pleasure or to particular objects of wants, drives, or
needs.

The things involved in our pleasures, satisfactions, and fulfillments vary
widely; they may be objects such as ice cream, a situation such as a job, an
event such as a graduation, or an emotion such as another's love. We speak
of these things also as goods, each of them being a good.

The phrase "the good" is an English language device with which we might start a sentence like "The good is . . . "—a sentence that we expect to complete with some identifying characteristics. The American logician C. H. Langford has pointed out that such phrases exemplify the "institutional use" of the word "the." We speak of "the horse," "the watch," or "the dictionary." "The horse is . . ." is completed by identifying characteristics such as "a four-legged, herbivorous, solid-hooved animal." "The watch is a mechanical device for keeping time" and "The dictionary is a word list with definitions and/or uses given for each entry" are sentences exhibiting the institutional use of "the." (Not every use of "the" is institutional, however. For example, "The horse is in the barn" is not; here "the" is a definite article used to pick out a particular animal.)

This institutional use of "the" preceding other words such as "horse," "watch," "dictionary," and "good" makes us treat these words as general terms. Thus there are race horses and draft horses, old horses and young horses, wild horses and tame horses, but in the institutional use of "the horse is . . ." we disregard these distinctions; we retain only those features that apply to all horses. They are characteristics we use to distinguish horses from non-horses. If we know how to complete "The horse is . . ." we will be able to say correctly, "This is *a* horse" and "That is *a* horse." Similarly, if we know how to complete "The good is . . ." we will know when to say "This is *a* good" and "That is *a* good"; we will know when to say that "pleasure is *a* good" and "gratification is *a* good."

Also, "the" may be used to particularize—to designate a particular person or thing. This comes from the use of "the" in definite descriptions, which is not institutional. "The" is a definite article, while "a" and "an" are indefinite articles. If I see a group of workers and want to say something about one and only one of them, I use a definite description because I intend it to apply to one and only one. Thus if among the workers there is one and only one with a checkered cap, I can say, "*The* one with the checkered cap is the one I want you to fire." "The one with the checkered cap" is the definite description.

The institutional use of "the" particularizes not an individual but a *class* of individuals. Thus "The horse is . . ." is completed by a phrase intended to identify the entire class of horses, but nothing else. Similarly, "The good is . . ." is completed by a phrase intended to identify the entire class of goods. Individual horses and goods are members of the class designated by "the horse" and "the good."

We can get sub-classes particularized by being more specific. For example, "The *race* horse is . . ." and "The *moral* good is . . . ." There are non-moral goods as well as the moral goods (and evils) that are our main interest here, but Socrates' argument applies to both kinds.

Now to pick out horses and goods, we have to have concepts in mind. Concepts are expressed by whatever we think completes "The horse is . . ." and "The (moral) good is . . .," etc.; thus the concept we have in mind when picking out horses is expressed by "a four-legged, herbivorous, solid-hooved animal."

Right now you may want to ask: What completes "The moral good **89** is . . ."?—which is the same as asking, "What is the moral good?" This, of course, is a central question in moral theory. I will give several philosophers' answers to this question in succeeding chapters. For our present purpose of accounting for the implausibility of Socrates' argument in *Gorgias,* we need only note that there is a distinction between "goods" and "the good," indicate how Plato asks us to think about it, and explain why the neglect of this distinction accounts for the apparent implausibility of the argument.

In summary, "goods" is a plural term that refers to such items as particular pleasures, achievements, and satisfactions, and to such general goods as pleasure, achievement, and satisfaction; "a good" is a term used to refer to some individual good or other; "the good" refers to the *class* of goods. To form this class and pick out individual goods, we have to have a *concept* of the good. If there is a single class answering to "the good," there must be a single concept of the good.

3.8 Why We Need the Concept of the Good

In this section I will state several reasons why we cannot do without the concept of the good. Basically, we need it to account for our ability to make certain kinds of judgments that we all make all the time.

First, let us deal with "goods." Saying that there are goods commits us to believing that, if we knew enough, we could give a list of goods on demand. What goes on the list? This question came up in section 3.2, when I asked the Gyges advocate how one would know which acts to list as being in our self-interest. Unless we have some concept of the good, we won't know whether something belongs on the list of goods or not.

It is easy to think that we don't need the concept of the good because, even without it, we can all give a pretty fair list of goods. However, our lists may be a mere mimicking of lists we heard our elders give when we were children; if so, you and I may have memorized different lists, and therefore will disagree about whether or not something is a good. For example, suppose fame is on your list but not on mine. Is it a good or not? Without some conception of the good, we have no way of beginning, carrying on, or concluding a discussion about fame's goodness. Armed only with a memory list, in the face of disagreement we either stand mute or merely repeat the list, neither of which responses is the least enlightening.

Actually, everybody has something to say by way of judgment about the goodness of something. They do not stand mute nor merely parrot what they've heard somewhere else. We can illustrate this with some answers received by the *San Francisco Chronicle*'s Question Man when he asked, "Would you rather be rich or smart?" [18] Here, of course, the question concerns the relative goodness of intelligence and money, but the young people who answer don't merely repeat what they've heard about which is better;

they give reasons. They could do so only because they have some conception of the good. Even an inadequate conception frees us from mere mimicry.

One answers: "Rich. Definitely rich. You could always go hire somebody smart to figure things out for you. If you're smart and you don't have any money, where are you? You're nowhere." Another answers: "Smart, of course. Intelligence you have forever. It grows. It increases. You don't have to worry about losing it. Intelligence would make your life much more fulfilled." A third replies: "Rich, because you get to travel and have a lot of clothes and don't have to be always worrying about money. It doesn't matter to me if I'm smart or not."

Each of these persons gives a reason or reasons for his or her preference. To do this, they have to have something in mind. What they have in mind, although perhaps not explicitly or adequately, is a concept of the good.

This argument for the need of a concept of the good might be countered by claiming we can construct a list by consulting our wants. We know what our wants are; our wants determine our goods; therefore we have a way of knowing what the list of goods is without copying others.

This argument has a premiss, "Our wants determine our goods," which was Link 1 in the Gyges assumptions; but this has already been shown to be false (pp. 86–87). The fact that we make mistakes shows that our wants do not always determine a good. Now we can't know we have made a mistake, if we don't have some idea of the good over and above the supposed goodness conferred by the want.

It might be replied that unless there were wants—pleasures, satisfactions, felt needs, desires, achievements, and so forth—there would be no goods. In a world in which there were no creatures with wants, there would be no goods. Therefore there is an important link between wants and goods.

We may concede this point. However, it only shows that wants are a necessary factor in determining goods; but it doesn't show they are sufficient. If they were sufficient, there would be no basis for acknowledging that we make mistakes. Wants determine goods at first glance only; what is wanted needs further evaluation. We have to consider the long run, not just the immediate circumstance of having a want. John Dewey puts this forcefully in *Human Nature and Conduct*. He links self-deception with mistakes, using the example of an angry child who initially confuses a short-run with a long-run good; later the child makes a more accurate long-run judgment. To do this, it must have some conception of the good over and above the immediate experience.

> Most so-called self-deception is due to employing immediate organic [bodily] states as criteria of the value of an act. To say that it feels good or yields direct satisfaction is to say that it gives rise to a comfortable internal state. The judgment based upon this experience may be entirely different from the judgment passed by others upon the basis of its objective or social consequences. As a matter of even the most rudimentary precaution,

therefore, every person learns to recognize to some extent the quality of an act on the basis of the consequences in the acts of others. . . . Even a young child sees the smash of things [occasioned] by his anger, and the smash may compete with his satisfied feeling of discharged energy as an index of value.

A child gives way to what, grossly speaking, we call anger. . . . In one case, anger is directed say at older, stronger playmates who immediately avenge themselves upon the offender, perhaps cruelly.[19]

A person who still had doubts about the need for a concept of the good might claim that the only important factor in both short-run and long-run judgments of goods is wants; in pitting long-run against short-run goods, we simply pit present wants and goods (or evils) against other wants and future goods (or evils). Dewey's child is pitting a present good, the discharge of energy, against a future evil, getting beat up by the stronger playmates. Having learned its lesson, the child is simply aware of two wants, where before it was aware of one. Or perhaps it is aware of one present good and two future goods.

We can point out, in response to this interpretation of Dewey, that if we have conflicting wants, we will apparently have conflicting goods. Unless the child has acquired a concept of the good, it will have no basis for choosing which is the real good. On the surface, each good is as good as the other. The problem of conflicting wants was stated in Reflection 20 of Chapter 1.

A person who doubts that we need a concept of the good might answer this "conflict of wants and goods" argument by claiming that features of our wants are sufficient to determine our choice of goods. Something may be more strongly wanted than something else; one thing may give a sweeter pleasure than another, and so forth.

However, the above argument can be shown to be suspect. The strongest want may often determine our choice, but does that make its object a good, or the act that it causes right? A drug called Depro-Provera "turns down the thermostat on the sex drive," according to a medical researcher. An imprisoned rapist recently went to court, asking to be put into a program where the drug is used. Because his sex drive was the strongest of his wants, he raped. But if rape is wrong, and his sexual satisfaction is not a good, then a feature of a want, such as strength, is not a basis for choosing a good; hence it cannot replace a concept of the good. The rapist himself reportedly said to the judge, "I'd just like to tell you how important it is that my sex drive be cut down, because it's inconvenient, because it's always giving me a problem." [20]

The arguments that I have given to show that judgments about "goods" depend on a concept of the good hold for "a good" as well, because "goods" is simply the plural of this good and that good. A list of goods is a list of individual things, each of which is considered "a good."

However, another argument applying to judgments about "a good" shows an additional reason why we need a concept of the good. Something may be judged a good on one occasion and not a good on another occasion, even though it may be wanted on both occasions. We can account for this difference of judgments if, in making them, we use a concept of the good rather than merely our wants. Since we want this thing on both occasions, if wanting were sufficient to determine a good, then we would judge it a good on both occasions; because we do not, we don't think wanting is a sufficient basis for judging something a good.

For example, exercising may be a good for a sound body, but not a good for a body with a back injury. Yet you may well want to exercise on either occasion; in fact, you may want all the more to exercise when it is least good for you, since one misses the invigoration of a good workout especially after one has had to be inactive.

In summary, I have argued that we need a concept of the good to account for our ability to make a list of goods; to explain how we are able to argue when we disagree about our lists of goods; to understand how we realize that we have made a mistake about a good; to grasp what is involved in our choosing between short-run and long-run goods; and to show how we are able to judge that something is a good on one occasion but not on another.

3.9 Evil and Ignorance of the Good

Summarizing this chapter, we saw Thrasymachus propose that injustice is more profitable than justice, using the example of a ruler who bases his decisions on what he believes to be his egoistic self-interest. Socrates made Thrasymachus retreat, but Glaucon took up the argument because he wasn't satisfied with Socrates' easy triumph. Glaucon claimed that Thrasymachus' view is held by most people, even by the just, who only appear to be just because they fear detection and punishment; everyone, the just as well as the unjust, would act in their own interests if rendered invisible by a Gyges ring.

I took the Gyges ring story as a thought experiment and set it out in the form of an argument, so we could distinguish its various elements clearly. Our examination of it led to a fuller Second Version of the argument that made certain assumptions explicit. I then outlined Socrates' argument against the assumption (G3.1) that wants determine our goods.

Next I tried to explain why the Gyges point of view is so plausible and has such a wide appeal, even though it leads to monstrous results. I suggested that the key to the explanation is in Link 1—the view that our wants, alone and always, determine our goods. Socrates pointed out that what we want is in our self-interest only if it is a good. The distinction between the appearance and the reality of good, which underwrites the possibility of making mistakes, broke the "alone and always" link between wants and goods.

We have also sought an explanation of why Socrates' argument seems like reaching for an "impossible dream." What would make his argument plausible? We are now in a position to say. Because of the distinction between "goods" and "the good,"and because it is a concept of "the good" that enables us to identify "goods" or "a good," we can say that we don't do evil voluntarily but rather because we have an inadequate concept of the good. Being ignorant of the good, we mistakenly take an evil for a good.

Socrates concedes that we always act in our self-interest; but, he points out, only the good is in our self-interest, and we know this, so we always act to secure a good. But we know that people sometimes pursue what is not a good. Why? There are two possible explanations: (1) Perhaps we do not always seek what is a good. (2) We do not know that what we seek is not a good.

The strong psychological egoist rejects the first explanation in the belief that people are *compelled* to seek their good; the ethical egoist rejects it in the belief that people *ought* to seek their good. The self-interest thesis cannot be given up by either kind of egoist. So, (1) can't be the explanation.

That leaves the second alternative. People mistake the bad for the good because they do not have a clear concept of the good; without a clear concept, they cannot identify what is a good (as I argued in section 3.8).

Do you want to lead a good life? Do you want to make the fewest mistakes possible about what the moral and non-moral goods are, and to avoid a mistake about your whole life (the kind that Ivan Ilyich made?) Of course you do. Then, according to Socrates' argument, you had better spend some time trying to learn about the concept of the good.

In the next chapter I will complete my account of Plato's refutation of the Gyges Argument. We found that egoists based their view on their idea of human nature; to complete the refutation, Plato proposes a different, fuller idea of human nature, an idea that includes some human features often left out by Gyges advocates. Plato supplements Socrates' argument in *Gorgias* with a more complete view of human nature in *The Republic*. He tries to show that acting justly is more in accord with this fuller human nature than acting egoistically.

STUDY QUESTIONS

1 What is the Gyges Argument supposed to prove? State the argument in its first version. What additional premises assumed in it were added to the first version to create the second? State the argument in your own words to avoid straight memorization (and fading memory and knowledge).

2 What is the difference between psychological and ethical egoism? Between the strong and weak forms of each? Is it logically consistent to believe in both strong psychological egoism and strong (or weak) ethical egoism?

3 Distinguish between "a good," "goods," "the good," and the concept of the good. Explain why we need the concept of the good.

4 What distinction does Socrates use to break Link 1, the link between wants and goods? And if he successfully breaks that link, why does this refute the Gyges point of view about the way we live and/or ought to live?

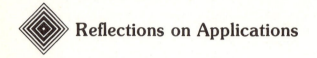 **Reflections on Applications**

1 Psychological egoism, in both its strong and weak versions, is a factual claim about human actions. A factual claim's truth is established on the basis of evidence. In the Goad family, daughter and father accuse each other of acting selfishly. But are they correct? Identify the reasons given by each to support the claim that the other is selfish. Do you think these reasons support their claims?

2 You may think that Mr. Goad didn't act as a father should. If your father acted similarly, would you think him wrong? If you do, you probably think fathers ought to act in the interests of at least certain others—namely, their children—rather than in their own interests exclusively. You may concede that out in the world it is dog eat dog, but maintain that the family should be a sanctuary from this otherwise universally hostile selfishness.

If you either condemn Mr. Goad or have a "sanctuary" view of the family, what does this imply about your position on ethical egoism, whether strong or weak? And your position on psychological egoism, strong and weak?

3 Imagine a society in which everyone has a Gyges ring. In that society, would injustice be more profitable than justice? Would people be likely to believe that injustice is more profitable than justice? Would you?

4 Do you draw any conclusions about the truth of the premises in the Gyges Argument from the following answers to the Question Man? The question was: If you were invisible where would you go?

"Run into a bank and get some money. No, that sounds bad. One thing good about being that, being invisible, is that you can just cruise around anywhere. I guess the only thing would be to steal stuff and that wouldn't be nice. You know, actually it would be nice to cruise around invisible. You wouldn't have to buy admittances to anything."

"I would go to the bank vault. I'd make a few withdrawals. Take a few million dollars. Then I would go out and find ways to spend it. Like a couple of yachts. A couple of penthouses. Make some investments. Invest in a parking lot in San Francisco. Charge a high price and make lots of money. Then just settle back to a basic easy life. Lots of booze and women."

"To the bank. Directly to the deposit area. See how much I could make invisible to go with me. Being invisible, I'd probably play a few jokes on a few friends. Nice jokes, of course. . . . There are a few girls I would like to check out."

"To the Mediterranean. I could go a lot of places where I wouldn't have to pay the fare. Wouldn't have to stand in line. . . . I would like to go visit some of my old friends to compare what they are doing with what I am doing."[21]

A similar question was asked at a *Dracula* intermission.

One theater-goer said she would play Robin Hood, taking from the rich to give to the poor. Her husband preferred to play executioner, claiming he could "clean up the world" by wiping out all psychopathic criminals, Mafia heads, evil cult leaders and corrupt dictators—to name but a few. . . .

"I'd go to [anti-feminist] Phyllis Schlafly's house," declares management consultant Jayne Townsend, "to see if she actually does get home every night to fix dinner for the family as she claims. Considering that she leads rallies, writes a newsletter, comments on CBS, lectures and attends law school—one tends to wonder."[22]

Which of the above answers do you believe—especially since none of the people answering were invisible? Would they answer the same way if they were?

5 Do you think the following argument shows what it claims to show?

If people are psychological egoists, then anyone who interferes with our pursuit of our self-interests becomes an object of dislike. Except for people who get favors from them, everyone dislikes the police and government officials. The duty of the police and government officials is to enforce laws intended to benefit the common good rather than our personal good. Therefore the fact that we dislike police and officials proves that we are interested in our personal rather than the common good, which is simply psychological egoism.

6 Lily Ehrlich, an advocate of the Austrian psychiatrist Alfred Adler's views on social psychology, says, "There is a lack of social feeling. We don't trust one another. The recent Watergate scandals have led people to believe that you can't trust government officials, even in the highest circles. There is too much competition in our society. Everyone wants to get to the top."[23]

How would a psychological egoist comment on Ehrlich's remarks? An ethical egoist? Would an egoist of either kind be surprised by Watergate or by anyone's misuse of governmental powers for their own ends? The fact that political scandals still shock and offend us must mean that not everyone believes in or defends an egoist theory of human nature. If you told Glaucon that you knew an honest politician, what kind of answer would he make?

7 Lily Ehrlich also says, "Children, like adults, want to feel significant. They want to fit in, to belong, to count for something. To be somebody to others is important to all of us. A misbehaving child is a discouraged child." She says that each person has one or more of four basic goals they are trying to achieve by their misbehavior: attention, power, revenge, or to make themselves feel adequate. "The objective of the Adlerians is to help everyone—parents, teachers, and children—understand the 'whys' in the bad behavior and to help the misbehaving individual deal with them."[24]

To what extent, if any, do you think Ehrlich's view is similar to Socrates' claims (a) that no one does evil willingly, and (b) that the reason people do evil is their ignorance of the good? Might a person think those "four basic goals" are goods?

8 Norman L. Heap, Vice President for Administrative Affairs at San Francisco State University, wrote in a university publication: "Ideally no human being ought to exercise power or influence over another except by persuasion, without hypocrisy or guile, showing patience, long suffering, gentleness, kindness, and love unfeigned toward the governed. However, history teaches us by sad experience that it is the nature and disposition of almost all human beings, as soon as they get a little authority, as they suppose, they will begin to exercise unjust, unmerited, or inequitable dominion over others."[25]

This sounds like a reluctant Gyges advocate speaking. Consider the last sentence, which begins, "However, history teaches . . ." Let's divide it into two things that history supposedly teaches: (1) that people in authority exercise unjust, unmerited, or inequitable dominion over others, and (2) that it is the nature and disposition of almost all human beings to do this. Would Socrates agree with (1)? With (2)? If not, why would he disagree?

9 In section 3.8 I cited some answers that people gave to the question about whether they would rather be rich or smart. How would you answer the question? What reasons would you give for one being a better good than the other? And what concept of the good do you think you have that leads you to give the reasons you give?

 ## Reflections on Theory

10 *Why moral reasons are better than egoistic reasons.* Are you satisfied that the following argument is a sound basis for rejecting weak and strong ethical egoism? And for subscribing to ethical altruism? In the Preface to *The Moral Point of View,* Kurt Baier says:

I must mention a reason why any and every agent *should be* a moral and not an immoral agent. . . . The reason is that a general acceptance of a system of merely self-interested reasons would lead to conditions of life well described by Hobbes as "poor, nasty, brutish, and short." These unattractive living conditions can be improved by the general adoption of a system of reasoning in which reasons of self-interest are overruled, roughly speaking, when following them would tend to harm others. Such reasons are what we call "moral reasons," and we rightly regard them as overruling reasons of self-interest, because the acceptance of self-interested reasons as overruling moral ones would lead to the undesirable state of affairs described by Hobbes. This is the reason why moral reasons must be regarded as superior to self-interested reasons and why everyone has an excellent reason for so regarding them. [26]

11 *Baier's "moral reasons" assume psychological egoism.* Suppose you subscribed to Baier's refutation of ethical egoism and his affirmation of ethical altruism. Suppose also the soundness of the argument in section 3.3 showing the unreasonableness of ethical altruism if strong psychological egoism is true. If you did subscribe to Baier's argument, it appears that you would have to maintain the falsity of psychological egoism. However, a defender of strong psychological egoism might argue that Baier's point of view is perfectly compatible with this egoism; he might even claim that Baier's argument presupposes the truth of psychological egoism. Evaluate the following argument for this claim.

People can be forced to perform acts that are in the interests of others by the threat of punishment. The anticipation of punishment transforms an act that otherwise would not be in your self-interest into one that is. In that case, the motive to perform the act is a self-interested one. Punishment could not have the force that it has if we were not self-interested; if someone didn't care what happened to him, the threat and pain of punishment would not force him to perform the acts that we know it does. Thus punishment's effectiveness presupposes self-interested agents. In making his argument, Baier cites the "unattractive" consequences of acting for self-interested reasons—namely, Hobbes's deplorable state of affairs. Now this state of affairs plays the same role as punishment does, differing only in that there need not be someone to inflict it. Predicting this state of affairs would not convince a person that "moral reasons" are superior to reasons of self-interest, if a person were not interested primarily in his or her own welfare. Thus the effectiveness of Baier's argument presupposes self-interested agents; the threat of Hobbes's state of affairs would not *impel* one to subscribe to Baier's position, unless strong psychological egoism were true.

12 *Baier's advocacy of altruism contains an empty "Should."* Evaluate the following argument, which is a follow-up to the arguments in Reflections 10 and 11.

Ought implies *Can* because it is reasonable to oblige persons to perform only possible tasks (section 3.3). But there is a reverse point to consider: *Must* makes *Ought* or *Should* empty—that is, an act we are impelled to do makes an obligation to perform that act superfluous. For example, if my human nature impels me to perform an act that I believe will bring pleasure, it is superfluous to tell me, "You ought to perform the act that brings you pleasure." The *Ought* is empty. If strong psychological egoism is true, we are impelled to perform those acts we think to our self-interest; now notice how empty it is to add: "You ought to (or should) perform those acts you think to your self-interest." Baier's urging for ethical altruism—"every agent *should be* a moral" agent—contains an empty *Should*. It is empty because the reasons he gives us for doing so are the egoistic Hobbesian reasons. If these reasons are the true and only reasons that we "should" be ethical altruists, then, because his argument presupposes the truth of strong psychological egoism, we are forced to be altruistic anyway. Furthermore, since Baier's plea *for* ethical altruism has an empty *Should,* the *Ought* (or *Should*) *in* the principle of ethical altruism is also empty.

13 *Arguments pro and con altruism.* A familiar argument is often offered as a refutation of psychological egoism, weak or strong. Here it is.

Weak psychological altruism is the claim that at some time we all *in fact* perform acts that we think are not in our self-interest (because in the interest of others). Psychological egoism is false because psychological altruism is true. Psychological altruism is true because it is human nature to have altruistic wants. Everybody at some time wants others' interests to be satisfied. For example, parents want their children's interests satisfied and vice versa. Furthermore, at some time everybody acts in such a way that they satisfy this want to have others' interests satisfied; everybody has at some time sacrificed their welfare in the interest of others.

The following counterargument is often offered by defenders of psychological egoism.

Altruistic wants are wants of an ego—my ego, your ego, her ego, and so forth. Since they are wants of an ego, their satisfaction is as much in that ego's self-interest as any other want; therefore the truth of psychological altruism is really just further evidence of the truth of psychological egoism.

Which of these two arguments do you accept, if either? Say why.

14 *Against Nietzsche?* Up to now I have spoken only of the interests of individuals. Some think there are "group" interests as well. For example, a labor union is said to have an interest because its members share an interest; this interest may differ from the employer's. You are undoubtedly familiar with the notion of a "class interest," the proletariat versus the bourgeoisie. One may ask whether one group interest can be shown to be superior to another. Think about the following remarks by Max Weber, a German sociologist, and see if you can fashion an argument against Nietzsche out of it.

In our subsequent discussion of castes and classes we shall have a good deal to say about the sense of honor or superiority characteristic of the non-priestly classes that claimed the highest social privileges, particularly the nobility. Their sense of self-esteem rests on their awareness that the perfection of their life pattern is an expression of their underived, ultimate, and qualitatively distinctive *being;* indeed, it is in the very nature of the case that this should be the basis of the elite's feeling of worth. On the other hand, the sense of honor of disprivileged classes rests on some concealed promise for the future which implies the assignment of some function, mission, or vocation to them. What they cannot claim to *be,* they replace by the worth of that which they will one day *become,* to which they will be called in some future life here or hereafter. [27]

15 *Ultimate wants determine ultimate goods.* In section 3.6 I argued that wants are not sufficient for determining goods because, if they were, we wouldn't make mistakes about goods; we do make mistakes; therefore wants aren't sufficient. Here is a counter-argument to this argument.

It's true that I may mistakenly believe that something I want is a good. For example, I may have been mistaken in wanting to earn a teacher's credential. I thought it was a good because I thought it a means to a career that would be fulfilling and contribute to my happiness. However, I found out during my practice teaching that I was unsuited to teaching children, that it wouldn't be fulfilling or contribute to my happiness. This mistake was learned only because ultimately my wanting was sufficient to determine a good. The goodness or badness of a teaching career was measured against the basic want to be happy. Because my wanting happiness is what makes happiness a good, wanting is shown to be a sufficient test for goodness.

Do you subscribe to this counterargument? To do so, do you have to maintain that a person couldn't be mistaken in wanting happiness?

16 *"Bad" wants show goods are not determined by wants.* Consider the following argument: The concept of the good may be used to evaluate anything in the world, including wants. We know that there are some circumstances under which a want has a bad end in view; when this is the case, it is a bad want. If a want by itself always determined that its end in view is a good, then there could not be such a thing as a bad want. However, there *is* such a thing as a bad want; therefore a want by itself does not always determine a good.

Supply an example of a "bad" want. Do you think this argument might be used to show the falsity of a key claim in the Gyges Argument? Which one? In the light of this argument, are you prepared to give up the Gyges point of view? If not, can you answer this argument?

17 *Do stronger wants make better goods?* We often make a choice between two goods on the basis that one is a better good than another. In section 3.8 and in Reflection 20 of Chapter 1, I pointed out that we sometimes have conflicting wants and asked how we can choose which one to pursue. One answer is that there is some feature of wants, such as being stronger, that compels us to pursue one want rather than the other. We can ask: Does having a stronger want for something always mean it is a better good? Try to formulate an argument parallel to the one in Reflection 16

100   of this chapter that shows we should answer "No" to this question. (Hint: Substitute "a worse end in view" for Reflection 16's phrase "a bad end in view.")

18 *Are two satisfactions better than one?* Suppose you have three wants, and that one of them conflicts with the other two. It might be claimed that one should perform the act that satisfies the two rather than the conflicting one, on the grounds that two wants satisfied is *better* than one want satisfied.

    Notice the use of "better." Do you think the use of "better" shows that a concept of the good is assumed in thinking about which act to perform? How else would you decide to perform the act with the greatest number of satisfactions, unless you assumed that "more is better, and better is a greater good"? (The notion of better requires that an adequate concept of the good must provide for degrees of goods.)

19 *Epictetus on rational self-interest.* Show how the following quotation from the Roman philosopher Epictetus' *Discourses* relates to some views presented in this chapter.

> Every error comprehends [involves] contradiction: for since he who errs does not wish to err, but to be right, it is plain that he does not do what he wishes. For what does the thief wish to do? That which is for his own interest. If, then, the theft is not for his interest, he does not do that which he wishes. But every rational soul is by nature offended at contradiction, and so long as it does not understand this contradiction, it is not hindered from doing contradictory things: but when it does understand the contradiction, it must of necessity avoid the contradiction and avoid it as much as a man must dissent from the false; but so long as this falsehood does not appear to them, he assents to it as to truth.
>
> He, then, is strong in argument and has the faculty of exhorting [encouraging] and confuting [refuting], who is able to show to each man the contradiction through which he errs and clearly to prove how he does not do that which he wishes and does that which he does not wish. For if anyone shall show this, a man will himself withdraw from that which he does. [28]

20 *Who to blame?* While reading the following quotation from Robert Olson, suppose that it is applicable to a car salesman who sold you a "lemon."

> The simple fact is that moral censure is not often an effective means of promoting the general welfare, when an individual performs an act dictated by rational consideration of his own best long-range interests. . . . The best thing to do at this point, if we wish to promote the general welfare, is to remind ourselves of the social imperfections that have given rise to the conflict, and to censure ourselves and others for having tolerated the conditions producing these tragic cases. [29]

    Do you think that Olson's point supports Socrates' position? Why?

4

On Human Nature:
Plato, Hobbes, Hume,
and Rousseau

4.1 Plato: The Three Parts of the Soul

In the previous chapter we found why the egoists' Gyges Argument is both plausible and abhorrent, and why Socrates' refutation in *Gorgias* is both implausible and attractive.

The Gyges Argument is plausible because it contains an implicit link between wants and goods: Link 1 asserts that the wants of human nature, always and alone, determine our goods. The argument is abhorrent because our wants, as in the case of a rapist, can lead us to evil acts.

Socrates' refutation of the Gyges egoist appears, at first sight, to be implausible because he seems to ignore the fact that humans seek their self-interest; yet his argument is attractive because he shows how we can be both self-interested and moral. Upon further scrutiny, moreover, we find that Socrates does in fact agree that we all seek our self-interest. His refutation begins to look plausible once we follow his distinction between "a good" (or "goods" in the plural) and the concept of "the good," and recognize that it is our ignorance of the concept of the good that may account for evil acts. People don't, in his view, voluntarily do evil acts because that's what they think they want; instead, they do them because they don't know what is *really* good for them. Because we sometimes don't know what is really good for us, we make mistakes.

This chapter will show, in sections 4.1–4.3, how Plato tries to use our knowledge of the concept of the good to persuade us that our self-interests are identical to the interests of others. This accounts for the attractiveness of Socrates' argument; we don't have to criticize ourselves for our "rotten" human nature. Here now is a summary of the reasons why we need the concept of the good, with italics to draw attention to another aspect of human nature that Plato emphasized.

> We need a concept of the good in order to account for our ability *to make a list* of goods; to explain how we are able *to argue* when we disagree about our lists of goods; to understand how we *realize that we have made a mistake* about a good; to grasp what is involved in our *choosing* between short-run and long-run goods; and to show how we are able *to judge* that something is a good on one occasion but not on another. (3.8)

Notice that all the phrases in italics refer to intellectual operations; they presuppose a mental capacity, sometimes referred to as the faculty of reason.

Socrates points out that if egoists want to act in their real self-interest, they have to act to obtain a good, not the unevaluated object of a want. This introduces the notion and leads us to see the necessity for the concept of "the good." This in turn, as just pointed out, leads us to recognize that part of our human nature is our capacity to reason; our human nature includes more **103** than just psychological and biological wants.

In *The Republic* Plato provides an analysis of the well-run state as a prelude to his analysis of human nature. He maintains that the state should have three parts, each with its function and its virtue. One part consists of the artisans, workers, and moneymakers, who provide goods, services, and luxuries. This part's virtue is temperance: moneymakers must refrain from excesses. The second part consists of the guardians—the soldiers, who must provide for defense. This part's virtue is courage. The third part consists of the rulers or philosopher-kings, whose virtue is wisdom. The rulers should rule the state because they have the wisdom to know the concept of the good. Knowing this, they can discern which things are goods and which are not; determining what is in the real interest of the citizens of the state, they can direct the citizens' actions.

When each of these three parts of the state is performing its function in accord with its specific virtue, the state will be just, which is a form of harmony. Justice is the virtue of the well-run state as a whole. Harmony occurs when each part does what it does best and doesn't perform another part's function; the lack of conflict among the parts is harmony.

Plato has Socrates argue that it is more profitable to live in a just state than an unjust one, because in a just state citizens cooperate functionally to pursue their real self-interest rather than the wants of the stronger. Wise rulers know that the objects of citizens' wants are not always goods, in which case these objects are not in the real self-interest of the citizens.

Plato's psychology—his theory of human nature—is a political theory. He says that the state is man "writ large." If the human soul has the same three-part structure as the state, then, by determining the nature of a well-run state, we can infer by analogy the nature of a well-run soul.

Plato's first step in learning about the well-run soul is to prove that the human soul has three parts that perform functions similar to the three parts of the state. On pages 5–6 I quoted from *The Republic* a portion of the dialogue that exhibits Plato's proof that the appetitive part of the soul—the part that has appetites or wants—is to be distinguished from the reasoning part. By a similar method, Plato shows that there is a third part of the soul, the spirited part; this part may act contrary to both the appetites and reason, although in a well-run soul it takes the side of reason. [1]

Plato matches the state's artisans with the soul's appetites, the guardians with the soul's spirited part, and the rulers with the soul's reason; they have similar virtues—respectively, temperance or moderation, courage, and wisdom. And precisely as justice in the state is the harmony of each part performing its proper function, so a just soul is one in which each part likewise performs its proper function. Justice in the soul

> does not lie in a man's external actions, but in the way he acts within himself, really concerned with himself and his inner parts. He does not allow each part of himself to perform the work of another, or the sections

of his soul to meddle with another. He orders what are in the true sense of the word his own affairs well; he is master of himself, puts things in order, is his own friend, harmonizes the three parts like the limiting notes of the scale. . . . He binds them all together, and himself from a plurality becomes a unity. [2]

Plato then suggests that from the character of this inner governance we can learn which actions are just and which are unjust: "They are no different from healthy and diseased actions; what those are in the body, these are in the soul. . . . Healthy actions produce health, diseased ones, disease. . . . Therefore just actions produce justice in a man, and unjust actions, injustice. . . . Excellence then seems to be a kind of health and beauty and well-being of the soul, while vice is disease and ugliness and weakness." [3]

We have reached Plato's final refutation of Thrasymachus and egoistic Gyges advocates. They claimed that injustice is more profitable than justice, because they thought that unjust acts allow a person to satisfy more wants. Plato's psychology is more elaborate: There is more to a person than the appetitive part with its many wants; we also have spirited and intellectual parts. Unless the intellectual part governs the appetites with wisdom, aided by the spirit, a person will have acted contrary to this more complicated human nature; appetites, having no wisdom, cannot by nature govern one and guide one to goods. Acting contrary to our human nature produces an unhealthy soul, just as abusing the proper function of our bodily parts produces a unhealthy body.

Plato's answer to the Gyges advocates, then, depends on his psychology of human nature, just as their view does. And if Plato's psychology is superior to theirs, this gives him the advantage in saying how we should conduct our lives. Justice is more profitable than injustice because to live as Plato suggests is to live in accord with our nature; living otherwise is living out of accord with our nature. An inadequate theory of human nature leads to inadequate morals.

Plato provides a dramatic image of an unjust person's soul at the end of Book IX of *The Republic*. [4] He asks us to imagine a creature whose outward appearance resembles a human. Inwardly it is made up of three parts. The appetites are fashioned like a many-headed beast, some the heads of tame animals and others the heads of wild ones. The spirited part resembles a lion, and the rational part resembles a man. Anyone—such as Thrasymachus— who maintains that injustice is profitable simply means

that it benefits the man to feed the multiform beast well and make it strong, as well as the lion and all that pertains to him, but to starve and weaken the man within, so that he is dragged along whithersoever one of the others leads. He does not accustom one part to the other or make them friendly, but he leaves them alone to bite and fight and kill each other. . . . Then do you think that licentiousness has long been condemned because in a licentious man that terrible, that big, that multiform beast is let loose more than it should be? Clearly.

Only the reasoning part of humans is capable of apprehending the con- **105** cept of the good; thus it and it alone is capable of ordering a person's life. Wants—the appetites, the many-headed beast—cannot know the good; this beast is blindly attracted to the objects of wants like iron filings to a magnet, and therefore this beast should not be in charge of our lives. To live the good life, one must come to knowledge of the concept of or form of the good. "The Form of the Good is the greatest object of study, and it is by their relation to it that just actions and the other things become useful and beneficial." [5]

4.2 Conflict of Interests

We may characterize Plato's views about a well-run soul as a warning to be prudent. He has tried to show that we should not let our wants rule our life. These wants conflict; they lead us first in one direction, then in another. If they are untamed by reason, they will "bite and fight and kill each other." A well-run soul is governed by reason, because wisdom enables us to determine which objects of wants are goods and which are not. In short, we should be prudent: we should determine what is really in our self-interest and do only that. Even a hungry person doesn't eat spoiled meat; he or she wants to eat, but also wants to live and be healthy.

Plato does not reject acting in our self-interest. He is not at odds with the rational egoist at this point; he is at odds only with thoughtless egoists such as Thrasymachus. So Plato has thus far not refuted the egoist, but only the mindless, want-dominated egoist. Has the egoist won, then? It is too soon to tell. There is more to the Gyges Argument than we have considered so far.

Consider John and Joan, each of whom is a prudent person—that is, they are rational egoists pursuing those goods that are in each one's real self-interest. Isn't it possible that what is in John's self-interest may not be in Joan's, and vice versa? It doesn't appear to be self-contradictory to suppose that their self-interests conflict. What is a good for John may be a bad for Joan and vice versa. Suppose the two of them are in a situation where both are starving, and there is food enough for only one to survive until rescue comes. If John eats the food, Joan starves, and vice versa. Eating the food is a good for each one, but each one's eating it is the opposite of a good for the other. We assume, of course, that self-preservation is in the real interest of each; in such a situation it would be hard for either to prove to the other that starving to death is in his or her best interest, although it is not inconceivable that one might persuade the other of this.

We know that members of groups believe they have conflicting interests. When the harvest is small, the rulers, backed by the guards, may decree that no one is to hoard food, attempting thus to spread the food evenly

106   among the populace so as to prevent starvation. The farmers, however, may wish to hoard, because that increases the price of their produce; they think that high prices are in their self-interest.

Suppose a farmer is a rational egoist, prudently looking after her interests. She will cite premiss G2.1 of the Second Version of the Gyges Argument: "It is human nature to pursue one's self-interest." She will go on to claim that high prices are in her self-interest; therefore it is to her self-interest, and in accord with human nature, not to share but to hoard.

Plato recognizes that he has to deal with conflict between citizens. In his view the state has to be prudent, just as an individual has to be prudent. The members of the various parts of the state have wants; for example, farmers want higher prices, but consumers want food at lower prices. The wants of these groups conflict, just as the wants of an individual conflict. And according to Plato, just as the individual must use the concept of the good to evaluate his or her wants, so as to determine which are goods and which are not, so too the rulers must use the concept of the good to evaluate the wants of the citizens, so as to determine which objects of their wants are goods and which are not.

We can infer what Plato's answer to the farmer-consumer conflict would be from a remark of Socrates in *The Republic:*

> It is not the law's concern to make some one group in the city outstandingly happy but to contrive to spread the happiness throughout the city, by bringing the citizens into harmony with each other by persuasion or compulsion, and to make them share with each other the benefits which each group can confer upon the community. [6]

Plato would decree that the farmers may not hoard but must share, because this will "spread the happiness throughout the city." He would conclude that high food prices are not a good.

4.3 Individual Good and the Common Good

Notice that Plato mentions two ways to bring citizens into harmony— "by persuasion or compulsion." Let's formulate an argument for persuading the farmers not to hoard: We ought to do that which is to the common good when it clashes with an individual or group good; not hoarding is to the common good ("spreading the happiness"); therefore you should not hoard.

This argument addressed to the farmers is intended to persuade them by pitting the common good against their individual goods. Since we are still trying to evaluate the Gyges Argument, let's assume that the farmer who answers this argument is a Gyges advocate. The counterargument could go like the following, which is an attempt to weaken the force of the common (or general or public) good:

In trying to show me that I should not hoard, and thus should give up **107** the action that will yield me higher prices for my grain, you appeal to the common good. I reject this appeal because the common good is just the individual goods of others. Nothing is a good except to individual persons. States or groups or classes don't have goods, only the persons in them do; states can't feel and don't have wants, but persons do. What you are arguing, in reality, is that I should act in the interest of others rather than myself. This is unprofitable to me. I realize that what goes by the name of "justice" is supposed to be ethical, and that what is said to be ethical is acting in the interests of others; but this justice is not as profitable to me as injustice. Since it is human nature to perform those actions that are in our self-interest, rather than in the interest of others (G2 of the Gyges Argument), your argument does not persuade me that I ought to act for the so-called "common good." The appeal to the common good is just an appeal to the good of the majority; there are more consumers than farmers, and naturally they want what is in their self-interest, which is more food at lower prices. This appeal to the common good is just a disguised form of egoist self-interest on the part of the consumers.

With the farmer holding this point of view, persuasion has failed to produce the harmony Plato advocates. Should other arguments be no more persuasive, the ruler will have to use compulsion to bring harmony to the state.

Up to this point in his refutation of the Gyges Argument, Plato has attacked Link 1, showing that we need the concept of the good to mediate between wants and goods. This first stage of Plato's refutation has moved us from the thoughtless Thrasymachus to the prudent egoist. Plato's first modification of the Gyges links diagram in this:

Plato will now be forced to deal with Links 2 and 3 because of problems like the John-Joan conflict and high food prices. Up until now we have seen Plato concentrate on the rational goods of a single person. Sugar may be a good for Jack, but not for Jill because she's a diabetic. Here one and the same thing, sugar, is a good for one but not for another. Yet they aren't conflicting, because Jack's and Jill's ends are independent of each other. However, the ends involved in the problem of high food prices and in John's and Joan's survival dilemma *are* related; John can't decide on his own ends and goods without also deciding on Joan's, nor does the farmer's hoarding affect only her own interest.

We move now to a second stage of Plato's argument, a more typically moral one because we have to deal with two or more person's *related* ends and goods—our own and others'. How do we manage to achieve both our own and someone else's rational good? It appears impossible, if they conflict.

108   Plato tries to deal with this difficulty by appealing to a common good—"to spread happiness throughout the city." He can't solve the difficulty, however, unless he can refute the farmer's claim that the common good is merely a trick used by others to persuade us to put their rational good before our own. Further, Plato has to reckon with the farmer's claim that it is human nature to perform the act that will obtain our own good rather than the conflicting act that will provide the good of others; we are psychologically compelled to choose our own good over that of others.

Acknowledging the distinction between our own rational goods and those of others, we find our links diagram doubling into two lines:

```
            concept of the good      Link 2a              Link 3a
          ┌──────────────────┐
OWN WANTS       OWN GOODS    →     OWN ENDS      →    ACTS FOR SELF
OTHERS' WANTS  OTHERS' GOODS →  OTHERS' ENDS   →    ACTS FOR OTHERS
          └──────────────────┘
            concept of the good     Link 2b              Link 3b
```

The question before us now, at the second stage of Plato's argument, is this: Is it possible to show that, at least on some occasions, we should and can go through Links 2b and 3b rather than Links 2a and 3a?

The strong psychological egoist maintains that we are always impelled to follow Links 2a and 3a. To be refuted, the egoist will have to be shown that it is possible to follow Links 2b and 3b as well. And if the Gyges advocate is to be refuted, it will have to be shown that following Links 1b, 2b, and 3b—the "just" path—is sometimes more profitable than following Links 1a, 2a, and 3a. This requires snapping Link 2a.

One way to snap Link 2a would be to bring our own and others' goods into harmony by showing that they are identical. This is Plato's tactic. He maintains that the individual and the common good are one and the same. This is the second-stage use of the distinction between real and apparent self-interest. Plato has taught us that the objects we want may not really be in our self-interest. Now he argues that, when we find a conflict between our prudent goods and other persons' prudent goods, we may, with the concept of the good, determine the one good, and therefore the one end and the one enabling act (the act enabling us to achieve our end) that is in the real self-interest of all. With a single good in the interest of all of us, the conflict between individual goods and the common good disappears. It becomes the harmony of unity.

Our links diagram should look like this, according to Plato:

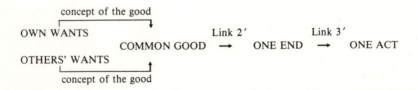

```
            concept of the good
          ┌──────────────────┐
OWN WANTS                          Link 2'          Link 3'
              COMMON GOOD   →    ONE END    →    ONE ACT
OTHERS' WANTS
          └──────────────────┘
            concept of the good
```

Because our own goods and others' goods are identical, they converge into unity. This means that in every situation we all have one common end, and so we can perform one common enabling act (or coordinated acts) to **109** secure this one end. The egoistic Link 2a disappears and becomes the egoistic-altruistic Link 2′. It is egoistic-altruistic because both our own and others' goods are secured, and it is to this that we are motivated.

Let us use this to reason with the hoarding farmer. Notice that this argument does not assume psychological altruism, nor does it use the altruistic moral rule that we ought to act sometimes in the interest of others rather than ourselves; nor does it assume that we are able to make free choices of alternative goods. The argument:

Farmer, you have not considered fully enough the consequences of hoarding your grain. While high prices may appear to be in your interest, you have to weigh that good against some ills. For example, with prices too high, people cannot afford to buy as much. Because they have a limited amount to spend, whether you sell little at high prices or a lot at low ones, you will get the same amount of money; the remainder of your high-priced grain will go unsold and may spoil in storage. Further, by selling little at high prices you will arouse the consumers' anger; when *you* wish to buy clothing, machinery, seed, and tools from *them,* this will prove to your disadvantage. These considerations show that by examining more things with your reason, you will see that the interest of others—lower prices for food—is also *your* real interest.

You can appreciate that there are an indefinite number of long-run and pond-wide considerations that can be brought forward in the rational evaluation of an act. This makes it impossible to disprove conclusively the Platonic thesis that in every situation there is an end and an enabling act (or acts) that are in the self-interest of all affected. But it cuts both ways. This indefiniteness also enables the egoist always to bring forward a new consideration to reestablish any conflict of interests that may have been resolved Platonically. For example, the farmer may point out that city grain speculators, food processors, and exporters make more money, with less risk, than she does on the grain she raises; besides, they don't work in hot, dusty fields. Unless she protects herself, others will continue to take advantage of her and other farmers. Thus each time the conflict is reestablished, the egoistic psychological spring to act in one's own self-interest, rather than in that of others, is released. So we are back where we started; Link 2a holds secure, and the Gyges Argument appears not to have been refuted.

4.4 Hobbes on War and Peace

We appear to be at a theoretical impasse because it seems impossible to show that our own and others' interests are identical, or at least complementary, and it also appears impossible to prove they are not.

110   At base, the commonly received notion of morals is ethically altruistic; it requires that any proposed system of morals contain some rules that lay obligations on us to act, on some occasions, against our own welfare and for that of others. Egoism is a form of moral skepticism. Psychological egoists are skeptical because they believe that our human nature impels us always to choose our own interests over others'; thus it is absurd to lay altruistic obligations on us that we are incapable of fulfilling. Ethical egoists are skeptical because they doubt that a moral system should contain rules obligating us to act in the interests of others; the only rules that we should follow in life are those that obligate us to act in our own interests; there are no such things as scoundrels.

Plato tried to refute moral skepticism in both varieties by arguing that a full rational examination shows that our own and others' interests are identical. This identity eliminates conflict between different persons' interests. Thus psychological egoists, being driven to act in their own interests, will simultaneously act in others' interests as well. Similarly, ethical egoists find themselves automatically acting in the interest of others when they act in their own interest, so their denial of obligations to others is pointless.

Given the theoretical impasse, however, moral skepticism is still plausible. Failing our ability to prove we all *always* have a common good, as Plato thought, it seems advisable to seek more modestly for some *one* common good. Then we could inquire whether this one common good would lead rational egoists to a moral system containing altruistic features. Maybe this is a way to escape our impasse.

That was the approach adopted by the seventeenth-century English philosopher Thomas Hobbes. Hobbes's strategy was, first, to suppose that persons are strong psychological egoists; second, to maintain that in common they prefer a state of peace to a state of war; and third, to deduce altruistic moral theorems from these assumptions.

Hobbes is celebrated for his distinction between the "natural state of men" and their "civil state." In the natural state there are no cultural restraints such as laws, morals, or manners. Hobbe's remarks may be interpreted to mean that he thought humans once lived in the natural state prior to the establishment of a civil society. We do not need to adopt this interpretation, however, to learn how he proposes to justify the civil state with its altruistic features. We need only suppose that the natural state is one in which our natural inclinations, unaffected by the restraints or conditioning of the civil state, direct our behavior.

The natural state can be conceived as a negation or denial of the civil state, not in the sense that it goes against laws and morals, but in the sense that it signifies the absence of them. In the absence of morals and laws, nothing is right or wrong.

> This is thus to be understood: what any man does in the bare state of nature, is injurious to no man; . . . for injustice against men presupposeth human laws, such as in the state of nature there are none. [7]

Hobbes vividly describes what our lives would be like in the natural **111** state. It would be "a war of all men against all men." In that state our years would be "few, fierce, short-lived, poor, nasty, and deprived of all that pleasure and beauty of life, which peace and society are wont to bring with them." [8]

Hobbes's state of war is a consequence of psychological egoism, a consequence of "a certain impulsion of nature."

> For every man is desirous of what is good for him, and shuns what is evil, but chiefly the chiefest of natural evils, which is death; and this he doth by a certain impulsion of nature, no less than that whereby a stone moves downward. . . . Therefore as the first foundation of natural right is this, that *every man, as much as in him lies, endeavour to protect his life and members.* [9]

Hobbes, like Plato, finds that our faculty of reason can lift us out of this "nasty" natural state, when it starts from a want common to all of us. Notice that Hobbes takes the common desire as given *prior* to the operation of reason, rather than as something derived *by* reason. This common want is for peace, a respite from the war of all against all, a respite from conflicts that cannot be harmonized.

> For every man by natural necessity desires that which is good for him: nor is there any that esteems a war of all against all, which necessarily adheres to such a state, to be good for him. And so it happens, that through fear of each other we think it fit to rid ourselves of this condition, and to get some fellows. [10]

The manner by which we "rid ourselves of this condition" is the construction of laws that reason proposes as necessary to obey if we are to secure this peace we desire in common.

> The passions that incline men to peace, are fear of death; desire of such things as are necessary to commodious [comfortable] living; and a hope by their industry to obtain them. And reason suggesteth convenient articles of peace, upon which men may be drawn to agreement. These articles, are they, which otherwise are called the Laws of Nature. [11]

Hobbes then goes on to distinguish between a "right of nature" and a "law of nature." A right is the "liberty" to preserve ourselves.

> A LAW OF NATURE, *lex naturalis*, is a precept or general rule, found out by reason, by which a man is forbidden to do that, which is destructive of his life, or taketh away the means of preserving the same. . . . And consequently it is a precept, or general rule of reason that every man ought to endeavour peace, as far as he has hope of obtaining. [12]

Hobbes then derives various "precepts" that are conditions for peace. Notice that the terms he uses for these precepts are normally names of altruistic moral virtues.

> All men agree on this, that peace is good, and therefore also the way or means of peace, which as I have showed before, are *justice, gratitude, modesty, equity, mercy*, and the rest of the laws of Nature, are good; that is to say, *moral virtues*.[13]

At the end of Chapter XV of the *Leviathan*, Hobbes speaks of these "dictates of reason" as "theorems" rather than laws; they do not become laws until someone in authority gives them as commands for others.

So Thomas Hobbes seems to reassure us that psychological egoism isn't so bad after all; persons with reason can arrive at the same altruistic morality by starting with a common desire for peace. Furthermore, this is a more modest base on which to rest than Plato offered: we need only *one* common desire—peace—and therefore don't need to show that every interest of ours, in the long run, is identical to every other affected person's interests. Hobbes's links diagram is as follows:

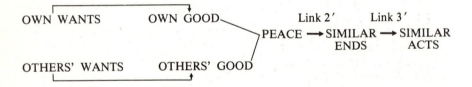

The common goal of peace transforms the egoist Link 2 into the egoistic-altruistic Link 2´.

It is time to return to Joan and John, still starving and with food enough for only one to survive until rescue. Theirs is a situation in which, using Hobbes's terminology, the first *law* of nature, to seek peace, may be overridden by the first *right* of nature, "to defend ourselves": "and when he cannot obtain it [peace], that he may seek, and use, all helps and advantages of war."[14] For Joan and John, all civil-state bets are off; our egoistic human nature and the "right of nature" put limits to our altruistic moral acts. We cannot go beyond those limits; we act in self-defense by an inevitable "impulsion of nature, no less than that whereby a stone moves downward." In this survival case, Link 2´ splits back into Links 2a and 2b again (see p. 108).

Hobbes makes a factual claim about humans' nature; he says that the rational convergence of human ends and acts that emerges from the one common good of peace ceases when self-survival is at stake. Is this factual claim true?

The psychological egoists' claim is universal; it is meant to be true of all persons. That is the point of the Gyges ring. Even the hitherto just humans will act unjustly if they possess the ring. Hobbes clearly intends the drive for self-preservation to be a natural law whose form is universal; *all* stones move downward in the absence of a stronger upward force; *all* humans act to **113** preserve themselves in the absence of civil-state laws.

But maybe this universal-natural-law claim is false. A universal statement is false if there is at least one entity that does not behave as claimed. "All persons get high on marijuana" is false if there is one person who doesn't. Similarly, "All persons will act for their survival" is false if there is one who doesn't. Thus if Joan or John insists on the other eating the remaining food, knowing that act will cause his or her own death, then he or she will have falsified the claim of Hobbes and all other psychological egoists.

But rather than imagine what Joan or John will do, as those who push the Gyges Argument invite us to do in their thought experiment, we can take Socrates as an actual exception to Hobbes's natural law about survival. Socrates' choosing to die rather than to escape is philosphically interesting not just because he falsifies Hobbes's psychological egoism but because, by his act, he demonstrates the possibility of leading one's life in accord with the belief that our own and others' goods are identical. The revelation of this identity may, of course, require extensive and careful thought.

While in prison Socrates gave this kind of thought to his situation. He could escape, for friends were ready to help him, and the officials were anxious to look the other way. The power of the Gyges ring was his. But Socrates argued against those friends who urged him to escape; he concluded that he should not escape, that it would be wrong. It would wrong his city, Athens, which had given him his culture and education, and it would also wrong and harm himself. Drinking the hemlock was the one act that would secure the identical good of both himself and Athens. Survival was not the only good: "Not life, but a good life, is to be chiefly valued." [15]

Even if he were unjustly put to death by the Athenians, Socrates thought that to return evil for evil would be unjust; it is better to "depart in innocence, a sufferer and not a doer of evil." [16] To harm others is wrong, even if done in retaliation for a wrong. And as we have seen in this and the previous chapter, Socrates argued that to be unjust is to harm oneself; it makes the soul unhealthy. Socrates' reasoning revealed to him that drinking the hemlock was a good; further, it was a good both for Athens and for him. He found no conflict between his own and others' goods; there was but one good because their goods were identical. Contrary to Hobbes's view, Socrates' death showed that reason, helped by courage, can lead a person to choose to die.

If one is serious about the identity of our own and others' goods, then one must be prepared not to make an exception when our death is required. Socrates was serious. That is one reason why he thought that all of life should be a preparation for dying. The doctrine of the identity of individual and common good is difficult to practice. But in demonstrating the doctrine by dying, Socrates showed that not even death could be used to confirm the psychological egoist's view of human nature. Rather, his death confirmed Plato's theory of human nature as expressed in *The Republic*. And disproved Hobbes! So Hobbes's way of finding altruistic rules by robbing eggs from the egoists' nest appears to fail. Where can we turn now?

114 4.5 Hume and Rousseau on Compassion in Human Nature

We have seen how Plato and Hobbes, holding that each person seeks what he or she thinks good, attempt to show that through the agency of reason it is possible to forge a moral system that contains altruistic rules. We have also noted some of that strategy's difficulties.

A different way of accounting for altruistic morals (which, like egoism, has a long philosophical tradition) is to base them on an altruistic theory of human nature. This alternative we may call "psychological altruism"; in this view, human nature contains not only a spring to act for our own interest but also a spring to act in the interest of others, because we by nature show compassion, pity, or sympathy for the welfare of others. One of our natural wants is to see other sentient creatures well off.

I will outline David Hume's and Jean-Jacques Rousseau's views on psychological altruism. Hume was an eighteenth-century English philosopher; Rousseau, his contemporary, was born in Geneva, Switzerland, and lived in France and other European countries. I choose these two advocates of psychological altruism because each also has clear and critical, but differing, views on the role of reason in morals. Both come down on the side of the heart. (Hume's ethics will be stated at greater length in Chapter 12.)

Hume thinks that we teach morals in order to influence actions. He insists, however, that the only thing that can move us to action is passion; therefore morals must be essentially connected to passion. "Morals excite passions, and produce or prevent actions. Reason of itself is utterly impotent [powerless] in this particular. The rules of morality, therefore, are not conclusions of reason."[17]

Hume adds that "reason is, and ought to be the slave of the passions, and can never pretend to any other office than to serve and obey them."[18] To underscore passion's dominance of reason, Hume remarks, "'Tis not contrary to reason to prefer the destruction of the whole world to the scratching of my finger."[19] Reason, then, is an instrument rather than the master of our passions.

Hume does allow, though, that passions may be called unreasonable, reflecting something of Plato's recommendation to reflect on our wants and not to accept their absolute dictates about goods. Our passions—such "as hope or fear, grief or joy, despair" —are unreasonable when they drive us to seek or avoid things that don't exist (he might have suggested ghosts or poltergeists), or to persist in an action that cannot achieve our end (he might have cited rain dances). But "where a passion is neither founded on false suppositions, nor chuses means insufficient for the end, the understanding can neither justify nor condemn it."[20]

Hume rejects Hobbes's program of deducing moral "theorems" by the operation of our reason. Instead, altruistic moral rules have their source in an altruistic operation of our nature, namely, sympathy for others.

Rousseau takes a stronger position than Hume on human reason; he thinks it corrupts our moral state. It does so by overwhelming the sentiment of compassion, which is the true source of morals. The civilized state established by our reason has ruined our natural state. In his prize-winning essay on a subject proposed by the Academy of Dijon in France— "What is the Origin of Inequality among Men, and is it Authorised by Natural Law?"—Rousseau cites with approval the English writer Mandeville's description of the agitation felt by a man who witnesses a wild beast tearing a child from its mother's arms and grinding it in its jaws.

> Such is the pure emotion of nature, prior to all kinds of reflection!. . . Mandeville well knew that, in spite of all their morality, men would have never been better than monsters, had not nature bestowed on them a sense of compassion, to aid their reason. . . . Compassion must, in fact, be the stronger, the more the animal beholding any kind of distress identifies himself with the animal that suffers. Now, it is plain that such identification must have been much more perfect in a state of nature than it is in a state of reason. . . it is reason which turns man's mind back upon itself, and divides him from everything that could disturb or afflict him. It is philosophy that isolates, and bids him say, at sight of the misfortunes of others: "Perish if you will, I am secure."[21]

The origin of inequality, according to Rousseau, lies in the social arrangements that human reason has invented. "There is hardly any inequality in the state of nature, all the inequality which now prevails owes its strength and growth to the development of our faculties and the advance of the human mind, and becomes at last permanent and legitimate by the establishment of property and laws."[22]

Rousseau finds that compassion is the basis for decent treatment of others, including animals; that this is most apparent in a state of nature before it is corrupted by civil society; and that Hobbes's psychological egoism is falsified by psychological altruism. In the state of nature we find the "noble beast . . . wandering up and down the forests, without industry, without speech, and without home, an equal stranger to war and to all ties."[23] Rousseau criticizes Hobbes for maintaining that humans are egoistic in this natural state.

> Above all, let us not conclude with Hobbes, that because [in the natural state] man has no idea of goodness, he must be naturally wicked; that he is vicious because he does not know virtue; that he always refuses to do his fellow-creatures services which he does not think they have a right to demand; or that by virtue of the right he truly claims to everything he needs, he foolishly imagines himself the sole proprietor of the whole universe. . . . There is another principle which has escaped Hobbes; which, having been bestowed on mankind,. . . tempers the ardour with which he pursues his own welfare, by an innate repugnance [inborn dislike] at seeing a fellow-creature suffer. . . . I am speaking of compassion, which is a disposition suitable to creatures so weak and subject to so many evils as we certainly are.[24]

116   Hume maintains about the social virtues—such as justice, humanity, friendship, benevolence, and public spirit—that their "public utility" is "the chief circumstance, whence they derive their merit." What has utility or usefulness has it as a means to an end; therefore the value of utility depends on the value of the end. "It is impossible for anything to please as means to an end, where the end is totally indifferent."[25] "The end, which they [the social virtues] have a tendency to promote, must be some way agreeable to us, and take hold of some natural affection. It must please, either from considerations of self-interest, or from more generous motives and regards."[26]

How are we to decide whether the ends of the social virtues are agreeable to us from self-interest or from "more generous motives"? In his *Enquiries* Hume attempts to use the "experimental method" in a philosophical investigation of human understanding and morals, just as Sir Isaac Newton used it in the natural sciences. Hume cites the English philosopher Francis Bacon's suggestion that, if we are in doubt about which explanation of a matter of fact is the correct one, we should try to formulate a "crucial experiment" designed to provide clear, unambiguous evidence for one of the alternative, competing explanations.

Hume proposes a crucial experiment on this issue: Are there occasions on which we find ourselves approving an action or a person's character when our self-interest is not involved? He answers yes. When we review historically remote events and persons—events in which the living have no stake—we find that people universally praise or blame persons for their actions and approve or disapprove their character. Because self-interest has no stake in the judgment, the judgment must be due to sympathy.

> Usefulness is agreeable, and engages our approbation [approval]. This is a matter of fact, confirmed by daily observation. But, useful? For what? For somebody's interest surely. Whose interest then? Not our own only: For our approbation frequently extends farther. It must, therefore, be the interest of those, who are served by the character or action approved of; and these we may conclude, however remote, are not totally indifferent to us. . . . If usefulness, therefore, be a source of moral sentiment, and if this usefulness be not always considered with a reference to self; it follows, that everything, which contributes to the happiness of society, recommends itself directly to our approbation and good-will. Here is a principle [compassion or sympathy], which accounts, in great part, for the origin of morality.[27]

Hume finds evidence that sympathy is present in all of us, and that it is aroused by similar actions and similar character. According to Hume, these two features of sympathy—universal to all and similarly aroused in all—are features that any factor claimed to be the basis of morality must possess. "The notion of morals implies some sentiment common to all mankind, which recommends the same object to general approbation, and makes every man, or most men, agree in the same opinion or decision concerning it."[28] Hume therefore believes that he has shown, using the method of the natural

sciences, that sympathy is the foundation of altruistic morals. "And though this affection of humanity may not generally be esteemed so strong as vanity or ambition, yet, being common to all men, it can alone be the foundation of morals, or of any general system of blame or praise."[29]

That sympathy, to serve as a foundation of morals, must be common to all men and be aroused under similar circumstances, seems to be a reasonable requirement. Morals must apply uniformly to all; there cannot be one morality for me and another for you. If diversity existed, morals, instead of being a basis for maintaining society, would be a basis for disrupting it. Whatever cooperation existed among people would result from the stronger coercing the weaker. This would take us right back to Thrasymachus' position—"Justice is what is to the interest of the stronger"—a result that Hume wishes to avoid.

Hume allows that self-love is also a cause of human actions, as does Rousseau. What if self-love and sympathy conflict? Need the stronger prevail? Not if we discount the effect that proximity (nearness) has on us.

> Sympathy, we shall allow, is much fainter than our concern for ourselves, and sympathy with persons remote from us much fainter than that with persons near and contiguous [next to us] but for this very reason it is necessary for us, in our calm judgments and discourse concerning the characters of men, to neglect all these differences, and render our sentiments more public and social.[30]

4.6 Reviewing Chapters 2-4

Let us review how we got where we are now, and summarize. I proposed that self-realization is the escape route from Ilyich's ordinariness. But Nietzsche's way of avoiding the herd mentality plunges us into egotism and egoism. Marin maintained that Nietzsche's isolating individualism can be countered by stressing community and cultivating human relations. However, the Gyges Argument presents a powerful barrier to anyone who urges us to become communal: if we are driven by our wants, we are forced to act only in our self-interest, which makes it impossible for us to act deliberately in the interests of community. My analysis of the Gyges Argument showed that its

118   plausibility depends on an egoistic notion of human nature. Following Plato
in his attack on the Gyges Argument, first we severed the link between wants
and goods, interposing instead the rational evaluation of our wants guided by
the concept of the good. Second, we found that Plato believed that the conflict of interests among prudent egoists is an illusion because each person's
long-run and pond-wide true interest is identical with the interest of the
others.

Plato's proposal is subject to neither conclusive proof nor disproof, so
we turned to Hobbes, who thought that, starting from an egoistic human
nature and the single, common good of peace, he could derive a set of
altruistic moral rules for the civil state. Hobbes's claim that in a self-
preservation situation we would act egoistically, tossing altruistic moral rules
aside, appears to be rendered false by Socrates' willingness to die instead of to
escape.

Then we looked at Hume's and Rousseau's altruistic theories of human
nature, in which compassion or sympathy is attributed to humans; this view
denies the truth of psychological egoism and tries to found altruistic morals
on an altruistic account of human nature. Hume and Rousseau are critical of
the role of reason in morals—Hume because reason has not and ought not to
have the power to move us to action, and Rousseau because reason divides us
from others and lessens and eliminates the influence of compassion.

I will now use the ideas of Plato, Hobbes, Hume, and Rousseau to state
counterarguments to the Gyges Argument. Each of them yields a conclusion
that is incompatible with the conclusion of the Gyges Argument; each concludes that justice is profitable.

Plato

What is profitable to us is whatever is in our self-interest.
Our (true) self-interest is identical to the (true) self-interest of
others.
Acting justly is acting in the interest of others as well as oneself.

Therefore, it is profitable to act justly, since what is in the interest
of others is also in our interest, these interests being identical.

Hobbes

What is profitable to us is whatever is in our self-interest.
Peace is a common good, being in everyone's self-interest.
A state of peace requires the observance of altruistic moral rules,
rules obliging us to act in both our own and others' interests; that
is, a state of peace requires rules of justice.

Therefore, it is profitable to act justly, except when our self-
preservation is at stake.

Hume and Rousseau   **119**

It is human nature to pursue one's own interest and others'.
Acting justly is acting in the interest of others as well as oneself.
Acting in the interest of others is acting to secure what we want
(psychological altruism).

Therefore, by acting justly (acting in the interest of others), we act
to satisfy our compassionate want (which we would not satisfy, if
we always acted solely to satisfy our egoistic want).

The argument then continues:

What is profitable to us is whatever is in our self-interest.
An act is in our self-interest if and only if it has good consequences
for us (which includes satisfaction of our compassionate wants).

Therefore, it is sometimes profitable to act justly. (But both Hume
and Rousseau allow that sometimes we should act in our own interest rather than the interest of others.)

4.7 The Egoists' Last Stand

The rebuttal of the Gyges Argument based on Hume and Rousseau is
tricky, because it gives a different meaning to ''self-interest'' than the egoist
does. We can bring this out best, perhaps, by formulating the Egoists' Last
Stand:

We have wants that are egoistic.
True, we also have compassionate wants.
But both kinds of wants are always the wants of a self—that is, are
possessions of an ego.

Therefore, in satisfying our compassionate wants, we are satisfying
ourselves, hence acting egoistically.

In short, the Egoists' Last Stand is to maintain that ''self-interest''
always means egoistic interest, while Hume and Rousseau maintain that it
means both egoistic and altruistic or compassionate interest. Hume and
Rousseau can defend their meaning because the Egoists' Last Stand contains a
fallacy, one noted over two hundred years ago by Bishop Joseph Butler in one
of his sermons (Sermon XI). The fallacy, stated here as a variant of Butler's
refutation, is that egoists confuse (a) possession of a want and its satisfaction
by an ego with (b) an egoistic want. To confuse them is to embrace a con-

120 tradiction. If a compassionate want and its satisfaction are egoistic, then we are committed to saying that compassion is egoistic. But a want is differentiated by its object or end, not by the identity of the owner. The end of compassion is the welfare of others, not our own, whereas the end of egoism is the welfare not of others but of ourselves. So to maintain that a compassionate want is egoistic is to say that the end of compassion is the welfare of ourselves rather than others, which contradicts the very concept of compassion.

Further, while a compassionate want is indeed our possession, so that its satisfaction can become a matter of self-interest, still, it can be satisfied only when we benefit others, which makes it non-egoistic even though it may possibly be in our self-interest. Compassion and self-interest are not contradictory, even though compassion and egoism are. Hume asks rhetorically, "Now where is the difficulty in conceiving, that . . . from the original frame of our temper, we may feel a desire of another's happiness or good, which, by means of that affection, becomes our own good, and is afterwards pursued, from the combined motives of benevolence and self-enjoyments?"[31]

Of course, this refutation of the egoist depends on the truth of the claim that it is human nature to have compassion. But we have seen conflicting claims about human nature. Which one is true? Maybe none of them. When we have evidence for two different kinds of human nature, this may indicate it isn't something that everyone inherits by birth, but rather something that is learned. If it were inherited, we would have the same nature; we don't, and therefore it isn't inherited.

But surely we don't have to speculate. After all, a lot of scientific knowledge—psychology, sociology, biology—has come to light since Plato, Hobbes, Hume, and Rousseau wrote. Why not look at this knowledge and settle the question scientifically? That's what we'll investigate in the next chapter.

STUDY QUESTIONS

1 Plato says the soul has three parts. What are they and what functions do they have? And how does he use this three-part analysis to argue against the Gyges Argument? How does he connect the many-headed-monster image to the profitability of justice and the health of the soul? And to the health of a state? (For a more detailed proof that the soul has three parts, see Reflection 12, p. 126.)

2 Explain Hobbes's attempt to prove that there are altruistic moral rules of behavior, even though he is a psychological egoist. Contrast his attempt with Plato's.

3 Hume and Rousseau explain the existence of altruistic moral rules dif- **121**
ferently than Plato and Hobbes do. State what is similar and what is
different about Hume's and Rousseau's theories.

4 What is the fallacy in the Egoists' Last Stand?

Reflections on Applications

1 How would you argue against farmers who decide to hoard grain during
a period of short supply? Try to bring as many considerations forward
as you can. After formulating these, reflect on the considerations you
have used in an effort to become more self-conscious about your concept
of the good.

2 Plato believed that a person's true self-interest is not in conflict with that
of others, because he thought them identical in the long run. Do any of
the arguments you just formulated in response to Reflection 1 support
Plato's view? If none do, try to formulate an argument against the
hoarding farmer that does.

3 Below are some quotations from a news story. Reflect on them and list
the related issues discussed in this chapter. Would you be more inclined
to say that the mother was imprudent or that the doctor was egoistic?

> Dr. Dan F. Moorer said yesterday there was nothing unethical in his
> refusal to deliver a baby whose mother did not have enough money to pay
> him. "My conscience is clean," Moorer said. "I don't see why it
> shouldn't be."
>
> Moorer said that he had told the woman as early as November that
> he would not deliver the baby and had made preparations to have her case
> taken over by the county health department, but that she never went to the
> department. "She did nothing whatsoever to help herself," he said.
>
> Mrs. Abrams [whose baby was delivered in a parked ambulance] said
> she did not go to the health department because she had forgotten the doc-
> tor's suggestion.
>
> Moorer said he stopped treating Mrs. Abrams November 30 because
> she was behind in her payments of $7 per office call and hadn't saved the
> $350 he charges to deliver babies.[32]

4 Dr. Moorer reported having received several abusive telephone calls after
news of his refusal spread. Would you recommend the following advice to
him? This advice, contained in an advertisement for the book, is a quote
from *Looking Out for #1,* by Robert J. Ringer.

122

In deciding whether it's right to look out for Number One, I suggest that the first thing you do is eliminate from consideration all unsolicited moral opinions of others. No other living person has a right to decide what is moral (right and wrong) for you.

5 Below are selections from the Administrative Code of Ethics issued by William F. Quinn, ex-governor of Hawaii (as renumbered by me). If you were a government employee in Hawaii, would you support or oppose these rules? Give arguments for your stand.

1 All employees or officials will disqualify themselves from participation in any transaction where they have a personal interest.
2 No employee or official will use his position to secure special privileges or exemptions for himself or others.
3 No employee or official will use his position or office to give preferential treatment to any person.
4 All full-time salaried employees or officials will disclose to their appointing officers their outside employment including hours of work, employer, compensation and nature of the outside employer's business.

6 Do you think that the need to issue such government rules on "conflict of interest" as those above proves anything about human nature or gives support to the Gyges Argument?
7 Do you think the following story about Abraham Lincoln supports the Egoists' Last Stand? Lincoln and another man were riding in a coach, Lincoln maintaining that all men were prompted by selfishness in doing good. Along the way they noticed a sow in great commotion because its piglets were stuck in a slough. Lincoln asked the driver to stop, then got out, lifted the piglets from the mud, and put them on the bank. His companion then remarked, "Now, Abe, where does selfishness come in on this little episode?" "Why, bless your soul, Ed, that was the very essence of selfishness. I should have had no peace of mind all day had I gone on and left that suffering old sow worrying over those pigs. I did it to get peace of mind, don't you see?"[33]
8 Rousseau asserted that egoism holds sway over altruism in society because reason has weakened compassion. But isn't it possible that, with the proper rational restructuring of society, the strength of compassion may be restored, so that it can compete on an equal footing with egoistic wants? A study of shyness at Stanford University showed that this may be the case. Would this indicate that it isn't reason but bad reason that is harmful?

Professor Philip Zimbardo and his students found that, when they interviewed 2,000 persons, 42 percent labeled themselves shy. Typically, they had negative, self-critical thoughts about themselves. This is in strong contrast to Chinese children in schools, nurseries, and child-care centers, where psychologists have found no shy children at all.

Zimbardo is quoted as saying: "The ideology of selflessness and service to the group appears to have replaced the ego orientation that is the foundation upon which shyness seems to be built in our culture and others. Their ideal is group success. Our culture emphasizes individuality, individual achievement and success. Once you have a concept of success, you have to have another [of] failure. So you're always concerned about failing.'' (La Rochefoucauld and Gore Vidal are credited with saying, ''It is not enough to succeed. Others must fail.'') ''Shyness,'' says the professor,''could be better understood as a product of American values rather than something a person is born with.''[34]

9 Throughout this chapter I have talked about the conflict of goods; apparently, sometimes not both of two or more persons' prudent goods can be satisfied. Think of Joan's and John's starvation situation. We examined Plato's attempt to show the conflict was apparent rather than real. But there is another way of looking at the matter. Most of us might uncritically accept a ''democracy'' of goods, thinking that each person's good has just as much value as another's. However, if we assumed an ''aristocracy'' of goods, then the so-called conflict of goods disappears.

In an aristocracy of goods, in every conflict some one person's goods would be better than another's. Suppose, for example, that Joan is well educated, intelligent, and thoughtful, whereas John is retarded. Wouldn't you decide in this case that Joan's preservation is preferable to John's? You may balk at going counter to your conditioned democratic bias, but you shouldn't balk long because, unless you are a vegetarian, you practice an aristocracy of morals every day you eat meat. Animals are sentient beings, yet you consent to their slaughter and, by buying meat, encourage it. Unless you believe that your own goods are superior to those of animals, you aren't justified in eating meat.

Logically extending this practicing aristocracy to humans, we can dissolve the apparent conflict between goods. In any conflict one person's goods are intrinsically better than another's. Just as you apparently find no conflict between your goods and those of animals because yours are better, so there is no conflict between humans' goods because one is always intrinsically better than another's.

Are you willing to give up eating meat now, so you can stick to the democracy of goods?

10 Here are some excerpts from an interview with Irving Kristol, professor of urban values at New York University, that appeared in a publication called *Exxon USA*. The editor comments that Kristol ''votes for individual liberty with its inelegant shortcomings over the utopian fantasies planned for us by political zealots [fanatics].'' In reading these excerpts, keep in mind that it could be a counter to your arguments against the hoarding farmer, although some remarks show Kristol agreeing with Plato on at least one issue (see if you can spot it).

> Kristol: Today there is a new class hostile to business in general, and especially to large corporations. . . . This new class consists of well-

124   educated and intelligent professionals who work in all levels of government. . . .

Exxon USA: Why does the new class disapprove of the free market
system?

Kristol: From the viewpoint of the new class, the major cost of the
free market comes from its effect on what they call the "quality of life."
They deplore the materialism which a free market system tends to
produce. Ordinary people, who are not rich, have a lot of needs they want
to satisfy. They express these needs in the marketplace. This means
that the marketplace is primarily oriented toward satisfying the commonplace needs of ordinary people. This bothers the new class because
it tends to produce a society that is not very elegant or brilliant. It is
not a society that intellectuals and educated classes are likely to
admire. . . . They feel that society should not be shaped by the appetites of such people.

Exxon USA: Are these people [the new class] willing to sacrifice
freedom to achieve these ends?

Kristol: Of course they are. They tell themselves they are not. . . .
So, they say, we aren't going to use the political authority to intervene
more directly in the life of the nation to give it a better shape for the benefit
of all. . . .

Certainly the new class, through the media, has helped to excite expectations among Americans that would be unreasonable in any society.
It is in the nature of the media to excite expectations. They criticize
authority for failing to satisfy expectations. . . . All satisfaction must be
instant. All demands must be met now, regardless of cost. Our entire
society seems to be encouraging this trend.

Exxon USA: Is such a trend normal to a democracy?

Kristol: I don't think so. I think it is what happens when a
democracy goes soft and loses its moral fiber. We seem to have lost our
capacity to be reasonable. When our demands aren't immediately
gratified, we protest that our rights have somehow been violated. As a
consequence, being a politician today is not much different from being a
demagogue. . . .

Exxon USA: Do you think those of us in the private sector should
fight back?

Kristol: Absolutely. . . . In American politics, it is perfectly
legitimate for any group to defend its interests. Interest-group politics *is*
American politics. . . . When legislation or regulations are proposed that
will have an adverse effect on a corporation, shareholders should step forward into the political process and say, ouch! We're being hurt. We
want you to know that we don't like it. That's American politics. . . .

What is at stake is the question of individual liberty. You don't
have to like corporations in order to think that their existence is
important. . . . They are private. They constitute a sector beyond the
reach of government. Now, that's the sector of freedom. To the degree
that this sector shrinks, for any reason, to that degree individual liberty will
also shrink.[35]

Senator William Proxmire held a position that differs from
Kristol's. The U.S. Steel Corporation refused to deliver steel needed to

construct submarines, unless the government agreed to relax its cost-accounting standards. "This is out and out blackmail," Proxmire declared. "If U.S. Steel had its way, urgent defense projects would be held hostage until the company's self-interest prevailed at the expense of the national interest."[36]

Kristol and Proxmire differ about whether the corporations' (shareholders') or the government's (citizens') interest should prevail when they conflict. According to Kristol, if the government's interest prevails, freedom is lost; according to Proxmire, if corporations' interests prevail (corporate egoism), the national (common?) good is lost. With whose view do you agree? What arguments do you think support that view?

11 Plato knows that wants conflict. I may want two things, not both of which may be obtained. I may want both a savings account and a new car, but under certain conditions I can't have both. So I am forced to choose. I may want the new car more than the savings account. According to Plato, however, the prudent person is rational; having a savings account may be more in my self-interest than having a new car, in which case I will judge that, in this instance, a savings account is a good and a new car is not.

In this situation my stronger want for a new car conflicts with my rational judgment in favor of a savings account. Such conflicts, drawing us in opposite directions, are the very basis for Plato's argument for multiple parts of the soul. But when it comes to moral advice, Plato says we should come down on the side of our rational part rather than our appetitive part. Hume, however, as we saw, thinks this is bad moral advice because reason cannot move us, but only our passions or wants. "Reason is, and ought to be the slave of the passions, and can never pretend to any other office than to serve and obey them".

Whose advice should we follow? Plato's or Hume's? The following remarks of Dewey may help you in deciding. Be sure to make up your mind. (Where Dewey uses "desire," substitute "want.")

> Analysis of desire thus reveals the falsity of theories which magnify it at the expense of intelligence. Impulse is primary and intelligence is secondary and in some sense derivative [not original, derived]. There should be no blinking of this fact. But recognition of it as a fact exalts intelligence. For thought is not the slave of impulse to do its bidding. Impulse does not know what it is after; it cannot give orders, not even if it wants to. It rushes blindly into any opening it chances to find. Anything that expends it, satisfies it. One outlet is like another to it. It is indiscriminate. Its vagaries [whims] and excesses are the stock theme of classical moralists; . . . What intelligence has to do in the service of impulse is to act not as its obedient servant but as its clarifier and liberator. . . . Intelligence converts desire into plans, systematic plans based on assembling facts, reporting events as they happen, keeping tab on them and analyzing them.
>
> Nothing is so easy to fool as impulse and no one is deceived so readily as a person under strong emotion. . . .

126

The glorification of affection and aspiration at the expense of thought is a survival of romantic optimism. . . . Persons of a literary turn of mind are as subject to this fallacy as intellectual specialists are apt to the contrary fallacy that theorizing apart from force of impulse and habit will get affairs forward. . . .

Sometimes desire means not bare impulse but impulse which has sense of an objective. In this case desire and thought cannot be opposed, for desire includes thought within itself. The question is now how far the work of thought has been done, how adequate is its perception of its directing object. . . .

No issue of morals is more far-reaching than the one herewith sketched. . . .

The separation of warm emotion and cool intelligence is the great moral tragedy.[37]

 **Reflections on Theory**

12 *How many parts has the soul?* Plato, like many others, thought that a psychology of human nature was a necessary part of a moral theory. In his psychology he maintained that the soul has three parts. His argument for this was based on the principle of opposites: (1) No one thing can (2) act in opposite ways or be in opposite states (3) at the same time (4) with respect to the same part of itself and (5) in relation to the same object.[38] Nothing can satisfy all five of these conditions; they are incompatible.

Take his example of a spinning top. It is (1) one thing (5) in relation to the same object, the floor. And (3) at one and the same time it is (2) both at rest and in motion, which are opposites, because the top stays at the same spot on the floor and so is at rest, but also is spinning and so is in motion. Because the spinning top satisfies four of the five incompatible conditions—(1), (2), (3), and (5)—the condition that cannot be met is (4): the rest and the motion cannot be with respect to the same part of the top, but must be referred to different parts. And indeed this is true; with respect to the axis the top is at rest, while with respect to the circumference it is in motion. Plato's argument for the soul having parts is analogous to the example of the spinning top. As illustrated in section 1.2, one may find oneself in opposite states about the same object at the same time: You're so mad at the cop who gave you a ticket that you'd like to slug him but, contemplating the consequences, you think better of it.

Reflect on the following quotation from the French artist Eugène Delacroix, some of which appears to be in agreement with Plato and some in disagreement.

All men are bizarre and inexplicable composites of contraries; that is what those fellows who turn out novels and plays refuse to understand.

Their men are all of one piece. There are no such creatures. There are
ten men in one man, and often they all show themselves within one hour,
under certain circumstances.[39]

Does this quotation raise any questions or arguments in your mind about
the number of "parts" of our soul? Why three parts—or ten?

13 *Remaining yourself.* In that same newspaper column Charles McCabe
wrote: "For as long as I can remember, the strongest single moving
force in my personality has been to remain myself. That it has not
been an easy thing might be suggested by the words of the great French
painter [Delacroix] quoted above."

Do you think an argument can be given to show that McCabe
ought to have written "that it is an impossible thing" rather than "that
it has not been an easy thing," given the truth of the principle of opposites and of Delacroix's remarks?

14 *Social conditions, not human nature, explains crime.* You might be inclined to think that the need for conflict-of-interest rules and legislation
favors the advocates of the Gyges Argument, because in that argument
it is predicted that a ring possessor will perform crimes. There the
commission of crimes is thought to prove the egoism of human nature.
However, another explanation of crime is possible. A Marxist explanation, first offered by William A. Bonger, a Dutch professor of
sociology, is outlined in the following remarks. (Bonger's book is
Economic Conditions and Crime, published in 1916.)

> Step by step, he [Bonger] implicated the very spirit of capitalism in the
> genesis of criminality. Capitalism taught men to compete, to accumulate
> property at the expense of others, to exploit others. Crime involved the
> robbing or exploitation of other people. Under capitalism, the economic
> mechanism itself, since it set the interests of all in eternal conflict, made
> men more egoistic, less compassionate and less concerned about the good
> opinion of others, and hence more capable of crime.
>
> Capitalism also inevitably produced a class system, and that system
> added characteristic pressures towards crime at each level of society. For
> the wealthy capitalists there were avarice and ruthless competition. For the
> small bourgeoisie there was the precariousness of their position. For
> the proletariat [working class], above all the lumpenproletariat [bums and
> rabble], there were the injustices and degradations under which they
> lived. It was by these pressures that crime, as a mass phenomenon, was
> shaped.[40]

This alternative explanation of human behavior relies on the notion that our social conditions, their structure, pressures, training, conditioning, conflicting class interests, and so forth, determine how we
act. Thus when we find criminal and egoistic human behavior, we
should attribute it not to human nature but to social conditions. These
alternative explanations have been referred to as the "nature versus
nurture" explanations.

128   Has reading the outline of Bonger's theory altered your view about egoism in any way? Has it led you to be skeptical about an egoist picture of your nature? Forced you to elaborate your defense of ethical egoism? Helped you to understand better why someone would act egoistically?

15 *Egoism explains social conditions, not vice versa.* Weigh the following argument, which an egoist might use to defend the egoistic viewpoint.

Marxists and others argue that egoistic behavior is accounted for by social conditions. But they don't seem to realize that the existence of such conditions itself has to be explained. In my view these egoistic social conditions, such as capitalism and private property, are explained by my theory of human nature. Such social conditions have evolved precisely because humans devise social schemes that reflect their egoistic nature.

This doesn't prevent me from acknowledging, though, that social conditioning does affect people's specific behavior. In fact, I can use it to my advantage. Some try to refute me by pointing to exceptions to egoistic behavior such as Socrates' refusal to escape. (See section 4.4, p. 113.) However, when we find exceptions, rather than using them to disprove egoism, we should look for exceptional conditions that blinded the "exceptional" humans from truly understanding their real self-interest. They were blinded by clearer-sighted egoists who successfully conditioned them to believe they ought to act in other persons' interests. When such successful conditioning sets in permanently, the conditioners have imposed a "second nature" on the poor boobs.

16 *Compassion is not learned, but original.* You can readily understand that the second half of the above argument could be used against Hume's and Rousseau's belief that human nature has compassionate as well as egoistic passions and wants. The egoist could argue that compassion is a result of social conditioning. Hume anticipates such an argument and tries to meet it. Does he do so to your satisfaction?

> From the apparent usefulness of the social virtues, it has readily been inferred by sceptics, both ancient and modern, that all moral distinctions arise from education, and were, at first, invented, and afterwards encouraged, by the art of politicians, in order to render men tractable [manageable], and subdue their natural ferocity and selfishness, which incapacitated them for society. . . . But that *all* moral affection or dislike arises from this origin, will never surely be allowed by any judicious enquirer. Had nature made no such distinction, founded on the original constitution of the mind, the words, *honourable* and *shameful, lovely* and *odious, noble* and *despicable,* had never had place in any language; nor could politicians, had they invented these terms, ever have been able to render them intelligible, or make them convey an idea to the audience. . . .
>   The social virtues must, therefore, be allowed to have a natural beauty and amiableness, which, at first, antecedent to all precept or education, recommends them to the esteem of uninstructed mankind, and engages their affections.[41]

17 *Altruism displayed only when no self-interests are at stake.* Appraise and take a stand on the following argument that egoists might make.

Yes, it's true that human nature has compassion as well as egoistic wants, as Hume and Rousseau maintain. And the presence of compassion does account for the origin of altrustic moral rules and legislation. However, while our compassion leads us to accept altruistic rules, our egoistic wants, being stronger, lead us to violate them when these two kinds of want come into conflict. Thus, in sizing up and accounting for human behavior, we should always look for the egoistic motives. When we find people acting altruistically, it is because nothing egoistic is at stake; hence the existence of altruistic behavior proves nothing about the falsity of egoism. Don't listen to what people say but rather watch what they do, when compassion and egoism are competing for mastery.

5
Moral
Psychology
and Sociobiology

5.1 Of Rats and Men

Scene: A rat psychology laboratory. Liz, an experimental psychology major, and Gus, a philosophy student.

Liz: What're you doing over here in the psych lab, and why do you look so gloomy and depressed?

Gus: I look gloomy because I *am* gloomy. It's that discussion we had the other day. I just realized how awful the human implications of your rat psychology are. So I've come over to talk you into dropping your psych major and taking up philosophy instead.

Liz: You've got to be kidding.

Gus: I'm not kidding at all. You must have read what B. F. Skinner* says about humans, based on experiments he performed on rats and pigeons.

Liz: Of course. We have to know that to understand how rewards encourage rats to run through the maze, and how getting them to do it several times reinforces their learning. Skinner's very big on conditioning—giving rewards and punishments to get animals to learn a bit of behavior and then get them to modify it.

Gus: Do you know he thinks we can condition humans too?

Liz: Of course. It works very well and it's not a bad thing at all. It helps people stop smoking, for example, and that's good.

Gus: To stop smoking is fine—I did it myself. But it's the *way* a person does it that's important. I did it by *deciding* not to smoke anymore. I'm proud of that. But if I'd stopped smoking by Skinner's method, I'd feel no better than a rat, because somebody would have manipulated me into stopping. I bet you don't have much respect for your rats.

Liz: The more I work with them the more respect I have. They're a lot smarter than I once thought, and tougher, and boy, are they survivors!

Gus: But I'll bet you think you're better than they are, and that you respect yourself.

Liz: Well, sure.

Gus: That's because you're smarter and control them. You play God with them. Well, it's the same if you stop smoking by Skinner's reconditioning method. The psychologist plays God to the smoker, manipulates the smoker like you manipulate the rat. To have human dignity you have to do things on your own, of your own free will. Then *you,* and not the psychologist, ends your smoking.

Liz: I think they can share credit. After all, the person who stopped smoking had to learn new habits.

Gus: I'm talking about the pride and dignity that come from personal

* A behaviorist and experimental psychologist.

responsibility. Here's an example to show you what I mean. Engineers and **133** computer specialists can build very complicated machines now. I just read about one for sale that's got arms and legs. It knocks on your door, opens it when you say "come in," greets you, shakes your hand, and asks if it can work out any problems for you. Let's suppose some guy buys one, learns how to program the robot, and wants to get rid of a woman who's been blackmailing him. So he programs the robot to knock on her apartment door and enter; when she identifies herself, the robot whacks her on the head and kills her. Then it walks out the door, closes it, gets in the elevator—this is the dead of night so it isn't seen—and goes back to its owner's garage. So who's responsible for the killing?

Liz: The man that programmed the robot, of course.

Gus: That's what I think too. The robot can't take credit for what it did. Only the programmer can do that. Only he can take pride in his "work"—and feel guilt as well.

Liz: So your point is that the programmer is to the robot as the psychologist is to the smoker and the rats. Right?

Gus: Right. As I said, I'm depressed because Skinner made me realize this when I was reading some excerpts from *Beyond Freedom and Dignity*—a really chilling book. Listen to how he puts humans down. *(He reads aloud.)*

> Almost all our major problems involve human behavior, and we cannot solve them by physical and biological technology alone. We need a technology of behavior . . . . The role of natural selection* in evolution was formulated only a little more than a hundred years ago, and we are only beginning to recognize and study the selective role of the environment in shaping and maintaining the behavior of the individual. As the interaction between organism and environment has come to be understood, however, functions once assigned to states of mind, feelings and traits are beginning to be traced to accessible conditions, and a technology of behavior may therefore become available. It will not solve our problems, however, until it replaces traditional prescientific views, and these are strongly entrenched. Freedom and dignity illustrate the difficulty. They are the possessions of the autonomous† man of traditional theory, and they are essential to practices in which a person is held responsible for his conduct and given credit for his achievements. A scientific analysis shifts both the responsibility and the achievement to the environemnt.[1]

So what could be plainer than that? The environment's in control, not us. We've just had our "freedom and dignity" taken away! That's enough to make anyone feel depressed—even you. Right?

Liz: I don't see that it's so bad. After all, an automaton, or robot as you say, has some inside control. Missiles have guidance systems that allow them to change course when the outside target changes course. We have

*Survival of the fittest.
†Having free will.

134 *some* inner control. The robot certainly did. If the blackmailer hadn't said to come in, the robot would have gone away. It could respond to the environment.

Gus: Big deal! Besides, the programmer is part of the automaton's environment. The programmer is outside the robot and made its insides. And as you admitted, the responsibility shifts to the programmer, which is just what Skinner said.

Liz: You forget one thing—we can think. I'm my own engineer and can design my own inner mechanism. That makes me unlike an automaton. I'm autonomous; I can control myself. I've got feedback. I can watch myself, and use that to alter myself. For example, I can watch myself smoking, learn that it's bad for my health, and do exactly what behavioral psychologists can do—modify my own behavior just the way they do. To put it your way, I play God to myself.

Gus: There are two things wrong with what you just said. You want to know what they are?

Liz: Yes, though I don't like the way you put it.

Gus: Sorry. First, it's been proven that computers can design other computers and can learn to re-design themselves. Some already do. So your "feedback" defense doesn't make you different from automatons. Second, when you say how you can modify yourself you put some steps in there that involve thinking and deciding. Where do you think they come from? It's not *you* that's responsible for them, it's the environment, so you're not able to escape outside control after all. Here, I'll draw you some diagrams. *(He makes some quick sketches.)*

One. You perform some act, say smoking, A_1.

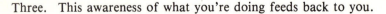

Two. You watch yourself smoking; you're aware of it.

Three. This awareness of what you're doing feeds back to you.

Four. You think and decide what to do.

Act$_2$: Stopping smoking

Five.   After thinking and deciding, you perform a different act, not smoking, A$_2$.

I say you're not able to escape control because of what happens in diagram four, where you're thinking and deciding.   You may think you're in control at this stage, but if Skinner is right in saying that we're the product of evolution, then when all is said and done, this thinking and deciding is done under the control of the environment.   The environment is out there trying to do us in all the time; we've got to adapt in order to survive.   Only the fittest survive, and the fittest are those who have evolved the equipment upstairs in the brain so as to figure out how to adapt to a hostile environment.

Liz: So you're saying our head is a black box and this black box is a product of evolution, and what's inside the black box is under the control of evolution and not us.

Gus: What do you mean, a "black box"?

Liz: A black box is anything that has input and output, that changes the input to the output.   The operations inside that make the changes can't be observed directly.   You can only infer them by noticing the difference between the input and output.

Gus: Give me an example.

Liz: A decoding machine that you can't open would be one.   The input would be some gibberish you can't read, the output would be something in English that you *can* read.   The decoding machine had some inside operations that changed the input into the output.   Since you can't get inside it, you have to infer how it makes the changes.

Gus: I get it. Okay, our head is a black box.   The input could be my awareness of my smoking, and the output the fact I stop smoking.

Liz: Right.

Gus: But a brain surgeon can open someone's head.   It's not closed to us like a black box.

Liz: True, but we can't observe the operations directly.   If we could, we'd know the mechanics of how people think and decide.   But we don't. We have to infer the mind's operations—that's what psychology's all about. You can't look at the brain and "see" memorization, but because we notice memorized outputs, we infer that there's some operation in the brain that stores information.

Gus: So in the end memory depends upon some physiological changes in the brain's nerves?

Liz: There has to be some chemical change, right.

Gus: That's even more depressing! If all the brain's operations are physical and they're the basis for thinking and deciding, then all our thinking

136 and deciding are controlled by chemical laws. This means we aren't in control for sure. Instead, the physical laws of the universe are in control of us. That's what depresses me about Skinner's psychology—it means the end of morality. He says freedom and dignity are "pre-scientific," as if they were myths told by ignorant people. That's because he thinks our moral output isn't controlled by us but by our physical brain, which was made by nature and not by us. Suppose I'm watching someone beating up a kid—that's my input—and I go over and stop him—that's my moral output. But I can't take credit for it—I'm not acting freely on my own, so I don't have any moral dignity.

Liz: So what's new? Weren't there always people who thought we weren't in control of ourselves? The black box theory has been around a long time. The old name for it was "human nature." People do what they do, including moral and immoral things, because that's the way they are—that's their nature. All Skinner's doing that's new is learning more about the nature of the black box. That should cheer you up, not depress you. Getting more knowledge is useful. Think of it—by conditioning, we can modify immoral behavior tendencies and replace them with moral ones.

Gus: But humans as we've known them are being abolished, which is what Skinner thinks he's doing. He says so himself.

Liz: You haven't got it quite right. The mythical, prescientific human is abolished, not the scientific one. And besides, you just agreed that a lot of thinkers long before Skinner believed human nature was the cause of our actions. So the human-nature human hasn't been abolished. What's new is that we've learned that we're products of evolution, we've learned where human nature comes from, which is an advance in knowledge. Look, I think you ought to be more scientific about this, to have more faith in science. I do. That's why I'm taking experimental psychology, and why my adviser has me taking biology courses. I suggest you take some, too, instead of just reading all those literary and philosophical types. You may not like the truth about human nature, but you'd better face it. If you knew the truth, you might not feel so glum about the loss of freedom and dignity; you'd feel more resigned and at peace with yourself. And you would't take all those phony moral burdens on yourself. Maybe it's time you abolished the Old Adam, Gus.

Gus: Maybe. But I'd sure like to be in control of who I am and what I do. I'd rather be a depressed, free, autonomous person than a happy automaton. Look, I'll make a deal with you. I'll agree to learn something about evolution and what psychologists and sociologists and biologists say about it and human nature, if you'll agree to learn some philosophy of morals.

Liz: You're serious?

Gus: Absolutely!

Liz: Okay, that makes sense. You learn more about the input and I'll learn more about the output. Maybe then we can figure out what's inside the black box. And maybe I'll know what to think about my roommate. When

she went home at the end of the semester, she took some of my clothes and   **137**
records with her!

Gus: Right.   Should you blame her because she decided freely to grab
your stuff, or should you blame her home environment for making her what
she is?

Liz: I'm not sure it's that simple.

Gus: Maybe it *is* more complicated, but that's what it comes down to in
the end.

This chapter is dedicated to Liz, and section 6.10 is dedicated to Gus.

5.2 The Relevance of Human Nature to Morals: Five Features

Psychology is the branch of science that studies beings with a psyche or
mind—especially humans.   Moral psychology is that branch of psychology
that tries to explain moral behavior—any behavior that on some occasion is
considered either right or wrong, good or bad.   Moral psychology's explanation of human behavior is based on human nature: we do what we do because
we are what we are.   According to moral psychology, human nature has five
features that are relevant to morals.

First, human nature is claimed to be *uniform:* given the same situation, we all make the same response; therefore, we must all share the same
nature.   This assertion underlies the Gyges Argument's claim that, if social
restraints were removed, we would all selfishly pursue our own interest.

Second, human nature is relevant to morals because no act of ours
escapes its influence; it is *comprehensive,* it comprehends all acts.   Every
act is allegedly motivated by a want; and every want comes from our nature.
A passage in Isaac Bashevis Singer's novel *Shosha* illustrates this point—that
every act of every human is caused by the "same powers."

> Somewhere I had had a trace of faith in free will, but this morning I felt
> sure that man possessed as much choice as the clockwork of my wristwatch
> or the fly that stopped on the edge of my saucer.   The same powers were
> driving Hitler, Stalin, the Pope, the Rabbi of Gur, a molecule in the center
> of the earth, and a galaxy billions of light-years distant from the Milky
> Way.   Blind powers? Seeing powers? It did not matter any more.   We
> were fated to play our little games and to be crushed.[2]

If human nature is comprehensive—if, that is, it causes all our
acts—then once again it is relevant to morals because some of these acts are
moral, others immoral.

138   Third, our human nature is said to be *causally powerful,* to have causal power. It is human nature to want sex, a desire that has driven humans to countless acts during thousands of years. When Paris abducted Helen to Troy, her beauty launched a thousand ships as the Greeks set sail for Troy to punish the abductors and get Helen back. The Greek poet Homer tells us in the *Iliad* about the rage and jealousy that started the Trojan War, which shows how causally powerful our human nature is. We haven't all acted like Paris, who abducted Helen, but we have flirted, cut our hair or let it grow, put on lipstick, given presents, gone dancing, punched rivals, and so forth—acts all motivated by our natural sexual want. If our nature is egoistic, we are driven to self-interested acts; if our nature is altruistic, we are driven to benevolent acts. Since our nature has causal power, the kind of nature we have is relevant to morals because it may impel us to moral or immoral acts.

Fourth, this human nature is said to be something *inherited* or *natural,* not something we make ourselves; its making is out of our control. So Skinner claims, as we saw in Liz and Gus's conversation. We are what we are because the environment made us that way; only the fit survive in a hostile environment. This is relevant to morals because it sets limits to our moral control. Ivan Ilyich wished he had become a different, unordinary person; Nietzsche urges us to change our values and stop being part of the herd; Marin recommends that to cure excessive egoism—that is, the idolatry of the self—we should become more communal. All these attitudes propose, in the most general terms, some form of self-realization. But if we are wholly natural, then we can't change ourselves, or if changeable, we are so only within limits. We are prisoners of nature.

Fifth, our nature is *fixed.* Says newspaper columnist Charles McCabe: "It has always been one of my deepest-held convictions that human nature changes very little through the centuries, that the Athenian and the New Yorker would react similarly to the same kind of stimuli."[3] If somebody abducted your wife or husband, you would feel today just the way Helen's husband felt when Paris kidnapped her. Shakespeare's *Othello* recounts the jealousy Othello felt because he thought his wife, Desdemona, was having an affair with another man; Othello smothered Desdemona in rage. This hasn't changed; men today feel the same way. The relevance of human nature to morals—to warring and killing—is evident.

We can sum up this discussion in one sentence: *Every act of every human (our nature is comprehensive), in any historical period (it is also fixed), when facing a similar situation, will, regardless of culture or upbringing or education (it is naturally inherited), be caused by wants (it has causal power) to act the same way (it is uniform).* So human nature is uniform, comprehensive, causally powerful, natural, and fixed.

Let's call this theory of human nature and its account of human acts, including moral conduct, "simple moral psychology."

5.3 Simple Moral Psychology   139

By adding human nature to our Links diagram, we get this diagram of simple moral psychology:

Link 0	Link 1	Link 2	Link 3
HUMAN NATURE →	WANTS →	GOODS →	ENDS → ACTS
	Natural Link	Endowment Link	Selector Link / Purposive Link

Link 0 is the "natural" link. Our human nature has inherited certain wants and drives. Conduct is performed to satisfy them: we run to catch the bus, win the race, or trim the fat from our body. We are naturally mobile; we begin to move in the womb. We are naturally competitive, according to defenders of capitalism. We naturally want to be slim and attractive, according to health enthusiasts; to be overweight is unnatural, unhealthy.

Link 1 is the "endowment" link. Our wants endow objects with goodness; food is a good because we get hungry. The motivating energy of our wants presses through the links to activate us; my hunger, present or anticipated, motivates me to get a job.

Link 2 is the "selector" link. We select our ends on the basis of what we take to be their comparative goodness. Tonight I'm really hungry, so I order the full-course meal rather than just the entrée.

Link 3 is the "purposive " link. Given that I have an end—a purpose I want to accomplish— I have to figure out the means of attaining it. These means are the acts we must peform.   If my end is to eat a lot of very good full-course meals in the best restaurants, I have to do those things that will get me the money needed.

Let's work through the Links diagram of simple moral psychology with a single example. Your human nature has sexual wants, the natural link. These wants *endow* persons of the opposite or same sex with goodness, give them value. Some person may be desired more than another and/or be thought preferable, which leads us to select one of them. Your end is to get him or her to consent to be your lover or spouse. Now you have to figure out the acts that will accomplish your *purpose*, such as asking him or her to go out, showing affection, giving presents, and so forth.

This is a tidy, simple way to explain human behavior. People use it a lot. How often have you heard someone say, "Well, that's just human nature. What else can you expect?" But is simple moral psychology true?

Gus thought it spelled the end of freedom and dignity and reduced us to the level of rats—a gloomy conclusion. But as Liz said, not wanting it to be

140   true doesn't make it false. She suggested looking at the scientific evidence, which is one thing we'll do in this chapter. However, we might be suspicious of its truth, since there seems to be a long-standing controversy about the kind of nature we do have—egoistic, altruistic, or a combination. All sides provide evidence for their view. The fact that there's something to be said for an egoistic *and* an altruistic nature might incline one to think that our nature isn't wholly inherited and fixed; perhaps nurture—upbringing, education, culture—can explain this mixed evidence better than nature.

Some, like B. F. Skinner, think human behavior patterns can be modified to a great extent: we can be conditioned to be egoists or altruists. Yet even for such theorists, there are limits to modification. You might be able to get people to eat less if they're overweight, but you can't cut out their food entirely and still have a live patient. Wet clay and granite can both be shaped, but they have different limits because of their nature; you can poke your finger in wet clay but not in granite. The range of possible behavioral patterns for humans and rats differs as well.

5.4 Challenging Simple Moral Psychology

Simple moral psychology can be subjected to many challenges. In this section I shall show how these challenges force defenders of moral psychology to make their theory more sophisticated. My aim in this and the next section is to push anyone who thinks moral conduct can be explained by human nature past the easy, glib use of phrases like "That's just human nature," as if they explained jealousy, selfishness, aggressiveness, competitiveness, pity, gratitude, envy, and so forth.   Serious inquiry into the existence and influence of human nature has to go beyond casual, half-baked conclusions drawn from superficial observation of a few people in one's own narrow circle; it has to go beyond repetition of a handy phrase.

CHALLENGES TO THE UNIFORMITY OF HUMAN NATURE. Simple moral psychology claims that everyone has the same human nature.

Challenge. Anthropologists report the variable conduct of peoples at different times and/or different places. If human nature is universally uniform, as simple moral psychology claims, then the conduct caused by it should be uniform. However, it is not; therefore, human nature is not uniform.

Response. We have to distinguish between external and internal causes of acts. Human nature is the internal, and our environment the external, cause. Skinner showed how much influence our environment has. Both causes contribute to the conduct of humans that results. For example, the environment of a South Seas island will cause food-gathering conduct and related activities quite different from those caused by an Arctic environment; however, persons in both environments uniformly gather food because their internal conditions are universally uniform. The Eskimo learns how to lure seals to breathing holes in the ice, of which a Trobriand Islander need know nothing.

By distinguishing between internal and external causes, moral psychology is rescued from its first challenge. Now, however, it will have to deal with a new challenge, this time to the universal uniformity of the *internal* condition.

Challenge to the response. If human nature, the internal cause, is uniform, then humans would have the same wants everywhere at all times, even if the acts designed to satisfy those wants—such as those of the Eskimos and Trobriand Islanders—are different. But we notice that people's wants differ enormously. Even identical twins who grow up in the same family environment and have the same education—in other words, similar nurture—don't have the same wants. Ann is fascinated by medicine, but it disgusts Andrea.

Response to the new challenge. This challenge can be met by pointing out that there are two kinds of wants—original or basic, and acquired wants. It's true that not everyone has the same wants, but this difference applies only to *acquired* wants; we all have the same basic wants. Ann's desire to study medicine is an acquired want, not a basic one like food or sex. And of course, different acquired wants cause different actions: Ann will study different subjects than her twin sister, Andrea, will. Despite the differences in acquired wants, Ann and Andrea have the same basic wants determined by their biological and psychological nature.

CHALLENGE TO THE COMPREHENSIVENESS OF HUMAN NATURE. Simple moral psychology claims that every act of humans can be explained by human nature.

Challenge. The claim is false because moral psychology can't use human nature to explain conduct caused by the acquired wants. Unlike basic, original wants, these acquired wants are not determined by our human nature but by our nurture. Therefore moral psychology is incomplete; it needs a supplement.

The challenger to moral psychology might think this supplement should be a moral theory that prescribes what conduct we ought to perform, and what moral education we ought to undergo, in order to acquire the suitable motivating wants that will become our "second nature." For example, if a moral psychologist maintains that our nature is originally egoistic, then the moralist may prescribe practising altruistic behavior and invent a moral education—Sunday school, social work, a course in ethics, some Platonic dialogues, or a tour of the solitary cell blocks in a maximum-security prison—that will enable us to acquire the motivating want to be less egoistic

142 and to wish to help others. Thus benevolence could be an acquired want, suitable to motivate us to do good for others. If this were to occur, the acquired want wouldn't come from our human nature—quite the opposite; it would have come from prescribed conduct and education, which works against nature.

The opponents of the moral psychologists—let's call them the moralists—might completely reverse the way to look at human conduct. The moralist might argue that the correct understanding proceeds in the opposite direction from the way the moral psychologist puts it, and might redraw the links diagram like this:

$$ACTS \rightarrow ENDS \rightarrow GOODS \rightarrow \begin{array}{c} ACQUIRED \\ WANTS \end{array} \rightarrow \begin{array}{c} ACQUIRED \\ HUMAN\ NATURE \end{array}$$

An example: My moral rules tell me that cheating a friend is wrong, so I reject the end of getting more money than it's worth from the sale of my car to a friend, which shows that money gotten that way isn't a good. By finding that cheating is wrong, I acquire a new want—to be honest with my friends, which means that I've acquired a new, second human nature. Consequently my human nature is the *result rather than the cause* of my acts.

This is an important re-orientation of our theoretical perspective. I will elaborate this and the following challenge when we come to the ethics of Immanuel Kant.

CHALLENGE TO THE CAUSAL POWER OF HUMAN NATURE.
Simple moral psychology claims that human nature's wants *and they alone* have the causal power to move us to act.

Challenge. The challenge to this claim is not that human nature has *no* causal power; the moralist can grant that some acts are caused by basic wants, but emphasizes that they are *not the sole cause* of our acts. This is shown by the previous challenge, in which human nature is viewed as the result, not the cause, of acts. But to make this point stick, the moralist has to provide another causal force for our acts. This could be some such faculty as will, or God's or the devil's power moving through us.

Suppose, however, that the causal power is not God's or the devil's, but our own. Here, too, the moralist's view differs from the moral psychologists: where the moral psychologist tries (a) to *explain* conduct by (b) tracing it causally to what we *are,* the moralist attempts (a) to *guide* and *justify* conduct by (b) suggesting what we *ought to be.* The moral psychologist finds us (at least partially) *made;* the moralist finds us (at least partially) *unmade.* The moral psychologist asks "Why do we act as we do?" whereas the moralist asks "What ought we to do?" or "What ought we to be?" The moralist tells us to exercise our will to do the right thing—not sell our car to a friend at an unfair price—rather than to give in to our natural want to get all we can for ourselves. The moralist tells us to develop a character that can compete with the natural self, and to give it the will power to defeat the causal power of human nature. Human nature may indeed be rotten and lead us to commit wrong acts; this is all the more reason to develop a good, strong character that can counter our natural tendencies.

CHALLENGES TO THE INHERITANCE OF HUMAN NATURE.

Simple moral psychology claims that our nature is inherited by us at birth.

Challenge. The moralist points out that the moral psychologists defend their theory against the first challenge—the challenge to the uniformity of human nature—by distinguishing between original and acquired wants. Once the moral psychologists grant that we have acquired wants, they have acknowledged that we don't inherit a full set of wants with our human nature. Each acquired want implies that there is some non-natural aspect of our nature—for example, wanting to be honest with our friends. Human nature, in short, is at least partially an artifact, something made by humans. Further, which kind of artifact we become depends on which morals we adopt as our guide to self-realization. St. Francis of Assisi gave up his inheritance because he wanted to be something other than a rich, idle fop; he made himself into what he willed to be.

Response. Our acquired wants can be explained by tracing them back to wholly natural original wants. We can do this by making use of psychological and sociological laws. Humans and other animals can be conditioned to behave in certain ways by giving rewards (positive conditioning) and by punishing (aversive conditioning). This is a well-attested psychological law. These rewards and punishments are based on original wants. For example, Ivan Pavlov conditioned dogs to raise their foot at the sound of a bell. He did it by ringing a bell at the same time that he gave an unpleasant electrical shock to the dog's foot. The dog learned to associate the bell with the shock. The shock was something the dog didn't want, but the dog didn't have to learn this, since to be free of pain is an original want. When the bell sounded, the dog lifted its foot to avoid the shock. More complicated conditioning is simply an elaboration of this simple conditioning situation, nothing different in principle. Thus the acquired behavior of lifting the foot is traceable by psycho-physiological laws to an original want to be free of pain.

Similarly, some sociologists have claimed they can give mathematically precise formulae to predict the numerical ratio of leaders to followers in groups of differing sizes. But these laws relate to needs for organization and order dictated by social survival, which is getting back to original needs.

So, given (a) certain environmental conditions, (b) certain social conditions, (c) certain psychological, physiological, and sociological laws, and (d) certain original wants, then such-and-such acquired wants will occur.

Challenge to the response. To defend moral psychology, its advocates have to make the simple theory more complex. At this point, we have a

144 "psychosociology" of human conduct, because we have both psychological and sociological laws introduced to explain our actions. This enrichment creates a demand for more investigation and data. But already the evidence for moral psychology begins to look thin. No well-attested laws enable us to predict which acquired wants result from particular environmental and social conditions and our original wants, nor have the original wants been identified conclusively. Novelists' imaginative constructions are as plausible as those of the moral psychosociologists.

Further, given the immense complexity of environmental and social conditions, it is foolish to claim that in the present state of our knowledge we can express these conditions with enough exactitude to use them as laws about acquired wants. Remember that to state a natural law we are required to specify conditions precisely: "If such-and-such conditions are present, then . . ." If these conditions can't be precisely specified, then no law can be stated.

CHALLENGE TO THE FIXITY OF HUMAN NATURE. Simple moral psychology claims that human nature doesn't change; its wants remain the same and cause similar actions when given similar situations. It changes only under evolutionary pressures.

Challenge. In order to defend their claim that human nature is inherited, in the preceding response the moral psychologists argued that acquired wants are predictable offshoots of original, naturally inherited wants. But this assumes that original wants remain fixed. The belief that human nature can explain human conduct would have to be given up, if it could be shown that original wants aren't fixed but changeable; there simply wouldn't be any human nature left to cause any conduct.

Now in fact we find that all wants, including original wants, are changeable rather than fixed. While moral psychosociologists differ widely on the list of original, fixed wants, there does seem to be wide agreement that the want for nourishment is one; our common biological nature creates the want for food. But we find actual instances in which this original want does not lead to eating behavior, even when food is available. People have deliberately starved themselves to death. Because the food want, according to simple moral psychology, must cause eating behavior, the fact that the person doesn't eat shows that the food want has been modified and turned into its opposite. Surely, if such a basic, original want as the one for food is changeable, then so is every other original want. Therefore, original wants and human nature aren't fixed.

Response. Wants don't *have to* cause specific behavior. The original wants can stay fixed and still be there as wants, without leading to action. You don't always eat when you want food.

Challenge to the response. But, the moralist might argue, you moral psychologists have now given up the heart of your theory. Human nature and its wants were supposed to explain behavior because it caused it. Now you say it doesn't have to cause behavior. Consequently, your explanation of **145** human conduct in terms of human nature is empty. So there must be some other cause of behavior such as free will.

Response to the new challenge. As was said in response to the last challenge, the fact that an active original want doesn't cause some behavior doesn't mean it has disappeared, or been turned into its opposite, or been otherwise modified. Even persons starving themselves to death for a cause continue to have chemical, physiological activity that disturbs their body; only food could stop this disturbance; thus the desire for food persists, which shows it is a fixed want. Additionally, the moral psychologists might say, we can explain why these self-starvers don't eat, nor are we forced to give up our belief that wants cause conduct; there is no need to bring in free will to account for our actions. Their starvation conduct is caused by an acquired, competing want or wants, which may be stronger than the original, fixed want for food. Perhaps they are starving to protect fellow revolutionaries, and do so because they want the revolution to succeed more than they want to eat. The fact that an acquired want is stronger than the original one need not make us give up the view that original wants are fixed. Further, this acquired want may draw its strength from the basic, fixed want from which it came, such as an emotional need for attention and approval.

5.5 Challenging Moral Psychology's Links Structure

The challenge tactic I employed in the prior section has forced moral psychologists to adopt a series of refinements in their theory, in order to maintain its plausibility. The back-and-forth of argument, with each new argument being a challenge or defense and an elaboration of the original opposite claims—a form of discourse known as dialectical process—has produced a more complex moral psychology. I continue the dialectical investigation, focusing now on the links that moral psychologists make in their account of human conduct (section 5.3). This dialectical pressure will force defenders of moral psychology to incorporate biological science into their theoretical account. In section 6.10 I shall investigate the success of this biological addition.

First challenge to the endowment link (Link 1). The target of this challenge is the same as Plato's in his first attack on the Gyges Argument (section 3.6).

Any object of a want is a good in simple moral psychology; if there were no wants, there would be no goods. By parallel reasoning, anything not wanted (shunned) is bad, is an object that is not a good. But wants conflict when it is not possible to obtain simultaneously the objects of two or more wants. Take the case of Rebella: She wants food because she is very hungry, but she also doesn't want food because she wants to starve to death so as not to betray her fellow revolutionaries who are under torture. Rebella cannot simultaneously both have and not have food; therefore her wants conflict.

But Rebella must decide: to eat or not to eat? Yet she can't decide by simply consulting her wants; for in this situation her wants conflict: one want endows food with goodness while the other endows it with badness. Therefore, to decide whether or not she ought to eat, she will have to consult something beyond her wants. It follows that want by itself cannot endow objects with goodness. Because every want may conflict with some other want, no want by itself may endow value. Without the endowment link, simple moral psychology can't account for human conduct.

Response to the first challenge. The moral psychologists' defense against this challenge must let them maintain their claim that wanting, always and by itself, endows things with goodness, and that not wanting endows them with badness. A defense could go like this: Rebella wants food; that's clear, therefore food is a good. But she also wants the revolution to succeed. Now these two wants conflict, because she thinks that the revolution will not succeed if she eats: eating will keep her alive and make it possible for her captors to extract information that will betray her fellow revolutionaries. Consequently, she can't simultaneously obtain both objects of her wants—namely, food and revolutionary success.

However, both food and revolution are goods for her, because each is an object of a want. The problem of deciding on conflicting wants doesn't force us to give up the endowment link; moral psychology provides for this possibility. For competing goods, the Links diagram provides the selector link, Link 2. Rebella can select among competing goods in order to determine which end to pursue and which acts to perform. She can select the *better* of two goods. There is no irresolvable conflict between two goods when one is better than the other.

Second challenge to the endowment link. Here now is another challenge to the endowment link that moral psychologists must answer. We may have conflicting wants between two persons rather than in a single person; the logic of the argument is similar. Rebella wants the revolution to succeed, but her captors do not; whose want is to be satisfied? The conflicting wants of Rebella and her captors make the wants themselves an insufficient basis for deciding. Therefore something else has to be introduced into the situation that will help decide on a revolution's goodness or badness; wants by themselves are not enough. This shows that the endowment theory of simple moral psychology is inadequate.

Response to the second challenge. Again, moral psychologists might defend themselves by claiming that both of two persons' conflicting wants endow their objects with the appropriate value. The selected end however, depends on which of the endowed goods is better—the goods secured by the revolution or the goods secured by the status quo.

Challenge to the selector link (Link 2). The defense of the endowment link has shifted the argument to the selector link. A critic of moral psychology may now wonder about the source of the "better" of two goods. **147** The notion of "better" must be related to wants in some way, if the theory of moral psychology is to maintain itself. This is so because if "better" relates to something besides wants, then something additional to wants and human nature must, at least partially, influence human conduct, thus falsifying the claim of moral psychology that all human conduct relies ultimately on human nature only.

The critic's challenge to the selector link proceeds by a process of elimination. First, there is no want tied to the notion of "better" or "best." A want has to have an object; but "better" and "best" aren't objects, as food is an object for hunger; rather they are comparisons of the goodness of two (or more) objects of two (or more) wants. (For brevity, I shall drop "best" from the ensuing discussion.)

Second, "better" can't be tied to the strength of a want, unless the moral psychologist claims that the selected end is always the better end. Presumably one end is selected over another because its associated want is stronger than the one not selected; the stronger want overcomes the weaker one and so causes the act that occurs. However, we know that this explanation is wrong, because often we realize that the worse end was selected, not the better one. Hence "better" can't be explained by "stronger."

Third, "better" can't be tied to an army of wants. We recognize that wants don't always conflict—sometimes they are allies. Rebella wants more social justice, a better distribution of income, better health care for the poor, and so forth; these wants are compatible, they are allies. The want for a revolution, when analyzed, is an army of wants. So we can imagine each conflicting want having its army. Arguing that the better want has the larger army won't work. Apart from the difficulty of actually determining the relative size of the armies of two wants, "more" may be worse, not better. For example, Hitler was an ambitious man; he probably had a larger army of wants than you have. But probably his "more" was worse than your "less." Further, a want may have the same number of allied wants as its exact opposite: Rebella's captors want to maintain social injustice, keep the wealthy wealthy and the poor poor, don't want to spend tax money for health care, and so forth. Surely we should be able to say which is the better set of wants, which would be impossible if "better" depended on size alone.

Fourth, "better" can't be tied to one kind of want favored over another when they conflict. A defense that tried this could, for example, divide wants into two kinds, egoistic and benevolent, and then claim that, because benevolence is the better kind of want, this gives us a selector principle based on wants. This won't do because, considered as wants, an egoistic and a benevolent want are on the same footing; to say that one is better is to go outside wants for the source of judgment, which of course goes outside the boundaries within which moral psychology claims to operate; this in turn shows that moral psychology fails to explain our selections and consequently our conduct.

The attack on the selector link boils down to this: the moral psychologist

148   cannot account for the comparative value of the objects of wants. A wants-account of goods alone isn't enough to explain conduct when two wants conflict; the account needs to be supplemented with a theory of "better."

At this point the moral psychosociologist becomes a psychosociobiologist whose basic defense is to explain the selection of better goods by the theory of evolution, which will taken up in section 5.7, after a summary of our dialectical exploration.

5.6 Summarizing the Dialectical Elaboration of Moral Psychology

We started with simple moral psychology and examined the challenges to it; defenses against these challenges made the simple theory become more complex. To help you grasp this dialectical exchange, here is a brief summary.

Challenge: Human nature doesn't uniformly cause acts, because human acts vary.

Response: Moral psychology counters by distinguishing between internal and external conditions, each being part of the cause of our conduct; the variations are due to the variety in external conditions rather than variety in human nature.

Challenge: A further challenge to the uniformity of human nature is the existence of varying wants.

Response: The defense against this challenge to the natural link, Link 0, is that we have both original and acquired wants; the variation is attributed to acquired wants.

Challenge: The comprehensiveness of moral psychology is the next feature attacked. Human nature doesn't explain all of human behavior if we have acquired wants. To obtain an understanding of human conduct, we need to supplement moral psychology; some philosophers think this supplement is a moral theory, and that a "moral" understanding of conduct starts rather than ends with acts we are obligated to perform.

Challenge: This reverses the direction of understanding and challenges the causality feature of moral psychology. Morals don't explain our acts by tracing them causally to wants; instead, morals guide and justify our acquisition of wants, these acquired wants being our "second" nature.

Challenge: This in turn shows that acquired wants aren't natural, but are artifacts; so the naturalness or inheritance feature has to be relinquished, too.

Response: The defense against these challenges to comprehensiveness, causal power, and naturalness is that we can explain the existence of acquired wants by showing that they are modifications or changes of original wants. This defense must be declared an article of faith, because we don't have sufficient knowledge to verify the defense's claim.

Challenge: Trying to explain acquired wants as modifications of original **149** ones opens moral psychology to a challenge to the fixity of human nature. If all original wants can be changed into acquired ones, then there are no remaining fixed wants. Rebella's revolutionary fervor shows also that acquired wants may become stronger than original ones; therefore we can't explain all human conduct by reference to an original, natural human nature.

Challenge: The endowment link, Link 1, can be attacked. Rebella wants food, but also wants the revolution to succeed; hence, according to moral psychology, they are both goods. But at the same time they conflict, and a choice between them is inevitable. Which is the better good?

Challenge: This moves the dialectic to focus on the selector link, Link 2. Four challenges to it show that wants by themselves can't account for a comparison of goods. The following sections (5.7–5.10) elaborate one defense that moral psychologists can offer to the attack on the selector link: to make nature the selector. This defense has species' survival depend on selector mechanisms: the better is simply what promotes survival; it is picked *for* us, not *by* us, through natural selection, through survival of the fittest.

5.7 Human Nature and Evolution

Moral psychologists start with the view that humans are natural creatures, that human conduct is caused by natural internal and external conditions, and that humans and human conduct are scientific subject matters just like other natural things such as fish, rocks, ants, trees, clouds, and their respective behavior.

To help us fully appreciate the naturalness of humans, they remind us of a larger process—the evolution of life on earth. Humans and other living things emerged, and are what they are and have the natures that they have, because their natures were suited to survive in the given environment. Ultimately, nature is the great selector; and like it or not, the moral psychosociobiologists tell us that "better" has to be understood in terms of individual and group survival: the better is what enables humans to survive.

Setting sentiment aside, they tell us nature has the last word on which are the better goods. It's true that we make decisions about which of two conflicting goods is better, and that we adopt and use standards of better to guide us in making our decisions. But the standards themselves have to be tested. Only time will tell if our adopted standards enable us to pick out the better; if they do, we survive; if they don't, we perish and become extinct. The ultimate standard, then—the standard of standards—is survival. Environment allegedly shapes us and our standards of behavior, as Gus discovered in reading Skinner. We are warned not to overemphasize the role of reason in adopting standards for choosing the better. According to Edna

150   Heidbreder, the great Viennese psychoanalyst Sigmund Freud took this position, giving the survival standard an even more dominant role.

> At the hands of Freud the intellect receives scant respect. The notion of "reason enthroned" disappears into myth, and the rational man collapses in the midst of Freudian desires. Thought and reason are anything but dominant forces in man's nature; they exist only to serve the great primal urges and desires that are the real masters of human conduct. The intellect is their servant, and a corruptible servant, not above twisting and concealing and manipulating the truth in the interests of its powerful masters. Always reason is motivated by affective [emotional] needs; it exists to do their bidding; directly or indirectly it works to procure their satisfactions. . . .[4]

> Another practice that indicates the secondary role of the intellect is one which Ernest Jones calls rationalization. Rationalization consists in finding *good* reasons for a deed, when the doer is unwilling to reveal or recognize the *real* reason—or when, as is entirely possible, he does not himself know what the real reason is. The occurrence of rationalization means that we do things primarily because we want to, and find reasons secondarily. The man who really *wants* to play golf can find plenty of good reasons why he should do so, both in and out of business hours. . . . Human beings like to think of themselves as ruled by reason, and rationalization is a device that fosters the illusion.[5]

Thus the "great primal urges and desires" are products of evolution and account for our choices; reason merely clothes these naked wants with respectable dress.

This survival standard does not imply that a conscious being like you or I deliberately adopted it as a means of measuring the worth of something. No claim is made that nature has a conscious design or that any planning process is at work. This is a "natural" standard, in contrast to a reasoned "human" standard; it consists of the complex biological relationship between living beings and their environment, as described in Darwin's theory of natural selection. The natural standard of natural selection operates without conscious purpose in the evolutionary process. It produced among other things the human species and with it the internal conditions out of which human standards could emerge. These internal conditions are our inherited nature, including our wants, capacities, and brains. Out of wants and mental calculations have come the standards that we use to decide which of two or more conflicting goods is the better or best.

Here moral psychology tries to meet the challenge that claims it can't produce an account of "better." It's true that such an account can't be created out of elements within the links diagram alone, but by placing the links within the larger context of evolution, an account of "better" can be formulated. Humans have been programmed through their genes to choose the better of the several goods available; if they had not been, they would not have survived as a species. We can understand this more clearly after considering the notion of natural selection and noting how the moral psychologist argues that

survival, the natural standard of "better," worms its way inside the links 151
schema (p. 139) to select human standards of better.

5.8 Natural Selection: Survival of the Fittest

There are four propositions central to natural selection.

(1) *Genetic inheritance.* Offspring in the main resemble the parent. The physical character of living things is determined by the genetic code inherited from parents; the color of your hair, the length of your nose, the shape of your toes are directed by the coded information in your genes. The collection of human genes forms a gene pool. The moral psychosociobiologist points out that the genes and gene pool are the source of human nature's naturalness, fixity, and universality.

(2) *Variation.* While it is true that members of a species resemble one another more than they resemble other things—that is, share a phenotype—even so they are not identical. The characteristics of members of a species vary because of mutations (changes) and differences in the genes; my children don't look exactly like me.

(3) *Species increase.* The membership size of a species, given the rate of reproduction, increases geometrically over time, all other things being equal.

(4) *Limited resources.* The resources of the environment on which members of a species depend do not increase geometrically.

Points 3 and 4 make members of a species "struggle for existence." Because populations increase faster than resources, there are not resources enough for all to survive; those "fittest for survival" continue to exist. Evolutionary change is carried by those fittest to survive, which is to be understood in terms of "natural selection." This occurs through the agency of genetic inheritance and variation (points 1 and 2). Darwin expresses it as follows near the beginning of Chapter III of *The Origin of Species:*

> Owing to this struggle, variations, however slight and from whatever cause proceeding, if they be in any degree profitable to the individuals of a species, in their infinitely complex relations to other organic beings and to their physical conditions of life, will tend to the preservation of such individuals, and will generally be inherited by the offspring. The offspring, also, will thus have a better chance of surviving, for, of the many individuals of any species which are periodically born, but a small number can survive. I have called this principle, by which each slight variation, if useful, is preserved, by the term Natural Selection, in order to mark its relation to man's power of selection. But the expression often used by Mr. Herbert Spencer of the Survival of the Fittest is more accurate.[6]

152   The following example would illustrate the principle of natural selection. Imagine a population of woodpeckers living upon insects that burrow in the bark of trees. Unusually heavy rains wipe out the insects that live near the bark's surface, leaving the deeper-burrowing insects as the sole food for the woodpeckers. Suppose now a slight variation in the length of woodpeckers' bills; the birds with the longer bills can get to the remaining insects and survive, while the shorter billed birds starve to death. The next population will be largely offspring of the longer billed and will themselves be longer billed because of genetic inheritance; further, these longer billed ones will, in turn, be more likely to survive than any remaining shorter billed ones. In this way, nature by the natural survival standard will have "selected" which of the birds have the "better" bills.

Natural selection applies not only to physical characteristics of species, as in our woodpecker example, but also to instinctive behavior. This is where the moral psychosociobiologist makes the connection between evolution and the selector link to explain the origin of standards of "better."

Living beings have a physical nature; they have certain imperative or unavoidable needs, each being necessary to survival. Humans need to ingest food for individual survival and need sex for species survival. Mobile living creatures have to perform some behavior in order to satisfy these needs. Behavior, in the most general sense, is the net result of the complex interaction of many nerve cells.

How does this complex interaction come into existence? Either by learning or by instinct. We may learn that some behavior will obtain our ends and learn how to perform the behavior; the physical state of Liz's rats after learning to get through the maze is different from what it was before, and this changed state makes possible a new "complex interaction." Brains become storehouses of information, because their physical state is chemically altered by learning.

Some behavior is instinctive. Negatively, this means that it was not learned. Positively, this means that the "complex interaction" necessary for the performance of behavior may occur because the nerve cell structure for it is already in place; the structure is inherited, which means that the genetic code provides a creature with the information needed to begin, guide, and complete the performance of the behavior in question. Examples of instinctive behavior are web-weaving by spiders, slave-making by ants, and honeycomb construction by bees, both of the latter nicely described by Darwin in his chapter on "Instinct" in *The Origin of Species*. The complex behavior of building a honeycomb appears to depend on the bees' nerve cell interactions, which are genetically pre-programmed.

Darwin argues that instincts, like physical characteristics, are subject to natural selection.

> Under changed conditions of life, it is at least possible that slight modifications of instinct might be profitable to a species; and if it can be shown that instincts do vary ever so little, then I can see no difficulty in natural selec-

tion preserving and continually accumulating variations of instinct to any extent that was profitable. It is thus, as I believe, that all the most complex and wonderful instincts have originated.[7]

One can view the instincts "as small consequences of one general law leading to the advancement of all organic beings,—namely, multiply, vary, let the strongest live and the weakest die."[8]

By natural selection, then, which includes the natural standard of survival, the "better" instinct will have been preserved. Let's see how this natural standard, external to the links schema, invades it. Let's suppose the external, natural standard of survival of the fittest will "select" for continued existence those creatures with Nature$_1$ rather than Nature$_2$. These two natures are genetically inherited and their instinctive behaviors are genetically programmed ; the natures causally determine which action is to be performed, and when. Nature$_1$ and Nature$_2$, differing slightly genetically, will cause variations in instinctive behavior. Suppose the flies upon which a spider feeds become larger; this could doom the Nature$_2$ spiders that spin webs with fewer and weaker threads, while enabling Nature$_1$ spiders with the instinct to spin stronger webs with more threads to flourish. Thus the spiders that instinctively "select" the stronger webs will survive; "stronger" is better; "better" is now inside the links structure of spiders with Nature$_1$ because if it weren't, the spiders would no longer exist.

5.9 Natural Selection and Human Nature

It takes only two additional premises to enable the moral psychosociobiologist to apply the above account of "better" to the human selector link.

First: Higher animals display instinctive behavior.

Second: Humans too, having evolved like and from other animals by natural selection, must have instinctive behavior, although the percentage of instinctive behavior is smaller. Darwin remarks that "the difference in mind between man and the higher animals, great as it is, certainly is one of degree and not of kind."[9]

The second point shows we can explain human conduct as we explain animal conduct. We, like they, have an evolved nature with its imperative needs. The behavior of the ancestors from which we evolved was directed, partially at least, by genetically programmed information. Because we inherited some genetic information from our animal ancestors, causing instinctive behaviors that had survival value, we may infer that humans too have behavioral instincts. The basic idea here is that there is a continuous link or continuum between our animal ancestors and us.

The human nature account of our conduct is not a mere historical curiosity; Hume and Darwin have their contemporary followers, who have had a widespread influence on people's conception of humans and of what it

154   is reasonable to expect in the way of moral behavior. With the advance in science, these spokesmen have become more sophisticated in their theories. We pursued the dialectical path to this sophistication by the series of challenges in sections 5.4–5.5. The final grounding of human nature is in the genetic inheritance of instincts evolved by natural selection.   Today ethologists and sociobiologists carry the flag of human nature; for them there is a continuum between animals and us that enables us to learn about human behavior by studying animal behavior.   Their fields of ethology and sociobiology study the physiological basis of animals' individual and social behavior; that basis, as we have seen, is the genes and gene pools.

If challenged, could ethologists defend their claim that humans have behavioral instincts? It isn't possible to verify this by direct inspection of the genes. This is where the assumed continuum between animals and us becomes important: because we observe instinctive behavior in animals, ethologists argue, and because animals are similar to us, humans too must have instinctive behavior. Animals and humans are similar because humans evolved from other species and carry some of their genetic code with them. By identifying these ancestor species and their instincts, we can identify our genetically inherited instincts.

To the challenge that some of our ancestors' instincts might have been extinguished in us as we evolved, the psychosociobiologist replies that they will not have been extinguished if they still help us survive. In fact, it is from this functional value that we can draw our explanation of how we select the better of two goods. But obviously, the best defense against the "extinguished" challenge is to study human behavior that resembles our ancestors'; we can infer that it is instinctive if we can show that (a) it is not learned, (b) it is universally displayed, and (c) it is incapabable of modification—that is, it is fixed (Section 5.2). These features let us infer backward through the links diagram, starting with acts and going on to selected ends to goods to imperative wants to human nature to the genetic code, because only a stable genetic structure can account for preprogrammed, universal, enduring behavior.

Well, *do* humans have behavioral instincts? At a conference on sociobiology George Pugh, author of *The Biological Origin of Human Values,* remarked: "Our primary human values are innate. They are the product of human evolution and genetics." For him the human brain is a "biological decision system" formed by evolutionary processes that "control human social behavior."[10] Gus's fears about the loss of autonomy and reinforced by Pugh's remarks.

At that same conference David Barash suggested that our having leaders is due to instinctive behavior. While softening the attack on autonomy, he said: "Sociobiology does not say we must surrender our autonomy to the despotism of DNA [the genetic code in cells]. It doesn't say why some of us vote for Jimmy Carter or Gerald Ford—but it may help say why we choose to have leaders in the first place. In a sense successful cultural conditions [e.g., having leaders] are those which have withstood a process analogous to natural selection; accordingly, they tend to be adaptive, at least for societies if not for individuals.''[11] **155**

But specifically, what instincts if any do we have? The list varies with the theorist, as does the list of innate wants. It is important to keep instinctive behavior, innate want, and innate values distinct. It has been claimed that we have innate *wants* for food, sex, peace, love, life, security, and territory; hence, by the endowment link, they are innate *goods* or values. However, not all instinctive behavior may be connected to innate wants. In humans, suckling is said to be instinctive behavior suited to the innate need for food; but it may be doubted, for example, supposing a sexually innocent childhood, that intercourse is instinctive behavior, even though suited to the innate desire for sex.

The instinctive behavior most discussed recently is aggression, which is said by some to be suited to the innate want for territory. According to ethologist Konrad Lorenz, aggression against one's own kind, which humans practice, is a spontaneous instinctive drive—as much so as in other higher animals.

Lorenz defines aggression as violence directed against a member of the same species [intra-specific]. Thus, strictly speaking, killing a member of another species for food is not an aggressive act. This distinction is important because a predator is not the same as an aggressor. When a predator is hungry he may kill, but his motive is quite different than that of an aggressor, who attacks a member of his own species.

Instincts exist, according to ethologists, because they are survival enhancing. Among other things, the aggressive instinct leads to the distribution of animals over wider territories, selective breeding, and the more efficient use of food resources. Within a given territory, there will always tend to be an equilibrium between predators and their prey. When members of one species become too numerous for the available sources of food, it is not the prey that they decimate [kill in large numbers], but rather their own kind. Hence the most important function of the aggressive instinct is population control.[12]

You may have wondered whether instinctive behavior might not be curbed by our reason or by cultural conditioning. After all, instinctive behavior may on some occasions be harmful to our survival chances; the fact that we have evolved into large-brained creatures with a capacity for reasoning is evidence that brainy reasoning also promotes survival; by natural selection, an intelligent human species has evolved.

Two kinds of responses have been made to this. The first is the kind that Heidbreder attributed to Freud (section 5.7) and that Hume also expressed: reason has no power; our passions and our drives alone have the power to move us. The other response is that of Lorenz, which he shares with Rousseau: reason operates against our interests and survival. (You can see that modern science has added few new ideas to moral psychology.) Lorenz says:

156

> It is a curious paradox that the greatest gifts of man, the unique faculties of conceptual thought and verbal speech which have raised him to a level high above all other creatures and given him mastery over the globe, are not altogether blessings, or at least are blessings that have to be paid for very dearly indeed. All the great dangers threatening humanity with extinction are direct consequences of conceptual thought and speech. They drove man out of the paradise in which he could follow his instincts with impunity [without injury] and do or not do whatever he pleased.[13]

Reason is a threat to our survival for several reasons: first, it enables the weak to survive and propagate; second, it gives us unlimited capacity for self-destruction through advanced technology; and third, it undermines the natural hierarchy by frustrating the superior and preserving the inferior.

Not all is lost, however: according to Lorenz, there is an instinct complementary to aggression—namely, ritualized aggression as in competitive games. Ritualization enables aggressive creatures to satisfy symbolically the urge that triggers aggression. Aggression is not eliminated but rechanneled by ritualization. Unless there were such an instinct, the species would simply wipe itself out. Now that we realize the danger of reason, we can encourage the increase of ritualization so as to blunt aggressive behavior. Humor helps, too, for it releases aggressive tensions. Natural selection has insured our survival because we have acquired the ritualization instinct along with the aggressive instinct.

Lorenz is a contemporary moral psychosociobiologist, an heir of the Gyges Argument's advocates. On the other hand Erich Fromm, another contemporary moral psychosociobiologist, tries to ground moral conduct in a psychological aspect of human nature. His strategy is to point out an imperative psychosocial human need, as for example avoiding aloneness, then to outline what will satisfy this, and to conclude what kind of moral society will satisfy it. It isn't clear whether Fromm thinks there is any instinctive behavior suited to the innate imperative need or not. It is clear, however, that he thinks human nature has an imperative need. Failure to satisfy that need puts an end to our mental survival.

> The physiologically conditioned needs are not the only imperative part of man's nature. There is another part just as compelling, one which is not rooted in bodily processes but in the very essence of the human mode and practice of life: the need to be related to the world outside oneself, the need to avoid aloneness. To feel completely alone and isolated leads to mental disintegration just as physical starvation leads to death. . . .[14]

> There are certain factors in man's nature which are fixed and unchangeable: the necessity to satisfy the physiologically conditioned drives and the necessity to avoid isolation and moral aloneness.[15]

This psychosocial need, suggests Fromm, is in us, first, because we require cooperation for survival, and second because, being self-conscious beings and aware of death and the whole of nature, we feel insignificant; we your examination copy of

LIFE AND MORALS: AN INTRODUCTION TO ETHICS

sent with the compliments of your Harcourt Brace Jovanovich representative

We would very much appreciate it if, after you have had an opportunity to examine the book, you would take a few minutes to give us your comments on this postage-paid reply card. Your response will be most useful in helping us determine how we can better meet your needs and those of your students.

Comments:

Name _____ may we quote you? yes ☐ no ☐

School _____ Department _____

Street Address _____ City _____ State _____ Zip Code _____

Course title _____ approximate enrollment _____

Current textbook _____ I do ☐ I do not ☐ plan to adopt this book

need to belong to something in order to acquire meaning and to lend impor-   **157**
tance to our life.

> Sanity and mental health depend upon the satisfaction of those needs and
> passions which are specifically human and which stem from the conditions
> of the human situation: the need for relatedness, transcendence,
> rootedness, the need for a sense of identity and the need for a frame of
> orientation and devotion. . . . Man's solution to his own needs is ex-
> ceedingly complex and it depends on many factors and last but not least on
> the way society is organized and how this organization determines the rela-
> tions within it.[16]

5.10 Natural Selection of the Better

We can now give a moral psychosociobiological account of how the
standards of "better" that we use to select one good over another are a product of natural selection.   The aim is to show how natural selection invades
the links schema to deposit in species' members one standard rather than
another one for selection of comparative value.

Consider two goods, $Good_1$ and $Good_2$, that are objects of conflicting
wants.   Either $Good_1$ is better than $Good_2$, or $Good_2$ is better than $Good_1$;
both cannot be better in a particular context, although they can be equally
good.   If one is the better good, it is either the only one that promotes or
enhances survival of the species, or the one that promotes survival more.

If the M_1 members of a species are genetically pre-programmed so that
they instinctively prefer the better good, then the M_1s will tend to survive.   If
the M_2 members are genetically pre-programmed either to be indifferent to the
goods or to prefer the worse good, the M_2s will tend not to survive.

Because the M_1s survive, the instinctive preference for the better good is
preserved; this builds a standard of preference into the species that becomes
part of the links schema.   On the other hand, because the M_2s don't survive,
the instinctive preference for the worse is extinguished; this standard of
preference ceases to be part of any links schema.

This is exhibited in the two links diagrams below, where we suppose that
$Nature_1$ is possessed by the M_1 members of a species and that $Nature_2$ is
possessed by the M_2 members.   Suppose further that $Want_1$ and $Want_2$ are
conflicting because $Good_1$ and $Good_2$ are not both obtainable on a given occasion, although M_1 and M_2 members want both $Good_1$ and $Good_2$.   Suppose
additionally that M_1 members have a preference mechanism that selects End_1
and that this selection triggers the instinctive Act_1; on the other hand, M_2
members have a preference mechanism that selects End_2, which triggers the instinctive Act_2.   If it turns out that Act_1 enables the M_1 members to survive,
then the M_2s with the "incorrect" selector trigger become extinct; that leaves

158   only the M_is with the correct selector trigger.   There is now a built-in standard of "better" in the M_i members.

$$M_1: \text{Nature}_1 \begin{cases} \text{Want}_1 \rightarrow \text{Good}_1 \rightarrow \text{Selects End}_1 \rightarrow \text{Act}_1 \rightarrow \text{Survive} \\ \\ \text{Want}_2 \rightarrow \text{Good}_2 \rightarrow \text{End}_2 \rightarrow \text{Act}_2 \end{cases}$$

$$M_2: \text{Nature}_2 \begin{cases} \text{Want}_1 \rightarrow \text{Good}_1 \rightarrow \text{End}_1 \rightarrow \text{Act}_1 \\ \\ \text{Want}_2 \rightarrow \text{Good}_2 \rightarrow \text{Selects End}_2 \rightarrow \text{Act}_2 \rightarrow \text{Extinct} \end{cases}$$

Notice that I used the term "preference." The moral psychologist's account of "better" does not depend upon any special interpretation of "preference."   In section 5.5   (p. 147) the critic of moral psychology's selector link pointed out that neither a want's strength, nor its army of allied wants, nor a particular kind of want such as benevolence, was sufficient to provide an adequate account of " better."   The moral psychologist may point out that he doesn't need any specific one of these as an interpretation of "preferred"; nor does he need something like the vividness of wants or their enduringness, as Darwin suggested.

Any one or a combination of such features of wants might be the factor that operates as the selector mechanism, as the preference trigger, but in themselves, singly or in any combination, they cannot be equated with "better" any more than "prefers" can be.   It is their connection with survival and natural selection that makes them indications of "better".   It is their causal effect inside the links schema as the selector link trigger that makes them the standard of "better" inside that schema.   Strength or enduringness of wants, or any other interpretation of "preference," can equally become a standard of "better" so long as it helps a species survive.   It can do this because it is tied through natural selection to the standard of survival, which is the standard of "better" outside the links schema.

This can be illustrated with Lorenz's aggression instinct and with Fromm's innate psychological need.

Lorenz first.   In explaining Darwin's conception of natural selection, we saw that a species increases in numbers faster than the resources on which it lives.   If this continued unchecked, all species would exhaust their resources and become extinct—unless they killed some of their own kind, which, Lorenz claims, is the solution to the problem.   Only species that exhibited aggression would kill their own kind and so survive.   Thus survival, the outward standard of " better," gets connected through natural selection with a selector mechanism that triggers instinctive aggressive behavior.

Animals have two sources of information for behavioral decisions, the genetic code and the brain.   The lower animals do not have brains adequate enough to acquire the judgment needed to decide to decimate their own kind;

By Phil Frank, Chronicle Features, © 1979

therefore the information must be genetically programmed, which makes aggression an instinct.

We also note that animals live in groups. This too is instinctive. It guarantees that the young, who cannot survive unaided, will have aid. Were group living not instinctive, many species would not have survived.

The aggressive and group instincts may conflict on occasion, in which case one only is better than the other, although this betterness may shift with circumstances; which is the better on a given occasion depends upon which enhances the species' survival. Proper programming for the better obviously should be tied to circumstances. But if a species still exists, we can infer that in the main the proper programming is in place; that is, the external survival standard of "better" has been linked to a sufficient number of internal links standards of "better." On the appropriate occasion, the selector mechanism correctly picked one of the conflicting goods— for example, aggressive behavior rather than group behavior, when the species needed decimating.

Now let's look at Fromm for another illustration of how a survival standard of "better" gets inside the links schema. Fromm, unlike Lorenz, doesn't use an instinct to connect our acts to our human nature. Instead of acts being instinctively selected for their betterness, he thinks of them as being consciously selected. However, he does connect this consciousness of our acts to the survival standard, which he thinks provides a standard of "better" that is objective rather than relativistic.

Fromm is convinced that the objective source of standards for ethical conduct is found in human nature; this is because they are based on humans' " inherent qualities." If these standards, such as the requirement of human relations (the avoidance of aloneness), are violated, we will fall apart mentally and emotionally; our psychic survival will be doomed.

> I shall attempt to show that the character structure of the mature and integrated [unconflicted] personality . . . .constitutes the source and the basis of "virtue" and that "vice," in the last analysis, is indifference to one's own self and [is] self-mutilation."[17]

Fromm's view is that there are conditions, standards, for the survival of the mental and emotional self; these conditons are part of our human nature. When, singly or with others, we consciously choose acts that violate these conditions, we fall apart. The built-in selector standards of our human nature are nature's and not our own consciously chosen ones.

160   Meeting these mental and emotional needs is necessary for not only psychic but also physical survival. Ronald Kotulak reported for the *Chicago Tribune* on the effects of loneliness observed by doctors.

> Most people spend their lives trying to keep one step ahead of loneliness. They don't always succeed . . . What makes loneliness so terrifying?
>
> Explanations range from the ageless search for the meaning of life to the feeling of being an infinitesimal speck in an infinite universe. People have long known of this powerful stranger within, and some have used it to destroy others.
>
> Solitary confinement, for instance, an ancient technique used to break down the human spirit. . . . Those who have undergone some type of isolation call it "naked horror." Body functions go awry. A person becomes fidgety and irritable. He may start to tremble, his blood pressure may rise, his hair may stand on end and he may develop stress ulcers. . . .
>
> "It is in the nature of human beings to try and avoid loneliness. That is one reason why we cling to our parents, have friends, get married, have our own children and have jobs and other social activities," said Dr. Melvin Prosen, a psychoanalyst at Chicago's Rush-Presbyterian-St. Luke's Medical Center.[18]

Kotulak reported on studies which suggest that having a pet can prevent "the lonely from drifting off to an early death." Eleven out of thirty-nine patients in a hospital who didn't have pets died within a year after being admitted; only three out of fifty-three who had pets died during the same period. Thus it is "better" to avoid loneliness because it literally leads to survival.

To summarize, thus far in this chapter I have outlined the minimum moral psychology, which I call "simple moral psychology," and the five features which this theory attributes to human nature ; I have also shown how this fits in with the links schema. Then I proposed a series of challenges —many of them traditional—to the features and links. The defenses that moral psychologists could make were stated, which produced a "complex" moral psychology that seemed more plausible.

This increased plausibility involves three things. First, the claim that we humans are natural creatures because we are products of evolution. We aren't unique beings who turn up willy nilly without any resemblance to other creatures. Any account of human conduct that ignores this evolutionary factor, says complex moral psychology, is out of touch with an important source of information about us. Second, moral psychology's plausibility is increased by an understanding of natural selection, inherited genetic structure, and instincts; ultimately, human nature is contained in a genetic code. And third, moral psychology appears plausible because it suggests a way to deal with value preferences. Everyone has to recognize that preference plays a role in human conduct. Moral psychology shows how, through the process of natural selection, the natural standard of survival produces an internal standard of "better."

5.11 Is Survival Always a Good?   161

I have devoted considerable space to discussing how moral psychologists can account for "better." I have done so, first, because their opponents often concentrate their attack on moral psychology's supposed inability to give a wholly natural account of a hierarchy of "better" goods. Furthermore, since moral psychologists locate the final source of human nature in our biological makeup, we need to understand how natural selection operates to evolve creatures who make value choices. Moral psychosociobiologists explain this by tying a selector mechanism to species survival. The tie between survival and value choices should be understood by us as clearly as possible, because survival value is used so often to explain or justify human behavior, and because it is the ultimate grounds for moral psychology's explanation of that behavior. Listen again to B. F. Skinner in *Beyond Freedom and Dignity:*

> A culture that *for any reason* induces its members to work for its survival, or for the survival of some of its practices, is more likely to survive. Survival is the only value according to which a culture is eventually to be judged, and any practice that furthers survival has survival value, by definition.[19]

At this point, however, Gus could reasonably ask: "But is survival the only good, or even the highest good? Aren't choices to preserve our freedom and dignity, freely made, more justified than survival? Are the prisoners who inform on co-revolutionaries to save their own lives more admirable than those who refuse to do so?" Gus might continue by asking: "If the informer is morally inferior to the loyal, tightlipped prisoner, then survival can't be a standard of the better value, can it?"

In section 6.10 I will sketch some criticisms of the sociobiological extension of moral psychology, but the point that Gus might raise—is survival always a good?—is so basic as to merit immediate treatment.

The argument against moral psychology on this point could go as follows: We distinguish between means and ends. Some goods are means goods and others are end goods. For instance, Aristotle thought that happiness or well-being is an end good, and that having friends is a means good to that end good. The goodness of means depends on the goodness of the ends to which they are means. The end justifies the means, although not necessarily every means. Moral psychology's biological account of "better" is inadequate because it applies only to means goods; it gives no explanation of end goods, yet without end goods there are no means goods. This account simply *assumes* that survival is an end good; if it isn't, then the means to survival aren't means goods. Additionally, an account of "better means goods," is empty unless based on an account of "better end goods," regardless of whether the end goods are moral or non-moral goods. The most this biological account can conclude is that one means is more efficient or effective than another, which doesn't make it morally better. For example, you

162   can have better napalm, better poison, or effective rather than incompetent torture. Thus the moral psychologists' account of "better" depends on the truth or falsity of the statement, "Survival is an end good." And of course, if the account is to be morally relevant, it depends also on the truth or falsity of the statement, "Survival is a morally good end."

The critic continues by pointing out that, although it may be a fact that animals struggle for survival and that this explains animals' behavior, we can't conclude from this that survival is an end good, moral or non-moral; nor can we conclude that behavior which promotes survival is morally right. We can't infer from what *is* to what *ought to be*. We can do so only if we establish that survival is an end good and that sometimes it is the supreme end good. (How moral psychologists think we can go from *Is* to *Ought* will be discussed in section 12.5 of the chapter on Hume.)

The next step in the criticism of moral psychology's account of "better" is to maintain that it is false that survival is an end good, and false that it is the supreme end good.

Consider this argument against survival's being an end good and against its being a standard of better goods. There are a great number of species whose members supposedly are struggling to survive, and some of these species are in competition with each other. For example, in Europe during the plague years of the late Middle Ages, when hundreds of thousands of people died, the rats that were carrying the bubonic plague were winning out against humans. It's still conceivable that the rat species might survive and humans not. A news story has reported that on Sumba Island near Java more than 70,000 people "are struggling to survive a famine after rats destroyed their ricefields"; many schools closed because teachers and students were too weak to attend.[20] If bare survival is an end good, then the good of the rats will have been achieved, but not the good of humans. But it's pretty obvious that, should that happen, a better good will have gone out of the world by natural selection. Thus we can see that the biological account of "better," when applied to end goods, leads to an absurd conclusion: the better good that survives is that of the rats! Just whose side are moral psychosociobiologists on—rats or humans?

The moral psychosociobiologists could make this defense against the preceding argument. You *assume* that humans' survival is a better good than rats' survival. Nothing you can refer to will show this to be so. Outside of the biological theater there is nothing from which you can draw value. Your thinking that humans' survival is better than rats' is just another instance of the point we're making: you're simply reflecting your species' competitive struggle for survival.

Further, they might say, you're clinging to a distinction between explanation and justification that can't be defended. You say we can't infer from *Is* to *Ought*—that is, from the explanation of behavior we can't get a justification of it. But since there is nothing outside the biological arena from which to draw value, there can be no values on which to base justification; there is only biological explanation, and we've given you that. The world is a

purposeless play of indifferent forces; there is no outside justification of its **163**
being the way it is, nor is there any justification from inside either. The most
that we can do is explain how "better" evolves, while you are foolishly
looking for a justification theory of "better."

To show that I am not inventing this position of the psychosociobiologists, I quote from ethologist Edward O. Wilson:

> . . . No species, ours included, possess a purpose beyond the imperatives
> created by its genetic history. Species may have vast potential for material
> and mental progress but they lack any immanent purpose or guidance from
> agents beyond their immediate environment or even an evolutionary goal
> toward which their molecular architecture automatically steers them. I
> believe that the human mind is constructed in a way that locks it inside this
> fundamental constraint and forces it to make choices with a purely
> biological instrument. . . .
>
> The essence of the argument, then, is that the brain exists because it
> promotes the survival and multiplication of the genes that direct its
> assembly. . . .
>
> The [human] species lacks any goal external to its own biological
> nature. . . . Traditional religous beliefs have been eroded, not so much by
> humiliating disproofs of their mythologies as by the growing awareness
> that beliefs are really enabling mechanisms for survival. Religions, like
> other human institutions, evolve so as to enhance the persistence and in-
> fluence of the practitioners. Marxism and other secular religions offer lit-
> tle more than promises of material welfare and a legislated escape from the
> consequences of human nature.[21]

To challenge all this, the critic of the biological theory of "better" could
make a flat statement that survival can't be a good end because in fact it is not
an end. He could then cite instances where both animals and humans
sacrifice their lives for their offspring. From this we can conclude that the
animals don't take survival to be an end, or that if they do, they don't consider it a supremely good end.

The moral psychosociobiologist could point out in defense that it is
necessary to distinguish between species and individual survival. Animals'
sacrifices of life for the offspring are instances of species survival. Natural
selection has provided them with a built-in mechanism for choosing sacrifice
as a means for preserving offspring, and so of preserving the species; hence individual sacrifice is the better good because it is a means to species survival.

The critic may grant this point, but may add that this doesn't apply to
humans. We don't have built-in mechanisms or instincts like animals; we are
cultural products; our behavior is learned rather than inherited. And clearly
humans do not universally take survival to be an end good, let alone the
supreme end good. People have chosen death rather than perform what they
believe are immoral acts. There have been a lot of Rebellas in the world,
preferring to act consistently with their beliefs in what is morally good rather
than to merely live. Socrates, we saw earlier, was an example. And today,

164 with all the liberation movements in the world, many obviously think it better to die than to live in political bondage. Additionally, even when a moral good isn't at stake, when people have to live in great pain, unable to live normal lives or enjoy even simple things such as food, they choose to die. This shows us that living morally or living happily are ends, isn't merely living. Hence it is the moral or the happy parts of life, not just life, that are our ends. Life itself is merely the vehicle, a kind of means, for carrying the moral and the happy, but is not in itself an end, let alone an end good. The fear of and the struggle against dying are not caused by the anticipated loss of life, but by the anticipated loss of experience.

This last criticism brings the discussion to the topic of the highest or supreme good, which I defer until section 11.1.

Here in summary is the argument against a purely biological account of "better" in terms of survival.

(1) We distinguish between end goods and means goods.
(2) Biologists use survival as an end good.
(3) But survival by itself is not always an end good nor even the highest end good on some occasions.
(4) The truth of (3) implies that there is a standard *outside* biology that we use to judge the goodness of biological survival.
(5) But sociobiology claims to explain all value by remaining within the bounds of biology and survival.
(6) Therefore, sociobiology cannot fully account for standards of goodness.

With regard to (4), to be sure, the sociobiologists can tell their critics to put up or shut up: just where are you critics going to find another source of value except in nature? What is this "outside" standard you say is implied in your criticism, and why should anyone accept it? This is a fair challenge to critics of sociobiology, and not an easy one to meet. Kant clearly saw the relevance of this challenge and the difficulty it posed. He was a direct and honest thinker as well as a profound one, as we'll see when we come to his ethics.

STUDY QUESTIONS

1 Why did Gus object to Skinner's view?
2 Explain the relevance of human nature to morals, using the moral psychologists' links schema to do this.
3 What contribution has the theory of evolution made to moral psychology?
4 Simple moral psychology attributes five features to human nature: uniformity, naturalness, fixity, causal power, and comprehensiveness.

Briefly state the claims made for each of these features. Then state one **165** challenge to each of them and the defense a moral psychologist can make to it.

5 Explain how natural selection may be used to account for animals having a selector mechanism for picking the better of two conflicting goods.

6 Why is the claim that bare survival is not an end good a challenge to the biological account of which of two goods is the better good?

Reflections on Applications

1 If you were a defender of moral psychology who thought human conduct is a causal product of human nature, would you agree with the following remarks of Neysa Moskowitz, whose daughter was shot and killed by "Son of Sam"? Mrs. Moskowitz said of the killer, who had slain several other young women: "An animal like this has to be caught, not to die or be killed but to be tortured for life. He's not human, he's not human. He's not human to do this to young people."[22]

David Abrahamsen was a psychiatrist who examined "Son of Sam," David Berkowitz. Berkowitz had claimed that he killed because demons, speaking with the voices of barking dogs had ordered him to kill. Abrahamsen's task was to find out if Berkowitz's demons were "real."

Do they have an independent existence in the defendant's mind and control his actions, which would mean he is psychotic and unable to stand trial? Or are they simply a conscious invention, which he himself controls?

Abrahamsen concluded that Berkowitz was faking his demons, which was subsequently confirmed by Berkowitz at a news conference at Attica, a New York State prison, and in a letter he wrote to Abrahamsen, saying: "Yes, it was all a hoax, a silly hoax, well planned and thought out. I just never thought this 'demon' story would carry so much"[23]

Reflecting on Abrahamsen's conclusion, do you think it throws doubt on Mrs. Moskowitz's view that Berkowitz isn't human but an animal? And, supposing the demons had been real, how would you relate them and their effect on Berkowitz's behavior to Liz and Gus's discussion?

2 Do you think the following statement, if true, shows that human nature is not fixed? The statement was made by Sgt. Jim Higgins of the San Francisco Police Department. "A man can get a heart of stone doing police work and his love for others shrivels up and drifts away."

Higgins and other police officers are trying to spread the Christian

166   gospel among fellow police because they think it will change them, help restore their love of others, and help get rid of the "macho image" that leads them to be insensitive, hard-drinking, and boisterous.[24]

Higgins could be interpreted as saying that something like Hume's and Rousseau's natural benevolent sentiment may stop functioning under certain circumstances. Do you think that it would be equally plausible to suppose that egoistic sentiments too might stop functioning under certain (for example, noncompetitive) circumstances? What would the lapse of a "natural" sentiment imply about the truth of moral psychology?

3 I noted that theorists of human nature differ about which and how many instincts humans possess, and carefully distinguished instinctive behavior from innate need. Consider the following quotation and decide if the Catalonian bookseller in Marquez's novel has identified an instinct that would have to be acknowledged by a moral psychologist. A group of young men were having a heated argument about the methods used to kill cockroaches in the Middle Ages. The bookseller enters the discussion.

> He [the bookseller] explained that the cockroach, the oldest winged insect on the face of the earth, had already been the victim of slippers in the Old Testament, but that since the species was definitely resistant to any and all methods of extermination, from tomato slices with borax to flour and sugar, and with its one thousand six hundred three varieties had resisted the most ancient, tenacious, and pitiless persecution that mankind had unleashed against any living thing since the beginnings, including man himself, to such extent that just as an instinct for reproduction was attributed to humankind, so there must have been another one more definite and pressing, which was the instinct to kill cockroaches, and if the latter succeeded in escaping human ferocity it was because they had taken refuge in the shadows, where they became invulnerable because of man's congenital [inborn] fear of the dark.[25]

What arguments do you think a moral psychologist might bring forward to show that humans don't have an instinct to kill cockroaches?

4 It might not always be apparent that we possess instincts, even though the possession has to be universal. (Naturally we allow for the variations that are an important feature of the theory of natural selection.) Our instinctive behavior might manifest itself only under some external conditions, and then in only some portion of humanity. Do you think this makes the notion of instinctive behavior useless for moral psychology? Think of this in terms of the following explanation.

> But when we were past the coast of Portugal, things began to go wrong. One morning we woke up to find ourselves overcome by a breathless sort of stove atmosphere, disquieting and frightful. The drinking water, the sea, the air, the sheets, our own sweat, everything was warm, sticky. . . .

It didn't take long. In this maddeningly unchanging temperature the whole human freight of the ship clotted together in one vast tipsiness. People walked wantonly about the deck, like jellyfish at the bottom of a pool of stagnant water. It was then that one saw the whole of the white man's revolting nature displayed in freedom from all constraint, under provocation and untrammelled [unrestrained]; his real self as you saw it in war. This tropic stove brought out human instincts in the same way as the heat of August induces toads and vipers to come out and flatten themselves against the fissured walls of prison buildings. In the cold of Europe, under prudish northern fogs, except when slaughter is afoot, you only glimpse the crawling cruelty of your fellow men. But their rottenness rises to the surface as soon as they are tickled by the hideous fevers of the tropics. It's then that the wild un-buttoning process begins, and degradation triumphs, taking hold of us entirely. A biological confession of weakness.[26]

5 Social Darwinism was an influential view in the nineteenth century. It was popular among persons who opposed government regulation of business and trade. Although Darwin himself wasn't a Social Darwinist, advocates of this view maintained that the lessons learned from his theory of evolution should be applied to our moral and social life. The argument went like this.

The course of evolution shows a progress from lower to higher forms of life; humans are, to date, the highest form evolved. This pro-gress occurred because of natural selection, which is the survival of the fittest in the struggle for existence. This arrangement of nature has resulted in progress in nature. We want progress to continue, including progress within our social arrangements. Because progress has occurred in nature by survival of the fittest, we *ought* to model our social ar-rangements on nature's. This can be done by an unregulated competi-tion between workers and other workers, between businesses and other businesses, and between workers and businesses. The best person or organization will survive, guaranteeing continuing progress.

Robert Ardrey, a student of ethology, has been called a contem-porary Social Darwinist. He thinks that our social arrangements should suit our human nature. This nature is written in our genes, which were selected when our animal and human ancestors lived in hierarchically ar-ranged societies. Selection processes under this arrangement implanted certain expectations and needs in us which, if not met and satisfied, threaten our psychosociobiological health. A society that democratically sweeps away the hierarchical arrangements is unsuited to our inherited nature, therefore we *ought* to arrange our societies in hierarchies so as to avoid leveling.

According to Ardrey, it is only within the framework of a properly hierarchical social structure that a human being can realize his most fun-damental needs: identity, security, and stimulation. By assigning each individual a well defined position within the hierarchy, a society secures his identity against anonymity, protects his position not only against external but also internal threats, and provides him with stimuli appropriate to his talents. To destroy this natural hierarchy is to leave human beings at the mercy of anonymity, anxiety, and boredom.[27]

A society might be hierarchically arranged either by wealth or by merit—standards that may put an individual at different levels. A person might end up at the top by one criterion and at the bottom by the other. Does this disprove Ardrey's thesis?

Do you think that Ardrey accepts a form of Social Darwinism? Or do you think, instead, that he is a "pure" advocate of the science of moral psychosociobiology?

A "pure" moral psychologist might attempt scientifically to explain human conduct by showing its causal connection with a genetically inherited human nature. Do you think such a moral psychologist would advocate what we "ought" to do? For example, would a physicist or a chemist advocate how matter ought to act? That would be absurd. Matter has to act according to natural laws. This is true for humans as well, if we are scientific objects. If our conduct is explained by natural laws that reach back to our genes, then, recognizing that genes are chemical entities that act according to natural laws, we have to acknowledge that humans are matter that must act in accord with natural, physical laws. Auguste Comte, for example, one of the founders of modern sociology, spoke of sociology as "Social Physics." It is as absurd to tell humans how they ought to arrange themselves as it is to tell rocks how to do so.

6 Relate the following remarks of Dr. Val Woodward to the issue raised above. These remarks were made at a conference on sociobiology held at San Francisco State University in June 1977, after a group of chanting protesters had vocally maintained that sociobiology is an effort by science to justify racism, sexism, and political oppression. According to the news story, Woodward "voiced the group's view to the audience more calmly."

> Modern society, Woodward argued, does in fact limit women to sex-defined roles, and "it's not surprising that some scientists have now discovered an evolutionary justification for sexism." He insisted that sociobiology is a scientifically invalid effort to justify class domination and even war by making them appear to be genetically inevitable.[28]

Do you think that Woodward is saying that sociobiologists (and ethologists) are Social Darwinists? (Note "inevitable" above.)

7 The "eugenics" movement has been associated with the theory of an inherited human nature. Its influential early leader was Sir Francis Galton, who believed in genetic engineering and who gave psychometry its first respectable prominence. Psychometry is a school of psychology that tries to make psychology more "scientific" by making it quan-

titative—that is, by orienting it toward the precise measurement of human qualities (hence the -*metry,* meaning "measure," in "psychometry").

IQ tests are among the best known psychometric devices intended to yield quantitative psychological information. They were used as early as World War I to determine who should go to officer training school. The most controversial conclusion drawn recently from IQ tests has been that blacks are genetically inferior to whites because they score lower on IQ tests than whites. From the fact that blacks have scores on an average 15 points less than whites, and that blacks do better on simple than on complex tasks (rote memory versus verbal reasoning), some people have concluded that intelligence is a hereditary quality. Among such claimants have been Sir Francis Galton, Arthur Jensen, Roger Herrenstein, and E. J. Eysenck. Others, however, question whether IQ tests show intelligence to be genetically determined. These critics point out that several factors other than heredity could account for the different performance, such as the influence of home and social environment, including the effect of prejudice; lack of proper diet during pregnancy and early youth; test questions slanted toward information familiar to a certain socio-economic class; and hostile test conditions.

The psychometric model, together with the claim that intelligence is hereditary, may be used as grounds for justifying a social policy that champions a hierarchical class system with people and their children assigned to a class level corresponding to their IQ: the higher the IQ, the higher the class to which they would belong. Such a social system would be defended as follows.

(1) Some jobs demand higher intelligence than others. (2) For maximum efficiency, persons' abilities should be suited to their jobs. (3) To survive, a complex society must make the best use of its members by maintaining a division of labor. (4) Therefore, jobs requiring a higher intelligence should be performed by those with a suitable intelligence. (*Meritocracy*) (5) Further, because intelligence is hereditary and because some classes of persons (for example, blacks and poor whites) have lower intelligence, these classes should be trained for and assigned to lower-class jobs. (*Sorting*) (Think here of the Scholastic Aptitude Test, or SAT, which you probably took and which is used to sort you.) (6) Additionally, because we can expect jobs to become more complex in the future and therefore demand higher intelligence, we should pass laws governing who may and who may not mate for purposes of conceiving children; we should allow mating only between people with similar IQs. (*Eugenics*)

Supporters of a democratic social policy proudly point out that such a policy is basically egalitarian, in that it is against the permanent assignment of persons to a particular class because of their origin. But eugenicists, they assert, who use an inherited human nature to justify

170   social policy involving a meritocracy, sorting, and eugenics, are undemocratic.

Do you think that a person who advocates a meritocracy is a Social Darwinist? Is one who advocates sorting a Social Darwinist? Is a person who advocates eugenics?

If it were true that intelligence is an inherited part of our human nature, would you agree with a social policy involving a meritocracy, sorting, and eugenics? Would you give the same answer if you were a member of a white minority in, say, Nigeria, who on the average scored lower on Nigerian IQ tests than blacks? This could be particularly important to Nigeria, since such a policy would enable it to pick out the best and brightest, now and in the future, to promote its fortunes.

8 Consider the following quotation, which recounts how a theory about an inherited human nature was used to justify a social policy in American history. If you believed in the biological theory of "better" that I developed for the moral psychosociobiologist in this chapter, and also were a Social Darwinist, would you have agreed with this policy?

> Then, in 1924—the year the Statue of Liberty was designated a national monument—Congress passed a permanent-quota law. It was the first piece of major immigration legislation and as amended in 1929, rigidly regulated the flow of immigrants to this country for thirty-six years. . . . Immigrants from the countries of northwestern Europe were, in effect, granted an allotment of more than seventy percent of this so-called national-origins quota, while those from the countries of Southern and Eastern Europe . . . were allotted proportionately low quotas. Historians usually give at least two reasons for the passage of the 1924 act: fear of political radicals, and the influence of contemporary theories of eugenics. At the time, there was much left-wing agitation in the trade unions, and part of the blame for this was placed on Poles, Italians, and Jews; Poles, Italians, and Jews also became targets of eugenicists, who called them "undesirables" and "biological degenerates," and whose ideas loomed prominently in the congressional hearings and debates on the bill. The eugenicists tried to show through laborious research that the human race was divided into superior and inferior types, and that America had been built up by superior types, who originated in Northern Europe, and was now being inundated by the inferior types, who originated in Southern and Eastern Europe. The eugenicists claimed that the inferior types were genetically incapable of performing "decently" in a free, democratic society, and that they or their children would end up by destroying it.[29]

9 Another social policy that may be related to the foregoing discussion was advocated recently in California; it proposed to do away with the law that made confidential any records that could be used to identify the

biological parents of adopted children. The new policy would enable adopted children to look at those records, so they could trace their biological parents. Jerome Lackner, then head of the California State Health Department, said: "Adopted persons should be able to learn more about their biologic and genetic heritage, if they wish, to become more familiar with their antecedents to help them fulfill their human potential."[30]

On the basis of Lackner's statement, do you agree that the new policy (finding biological roots) is desirable? Do you think that such agreement commits you to a belief in inherited human nature?

If we all have the same human nature, what difference would it make who our biological parents are? Do you think that Lackner's "human potential" includes "moral potential"? (Like father/mother, like son/daughter?) Do you notice that it is still a common practice for one parent to blame the other's nature for some defect in a child? For instance: He's shiftless, just like his father (whom he resembles)! She's messy, just like her mother (whom she resembles)!

10 Would you conclude anything about human nature from the fact that offering a reward leading to the apprehension and conviction of persons found guilty of a crime often brings forth information from persons that would not otherwise be forthcoming? Particularly if the informants are promised anonymity? Are we dealing here with one of those special external conditions under which our "true" nature reveals itself, like Céline's tropical temperature or the possession of a ring of Gyges? If so, what innate need would you name that causes informant behavior? And how would you prove it innate?

11 Can you relate the points made in the following quotation from Skinner to the moral psychologists' and the moralists' opposed links diagrams (pp. 139 and 142, respectively)? This is relevant also to Liz's and Gus's different ways of looking at humans.

> Science probably has never demanded a more sweeping change in the traditional way of thinking about a subject, nor has there ever been a more important subject. In the traditional picture a person perceives the world around him, selects features to be perceived, discriminates among them, judges them good or bad, changes them to make them better (or worse), and may be held responsible for his action and justly rewarded or punished for its consequences. In the scientific picture a person is a member of a species shaped by evolutionary contingencies [chance events] of survival, displaying behavioral processes that bring him under the control of the environment in which he lives, and largely under the control of a social environment that he and millions of others like him have constructed and maintained during the evolution of a culture. The direction of the controlling relation is reversed: a person does not act upon the world; the world acts upon him.[31]

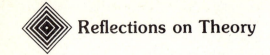 Reflections on Theory

12 *Arguments against Lorenz's evaluation of reason.* In section 5.9 (pp. 155–56) I reported three reasons why Lorenz thought that, paradoxically, reason is a threat to survival. (1) It enables the weak to survive and propagate; (2) it gives us unlimited capacity for self-destruction through advanced technology; and (3) it undermines the natural hierarchy by frustrating the superior and preserving the inferior.

The late Jane English, a young philosopher, pointed out the following to me: Regarding (1): anything, including reason, that aids survival is not a threat to survival. Regarding (2): Technology also aids the self-preservation of individuals and therefore of a species. Regarding (3): People who are superior in reasoning are superior.

Do English's remarks show the falsity of Lorenz's view that conceptual thought and verbal reasonings aren't altogether blessings? Is there anything in the world that is wholly a blessing? If something, such as reason, is not altogether a blessing and is an evolutionary product, does this show the biological account of "better" to be false?

13 *Against Social Darwinism.* Richard Hofstadter writes about Lester Ward's criticism of Social Darwinism and of defenders of scientific psychosociobiology. Ward was an early American sociologist.

> Of critical importance in everything Ward wrote was a sharp distinction between physical, or animal, purposeless evolution and mental, human evolution decisively modified by purposive action. . . . Unable to find in society the crude processes he saw at work in nature, Ward evolved a twofold criticism of Social Darwinism. He first debunked nature itself, displayed its wastefulness, and tore it from the high place it occupied in the popular mind. Then, by showing how the emerging human mind was able to mold the narrow genetic processes of nature into vastly different forms, Ward demolished the central feature of the monistic dogma . . . [that the process in nature and society are one and the same].[32]

Do you think that Ward's criticism can be refuted by the moral psychosociobiologist? What evidence would you give that the human mind is free of human nature's causality?

14 *Huxley against Social Darwinism.* T. H. Huxley, the English biologist, also was critical of Social Darwinism. Consider the following summary of his argument (in his famous Romane Lectures), which can be seen as a criticism of the account of "better" that I developed earlier for the moral psychologist. Construct an answer that the moral psychologist might make to Huxley.

Huxley accepted at its face value the Hobbesian interpretation of
Darwinism and acknowledged that "men in society are undoubtedly
subject to the cosmic process," which includes, of course, the struggle
for existence and the elimination of the unfit. But he flatly rejected the
common practice of identifying the "fittest" with the "best," pointing
out that under certain cosmic conditions the only "fit" organisms would
prove to be low ones. Man and nature make altogether different
judgments of value. The ethical process, or the production of what
man recognizes as truly the "best," is in opposition to the cosmic process. "Social progress means a checking of the cosmic process at every
step."

In a companion essay Huxley compared the ethical process to the
work of the gardener: the state of the garden is not that of "nature red
in tooth and claw," for the horticultural process eliminates struggle by
adjusting life conditions to the plant instead of making the plants adjust
to nature. Instead of encouraging, horticulture restricts multiplication
of the species. Like horticulture, human ethics defies the cosmic process; for both horticulture and ethical behavior circumvent [bypass] the
raw struggle for existence in the interest of some ideal imposed from
without upon the processes of nature.

The more advanced a society becomes, the more it eliminates the
struggle for existence among its members.[33]

15 *Aristotle on the highest good.* Aristotle says in his *Nicomachean Ethics*
that we should

state, in view of the fact that all knowledge and every pursuit aims at
some good, what it is that we say political science aims at and what is
the highest of all goods achievable by action. Verbally there is very
general agreement; for both the general run of men and people of
superior refinement say that it is happiness, and identify living well and
doing well with being happy; but with regard to what happiness is they
differ, and the many do not give the same account as the wise. For the
former [the many] think it is some plain and obvious thing, like
pleasure, wealth, or honor; they differ, however, from one
another—and often even the same man identifies it with different
things, with health when he is ill, with wealth when he is poor; but,
conscious of their ignorance, they admire those who proclaim some
great ideal that is above their comprehension.

To judge from the lives that men lead, most men, and men of the
most vulgar type, seem (not without some ground) to identify the good,
or happiness, with pleasure; which is the reason why they love the life
of enjoyment. For there are, we may say, three prominent types of
life—that just mentioned [enjoyment], [secondly] the political, and
thirdly the contemplative life. Now the mass of mankind are evidently
quite slavish in their tastes, preferring a life suitable to beasts, but they
get some ground for their view from the fact that many of those in high
places share the tastes of Sardanapallus [a high-living king of Assyria].

A consideration of the prominent types of life shows that people of superior refinement and of active disposition identify happiness with honor; for this is, roughly speaking, the end of the political life. But it seems too superficial to be what we are looking for, since it is thought to depend on those who bestow honor rather than on him who receives it, but the good we divine to be something proper to a man and not easily taken from him.[34]

Aristotle points out that three different things have been thought to be the highest good, and that each has its supporters; he observes that generally the most vulgar natures prefer pleasure as their highest good. This suggests not a single human nature but a plural number, each leading to a different conception of moral conduct. If the selection of none of these makes any difference to survival, what consequences does this have for the "natural selection" theory of how "better" gets inside the links schema?

16 *Innate needs do not imply instinctive behavior.* Below are some quotations from one of psychiatrist Erik Erikson's books in which, on the basis of some features of animal instincts, he throws doubt on the existence of instincts in humans. He doubts that innate "drives" (needs) have corresponding instincts for behavior. If his comments are true, what does this imply about the acceptability of moral psychology in whatever form, as stated by Hobbes, Hume, Rousseau, Gyges advocates, Lorenz, Freud, Darwin, or anyone else? If Erikson's view is correct, can we make any use of human nature in formulating a moral theory?

When we say that animals have "instincts," we mean that at least the lower forms have relatively inborn, relatively early, ready-to-use ways of interacting with a segment of nature as part of which they have survived. These patterns vary widely from species to species, but within one species they are highly inflexible; animals can learn little.[35]

In the higher forms of animals we observe a *division of instinct* (a term here used in analogy to "division of labor"). Here it is the mutual regulation of instinctive contact seeking in the young and of instinctive contact giving in the parent which completes adaptive functioning in the young. It has been observed, for example, that certain mammals can learn to defecate only by having the rectum licked by the mother animals.

We could assume that human childhood and human child training are merely the highest form of such instinctive reciprocity. However, the drives man is born with are not instincts; nor are his mother's complementary drives instinctive in nature. Neither carry in themselves the patterns of completion, of self-preservation, of interaction with any segment of nature; tradition and conscience must organize them.

As an animal, man is nothing. It is meaningless to speak of a human child as if it were an animal in the process of domestication; or of his instincts as set patterns encroached upon or molded by the autocratic environment. Man's "inborn instincts" are drive fragments to be assembled, given meaning, and organized during a prolonged childhood by methods of child training and schooling which vary from culture to culture and are determined by tradition.[36]

17 *A biological account of "better" is logically absurd.* Here is an argument that seems to prove that the moral psychosociobiologist's theory of "better" is self-defeating. It shows that the survival standard of "better" will lead to self-destruction, which is exactly contrary to the very basis on which the moral psychosociobiologist builds his theory of "better."

   (1) According to the theory, whatever internal standards of "better" a member of a species has are there because they are the residues left by the natural selection standard of survival. (2) Instincts for selection are among the internal standards for selection. (3) Such instincts must include instincts for self-preservation of the individual member of the species; indeed, without such instincts in the individual, there would be no survival of the species. (4) It is possible, and in our time it is becoming plausible and perhaps probable, that in the interests of individual self-preservation, the growing number of humans are despoiling "spaceship earth" to the point where it may leave no resources for the survival of future generations. (5) The conclusion is clear: self-preservation instincts selected by nature for survival of the species, which supposedly are a standard of the better, lead to the extinction of the species by robbing future generations of the means for survival. (Will cockroaches inherit the earth?) (6) Which leads to the further conclusion that the evolutionary standard of "better," namely, survival, leads to extinction, which logically is the standard of worse; that is, the better is worse. (7) "The better is worse" is self-contradictory and therefore logically absurd; which shows that any attempt to find a natural, biological standard for comparative value is logically absurd, and consequently false and to be rejected.

   Formulate a refutation of this argument that will protect moral psychology's theory of human conduct.

6
Romantic versus
Existential Authenticity
and Trouble for Sociobiology

6.1 Looking Back and Looking Ahead

We learned about problematic situations in the first chapter. We are in a problematic situation when we have two or more thoughts or theories that are contradictory or contrary and when, after reflection on these thoughts or theories, we find that each is plausible.

Our thoughts about morals up to this point have put us in a problematic state. On the one hand, our reflections on Ivan Ilyich made us want to live lives such that, unlike Ivan, we won't regret at the end how we lived; it is advisable to realize a self that isn't ordinary. This assumes that we *can* make ourselves. On the other hand, a long and persuasive tradition says that we are born with an unalterable human nature; as we saw, this tradition stretches from Plato's time (the Gyges Argument) down to the present. This theoretical tradition holds that we come into the world ready-made; moral psychology attributes to us innate needs and/or instincts that determine our behavior.

Thus one school of moral thought urges us to make or remake ourselves, while the other tells us that we cannot do this because nature alone makes us. Which of these moral theories, if either, should we believe? We can't accept both if they claim exclusive theoretical truth about our moral conduct. Let's see why this is so.

Assume that a moral psychology that attributes nature N to humans is true. Given that N is fixed and universal, and that all our behavior can be traced to N, a self-realization morals that urges us to realize a different, better nature than N, so that we will act differently and better, is pointless, because we cannot change our nature from N to some other nature M. For example, suppose that a moral psychology that attributes egoism to our nature is true; self-realization morals that urged us to realize an altruistic self would then be irrelevant.

The problematic choice we face can be shown also by approaching it from the self-realization side. One might claim that no matter what characteristic a moral psychologist attributes to our nature, there is some human who on some occasion can realize a contrary characteristic in his or her self. For example, Socrates and Joan of Arc had the courage to act honorably, even though it led to their deaths. This contradicts Hobbes's moral psychology, which claims that we always act to preserve ourselves. Realizing any characteristic of a self that we think is good falsifies a moral psychology that claims we have a fixed, universally similar nature.

The problematic tension between the denial and the affirmation that we

have the power to develop a chosen moral nature has a long history in $\quad$
Western culture, scarred by a persistent competition between the two schools
of morality. One school finds the source of moral conduct in a given human
nature, while the other urges us to rise above a natural state to true human
dignity.

This chapter is a turning point in our exploration of these two dominant
schools of thought about morality. So far, we have been occupied mainly in
stating the position of those who base morality on human nature. In this
chapter I prepare the ground for stating the opposing view of those who
believe that we can choose and realize our own nature. I do this, first, by
placing these two schools of ethical thought in a larger historical context that
emphasizes the contrast between Romanticism and Classicism; second by ex-
ploring the concepts of artificiality and authenticity; and third, by challenging scientific attempts to give a biological account of human nature.

First, let's see briefly how an examination of the meanings of
"artificial" and "authentic" will contribute to our understanding of the difference between these two ethical schools.

A word doesn't acquire its meaning in isolation; it depends in part on its
relations to other words—relations that transform a set of spoken sounds and
marks on paper into a language. For example, the mark "second" has the
meaning it has because it comes between the marks "first" and "third" in a
series. If "third" came between "first" and "second," then "third" would
have the meaning that "second" has now. Also, we can distinguish the two
or more meanings that a single word may have by contrasting it with its opposite for each meaning. For example, "tall" has different meanings in
"John is tall" and "That's a tall story." The opposite of the first instance of
"tall" is "short," and the opposite of the second is "true." Words travel in
groups, not alone.

Applying this to our present topic, we can get a clearer idea of the meaning of "natural," which figures so prominently in the meaning of "human
nature," by finding its opposite meaning or meanings. The opposite of
"natural" is "artificial." It turns out that "artificial" has several meanings;
hence, given the conditions for a word's meaning oulined above, "natural"
too, must have several meanings. Beneath the deceptively simple surface of
the natural/artificial contrast there is a complex structure. In uncovering this
complexity, we will be led to the connected concept of authenticity and of
course to its opposite, inauthenticity—concepts that play central roles in
Romanticism and Existentialism.

After analyzing the natural/artificial contrast and authenticity, I will
outline some criticisms of sociobiology and will isolate the most fundamental
differences between moral psychologists and their opponents. This will give
us a springboard for our examination of Immanuel Kant, the great eighteenth-
century German philosopher, who is the preeminent rational will moralist and
opponent of moral psychology. His is the best worked-out theory of moral
self-realization.

180 6.2 Romanticism and Classicism

Before examining the natural/artificial contrast, it will be useful to see it in an historical context; each side of the contrast has had its advocates, who were Romantics and Classicists respectively.

Romanticism and Classicism are terms used to divide two main schools of literature, but the terms also spill over into morals and politics. In their literature Romantics favor nature and feeling, while Classicists celebrate civilization and thought. Simply put, Romanticism is love of physical nature—rocks, trees, sky, mountains, wilderness,—versus Classicism's love of the city and social intercourse; a respect for children, peasants, madmen, and "noble savages"—all nonrational and "spontaneous"—versus Classicism's interest in civilized rational adults in society; a trust in our own inspiration, intuition, feeling, and spontaneity versus Classicism's respect for rules, tradition, reason, and the claims of society on us. The poet Shelley identifying with the west wind, or Wordsworth being inspired by daffodils in the English countryside, as opposed to Voltaire holding forth with genial or mordant wit in a Paris salon, say a lot about Romanticism and Classicism, respectively. Listen to how Shelley, invoking the "wild West Wind" in a moment of personal discouragement, becomes inspired by it and commands:

> Be thou, Spirit fierce,
> My spirit! Be thou me, impetuous one!
>
> Drive my dead thoughts over the universe
> Like withered leaves to quicken a new birth;
> And, by the incantation of this verse,
>
> Scatter, as from an unextinguished hearth
> Ashes and sparks, my words among mankind!
> Be through my lips to unawakened earth
>
> The trumpet of a prophecy! O Wind,
> If Winter comes, can Spring be far behind?

In a letter to his friend Eckermann, the German poet Goethe expressed the Romantic's fear of suppressing our natural feelings: "With us [Germans], everything pushes toward taming our dear young people early and driving out all nature, all originality and all wildness, so that in the end nothing remains but the Philistine [a smugly commonplace person]".[1]

On the other hand, Classicists see reason as a faculty freeing us from the bonds of ignorance and feelings. The Enlightenment was a Classical movement that had an important influence on Kant, who, as we will see in following chapters, was a penetrating critic of the human-nature school of morality.

The political thrust of Romanticism and Classicism— the Enlightenment in eighteenth-century Europe being a social and political expression of Classicism—was similar: toward the freedom of the individual. But each took a characteristically different pathway to this freedom. Partisans of the Enlightenment advised that we follow the path of reason as a way to free ourselves from the bonds of blind prejudices and impulsive feelings, whereas Romanticists urged that we follow the path of feeling so as to free ourselves from the bonds of dry, dead reason.

According to the American philosopher Theodore M. Greene, the Enlightenment "was essentially revolutionary, directed against the authority of intellectual and religious tradition. The positive force at its core was a determined assertion of the freedom of the individual—freedom in affairs social and political, intellectual and religious. This spirit expressed itself most emphatically in a new and extravagant belief in the power of reason. . . . Whatever, from the point of view of reason, had about it an air of mystery fell under suspicion; man's feelings, passions, and sentiments were in ill repute."[2]

Kant himself explained what he thought the "enlightenment" meant.

> *Enlightenment is man's emergence from his self-incurred immaturity. Immaturity* is the inability to use one's own understanding without the guidance of another. . . .The motto of enlightenment is therefore: *Sapere Aude*! Have courage to use your *own* understanding! . . .
>
> It is so convenient to be immature. . . . Thus it is difficult for each separate individual to work his way out of the immaturity which has become almost second nature to him. He has even grown fond of it and is really incapable for the time being of using his own understanding, because he was never allowed to make the attempt. . . .
>
> For enlightment of this kind, all that is needed is *freedom*. And the freedom in question is the most innocuous form of all— freedom to make *public use* of one's reason in all matters. But I hear on all sides the cry: *Don't argue*! The officer says: Don't argue, get on parade! The tax-official: Don't argue, pay! The clergyman: Don't argue, believe! (Only one ruler in the world [Frederick the Great of Prussia] says: *Argue* as much as you like and about whatever you like, *but obey*!)[3]

As for the Romantic/Classical division, it is still with us. Two recent motion pictures confirm this. Representing the Romantics is Werner Herzog's "Every Man for Himself and God against All" (also titled "The Mystery of Kaspar Hauser"); François Truffaut's "The Wild Child" represents the Classical-Enlightenment viewpoint.

In each picture, the central character grew up outside normal culture, Hauser chained in a dungeon and the Wild Child running with the animals in the forest. Both are factually based variations of the Tarzan myth, the story of a well-born Englishman raised by apes in "Darkest Africa." Film critic Pauline Kael notes the different treatment that Herzog and Truffaut give to the subsequent changes in their heroes' characters when introduced into nor-

182   mal human society. "Kaspar is the only one [among the movie's characters] who hasn't lost his innocent responses to the world about him, who hasn't been blighted by society. He's still got his soul. . . . Herzog is a film poet, but he's a didactic [moralizing] poet, and what he has to say is extremely fashionable right now. The film says that society stultifies [hobbles] you under the guise of civilizing you, and that education destroys your innocent, true perceptions. In Truffaut's account of a lost boy, "The Wild Child," he regarded the boy's learning pains as necessary if the howling, frightened animal-child was to come into his human heritage; Truffaut cast himself in the role of the doctor who became the boy's teacher and guide. Herzog says that society puts you through the pain in order to deform you, and he makes it absolutely impossible for you to identify with anyone but Kaspar."[4]

6.3 The Natural/Artificial Contrast

To understand how this wider cultural contrast between Romanticism and the Enlightenment phase of Classicism can be associated with the two moral viewpoints in our problematic situation, we should start with an understanding of the natural/artificial contrast. This is a contrast that Rousseau made clearly and explicitly in his essay on the origin of inequality.

> For it is by no means a light undertaking to distinguish properly between what is original and what is artificial in the actual nature of man, or to form a true idea of a state [of nature] which no longer exists, perhaps never did exist; and of which, it is nevertheless necessary to have true ideas, in order to form a proper judgment of our present state.[5]

An artifact is something made by an artisan; it is human-made; a self that is the product of our own making (or remaking) would be an artifact and so an artificial (self-realized) self. A natural object, on the other hand, is a product in which humans had no effective role. We are familiar with natural versus artificial bridges; natural bridges are formed by the effect of water, wind, and erosion, while artificial bridges are constructed by human labor and skill. Moral psychology characterizes humans as "natural" because they are the product of genetic laws and natural selection. The basic idea behind the natural/artificial contrast is that objects are traced to one of two different kinds of origins.

The natural/artificial contrast can unfairly load the case for moral psychology and against self-realization ethics, because these terms are often used not only to indicate a difference in origin but also a difference in reality. The artificial is often thought of as equivalent to the bogus or counterfeit; thus paper flowers are bogus flowers, not "real" flowers; here the natural/artificial contrast turns into a real/unreal contrast, although no one

© Universal Press Syndicate

would think a car, house, or computer "unreal" just because they are artificial.

Imagine a clever fellow who is convinced of but unhappy with the view that humans are by nature egoistic. To refute psychological egoism, he constructs an object that looks, feels, sounds, tastes, and smells just like a human and he christens it "Frank Goodbody." He programs Frank always to act altruistically, and then in triumph points to Frank's conduct as a refutation of psychological egoism. If it were subsequently discovered that Frank Goodbody was constructed, "he" would be seen as an artifact, a counterfeit human; being such, Frank isn't a "real" human, and thus would not be a valid disproof of psychological egoism. Frank Goodbody is just a robot. Again, the natural/artificial contrast becomes a real/unreal contrast.

When one moves from using the natural/artificial contrast to indicate a difference in origin, to using it to indicate a difference in reality, there is a shift from a neutral stance regarding the comparative value of natural versus artificial objects to a preference for the natural. "Counterfeit" and "bogus" are not bare synonyms for "unreal"; they contain a built-in value component that favors the natural over the artificial. Real flowers are better than bogus or artificial flowers; real money is better than counterfeit money; and real humans are better than robot humans.

When this built-in value component of the natural/artificial contrast goes unnoticed, unfortunately it can make people unconsciously favor the natural selves of moral psychology over the artificial selves of self-realization morality. Kaspar Hauser untutored is better than Kaspar Hauser tutored. We should not be fooled into automatically taking this stance, however, because it is a mistake to jump from the origin use of the contrast to the use of it to express reality and value. After all, regardless of their origin, artificial flowers are real paper flowers; counterfeit money fills the wallet; robots are

184 real machines; and false teeth are far better than nothing. Everything that exists is real, and everything that is real is as real as anything else. The natural/artificial contrast is not a contrast in reality after all; consequently, it doesn't automatically invest the natural with more value than the artificial. It could be plausibly maintained that an altruistic robot is morally better than a real but egoistic human. Less controversially, it is obvious that an artificial bridge may well be better than a natural one; steel knives are certainly better than bone or stone; and glasses aid the eyeballs. It is important not to jump to the conclusion that the "natural" human of moral psychology and Romantic artists is better than the "artificial" human of Classicists and self-realization advocates—an easy conclusion that overlooks the value assumption hidden in the natural/artificial distinction.

To summarize, I have noted three different meanings in the natural/artificial contrast: (1) origin difference, (2) reality difference, and (3) value difference. It is invalid to jump from the first meaning to the second or third. A theory about the origin of human nature doesn't allow us to infer anything about the reality or value of humans.

A useful curb on thoughtless acceptance of the second and third interpretations is provided by the reminder that while moral psychologists agree on the origin of humans and their wants, they may differ about the moral goodness of the natural human. Advocates of the Gyges Argument recognize that the artificial self is better than the natural human, because the latter is so interested in his or her own wants that he or she will perform crimes if sure of being undetected. That this view of natural evil is still current is shown by the following letter to the *New York Times,* commenting on a *Times* editorial about the looting that took place during the power outage in New York City in 1977. The outage gave the cover of darkness to humans, a condition equivalent to the invisibility conferred by the Gyges ring. The letter: "Oh, yes, says the *Times,* looting is to be deplored, but 'We did not spend enough of our ingenuity and affluence to solve the problems the riots of the '60's made evident.' Bah! Looters are born, not made."[6] The "hard-headed" business man and city police tend to agree about the human animal: humans need to be forcibly civilized, to be restrained.

On the other hand Rousseau's natural humans, with their natural sympathetic response, are better than artificial humans. Recall that for Rousseau the artificial human is formed by society; the sympathy that operates freely and effectively in a natural state is stifled by reason and the civil state with its laws of property and its hierarchical structure.

> If the reader thus discovers and retraces the lost and forgotten road, by which man must have passed from the state of nature to the state of society. . . he will explain how the soul and the passions of men insensibly change their very nature; why our wants and pleasures in the end seek new objects; and why, the original man having vanished by degrees, society offers to us only an assembly of artificial men and factitious [forced, artificial] passions, which are the work of all these new relations [of society], and without any real foundation in nature. (*Inequality,* p. 362)

6.4 Food and Wine Romanticism   185

The use of the natural/artificial contrast is probably most common to-day in food and wine discussions.   There is presently a Romantic upswing regarding food; nearly everyone claims to favor "natural" foods and "natural" ingredients.   This isn't explainable by a growing belief in the superior healthfulness of so-called natural foods alone, because many natural substances can kill you or make you seriously ill.

Upton Sinclair's *The Jungle* (1906) was a book that shocked America. In it he reported on the meat packing industry, describing in rich detail the disgustingly unsanitary methods used in it.   The book sparked legal interven-tion that produced government inspection and regulation.   Here were con-ditons that certainly made the natural look better than the artificial.   Who would want sawdust sausages (the first "junk" food?) or human lard? Sinclair told of huge vats at floor level into which workers sometimes fell and from which they could not be rescued, coming out later as part of the in-dustry's produce.   What could be more artificial than beef with humans in it?   Aversion to the artificial is quite understandable, given these gruesome revelations; the natural/artificial contrast obviously has moral dimensions.

But suppose the artificial in food isn't harmful, perhaps even useful, maybe healthier.   Is it to be shunned then?   Orville Schell wrote an amusing article[7] slanted toward the reigning food Romanticism after attending a con-vention of the Institute of Food Technologists (IFT).   On display were gadgets "whose job it is to flavor, color, fumigate, texturize, moisturize, stabilize, emulsify, propel, preserve, sequester, dehydrate, rehydrate, fortify, leaven, bleach, crisp and ripen the food we eat" (a list that leaves little doubt about food being an artifact).   Schell tasted "synthetically" produced flavors—"synthetic" being a currently popular synonym for "artificial." The advertising on the booth of the Norda Company which makes the flavors, showed how aware it was of the current Romanticism: "Next to Nature, Norda."   The company's director of research claimed any flavor could be duplicated "synthetically" and defended "artificial" flavoring : "We just can't buy natural botanics the way we used to.   Cherry bark for cherry extract is the same [as ginger, which is unavailable].   And it's much more economical to use artificials.   You don't need to refrigerate.   No insect infestations. You don't have the bulk to ship.   I'd hate to tell you about the bacteria and mold in some of this natural stuff."   Are there hints of Sinclair's *Jungle* here?

At the same convention Schell saw "engineered meat," or "meat analog," these being somewhat more contrived synonyms for "artificial." An Extrusion Cooker turned a high-protein vegetable flour into meat analog called Uni-Tex that may be "richly flavored, colored and given texture like that of ham, beef, chicken or seafood."   Schell asked the manufacturer's representative, "Why would people living in the wealthiest nation in the world want to eat these imitations as long as the real thing is available?"   (Notice "imitation" and "real.")   The representative had a ready answer, pointing

186 out that Uni-Tex was good for vegetarians and people on low-fat diets, that it was low in cholesterol and at 15 cents a pound, cheaper than meat.

Another manufacturer invited conventioneers to think about tomato juice in bottles. "Natural" tomato juice tends to separate, the heavier solids sinking to the bottom and making the top look thin and watery, which is unappetizing to the customer. A chemical is manufactured that stops the separation without either adding to or detracting from its healthfulness. But as this chemical company's salesman put it, "Maybe our consumer just doesn't want separated tomato juice. . . . When it's separated, it looks deformed to them. Maybe people don't want reality. Maybe what they're looking for is fantasy."

Perhaps the salesman slips too easily into the fallacy of thinking like customers who believe the natural in origin is more real and better than the artificial—a fallacy that I warned against in Section 6.3. But even the "origin" way of distinguishing between the natural and artificial becomes suspect, as Hank Rubin notes in his discussion about wine. In his column "The Wine Master"—this one titled "Is Wine Natural?"—he lists some "additives" used in making wine, which, to keep our perspective, is obviously not a natural product but an artifact. Already the line between the natural and the artificial starts to blur when one talks about "natural wine," which really is "natural/artificial wine." Rubin first isolates the "natural" in wine making by calling attention to the "process."

> In these days of the veneration of "naturalness" in food, wine is hallowed by some because it is a "natural" beverage, because it is the result of a pure, organic process that converts grapes into liquid delight. However, if the winemaker does not intervene, often with "unnatural" but legally permissible additives, the result might not be the desired ambrosia but something closer to salad dressing, or even worse. One or more of these additives are used almost universally to prevent spoilage or to improve quality. So the word "natural," when applied to wine, is not wholly apt.[8]

Rubin lists these additives: tartaric acid, sugar (before and after fermentation), egg whites or gelatin, sulfur dioxide, and oak extract. Tartaric acid and sugar are substances that the grape contains "naturally," but sometimes in insufficient amounts for good fermentation and alcoholic content. The sugar added before fermentation is in the form of sucrose, which splits into glucose and fructose,"the natural grape sugars. If sucrose splits into natural grape sugars, is it a 'natural addition'?" Egg whites obviously aren't grape parts, but they don't remain in the wine, being used only to get rid of tiny particles that won't settle out. Sulfur dioxide does remain to prevent spoilage and color change, but can't be tasted if used properly. And who wants to forego the addition of oak extract, which in moderation improves the flavor of wine just as the flavor of wine aged in oaken barrels is improved? Not I, no matter how artificial it is.

The longer one reflects on the natural/artificial distinction, the less precise it becomes and the less useful as an evaluative tool. Perhaps it's time to retire Romanticism.

6.5 Artificial, Inauthentic Humans: Acts and Motives   187

While it seems apparent that the natural isn't always better than the artificial, some would claim that the natural is superior to the artificial by using still another interpretation of "artificial" to defend their position: they see the artificial as inauthentic. In the following passage notice how Rousseau first sets up the difference between natural and civilized (artificial) humans, then attributes the difference to an inside/outside contrast—an important factor for understanding the idea of inauthentic.

> The savage and the civilized man differ so much in the bottom of their hearts and in their inclinations, that what constitutes the supreme happiness of one would reduce the other to despair. The former breathes only peace and liberty; he desires only to live and be free from labor. . . . Civilized man, on the other hand, is always moving, sweating, toiling and racking his brains to find still more laborious occupations. . . . He pays his court to men in power, whom he hates, and to the wealthy, whom he despises. . . . In reality, the source of all these differences is, that the savage lives within himself, while social man lives constantly outside himself, and only knows how to live in the opinion of others, so that he seems to receive the consciousness of his own existence merely from the judgment of others concerning him. (*Inequality,* p. 362)

The concept of the inauthentic human depends upon a distinction not explicitly introduced up to this point. This distinction is between an act and its motive, or to put it more carefully, between a moral agent's act and the agent's motive for performing the act. Rousseau distinguishes between "inside" and "outside" motives. Outside motives are those imposed by or acquired from others; they are not our own. We become inauthentic in a state of society because it lures us into living in accord with the opinion of others. This divorces us from our own natural—that is, inside—motives, which include our natural sympathy and compassion for others. The late philosopher Hannah Arendt remarks that Rousseau was the theorist of intimacy, which he discovered "through a rebellion. . . . against society's unbearable perversion of the human heart, its intrusion upon an innermost region in man which until then had needed no special protection."[9]

You may have heard echoes of Ivan Ilyich in Rousseau's remarks about the inside versus the outside man. Recall Ilyich's musings (2.2, p. 45): "It struck him that those scarcely detected inclinations of his to fight against what the most highly placed people regarded as good, those scarcely noticeable impulses which he had immediately suppressed, might have been the real thing and all the rest false."

Notice the contrast between the "real" and the "false," the real being Ilyich's own internal (inside) inclinations, impulses, or wants and the false being the externally derived (outside) inclinations. Ilyich, by living in accord with others' inclinations rather than his own—by following what Nietzsche called the "herd instinct"—was inauthentic; he wasn't "true to himself." For

188   Rousseau, the artificial human isn't true to himself; he lives on outside, borrowed motives. If only Ilyich had followed his own inclinations and realized them, he would not have ended up despising himself; he was ordinary because he became like others wanted him to be.

Although Gyges advocates and Rousseau differ on the moral character of human nature, they do agree that the artificial human is inauthentic. Gyges advocates see humans in society as inauthentic because, while their natural, inside inclinations or wants are directed toward their self-interest, society's laws with their accompanying enforced punishment introduce new, outside wants that force humans to act altruistically rather than egoistically. This is inauthentic because humans are forced to dissemble, to pretend that they are interested in the welfare of others; they are not really so inclined inside, but are forced to be "phonies." They are acting with prudent, reasoning guile rather than "truly"—that is, in accord with their inside feelings.

Such Gyges advocates did not die out with Thrasymachus. Some quotations from Michael Korda's *Success* (Random House, 1977) give us ample evidence of this. "The fastest way to succeed," writes Korda, "is to look as if you're playing by other people's rules, while quietly playing by your own." Korda advises you to memorize these rules: "It's O.K. to be greedy. It's O.K. to be ambitious. It's O.K. to look out for number one. It's O.K. to be Machiavellian (if you can get away with it). It's O.K. to recognize that honesty is not always the best policy (provided you don't go around saying so). It's O.K. to be a winner. And it's O.K. to be rich."[10]

An inauthentic human, according to some, is a pretender, a dissembler, a hypocrite, a person of guile. Anyone of whom this is true is not admirable, says conventional wisdom. Suddenly, with the addition of the "inauthentic" interpretation of "artificial," Gyges advocates are in the same camp as Rousseau and other Romantics: the artificial is the inauthentic is the bad; while its opposite, the natural, is authentic and good. Humans acting under pressure of civilization and its laws are as artificial and inauthentic as the robot Frank Goodbody, because they are formed by others and motivated from the outside.

Parenthetically, a moral psychologist need not hold that civilized humans and laws are artificial; he may consider them natural products, as Hume does. (See *Enquiries,* p. 307; we will examine his view in Chapter 12.)

The distinction between an agent's act and the motive for the act is illustrated in a newspaper story headlined as "Researcher Doubts Altruism of Public TV Sponsors." The article reports on a paper by M. David Ermann, delivered at the 1977 American Sociological Association meeting.

> They claim it's altruism and "social responsibility," but major corporations give $12 million a year to the Public Broadcasting Service (PBS) "not for the public but for themselves," according to a sociologist. A company's contributions are intended to create a social climate less hostile, even charitable, to themselves—and thus mute criticism—by associating their names with excellence. . . . This explains why four of the top five

contributors are oil companies (Exxon, Mobil, Arco and Gulf) with years of fast rising profits, Ermann said, and why, in turn, "PBS has sarcastically been called the petroleum broadcasting system."

In a brief discussion following the report, Bernard Greenblatt of the State University of New York at Buffalo objected somewhat to Ermann's implicit premise that PBS contributors were engaged in "socio-economic imperialism." But Greenblatt, a highly respected and experienced sociologist, also commented that company claims of altruism were "sublime rationalization" at times, and that such contributions were "public relations in the guise of philanthropy."[11]

Ermann and Greenblatt judge that the *act* of giving funds to PBS (philanthropy) is right, but they note that the *motive* (public relations) is not altruistic but selfish. Thus the rightness of the act is not matched by the goodness of the motive: a selfish motive is not to be praised. The oil companies and other corporations are inauthentic because, despite the right nature of the act, the motive that caused it is selfish. Note Greenblatt's use of "guise," implying trickery.

In distinguishing between an act and its motive and examining the possible variation in their moral nature, we can have four possibilities:

Right act - good motive
Right act - bad motive
Wrong act - bad motive
Wrong act - good motive

To be authentic is to be genuine, committed, engaged, sincere; it is to have integrity. To be genuine is to have one's acts and one's motives match; it is to be "up front" so that, if the act is right, the motive is openly good rather than secretly bad; or if the act is wrong, the motive is openly bad, as the Gyges advocates claim our motives always are.

Civilization makes it possible for us to be inauthentic in the Romantics' view because, as Rousseau notes (p. 184), it introduces new wants and "factitious" passions. These come with the new, artificial self created by society, and add artificial motives to our natural motives, making possible a mismatch between our acts and motives. To reflect this in the links diagram, we introduce artificial human selves with their artificial wants (motives), goods, and ends.

$$\begin{array}{lll}
\text{ARTIFICIAL} & \text{ARTIFICIAL} & \\
\text{SELF} \rightarrow & \text{WANT} \rightarrow & \text{GOOD}_1 \rightarrow \text{END}_1 \\
& & \hspace{3cm} \rightarrow \text{ACT}_n \\
\text{NATURAL} & \text{NATURAL} & \\
\text{SELF} \rightarrow & \text{WANT} \rightarrow & \text{GOOD}_2 \rightarrow \text{END}_2
\end{array}$$

Because it is possible that a right act can have either a good or a bad motive, and because the creation of artificial selves creates a second set of motives, the path to inauthenticity opens. Suppose ACT_n is a philanthropic

190 one; as such it is right.   However, such an act may benefit the agent who performs it as well as the person receiving the philanthropy.   Thus someone may perform a philanthropic act from a hidden, selfish motive while professing an altruistic motive; the hidden motive is bad, the professed one is good.   The result is a mismatch between the moral value of the act and of the real motive, and this is inauthentic.   If there were not artificial selves with their artificial wants and motives, such mismatches and therefore such inauthenticity would not be possible.

The natural want is our own "inside" want; the artificial one is the "outside" want imposed on us by indoctrination or by threats from others in society more powerful than we.   As Goethe remarks, our inside nature—originality, wildness—may be driven out of us until only the "outside," dominated Philistine remains, as it did in Ivan Ilyich.   If we wish to remain "true" to our natural "inside" self and keep from becoming wholly artificial, we have to learn to suppress the artificial motives.

Had we retained our original, natural self—our human nature uncorrupted by an imposed, artificial self—there would be no inauthentic humans, because inauthenticity requires the dualism of a natural and an artificial self. Without this dualism, we could not exploit a guileful mismatch between our acts and our motives; instead we would have an "appropriate" motive for each act.

6.6 Acts Requiring Authenticity

Regardless of whether or not you subscribe to their theory, the Romantics' condemnation of inauthentic, artificial humans finds support in some moral considerations that appear to be independent of contending moral theories and psychologies.   To see why this is so, let's first summarize what we've learned about inauthenticity, and then examine some very familiar kinds of acts to see how inauthenticity and immorality are linked together in them.

Persons are inauthentic when their acts don't have an appropriate motive—that is, when the moral qualities of the acts and their motivation don't match.   This mismatching is deceptive, which is a form of lying; lying is morally wrong; therefore, inauthenticity is immoral.   This summarizes the Romantics' theory of the link between inauthenticity and immorality.

Human acts are not well understood.   Philosophers disagree about when acts do and don't occur, and about how to distinguish between one kind of act and another, and about how to determine just what act has in fact been performed.   Philosophers' disagreements about acts lead to two different theories about the linkage between inauthenticity and immorality.   Let us take as our preliminary example the purported act of forgiving someone by uttering the words "I forgive you." Assuming the appropriate motive is absent, **191** the utterance of that sentence could be immoral either (a) because the act of forgiving is not really performed (deception) or (b) because, although the act is really performed, persons are deceived about your moral nature, expecting you to perform ensuing acts because they believe you forgave from appropriate motives (deception again). Let's look at this in more detail.

Acts that appear to require authenticity are forgiving, apologizing, praising and blaming, and thanking. In each of these acts we think that some feelings are appropriate motivations and that others are not. I have not acted from the appropriate motive of mercy if I say to someone who has asked for my forgiveness, "I forgive you," but feel no mercy, harboring hate or resentment instead, and knowing that these feelings will someday probably lead me to avenge myself. I may say "I forgive you" out of an inappropriate motive such as hate, because I plan to lull you into a false sense of trust in me. This inauthenticity may be immoral on either of the two grounds stated above. (a) It may be immoral because, while I appeared to forgive you, I actually did not do so. I appeared to forgive because I uttered "I forgive you"; I didn't however, actually forgive you because I didn't have the appropriate feeling of mercy, but rather the inappropriate feeling of resentment. The immorality of this inauthenticity is linked to my deceiving you about the actual performance of the act. (b) In the second theory of the linkage between inauthenticity and immorality, we suppose that uttering "I forgive you" is sufficient to perform the act of forgiving, even though I don't have the appropriate feeling. But, lacking the appropriate feeling, I deceive you about other acts you can expect me to perform as a result. For example, you may trust me to treat you like a friend again and to repay money I borrow from you; however, my resentment motivates me to welch on my repayment. If you think that I sincerely forgave you, you won't expect me to default on my debt; but I misled you.

In either the (a) or (b) theory of what is required to perform the act of forgiving—the first requiring the presence of the appropriate feeling, the second not requiring it—the act is inauthentic because it involves deception or pretense, which is a form of lying and wrongdoing.

To apologize for an act without feeling regret or guilt (the motives ordinarily deemed appropriate for apology) is to pretend. Genuine apology requires that it be motivated by a regretful heart. One may say "I apologize," for example, in hopes of gaining the approval of others for being morally sensitive, but this motive marks you as an impostor.

Many of our acts done from inappropriate motives do not have names of their own; pretending to forgive and to apologize, for instance, do not. We do, however, have a name for false praise: flattery. Genuine praise is motivated by admiration. Someone I know may have sacrificed a great deal of personal comfort in order to help another attain a worthy objective; this may have aroused my admiration for his or her character, motivating me to praise. But should I praise someone without feeling admiration, I would be flattering, which could be motivated by the desire to gain some favor or good will from another for an end of my own. Inauthentic praising is wrong; it

192　misleads the person praised about my attitude and becomes scheming flattery.

What feeling is appropriate to blame? Benedict Spinoza, the seventeenth-century Dutch philosopher, says: "The joy with which we imagine another person's action, the purpose of which is to delight us, I call *praise,* and the sorrow with which we turn away from an action of a contrary kind I call blame."[12] While Spinoza here does not distinguish the feelings (joy and sorrow) of praise and blame from acts of praising and blaming, he does suggest how to determine the appropriate motivation for acts of blaming. Because blame is the contrary of praise, the appropriate motive for blaming must be the contrary of the appropriate motive for praising; thus despising, being the contrary of admiring, must be the appropriate motivation for blaming. In cases when we blame someone, then, but do not despise them, we have simulated (pretended) blame. Because blaming is a form of moral censure, it has a powerful effect on most persons; so to simulate blame is to try to affect them, to get them to feel guilty, without the appropriate motive; it might be undertaken to manipulate the persons' feelings and thereby gain power over them, or needlessly to torture them mentally, either of which is immoral. Thus inauthentic blaming, whether or not it is actual blaming, is immoral.

My last example of a kind of moral act that requires appropriate motivation if it is to be authentically performed is thanking someone. Obviously, a feeling of gratitude toward a donor is the appropriate motive for thanking. However, in this case we don't always condemn inauthenticity. Suppose that as a birthday present Aunt Em gave you something ugly and useless that definitely and obviously does not arouse a feeling of gratitude in you; if you thank her inauthentically, you'll be less severely judged by your family than if you don't thank her at all. You are supposed to hide your lack of gratitude; your finest acting (Geez, Aunt Em . . .) is most suitable. In fact, the more inauthentic you are, bringing tears to Aunt Em's eyes, the better you are judged to be. Here the forms of society normally have a stronger hold on us than authenticity.

Even so, the pure, wholly authentic person who displays no guile—who acts solely and innocently from actual feelings, even though violating the forms of society—has been an object of admiration. In *The Idiot* Dostoevsky draws such an admirable character, Prince Leo Nikolayevich Myshkin. The novel's title expresses the conventional person's view of this kind of character, which is that perfect innocence carries authenticity to an idiotic extreme. But usually, were a person to look innocently right into the eyes of a blood donor and, feeling no gratitude, say, "I cannot thank you for the blood that saved my life; I cannot authentically do so because I feel no gratitude," we would think the person monstrous—authenticity be damned! Furthermore, not only should he have thanked the donor, but he ought also to have felt gratitude. The argument goes like this: the act merited thanking; thanking should be authentic; to be authentic, it has to be motivated by gratitude; to be so motivated, one must feel gratitude.

6.7 Appropriate Motives and Spontaneity   193

Throughout this discussion of acts that may require authenticity for their actual performance, and of their linkage to morality, I have relied on the claim that there are "appropriate" feelings that motivate authentic acts, or more briefly, that there are appropriate (and inappropriate) motives.

How can we distinguish between an appropriate and an inappropriate motive? According to Romanticism, an appropriate motive is one that spontaneously causes an agent to perform an act. To act spontaneously is to act without the intervention of thought; if thought is allowed to mediate between feeling and action, the act is calculated rather than spontaneous. The Romantic favors spontaneous acts because they express us; they express us because they are undistorted. Calculated acts are performed with an eye on others and their opinions, and are not free; only spontaneous acts allow us to express freely our "inside" life. Gene Kelly dancing in the streets of Paris in the rain to express his joy at finding love is unconventional, uncalculated, crazy, wonderful, infectious—and spontaneous. Those who, after seeing Kelly in "An American in Paris," come out of the cinema wanting to tap-dance down the street, know the appeal of spontaneity that Romanticism celebrates. Those who don't dance down the street because they fear "what people will think" have let thought intervene between their feeling and their actions; they aren't letting go, aren't letting themselves freely express their inward feelings. Instead, they are inhibited by a feeling of embarrassment—a motive with an "outside" source. Persistent, excessive inner control exercised to please others, the Romantics warn us, will eventually dry up the springs of feeling and make our souls as dry as desert dust. The tug of Romantic spontaneity and the authenticity it claims should be familiar.

You can appreciate Romanticism's emphasis on spontaneity in strictly moral actions as well. In the acts considered in 6.6 above, when the agent calculates the effect that such and such an action will have, he or she increases the chances for an inappropriate motive to enter and cause the act, which is the very condition that makes inauthenticity logically possible. Were we only our natural selves, then we would have only natural wants, with their associated goods and ends, to motivate our acts. For example, we would apologize only spontaneously from feelings of regret or guilt. We could not then apologize inauthentically, because there would be no other motive but these. If, however, we allow thought to intervene, then we might apologize from some feeling other than guilt or regret; this other feeling might be associated, for instance, with a devious end such as gaining the trust of a business partner to make it easier to cheat that partner later. Romantics often trace such intervening thoughts to society's attempts to indoctrinate us into constructing artificial selves.

To summarize: this Romantic account of inauthentic humans depends, first, on the distinction between an agent's act and motive; second, on possi-

194 ble mismatching of the moral worth of acts and motives; third, on society's creation of an artificial self with its artificial wants; fourth, on our being forced or indoctrinated to choose artificial over natural wants; and fifth, on the lack of spontaneity that enables us to act calculatingly from artificial, inappropriate motives (wants).

This fifth point reveals the connection between Romanticism and moral psychology. Romanticism advocates what simple moral psychology claims is a fact. Romanticism urges us to avoid inauthenticity; this can be done if our conduct is caused by the feelings aroused in humans uncorrupted by "outside" artificial influences. To act spontaneously as Romantics would have us do, is to behave exactly as simple moral psychology says we do in fact behave.

To appreciate the continuing influence exercised by Romanticism, you need only think of a typical justification for sexual availability. It is based on the appeal to act "naturally" without the forced, anxious suppression of your true desires. Witness this letter in Beth Winship's column, "Ask Beth": "I'm 16 and my boyfriend is 17. We care too much for each other. . . . . I know he won't force intercourse on me, I was brought up that it is morally wrong. But I also know we won't last too long. He says sex is not bad, it is natural. . . .—Exposed to a World of Experience."[13] To feel sexually free is to let your natural self lead to spontaneous acts of mutual joy; to try to make yourself over in the image of Puritan killjoys is to construct an artificial self that stifles the expression of your healthy, natural self. So goes the Romantic appeal.

6.8 Romantic Love and the Sleep of Reason: Shakespeare

Let's summarize how we got to Romantic authenticity and what it is, then consider an interpretation of Shakespeare's *A Midsummer Night's Dream* that questions the best that Romanticism has to offer—namely, romantic love.

To try to understand "nature" in the phrase "human nature," we explored the opposite of "natural," which is "artificial." We discovered that "artificial" has three meanings; consequently, "natural" has three corresponding opposite meanings.

(1) Origin: The natural is anything whose existence does not depend upon human artifice; the artificial is what is made by humans.

(2) Reality: The natural has reality; the artificial is unreal, bogus, counterfeit.

(3) Value: "Real" natural objects have more value than "unreal," bogus, constructed objects.

We found that it is fallacious to infer from meaning (1) to meanings (2) **195**
and (3). Bogus flowers are real paper flowers; artificial bridges are better
than natural ones.

For those who want to value the natural over the artificial, the next
move is to give "natural" a fourth meaning, "authentic," and to give "artificial" the meaning of "inauthentic." The Romantic concept of the authentic person has four components.

(4) Authenticity:

(a) *Naturalness.* Authentic persons do not inhibit their human
nature, which is fitted to respond emotionally to various kinds of
situations. Inauthentic persons have been "civilized" to respond
with artificial feelings, as Rousseau thought.

(b) *Freedom.* Authentic persons act from the natural "inside"
motives that are truly their own. Inauthentic persons act from
"outside" motives imposed on them by others, and so conform
to the "herd" instead of acting freely, independently of the
wants of others.

(c) *Genuineness.* Authentic persons' motives and acts are morally
matched—good motives and good acts, bad motives and bad
acts. Authentic persons are genuine and "up front," even
openly acknowledging bad motives if their acts are wrong. Inauthentic persons dissemble and pretend.

(d) *Spontaneity.* Authentic persons act spontaneously from their
natural, inside, appropriate feelings; inauthentic persons
shrewdly calculate their acts. This spontaneity expresses our
unique individuality; calculation distorts it.

Authentic, natural persons are better than inauthentic, artificial persons
because they are uninhibited in their feelings, are free and genuine, and spontaneously express their own individual selves. This Romantic theory is attractive doctrine, but not without its difficulties, as my interpretation of *A
Midsummer Night's Dream* will show.

Romantic love has been touted as a basis for morally praiseworthy
human relations between men and women. It is supposed to illustrate
perfectly the four components of authenticity above. (a) Love is a *natural*
phenomenon, not being generated at will or by instruction; love "strikes" us,
we are "meant" for each other. (b) The bondage of love is borne willingly
because each gives that love *freely,* without demands from the other; love is
truly an "inside" motive. (c) Supposedly, when a man and a woman love
each other, they are motivated to treat each other thoughtfully, regardfully.
Love tends to motivate right acts toward the other, insuring a match between
the morality of motive and act. Because romantic love is openly displayed to
the lover, it makes us as *genuine* as we can be. (d) And certainly acts
motivated by love are *spontaneous;* there is no calculation of the effects of
acts: they are pure expressions of ourselves.

This rosy peak of authenticity, however, may not be all it is touted to
be. Shakespeare had a pretty good go at criticizing its four components.

First, love may have origins that aren't wholly implanted in our nature. In Shakespeare's play Oberon plans to manipulate the loves that others feel; he does so with a drug, the juice of a flower struck by one of Cupid's arrows. The chemistry of love may be set bubbling by an outside agent. The *Dream* is a science fiction play: in it, a drug dispensed by human intervention induces romantic love not naturally but artificially; love is subject to push-button control. If Cupid and his arrows strike you as fanciful inventions, remember that love potions have been offered to the loveless for ages and still are today, when aphrodisiacs are advertised in "nudie" magazines. And on a less literal level, observe how clothes and toiletries and cosmetics—as a glance at the ads will tell you—are purveyed to the public as products all but guaranteed to stimulate love.

Second, the inside motive of love is produced chemically by the outside motive of someone else—Oberon. Hence, we aren't acting as freely as Romantics think authentic persons do when they act from love.

Third, love may be genuine but it is inconstant, fickle; when it changes, it also means being unfaithful to the former lover, which brings harm as well as good. Genuineness—the authentic matching of motives and acts—doesn't guarantee that all acts motivated by love will be right.

Fourth and finally, love makes reason its slave and comes when reason sleeps, as amply illustrated in *A Midsummer Night's Dream*. The celebrated spontaneity of love is akin to madness.

Let's see how Shakespeare makes these points.

Oberon, the King of the fairies, is jealous of his Queen, Titania, because she dotes on a young boy. He decides to avenge himself by making her fall in love with an animal. He sends Puck, also called Robin Goodfellow, for Cupid's elixir of love, which Oberon plans to place on Titania's eyelids while she sleeps (while reason sleeps). Oberon has observed Cupid shoot an arrow, and says,

> Yet mark'd I where the bolt of Cupid fell:
> It fell upon a little western flower,—
> Before milk-white, now purple with love's wound,—
> And maidens call it love-in-idleness.
> Fetch me that flower; the herb I shew'd thee once:
> The juice of it on sleeping eyelids laid
> Will make a man or woman madly dote
> Upon the next live creature that it sees. (Act II, Scene i, lines 165–73)

When Titania awakens she will fall in love with the first creature she sees, whether her eyes fall on a "lion, or wolf, or bull, on meddling monkey, or on busy ape."

The first creature Titania sees upon awakening is Bottom, a rough workingman from Athens who happens to be in the woods, and to whom Puck, for a joke, has given an ass's head, although Bottom doesn't know it. By having Titania fall in love with this new, absurd Bottom, Shakespeare lampoons romantic love. Poor Titania is blinded by it; she tells Bottom, with his ass's head:

Come, sit thee down upon this flowery bed,
While I thy amiable cheeks do coy,
And stick musk-roses in thy sleek smooth head,
And kiss thy fair large ears, my gentle joy. (IV. i. 1-4)

Oberon now takes pity on Titania and touches her eyelids to release her from the power of Cupid's flower. Titania awakens from her love-struck "dream" to announce: "My Oberon!what visions have I seen!/ Methought I was enamour'd of an ass." Pointing to the sleeping ass-headed Bottom, Oberon tells her, "There lies your love," and Titania exclaims: "How came these things to pass?/ O, how mine eyes do loathe his visage now! (IV. i. 79-83).

Shakespeare has great fun with Titania and Bottom, but puts the juice of Cupid's flower to more serious use in dealing with four young lovers who also come to the woods. At the play's opening Hermia loves Lysander, Helena loves Demetrius, Demetrius and Lysander both love Hermia, but no one loves Helena. Hermia's father Egeus has ordered Hermia to marry Demetrius, which she doesn't want to do because she loves Lysander. Egeus appeals to Theseus, Duke of Athens, for permission to kill Hermia, if she refuses to marry Demetrius. (To our romantic age, of course, hardly anything is as inauthentic as marrying without love—a real mismatch between act and motive.)

In the woods Oberon overhears Demetrius rejecting Helena—"I am sick when I do look on thee"—and she professing her love for him: "And I am sick when I look not on you." Wanting to help set things in order, Oberon commands Puck to put love's chemical on Demetrius' eyelids and make sure that the first person he sees upon awakening is Helena. Unfortunately, Puck mistakes Lysander for Demetrius and puts the juice of love on Lysander's eyelids while he sleeps. When Lysander awakens, Helena is the first person he sees, so he promptly falls in love with her and out of love with Hermia. Lysander professes his love of her to Helena, who wants him to keep loving Hermia because Hermia, her friend, still loves Lysander. The fickleness of what Lysander takes to be spontaneous, natural love for Helena is nicely put by Shakespeare:

Content with Hermia! No: I do repent
The tedious minutes I with her have spent.
Not Hermia but Helena I love:
Who will not change a raven for a dove?
The will of man is by his reason sway'd;
And reason says you are the worthier maid.
Things growing are not ripe until their season:
So I, being young, till now ripe not to reason;
And touching now the point of human skill,
Reason becomes the marshal to my will
And leads me to your eyes, where I o'erlook
Love's stories written in love's richest book. (II. ii. 111-12)

Poor Lysander. While he and reason slept, an outside agent by artificial, chemical means induced love in him for another. Not knowing this, he

198   believes that on his own he loves Helena rather than Hermia, and thinks that his reason accounts for his newfound love. But because reason slept, in reality his feelings have priority, and reason follows docilely in tow. So he abandons Hermia, who still loves him. And, so, Shakespeare puts a crimp in the theory that acts motivated by matching love are a secure base for stable, moral relations. Professions of "authentic" love are as suspect as a dream.

But *A Midsummer Night's Dream* is a comedy, after all, so Oberon orders Puck to set things straight, suspecting him of mischievous knavery in the garden of love. Puck is to apply Cupid's chemical to Lysander and Demetrius' eyelids, making sure that the first persons they see are Hermia and Helena respectively. This will insure that Lysander falls back in love with Hermia, who wants to marry him, and that Demetrius will return Helena's love and not try to marry Hermia as Egeus wishes him to do. Puck does as he is told, speaking thus as he squeezes the juice on Lysander's eyelids:

> When thou wakest,
> Thou takest
> True delight
> In the sight
> Of thy former lady's eye:
> And the country proverb known,
> That every man should take his own,
> In your waking shall be shown:
> > Jack shall have Jill;
> > Naught shall go ill;
> The man shall have his mare again, and all shall be well.   (III. ii. 453-60)

Puck remains the alert one throughout, unfooled by romantic love and deploring it somewhat: "Cupid is a knavish lad,/Thus to make poor females mad" (III. ii. 440-41). Shakespeare deals another blow to the unreliability and inconstancy of romantic love when he has Demetrius observe to Egeus:

> But, my good lord, I wot not by what power,—
> But by some power it is,—my love to Hermia,
> Melted as doth the snow, seems to me now
> As the remembrance of an idle gawd [ornament]
> Which in my childhood I did dote upon;
> And all the faith, the virtue of my heart,
> The object and the pleasure of mine eye,
> Is only Helena.   (IV. i. 168-75)

Hermia, Helena, Demetrius, and Lysander are understandably confused by these sudden turns of love. Is this midsummer madness, and is love a product of it? Demetrius asks: "Are you sure/That we are awake? It seems to me/That yet we sleep, we dream." (IV. ii. 196-98).

Theseus concludes for Shakespeare with these observations on the **199** strange goings-on.

> Lovers and madmen have such seething brains,
> Such shaping fantasies, that apprehend
> More than cool reason ever comprehends.
> The lunatic, the lover, and the poet
> Are of imagination all compact:
> One sees more devils than vast hell can hold,
> That is the madman: The lover, all as frantic,
> Sees Helen's beauty in a brow of Egypt:
> The poet's eye, in a fine frenzy rolling,
> Doth glance from heaven to earth, from earth to heaven:
> And as imagination bodies forth
> The forms of things unknown, the poet's pen
> Turns them to shapes and gives to airy nothing
> A local habitation and a name.   (V. i. 4–17)

Shakespeare has good business sense; he knows he has to please the audience.   Whatever offense he might have given to an audience partial to romantic love, he tries to remove when Oberon assures all that the last application of the herb to Lysander and Demetrius' eyelids will remove all error and fix their love forever, banishing mischievous Puck from their future lives.

> Then crush this herb into Lysander's eye;
> Whose liquor hath this virtuous property,
> To take from thence all error with his might,
> And make his eyeballs roll with wonted sight.
> When they next wake, all this derision
> Shall seem a dream and fruitless vision,
> And back to Athens shall the lovers wend,
> With league whose date till death shall never end. (III. ii. 365–73)

Shakespeare-Puck's last speech asks the audience's forgiveness for this assault on love as a motive for "authentic" lovers.

> If we shadows have offended,
> Think but this, and all is mended,
> That you have but slumber'd here
> While these visions did appear. . . .
> So, good night unto you all.
> Give me your hands, if we be friends,
> And Robin shall restore amends.   (V. i. 430–45)

Thus ends Shakespeare's commentary on the vagaries of love, which may be neither natural nor free, and genuine but fickle, spontaneous but crazy.

200   6.9 Existential Authenticity

We have found the concept of the "natural" person rather elusive. Our search for it moved from the "natural/artificial" contrast to the Romantics' "authentic/inauthentic" contrast. Romantics favor authentic humans because they are natural, free, genuine, and spontaneous. In this section we will find that authenticity, too, is an elusive concept. Existentialists provide another and different meaning for "authentic" than the Romantics—a meaning that comes out of a philosophy of humans that is resolutely opposed to moral psychology.

We should not assume that "Existentialism" is a philosophy shared in every respect by all who are called "Existentialists." But there is one central claim they do all share, which I will presently explain: namely, that existence comes before essence, whence the name *"Existent*ialism." In discussing Existentialism I will concentrate on the German philosopher Martin Heidegger and his analysis of "authenticity." My quote from Robert Coles's remarks on Heidegger (2.2, p. 46) showed the connection between Heidegger's concept of authenticity and Ivan Ilyich's reflections on his life and approaching death. Heidegger's theory of authenticity is important to us here because he presents passionate opposition to moral psychology and to the Romantics' belief that the foundation of authenticity is the natural self. Heidegger moves resolutely in the same direction that advocates of self-realization and self-determination such as Nietzsche do: we are not strapped to nature's plan, we are free to make ourselves. For Heidegger, to be authentic is to affirm and face our freedom to be what we decide to be. To our second theme question—To what extent am I free to determine what I ought to do and to become? (p. 42)—Heidegger answers, "We are wholly free."

To develop this basic Existentialist position, I will contrast and compare Existentialist authenticity with the four components of Romantic authenticity: naturalness, freedom, genuineness, and spontaneity.

NATURALNESS. Existentialists deny that humans are natural. To understand why they think this, let's explore their central claim that existence comes before essence.

The existence/essence distinction is of particular importance in characterizing humans, to whom Heidegger refers by the term *Dasein,* meaning literally, "being there" (*sein* means "to be" or "to exist" in German). Humans first exist, then they have an essence or a nature. "Essence" is a term used in reference to groups or kinds of things; an individual thing's essence is made up of the properties it shares with others of its kind. These properties are "essential" to it; without them, it wouldn't be that kind of thing. For example, Plato and Aristotle thought the essence of humans is expressed by saying they are rational animals. Animality is their **201** genus property—that which makes them resemble other animals; rationality is their difference property—that which makes them different from other animals. In this view, nothing can be human unless it has the properties of animality and rationality. Moral psychologists too are "essentialists": they think humans have a shared "nature," which can be specified by listing the properties that all humans have. Ethologists and sociobiologists and psychologists study the human species to determine what our nature is and what caused it to be that way, and to determine what part of it is fixed and what part variable.

Existentialists, on the other hand, deny that we have a nature, deny that we have an essence that is given to us. For them, the basic characteristic of humans is that they exist first and then acquire a nature. Existentialists emphasize the individuality of our existence rather than a group nature. To suppose that we have a nature and that it dictates what we are, Existentialists think, allows us to excuse ourselves for what we do. We say, "I (he, she) couldn't help myself because that's the way we humans are," and by saying this we deny having the power to make ourselves otherwise and do otherwise; this is what Jean-Paul Sartre calls "bad faith." We deny what we are. The "human nature" essentialist orientation toward ourselves and others fosters irresponsibility for ourselves and our acts; we use "human nature" as an excuse. Instead of looking for an inherited nature, we should be oriented toward the future and what we will make of ourselves from the possibilities we have.

> The essence of Dasein lies in its existence. Accordingly those characteristics which can be exhibited in this entity are not [essential] 'properties' present-at-hand [observable] of some entity which "looks" so and so and is itself present-at-hand; they are in each case possible ways for it to be, and no more than that. . . . So when we designate this entity [humans] with the term "Dasein," we are expressing not its "what" (as if it were a table, house or tree) but its Being.[14]

Dasein (humans) isn't natural, isn't defined by its essence, for several reasons. First, its own Being is an "issue" for it. We, unlike natural things, can reflect on ourselves, take ourselves for an object of thought; this gives us selfhood. Second, this selfhood brings with it "mineness"; our Being is in each case personal—my Being is *mine;* we are not indifferent to our existence, we care about it. Third, our Being is forward looking; we are not locked into the present but can project the future and think about what we *will* be. This is what provides us with possibilities and the freedom to choose; without possible alternatives, choice isn't possible.

> Dasein always understands itself in terms of its existence—in terms of a possibility of itself; to be itself or not itself. Dasein has either chosen these possibilities itself, or got itself into them, or grown up in them already.

> Only the particular Dasein decides its existence, whether it does so by taking hold or neglecting. (p. 33)
>
> And because Dasein is in each case essentially its own possibility, it *can,* in its very Being, "choose" itself and win itself; it can also lose itself and never win itself; or only "seem" to do so. But only in so far as it is essentially something which can be *authentic*—that is, something of its own—can it have lost itself and not yet won itself. As modes of Being, *authenticity* and *inauthenticity* . . . are both grounded in the fact that any Dasein whatsoever is characterized by mineness. (p.68)

Because humans are not natural, having no essence other than what they give themselves, the authentic/inauthentic distinction can no longer be based on the natural/artificial distinction stressed by Romantics. Humans, according to the Existentialists, are wholly non-natural. Therefore, the distinction between authentic and inauthentic is between two kinds of artificiality.

FREEDOM. Romantics prize freedom from conformity and emphasize acting on our natural, "inside" motives rather than on acquired, "outside" motives. Because Existentialists deny we are natual in any way, the inside/outside motive contrast can't be their way of explaining human freedom. They do have something akin to the Romantics' inside/outside contrast, however. It is a contrast between two kinds of artificiality.

For Heidegger, an inauthentic human is an entity that "falls away from" itself; it conceals its Being from itself, basically, denying that it can itself choose its own Being. Instead, it is content to lead an "everyday" life, much as Ilyich did, taking pseudo Being from others, who steal individuals' own Being away from them. These "others" are "they," in Heidegger's term. "They" exist with an "averageness" that is similar to Nietzsche's "ordinariness." By living in an everyday way, we lose our freedom to determine our own Being. (See also Rousseau's remarks, p. 184.)

> Dasein, as everyday Being-with-one-another, stands in *subjection* to Others. It itself *is* not; its Being has been taken away by the Others. Dasein's everyday possibilities of Being are for the Others to dispose of as they please. These Others, moreover, are not *definite* Others. On the contrary, any Other can represent them. What is decisive is just that inconspicuous domination by Others which has already been taken over unawares from Dasein as Being-with. One belongs to the Others oneself and enhances their power . . . .The "who" is not this one, not that one, not oneself, not some people, and not the sum of them all. The 'who' is the neuter, *the "they."* (p. 164)

Heidegger's emphasis on freedom from "the they," and the call to be authentic by making oneself, urges us to be our own artifacts rather than society's; if we passively let society construct us, we fall away from ourselves and let others choose our essence for us; we get swallowed up in the neuter.

You can see here the striving for individuality that Existentialists and   **203**
Romantics both advocate; for both, at least part of the value of freedom stems
from its being the means to individuality, to being your own rather than society's. The following remarks of Ferdinand Buisson, a professor of pedagogy
at the Sorbonne in the early nineteenth century and national director of
elementary education in France, will give you some idea of what European
Existentialists were opposing, and why authenticity should seem precious by
contrast.

> If . . . the primary function of education is collective in character, if its
> object is to adapt the child to the social milieu in which he is destined to
> live, it is absolutely indispensable that society take an active interest in
> educational matters . . . . Thus it behooves society to constantly remind
> the teacher of the ideas and sentiments which must be inculcated in the
> child, so that he will be well adjusted to the milieu in which he is going to
> live. If society were not constantly keeping watch . . . the great soul of
> the Fatherland would split up into an incoherent multitude of little souls,
> each in conflict with the others.[15]

Of course, being made by others may be the course of least resistance;
Ilyich found it so. He became aware of having fallen into an "ordinary,"
"everyday" life only when he realized he was going to die. Heidegger and
Tolstoy give death a similar function; death can do this because it is our
"ownmost." *Dasein* is always personal; Being is "mine"; the cessation of my
Being is "mine" in a very personal way. In authentically facing death, we experience "anxiety," sometimes translated as "dread," which is not the same
as fear of death. In facing *my* death, I am wrenched away from the "they,"
thrown on my own, providing I face death authentically.

> *But the state-of-mind which can hold open the utter and constant threat to*
> *itself arising from Dasein's ownmost individualized Being, is anxiety.* In
> this state-of-mind, Dasein finds itself *face to face* with the "nothing" of
> the possible impossibility of its existence. (p. 310)
>   We may now summarize our characterization of authentic Being-
> towards-death as we have projected it existentially: *anticipation reveals to*
> *Dasein its lostness in the they-self, and brings it face to face with the*
> *possibility of being itself, primarily unsupported by concernful solicitude,*
> *but of being itself, rather in an impassioned* **freedom towards**
> **death**—*a freedom which has been released from the Illusions of the*
> *"they", and which is factical, certain of itself, and anxious.* (p. 311)

Death, because it marks an end, makes our life a "whole," and by
releasing us from the hold of "they," "individualizes" us (p. 233). Provided, that is , that we don't take the "everyday," inauthentic attitude toward
death.

In the publicness with which we are with one another in our everyday manner, death is "known" as a mishap which is constantly occurring—as a
"case of death". . . . The "they" has already stowed away an interpretation for this event. It talks of it in a "fugitive" manner, either expressly or
else in a way which is mostly inhibited, as if to say, "One of these days one
will die too, in the end; but right now it has nothing to do with us." (pp.
296–97)

Once the anxiety of death has retrieved us from the "they," we are open
to our potentiality-for-Being, which for *Dasein* is a "potentiality-for-Being-
its-Self." The "voice of conscience" attests to this potentiality. Conscience
summons us to "Being-guilty," which is not the everyday moral guilt for
having done something we ought not to have done or not doing something we
ought to have done. Rather, it is more basic: it reminds us that we have
"fallen away" from our authentic self and haven't taken responsibility for
what we are.

GENUINENESS. To be genuine in the Romantic sense is to match the
morality or immorality of our motives with the morality or immorality of our
acts; we are open, forthright, without pretense. Even if one does wrong, it is
better to be forthright about it than to conceal the motive for the act. The
honesty that Romanticism advocates is primarily honesty toward others, while
Existentialists emphasize honesty with ourselves. According to Sartre, we act
in bad faith when we lie to ourselves. Further, the lie doesn't involve conceal-
ing a "natural" motive for an act, since we are not at bottom natural
creatures. Instead, to conceal oneself existentially is to take no responsibility
for having chosen what you are, but to "blame" it on something else; you
conceal your free self from yourself.

> In introspection I try to determine exactly what I am, to make up my mind
> to be my true self without delay—even though it means consequently to set
> about searching for ways to change myself. But what does this mean if
> not that I am constituting myself as a thing? . . . Shall I uncover in myself
> "drives," even though it be to affirm them in shame? But is this not
> deliberately to forget that these drives are realized with my consent, that
> they are not forces of nature but that I lend them their efficacy by a
> perpetually renewed decision concerning their value? Shall I pass judgment
> on my character, on my nature? Is this not to veil from myself at that mo-
> ment what I know only too well, that I thus judge a past to which by defini-
> tion my present is not subject? . . . Have we not shown indeed that in bad
> faith human reality is constituted as a being which is what it is not and
> which is not what it is?[16]

To be existentially genuine, then, is to take responsibility for our acts and not
to conceal this responsibility from ourselves.

SPONTANEITY. The Romantic advises us not to inhibit our natural motivations with calculations of reason. If humans are naturally good, then this seems like good advice; but if they are naturally bad, it is morally ridiculous. Existentialists are generally antinomian: they doubt that there are any moral laws that are objectively grounded. (On antinomianism, see Chapter 1, p. 30.) Consequently, responsibility cannot be defined in terms of acting in accord with the moral laws of God, nature, or reason.

Karl Jaspers, the German philosopher, says of two pioneer Existentialists, the nineteenth-century Danish philosopher, Søren Kierkegaard, and Nietzsche: "Both questioned reason from the depths of Existenz. Never on such a high level of thought had there been such a thorough-going and radical opposition to mere reason."[17] Kierkegaard, a Christian Existentialist, thought we could not reason out why we should live a Christian life; since to rationalize religion is impossible, we must make a "leap of faith" instead. (See Chapter 1, pp. 28–29, for Socrates' different view.) For Nietzsche, our action is chosen by naked will. Neither, however, was a partisan of reason's traditional opposite, feeling.

Having no natural essence upon which to ground our action, nor any ground revealed by reason, and rejecting feeling as a source of value, the atheistic Existentialist can tie responsibility to no other human faculty than Will. The Romantics' spontaneity of feeling is transformed by such atheistic Existentialists as Nietzsche and Sartre into spontaneous, ungrounded choices of the will; it is a radical kind of freedom. But it doesn't abandon responsibility; rather, it looks at it in another way. Michael Zimmerman has stated Nietzsche's idea of responsibility:

But we must be careful to distinguish between the ordinary idea of "responsibility" and Nietzsche's idea of it. Responsibility is often associated with "guilt," the self-destructive emotion which arises when someone breaks a taboo, or tries to act outside the normal table of values. But Nietzsche rejects this notion as being of a form of the "spirit of gravity," . . . .The "herd" does not want to assume responsibility for its existence; it would prefer to believe that God grants the ultimate meaning to human life, and (even if belief in such a God is lacking) that "real" responsibility involves slavish obedience to whatever norms and standards are in force at the moment. But for Nietzsche, responsibility only arises if a person takes over the burden of giving himself the meaning of his own life. As he asks in *Thus Spoke Zarathustra:* "Can you give yourself your own evil and your own good and hang your own will over yourself as a law? Can you be your own judge and avenger of your law? Terrible it is to be alone with the judge and avenger of one's own law. Thus is a star thrown out into the void and into the icy breath of solitude."[18]

The weight of Existentialist responsibility increases beyond what Nietzsche gives it, if the law that we will is not to be a law just for ourselves but for

206   *everyone,* as Sartre maintains.   No fixed human nature, no God, no law of reason; just our free, spontaneous will, which is a will *for all.*

> But if existence really does precede essence, man is responsible for what he is.   Thus, existentialism's first move is to make every man aware of what he is and to make the full responsibility of his existence rest on him.   And when we say that a man is responsible for himself, we do not only mean that he is responsible for his own individuality, but that he is responsible for all men. . . . I am creating a certain image of man of my own choosing.   In choosing myself, I choose man.
>
>   This helps us understand what the actual content is of such rather grandiloquent words as anguish, forlornness, despair.   As you will see, it's all quite simple.[19]

Anxiety comes from the contemplation of "everyone acting that way," of universalizing your own chosen act and all that it entails.   Forlornness is ours because God does not exist and we have to face all the consequences of this in solitude.   We live in a world of probabilities; because there is no certainty, all our acts have an uncertain outcome, which may lead to despair that we cannot "set things right."

Existentialists uncompromisingly oppose the view that scientific knowledge about an essential human nature enlightens us about human life or morals because, not being natural creatures, we have no such nature. According to them, we become inauthentic when we shift our moral responsibility from ourselves to something such as human nature which we "scientifically" declare to be not wholly under our control, but a product of cosmic evolution.   Yet Existentialism, which proclaims that we can be in control, and authentic, is merely a subjective prose poem celebrating a phantom self, if sociobiology's evolutionary account of human nature is true.

In the next section I will outline some arguments against sociobiology. If they are sound, it leaves open the possibility that Existentialism is true and not merely a subjective prose poem.   However, the arguments also isolate some factors—will and reason—that can be used to formulate a profound challenge not only to moral psychology and its extension, sociobiology, but also to Existentialism.   If humans have interlocking will and reason, a rational will, as Kant thought, then both sociobiology and Existentialism are false theories of humans and their moral conduct.   The next section, therefore, provides both challenges to moral psychology and a springboard for our examination of Kant's rational will ethics, which is opposed to and by Existentialists.

I conclude this section by stating Existentialism's view about the dreadful spontaneity of will—dreadful because of its separation from reason, because of reason's limitations, and the "absurdity" of the world.

Existentialists are opposed not only to and by moral psychologists, but also to and by philosophers such as Kant who believe that the human faculties of will and reason are not separate from each other but are essentially a **207** unity. Existentialists think our will functions independently of our reason, and further, that reason can provide no more basis for morality than moral psychologists' human nature can.

This freedom of will, operating independently of reason, is an important aspect of the Existentialists' view. This is their version of spontaneity. Whereas Romantics prize the spontaneity of acting without the intervention of calculating reason, the Existentialists' spontaneity of will, acting independently of reason because reason can provide no guidelines, is not something to be prized. Instead, it is rather awful because it means we live in an absurd world.

For Existentialists, our dreadful freedom exists in the absence of any objective moral laws on which we can lean; they are deeply antinomian in that they think, first, that we cannot "discover" any laws by reason but must make them ourselves, and, second, that we cannot justify the laws we make, only arbitrarily will them. Sartre thinks that when we make laws for ourselves we also make them for others; this universalization of our willfulness burdens us with an awful responsibility: we can find no "reasons" for them either in ourselves, nor in a now-dead God, nor in our nature. The world is, in Albert Camus's word, "absurd."

> With the exception of professional rationalists, today people despair of true knowledge. If the only significant history of human thought were to be written, it would have to be the history of its successive regrets and its impotences.
>
> Of whom and of what indeed can I say: "I know that!" This heart within me I can feel, and I judge that it exists. This world I can touch, and I likewise judge that it exists. There ends all my knowledge and the rest is construction. . . .
>
> Hence the intelligence, too, tells me in its way that this world is absurd . . . . A horde of irrationals has sprung up and surrounds him until his ultimate end. In his recovered and now studied lucidity, the feeling of the absurd becomes clear and definite.[20]

Kant, as the champion of the Enlightenment, would reject this collapse into absurdity. He believes, first, that reason is a source of morality; second, that reason can move us to action; and third, that we are free because we can freely give ourselves these laws and freely place ourselves under our own laws' rule. For him, contrary to the Existentialists, we are free only in relation to laws. We are our own guarantors against absurd, lawless freedom. As I said at the beginning of this chapter, Kant's position marks a turning point in our investigations. Kant's aim is to get the lions of freedom, self, and individuality, so beloved by Romantics and Existentialists, to lie down with the lambs of reason, others, and sociality.

6.10 Trouble for Sociobiology

So far in this book I have given the moral psychologists the major voice. They trace our behavior, including our "moral" behavior, to human nature. Sociobiologists belong to the moral psychological school of thought, because they claim to explain what our human nature is and how it got that way, relying upon the evolutionary theory of natural selection.

If sociobiology's ambitious program is true, it falsifies Existentialism and also forces Gus to concede to Liz (5.1) that "freedom and dignity" are outmoded "pre-scientific" thinking, as Skinner claims. If you sympathized with Gus, you have a stake in this section; if the arguments here are unsound, you can't continue to believe that we have a free will, without which we have no dignity. Your self-image is at stake. Are you an input-output black box mechanism programed by your environment, or do you have ultimate self-control and autonomy? In this section I represent Gus's viewpoint that the newest "science" isn't able to give an adequate theory of humans and their conduct.

Sociobiology is a very controversial movement. People have called it racist and sexist, demonstrated against its proponents, literally dumped water on its advocates at meetings, and gotten into fist fights over its claims. Its basic orientation is that we can learn about human conduct and society by inferring from what can be learned and is known about animal and insect conduct and "social" organizations.

The chief spokesperson for sociobiologists is Edward O. Wilson, whose views have been most extensively expressed recently in his book *On Human Nature*.[21] I direct the arguments against sociobiology at the views expressed by him.

Wilson straighforwardly believes that sociobiology has the last and hence the first informed word on morals.

> Innate censors and motivators exist in the brain that deeply and unconsciously affect our ethical premises; from these roots, morality evolved as an instinct. If that perception is correct, science may soon be in a position to investigate the very origin and meaning of human values, from which all ethical pronouncements and much of political practice flow. (p. 5)
>
> Like everyone else, philosophers measure their personal emotional responses to various alternatives as though consulting a hidden oracle.
>
> That oracle resides in the deep emotional centers of the brain, most probably within the limbic system, a complex array of neurons and hormone-secreting cells located just beneath the "thinking" portion of the cerebral cortex. Human emotional responses and the more general practices based on them have been programmed to a substantial degree by natural selection over thousands of generations. The challenge to science is to measure the tightness of the constraints caused by the programming,

to find their source in the brain, and to decode their significance through **209**
the reconstruction of the evolutionary history of the mind. (p. 6)

Let us examine four arguments against sociobiology.

6.10a. THE POLITICAL ARGUMENT AGAINST SOCIOBIOLOGY.

Theories that explain human societies by biological forces justify the status
quo. They legitimate past and present social institutions—war, capitalism,
upper and lower social classes, the inferior status of women—by claiming that
they are adaptive to a pitiless environment, and have been sorted out by
natural selection from other cultural forms that proved less capable of preserving human societies. Biological determinism is a new form of "social
Darwinism." (See Reflections on Applications 5–8, Chapter 5.)

> It is not surprising that the model of society that turns out to be "natural"
> bears a remarkable resemblance to the institutions of modern market soci-
> ety, since the theorists [such as Wilson] who produce these models are
> themselves privileged members of just such a society. Thus we find that
> aggression, competition, extreme division of labor, the nuclear family, the
> domination of women by men, the defense of national territory, in-
> dividualism, are over and over again stated to be the result of "human
> nature."[22]

Let us suppose, however, that biological determinists are not so culture-
bound that they uncritically impose their own values on their descriptions of
the social results of evolution. Then they can reply to this argument that
disapproval of the status quo doesn't prove that biological determinism is
false.

However, Wilson leaves a chink in his argument through which
biologically *un*determined values may enter. After he states "the challenge to
science" in the last sentence of the passage quoted above, Wilson says this:

> Success [in meeting the challenge] will generate the second dilemma, which
> can be stated as follows: Which of the censors and motivators should be
> obeyed and which ones might better be curtailed or sublimated? These
> guides are the very core of our humanity. They and not the belief in
> spiritual apartness [a human soul] distinguish us from electronic com-
> puters. (p. 6)
>   Pure knowledge is the ultimate emancipator . . . . We can hope to
> decide more judiciously which of the elements of human nature to cultivate
> and which to subvert, which to take open pleasure with and which to han-
> dle with care. We will not, however, eliminate the hard biological
> substructure until such time, many years from now, when our descendents
> may learn to change the genes themselves. (pp. 96–97)

Here Wilson pictures us looking on the results of evolution, the status
quo, and evaluating it, finding some good and some bad. He also imagines
us as someday capable of altering our human nature by altering our genes.

210 But since this stance is *outside* evolution, the values we use cannot come from *inside* it; therefore, they must come from some other source. Since they do, they can't be the product of "censors and motivators" and consequently aren't the product of evolution. So where do they come from?

Let us take an example. Suppose we stand back from our society and notice that women are not treated as well as men: they are thought to be inferior, receive lower salaries for the same work, and don't get promoted or elected to political office as often. Suppose also that we deplore this status of women, although most people accept it as the "natural" outcome of the way things are. Because we deplore, we decide to control human mating, allowing only those who dislike treating women unequally to have children in order to "breed out" the "censors and motivators" that produce sexism. This decision comes from outside the biological course of events. But where *does* it come from? Since it isn't biologically evolved, there must be another source of moral values, which shows the inadequacy of the so-called science of sociobiology.

6.10b. THE NURTURE AND CULTURE ARGUMENT AGAINST SOCIOBIOLOGY. This argument emphasizes the role that culture plays in shaping human behavior. The argument is pressed chiefly by anthropologists, who (a) note a variety in social customs that they think cannot be attributed to a single genetic cause, and (b) also maintain that the human genes do not contain enough information to explain adaptive behavior. Clifford Geertz, who expresses this argument well, first points out that humanity's varied and complex behavior can be explained only in terms of culture and its transmission. We are made by culture, not genes.

> Modern anthropology is firm in the conviction that men unmodified by the customs of particular places do not in fact exist, have never existed, and most important, could not, in the very nature of the case, exist.
>
> By the same token, it is extremely difficult to draw a line between what is natural, universal, and constant in man and what is conventional, local, and variable. In fact, to draw such a line is to falsify the human situation . . . .
>
> . . . Cultures are best seen not as complexes of concrete behavior patterns—customs, usages, traditions, habit clusters—but as sets of control mechanisms—plans, recipes, rules, instructions, what computer engineers call "programs" for the governing of behavior. The second [idea] is that man is the animal most desperately dependent upon such extra-genetic [non-genetic] control mechanisms for ordering his behavior . . . .
>
> . . . Undirected by cultural patterns, man's behavior would be virtually ungovernable, a chaos of pointless acts and exploding emotions, his experience virtually shapeless. Thus culture is not just an ornament of human existence, but an essential condition for it.

Geertz then points out that genes don't contain enough information to explain our behavior.

We live, as one writer has put it, in an "information gap" between what **211**
our body tells us and what we have to know in order to function. There is
a vacuum we must fill ourselves, and we fill it with information provided
by culture.

Between our inborn behavioral capacities and what we actually do
lies a complex set of significant symbols under whose direction we
transform the first into the second. Our ideas, values, action, even our
emotions, are, like the nervous system itself, cultural products.[23]

Geertz carries the argument deep into the sociobiologists' camp by
claiming that our "nervous system" is a product of culture; thus culture explains our physical nature, and not vice versa. Culture produces nerve
pathways in the brain. Sympathy for the plight of others is learned, not
natural. But the neurological argument need not be put quite as strongly as
this to score. Aram Yengoyan notes a difference in levels in our neurological
apparatus, and points out that human culture comes from a different, higher
level than the hypothalamus and limbic level on which Wilson chiefly relies.

The hypothalamus and limbic system are found throughout most reptilian
forms and occur at a relatively early phase in the evolution of higher
animals. Both centers are controlled by the cerebral cortex, but in man
most of our thought and reason occurs in the higher parts of the brain, not
in the lower areas. By linking man to other living forms along these
parallels, Wilson has consciously relegated the most human elements of
thought to secondary causes which have no bearing on this theoretical
argument. It is exactly for this reason that Wilson can collapse all reason
and thought to the realm of experience and maintain his contention that
humans are just another form of life. Modern neurology demonstrates,
however, that the real source of human thought lies in the higher reaches
of the two lobes which govern man.[24]

Wilson is fully aware of the long controversy between those who trace
the causes of human behavior to nature and those who trace it to nurture and
culture. He acknowledges that culture accounts for a great deal in human
behavior, but at bottom there remains the issue of whether or not culture
itself is explainable in terms of biology. Are biological or anthropological
categories the most basic? Chemical laws are less basic than the laws of
physics; chemical bonding and reactions can ultimately be analyzed in terms
of atomic laws. In the same way, sociobiologists think biological laws are
more basic than sociological and anthropological laws (if any such exist).

To anticipate a common objection raised by many social scientists and
others, let me grant at once that the form and intensity of altruistic acts are
to a large extent culturally determined. Human evolution is obviously
more cultural than genetic. The point is that the underlying emotion [of
altruism], powerfully manifested in virtually all human societies, is what
is considered to evolve through genes. The sociobiological hypothesis
does not therefore account for differences among societies, but it can explain why human beings differ from other mammals, and why, in one narrow aspect, they more closely resemble social insects. (pp. 153–54)

Wilson then makes what I take to be the most important statement in his book about morals and his theoretical enterprise:

> Can the cultural evolution of higher ethical values gain a direction and momentum of its own and completely replace genetic evolution? I think not. The genes hold culture on a leash. The leash is very long, but inevitably values will be constrained in accordance with their effects on the human gene pool. The brain is a product of evolution. Human behavior—like the deepest capacities for emotional response which drive and guide it—is the circuitous technique by which human genetic material has been and will be kept intact. Morality has no other demonstrable ultimate function. (p. 167; see also p. 125 on limits of "flexibility")

Wilson also says: "The question of interest is no longer whether human social behavior is genetically determined, it is to what extent" (p. 19). This last statement is remarkably confident. How can Wilson be so sure? It depends on his method, which brings us to the next arguments against sociobiology.

6.10c. THE METHODOLOGICAL ARGUMENTS AGAINST SOCIOBIOLOGY.

How can we link social behavior to the genes? It cannot be done by the method of direct inspection of genes; we don't have any way of looking at a gene and saying "Yes, this one has 'altruistic' properties and this one doesn't." Further, as Wilson acknowledges, few "behaviors are under the control of one or two genes"; we don't know what connections between genes to look for. (Even so, Wilson is optimistic about the future of direct inspection; see his p. 47.)

If the genetic basis for human behavior can't be verified by direct inspection, then it has to be done by the method of inference from some other data. Wilson uses analogy because he notes two important similarities between animals and humans.

I		II
Animals' genes are products of natural selection.	SIMILAR TO	Humans' genes are products of natural selection.
Ethology shows many behavioral traits are shared by members of a species.	SIMILAR TO	Anthropology shows many behavioral traits are shared by members of the human species.
This shared behavior is explained by gene duplication.		By analogy, because of the above similarities between animals and humans, we can infer that humans' shared behavior is also explained by their gene duplication.

It has probably occurred to you that the preceding nurture and culture **213** argument against sociobiology seriously weakens this argument by analogy because of the vast difference between the amount of culture humans and animals have. Since animals have a negligible amount of culture, it is highly plausible to explain their shared behavior by their similar gene structure. But, as Geertz pointed out, humans have an enormous amount of culture; therefore, it is highly plausible to explain humans' shared behavior by their shared culture rather than just by their similar genes. Wilson too recognizes this dissimilarity between animals and humans, and tries to overcome it by giving evidence of a strong behavioral similarity between humans and "our closest living evolutionary relatives," the Old World monkeys and the great apes.

> Human social behavior can be evaluated in essentially the same way, first by comparison with the behavior of other species and then, with far greater difficulty and ambiguity, by studies of variation among and within human populations. The picture of genetic determinism emerges most sharply when we compare selected major categories of animals with human species. Certain general human traits are shared with a majority of the great apes and monkeys of Africa and Asia, which on grounds of anatomy and biochemistry are our closest living relatives. (Wilson, p. 20)

Wilson then lists these shared traits: intimate social groups of 10 to 100, rather than two as in birds or thousands as in many kinds of fish; males larger than females; the young molded by a long period of social training; and social play as a developed activity to provide role practices, mock aggression, sex practice, and exploration. Wilson finds this similarity of social traits so strong that, when joined with anatomical and biochemical evidence, he thinks we can infer that "they are based at least in part on the possession of identical genes"(p. 31). This is as strong a statement as can be made; Wilson goes beyond similarity of apes and humans to partial identity.

Wilson leans very heavily on George Murdock, the American anthropologist, for evidence that humans, like the great apes and monkeys, exhibit universal social and behavioral traits. They "are as diagnostic [indicative] of mankind as are distinguishing characteristics of other animal species" (p. 21). Discussing Murdock's list, he says, "Few of these unifying properties can be interpreted as the inevitable outcome of either advanced social life or high intelligence" (p. 22). Murdock's list of traits includes athletic sports, bodily adornment, courtship, education, hair styles, incest taboos, mealtimes, postnatal care, property rights, tool making, visiting, weaving (Wilson, p. 22) .

The methodological arguments that I will give here against sociobiology—and these are not the only ones that have been or could be given—turn around the concept of function. Function is important to sociobiology because its advocates rely upon it to infer that a behavioral trait can be traced to the genes rather than to culture alone. Wilson's "functional" phrase in the following remarks is "superior fitness."

> The process, which Darwin called natural selection, describes a tight circle of causation. If the possession of certain genes predisposes individuals toward a particular trait, say a certain kind of social response, and the trait in turn conveys superior fitness, the genes will gain an increased representation in the next generation. If natural selection is continued over many generations, the favored genes will spread throughout the population, and the trait will become characteristic of the species. In this way human nature is postulated by many sociobiologists, anthropologists, and others to have been shaped by natural selection. (p. 33)

In short, a trait is functional if it contributes to individual and/or species survival; the predisposition to the trait will become genetically preserved because of its survival value.

Let's take Wilson's incest taboo example to illustrate this Darwinian claim (pp. 36ff). Wilson points out that such taboos are one of the universals of human behavior; all societies forbid sexual intercourse between brothers and sisters, and parents and their children. Incest has results that are unfavorable to survival: smaller bodies, less muscular coordination, and lower learning capacity. Outbreeding—the opposite of incest—doesn't have these unfavorable results. Consequently, outbreeding has a survival function. Natural selection insures that outbreeding will be a trait preserved in the genes, which explains the existence of a universal social taboo against incest.

To trace a trait to genetic causation, the sociobiologist has to find a survival function for it. When he finds it, the sociobiologist then infers that the trait has a genetic basis. Let's see why this is methodologically not as conclusive as the sociobiologist thinks it is.

I will first state the argument against the sociobiologists' method in a very simple way, then show in a more detailed way why the argument works. The sociobiologists' hypothesis is that a species' widespread behavioral trait is genetically determined because the trait is functional for survival. But contrariwise, if a trait is *known* to be functional, then we can explain its existence by intelligence; hence there is no need to trace it to genetic causation. The sociobiologists commit a methodological fallacy by tracing the behavioral trait to one cause (genes), when it can just as plausibly be traced to another and different cause (intelligence).

This argument can be seen to work for humans and other higher animals if we are careful to distinguish, first, between the cause-effect relation and the means-end relation, and, second, between a functional relation seen from the outside and seen from the inside.

Let's look first at the cause-effect relation and its methodology. When we observe an event, say an instance of eye-blinking behavior, and suppose that it has a cause, we try to isolate the conditions preceding the effect that are sufficient and necessary to cause it, such as a stone heading toward our eye. Conditions are *sufficient* when their presence is always followed by the effect, and *necessary* when the effect never occurs in their absence. This way of looking at the cause-effect relation is mechanistic, because the mere presence of the cause (sufficient and necessary conditions) guarantees the occurrence of the effect; there is no need for any awareness of the cause-effect relation to **215** bring about the effect, just awareness of the flying stone.

Applying this mechanistic notion of causation to one of Wilson's examples, the mosquito, allows him and us to call the mosquito an automaton. "The only way [for a mosquito] to run accurately and successfully through a life cycle in a matter of days is by instinct, a sequence of rigid behaviors programmed by the genes to unfold swiftly and unerringly from birth to the final act of oviposition [laying eggs]" (p. 56). The mosquito need not know the antecedent conditions and the effect they will have; the behavior it performs is independent of this. The genes program the neural machinery to operate and automatically perform the behavior. For example, the odor of lactic acid emanating from the skin activates a search and homing behavior toward creatures with blood. This is how mosquitos find you.

Let's look now at the means-end relation. This is a functional relation. Given an end to be attained, certain behavior is a means to that end if it enables the creature to attain it. There may be more than one means to attain a single end. Let's put these two things—cause-effect and functional relations—together now as the sociobiologist does.

$$
\begin{array}{c}
\ulcorner \text{Mechanistic} \urcorner \\
\text{Cause} \;\rightarrow\; \text{Effect} \\
\downarrow \\
\text{Means} \;\rightarrow\; \text{End} \\
\llcorner \text{Functional} \lrcorner
\end{array}
$$

Using the mosquito example, we have:

$$
\begin{array}{c}
\ulcorner \text{Mechanistic} \urcorner \\
\text{Odor of lactic acid} \;\rightarrow\; \text{Search and homing behavior} \\
\downarrow \\
\text{Finding blood} \;\rightarrow\; \text{Survival} \\
\llcorner \text{Functional} \lrcorner
\end{array}
$$

You can see that the functional relation plays an essential role in the sociobiologists' account of natural selection and the spread of genes through a population, because its survival contribution preserves those creatures with the appropriate genetic transmission of the mechanistic cause. (See Wilson's remarks on p. 214.) But notice two things. First, the odor of lactic acid mechanically explains the search and homing behavior; the mosquito does not conceive its behavior as a means to an end, does not understand the functional relation. Second, the functional relation is understood by the sociobiologist, but that relation doesn't explain the effect, which is explained mechanistically. What the functional relation explains to the sociobiologist is the natural selection of the mechanistic relation. Here the functional relation is seen by a human from *outside* the mechanistic relation; it is in the sociobiologist's mind, not the mosquito's.

Humans and other higher creatures are not automatons because, unlike mosquitos, we are conscious from the *inside* of the functional relation. Fur-

216 ther, because there are several means to attain an end, we can run through them and select the most efficient one or the one most likely to succeed; this isn't mechanistic; therefore, the sociobiologist cannot infer backwards from function to a genetic cause of our behavior. Instead, he should infer that our intelligence and culturally acquired information are the cause of our behavior.

Wilson is quite aware that humans are not automatons and that a large part of our behavior is traceable to our intelligence and cultural accumulations. Given this awareness, shouldn't he abandon his claim that human behavior is "genetically determined"? He tries to defend his claim by saying that genes determine our "capacity" to have traits.

> The channels of human mental development, in contrast [to the mosquito's], are circuitous and variable. Rather than specify a single trait, human genes prescribe the *capacity* to develop a certain array of traits. In some categories of behavior, the array is limited and the outcome can be altered only by strenuous training—if ever. In others, the array is vast and the outcome easily influenced. (pp. 56–57)

The last two sentences from this passage leave a hole in the sociobiologists' theory of genetic determinism through which you can drive practically the whole of culture. If genes determine few if any *specific* kinds of behavior, then they don't explain much behavior at all; if they explain the *limits* of our capacity for behavior, they obviously leave the determination of what exists within those limits to something other than genes, as Geertz pointed out (pp. 210–11). This of course includes moral behavior, so genes are inadequate to explain what we are most interested in understanding. The genes are underdetermined; while they explain all of a mosquito's behavior, they explain practically none of human behavior. I will explain this in 6.10d after the next argument against the sociobiologists' method.

Because the sociobiologists' method for proving genetic determinism relies on the theory of natural selection, they concentrate on the basic function that behavior has, namely, to enable creatures to survive. For them, all functional relations are tied ultimately to survival. Any trait that they claim is genetically determined, then, must be shown as a means to individual and/or species survival. However, they allow that within genetic limits there is an array of possible behavior, and that this array is available to intelligent, conscious formation; therefore, humans may project several ends other than survival. Further, a single kind of behavior can be seen as having different functions because it may be means to different ends. If some of these functions are not survival functions, then there can be no explanation of the behavior in terms of natural selection, nor consequently in terms of genetics. Therefore the sociobiologists' methodology cannot be applied to all of human behavior, nor can they show that all of it is genetically determined.

Let's apply this criticism to Wilson's account of homosexuality—a kind of behavior that for many falls within the moral domain, some considering it immoral and others moral. Wilson takes the Judeo-Christian condemnation of homosexuality to task, saying that this religion has "mis-interpreted" the biological significance of homosexuality. This mis-interpretation consists of thinking that the primary function of "sexual behavior is the insemination of wives by husbands" (p. 141). This error by writers of the Old Testament is understandable, because they belonged to an "aggressive pastoral nation whose success was based on rapid and orderly population growth enhanced by repeated episodes of terrritorial conquest" (p.142).

Wilson thinks that the real function of sexual behavior is "bonding," or the cementing of human relations, which helps a group maintain its social cohesion and in this way has a survival function.

> Human beings are connoisseurs of sexual pleasure. They indulge themselves by casual inspection of potential partners, by fantasy, poetry, and song, and in every delightful nuance of flirtation leading to foreplay and coition [intercourse]. This has little if anything to do with reproduction. It has everything to do with bonding. (p. 141)

This "bonding" interpretation of sexual behavior provides Wilson with an interpretation of homosexual behavior that enables him to give it a survival function. Remember that he needs to tie this behavior to a survival function in order to produce a genetic explanation of it. He is tentative in his explanation, which shows his awareness of the methodologically thin ice on which he skates.

> There is, I wish to suggest, a strong possibility that homosexuality is normal in a biological sense, that it is a distinctive beneficent behavior that evolved as an important element of early human social organization. Homosexuals may be the genetic carriers of some of mankind's rare altruistic impulses. (p. 143)

Homosexuality, like sexuality, is a form of bonding. All humans have a predisposition to bisexuality built into their brain, but some have chosen homosexuality; this has survival value because, not having children themselves, they are freed from parental duties so as to "operate with special efficiency in assisting close relatives," who can then have more children, thus contributing to the survival of a species. Wilson thinks that his "natural" explanation of homosexuality should alter the Judeo-Christian condemnation of it.

The condemnation of homosexuality may indeed be morally wrong, but the attempt to justify it by appeal to a genetic basis seems highly implausible, because it requires that homosexuality have *only* a survival function. An act may serve as a functional means to different ends, only one of which may be survival. That survival is homosexuality's sole function is pure speculation. Methodologically, to say that homosexuality then has a genetic basis is to go so far beyond the kind of evidence needed that the statement ranks little better than fiction.

218   **6.10d. THE UNDERDETERMINATION ARGUMENTS AGAINST SOCIOBIOLOGY.** Human behavior is complicated and various; it has subtle nuances and shadings. Since our genes govern our physiological structure, a theory of genetic determinism has to relate this physiological structure to complex behavior. There are principally three ways to do this: instinct, drives, and emotion. I will deal with each in turn, showing that genes are too crude and simple a base on which to erect the rich pattern of our behavior; alone, genes underdetermine complex human behavior. If my arguments are sound, Gus doesn't have to fear that sociobiologists have taken away our freedom and dignity.

(a) *Instinct.* Instinctive behavior is mechanistically determined; the genes dictate the neurological wiring, which when initially triggered sets off a chain of neural firing that causes physical movement of the body. This is automatic behavior; remember the mosquitos. When your doctor taps your knee in the right place and you make a small kick, there is a simple mechanical linkage that explains this "reflex" action. Wilson cites the smile also as an instance of instinctive behavior:

> In the terminology of the zoologist, it is a social releaser, an inborn and relatively invariant signal that mediates a basic social relationship . . . . The simplest and most automatic of such behaviors may well be genetically hard-wired into the cellular units of the human brain and facial nerves. (pp. 62–63)

There is very little other behavior that Wilson claims is "hard-wired" like the smile; the amount is so small that the genetic account of human behavior through the use of instinct is theoretically and practically of almost no interest. Left- and right-handedness is another example which he gives, but it doesn't seem to be "hard-wired." He gives it as an example of the limits genetic determinism places on our behavior repertoire; still, it can be overcome with training, in which case the genetic determinism isn't absolute and final.

The philosopher Michael Carella points out another difficulty for the use of instinct. If its use is sharply confined to "hard-wiring," it doesn't explain much of interest; however, Carella notes that if it is allowed to expand in its use, it starts to explain too much. He calls our attention to the widespread dispute about how many instincts there are and what their nature is.

> There exist no unequivocal criteria for what gets counted as a human instinct and why . . . . If one argues that human instincts can be inferred by observing human patterns of behavior, then any spontaneous pattern of behavior which cannot be ascribed either to learning or to previous experience becomes by definition instinctive. Hence the number of instincts must proliferate the more detailed the analysis of human behavior becomes, for there will be as many different instincts as there are logically different patterns of unlearned or unconditioned behavior . . . . In principle, then, the theory of. . . human instincts becomes scientifically self-defeating.[25]

In short, this argument contends that instinct explains either too little or too **219** much. You might wonder if cockroach extermination is a human instinct; look again at Reflection 3 of Chapter 5, p. 166.

(b) *Drives* (Wants). Sexual pursuit and food-getting activities are obviously not hard-wired instincts. Drives mediate between the neural wiring determined by genetic inheritance and the behavior. We say we feel the need for food, we get hungry; similarly, we feel the need for sex. But what is not so obvious is how such felt needs or drives determine behavior. The way an Eskimo gets food is so different from the way a South Sea islander does— although both feel the same need for food—that intelligent adaptation to the environment seems the only plausible explanation for their different food-getting behavior. The felt needs should be looked on not as "causes" of behavior having a genetic origin, but as "information" for the brain, on which we may or may not act. But this information is so underdetermined that it plays no role in explaining the different behaviors of the Eskimo and the South Sea islander.

Dewey has some interesting remarks about the sex drive and its underdetermination of behavior.

> The actual content and feel of hunger and sex are indefinitely varied according to their social contexts. . . .
>
> The treatment of sex by psycho-analysts is most instructive, for it flagrantly exhibits both the consequences of artificial simplification and the transformation of social results into psychic causes. Writers, usually male, hold forth on the psychology of woman, as if they were dealing with a Platonic universal entity, although they habitually treat men as individuals, varying with structure and environment. They treat phenomena which are peculiarly symptoms of the civilization of the West at the present time as if they were the necessary effects of fixed native impulses of human nature. Romantic love as it exists today, with all the varying perturbations it occasions, is as definitely a sign of specific historic conditions as are big battle ships with turbines, internal-combustion engines, and electrically driven machines. It would be as sensible to treat the latter as effects of a single psychic cause as to attribute the phenomena of disturbance and conflict which accompany present sexual relations as manifestations of an original single psychic force or *Libido*.[26]

The behavior associated with sex and romantic love in the West is so complicated and interwined with historical conditions, that citing a native sex drive as its sole cause is to oversimplify to an indefensible degree. This is because the drive is underdetermined in relation to its supposed effect.

(c) *Emotion.* Emotions, like drives, mediate between the genes and behavior. Suppose we have a theory that claims: Genes determine emotions, which in turn determine behavior. But suppose that the emotions underdetermine behavior, then it follows that genes underdetermine behavior, so that our actions aren't genetically determined. Wilson's theory clearly gives emotions this mediation role: "The point is that the underlying emotion, powerfully manifested in virtually all human societies, is what is considered to

220 evolve through the genes" (p. 153). The emotion to which he refers is the emotion of altruism. (See also Wilson, pp. 162–63.) He cites Hume favorably for his "conjecture that reason is the slave of the passions" (p.157). If the passion is soft-core altruism, then it will cause "altruistic" behavior.

The Sottish philosopher John Laird has a harsh criticism of such a view; he points out that a single emotion can be related to a variety of behaviors; hence, the emotion needs to be supplemented with other causal or reasoning factors, if it is to explain the different behaviors. If, for example, fear alone were the cause of behavior, then it would cause the same behavior on every occasion; it doesn't, therefore it underdetermines its effect.

> It must be confessed that any such theory leads to serious difficulties in its application. The very distinctive emotion we call fear, for instance, seems to be correlated with *several* modes of response. It may startle into flight, paralyze into immobility, rouse to desperate pugnacity . . . . A one-one correlation between a specific emotion and a specific channel of response, consequently, seems very unplausible.[27]

I can summarize this "underdetermined" argument against sociobiology in a rather devastating way; it makes their own theory turn on and destroy itself.

The brain is functional because it is an aid to survival. It is an aid to survival precisely because it isn't genetically deterministic as a mosquito's is. Its value lies in its superiority to instincts, drives, and emotions—that is, in determining a richer array of responses than our instincts, drives, and emotions do, all of which underdetermine our behavior.

Let's follow this up. If the brain is an adaptive mechanism, then it must contribute something over and above what is genetically determined. Part of its adaptive value must lie in the brain's ability to reason us into a set of relations with nature and other humans that is to our benefit. This requires thinking ahead of and independently of instincts, drives, and emotions. Thus, given that moral relations are included in human relations in the widest sense, our morals are not determined by our genes but by our brain. Therefore, morals must have their source and standards in reason and intelligence.

It should be conceded that Wilson does not present the best case for moral psychology in his sociobiological version of it, because he has a virtually nonexistent moral theory. If one is going to give an explanation of something, that "something" has to be identified clearly, and independently of and before the explanation of it. Suppose I said that I had a sociobiological theory of the phenomenon of sladoozle and proceeded to give you the explanation. You would not be in a position to judge the adequacy of my explanation, unless you knew independently of the explanation what sladoozle was. Similarly with Wilson: without a theory of his telling us what morals is, we don't know how to judge his contribution. David Hume, who is admired by Wilson, has worked out an ethics and provides the moral theory

that Wilson lacks. (A fuller discussion of Hume comes in Chapter 12 follow- **221**
ing most of my account of Kant's ethics.)

Wilson is our springboard to Kant, because we have found that genetic determinism is inadequate to explain the totality and variety of human behavior. Wilson's own theory about the usefulness of the brain points to a contribution from the side of reason to our understanding of human actions and morality. Kant's theory attributes three powers to practical reason that pertain to moral behavior: (1) Reason can prescribe values in an objective way that drives and emotions cannot; (2) reason can cause feelings in us that can motivate us to action, so emotions and feelings with genetic sources do not have exclusive claim over human motivation; (3) practical reason can choose between the motives of genes and reason because we do not stand wholly within the biological realm; reason is not fully explained by biological laws.

Kant gives reason powers that moral psychologists and sociobiologists do not. The latter give it an instrumental role alone; it stands in the service of the drives and emotions, which give us our ends; mind's role is to figure out the functional means to achieve those given ends.

As you will see, Kant presents a powerful challenge to the moral psychologists' attempt to confine reason to a functional role. Following him, we can point out that, given certain ends and allowing them to be determined by the emotions of our limbic system as Wilson would have it, there are usually several means to achieving them. So far as our limbic system is concerned, any one of them is as good as another, as long as each is effective. But Kant points out that some means are morally prohibited and others morally obligatory; yet, the limbic system is incapable of making these distinctions, only reason can do so; therefore reason makes a moral contribution over and above the drives and emotions wired into our limbic system by the evolutionary process. In physiological terms, the forebrain with its neocortex, which evolved after the limbic system and midbrain, makes a contribution that the midbrain and hindbrain can't make—namely, the concepts of the morally right and wrong, of obligation and prohibition.

When we turn to Kant's ethics, we enter another realm entirely. It is both demanding and exhilarating, difficult but rewarding. You may feel as others have felt before you—that for the first time you understand what ethics is, and that being moral is not just taking the most prudent means to a desired end. Proceed at your own peril. You may never be the same again after wrestling three falls with Immanuel Kant.

STUDY QUESTIONS

1 Distinguish the four meanings of "artificial" and "natural."
2 How does the distinction between natural and artificial selves relate to (1) Romanticism and Classicism, (2) authentic and inauthentic persons, and (3) good and bad human natures?

3 What are Shakespeare's criticisms of romantic love?

4 Explain how the distinction between an agent's act and motives contributes to the concept of authenticity. And what does the distinction between natural and artificial selves contribute to inauthenticity?

5 Give one argument why authenticity is a moral virtue and one argument why it is not. Give an example of each that supports the argument.

6 Summarize the four arguments against the sociobiologists' theory that human behavior is genetically determined.

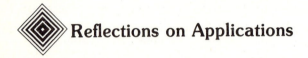 Reflections on Applications

1 Should we give authenticity first place among the moral goals to be sought after? According to the following remarks, there are some who think so.

> At Newton Junior High School in Boston there is a modern moral education course called "Man Alone" that, according to writer Jonathan Kozol, is "a whirlwind tour of alienation, loneliness, dying and narcotics with writings from John Donne to Bruno Bettelheim." In this class, says Kozol, a picture of one of the Hell's Angels was projected on the wall in gory, swastika-painted vividness.
> "Cool man, great," a voice shouted.
> "That's sick," said another.
> "He's honest anyway," chimed in another, "he's living out his own feelings."
> "He's not faking."
> Kozol goes on to say "the teacher then ventured the idea that an alienated person might not be able to be truly creative. A creative person is really alive and noncompulsive; alienation means the opposite."
> In this seminar the class has turned the virtues around 180 degrees so that the Hell's Angels are truly honest and creative, while the teacher uses psychological jargon about compulsivity and alienation to rotate the virtues back part way toward moral conformity.[28]

The virtue of authenticity, according to Romantics, requires matching our acts to our feelings, and openly professing those feelings. Do you have any reservations about this so-called virtue if it leads to admiration for Hell's Angels, many of whom favor violence and rule by terror?

2 George White was a narcotics agent. He set up a brothel in San Francisco for the Central Intelligence Agency (CIA), for purposes of secretly

watching what kind of behavior drugs induced in "clients." In a letter White told a CIA friend: "I toiled in the vineyards wholeheartedly, because it was fun, fun, fun. Where else could a red-blooded American boy lie, kill and cheat, steal, deceive, rape and pillage with the sanction and blessing of the All-Highest?"[29]

Is this a confession of inauthenticity? Is the statement itself an instance of authenticity? Apparently, White did what he did because it was "fun, fun, fun." Is this a bad motive? You need to decide this to determine if there is a mismatch between act and motive. Doing something because it's fun seems to be spontaneous, doesn't it? Could the same feeling or desire be a good motive on one occasion and a bad one on another? Is its goodness or badness tied to the moral nature of the act? Give an example of a right act that has "fun" as its motive.

3. In 6.5, p. 189, I set out the four variations possible between the moral nature of an act and its motive.

Right act: good motive Wrong act: good motive
bad motive bad motive

Give an example of each kind.

4 When a person performs a wrong act from a good motive, do you think the person is inauthentic? Use your example from Reflection 3 in your answer. Do you think mismatches between the moral quality of acts and motives is sufficient ground for saying a person is inauthentic? Give the reasoning that supports your answer. What would you think of a person who broke another's back while trying to rescue that person from a burning building out of humanitarian motives?

5 If there were no such thing as an "artificial self," could there be inauthentic acts? (Hint: Can a person simultaneously have two spontaneous, natural motives?)

6 Consider the following news report:

Phyllis Conti felt so guilty about her 25-year-old son's emotional problems in wanting to be a transsexual that she became a welfare cheat, court records show.

According to her probation report, Ms. Conti, 58, turned over to her son most of the $4,650 she earned as a live-in nurse over a two-year period so he could get clothes, hormone injections and electrolysis treatments. She then lived on her monthly general assistance benefits.

Kenneth, also known as Debbie, when approached by relatives about raising bail money for his mother after she was arrested September 29, reportedly said, "Let the b—— rot in jail."

Superior Court Judge John M. Sapunor, before imposing sentence Monday, was moved by the situation to quote from Shakespeare's play, *King Lear:* "How sharper than a serpent's tooth it is/To have a thankless child."[30]

While you may think initially that Kenneth was wrong not to help get bail money for his mother, don't you admire his honesty in expressing his true feelings? If you don't, does this imply that authenticity is not a virtue? Would it make any difference in your judgement of Kenneth/Debbie if it were established that Ms. Conti should feel guilty because she was responsible for Kenneth becoming Debbie against his wishes?

7 Alex Inkeles, a social psychologist at Stanford University, recently presented a paper to the American Sociological Association; he concluded that ten traits have remained continuously characteristic of Americans for two centuries, while three are changing.

Do the following remarks from Robert Toth's news story on the Inkeles paper show that authenticity is a value exhibited by Americans?

> Trust is the fourth characteristic [of Americans]. [Benjamin] Franklin made sincerity one of his basic precepts, and Harriet Martineau was struck by "the frank, confiding character" of Americans by 1837. Many others reported on the openness and friendliness of Americans, their casualness and spontaneity in chance encounters.
>
> In the mid-1960s, a poll asked whether "most people can be trusted."
>
> In Italy, only 7 per cent said yes, in Germany, 19 per cent, in the United States, 55 per cent. This answer came from all educational levels, from grade school through college. Americans were first by far among nine nations polled.[31]

8 Do you think that a case can be made for linking permissiveness and authenticity? The judge in the following case seems to suggest this.

> A judge yesterday sentenced 18-year-old David Smith to four concurrent life prison terms for the shotgun slayings of four youths.
>
> "This crime represents nothing less than permissiveness carried to the ultimate extreme—murder for fun and excitement," Circuit Court Judge Michael Kanne said. "There can be no more devastating proof of the depravity of the permissive philosophy than the horror disclosed by the evidence in this case."
>
> Kanne said the case represented two aspects of American culture "deemed acceptable in some quarters!" "One," he said, is "expressed by the notion that "if it feels good, do it," and the other is that society instead of the individual is made responsible for individual acts.[32]

According to the remarks in Reflection 7, many think that casualness and spontaneity are good traits in Americans. Do you think that this story of four murders shows the opposite?

9 Fyodor Dostoevsky, the Russian novelist, is celebrated for his insight into humans' inner life. In his novel *The Idiot* there is a scene where Keller, a rude, scheming fellow, bursts in on Prince Myshkin.

He told the prince, without beating about the bush, that he had come to tell him the whole story of his life. . . . Almost as soon as he had begun he skipped to the conclusion and declared that he had so utterly lost "every vestige of morality" (solely because of his disbelief in the Almighty) that he was even guilty of stealing. . . .

"Listen, Keller," the prince began, "in your place I shouldn't confess that if I didn't have to, but I expect you're probably making yourself out to be worse than you are on purpose."

"I'm telling you this—you alone—solely in the interests of my own spiritual development!. . ."

At last the prince felt not so much sorry for him as, somehow, ashamed of him. . . . Keller confessed with extraordinary readiness. . . .

"The main thing is," the prince said at last, "that you possess such a trusting, child-like nature and are so extraordinarily truthful. Do you realize, I wonder, that by that alone you atone for a great deal?"

"Noble, noble, chivalrously noble—that's me!" Keller assented, deeply moved.

The prince doubts that Keller can add to what he's already said, but Keller insists that he can.

"Why, have you really something more to add?" the prince asked, with timid amazement. "Then what did you expect of me; tell me, please, Keller; and why did you come to me with your confession?"

"Of you? What did I expect? Well, for one thing, it is a pleasure to have a look at so simple-minded a man as you. It is a pleasure to sit down and have a talk with you. At least I know that I'm dealing with a most virtuous person, and secondly—secondly—"

He stopped short and looked embarrassed.

"You didn't by any chance want to borrow some money, did you?" the prince prompted him very gravely and simply, almost a little shyly.

Keller gave a violent start. . . .

"Well, that's how you stump a fellow completely! Why, Prince, your simplicity and innocence are such as were never heard of in the golden age. . . . Of course, the whole object of my visit was to ask you for a loan in the end, but you asked me about the money as though you found nothing reprehensible in it, as though it were the most natural thing in the world."

"Well—coming from you it was the most natural thing in the world." . . .

"Now, will you believe the word of a most honorable man, sir? At the very moment I fell asleep, quite genuinely overflowing with internal and, so to speak, external tears,. . . a most fiendish thought occurred to me: 'And why, after all, shouldn't I ask him to lend me some money—after my confession, of course?' So I prepared my confession like, so to speak, some 'spiced sauce laced with tears,' so as to pave the way with those tears and, having softened you up, make you fork out one hundred and fifty rubles. Don't you think that was mean?"

"I'm sure it can't possibly be true, but that it's merely a coincidence. Two ideas occurred to you at one and the same time. This happens very often. It always happens to me. . . . It is terribly difficult to fight against these *double* thoughts. . . . But in my opinion it cannot be called simply meanness! What do you think? You were acting dishonestly so as to wheedle some money out of me? But you swear yourself that your confession was made with quite a different motive, an honorable and not a mercenary one. . . ."

The prince gazed at Keller with great interest. The question of double thoughts apparently occupied his mind for some time.

"Well, after that I simply can't understand why they call you an idiot!" exclaimed Keller.[33]

What difficulty does the occurrence of "double thoughts" create for confirming an instance of inauthenticity? Is Keller inauthentic? Is confession another one of those kinds of acts discussed in 6.6 that require authenticity?

10 Read the quotation from Buisson again (p. 203). Is what he says about education approximately true of education in the United States as you have experienced it? Or as you have come to see its "true" nature? Add to the influence of education that of television, as seen by Gunther Anders's remarks below.

As a German proverb has it, *Mensch ist was er isst,* "man is what he eats" (in a nonmaterialistic sense): it is through the consumption of mass commodities that mass men are produced. This implies that the consumer of the mass commodity becomes, through his consumption, one of the workers contributing to his own transformation into a mass man . . . . And this production takes place wherever consumption takes place—in front of each radio, in front of each television set.

Everyone is, so to speak, employed as a homeworker—a homeworker of a most unusual kind: for he performs his work—which consists in transforming himself into a mass man—through his consumption of the mass product offered him, i.e., through leisure . . . . To complete the paradox, the homeworker, instead of receiving wages for his work, must pay for it by buying the means of production (the receiving sets and, in many countries, also the broadcasts) by the use of which he becomes transformed into mass man.[34]

Which of the concepts that Heidegger uses to characterize Existentialist authenticity (see 6.9) do you think apply to Anders's notion of how mass media consumption transforms us?

11 Do you find the following advice from Paul Nizan, the late French Marxist philosopher, useful in rescuing yourself from becoming a mass man? An Ivan Ilyich? A member of Nietzsche's herd? A Heideggerian

they-self? Can you answer Nizan's questions when you ask them of
yourself?

> It is necessary to ask each man how he perceives the elements of his ex-
> istence: his actions, his happiness, his unhappiness depend on how he
> perceives them. Moreover, it is always necessary to know how, when,
> and where he learned to perceive things in this way, whether his percep-
> tion is derived from real experience or from lessons repeated ad
> nauseam by some teacher whose way of life was totally alien to his. It
> is necessary to ask each man whether there is a clear congruence [agree-
> ment] or a painful divergence between the judgments and ideas he
> mechanically mouths and what he actually sees and feels. Is your mar-
> riage causing you endless grief, even though you meekly assure
> everyone—even though you think you believe—that marriage is the most
> salutary [beneficial] of all social institutions? Did you suffer day and
> night when you were in the army, all the while blaming yourself for
> your wretchedness, and even believing that compulsory military service
> is an excellent idea? In your youth, you were trained to think and feel
> in a certain fashion—does this "training" make it easier for you to ac-
> cept things which, in the beginning, you naively mistook for great evils?
> If, some day, a particular experience causes you to question the dignity
> and infallibility of your customary way of perceiving events, which will
> decide the issue: your own first-hand experiences or the complicated
> precepts you learned by heart? . . .
>
> How do "they" brainwash men? Which men do they want to brain-
> wash? Why, and in whose interest, do they brainwash men? Who are the
> authors of this world-view? And how do they instill passivity, credulity,
> and respect for their values in the men they brainwash? (Nizan, pp.
> 112–13)

12 In his column "The Winemaster," Hank Rubin wrote: "So the word
'natural,' when applied to wine, is not wholly apt" (p. 186). After
reflecting on the various meanings of the natural/artificial contrast considered in this chapter, and noting how difficult it is to apply these
words, are you ready to give up the distinction? And are you ready to
give up a theory of morality to which the distinction is essential? Are
you looking forward to an alternative theory (such as Kant's)?

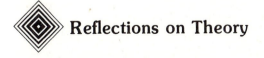 ## Reflections on Theory

13 *Underdeterminism of the genes.* Formulate an argument against genetic
determinism, using the following possibility that Wilson allows.

Genes determine a
capacity for behavioral
traits

$$\begin{cases} \text{Trait}_1 \text{ is a means to End}_1 \\ \text{Trait}_2 \text{ is a means to End}_1 \\ \text{Trait}_3 \text{ is not a means to End}_1 \end{cases}$$

Hint: Genes determine alternatives. What determines a selection of alternatives for intelligent beings?

14 *One, two, or no natures?* The dispute about the moral condition of natural humans, and whether good or ill is done them by society's influence, would be bypassed entirely if the natural/artificial distinction didn't apply to humans. The dispute between Hobbes and Rousseau wouldn't have to be taken seriously, if that distinction didn't apply. Consider the following analogy. Can you construct an argument based on it that shows the natural/artificial distinction is not a distinction between two kinds of natures?

Suppose that the adult/child distinction didn't apply to us, just as the natural/artificial distinction might not. Would humans then have either only an "adult nature" or only a "child nature"? Would all claims about a "child nature" be false because we have only an "adult nature"? Or in case we have only a "child nature," would all claims about our "adult nature" be false? Or would all these claims be true about some one "chidult" nature? And all true, not because we have two natures, but because there are two kinds of outside conditions operating on one nature, one kind of influence causing child behavior and another kind causing adult behavior? Think also of Wilson's belief that there is an array of behavior possible within genetically determined limits, and that this is our nature.

15 *The social monkey is the natural monkey.* In a news article Joel Greenberg reports Stephen J. Suomi's work with monkeys in carrying on the work of Harry F. Harlow. (See *Scientific American,* June, 1959, "Love in Infant Monkeys," by Harlow.) The work is considered significant because it might contribute to our knowledge about emotional development in children.

Harlow and Suomi's experiments vary "attachment factors." Harlow had isolated infant rhesus monkeys from their mothers. This led to emotional difficulties in later relationships. "Totally isolated monkeys would later sit huddled and crying in the corner of a cage and refuse to associate with other animals." Also, they developed severe interpersonal problems, frequently attacking dominant adult males and their own body. Then, as adults, they battered their own children. But cloth-covered wire figures, a mother substitute, provided sufficient attachment to encourage normal development.

Suomi isolated five- to eight-week-old monkeys from their peers. Normally the young monkey spends 70 to 75 percent of its first year of life swinging, running, chasing and wrestling with its mates. According to Suomi, "If deprived of interaction with peers, they (the monkeys) do not develop normal patterns of behavior. Later on, they become contact-shy around other animals, and hyperaggressive as well." Sexual "deviances" also develop. Greenberg writes that "when animals are separated from their cage-mates, they often become depressed. An immediate increase in vocalization is followed by self-clutching and a drop in locomotion and sexual activity."

According to Greenberg, "There has been considerable debate over the degree to which animal findings can be applied to humans. Suomi, for one, believes that 'in terms of patterns and developmental trends and how different social relationships form,' there are 'analogies with humans'."[35]

Do you think it would be valid to conclude that the isolation of young monkeys from either or both their mothers and peers reveals the "natural" monkey, and that the social attachments to mothers and peers produces the "artificial" monkey? If you have doubts about this—perhaps because you think that infant monkeys' association with their mothers and peers is natural—then shouldn't you have doubts about the way Romantics distinguish between "natural" and "artificial" humans? After all, what is the difference between these "natural" monkey attachment associations and our so-called "artificial" social associations?

16 *Innate needs for social contact.* What is your view of the following argument?

Harlow and Suomi's experiments reveal knowledge about the natural monkey, because they show that infant monkeys have a genetically determined innate need for mother love and peer play. When they don't have one or both, they exhibit abnormal behavior—depression, heightened aggressivity, and so forth. If love and play weren't innate needs, we wouldn't observe this abnormal behavior. But we do observe it; therefore, the needs are innate.

17 *Circularity of the prior argument.* Does the following argument refute the argument in Reflection 16?

The above argument needs the premiss that the isolated monkeys' behavior is "abnormal." The use of "abnormal" makes the argument circular and therefore invalid. This is because "abnormal" is roughly synonymous with "unnatural." Obviously you'll get the conclusion that the need for mother love and peer play are natural, if being denied them leads to "unnatural"—that is, "abnormal"—behavior.

18 *Moral uselessness of the natural/artificial distinction.* The person who argues as in Reflection 17 might go on in the following vein.

The natural/artificial distinction is useless in ethical discussions. In fact, it obscures the real issue, which is to evaluate behavior independently of whether or not you think it "abnormal."

230

Persons who keep to the natural/artificial distinction will be looking for natural needs, drives, characteristics, and so forth; when they think they've found them, any frustration or deprivation of the "natural," as in the case of the monkeys, will result in behavior that gets classified as "abnormal"—that is, "unnatural"—just because it is caused by frustration of something already labeled "natural." But this labeling is morally useless.

What we really want to know—the real issue—is whether the behavior is desirable or right. Being labeled natural or unnatural (artificial) doesn't help us to decide on the rightness or desirability of the behavior. The really important distinction isn't between natural and artificial monkeys and, by analogy, between natural and artificial humans, but between right and wrong conduct or behavior. Now it may be that certain conditions promote desirable conduct (love, play, sexual activity, and nonaggression in monkeys and human adults), and that other conditions promote undesirable conduct; it is more useful to think of these conditions this way than to wrangle about whether or not they are creating artificial monkeys or promoting "natural" monkeys (or humans). We should make a distinction in the moral effect of the conditions rather than in their contributions to the blurred categories of "natural" and "artificial" beings.

Does this argument persuade you that the natural/artificial distinction is wholly wrong? And that authenticity has been a red herring for all of us—including Hell's Angels? If it doesn't persuade you as a rational being, it must be because you have a counterargument either showing the invalidity of the argument or the falsity of one or more of its premises. What is your counterargument?

19 *Does sociobiology self-destruct?* We are dealing with complex matters, as our dialectic—the back and forth arguments in Reflections 14–18—shows. But there are still other considerations to deal with. Let me start by presenting one of them through an analogy.

It's true that different cultural conditions may lead to different behavior; it's also true that we might make distinctions between these conditions, rather than between our own artificial and natural nature, because of the conditions' effect on our behavior. However, this shouldn't lead us to deny the existence of "natural" natures. For example, a magnet attracts iron filings but not copper ones. Unless there were a difference in the nature of the filings, we couldn't account for their different behavior by the effect of the magnet alone. Part of the reason iron filings are attracted is because of their own inherent nature. Humans too have their own inherent nature. It is the combination of outside conditions *and* inherent, natural properties—not the outside conditions alone—that account for behavior.

This argument structure is analogous to the one proposed by Edwin O. Wilson in *Sociobiology: The New Synthesis.* Environmental conditions and natural selection produced humans with a certain nature, **231** as described in the quotations that follow. Wilson maintains that humans are wholly natural; what thinkers like Rousseau might refer to as a socially produced artificial nature is seen by Wilson as part of the nature of a "social species." A social species is wholly natural.

> Self-knowledge is constrained and shaped by the emotional control
> centers in the hypothalamus and limbic system of the brain. These
> centers flood our consciousness with all the emotions—hate, love, guilt,
> fear, and others—that are consulted by ethical philosophers who wish to
> intuit the standards of good and evil. What, we are then compelled to
> ask, made the hypothalamus and limbic system? They evolved by
> natural selection. That simple biological statement must be pursued to
> explain ethics and ethical philosophers. . . . The hypothalamic-limbic
> system of a highly social species, such as man, "knows," or more
> precisely it has been programmed to perform as if it knows, that its
> underlying genes will be proliferated maximally [duplicated to the max-
> imum] only if it orchestrates [programs] behavioral responses that bring
> into play an efficient mixture of personal survival, reproduction, and
> altruism. . . . Sociobiology is defined as the systematic study of the
> biological basis of all social behavior. (pp. 3–4)
> I argued that ethical philosophers intuit the deontological canons
> [obligatory rules] of morality by consulting the emotive centers of their
> own hypothalamic-limbic system. . . . Only by interpreting the activity
> of the emotive centers as a biological adaption can the meaning of the
> canons be deciphered.[36]

Against those who maintain that humans are artificial because they are the product of society, Wilson argues that we can trace culture back to the genes, which shows that culture is natural rather than ar-tificial. But only by assuming an inherent nature as we do for iron fil-ings, can we explain social and moral institutions.

> Only in man has culture thoroughly infiltrated virtually every aspect of
> life. Ethnographic detail is genetically underprescribed [undetermined],
> resulting in great amounts of diversity among societies. [That is,
> genetic organization doesn't have sufficient structural complexity to ex-
> plain the variety of cultural complexity.] Underprescription does not
> mean that culture has been freed from the genes. What has evolved is
> the capacity for culture, indeed the overwhelming tendency to develop
> one culture or another. . . . Culture, including the more resplendent
> manifestations of ritual and religion, can be interpreted as a hierarchical
> system of environmental tracking devices. . . . It is useful to hypothesize
> [suppose] that cultural details are for the most part adaptive in a Darwi-
> nian sense. (p. 560)

232   Does Wilson in this last paragraph perhaps unwittingly refute his
own earlier paragraphs, in which he claims to show that an "inherent"
human nature is genetically determined? Or is he showing that those
who maintain that our behavior is socially rather than genetically determined are wrong, because culture is natural—natural because genetically
determined, which has the effect of erasing the natural/cultural distinction and with it the natural/artificial distinction?

To help you understand this last question, look at the following
two arguments. By a simple substitution of one word for another, you
can get Wilson's argument out of them.

What word would Wilson substitute for "artificial" in these
arguments?

> Whatever is man-made is artificial.
> Culture is man-made.
> _____
> Therefore, culture is artificial.
>
> Humans are products of culture.
> Whatever is a product of something artificial is also artificial.
> _____
> Therefore, humans are artificial.

20 *"Culture is natural" is self-contradictory.* Father Ignace Lepp, a
Catholic philosopher, appears to agree with Wilson. He too
acknowledges that culture has contributed to the nature of humans. He
thinks culture exists because of humans' *natural* capacity for reflection
and creativity; further, humans are cultural products, therefore they appear to be manifestations of natural self-making. That is, humans
make culture naturally; culture makes humans; therefore humans make
humans naturally. Clearly, however, human self-making is an instance
of human artisanship, whose products are artifacts. Now, if we say
that human nature has self-making abilities to make an artifact, have we
talked ourselves into a contradiction? How can something's "natural"
nature be considered natural if, at some stage in history, it is an artifact
because it is a product of our self-making? In short, how can something
be natural and an artifact at the same time? Can contradiction be
avoided by talking, as Lepp does, about a natural capacity (potentiality)
and an actualization? Can we say consistently that the capacity is
natural and the actualization an artifact, and that they are two things,
although two aspects of humans?

Let's look at some passages from the chapter entitled "Natural
Morality and the Nature of Man" in Lepp's book, *The Authentic
Morality*.[37] As you reflect on them, ask yourself if Wilson doesn't have
to deal with the same questions that I raise about Lepp's position.

Lepp says that Christian moralists have found it important to claim that Christian morality is a natural one, because they want to maintain that it requires "nothing foreign to man's nature." So, Father Lepp points out, we have to define the nature of man. He deplores that, in the past, thinkers have used themselves as models. We should be more scientific. "Rigorously objective and scientific observation also obliges us to recognize that there exists in all men certain specifically common characteristics that enable naturalists to discern the evidence of a certain evolution. . . . Our [present] nature is only one of the many possible realizations of human nature and nothing authorizes us to consider it the most perfect or final realization" (p. 50). But isn't it contradictory to speak of more than one human nature with common characteristics?

Following up these remarks, Lepp says that paleontologists, scientists who study prehistoric life through fossils, could distinguish primitive man from other primates by "unequivocal signs of creativity, invention, and a break with the *established order* of nature. Paleontological evidence can be complemented with that of other anthropological sciences to indicate provisorily [conditionally] that human nature can be defined by its capacity for reflection, creative work, meaningful discourse, and morality. We say by its *capacity,* for reflective intelligence, language, freedom, and so forth were not in the beginning given realities but potentialities" (p. 50).

Lepp appears to be heading for a contradiction again in these next remarks:

Rousseau's idealization of the *primitive,* the *good savage,* cannot be scientifically supported. In order for man to be truly man, that is to say in order that he live in perfect conformity with his nature, he must not be stripped of all that centuries of evolution and civilization have added to what we can observe in primitive man. The most specifically human characteristic consists precisely in the impossibility of conceiving the nature of man as static. Either human nature is dynamic and dialectic[al] or there is no human nature. . . . The innumerable conquests of civilization are by no means foreign additions to our true nature; they are integral [essential] to this nature and have become authentic constituent elements. Our nature is therefore very different from that of the Peking or Neanderthal man. Even today human nature is different or, more exactly, differently actualized, depending upon civilizations, cultural evolution, and different collective and individual situations. (pp. 50–51)

Here is one more passage in a similar vein:

But we must take one fact as axiomatic: we must look for human nature more in the future than in the past. . . . It is man's nature to transcend continually or attempt to transcend his natural condition—not to free himself completely from nature but to acquire a new natural condition. . . . It is because it evolves and grows that human nature is

becoming richer and more and more complex. There is incontestably
an identity between primitive man and the evolved man of today.
And while the points of comparison may be few in number, restricted
almost entirely to fundamental potentialities, the identity is clear enough
to permit us to speak of a humanity that is one and indivisible. (pp.
51–52)

21 *Rousseau changes his mind.* Rousseau wrote *The Social Contract*
several years after he wrote *On the Origin of Inequality.* An extract
from the later book is quoted below. Would you say that Rousseau
had changed his mind about the relative merits of natural and artificial
humans? Would you say that Rousseau came to agree with Lepp's
criticism of his earlier position about the "good savage"? Note this
passage: ". . . did not the abuses of this new condition often degrade
him below that which he left. . . ."

> The passage from the state of nature to the civil state produces a very
> remarkable change in man, by substituting justice for instinct in his con-
> duct, and giving his actions the morality they had formerly lacked.
> Then only, when the voice of duty takes the place of physical impulses
> and right of appetite, does man, who so far had considered only
> himself, find that he is forced to act on different principles, and to con-
> sult his reason before listening to his inclinations. Although, in this
> state, he deprives himself of some advantages which he got from nature,
> he gains in return others so great, his faculties are so stimulated and
> developed, his ideas so extended, his feelings so ennobled, and his whole
> soul so uplifted, that, did not the abuses of this new condition often
> degrade him below that which he left, he would be bound to bless con-
> tinually the happy moment which took him from it for ever, and, in-
> stead of a stupid and unimaginative animal, made him an intelligent be-
> ing and a man. . . . We might, over and above all this, add, to what
> man acquires in the civil state, moral liberty, which alone makes him
> truly master of himself; for the mere impulse of appetite is slavery,
> while obedience to a law which we prescribe to ourselves is liberty.[38]

22 *Romantics betray science.* A recent event at a University of Hawaii
research laboratory where dolphins were being studied shows the strain
between Romanticism and Classicism/Enlightenment. Which side would
you favor?

Two young undergraduates were in charge of caring for two
dolphins; the dolphins had been the subject of several years' experi-
mentation under the direction of Professor Lou Herman. The students
took the dolphins and released them in the ocean. They were charged
and convicted of theft. The students called it a "liberation" of the
animals.

Dolphins are intelligent creatures. Arthur Lubow, in an article on
the event, writes that the current dolphin mystique owes

a great deal to John Lilly, who was an early experimenter on dolphins. In the 60s, Lilly released the dolphins he was studying. . . . In the foreword to a recent collection of his writings, he explains: "I no longer wanted to run a concentration camp for my friends and if they were as I found them to be, and if this was not only my imagination, then there was an ethical problem of maintaining them in a confined state in which they may not survive." . . .

Lilly is considered a lightweight by other scientists who study cetaceans. He committed the unpardonable sin: he let his emotions get the better of him. Even worse, he infected an entire generation with this poison. "You see it in applications for graduate school," says Santa Cruz' Kenneth Norris. "There's lots of this romantic view of life, all that kind of emotional stuff that happens when people of this cast of mind meet one of these animals. You hear about these peaceful creatures that live in a perfect society, blah, blah, blah, when in fact they can be aggressive as hell."

Among cetacean experts, the division between those whose approach is strictly scientific and those of a more "romantic" bent is a longstanding one. . . .

Herman says, "It's important also to distinguish between those who promote the death of the animals and those who study their life. Would you end cancer studies on laboratory rats? . . . Man's right to know—isn't that an ethical issue? If you give up the right to know, you're back in the dark ages of mysticism, religion and dogma. In all human history, I know of no era I'd less like to live in than the Dark Ages, when the mind of man was imprisoned."[39]

23 *John Austin on performatives. Feelings, thoughts, and intentions: Several kinds of inauthenticity?* In 6.6 we considered some acts that appear to require appropriate motivations; without such motivations, these acts appear to be inauthentic. I raised the question of whether such "inauthentic" acts were really acts or only appeared to be. Have you apologized by saying "I apologize" if you feel no regret, or have you only seemed to apologize? The late English philosopher J. L. Austin called sentences where "the issuing of the utterance is performing an action" by the name *performatives*. He thinks performatives are subject to "infelicities," some of which result in the nonperformance of an act, and others result in an act being performed but "unhappy"; he thinks "inauthentic" acts are performed but unhappy.[40]

Acts may be "unhappy" because the requisite (necessary) feelings, thoughts, or intentions are lacking. Note that we may be inauthentic if we don't have the appropriate thoughts or intentions, as well as if we don't have the appropriate feelings. Austin writes:

Examples of not having the requisite feelings are:
"I congratulate you," said when I did not feel at all pleased, perhaps even was annoyed.

"I condole with you," said when I did not really sympathize with you. . . .
Examples of not having the requisite thoughts are:
"I advise you to," said when I do not think it would be the course most expedient for you.
"I find him not guilty—I acquit," said when I do believe that he was guilty. . . .
Examples of not having the requisite intentions are:
"I promise," said when I do not intend to do what I promise.
"I bet," said when I do not intend to pay. (Austin, p. 40)

If someone said to you "I congratulate you" without feeling pleased, would you say you had been congratulated? If a judge said "I acquit you" even though he thought you guilty, would you consider youself acquitted? Or if someone said "I bet you five dollars" but didn't intend to pay, would you think you had a right to collect the bet? Are you more inclined to think that a bet has been made than that you have been congratulated? Perhaps some acts depend on having appropriate feelings and others do not. For example, it doesn't seem apparent that there is an appropriate feeling for betting. As for intentions, it doesn't seem necessary to have some intention in order to congratulate. Would this lead you to speculate that there are various kinds of inauthenticity?

24 *Hume on performative utterances.* And now for promises. After reflecting on the following quotation from Hume, say if you think he believes that intentions or thoughts or feelings are required, for a promise to have been made. What other factors would you say he thinks are involved in promising?

It is evident, that the will or consent alone never transfers property, nor causes the obligation of a promise (for the same reasoning extends to both) but the will must be expressed by words or signs, in order to impose a tie upon any man. The expression being once brought in as subservient to [expressive of] the will, soon becomes the principal part of the promise; nor will a man be less bound by his word, though he secretly give a different direction to his intention, and withhold the assent of his mind. But though the expression makes, on most occasions, the whole of the promise, yet it does not always do so; and one who should make use of any expression, of which he knows not the meaning, and which he uses without any sense of the consequences, would not certainly be bound by it. Nay, though he know its meaning, yet if he use it in jest only, and with such signs as evidently show, that he has no serious intention of binding himself, he would not lie under any obligation of performance; but it is necessary, that the words be a perfect expression of the will, without any contrary signs. Nay, even this we must not carry so far as to imagine, that one, whom, by our quickness of understanding, we conjecture, from certain signs, to have an intention of deceiving us, is not bound by his expression or verbal promise, if we accept of it; but must limit this conclusion to those cases where the signs are of a different nature from those of deceit.[41]

Perhaps the following further remarks of Hume's will help you to think of some other factors necessary for the issuing of performatives.

Were the interests of society nowise concerned, it is as unintelligible why another's articulating [uttering] certain sounds implying consent [for example, "Yes, you may have this"] should change the nature of my actions [say, from stealing to owning] with regard to a particular object, as why the reciting of a liturgy by a priest, in a certain habit and posture, should dedicate a heap of brick and timber, and render it, thenceforth and for ever, sacred. (*Enquiries,* p. 199)

25 *Sincerity.* "Somerset Maugham once said that sincerity in society was like an iron girder in a house of cards."[42]

Interpret Maugham's remark.

26 *Knockout argument against sociobiology?* Does this argument deal a knockout blow to sociobiology's claim that our behavior is genetically determined?

If an event is caused, then we say it is "determined." If anything is the cause of some event, E, it can't be the cause of its contrary, non-E or its contradiction, $-E$. For example, if we attribute John Iron's lifting 300 pounds to his muscular strength, we can't also attribute his not lifting 300 pounds to his strength. In short, if C is the cause of E, it can't be the cause of $-E$ or non-E.

Wilson says that genetic factors determine the capacity for traits.

Some of these traits are opposites of each other. For example, we can develop generous and miserly traits, honest and dishonest ones, friendly and unfriendly ones.

Therefore, genetic factors can't be the cause of traits.

Consequently, there is no evidence that we are genetically determined in our behavior.

7
Kant's Cosmos: Nature and Humanity

Man is the only animal that laughs and weeps; for he is the only animal that is struck with the difference between what things are and what they ought to be.

William Hazlitt

7.1 Kant's Vision

The full understanding of a philosophic theory of morals requires also an understanding of the larger philosophic theory into which the ethics fits. This larger theory will include a theory of the cosmos, a metaphysics of the world, and the place of persons in that cosmos. Essential to our outline of moral psychology is the understanding that this moral theory puts persons wholly into the world of nature: we are an evolved species subject to the same natural laws of biology, psychology, and physiology (chemistry and physics) that influence every other species of creature.

Moral psychologists think that to understand persons and their conduct we must follow the methods of natural science; therefore, a moral theory is part of natural science. A full understanding of moral psychology requires, then, a philosophy of the natural world and a philosophy of natural science that can comprehend the complex behavior of a highly intelligent species of that world. David Hume was the prime architect of moral psychology.

Immanuel Kant was the philosophic giant who developed the most powerful reply to Hume and moral psychology. More, perhaps, than with any other moral philosopher, the understanding of Kant's ethical theory requires a co-understanding of his theory of the place of humans in the cosmos. The following sketch of Kant's "vision" is intended to help you connect Kant's ethical theory with his theory of the cosmos. Of course this chapter's sketch is oversimplified; the next chapters will fill it out. However, this chapter's simplicity is its virtue: it will give you the heart of the matter and provide you with a map of a large, complex, and varied terrain that you can consult if you ever feel lost.

The first thing to note is that Kant, unlike moral psychologists, does not believe that humans are wholly natural creatures. Humans live in two worlds—the natural world and the supersensible world. The natural world is the sensible world, the world as given to our senses: grass, crickets, music, buildings, shadows, colors, sounds, shapes, and the furniture of the heavens.

These manifold sensory data that we experience are organized by our mind; **241** this organization makes the sensible world knowable. In the natural world everything is subject to natural laws of cause and effect; this covers those aspects of humans that are sensible, which includes the psychological, biological, and physiological aspects: desires motivate us; children grow into maturity; and our heart pumps the blood to move it through the plumbing of our veins and arteries.

But humans also have reason and will, according to Kant; these put part of us outside sensible nature and make us inhabitants of a supersensible world as well. As supersensible entities, we are like the gods; we are not subject to the laws of cause and effect. Rather, we give ourselves our own laws—not natural laws but moral laws. Further, because we have a rational will, we can cause ourselves to act in accord with these self-legislated laws. This supersensible capacity to (1) give ourselves laws and (2) cause ourselves to act gives us our autonomy, our freedom, and exempts us from the determined course of natural events. Our rational will, Kant thinks, gives us our dignity—a dignity he sometimes speaks of as a kind of divinity.

The supersensible and the sensible world intersect when we, as supersensible agents, cause our sensible selves to act in the sensible world: "The concept of freedom is meant to actualize in the sensible world the end proposed by its laws."[1] We are as gods, then; by acting in the sensible world, we change its course of events; by changing the course of events, we bring the order of moral laws into an otherwise non-moral sensible world. As human divinities, we re-create the world in a moral image. Were we to submit solely to natural laws, we would have denied our divine dignity and abandoned ourselves to a natural, animal existence in the sensible world.

Erwin Panofsky tells the following story about Kant:

Nine days before his death, Immanuel Kant was visited by his physician. Old, ill and nearly blind, he rose from his chair and stood trembling with weakness and muttering unintelligible words. Finally his faithful companion realized that he would not sit down again until the visitor had taken a seat. This he did, and Kant then permitted himself to be helped to his chair and, after having regained some of his strength, said, "Das Gefühl für Humanität hat mich noch nicht verlassen"—"The sense of humanity has not yet left me." The two men were moved almost to tears. For, though the word *Humanität* had come, in the eighteenth century, to mean little more than politeness or civility, it had, for Kant, a much deeper significance, which the circumstances of the moment served to emphasize: man's proud and tragic consciousness of self-approved and self-imposed principles, contrasting with his utter subjection to illness, decay and all that is implied in the word "mortality."[2]

Kant calls us to hearken to our divinity. He urges us to excercise our rational freedom and thereby realize our higher self. He asks us to put on our humanity:

The ultimate destiny of the human race is the greatest moral perfection, provided that it is achieved through human freedom, whereby alone man is capable of the greatest happiness. . . . The realization of the full destiny, the highest possible perfection of human nature—this is the kingdom of God on earth. Justice and equity, the authority, not of governments, but of conscience within us, will then rule the world.[3]

In this chapter I will give a larger overall outline of Kant's notions of the natural order, the moral order, and how they relate to each other. Subsequent chapters will draw a number of contrasts between the two dominant ethical theories, so that your reflections on morals are both deepened and sharpened. We live in an age dominated by a scientific mentality that has put humanistic and religious traditions on the defensive. Kant tried to put the scientific theory of humanity on the defensive.

7.2 Human Dignity, Moral Capacity, and Moral Realization

Kant would have approved of the remarks of the late Pablo Casals, the world-famous cellist, explaining his 1946 vow not to play in public again as long as Franco was dictator of Spain: "I am a believer in liberty, honesty, justice, brotherhood and plain human dignity. My decision to act in 1946 represented no great sacrifice on my part, nor have I suffered because of it. . . . I have no regrets, I am at peace with myself." Casals' emphasis on "plain human dignity" and his willingly acting to preserve it display the central concept around which Kant's moral philosophy turns.

Kant intends his moral theory to illuminate what human dignity is and how it is possible that we have it. This makes his theory relevant to our self-understanding. We all want respect. We don't want to be treated as common objects or as lower animals. We don't want to live as kept lap dogs or to remain as children. Except for Peter Pan fantasies, every child wants to become an adult. Children often are treated somewhere between pets and slaves. They are told what to do, as if they had little or no reason; they are threatened and beguiled as if they had no will. But everyone wants to be "somebody"; all of us wish to become worthy of esteem in both our own eyes and the eyes of others. Childhood and dignity are too often incompatible. That is why children do not want to remain children.

In ceasing to be children, we "grow up." To grow up, for Kant, is to realize oneself as a person; to realize oneself as a person is to become morally worthy, which you cannot be without exercising your freedom. To exercise your freedom is, first, to be self-governing, autonomous—to give yourself moral laws through your reason; second, to will those acts that are in accord with these self-given laws; and third, to will them just because they are in accord with them.

Kant thought that human dignity rested on our capacity to be moral persons; it is this that lifts us above the animals: "Autonomy is thus the basis of **243** the dignity of both human nature and every rational creature."[4] It also lifts us above the "noble savage." In Reflection 21 on p. 234, I quoted Rousseau's remarks about how humans are "ennobled" by their ability to act on principles of reason rather than on physical appetites and impulse. Rousseau's remarks summarize Kant's view well. This is not surprising, because Kant was deeply influenced by Rousseau and is said to have kept a copy of Rousseau's *Émile* on his desk and to have reread it every year. Kant too believed that humans have "moral liberty" and that "obedience to a law which we prescribe to ourselves is liberty."

This view, Kant believed, was at total odds with moral psychology. In the following chapters I shall contrast Kant's view with the views of moral psychologists. The contrasts will spell out the great divide that exists in ethical theory. Others share many of Kant's views, but none has been as uncompromising, forceful, and comprehensive in their treatment as he. Kant was probably the most important ethical theorist who ever lived. Not to know Kant's views on morals is to be seriously undereducated. Further, Kant was a theorist of self-realization ethics, as seen by the following key remarks:

> Man *himself* must make or have made himself into whatever, in a moral sense, whether good or evil, he is or is to become. Either condition must be an effect of his free choice[w]* (in German, *Willkür*), for otherwise he could not be held responsible for it and could therefore be *morally* neither good nor evil.[5]

To understand this quotation, we must note that it uses "moral" one way in the first sentence and a different way in the second sentence. "Moral" refers in the second sentence to our *capacity* to be moral; in the first, to our *realization* of that capacity. Unfortunately, in English we have but the single word "moral" to refer to these two distinct meanings, but fortunately we have two different words, "nonmoral" and "immoral," for their respective opposites:

Capacity:
$\begin{cases} \text{Moral—Capable of being good } or \text{ evil.} \\ \\ \text{Non-moral—Not capable of being good } or \text{ evil, as insects are not.} \end{cases}$

Realization:
$\begin{cases} \text{Moral—Having attained moral goodness.} \\ \\ \text{Immoral—Having lapsed into moral evil.} \end{cases}$

In the first sentence of the preceding quotation, Kant uses "moral" ("in a moral sense") to express his commitment to moral self-realization, to self-

* The use of the superscript *w* is explained on p. 277.

244   making; we make ourselves good or evil. This moral self-realization is the second stage of a two-stage notion of our moral personality. The first stage, referred to in the second sentence of the quotation, is the capacity stage. At this first stage of morality, the moral/non-moral distinction makes the same division for Kant as the human/nonhuman distinction does. Humans are moral creatures but animals are nonmoral. Animals can be neither morally good nor immoral. They lack the capacity for it because they do not have a free, rational will; they lack practical reason.

Although we humans do have moral capacity, we can take no credit for it; we inherit our moral capacity because we inherit the capacity of practical reason, just as we inherit the capacity to become strong or to play the piano or to walk. Kant thinks that animals lack practical reason because they lack the capacity for acting deliberately in accord with a rational conception of rules or principles.

The second stage of moral self-realization is the one at which we either realize or fail to realize our moral capacity. Here "moral" contrasts with "immoral." In this sense, to say we are "moral" is to say we are good, and to say we are "immoral" is to say we are evil. To be moral in the second sense or stage is to exercise our first-stage capacity—that is, our practical reason. In doing so, we self-realize what we have the capacity to become—rational, free, and morally worthy persons. In short, in the second stage we realize our first-stage moral potential. For Kant, our human "mission," our "ultimate destiny," is to realize our moral capacity, to become morally worthy. Although we all want to be happy, it is not our mission to become happy, but to become *worthy* of happiness.

We should note that in becoming evil we do not realize ourselves, because in that case we have *failed* to use our practical reason fully. Having the capacity to be morally good is analogous to having the capacity to become muscularly strong. Just as muscular weakness is not a realization of our capacity, but a failure to develop it, so too being evil is not a realization of our moral capacity, but a failure to develop that capacity. To practice Kant's theory, we are required by him to develop our character and strengthen our will. This development equips us with a disposition to act out of respect for the moral law and to overcome the opposing inclinations of wants and desires, as when we have sufficient strength of character to choose to tell the truth, even though it diminishes our happiness. Kant writes:

> We are not, then, to call the depravity of human nature *wickedness* taking the word in its strict sense as a disposition . . . to adopt evil *as evil* . . . we should rather term it the *perversity* of the heart. . . . Such a heart may coexist with a will which in general is good: it arises from the frailty of human nature, the lack of sufficient strength to follow out the principles it has chosen for itself. (*Religion,* p. 32. See also p. 31, where Kant traces the source of evil to giving priority to incentives for happiness over moral incentives, rather than tracing the source to any positively existing capacity for evil.)

Although I take Kant to be a moral realization theorist, Kant's moral **245** theory can be and has been classified in other ways. Some of these other classifications appear in this and subsequent chapters as bases for contrasts with moral psychology. I have chosen to emphasize the self-realization classification of Kant, because it is a useful way of organizing other aspects of his ethics. It also does justice to a central feature of Kant's view, namely, that nothing is without qualification morally good in this world or beyond this world except a "good will", and that such a will is not something given to us, but something which we must achieve by our own efforts (*Foundations,* p. 295).

As a self-realization moralist, Kant sets his face against moral psychologists, who see humans as made and natural. For Kant, moral psychology is fit to explain animals but not humans; to think it applies to humans is to think of humans as animals. To reduce us to this lower state, Kant believes, robs us of our dignity. Romain Gary, the French novelist, puts this point of view in modern terms:

> I even doubt if there are such things as natural good values and natural bad ones: Everything is of our own making. . . . The contemporary pseudo-Freudian crusade against inhibitions is another typical example of the oft-forgotten fact that any kind of dignity, decency, generosity or idealistic outlook is in no way a natural, beautiful golden fruit growing in the splendid garden of our being, but to a considerable degree the result of inhibitions, frustrations, discipline, restrictions, of a constant "rape" of our instincts, of a terrific, painful struggle against nature. Yes, against nature . . . civilization is man's attempt to control the facts of life and himself. The unrepressed, uninhibited individual can in no way be called civilized. . . . Civilization is, has always been and will always be, a struggle against nature, against what we *truly* are, an effort to strike some kind of balance between reality and unreality. . . . We are the result of a competition with reality. We are a creation of our own imagination, a culturally evolved image to which we are trying to conform, a myth of dignity, decency, fraternity, generosity, humanity that is pure poetry. There can be no scientific approach to our nature—cultural man is an artistic creation.[6]

7.3 Duty as a "Fact of Reason"

Kant thinks we have to take up, as Gary puts it, "a terrific, painful struggle against nature," because we all recognize that we have duties; we recognize that there are objective, moral laws that we are obliged to follow, even while being tugged toward satisfying our natural wants. Kant thinks this is a "fact of reason."[7]

246   This fact of reason he says, is recognized by the "commonest intelligence" and even by children.   They recognize the difference between acts done out of duty and acts done out of self-love to forward our happiness:

> And yet even the man of greatest limitations is capable of being impressed by respect for an action conforming to duty—a respect which is the greater the more he isolates it, in thought, from other incentives which, through self-love, might influence the maxim of conduct. Even children are capable of detecting the smallest trace or admixture of improper incentives; for an action thus motivated at once loses, in their eyes, all moral worth. (*Religion,* p. 44)

Kant gives some examples that illustrate, according to him, the common recognition of duty as a fact of reason.   He believes we are easily able to distinguish acting from duty and acting from the natural incentives to get what we think we need for our happiness.   Kant expects us also to confirm the fact of reason in reflecting on his illustrations:

> Suppose that an acquaintance whom you otherwise liked were to attempt to justify himself to you for having borne false witness, first by alleging the, in his view, sacred duty of consulting his own happiness; then by enumerating the advantages which he gained thereby, pointing out the prudence he had shown in securing himself against detection, even by yourself, to whom he now reveals the secret, only in order that he may be able to deny it at any time; and suppose he were then to affirm, in all seriousness, that he has fulfilled a true human duty; you would either laugh in his face, or shrink back from him with disgust. (*Practical Reason,* p. 305)

Kant offers a second illustration:

> Suppose some one recommends you a man as steward, as a man to whom you can blindly trust all your affairs; and, in order to inspire you with confidence, extols him as a prudent man who thoroughly understands his own interest, and is so indefatigably active that he lets slip no opportunity of advancing it; lastly, lest you should be afraid of finding a vulgar selfishness in him, praises the good taste with which he lives; not seeking his pleasure in money-making, or in coarse wantonness, but in the enlargement of his knowledge, in instructive intercourse with a select circle, and even in relieving the needy; while as to the means (which, of course, derive all their value from the end), he is not particular, and is ready to use other people's money for the purpose as if it were his own, provided only he knows that he can do so safely, and without discovery; you would either believe that the recommender was mocking you, or that he had lost his senses. So sharply and clearly marked are the boundaries of morality and self-love that even the commonest eye cannot fail to distinguish whether a thing belongs to the one or the other. (*Practical Reason,* p. 305)

As long as we have reason, we know we ought to follow the dictates of duty, even while we are not doing so.   We cannot escape knowledge of our moral duties except through madness; we cannot hide from the fact of reason unless we lose our reason, in which case we lose our personhood.   Our ability to grasp the fact of reason is what makes us persons, lifts us above animals, **247** and frees us from being confined in the sensible world. It is this wonderful ability that generates our troubled interior life:

> If man looks at himself objectively—. . . as his pure practical reason determines him to do—he finds that, *as a moral being,* he is also holy enough to transgress the inner law *reluctantly;* for there is no man so depraved as not to feel an opposition to this transgression and an abhorrence of himself on account of which he has to constrain [force] himself (to violate the law).[8]

Despite our self-abhorrence and the guilt and shame we feel when we do not obey the moral laws that we have given ourselves —even though our ability to grasp the fact of reason strips from us the pitiful fig leaf that we put on in the Garden of Eden— the existence and knowledge of moral laws elevates us into the awesome region of the supersensible world. Kant's excitement at our gloriously terrifying human condition shows through in the following famous passage:

> Two things fill the mind with ever new and increasing admiration and awe, the oftener and the more steadily we reflect on them: *the starry heavens above and the moral law within.* I have not to search for them and conjecture them as though they were veiled in darkness or were in the transcendent region beyond my horizon; I see them before me and connect them directly with the consciousness of my existence. The former begins from the place I occupy in the external world of sense, and enlarges my connection therein to an unbounded extent with worlds upon worlds and systems of systems, and moreover into limitless times of their periodic motion, its beginning and continuance. The second begins from invisible self, my personality, and exhibits me in a world which has true infinity, but which is traceable only by the understanding, and with which I discern that I am not in a merely contingent [conditional or accidental] but in a universal and necessary connection, as I am also thereby with all those visible worlds. The former view of a countless multitude of worlds annihilates as it were my importance as *animal creature.* . . . The second, on the contrary, infinitely elevates my worth as an *intelligence* by my personality, in which the moral law reveals to me a life independent of animality and even of the whole sensible world. (*Practical Reason,* p. 361)

7.4 The Intelligible and the Sensible Worlds

From the preceding remarks you can see how Kant thinks of us as living in two worlds—the sensible, visible, palpable world and the intelligible, invisible, supersensible world. The most awesome thing in the visible world is the starry heaven above, while the most awesome thing in the intelligible world is the moral law. For Kant as for Gary, we are in competition with the sensible world. Humans, as residents of the intelligible world, look upon the sensible

248 world, of which they are also residents, and find that the sensible world is not as good as it could be. The course of human events in the sensible world does not conform wholly to the moral law within. If the world is to improve, then the world's social and political events must conform more closely to the moral law within. Our knowledge of the intelligible world and its moral laws makes us critics of the sensible world, including our own sensible being, which too often follows our animal nature rather than our intelligible nature.

As beings in the intelligible world, we can know the sensible world is not as good as it could be, because we have knowledge of the moral law within. Further, once we recognize the moral law and know that we recognize it, we become aware that it is our reason that enables us to judge the world. Further still, recognizing that the moral law applies to us, we also recognize that the moral law obliges us to do something about it, which it couldn't do if we couldn't will to do something about it. Thus by these steps we are brought to acknowledge that through our free will we are able and ought to make the world better.

Kant holds that our consciousness of our freedom to change the world and our recognition of our obligation to improve it "reciprocally imply each other." Freedom and obligation together define our unique status in the world, and put us out of the reach of moral psychologists. Kant sometimes calls this status the "unconditionally practical": "unconditionally" because the moral law places a necessary, inescapable demand on us as long as we have our intelligence, independently of our life conditions; and "practical" because we are free to act—free to remake the world—and do not have to stand passively under the hammer of nature.

Kant then asks "whence *begins* our *knowledge* of the unconditionally practical, whether it is from freedom or from the practical law?" He answers that we first become conscious of the moral law, and that this "leads directly to the concept of freedom."[9] In another work Kant again puts the law first and our freedom second: "For when the moral law commands that we *ought* now to be better men, it follows inevitably that we must *be able* to be better men" (*Religion,* p. 46). Kant repeats his point: "Duty demands nothing of us which we cannot do" (*Religion,* p. 43). Again: "Duty commands him unconditionally: he *ought* to remain true to his resolve; and thence he rightly *concludes* that he must *be able* to do so, and that his will[w] [*Willkür*] is therefore free" (*Religion,* note, p. 45). This view is often expressed more succinctly: *Ought* implies *Can*.

Recognition of the awesome "moral law within" brings other knowledge with it: knowledge of the sensible world's imperfect moral condition; knowledge that we have a free will; and knowledge that we can change the world. Knowledge of these four things—moral laws, the world's moral condition, our free will, and our ability to change the course of the sensible world—makes humans *accountable*. We are accountable for the way the world is, for it is as it is either because we knowingly, deliberately, freely contributed our share to its course of events, or because we knowingly, deliberately, freely refrained from altering its course.

This accountability—the fact that we can impute or assign responsibility to humans—is what elevates humans above animals, and the four kinds of knowledge are what make us accountable:

> A *person* is a subject whose actions can be *imputed* to him. *Moral* personality is thus the freedom of a rational being under moral laws. (Psychological personality is merely the power to become conscious of one's self-indentity at different times and under the different conditions of one's existence.) (*Virtue,* p. 22)

We can summarize these recognitions or kinds of knowledge by saying that we recognize that we are *agents.* John Silber puts it this way:

> The moral law, according to Kant, reveals the fact and the meaning of the human personality. By telling us what we *ought* to do regardless of what our inclinations and desires may bid us to, the moral law forces us to be aware of ourselves as agents rather than as mere creatures of desire.[10]

7.5 Evil and the Best of All Possible Worlds

Kant became critical of the ideas of the early-eighteenth-century German philosopher Gottfried Wilhelm Leibniz, whose philosophy was dominant during Kant's younger years, although he owed to Leibniz his way of setting forth the problem of the moral strain between the intelligible and the sensible worlds. (See "Appendix" to the Transcendental Analytic of Kant's *Critique of Pure Reason*.) Leibniz is well known for his phrase "the best of all possible worlds," which Voltaire lampooned in his tale *Candide,* where as disaster after disaster befalls him, the hero nevertheless keeps reaffirming that this is "the best of all possible worlds." Voltaire's hero is a mental lightweight who fails to appreciate that the occurrence of so much evil in the world should show the absurdity of the assertion he keeps repeating.

Leibniz's doctrine that this is the best of all possible worlds was his attempt to deal with the "problem of evil." The problem of evil arises for Christians because their doctrine attributes the creation of the world to a deity that is all-powerful, all-knowing, and all-good. The problem can be stated by showing that the following four propositions are logically incompatible—that is, they can't all be true, although Christian doctrine says they are.

(1) God is all-powerful.
(2) God is all-knowing.
(3) God is all-good.
(4) In this world that God created, there is evil.

These propositions are thought to be incompatible because if the first three were true, the last would be false: there would be no evil in the world,

250   which would make it truly the best of all possible worlds. There would be no evil if God had these properties because, if God were all-good, He/She would not tolerate evil; if God were all-knowing, He/She would know how to keep evil out of the world and, being all-powerful, could arrange matters so that there would be no evil. However, there *is* evil; therefore, at least one of the first three statements is not true.

Leibniz conjectured that there were an infinite number of possible worlds from which God chose one to be the actual world. Because this actual world is the best of them, God is good. The best world for Leibniz is the one with the most variety combined with the greatest simplicity. The fact that such a world had evil in it would not show that God isn't all-good, all-powerful, and all-knowing. God could choose a world only from those that are possible; because God knows that among the possible ones ours is the best and chooses it, God is good.

Leibniz sets the stage for Kant's reflections on morals. The concepts of a possible world and of a world with evil in it are part of Kant's moral reflections. But instead of seeing the problem of evil from a theological perspective as Leibniz did, and trying to justify God's choice to humans, he put the problem in our laps. Because we have the "moral law within," we recognize that there is evil in the world. Because we are agents and therefore free and able to change the world, we have the task of making our world the best of all possible worlds or, at least, of making it a better world. The problem of evil isn't God's problem; it is ours.

Kant's moral theory may also be seen as his answer to the creator of the legendary Dr. Faustus, who alleged that a proud declaration of independence from God by us is a sure path to evil. Faustus is a fictional character with a long tradition, beginning in 1587 when Johann Spies published *The Historie of the Damnable Life and Deserved Death of Doctor John Faustus*. This is the story of a man who sold his soul to the Devil and renounced "all living creatures, and the whole heavenly host, and all human beings," in return for which he received the talents to extend his researches "to the uttermost parts of heaven and earth." The story is an allegory with a moral to the effect that our intellectual ambition, pride, and arrogance are manifestations of our submission to evil, symbolized by Mephistopheles. It locates the source of evil, the Devil in us,

> in the minds of men, [men] all of a sudden curiously suspicious of the instructions their Church had given them about their world and their place in it, and restlessly determined to probe forbidden depths. That time has passed, the mind has won its freedom, and the beast has not yet devoured us. Yet after centuries of free thought, free science, free testing, and free daredeviltry, there stood a doctor of nuclear physics, [Robert Oppenheimer] in an American desert, watching the first experimental explosion of the atomic bomb, and saying that for the first time in his life he knew what sin was.[11]

Kant was a fierce partisan of free, rational, independent humans. His moral theory is an attempt to show that we have within ourselves the moral equipment to be not only free but also good, and so able to avoid the fate of **251** Faustus, who had to become evil in order to know. Kant argues that humans can be free and good without relying on religion, but also without in any way violating traditional religious beliefs.

Kant puts us in the position of being a secular re-creator of the world, or at least of that part of it that we can re-create. This forces us to think about what it is to make a world, to make a totality.

7.6 Making a World

To understand what making or remaking a world is, we have to understand what a world is. We can begin by first answering this question: what would have to be true if there were only one world? Every thing that exists would have to be included in a single totality. We can put this as: everything that exists is either (1) the totality itself or (2) a part of the same totality of which every other thing is a part.

To determine that there is a single totality, then, we would have to be able to determine of any thing that it is a part of the same totality that any other thing is. What would enable us to say, for example, that this piece of paper, the furniture in your room, the moon, and the thought about your next meal are all parts of the same totality?

Leibniz's answer was that they are related to one another: our world is a world of change; it is dynamic, in constant change, and each thing in it is a force. The moon pulls the seas into waves that cause the tide to bring a fish that I plan to eat in my kitchen while sitting on my chair at my table. For Leibniz, the relations between all things can be stated in terms of laws that can be given mathematical form. The intelligibility of the universe requires a mathematical statement of the relations between all things. Thus the totality is a harmony of things in a set of relations; science, mathematically formulated, is the intelligible grasp of this harmony in a set of consistent laws governing every event in the totality. For Leibniz, there is a preestablished harmony among all parts of the totality; this preestablished harmony is grasped in its totality in the mind of God, but not, of course, in ours. The world is a mathematical system.

Kant too thought that the world is dynamic, and that its singleness and unity are due to laws governing change. But Kant thought that there were two worlds—the intelligible world and the sensible world of nature. About the sensible world of nature, he thought as Leibniz did: "Now, a system of nature, in the most general sense, is the existence of things under laws" (*Practical Reason,* p. 308). The natural world's laws are discovered by us. All natural things are subject to laws of causality; every event is an effect of another event that caused it. The natural world is the subject matter of natural science. We humans live in the world of nature as biological, psychological, physiological creatures, subject to its laws as are other material things.

But we also inhabit the intelligible world. This is a world beyond natural laws; in it, we are free. Yet the intelligible world is not a lawless, arbitrary world. In it, too, there are laws, but these are moral rather than natural laws. We do not discover these laws, *but give them to ourselves;* this is one important aspect of our autonomy, our freedom. In this intelligible world we are as gods, divine. From the perspective of the intelligible world, we have the task of creating a totality. This totality too must form a system under laws, as the sensible totality forms a natural system.

Think of this intelligible world as having parts and of each part as an existing, intelligent human, remembering that each of us has a free will. You can now ask youself, as Kant asked himself, what it would take to form a totality out of these free parts. This is the same as asking yourself how we free, individual human parts may create out of ourselves a comm*unity* of persons. A community of persons would be a social counterpart of Leibniz's idea of a natural harmony, with this important difference—namely, that a community of persons is not *preestablished* by God. Instead, it is our moral task to *establish* such a harmonious community. In this community we would relate ourselves together under moral laws; if we each give ourselves the same laws and obey them, then we will have formed ourselves into a social totality (community) without robbing ourselves of our freedom.

As beings in an intelligible world, we have our reason; to form a community of intelligent, moral beings, we have to use this reason to create a social totality. This social totality is forged when we inhabitants of the intellegible world give moral direction to our material bodies in the natural world; we act across worlds. Our mission is to transform moral laws into natural laws:

> We are, through reason, conscious of a moral law to which all our maxims are subject, as though a natural order must be orginated from our will. This law, therefore, must be the idea of a natural system, not given in experience, and yet possible through freedom; a system, therefore, which is supersensible (intelligible), and to which we give objective reality, at least in a practical point of view. (*Practical Reason,* p. 309)

Natural and moral laws, although different in kind, perform similar functions in the formation of totalities.

> The moral law is in fact a law of the causality of free agents, and, therefore, of the possibility of a supersensible system of nature, just as the metaphysical law of events in the world of sense was a law of causality of the sensible system of nature. (*Practical Reason,* p. 310)

It is important to underscore how Kant shifted the problem of an evil world from Leibniz's God to humans. This shift had reverberations that have echoed down the halls of time. Friedrich Engels, the friend and collaborator of Karl Marx, wrote:

"Wow—you mean you have your very own Private Moral Universe?"

> Hitherto the question has always stood: What is God?—and German philosophy has resolved it as follows: God is man. [Man must now] arrange the world in a truly human way, according to the demands of our nature—and then the riddle of our time would be resolved by him.[12]

Suppose, then, that our moral mission has the cosmic setting and task that Kant advocates and envisions; the next question is this: which laws should we humans adopt if we are to organize a social totality, if we are to create a new, better world, if we are to construct a community?

Kant thought the answer to this question should be modeled on the answer to the question: "What makes a natural totality?" Any totality, including a social totality, is a set of parts made into a whole under a consistent set of laws governing the relations between parts. A law expresses a relation between kinds of things; this relation must never vary from one instance to another of the kinds; the relation must hold *universally*. For example, the relation of dissolving must hold for every instance of water and every instance of sugar, when sugar is placed in the water; if there is an exception, then we do not have a "lawful" relation. The universality feature of laws provides the "self-consistency" of events in a totality; that is, nothing can occur in the relations between instances of two kinds of things that contradicts the law. A law does not have exceptions.

So in making a social totality, a moral law must specify a relation among persons that we could all universally follow. Kant thinks, for instance, that we can all tell one another the truth without exception. A moral law specifies a relation of behavior among persons that consistently regulates our treatment of one another. Any proposed moral law that cannot be universally obeyed

254　cannot be a moral law, for in that case we would necessarily have to act in contradiction to it; we would not be making a totality at all but negating and therefore canceling one another's efforts to make a new, better social world. Thus Kant thinks lying cannot be universally practical without contradiction.

Further, as moral beings we have *equal* responsibility for making a better world. This equal responsibility can be fulfilled only if the laws can be universally obeyed. Additionally, such laws would not abridge the freedom of anyone because everyone can (1) self-legislate such laws, (2) choose to act in accord with such laws, and (3) not interfere with other persons' rights to act in accord with them. The universality condition provides the basis for a totality of persons while maintaining the freedom of each.

Kant points out that happiness, which some moral psychologists take as the base for their ethical theories, cannot provide principles or laws for the construction of a social totality. It cannot provide a ground for action that can be universalized. Kant agrees that happiness is a good and thinks that "to be happy is necessarily the wish of every finite rational being" (*Practical Reason,* p. 300). "Happiness" he takes to be "only a general name" for the satisfaction of a group of ends; happiness is a secondary, not a primary, end because it signifies the satisfaction of such primary ends as to have food, to be clothed, to be famous, successful at our job, rich, and powerful: "A rational being's consciousness of the pleasantness of life, uninterruptedly accompanying his whole existence, is happiness; and the principle which makes this the supreme ground of determination of the will is the principle of self-love" (*Practical Reason,* p. 298). Because these primary ends vary, both within ourselves during our lifetime and from one person to another, they cannot form the basis for universal law:

> For it is every man's own special feeling of pleasure and pain that decides in what he is to place his happiness, and even in the same subject will vary with the difference of his wants according as this feeling changes, and thus a law which is *subjectively necessary* (as a law of nature) is *objectively* a very contingent practical principle, which can and must be very different in different subjects and therefore can never furnish a law. (*Practical Reason,* p. 300)

Kant gives an example of a plan of action, a maxim, that is suited to a man's happiness but which would, if made into a universal law, be destructive of a totality:

> Suppose, for example, that I have made it my maxim to increase my fortune by every safe means. Now, I have a deposit in my hands, the owner of which is dead and has left no writing about it. This is just the case for my maxim. I desire then to know whether that maxim can also hold good as a universal practical law. I apply it, therefore, to the present case, and ask whether I can by my maxim at the same time give such a law as this, that everyone may deny a deposit of which no one can produce a proof. I at once become aware that such a principle, viewed as a law, would an-

nihilate itself, because the result would be that there would be no **255** deposits. . . . I cannot adduce [bring forth] my inclination (e.g., in the present case my avarice) as a principle of determination fitted to be a universal law. (*Practical Reason,* p. 301)

To adopt happiness as a principle or policy of life, to adopt the universalized maxim that everyone should make their desire for their primary ends dictate to their will, means "the extreme opposite of harmony will follow, the greatest opposition and the complete destruction of the maxim itself and its purpose. For, in that case, the will of all has not one and the same object, but everyone has own (his private welfare)"(*Practical Reason,* p. 301). In short, to follow the maxim of happiness guarantees that there will be no social totality.

Kant thinks he has demonstrated that morals founded on natural laws, such as the universal desire for happiness, cannot provide the grounds for a communal, moral community. He thinks he has shown that this variant of moral psychology is inadequate to provide us with moral laws.

7.7 Exchanges Between the Sensible and Supersensible Worlds

Although Kant thinks humans occupy two worlds, these worlds are not sealed off from each other. Very briefly, the exchanges that take place between them do so through the medium of a maxim, which is a subjective, personal formulation of a policy of action when facing certain life situations.

Kant gives this example of a life situation, which we will examine more carefully later. You are in need of money and your only resource is borrowing it; however, your financial situation is so bleak that you know you won't be able to repay a loan. What should you do—promise to repay the money in order to get a loan, or refrain from such a "false" promise? There are two possible maxims to adopt here: (1) when in such a financial situation, I will promise to repay; (2) when in such a financial situation, I will refrain from such a promise.

This kind of situation occurs to us in the sensible world. Our sensible self is always motivated by self-love—that is, in a situation we always formulate an end that we conceive will satisfy the drive, need, want, or desire we are experiencing. Self-love, in short, leads us to formulate and contemplate an act that will achieve an end in that situation. This is expressed as a maxim.

If we acted only prudentially with an eye to our happiness, then we would adopt as our personal policy whatever maxim we believe will lead us to attain the desired end. But because we also participate in the supersensible world, there is more to our decision than prudential considerations. As residents of the supersensible world, we possess practical reason that enables

256 us to consider the morality of our maxim. As moral persons, we ask if the maxim can be a moral law. Can it be one that everyone can consistently adopt as their policy?

Because each act that we contemplate performing has an opposite—namely, not performing the act—maxims come in pairs. There are maxims of commission or of proposing an act, and maxims of omission or of refraining from the act. As moral beings, we have to make a choice between them. Should I promise to repay or should I refrain from promising? Kant thinks we ought to make a decision by asking which of these maxims may become a moral law for all. One of the issues we will take up later is Kant's theory of how we can determine whether or not a maxim can be a moral law.

As moral agents residing in the supersensible realm, we make a decision on the morality of a maxim and, if we are morally worthy and act out of respect for the law, we will will to do that act, select that maxim, which we believe is moral. Thus our supersensible existence affects the course of events in the sensible world when we act morally rather than prudentially. We can picture the exchange this way:

Sensible world: Coping with life, striving for happiness out of self-love, we formulate a pair of maxims which are sent to the ⎯⎯⎯⎯⎯⟶ *Supersensible world:* Here our practical reason determines which maxim may be made into a moral law; if we act morally, then we will an act that alters the course of events in

sensible world. ⟵⎯⎯⎯⎯⎯ the

7.8 Totality and Kant's Tragic Vision

Of course, if we are to improve morally the natural, sensible totality, it is not enough to find laws that may be universally followed without contradiction; everyone also has to follow them in their actions. According to the late Romanian philosopher Lucien Goldmann, this makes Kant's vision a tragic one. We cannot expect everyone to follow the laws to make the world into a new, morally perfect totality. To do that we would have to perfect ourselves. Further, in a perfect world, we would have to possess a happiness corresponding to our moral perfection; the degree of our happiness should match the degree of our moral worthiness. Alas, we are not, nor can we expect to become, morally perfect in this world; nor is there any guarantee that happiness would be distributed in proportion to this perfect worthiness to be happy.

To help us understand why Goldmann, as we shall see, thinks that

Kant's critical philosophy becomes "one of the great expressions of the tragic
vision of the world," we should look first at Kant's conception of the *summum bonum* (highest good), and second at why he thinks we cannot attain the *summum bonum*.

Humans possess reason. It is at once a blessing and a curse: a blessing because it ennobles us and a curse because it sets a task for us that we cannot attain. Pure practical reason ennobles us by setting the notion of *summum bonum* before us and frustrates us because it imposes on us the task of achieving it, of making a perfect world. Our intelligible existence, our reason, makes us try to reform the sensible world.

Kant notes that *summum* is ambiguous, since it has two meanings: "it may mean either the 'supreme' or the 'perfect.' (*Practical Reason,* pp. 337–40). Kant says he has shown that

> *virtue* (as worthiness to be happy) is the *supreme condition* . . . and therefore the *supreme* good. But it does not follow that it is the whole and perfect good as the object of desire of rational finite beings; for this requires happiness also. . . . There is one end . . . which we may presuppose as actual in all rational beings. . . . There is one purpose not only which they *can* have but which we can presuppose that they all *do* have by a necessity of nature. This purpose is happiness. (*Foundations,* p. 310)

Kant concludes that "virtue and happiness together constitutes the possession of the *summum bonum* in a person" (*Practical Reason,* p. 338).

Thus Kant embraces both meanings—"supreme" and "perfect"—of *summum* and thinks that both constitute the *summum bonum*. This gives Kant the notions he needs to conceive what is meant by the "highest good" in a world: "The distribution of happiness in exact proportion to morality (which is the worth of the person, and his worthiness to be happy) constitutes the *summum bonum* of a possible world" (pp. 338–39). From this, Kant can project a conception of what the highest good in the *best* of all possible worlds would be. Because "morality is the *supreme* good (as the first condition of the *summum bonum*), while happiness constitutes its second element" (p. 342), to make the *best* of all possible worlds will first require that each inhabitant of it act only and always in accord with moral laws. Without the harmony of consistent actions, without a community of ends of all persons, we could not have a moral *world,* a totality; but with it we will have a *moral world*—a supremely moral totality. And second, of course, in the *best* of all possible worlds the distribution of happiness is proportional to everyone's morality; since in this best of all possible worlds everyone will be supremely virtuous and therefore worthy of happiness, everyone should also be perfectly happy.

The tragedy of this vision of the "best of all possible worlds" should be as plain as the starry heavens above. Everyone supremely moral? And everyone perfectly happy? "What may I hope for?" asks Kant, recognizing that what we want most is to live in the best possible world. But this is

258 hopelessly impossible under our present conditions. Only if we were immortal could we hope to have the time to become supremely moral. Only if there is a benevolent, powerful deity that guarantees a happiness in proportion to our worthiness may we hope to be perfectly happy. However, Kant also shows that we can never prove we are immortal nor that God exists. So the very conditions that are necessary for what we most want to be realized are beyond assurance; hence, the basis for hope is unprovable and reduces our hope to just that—a mere hope. Still, our reason, which conceives of immortality and a God that doesn't suffer our limitations, confronts us with the "fact" that there are obligatory moral laws. Kant observes: "Thus the question: '*How is the summum bonum* practically possible?' still remains an unsolved problem" (*Practical Reason,* p. 339). The limitations of our intelligence and power that force the tragic on us are even more devastating than our inability to be perfectly moral. We could not bring about the *summum bonum,* even if we were perfectly moral and always willed only to act in accord with moral laws. We cannot bring it about because

> the practical connection of causes and effects in the world, as the result of the determination of the will, does not depend upon the moral dispositions of the will, but on the knowledge of the laws of nature and the physical power to use them for one's purposes; consequently, we cannot expect in the world by the most punctilious [strict] observance of the moral laws any necessary connection of happiness with virtue adequate to the *summum bonum.* (p. 340)

Achieving the best of all possible worlds requires complete knowledge and complete power, which only a deity could have; being perfectly moral isn't sufficient to make the best of all possible worlds.

Goldmann thought that because Kant emphasized the individual, the "I" rather than "*We,*" his philosophy was doomed to be an expression of the "tragic vision of the world"; but this emphasis, he points out, does give a grand vision of the meaning of individual existence:

> "What ought I to do?" It was only in asking this question—and by the way in which he asked it—that [Kant's] critical philosophy became one of the great expressions of the tragic vision of the world. . . . What can *I* do? If we reflect on the fact that we are here concerned with the overcoming of human limitations, then so long as the question is asked *in this form,* so long as the subject of the sentence is *I,* there is only one possible answer: *Nothing which can really overcome this limitation.*
>
> That is why in the critical philosophy (as in all tragedy) the question of *doing,* of action was no longer an attempt really to overcome the obstacles, really to resolve the problems; it no longer concerned the *realization of the whole,* but only the meaning of *individual existence.*[13]

But diverting our attention to the individual isn't of itself tragic. The tragic looms only for persons who can't exist without fulfilling themselves, who are driven to transform their projects into actions; it looms for them **259** because individuals through their actions can never by themselves carry out their moral mission, the mission of making a moral totality for everyone.

> For Kant the question "What ought I to do?" has only one sense: What ought I to do *to realize the absolute, the perfect totality, knowledge of the universe and the kingdom of ends?* This provides the only authentic meaning for human life whereby man can rise above the physical and the biological.
>
> Kant's reply is brief and straightforward, consisting of *one* premiss and *one* conclusion.
>
> The premiss: It must be shown (and is shown in the first two *Critiques*) that the totality is not [logically] impossible, that a hope exists—be it ever so small—of attaining and realizing it. For no man could consciously and unreservedly commit his existence to the pursuit of a goal which he knew to be necessarily unattainable.
>
> The conclusion: If there remains the *slightest hope* that somewhere, one day, in an intelligible world the absolute can be realized, then *act as if the maxim of your action were to become through your will a universal law of nature* [Kant's famous Categorical Imperative], that is, act *as if* the realization of the absolute depended only upon that single action which you are about to perform. . . .
>
> But Kant knows full well—and herein lies the tragedy—that in reality it does not depend only upon any single action. For the individual, for the man who acts, however, that is of no consequence. From the moment he accepts the existence of the slightest hope, he has no further choice. . . .
>
> "Through your will" expresses the grandeur of man. When he acts nothing external can determine his will or change its course, there can be no compromise, no distraction, for the fate of the community and of the universe, the absolute, depends upon that will alone.
>
> "As if"—that is the tragic limitation, for nothing essential in the external world really depends on this individual action. It will not change the world, still less other men. At most the individual will fulfill his own destiny, and even this only partially and imperfectly. He is now "worthy of happiness" but not really "happy," since for that the realization of the "highest good" would be necessary.

In a later book Goldmann writes that to understand a philosopher's views one needs to understand the structure of the philosopher's society and its effects on him or her: "Kant becomes more comprehensible if viewed as the philosopher of the tragic situation of the eighteenth-century German bourgeoisie, which aspired to a revolution that it was unable to bring about."[14]

Other historians of philosophy, searching for a connection between the social conditions and an individual's theories, connect Kant's emphasis on the role of reason in morals to the Enlightenment, which placed its bet on our rationality—a bet that Romantics thought was a sure loser.

It is a useful antidote to such historical speculations to note that Kant

260 may have learned from earlier thinkers. A contemporary Kantian scholar, Pepita Haezrahi, in an article entitled "The Concept of Man as End-in-Himself," calls attention to a passage in the Roman philosopher Marcus Aurelius' *Meditations* (Book IV, paragraph 4) that may have influenced Kant; we know Kant read the Stoics. The passage draws out the moral and political consequences of supposing that humans possess a common rationality.

> If our intellectual part is common, the reason also, in respect of which we are rational beings, is common; if this is so, common also is the reason which commands us what to do, and what not to do; if this is so, there is a common law also; if this is so, we are fellow-citizens; if this is so, we are members of some political community; if this is so, the world is in a manner a state. For of what other common political community will any one say that the whole human race are members? And from thence, from this common political community comes also our very intellectual faculty and reasoning faculty and our capacity for law; or whence do they come?[15]

STUDY QUESTIONS

1 Explain why Kant's distinction between the sensible and the supersensible (intelligible) worlds is important to his moral theory.
2 What relations did Kant think hold between dignity, autonomy, and rationality? Between a good will, freedom, and rationality?
3 Describe what Kant thinks is the best of all possible worlds.
4 State the "problem of evil."
5 What is Kant's "fact of reason"?
6 What exchanges take place between the sensible and supersensible world?

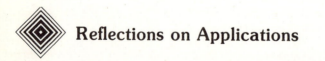 **Reflections on Applications**

1 Trader Vic is a successful restaurateur who, when interviewed by Ira Kamin, is reported to have said:

> I believe in the dignity of man. My relations to my fellow man are very important to me. It doesn't make a damn bit of difference whether he's got a million dollars or works for a living:—they're all human beings and we're forgetting too much about human beings. Greed has creeped into our economy and it's just spoiled our . . .
> You know, we recently had a Christmas party for our help.
> Three, four hundred people were there, with their children. It was

gratifying. All the kids were well groomed. They had nice cars. And they had a lot of dignity, and dignity to me is the whole goddam ball of wax.[16]

Is there anything in these remarks of Trader Vic that Kant would agree with, and is there anything he would disagree with? What and why?

2 What kind of comments do you think Kant might make on the following news story? Do you think that he might make use of the distinction between nonmoral and immoral?

> David Rachais, 22, has filed a complaint before the Commission for Racial Equality (in London) alleging that Toby, a mongrel dog, practices racial discrimination.
>
> "He always barks viciously at me," Trinidad-born Rachais charged. "White people walk past without being pestered, but as soon as he sees a black person it sets him off."
>
> Toby's owner, Jimmy Shelton, said it is true Toby barks only at blacks.
>
> "He never bites them, though. He just has a good bark. He ignores whites. We didn't train him that way. It was only after a few weeks that we noticed his prejudices," Shelton said.[17]

3 Rose Bird is Chief Justice of the California Supreme Court. Recently she wrote a column, "Philosophy," in which she made the following points:

> In America, racial intolerance has been, and is, one of the most divisive aspects of our society. We can deal with the problem legislatively, through civil rights acts and fair housing laws. We can deal with it administratively, through Fair Employment Practices Commissions and affirmative action programs. We can deal with it judicially, through school desegregation decisions.
>
> However, the ony way we can deal with racial intolerance directly is through the respect of one person for another person. . . .
>
> Another example of our lack of respect for each other is found in our treatment of the elderly. . . . And why do we treat the aged this way? Because we see them as something less than full persons, as somehow diminished. We lack respect for them as people.[18]

Relate Bird's comments to Kant's notion of a social totality.

Kant thinks that respect, dignity, and freedom are intimately related concepts. Can you use Bird's views as an illustration of the relations that Kant sees between these concepts?

4 Chief Justice Bird is fully aware that her remarks show that ours is not the best of all possible worlds. She is, of course, calling on us to make ours a better world. Our lack of respect for certain classes of persons

262   and the social problems this causes, such as the decay of inner cities, have to be corrected. She says:

> The key to dealing with these problems lies in the manner in which we deal with the precious resource of people. And that means education, which is an investment in people in the best possible sense of the word. Education teaches people to respect themselves, to respect each other, and to respect the world we all live in. Education is an ongoing experience, a life process.[19]

This reference to "education" is vague at best. If you were to make some suggestions about the nature of an education intended to increase our respect for ourselves and others, using Kant's point of view, what would you suggest?

5 The Question Man asked the following question of some young people: "Would you tell of an affair with a famous person?" Below are four answers. Which do you think reflect Kant's point of view and which reflect the moral psychologists' viewpoint? Think of "exchanges" between worlds. Explain the basis for your identification.

> Gail W.: Sure, I would. Like if I'd had an affair with Elvis or some movie star, sure, I'd tell my story. I'd go on the talk shows and sell my story to all the magazines. I think if it actually happened everybody would. They say they wouldn't because it hasn't happened, but if it really did happen, they'd think about the money.

> Liz R.: No, I would not tell if I had an affair with a famous person. I couldn't do anything like that because I believe in everyone having their right to privacy and I would not violate that right. I would have no respect for anyone who would take advantage of a personal situation. I would never betray a confidence.

> Edward F.: Yes, I'd have to tell. I'd have to be boastful. You just can't help your yourself on something like that. I don't know if I'd go and tell it on TV but I'd tell my fiancée or my mother. My mother would get mad and tell me I wasn't being a gentleman and then she'd go and tell my fiancée on me.

> Beverly L.: No, I wouldn't tell anything like that because that is personal. That isn't anybody's business. That is private and you don't go around talking about that no matter how famous the person is. Even if they offered me $5000 to write about it in one of the scandal magazines, I wouldn't.[20]

6 Even if one or more of the persons quoted above speaks from a moral psychological viewpoint, do you find that they reveal a knowledge of Kant's "fact of reason"? Explain.

7 What claim that Kant makes about us as rational beings does the following remark of President Nixon's aide John Ehrlichman, convicted for his role in the Watergate scandal, illustrate?

Ehrlichman said "an exaggerated sense of my obligation to do as I was bidden" had caused him to commit the crimes of which he was convicted. "In effect, I abdicated my moral judgment and turned it over to someone else," he said.[21]

8 How would you relate the aims of "liberation movements" to Kant's view that humans have dignity because (1) they have the capacity to give themselves laws and (2) they have the capacity to choose to follow those laws?

Notice that I used the word "capacity" twice in my question. Because the capacities in (1) and (2) are different, the conditions for their realization and for their frustration might be different; and, being different, the frustration of one might occur even though the other is realized. Below are some thoughts of Linda Phelps about the women's sexual liberation movement taken from her article "Female Sexual Alienation." From her remarks, what would you conclude about the separate realization and/or frustration of the two Kantian capacities?

Phelps thinks that the sexual revolution has produced nothing new at all. "What we have is simply a new, more sophisticated (and thus more insidious) version of male sexual culture":

> We have an "inner self" of reflection and thought but our body is part of the world "out there" of experience and material objects. This mind-body dualism is at the base of human power—our ability to reflect upon and then act upon the material world. Such power becomes destructive—as in schizophrenia—when the mind turns in on itself and never tests its perceptions in concrete reality.
>
> In this reverse process, the schizophrenic fails to develop the necessary unity between mind and body, takes refuge in a world of *symbols,* and thereby forfeits *experience.* In other words, a schizophrenic is someone who becomes accustomed to relating to symbol-objects rather than person-objects and in doing so loses all self-powers.
>
> I would argue that as females we are sexually schizophrenic, relating not to ourselves as self-directed persons, not to our partners as sexual objects of our desire, but to a false world of symbols and fantasy. . . .
>
> Sexual images of conquest and submission pervade our imagination from an early age and lay the basis for how we will later look upon experience and sex. . . . Rapunzel waits in her tower for years in hopes of the young prince who will free her body from imprisonment. . . .
>
> As females, then, we relate to symbol-objects rather than person-objects. Like the schizophrenic, we are alienated from our own experience and from our own self-powers of initiation. . . . The female is taught to be the object of sexual desires rather than to be a self-directed sexual being oriented toward another. . . . Caught between the demands of a male-dominated society and the demands of our own self-definition, we survive by fully accepting the masochistic symbol-world given to us by male society at the expense of our own experience.[22]

264   9 By a simple, straightforward argument, we can give a Kantian basis for children's liberation: persons are given their full dignity only if allowed to exercise their autonomy; because children are persons, they ought to be given their dignity; therefore children ought to be allowed to exercise their autonomy. Because Kant thinks that children can apprehend the fact of reason—that is, sort out acts done out of duty from those done out of self-love—perhaps they are capable of autonomy.

One consequence of this argument appears to be part of the view advanced by Dr. Alayne Yates, a psychiatrist and pediatrician. Her views were expressed in an interview with Philip Nobile, who said it was "probably the most controversial I have ever done."

> The controversy turns on Yates' revolutionary views on the sexual desires and behavior of children. Rather than repress the erotic instincts of the young, Yates urges total sexual liberation for them. In brief, she feels that kids should not only engage in sexual experimentation, but that parents should encourage them to do so. . . . Because, as Yates points out in "Sex Without Shame," sexual dysfunction afflicts half the nation's marriages, and such problems can be traced back to early childhood restrictions on this very natural and most pleasurable function.
>
>   Despite the utter amorality of her prescription, I believe Yates has an argument that should be heard. For she wants to save the children, too.[23]

Yates encourages masturbation ("reinforce the child's positive feelings about touching himself or herself"), does not discourage sibling incest ("I know a 4-year-old boy who had intercourse with a 6-year-old girl and neither seemed damaged by it"), and even thinks father-daughter incest may be beneficial ("The daughter must be young and therefore untouched by the religious and cultural taboos against incest").

Do you agree that children should be given autonomy over their sexual relations?

In thinking about this question, you should separate considerations about the right to autonomy from your views about the moral rightness or wrongness of Yates's views. After all, a child, in exercising its autonomy, might disagree with Yates and decide that sibling or parental incest is wrong. Further, although a child might think incest is morally right, this is not necessarily a good reason to restrict its autonomy; you wouldn't want your autonomy restricted just because you might make a moral mistake. The right to decide entails the right to decide wrongly.

Here are some of Kant's views on children and sex:

> All education must be free, so far as the pupil does not interfere with the freedom of others. The main ground of discipline on which freedom depends is that the child should recognize its position as a child and that its duties should all be derived from the consciousness of its childhood, age and limited capacities. The child ought not to exercise

greater powers than are in keeping with its years. It is a child and **265**
weak. . . .

The greatest care should be exercised that the passions, of which
the sexual passion is the strongest, are not abused. Rousseau asserts
that it is a father's duty to give his son at this age a complete conception of sex and make no secret of it, clearing his mind on the subject
and explaining the purpose of the desire and the harm that comes from
the abuse of it. He must represent to him on moral grounds the
heinousness [hatefulness] of the abuse of sex, and show him the
degradation of the worth of humanity in his own person which it entails. This is the last and most delicate point in education. It will be a
long time before schools recognize this, and in the meantime vice will
continue to be prevalent. (*Lectures,* pp. 249, 251)

Kant gives an argument against "self-defilement" or masturbation
that he thinks shows it to be immoral:

Just as the natural function of the love of life is to preserve the *individual,* so the natural function of sexual love is to preserve the *species;*
in other words, both of these are *natural purposes.* . . . Lust is called *unnatural* if man is aroused to it, not by its real object, but by his imagination
of this desire, since he himself creates its object by imagination. . . .

That such an unnatural use (and so misuse) of one's sexual power
is a violation of duty *to oneself* and, indeed, one which is contrary to
morality in the highest degree occurs to everyone immediately, along
with the thought of it, and stirs up an aversion from this thought to
such an extent that we consider it indecent even to call this vice by its
proper name. (*Virtue,* pp. 88–89)

10 Beth Winship, in her column "Ask Beth," gives an answer that may
have some Kantian elements in it. Do you think it does?

Dear Beth: From what everyone tells me, I'm beautiful and have a body
to match. I don't look 13, and guys of all ages go to bed with me. I
love it, but now it's got to be a habit I can't break. I have even gone
with some lesbians. Is there some kind of help I can get? I don't consider myself a tramp, I just want to break this habit. —Popular

It is good [Beth replies] you want to break the habit. Only the
young or foolish confuse sex with love. However, it takes tremendous
will power to stop sexual activity once you have started.

Think about where you are heading. Maybe you don't consider
yourself a tramp, but few people respect those who will bed down with
any and all comers. No relationship of mutual love or respect can
develop, and that is what makes people happy ultimately.[24]

11 Kant gave children and young people a lot of credit for their moral
discernment (ability to recognize the fact of reason). How would he
criticize the following remarks of William Allen White, taken from the

266   editorial he wrote upon the accidental death of his sixteen-year-old daughter?

> But the most fun she ever had in her life was acting as chairman of the committee that got up the big turkey dinner for the poor folks at the country home; scores of pies, gallons of slaw; jam, cakes, preserves, oranges, and a wilderness of turkey were loaded in the car and taken to the country home. . . . The poor she had always with her, and was glad of it. She hungered and thirsted for righteousness. . . .
>
> Above every other passion of her life was her passion not to grow up, to be a child. The tom-boy in her, which was big, seemed to loathe to be put away forever in skirts. She was a Peter Pan, who refused to grow up.[25]

12 Gordon King was a first-round draft choice to play tackle for the New York Giants. Although he agrees with Kant that we have a will and seems to agree that we humans have two aspects to our existence, do you think that Kant would agree with his attempt to break the will of his opponent? King says:

> There is an intangible entity, the "will," which imposes itself into any battle of the football pit. The competition down there is more than physical, more than big bodies on a collision course. If you can break your opponent, I mean break his will, you can make him give up. If you hit hard on every play as a pattern evolves, you can tell by the fourth quarter if a team is still in the game but has lost that mental edge.[26]

Somebody might argue that Kant could indeed agree, because football is only a game: nothing moral will be lost by breaking a person's will in that context. Furthermore, football is good training for the will, providing discipline and tests and will-strengthening exercises; it will hold a person in good stead when the moral going gets tough. (It was a familiar refrain that attributed the English success in wars to the training their officers got on "the playing fields of Eton.")

Do you agree that this argument shows Kant could agree with King's aim? After all, it is quite different from using torture to break a war prisoner's will, or to get a political opponent to give up his or her principles, or to make someone a pliable slave.

 **Reflections on Theory**

13 *Marx less optimistic than Kant.* There is an optimism in Kant about our ability to personally restrain the power of our desires, and thus there is an optimism about our ability to avoid doing wrong. Suppose,

however, that social forces in the sensible world are beyond our personal ability to change. Suppose further that the society in which people grow to maturity provides no instruction in the discipline needed to strengthen our will as Kant advocates. Karl Marx and Friedrich Engels describe such a society:

> [The bourgeoisie] has left remaining no other nexus [bond] between man and man than naked self-interest, than callous "cash payment." It has drowned the most heavenly ecstasies of religious fervor, of chivalrous enthusiam, of philistine sentimentalism, in the icy water of egotistical calculation. It has resolved personal worth into exchange value, and in place of the numberless indefensible chartered freedoms, has set up that single, unconscionable [unscrupulous] freedom, free trade. In one word, for exploitation, veiled by religious and political illusions, it has established naked, shameless, direct, brutal exploitation. The bourgeoisie has stripped of its halo every occupation hitherto honored and looked up to with reverent awe. It has converted the physician, the lawyer, the priest, the poet, the man of science, into its paid wage-laborers.[27]

Of course Marx and Engels advocated changing our world into a better one, just as Kant did. Their picture of capitalist society does not allow them, or us, to make a better world by personal acts of will; such change requires a social revolution and an alteration of the economic structure. They paint a pessimistic picture about our individual capacity to improve ourselves and the world.

Relate Marx and Engels's remarks to Goldmann's criticism of Kant (see pp. 258–59), and state what you think a Marxist would advocate as a necessary step to making a better world.

14 *Behaviorism against Kant.* Let us add to Marx and Engels's picture of bourgeois society certain aspects that have developed since they wrote. Since their time, behaviorist psychologists have learned a great deal about controlling animal and human behavior. This gives those in certain social positions and power a means of decreasing the personal freedom of others.

Vance Packard quotes the humanistic psychologist Carl Rogers: "We can choose to use our growing knowledge to enslave people in ways never dreamed of before, depersonalizing them, controlling them by means so carefully selected that they will perhaps never be aware of their loss of personhood."

Packard also quotes James McConnell: "I believe that the day has come when we can combine sensory deprivation with drugs, hypnosis and astute manipulation of reward and punishment to gain absolute control over an individual's behavior."

Packard continues:

> There are precise techniques for altering long-term behavior patterns in predictable ways. It was a Harvard psychologist named Burrhus

Frederic Skinner who did pioneer work on an aspect of behaviorism involving what is called operant conditioning.

Skinner conditioned pigeons to perform fairly complex feats by breaking each feat down into its component parts. The pigeon was rewarded with a food pellet for each correct move, no matter how slight. This gave the bird an incentive to repeat the move. To get a pigeon to walk in a circle, Skinner rewarded its first slight clockwise movement. Soon he had pigeons doing figure eights, dancing and playing a kind of table tennis. . . .

Skinner and others also conditioned animals to avoid certain prohibited behavior by setting up automatic punishments. . . .

To sum up: We fall into patterns of behavior desired by the controller because he gives us incentives (consequences) to repeat the pattern again and again. The incentives can be a positive reinforcer like candy, or a negative reinforcer like a whack from a stick. Negative reinforcers are also known as aversive stimuli.[28]

What would Kant's view of behavior control and modification be? Do you think that we are still free in Kant's sense, even if our behavior has been subjected to Skinner's operant conditioning? How would you relate psychological conditioning to "breaking the will"?

15 *Showing you understand Kant's theory.* Relate the following paragraph of Kant to as many points in this chapter as you can:

He who has *lost* at play may be *vexed* at himself and his folly, but if he is conscious of having *cheated* at play (although he has gained thereby), he must *despise* himself as soon as he compares himself with the moral law. This must, therefore, be something different from the principle of private happiness. For a man must have a different criterion when he is compelled to say to himself: "I am a *worthless* fellow, though I have filled my purse"; and when he approves himself, and says: "I am a *prudent* man, for I have enriched my treasure." (*Practical Reason,* p. 306)

16 *Kant as a marriage counselor.* Suppose that you were a marriage counselor with a Kantian outlook, and that you were faced with the following situation. Robert Coles found this situation in a book he was reviewing (Gerald Grant and David Riesman's *The Perpetual Dream,* concerning higher education). What advice would you give the couple?

They [students of St. John's college] also learn the importance of moral inquiry and ethical reflection. There is a decided emphasis on what the two sociologists [Grant and Riesman] describe as "the development of character." Young people are not asked, as part of the curriculum, to probe their fantasies, dreams, and free associations; they are asked to discipline their thinking and reflect upon the rights and wrongs of the world and how they may try to live a reasonably thoughtful, just, decent life. . . .

At a meeting of alumni, an attempt was made to find out how
their particular and unusual college education had affected those increasingly removed from it by time. One graduate remarked upon difficulties experienced in his marriage: "You must understand that I am a
chicken farmer and in order to make any money raising chickens you
must cheat. My wife blames St. John's for the fact that I won't."[29]

17 *Sexual liberation and the* summum bonum. Although Kant holds that
humans exist in two worlds, the sensible and the supersensible, each
with its respective ends of happiness and worthiness (the two parts of
the *summum bonum*), he also thinks these two worlds intersect.
Ideally, in fact, these two worlds should be unified and become one;
that is the point of achieving the *summum bonum*. We will deal with
the unification of the two worlds at more length later, for it poses a
problem. But for now, state how you think Linda Phelps's analysis in
Reflection 8 relates to this issue.

18 *Nietzsche and Kant's "tragic vision."* Below are some thoughts of
Nietzsche, taken from an article by Michael Zimmerman.[30] Zimmerman
says: "An essential presupposition for the concept of the Overman
[sometimes translated as "Superman"] is, of course, that man (or at
least *certain* men) can change and develop himself, i.e., that man can
create a way of existence for himself." Zimmerman then points out that
the obstacle to this creation comes not only from the "herd" but also
from ourselves: "Nietzsche claims that '. . . the worst enemy you can
encounter will always be you, yourself; you lie in wait for yourself in
caves and woods' " (p. 215). Zimmerman then quotes Nietzsche
(Walter Kaufman's translation of *Beyond Good and Evil):*

> The discipline of suffering, of *great* suffering—do you know that only
> *this* discipline has created all enhancement of man so far? That tension of
> the soul is unhappiness which cultivates its strength, its shudders face to
> face with great ruin, its inventiveness and courage in enduring, persever-
> ing, interpreting, and exploiting suffering, and whatever has been
> granted to it of profundity, secret, mask, spirit, cunning, greatness—was
> it not granted to it through suffering, through the discipline of great
> suffering? In man *creature and creator* are united; but in man there is
> material, fragment, excess, clay, dirt, nonsense, chaos; but in man there
> is also creator, form giver, hammer hardness, spectator divinity, and
> seventh day: do you understand the contrast?

This passage reads as if written by an excessively poetical Kant.
But it does appear to be good Kantian material.
However, another belief of Nietzsche's is quite un-Kantian. "For
Nietzsche," says Zimmerman, "the vast majority of human beings are
incapable of creating something with their lives" (p. 226). If this is true
and Kant is wrong, do you think this Nietzschean view provides an

270   alternative basis for thinking of Kant's philosophy as "a tragic vision"? Contrast this to Goldmann's basis for interpreting Kant's philosophy as "a tragic vision."

19 *Desires, interests, and inclinations cannot be universalized.* Does the following passage from R. N. Hare agree with any of Kant's views? Which?

> As was suggested earlier, we might say that to have an interest is for there to be something which one wants (or may want), or which is (or may be) a means, necessary or sufficient, for the attainment of something which one wants (or may want). Now it is . . . characteristic of desires that they are not universalizable. . . . Desires do not have to be universal. To want to have something does not commit the wanter to wanting other people, in the same circumstances, to have it. A moderately selfish man may want to have enough to eat without wanting everyone, or even everyone in like circumstances, to have enough to eat. It follows that interests likewise are not universalizable; what it is in one person's interests to have, it is not necessarily in his interest that anyone else should have.[31]

20 *Can you distinguish the sensible from the supersensible?* Concerning the sensible and intelligible worlds, Kant has written:

> *Sensuality* is the *receptivity* of a subject by which it is possible for the subject's own representative state to be affected in a definite way by the presence of some object [i.e., objects can cause us to have visual, auditory, and other sensations]. *Intelligence* (rationality) is the faculty of a subject by which it has the power to represent things which cannot by their own quality come before the senses of that subject. The object of sensuality is the sensible; that which contains nothing but what is to be cognised [known] through the intelligence is intelligible. In the schools of the ancients the first was called a *phenomenon* and the second a *noumenon*.[32]

This is going to be a difficult question. If you haven't had some epistemology (philosophy of knowledge), you probably can't answer it without the aid of your teacher; with that aid, the question will help you get at the core of Kant's ethics.

The question: Which of the items in the following list do you think are sensibles (phenomena) and which are intelligibles (noumena)? What standard (s) do you use to make your division?

Blue	Shape	Taste	Acrid
Color	Space	Part and Whole	Infinite
Existence	Substance	Regularity	Decency
Necessity	Obligatory	Tragic	Pleasant
Square	Cause	God	Sour
Air	Time	Totality	

21 *Kant's theory of morality is self-contradictory (Bradley).*   F. H . Bradley   **271**
agreed with a good deal of what Kant says about ethics. He wrote:
"The field of morality we find is the whole field of life; its claim is as
wide as self-realization." [33]

Not all of self-realization is morally relevant, however, because
"we come into direct collision with the moral consciousness, which
clearly distinguishes moral from other excellence, and asserts that the
latter is not in itself moral at all; and . . . we find the deliverance of
that consciousness in the emphatic maxim that nothing is morally good
save a good will" (p. 206).

Bradley describes the process of moral self-realization: "It has two
sides or elements which can not be separated; (1) the position of an
ideal self, and the making of that actual in the will; (2) the negation,
which is inherent in this, the making unreal (not by annihilation but
transformation) of the for ever unsystematized natural material, and the
bad self" (p. 211).

Bradley then proceeds to comment on this process. Do you think
that these comments do or do not show that Kant's (and Bradley's)
moral theory is wrong? Or is there a way of interpreting Bradley's
remarks that save the theory?

> Morality does involve a contradiction; it does tell you to realize that
> which never can be realized, and which, if realized, does efface itself as
> such. No one ever was or could be perfectly moral; and if he were, he
> would be moral no longer [but holy].
> Where there is no imperfection there is no ought, where there is no
> ought there is no morality, where there is no self-contradiction there is
> no ought. The ought is a self-contradiction. Are we to say then that
> that disposes of it? Surely not, unless it also disposes of ourselves; and
> that cannot be. At least from this point of view, we are a self-
> contradiction: we never are what we feel we really are; we really are
> what we know we are not; and if we become what we are, we should
> scarcely be ourselves. Morality aims at the cessation of that [imperfec-
> tion] which makes it possible; it is the effort after non-morality
> [holiness], and it presses forward beyond itself to a super-moral sphere
> where it ceases as such to exist. (pp. 211–12)

8
Kant's Theories
of the Will
and Moral Laws

8.1 Self-Realization and a Rational Will

Let us review our argument to this point, so that we can place it within a dialectical framework.

Ivan Ilyich was ordinary; he wished too late that he had not been ordinary. Nietzsche despised the "herd," whose members are ordinary. He advocated replacing a "herd-morality" with a "master-morality." Marin considers Nietzsche's solution too extremely egoistic because we ought to have a socially responsible point of view. But to avoid equating a social point of view with a herd morality, every member of a social group must be able to be "unordinary"; otherwise, we become one of Nietzsche's "despicable" persons, living a life of callow conformity as Ilyich did.

Implied in the reflections of Ilyich, Nietzsche, and Marin is the belief that we can make ourselves, in whole or in part; their views presuppose that people are capable of self-realization.

Initially, we may be sympathetic to Ilyich's despair. We may shun his fate, perhaps wish to become existentially authentic, scorn Nietzsche's despicables, and favor—maybe vaguely and abstractly—some form of Marin's solution for combining social responsibility with personal dignity. However, we found that these sympathies, avoidances, wishes, aversions, and favorings wilt before the theory that our ready-made human nature defies alteration by individual effort. Moral psychology makes self-realization of a wholly new, better self impossible: ultimately, we are evolutionary products of nature, and all our conduct is a causal consequence of the impact of our environment filtered through our human nature. This nature, locked in our genes, is alterable only within limits, which can be redrawn through the evolutionary process alone.

I argued, then, that moral psychology, in both its simpler and its more sophisticated sociobiological form, explains human behavior inadequately, because it cannot account for moral behavior. However, criticizing a theory of morals is easier than creating a better theory. Kant both criticized moral psychology and formulated an alternative theory that he claimed was better. Moral psychology, according to him, is a theory of happiness and prudential behavior rather than a theory of morals. Moral psychologists confuse happiness and worthiness, which are not the same; since only worthiness is a moral datum, moral psychology is not a theory of morals. Consequently, neither can it be a theory of moral self-realization.

Kant tried to show how to achieve moral self-realization. He provided a theory that, if correct, turns our wish not to be like Ilyich into an attainable end. Furthermore, Kant maintained a powerful belief that we should avoid being despicable; dignity and freedom and self-esteem were as important to him as to Nietzsche. (See the quote from Nietzsche in Reflection 18 on p. 269.) But, unlike Nietzsche, he thought that we could be both dignified and socially and morally responsible; being moral doesn't doom us to the herd. *Kant assumed the task of showing us both how to form a moral/social totality, and how to self-realize our freedom and dignity.* If he succeeded, then he will have supplied the moral theory to underwrite Marin's and perhaps your own hope for a better society that preserves the dignity that comes with freedom. While Kant's importance justifies the fairly extended discussion I give him, I stress his thought primarily because he has formulated a more adequate, straightforward, and uncompromising opposition to moral psychology than any other philosopher. At the same time, I have given moral psychology a lot of space, so the opposition, too, should be adequately represented.

I have said that Kant's ethics is an ethics of self-realization; it claims that the only thing that is morally good without qualification is a good will, and that our moral task is to attain a good will, to become morally worthy. I am going now to shift the emphasis from self-realization to will, and accordingly I shall refer to Kant's moral theory as a "rational will" ethics. The terms "rational will" and "practical reason" are interchangeable.

The point of this name shift is to emphasize Kant's view that morality and moral self-realization are possible only because we possess a rational will. Prior to my discussion of Kant in this book, I have not stressed the concept of the will, which some people equate with a "free" will. For many others besides Kant, there is no such thing as morality, if humans don't have a will; unless each of us wills an act freely, we aren't responsible for it or its consequences, and if we aren't responsible, then we can't be morally blamed or praised. Kant agrees: if we do not have a rational will—if our reason is not practical—then all morality is an illusion. Without a rational will, we are purely the creatures of nature that moral psychologists claim we are, and their theoretical approach to human conduct is the only possible and correct one; without a rational will, the "moral" factor that accounts for human behavior is our prudence in pursuing our happiness. Without a rational will, of the two components of the *summum bonum*—happiness and worthiness—only happiness remains as a human value. The discussion of human life can then be included solely within the discourse of happiness and striving for happiness, whether (as egoism would have it) only our own, or (as altruism would have it) the happiness of others as well. Every act is to be appraised solely in terms of its usefulness in gaining happiness—our own or others'. Any so-called ethical disagreements that remain—whether, for example, we are to pursue our own or others' happiness—can in the end be settled factually by an adequate psychosociobiological science. Without a rational will, which Hume denied we have, Hume's approach to ethics must be the correct one.

Here now is Kant's view of what is at stake: "Without this freedom of a rational will (in the latter and true sense), . . . no moral law and no moral imputation are possible."[1]

276   8.2 Kant's Theory of Will: *Wille* and *Willkür*

8.2a. THE RATIONAL ASPECT OF WILL (*WILLE*). I have said that "rational will" and "practical reason" are interchangeable. The central idea of these two phrases is that reason is practical because it, as well as our sensible inclinations (the feelings associated with desires, wants, and drives), can cause action. "Will" is the popular term for the faculty that some believe enables us deliberately to cause our bodies to move. Kant's "rational will," we should understand, is not two things, reason and will, but one thing with two aspects, which he calls *"Wille"* and *"Willkür."* Let's consider *Wille* first.

As *Wille,* practical reason does two things: (1) it is the faculty with which we give ourselves moral laws and so is our autonomy, our positive, legislating freedom; (2) when we think about these moral laws, it causes a feeling of pleasure in us that Kant calls "moral feeling." Feeling, Kant believes, moves our bodily, sensible selves to action; because reason *(Wille)*, as well as our desires, can supply us with feeling, we can simultaneously have two feelings, either of which can move us:

> In order to will that which reason alone prescribes to the sensuously affected rational being as that which he ought to will, certainly there is required a power of reason to instill a feeling of pleasure or satisfaction in the fulfillment of duty, and hence there must be a causality of reason to determine the sensibility in accordance with its own principles.[2]

Reason is practical because it can cause moral feeling in us, which in turn can cause action. The feelings of inclination may be present simultaneously with moral feelings, and they too can cause action.

Feeling, for Kant, is the capacity for pleasure and pain, which can be aroused in different ways. First, we can arouse them by mentally representing an object or end to ourselves. For example, I am hungry and imagine eating a three-star meal and so am filled with anticipatory pleasure; or I imagine it's being too expensive for my wallet and am filled with the pain of frustration. Second, the feelings can be aroused by actually eating a three-star meal: I am filled with pleasure if it is delicious or with pain if it is tasteless. Third, a pleasurable moral feeling is aroused when we mentally represent a moral law to ourselves, as for example when I think about my obligation to contribute to the happiness of others, perhaps by buying a hungry person a hearty meal.

Kant's advocacy of a rational will *(Wille)*, and its causal power to generate moral feeling, led him to revise the moral psychologists' links diagram of the connections between human powers and acts. It now reflects the dual nature of persons, incorporating both our sensible and supersensible (intelligible) aspects.

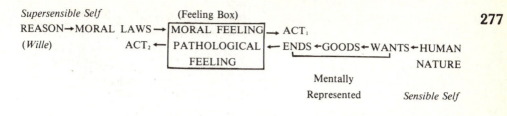

Supersensible Self

REASON→MORAL LAWS → │ MORAL FEELING │→ ACT₁

(Wille) ACT₂ ← │ PATHOLOGICAL │ ← ENDS ←GOODS←WANTS←HUMAN

│ FEELING │ NATURE

(Feeling Box)

Mentally
Represented   *Sensible Self*

8.2b. THE FREE CHOICE ASPECT OF WILL (*WILLKÜR*). In

the preceding section I outlined Kant's ideas of reason's practical powers
(Wille), which give us autonomy for legislating moral laws and causing moral
feeling—powers we must have if there is to be morality over and above
prudence. These powers are necessary also if we are to be capable of moral
self-realization.

Kant presents one of the most sophisticated theories of will; to his
theory of rational will *(Wille)* outlined above, we have to add his theory of
free choice, which he calls *Willkür*. Many English translators unfortunately
use the same word, "will," to translate Kant's *Wille* and *Willkür*. I will
follow the suggestion of John Silber (in his introduction to *Religion*) and
distinguish them by using "will" for *Wille* and "will^w" for *Willkür*.

In exercising *Willkür's* power we choose between two feelings, a
pathological and a moral feeling, represented in the "feeling box" of Kant's
links diagram. *Willkür's* function is to choose which one will cause an act.
Because we are sensible and supersensible beings, we can have these two kinds
of feelings simultaneously. By "pathological" feeling Kant doesn't mean
something diseased; he means the natural feeling aroused by the wants and
desires of our sensible self. For example, suppose I am in desperate need of
money. The thought of borrowing inclines me to promise to repay someone
who can lend me money, even though I know I won't be able to do so. This is
the pathological feeling of anticipatory pleasure. But at the same time I think
about this policy, this maxim of "falsely" promising, and realize that the
moral law bids me *not* to promise falsely, which causes in me a moral feeling
of pleasure at the thought of doing what I ought to do.

ANDY CAPP by Reggie Smythe. © 1975, Daily Mirror Newspaper, Inc. Dist. by Field Newspaper Syndicate

We are now faced with the presence of two feelings. The pathological one will cause me to promise falsely; the moral one will cause me to refrain from promising falsely. The act I will perform depends upon which feeling I choose. The power of *Willkür,* which is the power of free choice, enables me to pick one or the other. If I have a "good will," which Kant thinks the only thing that is without qualification morally good, then I will subordinate the pathological feeling to the moral one and restrain my sensible inclination. I will make myself morally worthy; my supersensible self will initiate a course of action in the sensible world that will improve that world.

Kant gives an example where our moral and pathological feelings would cause the *same* act, rather than different acts:

> For example, it is in fact in accordance with duty that a dealer should not overcharge an inexperienced customer, and wherever there is much business the prudent merchant does not do so, having a fixed price for everyone, so that a child may buy of him as cheaply as any other. (*Foundations,* p. 298)

The desire for profit may cause a prudent merchant, looking to his long-term interest, not to take advantage of an inexperienced customer; a moral feeling caused by the thought of honesty will also cause the merchant not to take advantage. Here the same act—not taking advantage of an inexperienced customer—may be caused by either a moral or a pathological feeling.

When our duty and desire cause the same act, Kant thinks it difficult to determine which feeling we have actually chosen; it could have been either: "For man cannot so scrutinize the depths of his own heart as to be quite certain, in even a single action, of the purity of his moral purpose."[3] Since we are morally worthy only if we have acted because it was our duty—an act caused by moral feeling alone—in such cases it is difficult to tell whether or not we have acted virtuously. Moral congratulations are not in order if we have treated a child honestly simply because we thought we would make more profit in the long run. In that event we have looked to our own happiness, acting out of self-love rather than out of fairness to the child; our act of honesty was caused by pathological rather than moral feeling.

There are times, however, when we do know which feeling caused the act. Suppose I am a fly-by-night merchant who does not have to worry about the consequences to my future profit if I charge a child more than I do a knowledgeable customer. In this case my desire for a quick profit, if unchecked, will cause me to cheat the child. I will know that I have acted from the pathological rather than the moral feeling, because the moral feeling of pleasure at the thought of honesty would have caused me not to cheat the child, had I chosen it over my wish for a quick profit.

Our tragic human condition arises because, in a conflict between duty and inclination arising from our dual nature, we are not always able to choose the moral feeling; our *Willkür* is sometimes too weak. The fly-by-night merchant has two feelings in conflict because each, if acted on, would cause an act contrary to the other: in one case he would treat the child honestly, in the other dishonestly. He would be responsible for either act; in one instance he would deserve praise and in the other blame; one act would make him morally worthy and the other morally unworthy. Since blame and praise presuppose *Can,* this means that we are free to be either morally worthy or unworthy, to act honestly or dishonestly, to be good or evil. In Kant's view, if we are to be free, we must have the freedom to choose to act from either the moral or the pathological feeling. If only the pathological feeling can cause an act, as Hume and other moral psychologists claim, then we are not free and consequently lack moral power.

279

It is our *Willkür* power, our freedom to choose whether to subordinate our pathological to our moral feeling or vice versa, that makes us moral beings. Animals, on the other hand, have no *Willkür* power; they act only and always from pathological feeling. Further, having no *Wille* power—no rational capacity to give themselves moral laws—they lack what is needed to cause a moral feeling.

Kant maintains that the distinction between good and evil persons depends on the tendency of choice. Virtue is the tendency to choose moral over pathological feelings:

> Hence the distinction between a good man and one who is evil . . . must depend upon *subordination,* . . . *i.e., which of the two incentives* [feelings] *he makes the condition of the other.* . . . He [the good man] adopts, indeed, the moral law along with the law of self-love; yet when he becomes aware that they remain on a par with each other [and therefore conflict], . . .he makes the incentive of self-love and its inclinations the condition of [subordinate to] obedience to the moral law.[4]

How does *Willkür* do it? It is a mystery (*Religion* p. 17). *Willkür* is pure spontaneity. This absolute spontaneity is what some people refer to as "free will," although it is more accurately called "free choice." Sometimes people who claim we have "free will" mean that some acts of ours are uncaused. This cannot be what Kant means, however, because every act for him is caused by a feeling, by either a moral or a pathological feeling. This power of free choice cannot be scientifically understood:

> But freedom [of choice] is a mere idea, the objective reality of which can in no way be shown according to natural laws or in any possible experience. . . . It holds only as the necessary presupposition of reason in a being that believes itself conscious of a will, i.e., of a faculty different from the mere faculty of desire. (*Foundations*, p. 337)

Although we cannot have a scientific, theoretical understanding of *Willkür*, practically we are not helpless. Because we are able to become virtuous, we can acquire a disposition to choose to act from the motive of moral feeling rather than inclination. We are born with a capacity for good moral

280 character, but its actualization requires that we strengthen our *Willkür* power so that when both a moral and a pathological feeling are present, we are able to subordinate the pathological to the moral feeling; we must do this whether the feelings conflict or not, in order to be morally worthy:

> Virtue here has as its steadfast maxim conduct *conforming to law*. . . . Virtue in this sense is won *little by little* and, for some men, requires long practice (in observance of the law) during which the individual passes from a tendency to vice, through gradual reformation of his conduct and strengthening of his maxims, to an opposite tendency. For this to come to pass a *change of heart* is not necessary, but only a *change of practices*. . . . But if a man is to become not merely *legally*, but *morally*, a good man, . . . that is, a man endowed with virtue in its intelligible [supersensible] character and one who, knowing something to be his duty, requires no incentive other than this representation of duty itself, *this* cannot be brought about through gradual *reformation* . . . but must be effected through a *revolution* in the man's disposition. . . . He can become a new man only by a kind of rebirth, as it were a new creation, and a change of heart. (*Religion*, pp. 42–43)

Ultimately our moral self-realization and worthiness depend upon acquiring virtue, which is the strength of character to choose moral feeling as the cause of our actions; this is the lonely moral task that Kant assigns us:

> Man *himself* must make or have made himself into whatever, in a moral sense, whether good or evil, he is or is to become. Either condition must be an effect of his free choice[w] [Willkür]; for otherwise he could not be held responsible for it and could therefore be *morally* neither good nor evil. (*Religion*, p. 40)

To summarize: morality and the self-realization of moral worthiness depend upon a rational will or practical reason, according to Kant. This practicality of reason is analyzed into three powers:

(1) the power to give ourselves moral laws, which Kant calls autonomy or positive freedom *(Wille);*

(2) the power of reason to instill in us a moral feeling, which is the feeling of pleasure at the thought of the moral law;

(3) the spontaneous power to choose whether a moral or a pathological feeling will cause our act, which Kant calls negative freedom or free choice *(Willkür).*

Caution yourself against a common misinterpretation of Kant. He does not share the Christian fundamentalist view that I recently saw expressed on a bumper sticker:

> The Devil gives Want/Power
> God gives Will/Power

This kind of thinking supposes that our sensible self is the source of evil; it **281** labels bodily wants, desires, and inclinations as moral misfortunes. Kant, on the contrary, thinks that satisfaction of wants is happiness, which is one of the elements of the *summum bonum*; thus wants and happiness are not in themselves evil or the Devil's work. We are evil only when we fail to subordinate to our moral feeling a conflicting pathological feeling of inclination. In that case we allow our pathological feeling to cause an act that we know is contrary to our duty; deliberately allowing this is what is evil:

> The proposition, Man is *evil*, can mean only, He is conscious of the moral law but has nevertheless adopted into his maxim the (occasional) deviation therefrom. (*Religion*, p. 27)

> Now the ground of this evil cannot be placed, as is so commonly done, in man's *sensuous nature* and the natural inclinations arising therefrom. (p. 30)

> Natural inclinations, *considered in themselves, are good,* that is, not a matter of reproach, and it is not only futile to want to extirpate [eliminate] them but to do so would also be harmful and blameworthy. Rather, let them be tamed and instead of clashing with one another they can be brought into harmony in a wholeness which is called *happiness*. Now the reason which accomplishes this is termed *prudence*. But only what is opposed to the moral law is evil in itself, absolutely reprehensible. (p. 51)

The only thing that can be opposed to the moral law is our will^w; only a will^w, then, and not inclinations, is evil. Or, more accurately, humans may be evil only because they have failed to develop a good will—that is, failed to develop a character disposed to put moral feeling uppermost. God, as represented in most Christian religions, doesn't have a good will, but a *holy* will. God is a purely intelligible being; as such, God has no pathological feeling; hence only the thought of the law can cause God to act. God, unlike humans, does not have to struggle against inclinations to realize a good will.

Although Kant's detailed theory is complex, his grand strategy is not; it is very simple. Kant proposed a dual nature of humans—sensible and supersensible—because he thought it was the only way that we could make sense of moral experiences. Without the supersensible world and without supersensible selves with rational wills, he believed there wouldn't be any morality. It's that simple.

Kant thought that if we humans are wholly sensible, natural creatures, we must be completely determined causally by natural laws, which means we are as unfree as insects to choose our acts and our moral character. He thought that we must say good-bye to morality if we aren't free to determine our acts and our character, and that we can determine them only if we partake of the supersensible world.

282   8.3 Natural Laws

You may wonder if Kant's supersensible world is anything more than an "airy nothing" to which his pen has given "a local habitation and a name." So you may well ask, "How can I understand the nature of these two worlds?"

The thread to follow in answering these questions is the concept of laws. Kant thought that natural laws are the threads that stitch the natural world together, and that moral laws bind supersensible selves into the supersensible world. Consequently, in inquiring into our sensible and supersensible natures, we are led to inquire into the sensible and supersensible worlds, from which in turn we are led to inquire into the nature of natural and moral laws. Persons, their worlds, and their worlds' laws are connected concepts; they cannot be understood separately, only jointly.

My strategy for the remainder of this and the next section is to examine four features of natural laws and to explain in what ways Kant thought moral laws were like them and in what ways not. I will also relate these laws to our sensible nature, which is causally determined by natural laws, and to our supersensible nature, which is free from natural laws and able to give itself its own moral laws and follow them.

There are four features of natural laws we should consider in seeing why our sensible selves are causally determined and unfree. These features provide Kant with his model for moral laws, some of whose features—conditional form and universality—are similar, while others—necessity and direction—are only analogous. When the true statement of a natural law is conditional, universal, necessary, and directional, then we can affirm the existence of a causal relation between events.

Conditional form. Natural laws have an "if . . . then . . ." form. What follows the *if* is a statement referring to and describing some antecedent condition or conditions, as for example, "if the water in a closed container is heated." What follows the *then* is a statement that refers to and describes the consequent event, as for example, "then the pressure in the container increases." This conditional form expresses a relation between events such that the occurrence of the consequent event is conditional upon the occurrence of the antecedent event or events (the conditions).

Universality. Natural laws cover *kinds* of events. Suppose that one event, E_1, is said to be conditionally related to another event, E_2. This gives us: if E_1, then E_2. To elevate this relation to a natural law, we now have to give it universality, which can be done by saying that every time an event of kind E_1 occurs, it will be the condition for the occurence of an event of kind E_2. This gives us: *always* when (or if) event of kind E_1, then event of kind E_2. For example: always when (if) the water in a closed container is heated, the pressure in the container increases.

Necessity. In a natural law, the conditional relation stated between events of kinds E_1 and E_2 is said to be necessary. This is a modal feature—a mode of connection—of natural laws; what it adds to the universalized condi- **283** tional relation can be intuitively grasped by contrasting two examples.

Suppose the following happens to be true: always when (if) someone names their male child "Edmund," then it rains in Monrovia. Now consider this example: always when (if) a sharp diamond edge is pressed with five pounds' pressure against slate and pulled across it, then a scratch is made on the slate.

(Notice that, although I have spoken of a single antecedent event of kind E_1 in natural laws, there might be a conjunction of antecedent events and conditions that have to be satisfied before we can truly assert a natural law relation between antecedent and consequent. Think of the complicated set of events and conditions necessary and sufficient to split an atom in a linear accelerator. Or think of the complicated and still undiscovered set of events and conditions sufficient for various kinds of weather to occur!)

Which of the following two statements, with the modal term "necessarily" prefacing them, would you be more likely to accept as true?

> Necessarily always when (if) someone names their male child "Edmund," then it rains in Monrovia.
>
> Necessarily always when (if) a sharp diamond edge is pressed with five pounds' pressure against slate and pulled across it, then a scratch is made on the slate.

Although the universal, conditional relation between all past Edmund-namings and rain in Monrovia might be true *in fact,* this is purely accidental; hardly anyone would suppose that naming someone "Edmund" is the *cause* of rain in Monrovia. What do you think the government in Monrovia would do during a drought if they believed that there was a causal relation?

Now contrast this with your confidence that, after a vandal had taken his diamond ring to it, a clean slate would surely (necessarily) have scratches on it. The basis of your confidence, according to some philosophers, is your belief in a causal connection between the moving diamond and the scratch on the slate.

Philosophers distinguish between causal necessity and logical necessity. For example, although it is true that "Necessarily always when (if) today is Tuesday, then tomorrow will be Wednesday," this relation between days of the week is said to be logically necessary but not causally necessary, because no one supposes that today's being Tuesday *causes* tomorrow's being Wednesday. Causal necessity is a mode of relation between events. Logical necessity is, according to one theory, a mode of relation between statements or concepts. For example, the two statements "Today is Tuesday" and "Tomorrow is Wednesday" are logically related in "If today is Tuesday, then tomorrow is Wednesday." The truth of the first statement necessarily entails the truth of the second.

Direction. Usually those who claim that causal relations are between events, distinguish the event referred to in the antecedent from the event

284 referred to in the consequent by speaking of the first as the "cause" and of the second as the "effect." Direction is a feature of natural laws because it is said that the causal relation, like time, goes in one direction. The effect can't cause the cause; for an event to be the cause event of an effect event, it must precede the effect event.

Let's relate these features of natural laws to the determinism of our sensible selves and its consequence for freedom and morality. Suppose there is a set of natural laws consistent with one another, and suppose also that *every* sensible event is described by the consequent of some natural law. What results? The events belong to the same totality, which is the sensible, natural world; and every event in this totality is predetermined necessarily to occur by an antecedent event.

Kant thinks this is true of our natural world. He thinks all events in the sensible totality, including the actions of sensible selves, are predetermined (*Religion*, note, p. 45). Because we had no control over the intertwined, indefinitely long series of causal relations that preceded the present state of the world, we have no control over the next set of events, including our own actions.

The conclusion is that we are not free—at least, our sensible selves aren't. But, Kant argued, if we are not free, then morality is an illusion, and praise and blame cannot justly be applied to us on the basis of our having freely chosen to be, respectively, morally worthy or unworthy. Yet Kant says that *morality is not an illusion;* therefore, there must be another, nonsensible aspect to ourselves that is free and not predetermined. (Kant's answer to the charge that it is inconsistent to say we are both predetermined and free is outlined in 13.3 and 13.4.)

Having learned something about natural laws, let us turn now to a discussion of moral laws. This discussion will tell us how Kant conceives the supersensible aspect of ourselves. I will explain later how Kant believes we can identify moral laws by the use of the Categorical Imperative.

8.4 Moral Laws

Kant emphatically denies that moral laws can be drawn from experience (*Practical Reason*, Theorems I and II). One reason for this is that moral laws share with natural laws the modality of necessity. Because necessity is not something we can experience through our senses, moral laws cannot be drawn from sensible experience. Further, necessity is a concept of our reason; therefore, moral laws must be a product of our reason. (See *Practical Reason,* pp. 301–05. For another argument against an empirical source of moral laws, which is based on the variation of our wants, see the first quotation from Kant on p. 254.)

With respect to necessity, it appears from the two arguments just stated **285** that moral and natural laws are similar. So far as that statement goes, this is true. However, there is also a difference between them; moral and natural necessity, although they both spring from reason, apply to different relations. Let's see why. The discussion will cover all four features of natural laws distinguished in the preceding section, 8.3, but with special emphasis on the modal feature of necessity.

Conditional form. Moral laws share the "if . . . then . . ." conditional form with natural laws. The various ingredients that go into the antecedent condition will be identified in my discussion of Kant's notion of maxims of action (9.4). The consequent of a moral law is a human act. Moral laws express a conditional relation between antecedent conditions and consequent acts.

Universality. A moral law is one that other things being equal, is to be obeyed always, regardless of person, whenever a certain kind of antecedent condition or conditions occur. A certain kind of antecedent calls for a certain kind of act—for example, a generous act or telling the truth. This feature is also called "generality" by some philosophers.

Universality is an important feature of moral laws, which express our duties. If duties didn't apply to *all* persons, then there would be persons excepted from following the moral law. But if some persons are excepted, they would be granted a privilege. Enjoying a privilege is having the license—that is, the freedom—of acting or not acting, whereas when we have a duty, everyone is enjoined to act or refrain and no one has the luxury of license. Therefore, if we are to distinguish between privilege and duty—a distinction which everyone acknowledges—then we have to allow that duty does not except anyone. That is, it applies universally. If it didn't, then a moral law would grant us a privilege rather than impose a duty. This is impossible; therefore, a moral law must apply to and be obeyed by *all,* when the antecedent conditions are satisfied. If it is a duty not to steal, then no one may steal; no one is excepted.

The following parable, adapted from R. M. Hare's *Freedom and Reason,*[5] shows the intuitive plausibility of claiming that moral laws are universal.

Deadbeat owes you $5,000; you owe Bankman $5,000. The loans are past due. It is a law in your country that creditors may have their debtors put in prison for nonpayment of overdue loans. Should you take this measure against Deadbeat in order to make him pay? You may no doubt be *inclined* to do this, or *want* to do this. Therefore, if there were no question of universalizing your prescriptions, you would readily assent to the *singular* prescription, "Let *me* put Deadbeat in prison." But if you intend to turn this prescription into a *moral judgment,* and say, "I *ought* to put Deadbeat in prison because he won't pay me what he owes," you realize that this would commit you to the principle: "*Anyone* who is in my position ought to put his debtor in prison if he doesn't pay." But now you reflect that Bankman is in the same position of unpaid creditor with respect to you that you are with respect to

286   Deadbeat. If anyone in this position *ought* to put his debtors in prison, then Bankman ought to put you in prison, too. Should you decide to take action against Deadbeat without acknowledging that Bankman can do the same against you, you are acting not on a moral principle but on an inclination or your desire. You have given yourself a privilege but have not prescribed a moral law.

Marcus Singer says that moral judgments and moral principles of action possess "implicit generality." He says this about the generalization principle for moral action:

> Thus the generalization principle can be formulated in any of the following ways. What is right for one person cannot be wrong for another, unless there is some relevant difference in their natures or circumstances. Or, what is right (or wrong) for one person must be right (or wrong) for everyone, if there is no reason to the contrary. This is obviously equivalent to saying that what is right for one person must be right for every similar person in similar circumstances.[6]

Singer's way of stating the universal feature of moral laws allows for factors that make a moral rule inapplicable, which is not the same as making an exception. A paraplegic is not similarly equipped to save a drowning child as an Olympic swimming chmpion is; so a moral rule that everyone ought to save a drowning child is not always applicable to the paraplegic, when we take care to specify the kind of person and the kind of circumstance under which the rule is to hold. Moral rules are not unqualified imperatives like the Ten Commandments. Shalt thou honor thy mother and thy father when they are cheating on their income tax, committing adultery or perjury, leaving the scene of an accident, displaying blatant prejudice, or making statements that they know to be untrue? Or are there circumstances when one should (or should not) honor them?

Necessity. Moral necessity is expressed by *ought*. When we say we ought to do so-and-so, we are saying that it is *required,* that it is necessary to do so-and-so. *Ought,* expressing moral necessity, contrasts with *may,* expressing moral permissibility. Compare "smoking is prohibited" (one *ought not* to smoke) and "smoking is permitted" (one *may* smoke). Kant uses the phrase "command of reason" to designate moral laws containing "ought." Since a moral law says that an act is *required* (necessary) and so, as we just saw, that it is required of *everyone* (universal), necessity and universality are distinct features of moral laws. We will see why this is so when we come to the discussion of Kant's Categorical Imperative and follow his application of it to maxims—that is, to proposed policies of action.

Some additional remarks about necessity will follow an explanation of direction, the fourth feature of moral laws.

Direction. The direction of a moral law is from antecedent to consequent and not vice versa, just as in natural laws. There is a difference, however, between these two kinds of laws. Although the direction of natural laws is given by the direction of causality, the direction of moral laws is given **287** by identity. This is because what is described by the consequent of a moral law is an *act* like signing a check, not an event like moving a pen on paper, and an act's identity depends upon the antecedent conditions and not vice versa. On the other hand, the event described by the consequent of a natural law can be identified independently of the antecedent event; cancer can be identified in a patient without knowing the antecedent conditions that caused it.

The dependence of an act's identity on the antecedent conditions makes it unlike motions or events. We can describe someone's *motion* by saying she moved her arm back and forth in an arc. But what *act* did she perform? Was she waving to a friend, exercising, giving a prearranged signal, or trying to get rid of an ache? A single motion may have alternative act-descriptions; this one-many relation can be turned into a one-one relation (one motion, one act) only by specifying the antecedent conditions. (One aspect of a theory of action is to classify the different kind of antecedent conditions that we need to consider in trying to identify an act.) This one-many relation of motion and action has consequences for moral theory. Let's consider the motion of driving a car with two different sets of antecedent conditions.

Antecedent Conditions One: A pedestrian has just been hit by a truck. You are a doctor; you judge that the person will die unless taken to the hospital immediately and given a blood transfusion. The accident took place in a town with no ambulance. There is a car nearby with keys in it; the owner isn't known and is not in the gathering crowd, so you don't have the owner's permission to drive the car. Nevertheless, you get the injured person in the car and drive to the hospital.

Antecedent Conditions Two: Your job is a long way from home. The public transportation in your town is poor, so you are often late for work. Your boss has threatened to fire you if you are late again. There is a car parked near your home one morning when you get up late. Although you don't have the owner's permission, you drive the car to work and get there on time.

What act did you perform in the first case and what act in the second, by driving the car? You might say that in the first case you performed an act of mercy and benevolence—which is morally right. On the other hand, in the second case you have come perilously close to stealing—which is morally wrong. Had you liked driving to work so much that you had the car repainted, scratched out the identification numbers, and moved to a new address, the accusation would get more plausible; the additional antecedents would weight the identification of your motion toward stealing.

Two different antecedents provide two different act-descriptions; different act-descriptions lead to different moral evaluations of your motion. Action theory is important because act-descriptions stand between our motions and moral laws. Moral laws don't apply directly to motions; they apply to acts, which are motions identified by their antecedent conditions. Thus morality and action theory are tied together. This is why directionality is an important feature of moral laws.

288   Let us now return to the necessity of moral laws.

Necessity (*continued*): Kant makes it clear that "the necessity involved in the [moral] law is not a physical necessity" (*Practical Reason,* p. 304). There is an obvious reason why the two necessities cannot be the same. Whenever the antecedent conditions specified by a natural law are satisfied, it is necessary for the consequent to occur; here there is no freedom about the occurrence of the consequent event. But obviously, a moral law may or may not be obeyed; we have freedom to follow the moral law or to follow our inclinations. The antecedent conditions of the tardy worker have been fulfilled many times, but that need not cause the consequent act of stealing a car to occur; under those same conditions, many people restrain themselves from driving a car without the owner's permission.

The necessity of moral laws has to allow for freedom of acting or not acting. Let's let an arrow represent the causal relation between the antecedent and the consequent events: antecedent event → consequent event. This arrow relation has the property of necessity, and so: antecedent event → consequent event must occur. Because the necessity of moral laws differs from that of natural laws, we get: antecedent conditions → consequent act need not occur. It need not occur because we are free to perform the act or not. This freedom of choice is the function of *Willkür,* according to Kant. Therefore, the relation in which moral necessity plays a part must stand between our *Willkür* and something else.

Kant gives us a clue to the relation by the use of the words "constraint" and "respect" or "esteem." He tells us that the moral law constrains our inclinations and that we have respect for it. Thus the relation we are looking for, in which necessity plays a part, holds between the moral law and *Willkür.* Further, it is a "double" relation; to reflect this, I will call it the "respect-constraint" relation. By adding to the appropriate place in Kant's links schema (p. 277), we get the following picture, where the thick double-headed arrow is the relation for which we have been searching. The left point of the arrow represents respect for the moral law, and the right point represents constraint of our inclinations by *Willkür.* "*Willkür*" has the location it does because it has to subordinate freely one of the feelings to the other when they conflict. We are worthy when we subordinate the pathological to the moral feeling, and unworthy when we don't.

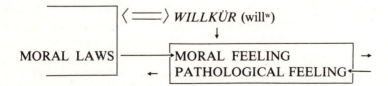

Kant is clear about the double nature of this respect-constraint relation and is certain that the relation stands between the moral law and *Willkür* (will^w):

The consciousness of free submission of the will[w] to the law, combined with an inevitable constraint imposed only by our own reason on all inclinations, is respect for the law. The law which commands and inspires this respect is, as we see, no other than the moral law, for no other law precludes [bars] all inclinations from having a direct influence on the will[w].[7]

Kant makes the same points quite clearly also in his earlier *Foundations:*

The conception of an objective principle [a moral law], so far as it constrains a will, is a command (of reason), and the formula of this command is called an *imperative.*

All imperatives are expressed by an "ought" and thereby indicate the relation of an objective law of reason to a will which is not . . . necessarily determined [causally] by this law. This relation is that of constraint. (*Foundations,* p. 308)

To sum up: moral laws are a product of our rational *Wille;* they are objective laws of our reason. They have an "if . . . then . . ." form and are universal: always when (if) the antecedent conditions are satisfied, then we *ought* to do act_1. Because "ought" expresses necessity, we can rewrite the form of a moral law, removing "ought" and putting "necessarily" at the front: *necessarily* always when (if) the antecedent conditions are satisfied, do act_1.

Finally, the direction from antecedent to consequent is the direction of identifying the consequent act; the descriptions in the antecedent enable us to pick out the appropriate act-description, not vice versa. Recall the example of driving a car without the owner's permission.

STUDY QUESTIONS

1 Why does Kant think morality is an "illusion" if we don't have a rational will?

2 Explain the different functions of *Wille* and *Willkür* in Kant's theory of the rational will. Relate them to his theory of moral worthiness and a good will.

3 State and explain the four features of natural laws. Explain how the four features of moral laws are similar and dissimilar to them.

4 Explain how the features of natural laws help characterize a sensible totality and our sensible nature. Also explain how the features of moral laws help characterize a supersensible totality and our supersensible nature.

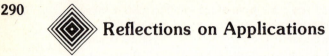

Reflections on Applications

1 In the news report that follows, how would you fit into the "feeling box" of Kant's links diagram (p. 277) the claims that Attorney Langford makes about "semi-willing" victims? What does Langford assert to be a pathological feeling and what a moral feeling? Is the judge's retort based on a claim that there are two pathological feelings, two moral feelings, or one of each?

> A Superior Court judge [in San Diego, California] was angered yesterday when a defense attorney with 50 years experience called his defendant's rape victims "semi-willing." Attorney Edgar Langford, representing admitted rapist Richard Verkaaik, 24, sparked the ire of Judge Edward Butler during Verkaaik's sentencing.
> "He could have bumped into some real tigers," attorney Edgar Langford had said. "He encountered several semi-willing victims."
> "Semi-willing victims, with a knife at their throats?" Judge Butler asked.
> "Oh, nonsense," Langford said. "Any girl who values her honor isn't going to be bothered by the fact that somebody has a knife."
> The judge retorted, "For you to say to the women of this community and elsewhere that honor is more precious than life, and that they ought to resist to the point of death or to death itself seems to me to be a proposition outrageous on its face."[8]

2 Hans Schnier, the main character in Heinrich Böll's novel *The Clown*, tries to telephone his brother Leo, who is a student in a Catholic college that trains men for the priesthood. A "crotchety deaf old fellow" whose voice "smells" of pipe tobacco and cabbage answers the phone. The old man won't put him through to his brother, because they never interrupt a meal unless it is an emergency. Hans insists that it *is* an emergency—he's had an "internal accident." He says to the old man, "Please tell Mr. Schnier that his brother's soul is in danger, and ask him to phone me as soon as he's finished dinner."
  The cabbage smell sets Hans Schnier to thinking:

> The cabbage smell was something I remembered from boarding school. A padre there had once explained to us that cabbage was supposed to suppress sensuality. I find the idea of suppressing mine or anyone else's sensuality disgusting. Evidently they think day and night of nothing but "desires of the flesh," and somewhere in the kitchen a nun sits drawing up the menu, then she talks it over with the principal, and they sit opposite each other and don't talk about it but think with each item on the menu: this one inhibits, that one encourages sensuality. To me a scene like that seems a clear case of obscenity, just like those con-

founded football games that went on for hours at school; we knew it was supposed to make us tired so we wouldn't start thinking about girls, that made football digusting to my mind, and when I think that my brother Leo has to eat cabbage so as to suppress his sensuality, I want to go to that place and sprinkle hydrochloric acid over all the cabbage. What those boys have in store for them is hard enough without cabbage.[9]

Would Kant approve of this method of suppressing sensuality in young men? Does Kant believe that sensuality is evil or the source of evil? If not, why should any of us suppress our sensuality? Are there circumstances when we should? When?

3 What views of Kant's can you connect to the following remarks of Robert Coles about one of the novelist Walker Percy's articles?

The entire direction of his [Percy's] thinking as it had developed for nearly two decades comes across in an article on America's "culture critics," its various social observers, written for *Commonweal* in 1959. "It is no doubt legitimate, for sociological purposes, to speak of a member of the upper-middle [class] who has his house done over in Early Federal with decorator's Picassos as status symbols," Percy wrote. "But let us not forget that this same class-member may have saved a comrade's life in battle, suffers from sinusitis, has a sick wife, and works like a dog to pay his debts. He cannot really be understood by a sociology of motivations but only by a larger view of man which takes account of what a man is capable of and what he can fall prey to. There is not really such a thing as a consumer or a public or a mass man except only as they exist as constructs in the minds of sociologists, ad men, and opinion pollsters."[10]

4 In this chapter I discussed the "direction" feature of moral laws. I pointed out the difference between a person's motion and a person's act, and claimed that a difference in antecedent conditions generates different act-descriptions of the same kind of motion. Below are three motions whose act-descriptions are disputed. Analyze each with the aim of clarifying how the disputed identity of the act depends upon a dispute about the antecedent conditions.

(A) In October 1977, California Governor Edmund G. ("Jerry") Brown, Jr., fired Dr. Josette Mondanaro from her post in the Health Department because she wrote a letter using sexually explicit terms; the letter criticized an article suggesting that more study was needed to determine whether sexual abuse of children harms them permanently. There is no doubt that Brown "fired" Mondanaro; a person with his power who performs the speech motion of saying, "You're fired, Mondanaro," is doing just that. But further act-descriptions are possible, which lead to opposite evaluations of this firing.

Mondanaro "contends Gov. Brown ordered her fired October 25 for political reasons, because she is a lesbian who might represent a threat to the governor's political future. She was fired four months after the letter was written and the day before her probationary period expired."[11] Democratic and Republican legislators critized Brown, suggesting that "Brown fired Mondanaro for the most ignoble of motivations, overweening self interest."[12] Here the act-description presents the firing as political hypocrisy.

The hypocrisy description was supported by two legislators who pointed out that when Brown was a member of a community college board in Los Angeles, "he had voted against firing a . . . teacher who used an allegedly obscene poem in the classroom in 1969." But Brown argued that "the two situations were not comparable":

> "The question before the junior college board was whether or not a tenured teacher should be fired—a community college teacher where all the students were adults over the age of 18—. . . and I believe that under the principles of academic freedom and the fact that she was an English teacher she should be given the benefit of the doubt. . . ."
>
> Brown said, "the standards for firing a teacher are not the same as for a $41,600-a-year director of a $40 million-a-year program, a high office in my administration."[13]

Brown claimed that the letter was "inappropriate" for a state official. This act-description asserts that the firing was to remove state officials who inappropriately use language that some would find offensive. After a hearing, Mondanaro was restored to her job.

(B) Kenneth Levasseur and Stephen Sipman were the young researchers who released two Atlantic bottlenose dolphins from a University of Hawaii facility. (See Reflection 22, pp. 234–35.) They were tried for theft. The young men claimed that they had liberated the dolphins:

> An anonymous note signed by the "Undersea Railroad" and left at the laboratory at the time called the dolphins "slaves" that had been freed after six years of "total isolation and remorseless experiments." . . .
>
> Circuit Court judge Masato Doi said he wouldn't allow testimony on the question of whether the dolphins' captivity was "evil" because the defense [pleading the choice of a lesser evil] can only be used in reference to human beings, not animals.[14]

Was the motion of releasing the dolphins an act of theft or liberation?

(C) Opponents of [public] funding for most abortions have a decisive argument that is logically independent of views about the general morality of abortion. The argument is that few abortions are, properly speaking, medical procedures, and so should not be subsidized by funds appropriated for medical programs.

Dr. Leon Kass of the University of Chicago argues for what he calls "the old-fashioned view" that health is the true goal of the physician's art. If his argument is correct (and it is not easily assailed), most abortions are not acts of medicine, properly understood. The vast majority of abortions are non-therapeutic, in that they are not performed to insure the health of the woman (who surely should not be called a "patient"). Although they are performed by persons licensed to practice medicine, they serve not the pursuit of health, but rather the woman's desire for convenience, absence of distress—in a word, happiness. . . .

Supporters of subsidized abortions argue that such relief is not only a social good, but also is an individual right that must, as a matter of equity, be subsidized for those who cannot afford it. But no such argument can establish the propriety of using funds appropriated for medical services to promote such a goal, which, whether defensible or indefensible, is not a true goal of medicine.[15]

Are abortions acts of medicine or acts of convenience and happiness? Explain.

5 People get labeled with different descriptive terms. Menachem Begin, the prime minister of Israel, was Terrorist No. 1 to the British administration of Palestine before the state of Israel was created. He founded the Irgun Zva'l Leumi army, which raided Arab villages, tortured British soldiers, and planted bombs. Begin said: "You call me a terrorist, but I call myself a freedom fighter. Everything I did was for the freedom of the Jewish people, which had never known mercy from any persecutor."[16]

Connect a dispute about labels for persons with a dispute about the correct act-description of some human motion. Do you think a Palestinian guerrilla attacking Israel could reply to Begin as Begin replied to the British when they called him a terrorist?

6 While reading the following news story, note the difference between the thoughts of the two strikebreaking substitutes quoted.

The sad-eyed little 35-year-old man with a Ph. D. in history and teaching experience at both the college and high school levels is out of steady work and needs money. So he has continued daily to defy both a cursing conscience and picketing teachers outside Fremont's Kennedy High School to pick up the $60 a day the strike-torn school district is using to lure 800 substitutes from all over the Bay Area.

"Morally, I think I'm wrong," he said. "But I have a family, and children, and I really need the money very badly."

Far from all the substitutes—striking teachers call them "scabs" and much worse as they cross picket lines—share his intensity of guilt. . . .

Another substitute was not apologetic about . . . his picket-crossing, although he said, "I feel they (the striking teachers) have a legitimate complaint." When "there are just not enough jobs for everybody," it becomes a dog-eat-dog world where strikebreaking is inevitable—and probably justifiable—he implied in subsequent comments. "I need money as bad as those teachers on the lines do," he said. "I need food as bad as they do."[17]

Using the remarks of the first strikebreaker, fill in the portion of Kant's links schema that appears on p. 288. Would you say that he is conscious of the respect-constraint relation?

Notice the second strikebreaker's use of 'inevitable," which is roughly synonymous with "necessary." Is his use of "inevitable" roughly synonymous with "causally necessary" or "morally necessary?" Would Kant accept his claim that scabbing is "inevitable"? Is there a natural psychological or sociological "law" governing scabbing?

7 Do you think that "A No-Good Guy," author of the following letter, has a moral or a psychological problem?

> Dear Abby: I've stolen all my life. I started taking small things from my friends. I've stolen money from my mother's purse and also my father's pocket. I've even shoplifted just to get away with something. . . .
>
> I'm also a terrible liar. I make up things just to get people to listen to me. . . .
>
> I'd like to be a good person but I don't have the will power to do what's right. Dishonesty seems to come more natural to me. I need some help before I end up in jail.[18]

Abby's reply seems to imply that "No-Good" has a psychological problem, because she advises him to go to a mental health clinic. Would Kant agree with Abby? Or would Kant think that "No-Good" has a moral problem? Could he have both, or does having one exclude having the other? Here is part of Abby's advice:

> Dear Guy: A guy who knows his faults as well as you know yours is no failure in my book. [Kant's *Wille*?]
>
> You are fair enough to blame only yourself for your weakness [of *Willkür*?], smart enough to know that you lie to attract attention, and sufficiently honest to admit you want friends and a clear conscience.
>
> If you have a school counselor, make tracks for that office. If not, tell your parents you have some personal problems you would like to talk over with someone at the mental health clinic. Once you get the help you need, I'll bet on you.

8 Make a rational will ethics criticism of the following remarks made by Robert Callison, who was treasurer of the city of San Jose, California. In 1962 he confessed to having stolen $80,000 of parking meter funds. Callison is quoted as saying:

It was childishly simple. It was as if you saw a $5 bill lying in the street. You pick it up. That's all. It was just a matter of it being so easy a system to take advantage of that I couldn't turn it down. . . . I got bolder as the years went by and nothing happened. I guess I just went overboard. As long as I live, I'll blame Dutch [A. P. "Dutch" Hamann, the city manager of San Jose]. He's at fault in letting this situation exist. . . . He never gave any of his department heads any supervision at all.[19]

9 How would you need to alter the feeling box in Kant's links schema (p. 288) to accommodate the following phenomenon, if it actually occurred?

A woman who claimed her alternate personality was responsible for passing several forged and bouncing checks has been acquitted by a Superior Court jury. The acquittal, which came Friday, is believed to be the first by a California jury in such a case.

Ester Minor . . . said after the verdict that her alternate personality no longer existed and that she would not commit the crimes again. "I plan not to disappoint anybody," Minor told her attorney and the jurors. . . .

During the trial, three psychiatrists and two psychologists testified that they believed Minor had an alternate personality who used the name of Raynell Potts. It was Potts, the experts contended, who passed the forged checks. . . . The doctors said at the trial they believed Minor had no knowledge, control or recollection of her actions when her alternate personality was in control of her body.[20]

What do you think of the following argument that someone such as Kant might make? If she was a real alternate, Raynell Potts was another person. As such, she had reason and both moral and pathological feelings; therefore, she knew she ought not to forge and had the freedom not to do so. Further, if Potts was a real alternate, she would remember what she did as Potts. Therefore, she ought to be held reponsible, found guilty, and punished.

10 Which feature or features of moral laws do you think the teacher was trying to get the pupils to learn in the following experiment in moral education?

In 1970, Jane Elliott, a teacher at Community elementary school in Riceville, Iowa, wanted to teach her third-grade students the injustice of discrimination. Instead of just talking about the arbitrariness and unfairness of race prejudice, she decided to appeal directly to the children's capacity for emotional experience and empathetic insight [insight from sharing in another person's feelings]. She declared a day of discrimination against children with blue eyes.

First Elliott "explained" the innate superiority of the "cleaner, more civilized, smarter" brown-eyed. When the children were disbelieving, she snapped sarcastically at a blue-eyed child, "Is that the way we've been taught to sit in class?" Then she moved all the blue-eyed children to the back of the room.

The brown-eyed snickered as she informed the blue-eyed that they would not be permitted to play on the big playground at recess unless they were invited by a brown-eyed child. Throughout the day she was conspicuously more tolerant of mistakes made by brown-eyed children.

The brown-eyed quickly started to enjoy lording it over the blue-eyed, who soon showed signs of growing insecurity and loss of confidence.

After reversing the rules for a day, Elliott had every child write about how it felt to be discriminated against. The profound impact of the experience was apparent.[21]

In the first paragraph above, it is said that Elliott "decided to appeal directly to the children's capacity for emotional experience and empathetic insight." Do you think that is all the experiment appealed to? What would a Kantian say about that phrase and how would a Kantian alter it?

 **Reflections on Theory**

11 *Finding the supersensible self.* In Chapter 7 I said that, for Kant, moral self-realization is the actualization of our capacity for freedom—both the positive freedom of giving ourselves moral laws (*Wille*) and the negative freedom of constraining our inclinations and of choosing to act on the pleasurable feeling (*Willkür*) prompted by the thought of the moral law. In this chapter I have tried to get across Kant's notions of *Wille* and *Willkür,* so we can understand how he thinks we realize our personhood through the exercise of our freedom. However, you mustn't think these are the outmoded thoughts of an antique thinker lost in a maze of philosophical meanderings. Because Kant has an eighteenth-century style and his language is often technical, he needs "translation" into a more contemporary idiom, if he is to be understood by a person making a first acquaintance with his writings. The translation failure of so many commentators and explicators of Kant haunts anyone who undertakes to rephrase his writings. It is important to recognize that much of his thought is embedded in our own and others' current thinking; because Kant's idiom isn't current, we can easily miss the currency of his thought in comtemporary writing and speech.

Following are some reflections of George Will on Robert Bolt's

play about Sir Thomas More, *A Man for All Seasons.* More was executed by England's King Henry VIII because More would not swear
that Henry rather than the Pope was the spiritual leader of the Roman
Catholic church in England. In reflecting on Will's excerpts from Bolt
on More, try to bridge the gap between Bolt's language and Kant's by
identifying the Kantian thoughts expressed by Bolt.

> More's reputation in our time derives primarily from Robert
> Bolt's play, *A Man for All Seasons,* in which More says to his daughter,
> "When a man takes an oath, Meg, he's holding his own self in his own
> hands, like water, and if he opens his fingers then—he needn't hope to
> find himself again."
> And in his argument with the pliable Duke of Norfolk, More
> says: "I will not give in because I oppose it—I do, not my pride, not
> my spleen, nor any other of my appetites but I do—I!" (More then
> grabs Norfolk in various places, testingly, as he would grab livestock.)
> "Is there no single sinew in the midst of this that serves no appetite of
> Norfolk's but is, just, Norfolk?"
> In the preface to the play, Bolt says of More: "He knew where he
> began and left off, what area of himself he could yield to the en-
> croachments of his enemies, and what to the encroachments of those he
> loved. . . . But at length he was asked to retreat from that final area
> where he located himself. And there this supple, humorous, unassum-
> ing and sophisticated person set like metal, was overtaken by an ab-
> solutely primitive rigor, and could no more be budged than a cliff."
> We try, says Bolt, to "assure ourselves that from the outside at
> least we do have a definite outline. But socially and individually it is
> with us as it is with our cities—an accelerating flight to the periphery,
> leaving a center which is empty when the hours of business are over."
> More's sense of self was not equivocal, and his modern admirers must
> ask whether his enviable sense of "where he began and left off" derived
> from convictions that the modern world is pleased to consider
> superstitious.[22]

12 *Plato's and Freud's notion of freedom contrasted with Kant's.* I have
called an ethics like Kant's a "rational will" ethics. Such an ethics
holds that moral self-realization, the development of a "good will,"
isn't possible unless humans have a rational will. Below are some excerpts from an article by Wright Neely.[23] For each excerpt, compare the
view stated by Neely with Kant's and decide if Kant would agree or
disagree with it. Explain why you decided as you did.

> (A) One of the earliest attempts in Western philosophy at understanding
> the correlative [mutually related] concepts of being slave to oneself and
> being master of oneself was made by Plato. In the *Republic* Plato
> makes two points about these notions. First, he brings out that such
> expressions as "self-mastery" and "self-enslavement" presuppose inter-
> nal complexity on the part of the self. Then he asserts that they

presuppose giving a special importance to certain elements of the self vis-à-vis the others. . . . [Recall that Plato divided the self into three parts: reason, passion or spirit, and appetite.] And he, in effect, asserts that reason is the dominant element in the sense that when its claims win out, the agent is free (master of himself); when it is subordinated to, say, the appetites as a whole or to some subset of them, the person is unfree (slave to himself). (pp. 41–42)

(B) Some contemporary Freudians . . . hold that, roughly, the man is free to the extent that the appetites win, the influence of what Plato called the rational element (superego) being construed [interpreted] as an alien intrusion into the self, thrust upon it from outside by parental training and social pressures.

The presumption behind each view [Plato's and the Freudians'] is that the element which it champions as being the source of true freedom is more truly the self than the other elements with which it may be, and usually is, locked in combat. (p. 42)

(C) If we are to progress beyond Plato, we must avoid the opposite errors of existentialism and a simple-minded naturalism—the errors, that is [respectively] of construing the real self as something over and above all its desires, desirelessly deciding which of them to satisfy, and of simply identifying the self with the totality of desires. We must find a way of saying that some desires are more intimately related to the self—are more its own—than others without adopting the "solution," with its attendant reduplication of the problem, of simply putting another man inside the man. (p. 43)

(D) Here the view of the moral libertarian is instructive. In its strong form it is very similar to Plato's own. According to the strong moral libertarian, we act freely only when we are confronted with a conflict between moral conviction and the rest of our desires. When we act according to the dictates of conscience, we overcome the pull of our strongest (other) desire and, thus, manifest our freedom. . . . What is right about moral libertarianism is that we are free only to the extent that we can resist the pull of desire. But we must, when we do resist this pull, act out of some desire; otherwise we cannot give the proper sense to the notion of being *pulled* by a desire, and we cannot avoid the absurdities of existentialism. (pp. 43–44)

In answering this question, the bulk of your reflections will be concentrated on Kant's notion of *Willkür* and the "feeling box" in his links schema (p. 288). To some extent, particularly with (B), you will have to compare the views stated with Kant's idea of *Wille,* although I still have to supplement my discussion of *Wille* with his theory of (1) how *Wille*'s moral laws get their authority and (2) why our moral worthiness depends on being motivated by respect for the law instead of by our inclinations.

9
Human Rights, Obligation, and Personal Policies

9.1 Two Theories of Duties

We come now to another major contrast between moral psychology and rational will ethics—a contrast, as we shall see, between teleology and deontology.

No one who follows political events abroad and at home can fail to appreciate how widely shared is Kant's belief that human dignity is beyond price, a dignity that is preserved and recognized only when human rights are respected. Think of all the places in the world where people are asserting and fighting for their "rights," much as the colonial revolutionaries did in fighting for what the Declaration of Independence asserted: "We hold these truths to be self-evident, that all men are created equal, that they are endowed by their Creator with certain unalienable Rights, that among these are Life, Liberty and the Pursuit of Happiness."

"Self-evident"?

Not everyone thinks so. Not even a majority of United States citizens responded favorably when unidentified excerpts from the Declaration of Independence were presented to them. "Too radical," said many. George III would certainly have agreed. A lot of powerful rulers in the world don't think these rights belong to everyone self-evidently, and they would vehemently disagree if you called them "dictators" and "tyrants." Some people claim the right to abortion because they think they have rights over their bodies; others passionately challenge this. Some think they have a right to welfare payments to help raise their children when the father leaves or becomes too ill to work or loses his job, or when the mother loses her job; others call them slackers and freeloaders. Some insist on the right of free speech, but others think Communists, Nazis, and the Ku Klux Klan don't have that right.

Rights, then, aren't self-evident to everyone. One person's self-evidence is another's absurdity. Is there a way of finding out what is and what is not a right, to make a true and correct list of rights based on some rational approach that doesn't need to rely on "self-evidence"? The most sustained effort at providing a positive answer to this question came from Immanuel Kant. He believed passionately in freedom but said we have no freedom unless we have rights respected by others. Having a right, however, isn't the same as having a license to do what we will, when we please, to whom we choose, for others too have rights. Every person's having rights is what places constraints on our behavior toward others. Knowing the boundaries of these constraints requires knowing what rights each of us has. That's what, at its most basic, Kant's ethics is about. My exposition of Kant is aimed at showing how his moral theory contributes to our understanding of human rights and provides us with a rational method for determining what **301** rights we have.

In this chapter I begin showing how Kant connects the notion of human rights to other essential notions—obligation, maxims, and human action. First, we need to define the deontic concepts—obligation, prohibition, permission—in terms that help us to understand human rights. ("Deontic" comes from the Greek *deon,* meaning "necessary," "binding" or "right.") Then we will examine the concept of a maxim, which expresses our consciousness of a personal policy for an act. It is our consciousness of the elements of a maxim or personal policy that turns a motion into an action; Kant's concept of a maxim is his theory of action. Clocks, engines, ants, and roulette wheels just move; humans move *and act.* It is our ability *to act* that makes us moral agents and gives us human rights; therefore, Kant thinks, we have to understand the relation between maxims and action, if we are to fully grasp the idea of human rights.

In the next three chapters we will examine and apply the principle of the Categorical Imperative, which is Kant's test for whether or not we have a duty to perform an act or adopt an end. Because of the logical relation he sees between a duty and a right, the Categorical Imperative is also Kant's test for human rights. The chief formulation of the Categorical Imperative is as follows: act only according to that maxim by which you can at the same time will that it should become a universal law.[1]

Let's proceed now to Kant's definitions of the deontic concepts.[2]

Obligation: Obligation is the necessity of a free action under a moral law.
Impermissible (Forbidden, Prohibited): An action which is contrary to obligation is impermissible.
Permissible: An action which is not contrary to obligation is permissible.
Merely Permissible (Morally Indifferent): An action that is neither commanded (obligatory) nor forbidden is merely permissible.

Regarding the last, Kant remarks that "an action of this kind is called morally indifferent" (*Virtue,* p. 22). Although he recognizes that some people think there are no morally indifferent acts, he disagrees:

> But that man can be called fantastically virtuous who admits *nothing* morally *indifferent* and strews all his steps with duties, as with man-traps; it is not indifferent, to him, whether I eat meat or fish, drink beer or wine, supposing that both agree with me. Fantastic virtue is a micrology [attention to petty, trivial matters] which, were it admitted into the doctrine of virtue, would turn the sovereignty of virtue into a tyranny. (*Virtue,* p. 71)

Kant thinks a deed is "right" when it conforms with duty or obligation, and "wrong" when it is contrary to duty.

302   Kant defines a person as "a subject whose actions can be *imputed* to him. *Moral* personality is thus the freedom of a rational being under moral laws." He helps us to understand his definition of "person" by going on to define "impute": "The agent is considered the *author* of the effects of his deed, and these, along with the action itself, can be *imputed* to him, if before he acts, he knows the law by virtue of which they come under obligation (*Virtue,* p. 22). According to Kant, then, we are persons rather than animals or insects because we are able to determine (through *Wille*) what our obligations are; it is our mastery of the basic deontic concept, obligation, that makes us human.

Kant thinks obligation or duty is the basic moral concept. This makes Kant a "deontologist," because he believes that our first moral task is to determine what is obligatory, and he believes also that we can do this without relying on the concept of good. Moral psychologists, by contrast, generally believe that good is the basic moral concept. They are teleologists, because they believe our first moral task is to determine which ends or goals are good; teleology is the theory of ends or purposes. Utilitarians too, of course, are teleologists. According to teleologists, once we know what ends are good, we can determine the deontic properties of acts by discovering their utility or lack of utility (uselessness) as means for achieving good ends and avoiding bad ones.

That Kant is a deontologist doesn't mean he thinks that ends are irrelevant to morality or that moral action is independent of ends. On the contrary, he says, "Every action, therefore, has its end" (*Virtue,* p. 43). However, what makes him a deontologist rather than a teleologist is his belief that ends can be *moral* ends if, and only if, they are *obligatory,* which is a deontic property. He doesn't think every good end is a moral one, for some are merely prudential ends that we associate with happiness.

Kant's theoretical task, then, is a deontological one; he has to explain how we can determine that an act or an end is obligatory. And, using other deontic terms, how we can determine that acts and ends are right, wrong, forbidden, prohibited, permissible, or impermissible.

In *Virtue* (pp. 43–54) Kant identifies two moral ends that are obligatory. First, one's own perfection is an obligatory end. This end has two parts: to perfect our natural, physical, and intellectual powers; and to perfect our moral power—that is, our will. In short, self-realization is an obligatory end. Second, the happiness of others is also an obligatory end. This end likewise has two parts: to act for the natural welfare of others, making sure they have sufficient food, clothing, shelter, good health, and so forth; and to help others achieve moral well-being by not tempting them to perform acts against their conscience.

As you will see, Kant thinks that the Categorical Imperative tests the obligatoriness of both acts and ends. Thus deontology has two parts: one part dealing with the obligatoriness of acts, which Kant calls the *doctrine of justice* (sometimes translated as the "doctrine of rights"), and the other part dealing with the obligatoriness of ends, which Kant calls the *doctrine of vir-*

tue. The first part determines obligatory laws of action for persons as citizens **303**
of states—a political task. The second part determines obligatory laws of
morality in which we attend to the motives and ends of the action as well as to
the action itself—a moral task. Kant sees both parts, justice and virtue, as
aspects of morality in the larger sense; politics is part of this larger morality.

Kant defines and states the relations between deontic terms so as to
clarify our moral vocabulary. He shows that we can define all other deontic
concepts in terms of obligation, which makes it the basic deontic concept.
Notice that "obligation" or "obligatory" occurs in the definition of the other
deontic terms. To be sure, one could take any other deontic term and use it
as the basic one to define the others, since deontic terms are interdefinable.
But Kant chooses "obligation" because it efficiently brings in the concept of
necessity.

Do you recall the discussion of the nature of moral laws in 8.4 and their
feature of necessity? To define "obligation" (p. 301), Kant uses that feature
and also the concept of freedom ("free action"). Given that Kant makes the
concept of obligation the basic moral and deontic concept, and that it rests on
the concept of necessity, it is of the utmost importance for Kant to provide us
with a means of knowing when we have the necessity needed to make a moral
law. He thinks that by means of the Categorical Imperative we can determine
the presence or absence of moral necessity, and so say when we do or do not
have a moral law: "The categorical imperative, which as such only expresses
what obligation is, reads: act according to a maxim which can, at the same
time, be valid as a universal law" (*Virtue,* p. 24).

9.2 Duties and Human Rights

Let's see now how we can connect these deontic concepts with the more
familiar notion of human rights or human freedoms. In the phrase "human
rights" we use "right" as a noun rather than as an adjective; "a right" is the
singular of "rights." "Rights" occurs as a noun in the famous statement I
quoted from the Declaration of Independence: "We hold these truths to be
self-evident, that all men are created equal, that they are endowed by their
Creator with certain unalienable Rights, that among these are Life, Liberty
and the Pursuit of Happiness."

We can define "a right" as follows:

That a person, *P,* has a right to do *A,* means:
(i) It is permissible for *P* to do *A.*
(ii) Any other person, *Q,* is forbidden to interfere with *P*'s doing *A.*

Thus if a person has a right to free speech (freedom of speech), then (i) it is
permissible for him or her to speak when moved to do so, and (ii) others are
forbidden to interfere in any way or to stop the person from speaking. In

304   other words, a person is *free to* (permitted to, may) speak and should be *free from* the hindrance of others, all of whom are forbidden to prevent speech. If someone, Q, did hinder, that hindrance would be wrong, for Q would be violating an obligation not to interfere.

The Declaration of Independence says we have a right to "life." In terms of the definition given, each of us has a right to perform those acts that will sustain our life, and others are forbidden to do anything that will end our life, such as shooting us, keeping food from us, or negligently driving their car where we are driving or walking. Insofar as housing and clothing are necessities for life, we have a right to obtain them.

You may see from this discussion that we can specify our rights only if we can specify our obligations to each other. This becomes more evident by defining "a right" with "obligation" as the only deontic term. This second definition is equivalent to the first because "permissible" and "forbidden" were defined by Kant (p. 301) in terms of "obligation." Definition 2:

That a person, P, has a right to do A, means:
(i) It is not contrary to obligation for P to do A.
(ii) Any other person, Q, is obligated not to interfere with P's doing A.

This definition shows us that the concept of "a right" and "rights," or "freedoms," is a deontic concept. Kant's moral theory is centrally concerned with the concept of human freedoms. He was intensely interested in the French Revolution, which was proclaimed as a struggle for human rights—liberty, equality, fraternity—and for freedom from tyrannical and arbitrary rule.

Here is a vivid recent example of a respect for someone's right. Alexander and Kyril Podrabinek are brothers who live in the Soviet Union. Both were arrested, although at different times. Kyril was tried and convicted for possession of a scuba diver's underwater gun and ammunition that didn't fit the gun. The brothers are convinced that the real reason for Kyril's conviction is their dissent from official Soviet policies.

Alexander Podrabinek had organized a Working Commission to Investigate the Misuses of Psychiatry for Political Purposes. He and several friends compiled a series of documented reports on psychiatric abuses in the Soviet Union. Alexander said that the K.G.B. (the Soviet police) had offered the brothers a deal: if they and their father would apply to leave for Israel and go there together, charges against Kyril would be dropped. But Alexander did not want to go to Israel. He explained why in a letter to a friend:

> I can give you the answer I gave to them [the K.G.B.]. . . . I explained: "All my contact is with this country; it is my motherland; it will be very hard to live without this country. And I consider myself a man who fights for human rights. In such a difficult situation, I have no right to escape. I would consider myself a coward. There are people here I can help.
> . . . I told my brother, "If you want me to emigrate with you and

our father, I will go.'' And Kyril answered, ''No. That is not your will.''
He would not press me to change—to act against my will.''[3]

Kyril refused to violate part (ii) of the definition of ''a right''; he
believes he should not interfere with Alexander's right to help others.
Alexander believes he has a right, even a duty (''no right to escape''), to help
others exercise their right not to be psychiatrically abused when they exercise
their right to dissent from official government policies.

Following is an example of government intervention to protect the right
to life:

> A 2-year-old boy with leukemia must undergo chemotherapy despite his
> parents' objections, the Massachusetts Supreme Court ruled yesterday.
>
> Chad Green, son of Gerald and Diane Green, has been the subject of
> a court battle since February over whether chemotherapy—urged by doc-
> tors—or a natural food diet pushed by his parents was the better
> treatment. Dr. John Truman . . . said throughout the court hearings that
> the boy would die without chemotherapy.
>
> But the Greens said that they would rather see him ''go to a better
> place than suffer with poisonous drugs and needles.'' . . .
>
> The decision said the ''the medically indicated treatment program
> offers the child his only real chance of survival. Consequently, the state
> interest in the preservation of life applies with full force.''[4]

Although Kant doesn't think the preservation of life always overrides all
other concerns, he could agree with this decision. First of all, he thinks the
state has a right to pass laws:

> For all right depends on laws. But a public law which defines for everyone
> that which is permitted and prohibited by right, is the act of a public will,
> from which all right proceeds and which must not therefore itself be able to
> do an injustice to anyone. . . . The basic law, which can come only from
> the general, united will of the people is called the *original contract.*[5]

The ''public will'' is that of elected legislators.

Second, Kant thinks the legislators may justly pass only laws that conform to the Categorical Imperative—laws that preserve the coexistence of
everyone's freedom. He calls such laws ''external'' ones. External laws
don't exhaust our duties; we also give ourselves laws—such as helping those in
distress, not lying to our friends, and being loyal to our family—which he
calls ''internal'' laws. (See Reflection 3, p. 320.)

> The body of those laws that are susceptible of being made into external
> laws, that is, externally legislated, [constitutes justice and here] is called
> jurisprudence (*Jus*). Where these laws have actually been externally
> legislated, the body of them is called positive Law. . . .
>
> ''Every action is just [right] that in itself or in its maxim is such that

the freedom of the will of each can coexist together with the freedom of everyone in accordance with a universal law.''

If, therefore, my action or my condition in general can coexist with the freedom of everyone in accordance with a universal law, then anyone who hinders me in performing the action or in maintaining the condition does me an injustice, inasmuch as this hindrance (this opposition) cannot coexist with freedom in accordance with universal laws. . . . Admittedly, this law imposes an obligation on me.[6]

That a person such as Chad Green has the right to undergo the chemotherapy acts that will preserve his life, and that the chemotherapy given by Dr. Truman is an act that does not interfere with others' right to life, seems obvious. So here we have a case of the coexisting freedoms that Kant requires. And in the last sentence of the preceding quote, Kant admits that the ''law imposes an obligation,'' which is expressed in part (ii) of our definition of ''a right.'' Chad's parents have an obligation not to hinder the life-saving acts; their resistance to chemotherapy, however, constitutes a hindrance to Chad's exercise of his right to life and to the doctor's right to save Chad's life. (Chad died in Mexico, where his parents took him off chemotherapy.)

Third, Kant thinks the state has the right to coerce—in this case, to coerce the Greens to let Chad have his chemotherapy. Kant has an argument justifying the state's coercion. Put simply, it is as follows: hindering others from exercising their right is wrong; hindering the hindering restores the freedom to exercise a right, which is just; therefore, the state may justly use coercion to enforce the rights that law provides:

Any opposition that counteracts the hindrance of an effect promotes that effect and is consistent with it. Now, everything that is unjust is a hindrance to freedom according to universal laws. Coercion, however, is a hindrance or opposition to freedom. Consequently, if a certain use of freedom is itself a hindrance to freedom according to universal laws (that is, is unjust), then the use of coercion to counteract it, inasmuch as it is the prevention of a hindrance to freedom, is consistent with freedom according to universal laws; in other words, this use of coercion is just. It follows by the law of contradiction that justice is united with the authorization to use coercion against anyone who violates justice. (*Justice*, pp. 35–36)

Here is another example. This right to invoke a government's coercion rights and the passage of a law by the ''general, united will of the people'' was utilized by some California citizens in the November 1978 elections. At that time they placed on the ballot an initiative measure (Proposition 5) that would restrict smoking and require smoke-free areas in stores, offices, restaurants, arenas, and other buildings. (The initiative did not pass.)

''We're not prohibitionists,'' said Dr. Robert W. Jamplis, past president of the Cancer Society's state branch. ''We're only trying to protect the rights of non-smokers in California.''

Dr. Nicholas Krikes, president of the California Medical Association, noted that the ballot measure insures the right to smoke, but protects the rights, and health, of non-smokers. "Second-hand smoke, the unfiltered smoke that comes from the burning ends of other people's cigarettes, can cause disease and discomfort in healthy non-smokers," he said. "Although we believe smokers have the right to risk their own health, we do not believe smokers have the right to risk the health of non-smokers," he added.[7]

The argument of the initiative's proponents clearly rests on the kind of rights analysis made above: (i) the initiative would permit non-smokers to pursue a healthy, comfortable life; (ii) smokers have an obligation not to hinder non-smokers in the exercise of their permissible acts. Smoking in public places open to non-smokers violates the obligation of smokers to non-smokers; therefore, it is wrong. By Kant's argument justifying government's coercion powers, a law that coerces smokers to respect non-smokers' right to a healthy life is justifiable. (Kant would not agree that people have the right to risk their own health and life.)

Deontic properties belong to *acts* and *ends*. Naturally, we want to know how to tell whether an act or an end has a deontic property and, if it does, how to tell which one it has. Kant thinks we can find out by using the Categorical Imperative. However, because the Categorical Imperative applies directly, not to acts and ends, but to maxims, we have first to understand the concept of a maxim. Because acts aren't simply motions, but motions related to other factors in the doers' minds, the Categorical Imperative is applied to the maxims of actions, which specify the elements in the doers' minds when contemplating an act. I turn now to maxims, which are the doers' personal policies for what they do.

9.3 Personal Policies (Maxims)

The concept of a maxim is central to what is distinctive and valuable about Kant's ethical theory. Strangely enough, he says very little about maxims directly. What I have to say about them I have gleaned from his examples, from things he says indirectly when he talks about other moral topics, and from various commentators.

Notice first that the Categorical Imperative applies to maxims of actions, not to actions themselves: act according to a *maxim* which can at the same time be valid as a universal law (my emphasis). Here now are two of Kant's direct statements about maxims:

A *maxim* is the *subjective* principle of action, the principle which the subject himself makes his rule (how he chooses to act). The principle of duty, on the other hand, is the principle that reason prescribes to him absolutely and so objectively (how he *ought* to act). (*Virtue,* p. 25)

A maxim is the subjective principle of acting and must be distinguished from the objective principle, i.e., the [maxim is a] practical rule which reason determines according to the conditions of the subject (often its ignorance or inclinations) and is thus the principle according to which the subject acts. The law, on the other hand, is the objective principle valid for every rational being, and the principle by which it ought to act, i.e., an imperative. (*Foundations,* footnote, p. 313)

A maxim is something that individuals propose to themselves. It expresses various elements that are in the mind of a person while he or she is contemplating whether or not to do an act; this is what makes it subjective. Further, what the person has in mind is what "the subject himself makes his *rule.*" So a maxim deals with a "policy" to act in a *kind* of way when appropriate; it has some generality for the doer.

Robert Paul Wolff, in his commentary on the *Foundations,* says:

It is Kant's view that whenever a man acts—indeed, whenever any rational agent acts—he acts on the basis of a policy which he adopted covering a class of relevantly similar cases. Examples of policies which a man might adopt and act on are: to maximize profits in economic transactions, to drink a quart of water a day, to revenge all insults ([Lewis W.] Beck's example) [and Kant's], to commit suicide when continued life threatens more evil than satisfaction (Kant's example), and never to send a boy to do a man's job.[8]

Three other of the four famous Kantian examples of maxims are in the *Foundations* (pp. 314–15). The first of the four is the maxim on suicide cited by Wolff. The other three follow.

Two: "When I believe myself to be in need of money, I will borrow money and promise to repay it, although I know I shall never do so."

Three: I shall neglect my talents and gifts and resolve to devote my life "merely to idleness, indulgence, and propagation—in a word to pleasure."

Four (an aid-to-the-distressed maxim): "A . . . man, for whom things are going well, sees that others (whom he could help) have to struggle with great hardships, and he asks, 'What concern of mine is it? Let each one be as happy as heaven wills, or as he can make himself; I will not take anything from him or even envy him, but to his welfare or to his assistance in time of need I have no desire to contribute.' "

Here now is a fifth example from Kant: "I have, for example, made it my maxim to increase my property by every safe means. Now I have in my possession a deposit, the owner of which has died without leaving any record of it. Naturally, this case falls under my maxim."[9]

The sixth and seventh examples of a maxim occur in a footnote where Kant claims that Aristotle's "principle which locates virtue in the *mean* between two vices is false." (*Virtue,* p. 65). (On Aristotle's "mean" see the **309** discussion of "Self-sufficiency of well-being" on p. 389.)

> What distinguishes *avarice* (as a vice) from thrift (as a virtue) is not that avarice carries thrift *too far* but that avarice has an entirely *different principle* (maxim): that of economizing, not for the sake of *enjoying* one's wealth, but merely for the sake of *possessing* it, while denying oneself any enjoyment from it. In the same way, the vice of *prodigality* is not to be sought in an excessive enjoyment of one's wealth but in the bad maxim which makes the use of wealth the sole end, without regard for maintaining the wealth. (*Virtue,* p. 65, footnote)

You will have noticed that Kant contrasts the "subjectivity" of maxims with the "objectivity" of the law. This makes it sound as if we have two wholly unrelated things, maxims and laws, which is not quite true; they are different but related. A maxim is one person's subjective, proposed policy of acting in certain circumstances. When, however, this maxim is universalized—that is, proposed as a maxim for all persons in such circumstances—and when this universalized subjective maxim passes the Categorical Imperative test of reason, then it becomes an objective moral law:

> Assuming that pure reason can contain a practical ground sufficient to determine the will [such as the Categorical Imperative], then there are practical laws. Otherwise all practical principles are mere maxims. In the will of a rational being affected by feeling, there can be a conflict of maxims with the practical laws recognized by this being. For example, someone can take as his maxim not to tolerate any unavenged offense and yet see at the same time that this is only his own maxim and not a pratical law and that, if it is taken as a rule for the will of every rational being, it would be inconsistent with itself. (*Practical Reason,* Beck, p. 17)

The aim of our inquiry in the remainder of this chapter is to determine as carefully as we can what the elements of maxim are (9.4, 9.5). Then, in the next chapter, we shall see how the form of a maxim changes when we universalize it and explain how Kant applies the Categorical Imperative test to universalized maxims, so we can tell when we do and when we don't have a moral law.

9.4 The Elements of Personal Policies

Whatever element belongs to a maxim has to be prefaced by a phrase indicating some subjective state of mind in the person entertaining the maxim. For instance, in our second example of a maxim, Kant has the phrase "when I believe"; here belief is the state of mind. The mental state in the third exam-

310 ple is "resolve," while in the fourth Kant says that the man "sees" others struggling with hardships but has "no desire" to help.

In our efforts to live a moral life, Kant recognizes that we have to start realistically with our own limited state of mind, not from some impossibly ideal standpoint. Thus we have to deal with what we *believe* is true, not with what is actually true; we are often mistaken in our beliefs. The most we can do is to try earnestly and honestly to be accurate; we are not omniscient gods, but fallible humans.

Let us examine the seven elements of maxims—end, circumstances, means, intent, duty, motive, and act. Each of them is an element in the state of mind of rational beings when they take thought of the motions they will or will not produce in the world. This state of mind is what transforms bodily motions into human actions. It separates humans from robots, insects, "lower" and "higher" animals, all of which may move but do not act. I identify these elements of maxims by extracting them from Kant's examples of maxims. I know of no statement in which he explicitly lists all of these as the elements of maxims. It is important to be clear about maxims because the major instrument of his ethics is the Categorical Imperative, which is applied *not to actions* directly, but *to maxims.*

Element 1: *Representation* of an *end.*

I use "representation" as a catch-all, neutral term for a mental state. It covers mental attitudes such as wishing for, desiring, hoping for, and entertaining an end. Each of these attitudes can occur only if we represent some end in our mind; we represent an end by thinking about or imagining it.

Kant explicitly holds that every action has an end (*Foundations,* p. 323). And since a maxim expresses our state of mind when we are contemplating an action, one of its elements has to be a representation of the end of our action. In the sixth and seventh maxim examples, he used the expressions "for the sake of" and "sole end." In short, we are purposive creatures: we act for a purpose.

Element 2: *Belief* about the *circumstances* in which we find ourselves.

Kant's second example of a maxim says, "When I believe myself to be in need of money. . . . " Of course the circumstances may be much more complex than in this example.

Element 3: *Belief* that a *means* will be a way of achieving the projected end.

Here we must have knowledge or beliefs about such things as natural laws, the behavior of others, social conventions and practices, and the properties of objects. For example, suppose our purpose is to drive a nail into a piece of wood. We have to know that a hammerhead is hard, that a nail is harder than a piece of wood, and that the force of a swinging hammer will drive the nail into the wood. In Kant's second example of a maxim, he points out that the person has a belief that borrowing money is a means of getting the needed money, and that people tend to lend money if they are assured that they will be repaid. Onora Nell (now O'Neill), a contemporary philosopher, points out: "Tests of the capacity of maxims to guide any human moral choices must assume those natural laws in whose context all human society operates—that men are mortal and learn from experience; that material goods are not infinitely abundant and are desired, and additional specific laws of this sort."[10]

Because an end is part of a maxim, we have to include the means as a part. "Whoever wills the end, so far as reason has decisive influence on his action, wills also the indispensably necessary means to it that lie in his power. This proposition, in what concerns the will, is analytical [logically contained]" (*Foundations,* p. 311).

Element 4: *Intent* to produce the *effects* we believe will follow from deliberate employment of the means, and intent not to produce other effects.

This fourth element is not, of course, belief about what effects will predictably occur if we set in motion the means to the represented end. Rather, it is the conscious intent actually to produce the effects we believe will occur, and to prevent those we do not intend. A look at Kant's definition of "impute" on p. 302 shows that intent is an element that must be in our state of mind, and consequently must be expressed by our maxim if we are to be considered the *authors* of our deeds. Our maxims, in other words, must reflect the factors of consciousness that make us responsible for our acts. If I hug an old friend whom I haven't seen for a long time, and he cries out in pain because, unknown to me, he has a broken rib, he won't hold me responsible if he believes that I intended affectionate rather than painful results. I caused the pain but didn't intend it. When we test a maxim's fitness to be a moral law by contemplating it as a universal law, it is important that we also intend that some results *not* occur; for example, we intend not to be arrested in our embezzlement. (See Nell, p. 71.)

Element 5: *Knowledge* of the *moral law.*

That this is an element of a maxim can be seen by looking at the last part of Kant's definition of "impute" (p. 302). We can impute responsibility to a person if, before acting, he or she has some knowledge or belief about the morality of the act and of producing the intended results. I believed there was nothing morally wrong about showing affection to my long unseen old friend; I also know it is morally wrong to inflict needless pain. Law courts recognize that people aren't legally responsible if they couldn't reasonably have known they were doing something wrong.

Kant doesn't think this is a fantastic, unreasonable element to include in our maxims. It is an element available to all, regardless of their education and intelligence. He says: "I should never act in such a way that I could not will that my maxim should be a universal law. . . . The common reason of mankind in its practical judgments is in perfect agreement with this and has this principle constantly in view" (*Foundations,* p. 301). "To be sure, common human reason does not think it abstractly in such a universal form, but it

"Of course what we're doing is wrong, but that doesn't make it indefensible."

always has it in view and uses it as the standard of its judgments" (*Foundations,* p. 302).

Further, we would never be conscious of our temptation to transgress our duty (crib from a fellow student's exam, for example), if we didn't know our duty (not to cheat); and we wouldn't know our duty, according to Kant, if we didn't know whether or not our maxim can be made into a universal law. But we are aware of our temptation as well as of our actual transgressions; therefore, we know the moral law and our maxim's relation to it.

Element 6: *Consciousness* of our *motives* in acting.

Here we need to remind ourselves that Kant thinks there are two kinds of motives: (1) moral feeling, which is generated by the thought of the moral law, and (2) the feeling of our sensible inclinations. With *Willkür,* our power of choice, we pick one or the other as the motive for our action.

This sixth element is essential to a theory of human action, because *Willkür*'s having a choice of motives is the very factor that makes our act a free one. Notice that Kant's definition of "obligation" contains the phrase "free action." Because maxims are candidates for obligatory moral laws, they have to contain an element that assures us we are dealing with "free" acts.

We do not use this sixth element to determine whether our maxim is fit to be a universal moral law but to determine our moral worthiness. We are morally worthy only if we choose moral feeling to be the motive for our action.

This "motive" element of a maxim is important also for Kant's distinction between the *legality* and the *morality* of an act, a distinction we commonly make. In determining the legal status of an act, we are not concerned with which kind of motive actually caused the act; we don't care, for example, whether a person refrained from embezzling because he was afraid he'd be caught or because he had respect for a moral law he knew he ought not to **313** transgress. Legally, he is in the clear simply by refraining from embezzlement. But if we want to know about his morality, we have to know whether he acted out of fear of detection or out of respect for the moral law. It isn't always possible to determine the morality because we can't always determine its motive. There is no doubt, however, that Kant thinks we should always strive to make moral feeling the motivating element of our state of mind and so of every one of our maxims:

> Freedom of the will^w is of a wholly unique nature in that an incentive can determine the will^w to an action *only so far as the individual has incorporated it into his maxim* (has made it the general rule in accordance with which he will conduct himself).[11]

> Man is *evil,* can mean only, He is conscious of the moral law but has nevertheless adopted into his maxim the (occasional) deviation therefrom. (p. 27; other related remarks occur on pp. 23 and 31)

Element 7: *Resolve* or decision or intent to perform an *act*.

Regardless of the variation of the first six elements, a motion that we don't resolve or intend to make is not an act and is not an element in a maxim. Suppose that during a power outage I strike a match to look for my flashlight and have a muscle spasm that makes me drop the match, which then sets the house on fire and so causes death and destruction. In this case, the motion of dropping the match is not an act, because I didn't resolve or intend to drop it; it is a reflex from a spasm-caused movement that I also did not resolve. My motion, then, cannot be called an act because I didn't "start a fire."

I have put down in barest outline the seven factors Kant thinks we need to consider when we honestly try to find out what we ought and ought not to do. More detailed examples will follow, to help you connect his theory with your actual everyday moral decisions. Kant's theory isn't just an academic exercise, but as conscientious an attempt as any ethical writer ever made to deal with our moral agonies. Other philosophers tend to slice life a bit thinner than he. Real moral wrestling isn't as textbook-simple as they represent it to be. Don't glaze over and don't flag; take an intellectual and moral voyage with the best.

9.5 Identifying a Maxim's Elements: An Example

I will now apply Kant's theory of the elements of a maxim to his second example: "When I believe myself to be in need of money, I will borrow money and promise to repay it, although I know I shall never do so." Although his citation of the maxim proper is much shorter than the full maxim I will extract

314   from his example, this fuller description of the maxim's setting provides all the elements I have identified:

> Another man finds himself forced by need to borrow money. He well knows that he will not be able to repay it, but he also sees that nothing will be loaned to him if he does not firmly promise to repay it at a certain time. He desires to make such a promise, but he has enough conscience to ask himself whether it is not improper and opposed to duty to relieve his distress in such a way. Now, assuming he does decide to do so, the maxim of his action would be as follows: When I believe myself to be in need of money, I will borrow money and promise to repay it, although I know I shall never do so. Now this principle of self-love or of his own benefit may very well be compatible with his whole future welfare, but the question is whether it is right. He changes the pretension of self-love into a universal law and then puts the question: How would it be if my maxim became a universal law? He immediately sees that it could never hold as a universal law of nature and be consistent with itself; rather it must necessarily contradict itself . . . it would make the promise itself and the end to be accomplished by it impossible. (*Foundations*, p. 314)

Element 1: Representation of an end.   He wants to acquire money.

Element 2: Belief about circumstances.   He knows he needs money; he knows he will not be able to repay a loan.

Element 3: Beliefs about the means.   He knows that one can get money by the practice of borrowing, that people normally lend money only if they believe they will be repaid, that promising (firmly, perhaps by signing an IOU) is a means of establishing belief of repayment in the mind of the potential lender.

Element 4: Intent to produce the effects caused by employment of the means.   In the example, Kant does not say that an intent was formed, but he pictures an internal struggle.   The man desires to make a false promise, but he has enough conscience to ask if it is opposed to duty.   When he universalizes his maxim, he realizes its effects—the destruction of promising, which would thwart the achievement of a generally desired end.   Kant catches what he takes to be the kind of considerations we mentally struggle with in the process of forming an intent.   In this example we find the man midway toward forming his intent, after duly considering his relevent beliefs about his circumstances and the probable effects of an act, his desires, and his conscience.

Element 5: Knowledge of the moral law.   The discussion of Element 4 amply highlights the presence of this element.

Element 6: Consciousness of motives.   The man desires the money to take care of his needs; it may be compatible with his whole future welfare or happiness.   This is clearly a motive of inclination.   That the motive of duty is present, Kant indicates by supposing that the man has "enough conscience" left to ask if a false promise is opposed to duty.   There is still enough respect (moral feeling) for the law to keep this man within the moral community.

Element 7: Resolve or decision to perform the act.   Kant does not say which act—to promise or to refrain from it—the man decides upon, but the **315** act is an obvious element in a maxim because this is the outcome of practical deliberations.

Let's remind ourselves that a motion isn't an act. A motion (or not making a motion) becomes an act (or refraining) when the first six elements are consciously present to the mover. Further, which specific act a motion is depends upon the specific nature of the first six elements. But in our present example, as in all actions, there must be a motion (or its restraint) that needs identification.

Just what motion must we consider here? It is, perhaps, the man moving his speaking apparatus in uttering the sounds "I promise to repay by October 1," or perhaps the moving of his hand guiding a pen that writes his signature on an IOU or loan contract. These motions would be acts of promising because Elements 1 through 6 are present, and because he utters the word "promise" or some synonym, or signs a promissory note. But more is involved: it is an act of *falsely* promising because, during the very uttering of "I promise," he knows that he will not repay (Element 2). This seventh motion-act element is what activates the means. Uttering "I promise" sets in motion the convention of lending upon promise to repay.

Let's give the following names to these seven elements (remembering that, although I drop "believes," "intends," etc., they are always conscious elements): End Element, Circumstance Element, Means Element, Intent Element, Duty Element, Motive Element, and Act Element.

In my discussion of the direction of moral laws, I talked about the vagueness of motions, pointing out that the single motion of a woman moving her arm may have several act-descriptions (p. 287); there is a one-many relation between descriptions of motions and descriptions of acts. Was the woman waving to a friend, exercising, giving a prearranged signal, or trying to get rid of an ache, I asked. Motions in themselves are vague with respect to their act-description. Think of what happens when you're watching a movie and the sound goes off.

Although a motion could have more than one correct act-description, for purposes of moral evaluation we should try to settle on a single correct one. In a theory of action, we should try to classify the different kinds of antecedent (or accompanying) conditions that we can use to settle on a single correct act-description. Kant's theory of maxims is just such a theory of action; the first six elements are those antecedent (or accompanying) conditions; when known, these elements remove the vagueness of motions. In Kant's example analyzed above, because of the presence of "I promise," we don't have much doubt about the act; however, if we don't know that the promiser won't be able to repay—which in this example the promiser *does* know—we won't know that it is an act of *false* promising. This shows we need information of the Circumstance Element and Intent Elements in the promiser's mind in order to arrive at the correct act-description.

Stuart Hampshire examines the vagueness of motions in his review of E. O. Wilson's *On Human Nature,* a book that I discussed earlier. Hampshire

316   criticizes Wilson for failing to appreciate that there is an important difference between the physical sciences and the so-called social "sciences" —a difference that he finds relevant to the distinction between motions and acts:

> When I go for a walk and wave to a friend, the scientific descriptions of motion and change in the language of physics and biology make no reference to the gesture of waving, or to friends, or even to going for a walk. These are concepts from the mixed descriptions of common sense, and common sense is not principally concerned with the purely physical mechanisms that will explain the observed physical events scientifically. This mixed vocabulary was not designed for the purposes of scientific theory or for adequate explanation. Rather it has developed to meet the needs of communication between persons, and, most important, to meet the needs of decision-making and of discussing intentions and sentiments with others.
>
> The beliefs, desires, sentiments, and intentions that initiate and guide my actions have been formed in my head, or heart, for some good or bad reasons, and often for reasons which I then explain to others. At the same time I see the behavior of others as indications of their beliefs, desires, and sentiments and as realizing their intentions. Our verbs of action and names and descriptions of persons and things—e.g., "waving," "friendly"—depend for their meaning largely on the social institutions, customs, and rituals to which they refer, or which provide a necessary context for them.
>
> A keen-eyed observer from outer space, where they have quite different ways of life, would not see the point of much of our behavior, and would not be able to infer the beliefs, desires, and sentiments which inspire it. He would not recognize the furniture, or classify patterns of behavior as we do. The options open to him in his planning would be correspondingly different. Similarly, an old man arriving in contemporary California from some backward area might not be able to identify what middle-aged professors are doing running [motion] through the streets in shorts: they are running, plainly, but with what intention or meaning? "Jogging" is the name of a new institution [action], with a particular context of belief and desire, and to identify someone's running as jogging implicitly invokes this background and setting.[12]

Here running is the motion, jogging the act-description. (From whom are they running? No one—they're jogging.) Hampshire's reference to beliefs, desires, intentions, and sentiments recalls the elements of Kant's maxims.

It is interesting to note that you can work backward from an act-description to the required elements in a maxim: if someone was truly blackmailing another, and if you understand the concept of blackmail, you already know what elements have to be present in the mind of the blackmailer. It is this conceptual knowledge that enables you to evaluate the justness of accusing someone of blackmail. I leave you to discover your knowledge of blackmail in Reflection 4 of this chapter. Without an ability to work backward, a detective or district attorney would not know what kind of evidence must be obtained to secure a guilty verdict. Further, this evidence has to support claims about the subjective state of mind of the black-

mailer—for example, that he or she knew and intended that threats to expose
the victim to unwanted public scrutiny would cause the victim great mental distress and emotional suffering, and would likely make the victim "cough up."

To summarize: in this chapter I have related Kant's definition of the deontic term "obligation" and have shown how he used "obligation" to define such other deontic terms as "impermissible," "permissible," and "merely permissible" (morally indifferent). Because Kant takes "obligation" (duty) as the basic moral concept, he is an ethical deontologist. A deontologist such as Kant and others can conceive "human rights" as a deontic term because they define "a right" in terms of obligation. Kant defines "obligation" with the help of "necessity," whose presence or absence will be tested by the Categorical Imperative. When this necessity is a feature of universalized maxims, they become moral laws, as we will see in the next chapter. To prepare ourselves for Kant's application of the Categorical Imperative to maxims, I made a seven-element analysis of them. We saw how the subjective consciousness of these elements transforms bodily motion into action; this transformation gives us our "moral personality" and makes us agents to whom moral responsibility may be imputed. By identifying these seven elements, we can supply act-descriptions of vague motions and be precise about what we can impute to persons.

The figure below pictures Kant's theory of the relations discussed in this chapter and the way deontic terms relate to moral laws, with the four features —conditional form, universality, necessity, and direction—discussed in 8.4.

	defined by		defined by	
Deontic concepts	⟶	concept of obligation	⟶	free acts under a moral law ⟶

which moral law must be ⟶	{ conditional in form, universal, necessary, and directional }	which are the necessary conditions for a social totality, and whose presence the Categorical Imperative requires.

It is interesting to note that Kant thinks the whole moral structure rests on the four features of a moral law and that none of these is a moral term; hence, Kant's definitions of deontic moral terms are not circular.

STUDY QUESTIONS

1 Which moral concept is basic for a deontological theory of morals? Which for a teleological theory? List the deontic terms and Kant's definitions of them, and explain why his theory can be said to make "obligation" the basic deontic term. Could a deontologist make a different term the basic one?

318

2 Explain why the notion of a human right can be considered a deontic one. Name a human right that wasn't listed in this chapter.

3 What does Kant mean by a maxim? What are the elements of a complete maxim? Choose your own example of a maxim and analyze it into its elements.

4 How do motions differ from acts? Your answer should explain the vagueness of motions and how we are to settle on an act-description. Relate this to Kant's idea of a maxim, and in this connection explain the concept of the "direction" of moral laws. Work with an example.

 ## Reflections on Applications

1 There are deontic terms other than those listed and defined by Kant. Here are some: "behooves," as in "It behooves you to keep your promises"; "due," as in "Give every man his due"; "fitting," as in "It is fitting that you remain faithful to your wife"; "binding," as in "Promises are binding"; "beholden," as in "Everyone is beholden to his or her benefactors."

Can you think of any other deontic terms? Of those mentioned, try to give a definition of each, using only Kant's deontic terms.

2 I connected "rights" and "a right" to deontic concepts in 9.2 when I defined "a right" in terms of "obligation." I applied this definition to some alleged rights: to dissent from a government's policies, to life, not to breathe the tobacco smoke of others. Make an analysis of the following examples of alleged rights, showing how they can be expressed in deontic terms:

(A) Former CIA Director William Colby told the *Playboy* magazine it would be "moral" for the Ugandan people to kill President Idi Amin and it would be moral for the CIA to morally aid in the assassination, it was disclosed yesterday.

In an interview in *Playboy's* July issue, Colby said he believes, "If a man is a total tyrant, then somebody under him has the right to shoot him. But that doesn't mean a separate country has a right to do it. If I am being oppressed by someone—my family has been destroyed, I've been sent to jail and all the rest—then I have a right to respond."

He noted, as an example, it would be a "moral act" for the Ugandan people to kill Amin. Asked whether the CIA would encourage such an act, Colby responded: "No, that's different. . . . But helping them in what they want to do? There it would be moral if the safety and welfare of the United States could somehow be related to it."[13]

(B) Thirty-five nations, including the United States and the Soviet Union, signed the Final Act of the Helsinki Conference on Security and Cooperation in Europe. This "Final Act" called for the observance of several fundamental human rights. One of them is the right to emigrate, at least for the purpose of reuniting split families.

(C) Medical advances help save the lives of babies born prematurely who weigh three pounds or less. However, there is still a high risk that such children will be severely handicapped. Decisions about whether to try to sustain the life of such infants have to be made within minutes, often with inadequate information about the normality of the infant. Should such small infants be kept alive, particularly since there are few places where sophisticated methods are available that increase the chances for normal development?

There are dismal cases of preemies [premature babies] saved only to turn out later to have cerebral palsy, to be blind, retarded or impaired in communication. . . .

Clearly not every couple has access to such sophisticated childbirth facilities, and that, said University of California School of Nursing Professor Anne Davis, is only one of the ethical problems raised by the neonatology (medicine of the newborn):

To underline possible moral conflicts she asked these questions:

What are the long term effects of saving children who otherwise would have died?

Do we have the duty to save the fetus regardless of the consequences?

Is parenthood a basic right under all circumstances? Do people have the right to produce a child that will have [a] larger than average drain on economic resources?[14]

(D) A judge ruled yesterday that the cousin of a critically ill man cannot be forced to submit to a bone marrow transplant, even though it might increase the patient's chances for survival.

"In our law, there's no duty to rescue someone or save someone's life," said Allegheny [Pennsylvania] county Judge John P. Flaherty. "Our society is based on the right and sanctity of the individual. . . . Forcible extraction of living body tissue causes revulsion to the judicial mind," said Flaherty. "You can picture the man strapped to the table and then the extraction. This is not our society. The rights of the individual must be upheld, even though it appears to be a harsh decision."

"I love my cousin, we're like brothers, but he has a fear in him," McFall [the man who needed the transplant from a compatible donor] said in a hospital interview after the ruling.

"I thought about it good and hard," he said. "I have a moral obligation to fight for my life. Whether you're religious or not, there is a moral obligation. I'm no philosopher, but I'd like to stick around for a couple more years."[15]

320

(E) The 6th Special UN General Assembly Session of April 9–May 2, 1974, met to consider the grave problems of raw material resources and "third world" economic development. It adopted a significant *Declaration on the Establishment of a New International Economic Order*. Expressly recognized is the right of every sovereign state to control all internal economic activity without foreign interference, and select its own economic and social system, including the right to begin non-capitalist development.[16]

(F) Sergei Polikanov is an important nuclear physicist in the Soviet Union. He was invited to spend a year in Geneva to work with Soviet-made equipment to do research. His superiors gave him permission to go, but with the proviso that his wife and 16-year-old daughter were to stay in Moscow. Polikanov said:

> What was my fault? Only that I love my wife and daughter and I do not want to live apart from them for a long time? I prize every day with my family. Isn't a man in charge of his own fate? Is my wish to cooperate with Western scientists criminal? How can someone unknown to me decide how I live my life?[17]

3 I pointed out on pp. 302–03 that Kant distinguished between the doctrine of justice and the doctrine of virtue. In the doctrine of justice he is concerned with external laws, in the doctrine of virtue with internal laws (see p. 305). Parallel to this distinction is his distinction between the "legality" and "morality" of an act (p. 312). In determining the legality of an act, we are concerned only with whether or not persons acted in conformity with external law, disregarding their Motive and End Elements; but when we want to determine the morality of their acts, we have to include their End and Motive Elements in our deliberations.

Apply this legality-morality distinction to the refusal of McFall's cousin to donate bone marrow [Reflection 2 (D), p. 319].

4 After identifying the elements of maxims, I took one of Kant's maxims—falsely promising in order to obtain needed money—and picked out its elements (9.5). Later I pointed out (on pp. 316–17) that if we have a summary name for an act, such as "embezzlement," "theft," or "blackmail," we can work backward and figure out some essential elements of the complete maxims for those acts—apart, of course, from varying particulars of different occasions. For example, one person may be blackmailed for infidelity, another for perjury. State complete maxims for theft or blackmail.

5 Conjecture complete maxims (the seven elements) for the fifth, sixth, and seventh examples of Kant's maxims (pp. 308–09).

6 Work out a complete maxim for Colby's claim that oppressed people have a right to assassinate a tyrant [Reflection 2 (A), p. 318]. Is such a maxim consistent with a right to life? Are tyrants exempt from the

right to life? Could killing in self-defense be an exercise of the right to life? Would killing in self-defense be a violation of another's right to life? Formulate a right-to-life maxim and a self-defense maxim. Can Colby's maxim be related to a maxim of self-defense?

7 "The Yippie Party, once known as a revolutionary band of anti-establishment malcontents, has a new maxim: Never commit 'a felony when a misdemeanor will do.'"[18] Conjecture the complete maxim for the Yippies.

8 Consider the motion of cutting open a person's abdomen. Make up two complete but different maxims that produce two different act-descriptions of that motion, which would nomally incline us to make two different moral evaluations of the agent's motion. Give a "summary" name to the two different acts.

9 Here is an interesting example of an attempt to influence our act-descriptions—in this case, act-descriptions of a whole set of motions of a lot of people. It is from an advertisement by Mobil Corporation called "Business and the Rational Mind, Part III."

Judging by some of what we read and hear, self-flagellation seems about to become the order of the day. Much of whatever Americans do or achieve or enjoy is termed immoral or otherwise indefensible, and what people in other countries do is hailed as the shape of the future, morally speaking.

Well, now.

A lot of this national guilt complex depends on how things are put.

Suppose, for example, we ask you, "Do you think it's right for the United States, with only 5% of the world's population, to consume 28% of its energy?" That might be your cue to beat your breast and cry, "Heavens to Betsy, no! How could we do such a thing? And how can we atone?"

Suppose, however, we rephrase that question and ask you, "Isn't it remarkable that the United States, with only a twentieth of the world's population, can produce a fourth of the entire world's goods and services? And that we have become the industrial and agricultural breadbasket of the world . . . a prime purveyor to the hungry and the needy abroad?"

"Gee," you might say, "Just shows you what the old Yankee ingenuity, along with hard work and clean living, can do." . . .

This is not a plea for devil-may-care hedonism. On the contrary, we are trying to make two points:

(1) Gratuitous martyrdom is an exercise in futility.

(2) When someone tries to make you feel guilty because our country has achieved to considerable degree what *all* countries strive for, don't leap to the bait. Remember, it's possible to state even the most positive accomplishments in a way that makes them sound like original sin. . . .

Life is short, and people who work hard and productively shouldn't reproach themselves over their rewards, especially since pro-

322   ducing for plenty makes society a lot more comfortable than sharing unnecessary shortage.   To some people pleasure may be a little sinful, but if there were no sin in the world, what would be the benchmark for virtue?

Which elements of a maxim do you think Mobil appeals to in order to persuade you that its act-description is correct and, consequently, to secure your agreement with their moral evaluation of a capitalist mode of life?

10 Kant thought that the state has a right to coerce us to conform to external laws (pp. 305–06).   Consider the following platform plank of Ed Clark, who was a Libertarian party candidate for governor of California in 1978.   Clark said that he would pardon all prison inmates in California that were convicted of "victimless" crimes.

"Government should be in the business of protecting rights, not legislating personal moral standards," said Los Angeles attorney Ed Clark, the first person to run for governor from the tiny Libertarian party.

Clark, 48, told reporters at the Hall of Justice [in San Francisco] that he considered the use and sale of drugs, prostitution and gambling to be "victimless" crimes, which he defined as "acts by consenting adults that do not use force or fraud."

As governor, he said that he would also cease enforcement of laws against "victimless" crimes that represent "a moralistic, paternalistic approach to government which is completely antithetical to the spirit of voluntary, individual choice."

Clark estimated that his pardon would affect about 4000 inmates in state prisons and "tens of thousands more" in county and local jails.   The largest group of such prisoners is probably those who have been convicted for violating marijuana laws, Clark said.[19]

Supposing that "victimless crimes" are those in which a person has not violated the rights of another (no "force or fraud," said Clark), is Clark's stand consistent with Kant's theory about a state's right to coerce its citizens?

 **Reflections on Theory**

11 *Davidson on agency and intention.*   How would you relate the following remarks by Donald Davidson to the distinction between motion and action (p. 313 and section 9.5)?   And how would you relate them to Kant's definition of "impute" (p. 302).

What events in the life of a person reveal agency; what are his deeds and his doings in contrast to mere happenings in his history; what is the mark that distinguishes his actions?

This morning I was awakened by the sound of someone practising the violin. I dozed a bit, then got up, washed, shaved, dressed, and went downstairs, turning off a light in the hall as I passed. I poured myself some coffee, stumbled on the edge of the dining room rug, and spilled a bit of coffee fumbling for the *New York Times*.

Some of these items record things I did, others, things that befell me, things that happened to me on the way to the dining room. Among the things I did were get up, wash, shave, go downstairs, and spill a bit of coffee. Among the things that happened to me were being awakened and stumbling on the edge of the rug. A borderline case, perhaps, is dozing. Doubts could be kindled about other cases by embroidering on the story. Stumbling can be deliberate, and when so counts as a thing done. I might have turned off the light by inadvertently brushing against the switch; would it then have been my deed, or even something I did?

Many examples can be settled out of hand, and this encourages the hope that there is an interesting principle at work, a principle which, if made explicit, might help explain why the difficult cases are difficult. . . .

Can we say what element is common to the cases of agency? . . . In the case of agency, my proposal might then be put: a person is the agent of an event if and only if there is a description of what he did that makes true a sentence that says he did it intentionally. . . .

Action does require that what the agent does is intentional under some description, and this in turn requires, I think, that what the agent does is known to him under some description.[20]

12 *Cornman: Negligence disproves the intentional theory of agency.*
Following is a criticism by James Cornman of Davidson's claim about intention and agency. Do you think it is a good one? Can it also be made a criticism of Kant's theory of action and agency?

I think there are cases of agency where there is no description, *x*, of the event such that "*P* did *x* intentionally" is true. The clearest class of cases are those of negligence, where a man is the agent of an event, although he intended to do nothing whatsoever. The man who starts a forest fire by absent-mindedly dropping a lighted match or by flipping away a cigarette out of habit often has no intention at the time at all. He may not intend to drop the match, throw it away, or anything else. He just failed to think about or pay any attention to what he was doing. He may, of course, sometimes have some intention at the time, but it may be irrelevant to what he did. He may be intending to cut down a tree, for example, and his concentration on that might explain his negligence. In such cases I would claim that the person is the agent of the event of the forest fire beginning, and that there is no description, *x,* of that event such that "He did *x* intentionally" is true.[21]

324

We can strengthen the plausibility of Cornman's case by reminding ourselves that persons are responsible for their negligent acts, and that responsibility can be imputed only to agents (authors of deeds); hence, negligence implies agency. Further, we hold persons responsible for negligence because they *failed* to do what they could reasonably be expected to do. In Cornman's example the person failed to take the precautions that would have prevented the forest fire; he failed to do so because he did not have the intent he ought to have had, namely, *not* to cause a forest fire by what he did. Recall that in the Intent Element I included the intent to produce some effects and also *the intent not to produce others.*

13 *Negligence in motion, not action.* Do you think the following defense against Cornman's argument is one that Kant could successfully use? True, we hold people responsible for their negligent acts, and, true, I claim intent is an element of a maxim whose presence differentiates acts from mere motions and happenings. It is also true that in negligence we do not have an intent. But this doesn't show, as Cornman thinks, that a negligent motion is an act. Thoughtlessly tossing away a lighted match in a tinder-dry forest counts as a mere motion. But its being a mere motion is precisely what makes a person responsible; the person ought to have *acted,* not merely moved. To have acted would have required an intent—in this case, an intent not to start a forest fire. Hence, we hold people responsible for their negligence because they didn't have an intent that, as agents, they could and ought to have had. In short, usually when people move, they have the responsibility to formulate a maxim that turns the motion into an act, which maxim must include the Intent Element.

Which comes down to this: the maxim "I will make motions in the world without thinking about them" doesn't pass the test of the Categorical Imperative. It doesn't do so because this maxim cannot consistently be made into a universal law of behavior for all humans on all occasions. Such a maxim, if valid, would require us to will that we not think; but since this willing requires thinking, this maxim would in effect require us to think that we not think. This is contradictory and so can't be made into a universal law. Because we can't consistently will not to think, we can't consistently will to be negligent. Since it is impossible to have a universal law that we should all be negligent, it is necessary that we not be negligent; that is, it is our duty not to be negligent, which is the same as saying that it is our duty to move thoughtfully in the world. Moving thoughtfully is acting, which includes having intentions.

In other words, *one can universalize the maxim that we ought to have maxims for most of our notions.* As agents, we can generate such maxims; this is why we can be held responsible for our negligence, and also why we can be held responsible for merely moving, as when we unintentionally toss away a lighted match in a forest. The argument proves that, although unintentional negligent motions aren't acts, we are responsible for them because agents' motions ought to be acts. Cornman incorrectly thinks that unintentional motions are acts, but he correctly thinks that we are responsible for them. This argument shows that we are responsible for them not because they are acts, but because they are mere motions. This argument provides the missing link between negligent motions and responsible agency that Cornman fails to consider: namely, the maxim to have maxims.

10
From Maxims
to a Morally
Perfect World

10.1 Getting Our Bearings

To remind you of our progress, I will relate Kant's views, as developed thus far, to some main themes of this book. This chapter will then explain in outline how Kant proposes to use the Categorical Imperative to move us beyond subjective maxims of personal policy to objective moral laws, and will explain how this differs from the Golden Rule and from the moral psychologists' search for moral laws through generalization. Generalization of our acts presses into view whenever we ask, "What if everyone did that?"

Kant thinks we humans occupy a moral realm rather than a natural, non-moral one because we are rational: our reason (i) provides moral laws and (ii) can cause us to act; it is *practical*. In the preceding chapter I examined the distinction between moving and acting. We act because we think before moving. This thinking is what makes us moral agents and therefore morally responsible for our acts. The "subjective principle" of this thinking Kant calls a "maxim." I have asserted that a maxim has seven elements (pp. 308–09).

At the beginning of this book I argued that theory is practical because it is reflexive, self-correcting thought about practical thought. Kant too believed this. In considering the morality of a contemplated act, we think about the maxim that expresses our proposed practice or policy. The self-correcting aspect of our theoretical thought is manifested by the application of a moral standard or test to our maxims. A familiar example of reflexive self-correction is using a yardstick to check our estimate of a length. Another example would be using the rules of arithmetic to check the addition and subtraction in our bank book.

What standard can we use to self-correct our moral estimations that is analogous to yardsticks and rules of addition and subtraction? Kant proposes the Categorical Imperative. Applied to maxims, it enables us to determine if our contemplated act is obligatory, permissible, forbidden, or morally indifferent.

Kant's proposed test for the deontic properties of acts and ends offers an answer to a question posed earlier (pp. 274–75): How can we (i) characterize a self-realization that enables us to escape Ivan Ilyich's ordinariness; that at the same time (ii) preserves the freedom and dignity that Nietzsche thinks separates Masters from Slaves; and that at the same time (iii) is a way of building the social community of persons that Marin recommends?

This question's relation to the three themes of this book (2.1) is clear as soon as we ask it. We can restate it as three questions: (1) What kind of a person must I be or become to be a worthy person? (2) To what extent am I free to determine what I ought to do and become? (3) What kinds of acts does a worthy person do?

To this three-part question, Kant gives a three-part answer. (i) Our self-**329** realization should be a moral one; we ought to develop our natural and moral powers into the kind of character that enables us to act morally. (ii) Moral self-realization is the actualization of our capacity for freedom, the source of our dignity, because self-realization is the activity of freely self-legislating and obeying moral laws through *Wille* and *Willkür*. (iii) The Categorical Imperative structures our values and acts as expressed in maxims so that they do not infringe on others' freedom, yet it generates a shared set of moral laws that, when obeyed by all, enables us to construct a social totality. We can be masters of ourselves instead of being chained to our own or others' inclinations, without being the master of anyone else.

Kant's program is impressive. He doesn't duck the fundamental moral questions. If he has successfully answered the three-part question posed, he is indeed a giant among humans. Kant fully realized that his answer should not be merely personal, idiosyncratic, or arbitrary; he intended it to be objectively valid. Let's see why he thought it was.

10.2 The Objectivity of Moral Laws and the Categorical Imperative

The Categorical Imperative makes objective judgments about deontic properties possible, just as yardsticks make objective measurement and arithmetical rules make objective calculation possible. Standards provide for both objectivity and mistakes. They provide for objectivity because they are the source or measure of correctness and incorrectness, right and wrong, true and false, valid and invalid. At the same time they provide for mistakes because they give us something to stray from; if something weren't objectively the case, we couldn't be wrong about it—nor right about it either.

Plato thought that the concept of the good was our moral standard; he was a teleologist. Kant thought it was the Categorical Imperative; he was a deontologist.

But, you may ask, why should anyone and everyone accept the Categorical Imperative as a standard of objectivity? First, because it deals with the stable form of laws rather than their changing content; second, because it uses the test of consistency, which is a logical feature of form that every rational person accepts as a standard of reasoning. Let's look at these two reasons more closely.

Form and content. This is an ancient distinction. Traditionally, it was believed that reason deals with form and that content (or matter) comes from sense experience, not from reason. The Categorical Imperative is an objective standard because it uses the standard of reason on the form of universalized maxims.

"And just how do you find out who's been naughty and who's been nice?"

You're familiar with the concept of form from algebra. Take these two equations: $2 + 3 = 3 + 2$ and $6 + 7 = 7 + 6$. They have the same form, which is $a + b = b + a$. By putting the letters (variables) in place of the numbers, we rob the equations of their number content and leave only their arrangement or form.

In 10.3a I will show how Kant exposes the form or arrangement of maxims posed as laws. His emphasis on the form of maxims contrasts with the moral psychologists' emphasis on their content, which Kant thinks a mistake. Form is stable but content varies, as our algebra example shows. The moral psychologists' content comes from the experiences of wanting, desiring, needing, taking an interest, satisfying, pleasing, and so forth. From such unstable content, Kant thinks we cannot get any objective laws.

The teleological theory that the deontic properties of acts are to be judged by their consequences, good and bad, is a moral theory that rests on content or matter rather than form. Teleologists don't look at the form of an act's maxim but at the anticipated or actual experiences of those persons affected by the act. For example, if thanking someone for a kindness produces pleasure, and if pleasure is a good, then the act of thanking is right. This "content" test of deontic properties does not rest ultimately on reason but on our affective-emotional life. The varying and uncertain nature of this content, however, doesn't provide the universality and necessity that Kant thinks attaches to moral laws, and which must attach if they are to be objective **331** rather than subjective.

Form and consistency. We can tell from form alone if a statement is inconsistent with itself or with another statement; we don't need to know anything about its content. This is why it has been held traditionally that form is reason's province. For example, "A white thing is not white" is inconsistent with itself; its form is "A is not A." This is self-contradictory and so necessarily false. "I am a man and I am not a man" are two inconsistent statements; their form is "A and not A," where "A" is a letter variable replacing the two occurrences of "I am a man." These two statements contradict each other; hence, it is necessarily false to state both simultaneously about the same thing.

We have just seen how the feature of necessity—necessarily false—gets attached to statements. Kant's Categorical Imperative test is just a search for this kind of necessity in the form of universalized maxims.

> If a universalized maxim is inconsistent with itself, then it is impossible for it to be true, which is equivalent to saying it is *necessary* that the maxim be false.

> If a universalized maxim is inconsistent with a true statement, then it is impossible for the universalized maxim to be true, which is equivalent to saying it is *necessary* that the maxim be false.

The move is from inconsistency to impossibility to necessity. Insofar as anyone aims at valid reasoning, they accept consistency as an objective criterion, and consequently also accept the Categorical Imperative as an objective criterion, since it is simply a test for consistency. Kant thinks that anyone who occupies the moral realm is rational; if they are rational, they accept consistency as an objective criterion of truth; consequently, they will accept the Categorical Imperative as an objective standard of morality.

10.3 Four Steps from Maxims to Moral Laws

In the next sub-sections I will show how Kant modifies maxims by (i) giving them a conditional form, (ii) universalizing them, and (iii) treating them *as if* they were causal laws (had causal direction), and then how he (iv) proceeds to determine their deontic status (obligatory, forbidden, permissible) by looking for internal or external inconsistency. Here I will only give a sketch of how to look for inconsistency, so as to provide the essence of Kant's theory. A fuller, detailed, and exact practical application of the Categorical Imperative to examples will be found in the appendix to this chapter.

10.3a THE FORM AND CONTENT OF MAXIMS. Maxims
have seven elements, and will have different content if any one of the elements

332   differs. Giving a maxim a conditional form is quite simple: take the first six elements and preface them with "if," then preface the last element, the act element, with "then." Assume that each element expresses some particular thought content, which I will abstractly indicate here with sub-numerals on letters. Thus we get:

> If   (1) I represent an end, E_1, and
>   (2) I believe that certain circumstances, C_1, prevail, and
>   (3) I believe that certain means, M_1, will achieve the end; and
>   (4) I intend to produce results, R_1, and not others, R_2; and
>   (5) I know the moral law, L_1, covering my act; and
>   (6) I consciously choose my moral motive, MM_1, and/or my pathological motive, PM_1;
> then (7) I will perform or refrain from act A_1.

10.3b UNIVERSALIZING A MAXIM. Laws are general; they hold of all similar cases. A law of acceleration for falling bodies applies to all such bodies, not just to some. Kant thinks that moral laws too must apply to all similar cases, not just to some. A moral law obligates all of us to act as it prescribes. "Thou shalt not steal" applies to everyone; if it didn't, it wouldn't be a law.

To illustrate this step in modifying a maxim, I shall replace "I" with "any person" in the example below, whose sample content is from one of Kant's maxims.

> *If*   (1) Any person represents an end, E_1, e.g., to obtain money;
> > *and*
>
>   (2) That person believes the circumstances, C_1, are such and so, e.g., he (or she) knows he needs money and will be unable to repay it;
> > *and*
>
>   (3) That person has beliefs about the means, M_1, that will help achieve the end, e.g., that people will lend money if promised repayment;
> > *and*
>
>   (4) That person intends to produce the results, R_1, and not others, R_2, e.g., to get the money but not to be punished for failure to repay;
> > *and*
>
>   (5) That person knows the moral law, L_1, e.g., that it is forbidden to make false promises;
> > *and*
>
>   (6) That person consciously chooses the moral motive, MM_1, and/or the pathological motive, PM_1, e.g., that he (or she) has a moral feeling caused by awareness of a duty not to falsely promise, and has the pathological feeling of being inclined to falsely promise to promote his (or her) happiness,

then (7) that person will perform some act, A_1, or its omission, not A_1,   **333**
e.g., uttering "I promise to repay you." (More on this later.)

To summarize: For any person, if elements 1–6, then act, A_1 (or not A_1).
I will refer to elements 1–6 as the antecedent-factors, and to element 7 as the
act-factor.

10.3c THE "AS IF" CAUSAL DIRECTION OF UNIVERSAL-IZED MAXIMS.

Earlier, I distinguished acts from motions (pp. 287,
310). What distinguishes acts from motions is the thought that precedes the
motion—a thought that is made up of the first six elements of a maxim, which
enable us to give an act-description of the motion. Since the act-description
depends upon the first six elements of a maxim, the direction of a moral law
goes from those first six elements, the antecedent-factors, to the act. The act-
description is dependent upon the six elements, and not vice versa; this is
made explicit by their order in the conditional form.

To understand Kant's Categorical Imperative test, we will have to be
clear about the difference between the direction and necessity features of
moral and natural laws, and must understand how the "as though" assumption of their similarity enables us to identify moral laws. This sub-section will
explain "as though" for direction; subsection 10.3d will explain it for necessity.

The difference between the direction of moral and natural laws is this:
the six elements of a maxim that precede an act enable us to *identify* what
kind of act a motion is, whereas the antecedent conditions that precede an effect *cause* the effect. The first gives us the direction of act-description and
identification, the second the direction of causality. What the antecedent-
factors of moral and natural laws have in common is that direction flows
from them to the act and the effect respectively.

Now let's take another look at Kant's "as though" formulation of the
Categorical Imperative.

Act as though the maxim of your action were by your will to become a
universal law of nature.

This time I want you to notice the phrase "by your will." Kant is asking you to assume the stance of a creator of the world. We assume that as a
creator you have the power to legislate the laws for events in the world you are
going to create. Kant knows we don't create the natural world; but because
he believes that we have the power of our will to create the social world, a
social totality, he thinks it appropriate here to assume the creative stance. We
can now say what the "as though" means for direction: to act "as though" is
to assume you decree that, whenever the antecedent-factors of some moral
law are present, they will (always) *cause* the occurrence of the act. For example, if you resolve to falsely promise to repay a loan with antecedent-factors as
in Kant's example on p. 332, then it is as though you decreed that whenever
those factors are present, they will *cause* everyone to say (falsely), "I promise
to repay." So when we ask, in accord with the Categorical Imperative,

334 whether my universalized maxim can be a moral law, we are to think "as though" the antecedent six elements of a maxim always cause the act to occur. Once we have done this, we then look to see if this universalized maxim does or does not have the modality of necessity, the fourth feature of moral laws. Let's turn now to consider the "necessity" of moral laws.

10.3d NECESSITY, INCONSISTENCY, AND THE CORRESPONDENCE PRINCIPLE.

Necessity is a truth modality, as are possibility and impossibility; they are modes of truth. A statement's truth may be necessary or possible or impossible. The truths of mathematics and logic are necessary; it is necessarily true that a = a. Statements of fact have the modality of possibility; it is possibly true that my dog has fleas; it is neither necessary nor impossible that my dog has fleas.

The truth modalities, like the deontic moral modalities—obligatory, permissible, and impermissible—are interdefinable: they can be defined in terms of one another. We saw earlier (p. 301) that "permissible" and "impermissible" can be defined in terms of "obligatory." Similarly, "possible" and "impossible" can be defined in terms of "necessary."

In this subsection we will learn how Kant uses his tactic of thinking about universalized maxims "as though" they were natural laws, so as to determine whether or not a proposed moral law has or has not the fourth feature of moral laws, necessity. Put at its simplest, we first determine the truth modality of a moral law considered as though it were a natural law; then, given a correspondence between truth and deontic moral modalities, we can tell what deontic modality the proposed moral law has. Kant connects the truth and deontic modalities as follows in what I will call the *Correspondence Principle:*

If as a natural law a maxim is necessary, then as a moral law it is obligatory; if it is impossible, then it is impermissible (forbidden); if it is possible, then it is permissible.

We can state the relations between truth modalities about nature and deontic modalities about morality in a succinct way:

Necessary Truth   corresponds to Moral Obligation
Impossible Truth corresponds to Moral Prohibition (Impermissibility)
Possible Truth   corresponds to Moral Permissibility

Kant's tactic is to move from the truth about natural totalities on the left, to the deontic properties of social totalities on the right.

Suppose that you are in the situation posed by Kant's false-promising example. You need money, you know you can get it by promising to repay, and you know you can't repay. You are faced with choosing between the positive and the negative maxim: are you going to promise to repay or to refrain from promising?

According to Kant, you are to ask if either maxim can or cannot be made into a natural law; this is his "as though" tactic. Thus you are to consider the universalized positive maxim and the universalized negative maxim "as though" they were natural laws. How will doing this enable you to determine the deontic modality of these alternative acts?

First, we determine the truth modality of these "as though" natural laws. Suppose we decide to make it a natural law that we will lie whenever we know that we can get away with it and that it will benefit us. In that case, everyone will do likewise. Because we have specified that one of the antecedent-factors is that we can get away with it, no one else will be the wiser. Since this ignorance is part of our proposed natural law, *no one* will be able to tell when someone else is lying; and knowing this, everyone knows they can no longer tell when others are lying or telling the truth. Consequently, everyone loses a hold on what is true and what is false in others' statements. Lying, which depends on being able to distinguish between truth and falsehood in others' statements, disappears; hence our resolve to lie under those universalized "as though" causal conditions becomes *impossible*. This "as though" natural law has the truth modality of impossibility.

Second, we use the Correspondence Principle stated above, which tells us that the impossibility of universal lying under those conditions corresponds to the *prohibition* of lying under those conditions.

In the example where we just dealt with lying, I said that our resolve to lie makes lying disappear and so become impossible when it is stated as an "as though" natural law. Now let's be more precise about how we find out if "as though" causal laws are impossible by explicitly tying this to the search for inconsistency. Natural laws may be *internally* or *externally* inconsistent.

Internal inconsistency and impossibility. A statement of a natural law is internally inconsistent if the antecedent-factors are self-contradictory. We know they are so when we find that at least two elements may be put in the form of "A and not A." Since it is impossible for "A and not A" to be true, then a maxim posing as a natural law has been found to have the feature of impossibility. Given the correspondence between the truth modality of impossibility and the deontic modality of impermissibility as stated in the Correspondence Principle, we will have discovered an objective moral law that forbids an act.

If everyone promises to repay a loan when the antecedent-factors are as in Kant's example, and if it turns out that this produces a contradiction within those factors—for example, that promising to repay ceases to be a means for getting a loan (M, and –M, Element 3, p. 332)—then this "as though" natural law has antecedent-factor conditions that are impossible to fulfill; so, necessarily, it can't have any instances. This means, given the correspondence between impossible and impermissible, that it is impermissible to promise repayment when those antecedent-factors are as stated in the maxim; or, it is obligatory not to promise when those factors are as stated.

External inconsistency and impossibility. In a single totality such as the natural world, the natural laws for events in it have to be consistent with one another. Here consistency is external because we are dealing with the con-

336   sistency of one law with another law outside of it.   If we find that universalizing a maxim and treating it "as though" it were a natural law results in a law that is inconsistent with a known natural law, then our proposed law is impossible; we can't will such a law to be true.   In other words, our proposed law is necessarily false.   Using the Correspondence Principle relating truth to deontic modalities once again, we will have found that it is forbidden to act on a maxim that is externally inconsistent when universalized.   I can't give you an illuminating example of a maxim that Kant thinks is externally inconsistent, until you understand the distinction between "act maxims" and "end maxims," which is the topic of the next section.   (See pp. 367–69, Appendix, for an example of the external inconsistency of an end maxim.)

What you should have learned from this sub-section is how Kant connects (i) logical inconsistency, (ii) the truth modalities of "as though" natural laws, and (iii) the deontic modalities of moral laws.   As supersensible, rational creatures, we use our logical abilities to assess the sensible results of universally acting on a maxim.   While our thoughts are in the supersensible world, our practice is in the sensible world.   As supersensible moral agents we are trying to create a sensible social totality; but we can't create willy nilly because there are logical limits imposed on this creative activity.   Moral laws draw these logical limits.   A social totality can exist only within the logical limits of internal consistency and external consistency with the natural laws governing the sensible world.

10.4 Maxims of Acts and Maxims of Ends

Strictly speaking, there are not two kinds of maxims, act and end maxims.   Rather, they are different combinations of certain elements in a "complete" seven-element maxim.   Let's sort them out.

Element 1: Representation of an end
Element 2: Belief about circumstances
Element 3: Belief about means
Element 4: Intent to produce certain results and not other results
Element 5: Knowledge of the moral law
Element 6: Consciousness of our choice of motives
Element 7: Resolve to perform or to refrain from an act

Act maxims consist of the circumstances, means, results, and act elements of a complete maxim; the end element is excluded.

End maxims consist of the end, circumstances, means, results, and act elements of a complete maxim; the end element is included.

Notice that the motive element, 6, appears in neither act nor end maxims.   We use it to determine the worthiness of the person; it contributes nothing to the deontic status of an act.   The moral law element, 5, likewise appears in neither act nor end maxims. This is because act and end maxims **337** consist of the elements that we use to determine *if* the maxim, when universalized, *is* a moral law.

Act maxims are what we need to determine the "legality" of a maxim; they are the concern of the doctrine of justice. End maxims are what we need to determine the "morality" of a maxim; they are the concern of the doctrine of virtue. (See Chapter 9, pp. 302–03 and 312–13 for discussions of these terms.) Thus the fifth element of a complete maxim, knowledge of the moral law, comes *after* we have considered the act and end maxims of the complete maxim; and the sixth element, the moral feeling motive, *follows* the thought of the law (see p. 276).

Act maxims are what we consider when we want to know if an *act* such as lying to save a friend's life is obligatory, impermissible, or permissible. End maxims are what we consider when we want to know if an *end* such as the happiness of others is obligatory, impermissible, or permissible.[1]

A legislator who has to decide if a proposed piece of legislation should be a law has to consider (a) what act the proposal prescribes (pay 20% of your income as tax) or forbids (no one under 21 years of age may be served alcoholic beverage in a bar), and (b) what its deontic status is; he determines the latter by applying the Categorical Imperative in the form stated in the Kant reference just cited. The legislator need consider only act maxims. He or she doesn't have to be concerned with what ends a person might have in mind when committing or omitting the act; the legislator—and sheriff too—is concerned only with the legality of the act. And when the law prescribes or forbids an act, our act's "legality" can be known without our having to think about an end we want to achieve by the act; here we are constrained by the "general" will of the legislators.

But when we come to ethics or morals in the narrow sense—an area of decision about what act to commit or omit that isn't covered by an enacted law—we have to constrain *ourselves,* and for this we have to represent an end. There is no occasion consciously to choose an act, unless we first represent an end to ourselves. This is because at any one time an indefinite number of acts are open to us; our decision to perform one of them depends on the end we have in mind; ends operate as criteria for selecting from among possible acts. As you read this you could continue to read, or get up and go to the grocery, or call a friend, water your plants. Which one you choose to do depends upon your choice of ends. Your willing an act not prescribed by others includes willing an end.

There are, of course, an indefinite number of ends that you can will. It is here that the deontic status of ends becomes relevant. Kant thinks there are some ends that are obligatory—that is, there are some ends from among all possible ends that you ought to choose; among these he stresses the self-realization of your natural and moral perfection, and the happiness of others.

Kant calls an obligatory end maxim a "wide" duty or sometimes an "imperfect" duty. This is because it doesn't specify any particular act; it only requires that we perform some universalizable act or other that will

338   enable us to achieve the obligatory end. To realize our natural perfection, for example, we have to cultivate our talents, but there is a "wide" latitude in this duty; no specific acts can categorically be prescribed to accomplish this. This is because there may be several universalizable ways to an end; which we choose depends on the circumstances in which we find ourselves. Thus to develop your talents, you may choose to study chemistry, history, accounting, or engineering.

Obligatory act maxims, on the other hand, are *narrow* duties or, as Kant sometimes says, "perfect" duties. "I promise to repay" is a specific act element in the false-promising maxim. A law that prescribes paying 20% of your income as tax to the government prescribes a specific act; here you have no latitude—only one "narrow" act will satisfy the law: paying 20%.

The Categorical Imperative for act maxims: "Act externally in such a way that the free use of your will is compatible with the freedom of everyone according to a universal law."[2] He also calls this formulation the "universal law of justice."

The Categorial Imperative for end maxims: "Act according to a maxim of *ends* which it can be universal for everyone to have" (*Virtue,* p. 55).

The distinctions made in this section can be summarized by a two-column list. This is a major division in Kant's theory of morals. His notion of morals in the wide sense includes both political and personal morality, both the public and the private; both are covered by the Categorical Imperative.

Maxims of Acts	Maxims of Ends
Elements: Circumstances, Means, Results, and Act	Elements: End, Circumstances, Means, Results, and Act
Deontic status of acts determined	Deontic status of ends determined
Doctrine of Justice	Doctrine of Virtue
Legality of acts	Morality of acts
Outer legislation (may be by others) ("outer duties")	Inner legislation (only we can adopt ends) ("inner duties")
Narrow (perfect) duties	Wide (imperfect) duties
Outer freedom (freedom of our wills can coexist together)	Inner freedom (constraint of inclinations in choosing ends and acts)
Categorical Imperative formulated for act maxims	Categorical Imperative formulated for end maxims

10.5 Contrasts with the Categorical Imperative

As we have seen, Kant's test for a moral law is logical consistency, internal or external. We universalize a maxim we are considering, treating it "as though" it were a natural law governing everyone's actions under the maxim's

antecedent-factor conditions.   Its consistency or inconsistency gives us its   **339**
truth modality; using the Correspondence Principle, we then learn what the
deontic modality of this universalized maxim is.   In effect, Kant bids us ask
for the *logical* outcome of *"What if everyone did that?"*

In the appendix to this chapter, I work out in detail how we go about
discovering the logical "consistency" results of "everyone doing that." Here,
however, to help you understand Kant's test, I will contrast it with two others
with which it might be confused: the Golden Rule and a generalization test.
Let's see how they differ in dealing, for instance, with lying.

10.5a LYING AND THE GOLDEN RULE. James Gould, a contemporary philosopher, has noted that "as an ethical standard 'The Golden
Rule' is not highly thought of by philosophers writing in the area of ethics.
They seldom mention it.   Surprisingly, neither do the writers in religious
ethics." [3]

Kant is among those philosophers who do not think highly of the
Golden Rule.   He mentions it only in a footnote,[4] where he says that, unlike
his Categorical Imperative, it can't serve as a test for laws. "Do unto others as
you would have them do unto you" (which is a common formulation of the
Golden Rule) can't be a test because (a) from this we can't get any duties to
ourself, but only to others; (b) we can't get from it a duty of benevolence to
others because, as he writes, "many a one would gladly consent that others
should not benefit him, provided only that he might be excused from showing
benevolence to them"; and (c) it could lead to the violation of duty, since the
criminal might argue that the judge punishing him should act as the judge
would like the criminal to act toward him, were their roles reversed.

The Golden Rule grows naturally out of the question "What if
everybody did that?"   Here are a couple of examples where this question is
asked.

There's this "truth machine" you can buy that looks like a cassette tape
recorder and is supposed to light up green when someone is telling the truth
and red when there's a good chance he's lying.

The makers expect to bring out a wristwatch-sized model, and that
could make universal truth-telling well-nigh compulsory—revolutionizing
our business and social lives, for better or for worse . . . .

The machine—called the "Hagoth"—picks up inaudible vocal
changes (an absence of normal voice tremors) caused by stress.   And telling lies causes stress, turning on the red lights.

When I first heard about this contraption it occurred to me that it
could come in handy for a reporter.   "The Senator denied he had ever met
Tongsun Park, but confronted with red lights on the reporters' truth
machine, he recalled that perhaps he had run into the lobbyist at some
Washington cocktail party and in fact knew him well."

340

But what if everyone gets hold of one of these Hagoth things? What would happen to privacy? Do you have a constitutional right not to tell the truth, or should everybody read your inmost thoughts as soon as you open your mouth?[5]

The second example is also about lying.

One Monday morning, the students in a Pittsburgh junior high school started their civics class with a brief "moral dilemma."
"Sharon and Jill were best friends. One day they went shopping together. Jill tried on a sweater and then, to Sharon's surprise, walked out of the store with the sweater under her coat. A moment later, the store's security officer stopped Sharon and demanded that she tell him the name of the girl who had walked out. He told the storeowner that he had seen the two girls together, and that he was sure that the one who left had been shoplifting. The storeowner told Sharon that she could really get in trouble if she didn't give her friend's name."
"Should Sharon tell?" the teacher asked.
One student suggested that Sharon should deny knowing Jill. Did the student approve of lying for a friend? the teacher wanted to know. "Yeah," was the answer. "What is going to happen to all of us if everyone lies?" the teacher inquired.[6]

There are several versions of the Golden Rule. Superficially, each of them appears to have a built-in principle that everybody is to be treated alike. The Golden Rules supposedly place a universalization criterion on the way we are to treat others and on the way they are to treat us. They tell everyone not to make exceptions. Here are the three versions.

Version One: Do unto others as *you* would be done to.
This version requires that you test what you are contemplating to do to others by asking if you would want others to do it to you. You want to secretly use your Hagoth wristwatch while asking your girl friend about her activities last week. Should you do it? No, not to her or anyone else, if you don't want anyone to do it to you. This version is a popular formulation of the rule attributed to Jesus Christ in his Sermon on the Mount (Matthew 7:12): "Therefore all things whatsoever ye would that men should do to you, do ye even so to them."

Version Two: Do unto others as *they* would be done to.
The first version asked you to consider how *you* wanted to be treated; this second version bids you ask others how *they* want to be treated. Does your girl friend mind your secretly using your Hagoth wristwatch on her? If she does, then, according to Version Two, you are not to use it.
Versions One and Two together provide a test in which all may participate. In the event that you and others agree on how you want to be treated, then the contemplated act has *universal approval.* But does it follow that the contemplated act is right? Does it, in other words, enable us to determine correctly the deontic status of the contemplated act? Henry Sidgwick, an eminent English moral philosopher of the last century, thought not.

Sidgwick cites the first version of the Golden Rule—"Do to others as you would have them do to you"—then remarks: "This formula is obviously unprecise in statement; for one might wish for another's co-operation in sin, and be willing to reciprocate it."[7]

Sidgwick's objection applies to the second version also: "reciprocation" could occur when others wish for and we agree to cooperate in a sin. Thus everyone might universally approve a sin; but, since a sin is morally wrong, universal approval is not a sufficient criterion for determining the deontic status of an act.

Sidgwick does think that the Golden Rule, in its first version, appeals implicitly to a universality test. He formulates this principle: "We cannot judge an action to be right for A and wrong for B, unless we can find in the natures or circumstances of the two some difference which we can regard as a reasonable ground for difference in their duties. If therefore I judge any action to be right for myself, I implicitly judge it to be right for any other person whose nature and circumstances do not differ from my own in some important respects" (p. 209). This principle explicitly introduces the terms "right" and "wrong," which are absent from the Golden Rules. This is an important addition, because otherwise you can interpret the Golden Rules to be merely about our wishes and wants: do unto others what you *want* done to yourself.

While universal approval of an act doesn't guarantee that it is morally right, might its *absence* guarantee that it is morally wrong? Suppose by Version Two that others don't mind your using the Hagoth wristwatch; then the second version of the Golden Rules justifies your using it on others. But suppose by Version One that you don't want others to use it on you; then the first version does *not* justify your using it. Here, Versions One and Two produce a contradiction. You could also describe this outcome as showing that using the Hagoth wristwatch is not universally approved; if the Golden Rules implicitly impose a universal test, and if we introduce "right" and "wrong" as Sidgwick suggests, then, since you don't want it used secretly on you, it would be wrong for anyone to use the Hagoth wristwatch, since you are "other" to them. In fact, others using Version Two would be forbidden to use it on you—unless differences in circumstances or natures provided a reason for departure from the rule.

Here now is the third form of the Golden Rule.

Version Three: What you do not want done to you, do *not* do to others.

This is a complement of Version One: Three deals with acts of omission and One with acts of commission. Version Three is a restatement of Rabbi Hillel's rule, "What is hateful to thee, do not unto thy fellowman."

Although, from the above reasoning, it appears that lack of universal approval shows it would be wrong to use the Hagoth, we can throw doubt on this conclusion by asking *why* you don't want it used on you. If you don't want it used on you because you're afraid you'll be caught lying about how you got your sudden wealth (perhaps by embezzlement), this hardly seems a *moral* basis for holding out against universal approval. Not every reason for invoking Version One, Two, or Three is a moral reason, therefore the Golden Rules do not by themselves reveal whether an act is wrong; the act may simply

342 be wanted or unwanted. The Golden Rules, then, are inadequate tests for the deontic status of acts. They tell us nothing about the basis for anyone's consenting or not consenting to be treated or to treat others in a given way.

That the Golden Rules, then, singly or in combination, are not the same as Kant's Categorical Imperative, is obvious as soon as one reflects that they do not hunt the same game: they do not claim to tell us anything about the modality of a proposed rule of action. They tell us nothing about necessity because they tell us nothing about the internal or external consistency of everyone following the proposed rule; they simply bid us be consistent in the way we want to be treated and in the way we treat others. Even if there is universal approval of an act, nothing about the necessity of it follows from this approval. It is perfectly possible that everyone might want everyone else to check their statements with the Hagoth machine, which would give them sanction to use it to check secretly the truthfulness of others. But this is merely a coincidental agreement of what everybody wants; the Golden Rules have not shown that this is what everybody ought (or ought not) to do. Clearly, if Kant is right when he demands that nothing can be a moral law unless it has the feature of necessity, the Golden Rules are inadequate tests of morality.

10.5b LYING AND GENERALIZATION. Marcus Singer is an important and influential advocate of a *generalization* test of moral rules. Singer makes it clear that this is different from the Categorical Imperative (though not everyone is as clear about this as he is). I will deal with the generalization principle only to the extent that it helps us understand the Categorical Imperative test better.

Singer points out that the generalization principle has also been called "the principle of fairness or justice or impartiality."[8] He distinguishes between the "generalization *principle*" and the "generalization *argument*"; the principle is a premiss in the argument. Here now are Singer's formulations of the principle; you will see that it is the same as Sidgwick's principle quoted above in connection with the Golden Rules (p. 341).

> Thus the generalization principle can be formulated in any of the following ways. What is right for one person cannot be wrong for another, unless there is some relevant difference in their natures or circumstances. Or, what is right (or wrong) for one person must be right (or wrong) for everyone, if there is no reason to the contrary. This is obviously equivalent to saying that what is right for one person must be right for every similar person in similar circumstances . . . . In the form especially appropriate to the generalization argument, the principle may be stated: If not everyone ought to act or be treated in a certain way, then no one ought to act or be treated in that way without a reason. (*Generalization*, p. 32)

"Similar natures" and "similar circumstances" are important conditions in the generalization principle. Two people might have different colored skin and so not be "similar persons"; but Singer thinks this by itself would not be morally relevant and would not give, for example, the light-skinned person a reason to act differently from the dark-skinned one. If they have different governmental positions, this could constitute a morally relevant difference. The president of the United States has a morally relevant different position from private citizens; we aren't "similar persons." We can't give an order ending a war but the president can, and he might well be under moral obligation to do so.

The generalization *argument* comes to the fore when the answer to "What if everyone did that?" is: "It would be disastrous (or undesirable)." The argument goes like this (*Generalization,* pp. 63–68):

(1) Principle of Generalized Consequences: If the consequences of everyone's doing x would be undesirable, then not everyone has the right to do x (without a morally relevant reason).

(2) Generalization Principle: If not everyone has the right to do x (without a morally relevant reason), then no one has a right to do x.

(3) From which it follows: If the consequences of everyone's doing x would be undesirable, then no one has a right to do x (including me).

> The application of the generalization argument presupposes, and does not itself determine, that the consequences of everyone acting in a certain way would be undesirable. (p. 11)

Singer here refers to the premiss (1) of the generalization argument. Notice that premiss (1) connects undesirability and the deontic phrase, "not everyone has the right." If the undesirability of an act is based on the inclinations of our sensible self, then the connection between desirability and right is one that rests on human nature. Kant cannot accept this; he rejects the moral psychologists' claim that morals have their source in human nature and its propensities and inclinations. Morals rest on reason alone; desirability and undesirability are not purely rational factors; therefore, they cannot be used to establish a moral law.

To push the difference further, "undesirability" is not a synonym for the truth modality "impossibility" or the deontic modality "impermissibility"; nor is "desirability" a synonym for "necessity" or "obligation." Hence, the generalization principle and argument do not provide the test for moral modality that Kant seeks. The undesirability of everyone lying is not the same as the impossibility of everyone lying.

Before turning to Kant's test for the moral modality of lying, let's see how the generalization test works. Singer would approve the teacher's asking her students, "What is going to happen to all of us if everyone lies?" Like Singer, she is directing attention to the consequences of everyone lying. If it is disastrous or at least undesirable, then no one ought to lie.

The use of the generalization principle and argument requires that we specify the "similar circumstances." A lie told to save a life is an act whose circumstances differ from a lie told to cheat. It is possible that the cheating

344 lie is wrong while the life-saving lie is right, because the cheating lie might lead to undesirable consequences while the life-saving lie might not. The teacher's question (p. 340) is, however, overly general. The specific circumstance her students were asked to consider was a shoplifting one where two friends were involved; but her question asks about the consequences of lies regardless of the circumstances. Her question is really this: What is going to happen to all of us if everyone lies *in every circumstance?*

Here the students should have to consider only the consequences of everyone intentionally denying knowledge of the identity of a friend who has shoplifted. It is doubtful that being a friend is a circumstance that gives one an excuse not to identify a shoplifter; so in predicting the consequences of everyone lying about a person's identity, let's open it to the circumstance that the shoplifter need not be a friend but anyone we know. (What if it's your mother? And it's a new sweater for your birthday present? And no one in the family has a job?)

One consequence of everyone refusing to identify a shoplifter might be an increase in the number of people who take advantage of us, leading to an increase in stolen goods. This would cut stores' profits; to compensate for the loss in profit, store managers might raise the price of their goods or increase the number of security officers, each of which would result in greater costs to those of us who buy our goods rather than "lift" them. Is this a disastrous consequence? Well, maybe not, but for us it's at least undesirable. Is it undesirable enough to lead us to say that "no one has the right to deny knowing a shoplifter's identity (without a morally relevant reason)"? This is the issue put to you by the generalization principle and argument, when you reflect on the morality of not identifying your friends.

J. M. Cameron reviewed Sissela Bok's book, *Lying: Moral Choice in Public and Private Life* (New York: Pantheon Books, 1978). He suggested that the consequences of lying differ when the liars have different kinds of work, which is related to Sidgwick and Singer's hedge about "similar persons."

> Hypocrisy, deceit, falseness to one's word, self-deception, the treachery of appearances . . . these have always been the staple of human life, as playwrights and novelists have known very well. But there are those for whom mendacity is a deeper wound, a heavier fall, than for others. Such are the professions, medicine, the law, scholarship, and teaching. For these the practice of lying is more wounding than for, say, those who live by the market or who get their living by entertaining the public. It is good that these latter should tell the truth; but if the former fall into mendacity they have destroyed the substance of their lives and made their professions useless for their formal purposes.[9]

A listing of Bok's chapter titles suggests the variety of circumstances and persons that many have thought relevant to differing judgments about the morality of lying: "White Lies," which includes "Letters of Recommendation''; ''Lies in a Crisis''; ''Lying to Liars''; ''Lying to Enemies''; ''Lies Protecting Peers and Clients''; ''Lies for the Public Good''; ''Paternalistic Lies''; and ''Lies to the Sick and Dying.''

Bok includes in an appendix Kant's article ''On a Supposed Right to Lie from Altruistic Motives.'' Kant thinks we have no such right. He says:

> To be truthful (honest) in all declarations, therefore, is a sacred and absolutely commanding decree of reason, limited by no expediency. . . . The duty of truthfulness . . . makes no distinction between persons to whom one has a duty and to whom one can exempt himself from this duty; rather, it is an unconditional duty which holds in all circumstances. (Bok, pp. 269, 271)

Kant doesn't think we have the right to lie even for the altruistic purpose of saving a life. The critics of Kant have been legion. Bok gives an example of a typical reply:

> Similarly, a captain of a ship transporting fugitives from Nazi Germany, if asked by a patrolling [German] vessel whether there were any Jews on board would, for Kant's critics, have been justified in answering No. His duty to the fugitives, they claim, would then have conflicted with the duty to speak the truth and would have far outweighed it. In fact, in times of such crisis, those who share Kant's opposition to lying clearly put innocent persons at the mercy of wrongdoers. (Bok, pp. 40–41)

The generalization principle doesn't seem necessary here. The consequences of the act of a *single* man's telling the truth in this circumstance are claimed to be so sufficiently undesirable that it seems unnecessary to ask for the consequences of *everyone's* telling the truth in a similar circumstance. Kant's claim, however, is that *no* consequences, singly or universally, are relevant when we consider the morality of truth-telling. This gets us closer to the teacher's question, which wasn't limited to any particular circumstances. In his review, Cameron sketches the anticipated consequences of universal lying under any circumstances.

> But the habit of truthtelling, an acquired disposition to speak the truth even in situations where something else we value could be safeguarded, as we suppose at the time, by a lie, this seems quite straightforwardly a virtue, and what binds together any tolerable society.
>
> After all, truthtelling has to be the norm; if it isn't, language, considered as nonfictive communication, stumbles and collapses. And since language may fairly enough be thought constituitive of human nature, the most evident sign of the rationality believed to set man apart from the other animals, lying resembles spiritual suicide. Truthtelling seems so necessary a virtue that it has been tied to peaceableness, and the disposition to observe the Golden Rule, as a part of the comprehensive virtue of civility. (Cameron, p. 6)

346   **10.5c LYING AND THE CATEGORICAL IMPERATIVE.** Cameron, following Bok, raises doubts about universal truth-telling as a virtue, but he begins to approach Kant's conclusion when, like Kant, he applies a consistency test to the special position of the physician.

> Physicians, in particular, as Dr. Bok is able to show, in general treat truth roughly and have good consciences about the deceptions they practice. Many of them are now coming to doubt the doctor's right to lie to his patient, and *Lying* may convert some more. It is after all clear, to put the matter at its lowest, that if physicians are known to lie to patients about their conditions they will not be believed when what they say is true; when for instance they say that the tumor is benign; and it is true that it is benign. (Cameron, p. 9)

Cameron approximates Kant's consistency test because he thinks that, if it is *known* that lying is a practice, truth-telling becomes impossible. To carry the point further, if truth-telling is impossible, then so is lying. Thus universal lying contradicts itself; it is not self-consistent. This is a somewhat loose way of talking in which Kant and his commentators often indulge; it is a short way of invoking the criterion of inconsistency. In the appendix to this chapter I will relate this consistency test to the Categorical Imperative test more explicitly. We can take steps toward this explicitness by elaborating Cameron's argument, using some of Kant's ideas.

(1) Suppose a doctor's maxim is: I will lie to my patients about their terminal cancer (from the altruistic motive, or end, that I wish to protect them).

(2) We universalize and put the maxim in conditional form: If a patient has terminal cancer known to the doctor, then every doctor will lie to the patient.

(3) Treat this universalization "as though" it were a natural law.

(4) As a natural law—that doctors always lie under these circumstances—it can become known to all just as any natural law can become public knowledge.

(5) Lying and truth-telling are social phenomena that relate to the transmission of knowledge. To transmit knowledge requires (i) stating what is true and (ii) inducing belief in those who read us or listen to us.

(6) Inducing beliefs in others depends on an important condition. Belief in another's statement (for example, you do or do not have terminal cancer) depends upon another more basic belief that a doctor will always say what he or she believes is true, regardless of the circumstances. (The basic belief is a necessary condition for inducing other beliefs.)

(7) But the knowledge assumed in (4), the "as though" knowledge that doctors always lie under the circumstance of terminal cancer, renders the basic belief in doctors' truth-telling impossible.

(8) Therefore, there will not be any belief in doctors' statements about cancer, because they depend on the discredited basic belief in doctors' honesty. This holds even if a doctor's statement is true.

(9) If doctors can't induce beliefs in their statements, then doctors' lying and truth-telling alike will have failed. They have lost their social effect.

(10) If doctors' statements lose their effect, then there is no more medical lying and no more medical truth-telling. Again, lying and truth-telling are not just knowingly saying what is false and true, respectively, but saying them to induce others to believe one's statements.

(11) Therefore, doctors' adoption of the universalized maxim to lie to patients if they have terminal cancer contradicts itself, because it results in *not* lying (and in no truth-telling either); it does this because it nullifies (makes inoperative) the condition for success in lying and truth-telling.

(12) If universalizing the maxim produces the truth modality of impossibility, then, by the Correspondence Principle, we have to say that it is impermissible (forbidden) to lie to patients about their terminal cancer; or equivalently, it is obligatory not to lie to them under that circumstance.

This argument is not like the generalization argument. It doesn't look to the undesirable consequences of every doctor lying and conclude that, because it is undesirable that everyone lie, no one ought to lie. It concludes, instead, on the impossibility, and so the impermissibility, of every doctor lying.

This is not a fanciful case. The very day I completed writing this argument, I was handed a copy of the pamphlet "Do Doctors Know Best?" by the author Stan Roberts, who publishes his views on various topics in a publication called *People's Ideas*. He recounted that he had recently passed blood, heard on the radio that it was a symptom of cancer of the colon, went to a doctor who took x-rays with uncertain results, and was later told he had hemorrhoids. However, he was not reassured because he knew "some doctors do not tell patients the extent of an illness as they have diagnosed it. This is often done in the effort to give mental comfort to the patient." He then goes on to give an argument against doctors' lying. His argument is an instance of the generalization argument, not of Kant's inconsistency test. He notes the undesirable consequences of "What if every doctor did that?"

Allowing doctors such liberties [of lying] has social consequences that cause or facilitate real cancers and other diseases known to be caused or increased by people's fears. People like myself, with hemorrhoids or other minor maladies, should not have these fears. Living with anxiety causes many physical illnesses . . . .

Two weeks ago I visited a friend of mine and told him my story. This friend personally knew someone [his uncle] who had committed

348 suicide because he thought he had cancer. It was found in his autopsy that he merely had hemorrhoids. We are, each and every one of us, especially doctors, responsible for that man's death.[10]

Kant agrees with Roberts to the extent that he thinks the doctor is responsible for the consequences. In his article "On a Supposed Right to Lie from Altruistic Motives," he writes:

> Therefore, whoever tells a lie, however well intentioned he might be, must answer for the consequences, however unforeseeable they were, and pay the penalty for them even in a civil tribunal. This is because truthfulness is a duty which must be regarded as the ground of all duties based on contract, and the laws of these duties would be rendered uncertain and useless if even the least exception to them were admitted. (Bok, p. 269)

In the appendix, I will give a fuller formulation of Kant's Categorical Imperative test and show how he uses logical inconsistency and consistency to discover the truth and deontic modalities of universalized maxims.

10.6 The Nature of a Morally Perfect World

Kant thinks we have a duty to move, as the Correspondence Principle states (p. 334), from truth to deontic modalities—from impossibility to impermissibility—because we have a moral duty to move from the actual, morally imperfect world to a morally perfect world. We have, for instance, a duty to move from a world of casual lying to a better world of reliable truth-telling. As citizens of the intelligible, supersensible realm, we rational beings may envision our world remade in the ideal image of a morally perfect world. Because we also live in the sensible world, we must use its clay to sculpt a morally perfect one. But just as a sculptor has to respect the limits of his clay in fashioning the sculpture that exists in the mind's eye, so we moral sculptors have to respect the limits of the actual world in fashioning a morally perfect world. The morally perfect world has to be a possible actual one; this possible one exists between the limits of the impossible and the necessary. Hence, no one seeking to fashion a moral world can ignore the modalities of the impossible and the necessary.

This ideal, morally perfect world is, for all its ideality, conceived as a *world;* it is an envisioned *totality.* As an ideal moral *world,* it too has its limits, drawn by the impermissible and the obligatory. Hence, sculptors of the morally perfect world have to observe both the modalities of the actual world and the modalities of the morally perfect world, and consequently, their correspondence.

Let's see what a morally perfect world is like for Kant—and for us. The nature of such a world is a summary way of stating the central beliefs in

Kant's morality. I will first quote Kant and then extract what I think are the **349** central ideas. Notice that Kant starts off with rational beings considered as creators or sculptors of a "realm of ends," a "morally perfect world."

> The concept of each rational being as a being that must regard itself as giving universal law through all the maxims of its will, so that it may judge itself and its actions from this standpoint, leads to a very fruitful concept, namely, that of a *realm of ends*.
>
> By the "realm" I understand the systematic union of different rational beings through common laws. Because laws determine ends with regard to their universal validity, if we abstract from the personal difference of rational beings and thus from all content of their private ends, we can think of a whole of all ends in systematic connection, a whole of rational beings as ends in themselves as well as of the particular ends which each may set for himself. This is a realm of ends, which is possible on the aforesaid principles [formulations of the Categorical Imperative]. For all rational beings stand under the law that each of them should treat himself and all others never merely as means but in every case also as an end in himself. Thus there arises a systematic union of rational beings through common objective laws. This is a realm which may be called a realm of ends (certainly only an ideal), because what these laws have in view is just the relation of these beings to each other as ends and means.
>
> A rational being belongs to the realm of ends as a member when he gives universal laws in it while also subject to these laws. He belongs to it as sovereign when he, as legislating, is subject to the will of no other . . . .
>
> Morality, therefore, consists in the relation of every action to that legislation through which alone a realm of ends is possible. This legislation, however, must be found in every rational being . . . . Duty pertains not to the sovereign in the realm of ends, but rather to each member, and to each in the same degree.
>
> The practical necessity of acting according to this principle, i.e., duty, does not rest at all on feelings, impulses, and inclinations . . . but rather [proceeds] from the idea of the dignity of a rational being, which obeys no law except that which he himself also gives. (*Foundations,* pp. 321–22)

Extracting from these remarks, we can say that at least the following would be true of a morally perfect world.

(1) *Dignity and autonomy.* Everyone ("each member") is capable of knowing and self-legislating ("he himself gives") what is obligatory, impermissible, and permissible. We all have *Wille*.

(2) *Objectivity.* Everyone agrees on what is obligatory, impermissible, and permissible ("common laws").

(3) *Co-existing freedom.* Everyone does what is obligatory and refrains from what is impermissible ("the practical necessity of acting according to"). That is, each respects others' rights and freedom ("subject to the will of no other").

350

(4) *Good will.* Everyone does what is obligatory from the motive of duty. (Moral feeling, rather than "impulses and inclinations," is always the motive chosen by *Willkür.*)

(5) *Justice.* Everyone's happiness is proportional to their worthiness. (While happiness is not a moral category for Kant, justice is. A morally perfect world is also perfectly just; because perfect justice requires that everyone's happiness be proportionate to their moral perfection, a world in which we are all perfectly moral would be a perfectly just one only if everyone is also perfectly happy. Remember that the *summum bonum* has two parts: worthiness and happiness.)

This sketch of a morally perfect world, a realm of ends, can now be linked to some points about Kant's ethics made earlier.

(1) *Dignity and autonomy.* The first part of this outline of a morally perfect world connects with Kant's belief that humans have the moral worth of dignity. We have dignity because we have the capacity of giving ourselves moral laws; it is our autonomy or positive freedom.

(2) *Objectivity.* Kant provides a formal, logical standard that all rational beings can use for reaching rational agreement on what we ought and ought not to do. This is the Categorical Imperative, which directs us to base our moral conclusions on consistency and inconsistency.

(3) *Co-existing freedom.* Achieving moral perfection is always doing what we ought to do (and refraining from what we ought not to do). Doing what is obligatory is doing what everyone can do without hindering others from doing the same. Hence, in a morally perfect world there is co-existing freedom, which is a necessary condition for all to achieve the obligatory end of moral perfection.

(4) *Good will.* In a perfectly moral world our actions are not caused by our personal inclinations but by our respect for duty, which frees us from those inclinations. This is what makes us morally worthy. In a perfectly moral world we would all be perfectly worthy; we would have a "good will." "Nothing in the world—indeed nothing even beyond the world—can possibly be conceived which could be called [morally] good without qualification except a *good will*" *(Foundations,* p. 295). Moral self-realization, which is an obligatory end, is building our character so that our *Willkür* always chooses moral feeling as the motive for our actions.

(5) *Justice.* In a morally perfect world everyone adopts the end maxim of everyone aiding other persons in their quest for happiness. We should note that, in a morally imperfect world, there is one cir-

cumstance in which we seek to diminish others' happiness: when

justice demands it. A world may be perfectly just without being morally perfect; a morally imperfect world would be perfectly just if the imperfect happiness of each person were proportionate to each one's imperfect worthiness. As we have seen (pp. 306–07), Kant thought the state has a right to coerce persons to respect the rights of others; it has a right to hinder an action that hinders others from performing what is permissible and what is obligatory. Part of this coercion takes the form of punishment. Punishment is doing something to wrongdoers that diminishes their happiness. They get what they deserve; this is just.

> In every punishment as such there must first be justice, and this constitutes the essence of the concept . . . . Punishment is physical harm which, even if not bound as a natural consequence to the morally bad, ought to be bound to it as a consequence according to principles of moral legislation.[11]

Legislation not only specifies acts that we ought to do, but it also specifies the punishment we deserve if we break the law. This punishment is the law's sanction, which should not be looked on, Kant thinks, as a threat to deter us from crime or as a means of controlling our behavior; this would be "a mechanism destructive of freedom" (p. 40). Rather, the punishment is specified and administered in order to make happiness (and unhappiness) proportionate to worthiness (and unworthiness). To make it proportionate is to make the world more just. It would be an unjust world in which the morally unworthy were the happiest of men and the morally worthy the unhappiest. Recall the discussion about the Ring of Gyges and the profitability of injustice; Socrates argued that unprofitability is a "natural consequence to the morally bad"; Kant doesn't believe this, but he thinks it *ought* to be a consequence.

To summarize: in a morally perfect world (1) everyone has dignity and autonomy; (2) there is no moral conflict that isn't resolvable by reason; (3) no one's freedom to do what is obligatory and permitted is hindered; (4) everyone has a good will; and (5) each can count on the good will and help of all to achieve happiness.

10.7 Summary

In this chapter we have seen that Kant believes the Categorical Imperative provides us with an objective test of moral laws. This test, unlike the moral psychologists' reliance on subjective responses of human nature with its wants and inclinations, relies on our reason's grasp of logical consistency and inconsistency.

352   We have also seen how Kant relates the forms of maxims and their universalizations to their contents. The antecedent-factors in complete maxims and their universalizations consist of the first six elements of a maxim. They give us the direction of identification of the act; the identification of the act is dependent upon the thought content of the antecedent-factors and not vice versa. When we treat a universalized maxim "as though" it were a natural law, then we treat the antecedent-factors as if they were the causal conditions for the occurrence of the act.

Kant groups together different elements of a complete maxim when he differentiates between maxims of acts and maxims of ends. The test for act maxims is internal consistency: if they are internally inconsistent when treated "as though" they were natural laws, then such acts are impossible. The test for end maxims is external inconsistency; if they are found to be externally inconsistent, then such ends are impossible to will. Now, given the relations between truth modalities, if an act is impossible, then it is necessary that the act not occur; and given the Correspondence Principle (p. 334), we can relate the truth modality of necessity to the deontic modality of obligation, and so can determine if a universalized maxim is a moral law or not. The contrasts between act and end maxims were summarized on page 338.

Kant's search for moral laws by means of the Categorical Imperative involves four steps.

(I)   Identify a maxim's elements.
(II) Give it a conditional form, universalize it, and treat it "as though" it were a natural law.
(III) Search for an inconsistency, internal for act maxims and external for end maxims.
(IV) Use the Correspondence Principle to obtain the deontic modality.

A more explicit formulation and application of these four steps will be presented in the appendix to this chapter.

We examined three versions of the Golden Rule and found that in any version, singly or combined, it is not the same as the Categorical Imperative, and that it is an inadequate criterion for determining moral laws. When more carefully formulated, as Sidgwick and Singer did, the Golden Rules become the generalization principle, but this principle is not similar to the Categorical Imperative either. Further, because generalization uses undesirability in its test for obligation, and because undesirability is not the same as impermissibility, Kant would reject the generalization principle because it is an inadequate criterion for moral laws. Generalization cannot supply a test for necessity, which Kant thinks is a required feature for moral laws.

Finally, we saw what a morally perfect world is for Kant. It is a world whose construction is guided by the Categorical Imperative. Kant's Categorical Imperative is the foundation principle in a "metaphysics of morals" precisely because it states the conditions for creating a moral

world *(The Foundations of the Metaphysics of Morals)*. The description of **353**
this world summarizes Kant's moral theory.

The following figures summarize the relations between the main concepts in Kant's ethics. If you can thoughtfully follow through the arrows,
you have a good outline understanding of his moral theory. This first figure
is a simpler version of the second, which is a more complete representation of
Kant's main ethical concepts and the relations between them.

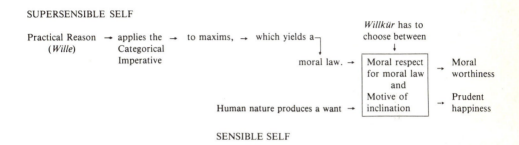

With the sketch of a morally perfect world—Kant's Realm of
Ends—and the Categorical Imperative, we have found a philosophy of morals
that supplies what Marin called for, which was for a human community in
which there is a web of reciprocity. Kant's conception of this community of
ends preserves our autonomy and dignity, and, so, escapes Ivan Ilyich's ordinariness; his conception also avoids Nietzsche's egoism and the "idolatry of
the self" because we respect others' freedom, and, at the same time, we do not
become slaves of others but remain our own moral master. You should now
have an understanding of Kant's answer to the question I posed at the beginning of this chapter, p. 328.

Practical reason for Kant consists of *Wille* and *Willkür*. *Wille* is the
legislative function that enables us to give ourselves moral laws; it is our
positive freedom. *Willkür* is the executive function, is free choice of moral
and/or pathological feeling; having the power to choose moral feeling as our
motive to action, it frees us from the dominance of inclinations and so is our
negative freedom from our sensible self.

I've drawn Kant's schema for the "sensible self" to be in agreement
with the moral psychologists' schema, and with sociobiologists who add
natural selection; like the moral psychologists, Kant includes an instrumental
role for reason to produce hypothetical, pragmatic imperatives. Kant differs
radically from them, however, in giving two roles to reason that they do not.
(1) *Wille:* Kant believes that practical reason as *Wille* can (a) determine values
by determining the deontic status of acts and ends, and (b) cause moral feeling
in us, thereby providing reason with a motive. (2) *Willkür:* Kant thinks that
practical reason as *Willkür* can freely choose between motives.

SUPERSENSIBLE SELF

Practical Reason *Wille* → Categorical Imperative: FOUR STEPS → Complete maxims: Seven elements → ⌈Act maxims⌉ / ⌊End maxims⌋ → ⌈Conditional / Universal / Directional / Necessary⌉ → Moral law → *Willkür* ⟨⟩ Respect-Constraint ⌈Moral feeling↑⌉ / ⌊Pathological feeling↓⌋

⌈Morally right act; and morally worthy person with good will⌉

Genes by natural selection → Human nature → Wants → Goods → Ends → (Continues from above) *Willkür* ⌈Moral feeling → Act₁⌉ / ⌊Pathological feeling → Act₂⌋

Utility: Instrumental reason's counsels of prudence

Happiness: A prudential act

SENSIBLE SELF

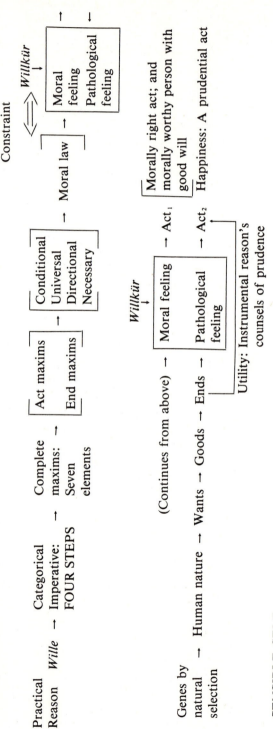

1 Why does Kant think that the Categorical Imperative is a test of moral laws that, if followed, will enable us to create a social totality? Think here of Kant's answer to the question: How is it possible for everyone to obey morally necessary laws while simultaneously maintaining their freedom and dignity?

2 What is the source of the Categorical Imperative? Why does Kant think that it has the power of objectively determining that subjective maxims can or cannot be turned into moral laws?

3 Can you take one of your own maxims and identify its elements? Put it in conditional form, universalize it, treat it as though it were a natural law, and find out whether it is inconsistent or not.

4 What are the truth modalities? The deontic modalities? What is the purpose of the Correspondence Principle? What role does inconsistency play in the use of the Correspondence Principle?

5 State the difference between internal and external inconsistency for universalized maxims. Explain this in connection with Kant's proposal to treat universalized maxims "as though" they were natural laws.

6 What are the four steps in using Kant's Categorical Imperative to find out if a maxim may be a moral law?

7 What is the difference between act and end maxims? Why do act maxims fall under legality (justice) while end maxims fall under morality (virtue)? Relate act and end maxims to internal and external inconsistency, respectively.

8 Why is the Golden Rule inadequate as a test for moral laws? Why can't Kant accept the generalization principle as the test for moral laws?

9 What are the main categories that Kant thinks are needed to describe the nature of a morally perfect world? Can you explain them to a friend?

10 Is it possible to have a perfectly just world and not to have a morally perfect world, according to Kant? Explain your answer.

Reflections on Applications

1 The Question Man once asked, "Who's getting more than a fair share?" Deanna Wieman answered:

> It's obvious that the lower income brackets have the advantage of a lot of resources that we don't. Resources like welfare, food stamps and so forth. They have those advantages that we in the middle income bracket don't have and are paying for them to have. On the other hand, I wouldn't want to switch places with them.[12]

356   If Wieman were to apply the Golden Rule to her answer, do you think
she would continue to think that they have "more than a fair share"?
Which version of the Golden Rule should she use?

2 Which feature of moral laws is affirmed by the following quotation?

> Like [the English playwright Tom] Stoppard, [Czech playwright Václav]
> Havel asks only to be allowed to work freely, without political
> surveillance. But that in itself is a political demand, and the man who
> makes it on his own behalf is morally bound to make it for others.[13]

3 Kant held that the Categorical Imperative was a standard to be used both
for the laws of political entities and the laws of personal morality; one
formulation of the Imperative was designed to identify external laws for
act maxims that legislators might pass, and another formulation was
designed for end maxims that we could personally adopt. The first provides for the "legality" of our actions and the second for their "morality." The distinction between the political and the personal is a familiar
one and seems to be what Kant has in mind. Where do the decisions of
corporations fit into this two-part division? Corporations are neither
political entities nor "real" persons. Although they are treated as persons in our legal system, it is obvious that they are institutions. Does
the Categorical Imperative apply to their acts and ends? Below are two
cases where corporate stances raise this question. How would you deal
with them in a Kantian manner?

> Business credibility might improve if more executives were willing to ad-
> mit—even to themselves—that the obligation to pay adequate attention
> to public needs has not yet become one of the requisites [requirements]
> of sound management. The problem is inherent in the system. The
> corporation's success depends on how well it employs capital, not how
> well it serves society. Although men of conscience do not want their
> money used for immoral purposes, a good investment does not have to
> be good for society; it just has to be gainful for the investor . . . .
>
>   Altruism, defined in Webster's as "uncalculated consideration for
> others' interests" is embarrassingly out of place in business. Indeed, the
> purpose of business is quite the opposite—to serve calculatedly the in-
> terests of those who have a stake in it. In this context, the business-
> man's best hope—which these days he dare not express in public—is
> what is good for the corporation is also good for the country.[14]

> Ten years ago, when psychologist Ed Lawler first began to approach the
> heads of corporations with his suggestions on how they could improve
> their firms' "quality of worklife," he had "to beg them to let me in the
> door."
>
>   Today, top management calls him . . . . Doors are opening up to
> him he said, because of the steady increase of a better educated, more
> diverse work force that is less willing to take orders . . . .
>
>   "People have rights to make their own decisions in our society;
> why can't they enjoy the same rights in a work situation?" Lawler
> asked.

"At home, a person can and has to make many vitally important
decisions every day. He has the right to vote, the freedom of speech.
But in the office, things are different. The worker virtually has no
decision-making power, cannot vote at board meetings and can easily be
fired for speaking out against his employer."[15]

4 How would you relate the following letter to the editor of *Phoenix,* a San
Francisco State University student newspaper, to the Generalization
Principle?

We in the minority community have become accustomed to and are
aware of the double standard of behavioral expectations applied to us
by the white community. Even terms are applied differently to similar
traits or activities dependent upon racial characterizations. For example, what is described as "dynamic, take-charge-guy, energetic" for
whites, becomes "aggressive, hostile, intruding" when applied to blacks.
A white group can have "good organizational ability," be "goal-
oriented," or know how to "cut through red tape"; but minority
groups exhibiting much the same behavior are looked upon as "con-
spiracies," having "sinister motives," or "ignoring the rules."[16]

5 Relate the following remarks to Kant's moral theory, particularly as they
relate to Ilyich, Nietzsche, and Marin.

The oppressed, having internalized the image of the oppressor and
adopted his guidelines, are fearful of freedom. Freedom would require
them to eject this image and replace it with autonomy and responsibility. Freedom is acquired by conquest, not by gift. It must be pursued
constantly and responsibly . . . .
   The oppressed suffer from the duality which has established itself
in their innermost being . . . . They are at one and the same time
themselves and the oppressor whose consciousness they have internalized. The conflict lies in the choice between being wholly themselves or
being divided; between ejecting the oppressor within or not ejecting him;
between human solidarity or alienation; between following prescriptions
or having choices; between being spectators or actors; between acting or
having the illusion of acting through the action of the oppressors; between speaking out or being silent, castrated in their power to create
and re-create, in their power to transform the world. This is the tragic
dilemma of the oppressed which their education must take into
account.[17]

6 Kant thought the Categorical Imperative a proper test both for our personal morality and for political legality. In the introduction to his
translation of Kant's *The Metaphysical Elements of Justice,* John Ladd
writes:

The treatise as a whole focuses on the fundamental problem of political
philosophy, namely, the justification and limits of the use of coercion
(or, in modern terms, the morality of power). Philosophically, this

358

problem in its many ramifications leads inevitably to the question of the relation of the ideal (Idea) to the actual in politics and law. These are the themes that run throughout the *Rechtslehre* [*Doctrine of Justice*] (p. xii)

We saw that in this treatise Kant stated the Categorical Imperative in such a way that we are to adopt only those maxims that assure our coexisting freedom. It has been more often maintained, however, that political and personal acts should not be governed by the same criterion; politics is a laxer realm than that of personal relations. Deception of one country's leaders by another's is not only excused but often praised; at the least, such deception is thought "necessary." It is said that in politics we have to be "realistic." The aim of successful political action is the possession of power; without power, a country is helpless before its enemies, and so forth. Here are some remarks from columnist David Broder on the topic. Do you agree with him or Kant?

> In his classic study of American foreign policy, "In Defense of the National Interest," Hans J. Morgenthau wrote that "the illusion that a nation can escape, if it wants to, from power politics into a realm where action is guided by moral principles rather than by considerations of power is deeply rooted in the American mind." . . .
> A re-emphasis on moral principles as the root of international policy was both necessary and proper after the massive cynicism induced in the American public by the contorted rationalizations successive Presidents used to defend the foredoomed American intervention in Indochina.
> [President] Carter's "Human Rights" foreign policy is the spiritual descendant of Woodrow Wilson's crusade to "make the world safe for democracy" and Franklin D. Roosevelt's espousal of "the four freedoms." . . . But as the earlier examples of Wilson and Roosevelt remind us, a heavy dose of moralism can lead a President either to the ruin or the redemption of his realistic aspirations in the international arena.
> The lesson has not been lost on Carter. In his Notre Dame speech, he said, "I understand fully the limits of moral suasion." He rejected any suggestion that "we can conduct our foreign policy by rigid moral maxims."
> . . . We are likely to be lulled into forgetting that while moral principles can provide a base for our foreign policy, they are not, in themselves, a policy. They become a policy only when they are applied to the practical problems of international affairs in a manner that not only reflects the values of the country but protects its interests as well."[18]

7 Questioned by Congressman Christopher Dodd (Dem-Conn), former CIA director Richard Helms said that he regretted not telling the Warren Commission—the commission that investigated President John Kennedy's

assassination—about secret U.S. plots against Fidel Castro, the head of
the Cuban government.

> When Dodd said he still found it difficult to understand "why you
> didn't inform the Warren Commission," Helms retorted: "I can under-
> stand your difficulty, Mr. Dodd. I'm just sorry, it's an untidy world."
>   The committee's chief counsel, G. Robert Blakey, asked Helms,
> "What possibly could be the moral justification for trying to kill the
> president of a foreign country?"
>   "There was none," said Helms. "I have apologized for this. I
> can do no more than apologize on public television. It was an error on
> my part. There was great pressure brought on me."[19]

Even if there is no "moral" justification for plotting Castro's
death, could there be a "political" justification? If there is no political
justification, is apologizing on public television all that Helms "can
do"? Is it all that he should do?

Helms was not punished beyond a $2,000 fine for what he admitted
had no moral justification. Is this evidence that Justice Department
authorities believe that there was political justification for what he and
others did?

8 Here is a letter to "Dear Abby." Do you agree with her advice to
"Wondering"? Do you think that the Golden Rule, the generalization
principle, and the Categorical Imperative would give the same answer
that Abby gave? Explain.

> DEAR ABBY: Your best friend is filing for divorce, and she asks you
> if you knew all along that her husband had a mistress for many years.
> You know it is true, and everyone else knows it. What do I tell her?
> WONDERING
>
> DEAR WONDERING: In the first place, common gossip is not
> necessarily fact. I would tell my friend that I have no reliable evidence
> to confirm her suspicions. (True, you haven't.)
>   A good friend spares unnecessary pain whenever possible. For
> you to join the others who said, "I knew it all along" would only add
> to your friend's misery.[20]

Reflection on Theory

9 *Conflict of duties and defense of Kant's view of lying.* The occurrence
of a conflict in duties has always posed one of the thorniest problems for
moral theorists. When we have two duties, but performing one will pre-

360   vent us from performing the other, and vice versa, how can we decide which duty to perform?   Kant too recognized this problem but did not, to my knowledge, give any specific procedure to follow in making a decision.   The following remarks state his view of the matter.

> A *conflict of duties* would be a relation of duties in which one of them would annul the other (wholly or in part).—But a *conflict of duties* and obligations is inconceivable . . . two conflicting rules cannot both be necessary at the same time: if it is our duty to act according to one of these rules, then to act according to the opposite one is not our duty and is even contrary to duty.   But there can, it is true, be two *grounds* of obligation both present in one agent and in the rule he lays down for himself.   In this case one or the other of these grounds is not sufficient to oblige him and is therefore not a duty.—When two such grounds conflict with each other, practical philosophy says, not that the stronger obligation takes precedence, but that the stronger *ground of obligation* prevails. (*Virtue,* p. 23)

Notice two things here.   First, Kant denies that there can be a conflict of duties; properly speaking, there is only a conflict between grounds for duties.   Second, the conflict between grounds is to be settled by selecting the stronger ground.   But Kant doesn't go on to tell us how we can tell which is the stronger ground.

Kant is correct in saying that a conflict of duties is "inconceivable," given that a universalized obligatory maxim has the feature of necessity.   Using truth modalities, if some universalized maxim, UM_1, is necessarily true and if another, UM_2, is necessarily true, they do not conflict; in order to conflict, the truth of one must entail the falsity of the other.   But since by hypothesis we have two truths, we do not have a conflict; nor could we logically have a conflict.   Hence, a conflict of duties is "inconceivable," that is, it is logically impossible.

Onora Nell, in her book *Acting on Principle,*[21] addresses the conflict-of-duties problem.   She provides an interpretation of Kant's undeveloped "stronger grounds," using an example taken from his article "On the Supposed Right to Lie from Altruistic Motives."   The example is a classic one in the history of ethical literature.   A man comes to a householder's door inquiring about the whereabouts of a person; the inquiring man lets the householder know that he intends to kill the person; the householder has earlier let the potential victim into the house. What is the householder to do?

Here we supposedly have a conflict of duties: I have a duty not to lie and I have a duty to prevent someone's death.   If I lie, I will have violated the first duty but observed the second; if I don't lie, I will have observed the first duty but violated the second.

Kant's claim is that the householder is not to lie; no altruistic motive such as the desire to save someone's life can be a ground for lying, because truth-telling is an inviolable duty.   Nell writes:

In his essay on the case Kant argues for the overriding duty of truth telling. Commentators have agreed that Kant's solution is repugnant and
uncharacteristic, but have not satisfactorily explained what his solution
should have been. (p. 133)

Notice that here we have an instance where commentators pit Kant's
theory against our common-sense moral judgment. Of course, it is
possible to argue that it isn't Kant's theory but its application that is
refuted. Kant may simply have made a mistake in applying his own correct theory.

Nell states the conflicting maxims and their universalization this
way (the labels "M_1," "UM_1," "M_2," and "UM_2" are mine):

M_1 One must tell the truth, even if it means allowing (failing to
prevent) a death.
UM_1 Everyone will tell the truth, even when it means allowing death.
M_2 One must prevent death, even if it means telling a lie.
UM_2 Everyone will prevent deaths, even when it means telling lies.

Nell's solution to Kant's problem is to compare the maxims'
universalizations and see which one brings us closer to a "Hobbesian
state of nature" (a war of all against all). "So the priority of conflicting grounds of obligation can be determined by seeing which of the two
maxims, balancing them, tends more toward a state of nature when
universalized" (p. 135). Nell thinks that the grounds of M_2 and UM_2
are stronger because they tend less toward a Hobbesian state of nature;
therefore, they are to be chosen over M_1 and UM_1.

No serious breakdown of trust or cooperation with others will arise if
we know that others will lie when it is required to save a life. But in
the case of simultaneously intending [M_1 and UM_1], we would intend
such a breakdown of trust and cooperation. If we know that others
will not tell a lie even to save a life, then we can hardly trust them in
any situation of potential danger. Intending [M_1 and UM_1] commits
any agent to intending a situation which tends toward a Hobbesian state
of nature, and so tends to impede or prevent all plans of action, including that envisaged in M_1 . . . . No rational agent will intend both an
avoidable state of nature and a plan of action. (p. 135)

In Victor Hugo's novel *Les Misérables*, Jean Valjean's housekeeper
was known never to have told a lie; at Valjean's request, however, she
lied about his presence to Inspector Javert, because she knew Valjean
was a good man and she trusted him. By telling her first lie, she saved
Valjean, and readers generally approve her for it.

I want to suggest a different interpretation of "stronger grounds"
than Nell's—one which supports a contrary judgment about the
householder's duty than is popularly given. I will defend Kant's answer,
using an interpretation of "stronger grounds" as "more probable

beliefs.'' Your assignment is to choose between the answers to the householder's dilemma and between Nell's and my interpretations. The answers and interpretations seem to be linked.

What can Kant mean here by "grounds of obligation"? My interpretation is that the grounds are the antecedent elements of a person's maxim, where the maxim is "the rule he lays down for himself." Our life is complicated. It can be complicated by a potential murderer unexpectedly knocking on our door and asking the whereabouts of our visitor. We are suddenly presented with antecedent elements that are mixed: they don't sort themselves into self-consistent sets; it is we who have to sort them. In the present example, we have to sort them into two sets: one antecedent set pertains to lying, and the other to saving a life. Here we have two "grounds," and so a division into two maxims, one about committing or omitting a lie, the other about saving or not saving a life. Furthermore, they appear to conflict. As Kantian moralists, we proceed to use the Categorical Imperative test: we universalize a maxim about lying, UM_1, and another about saving a life, UM_2.

But this gives rise to a problem. If both UM_1 and UM_2 are inconsistent, then their grounds give rise to: it is impossible that UM_1 (it is impossible to universalize lying) and it is impossible that not UM_2 (it is impossible to universalize not saving a life when we can); these are equivalent to: it is necessary that UM_1 (tell the truth) and it is necessary that UM_2 (save a life). Here, each of two grounds that lead to necessity have the same strength; therefore, there is no one stronger ground to select as Kant recommends.

We can deal with this problem, however, if we recall that beliefs about the circumstances and means are among a maxim's elements. These beliefs are beliefs about the truth of propositions. Some of these beliefs may be stronger than others, because it may be more probable that the beliefs in UM_1 are true than the beliefs in UM_2, or vice versa. If the beliefs in UM_1 are more probable than those in UM_2, then the grounds of UM_1 are stronger and we ought to choose to act on UM_1.

I suggest that Kant was correct in holding that the householder should not lie to the inquirer; the grounds for truth-telling are stronger than the grounds for lying. First, I think that the householder's dilemma is that he has to choose between lying and not lying; it is incorrect to say simply that he has to choose between truth-telling and saving a life. Saving a life is not an act; it is an end to be accomplished. Not being an act, saving a life has to be an End Element in a maxim rather than an Act Element. I think there is little doubt that the end of saving an innocent life comes under the more general obligatory end of promoting the happiness of others. Further, I think Kant believes that, *other things being equal,* an end maxim that has saving a life as its End Element is obligatory.

Notice, second, that I just qualified the end maxim with "other things being equal." But suppose that the probability of the beliefs in an end maxim are less probable than the beliefs in an act maxim; then, other things are not equal. Not being equal, the grounds of obligation for the act maxim are stronger than those of the end maxim; by Kant's recommendation, therefore, the act with the stronger grounds is our duty.

Applying this to the householder's dilemma, I think we can argue plausibly that the grounds of the truth-telling act maxim are stronger than those of the life-saving end maxim. Consider something Kant himself said in "On the Supposed Right to Lie." The householder may have a mistaken belief that the visitor sought is still in his house; the visitor may have heard the inquiry and, thinking that his host would tell the truth as usual, slipped out the back way, only to run into the inquirer, who shoots and kills him. The householder's lie, which sent the inquirer away and into the path of the one sought, is the very thing responsible for the murder, so the householder by his lie will have to share responsibility for the death.

Compare the probable truth of the householder's belief that he saw his visitor today with the probable truth of his belief that his visitor is still in his house. Obviously, the probability of the former is higher than the latter, and consequently is a stronger ground.

Another consideration supporting Kant's claim that the householder has a duty not to lie turns on correctly posing the householder's choice. I said his choice was between telling the truth and lying. Lying is only one means that the householder might believe he has for preventing the death of his visitor; surely, it is but one means belief in the "wide" duty of an end maxim whose End Element is preventing the death of the visitor sought. But consider other beliefs about means that a dutiful, reasonable person should have. He might engage the inquirer in conversation, perhaps loudly, thereby both delaying and warning his visitor, who could take what action he thought appropriate. Or he could wrestle him into submission, or shout to warn his visitor, or call to neighbors for aid. As we saw, an end maxim poses a "wide" duty; there are generally many acts that are means to the obligatory end. Thus, to suppose that the householder has a duty to lie ignores the fact that there are other equally, perhaps more, effective acts he can perform. Wrestling or delaying or calling for help may well be more probable deterrents than lying, particularly since lying may be the very act that, as Kant pointed out, leads to the visitor's death. It's true that wrestling with the inquirer or shouting may involve more danger to oneself than lying, but the issue here is one of morality and duty, not of prudence.

Appendix: Applying the Categorical Imperative

In this short appendix, I set out more precisely than hitherto the application of the Categorical Imperative, central to which is the search for internal or external inconsistency. I illustrate in detail the search for and discovery of inconsistency in two of Kant's maxims—an act and an end maxim. It is meant to show that a Kantian rational will ethics does have applicability, is practical, and can challenge the advantage enjoyed up to now by utilitarianism. While this effort lengthens the amount of space given to Kantian ethics beyond that normally given in ethics texts, it is important to do if students are to be given a fair picture of the two main ethical theories between which they may choose. Most philosophers—even moral psychologists—admire Kant and his impressive achievement, and acknowledge that his theory has delineated brilliantly one of the two main moral theories; but without practical applicability, it will remain a purely intellectual triumph, something that Kant would have thought insufficient. He thought, as I remarked before, that he wasn't creating a new theory, but simply giving a clear, explicit statement to the moral views of everyone. He claims in several places that in fact everyone *does* use his Categorical Imperative. This claim will lack support if it can't be shown how we really do, or can, use it. Let's see if we can give it that support in this appendix.

Kant's Categorical Imperative test has two different applications, one to act maxims and the other to end maxims. The first gives us the deontic modalities of acts, the second the deontic modalities of ends. In maxims of acts we look for internal consistency and inconsistency; in maxims of ends we look for external consistency and inconsistency. Internally inconsistent maxims of acts are "inconceivable"; externally inconsistent maxims of ends are "unwillable."

> We must be able to will that a maxim of our action become a universal law; this is the canon of the moral estimation of our action generally. Some actions are of such a nature that their maxim cannot even be *thought* [conceived] as a universal law of nature without contradiction, far from it being possible that one could will that it should be such. In others this internal impossibility is not found, though it is still impossible to *will* that their maxim should be raised to the universality of a law of nature. We easily see that the former maxim conflicts with the stricter or narrower (imprescriptible) duty, the latter with the broader (meritorious) duty. (*Foundations,* p. 315)

Let us see how Kant's theory can be used to show, first, the internal inconsistency and so the inconceivability of act maxims, and second, the external inconsistency and so the unwillability of end maxims.

I develop Kant's "inconceivability" claim by using his act maxim that I will (falsely) promise to repay a loan that I know I can't repay. (See pp. 307–08 for Kant's statement of the maxim and its elements, and pp. 310–13 for my analysis of its elements.)

We start by identifying the elements relevant to act maxims of which a person is conscious; these are the Circumstances, Means, Results, and Act Elements.

Beliefs in Circumstances, C_1: I believe I need money, *and* C_2: I believe I will be unable to repay.

Beliefs in Means, M_1: I believe that I can get money by borrowing; *and* M_2: I believe that firmly promising to repay will induce the belief in a lender's mind that I will repay; *and* M_3: I believe that, when I induce someone to believe I will repay, the person will lend me money (providing they have the money and want it to earn interest, or it's a friend, and so forth).

Intended Results, R_1: I intend to induce in a potential lender's mind the belief that I will repay the loan; *and* R_2: I intend to get the loan; *and* R_3: I intend the result of non-repayment; *and* R_4: I intend the result not to produce in potential lenders a future loss of confidence in me.

Resolved Act, B: I resolve to promise to repay.

I will now show that an internal inconsistency occurs if we universally promise to repay, when the antecedent of this universal law contains the elements listed above. I will produce a statement that is true under universalization and that contradicts one of the statements of the elements. Because we treat the universalization as a natural law, and so suppose that the antecedent elements are necessary and sufficient conditions for causing the "effect" of promising to repay, this internal inconsistency will falsify one of the necessary antecedent conditions; when this happens, the supposed law could have no instances. The impossibility of having any instances means that it is not a law governing any events in any possible universe. It is "impossible" for it to be nontrivially true of any possible universe.

In this proceeding we should assume that all agents are fully informed and wholly rational; they know all the premises set down and make all the inferences that I make.* This is both appropriate and necessary, because we are interested in the *rational* conditions required for a social totality; we are interested in a *perfectly* moral world, even though we recognize that it cannot be attained. Without a clearly apparent target, we won't know where to aim the arrow. Here now is the argument.

* See *Practical Reason* (Beck), p. 72, where Kant explicitly rules out "secret" and "unnoticed" acts in the search for inconsistency.

(1) We suppose that everyone knows the "as though" natural law that everyone will promise to repay a loan when the antecedent elements are as stated above. The law is public and not secret knowledge. We know it as well as we know that water runs downhill.

(2) This known law is in every person's mind who is asked for and promised repayment of a loan.

(3) The potential lender may not know C_2, that the borrower is unable to repay, or R_3, that the borrower intends the result of non-repayment of the loan; but that this is a possible circumstance and a possible intent is known by the potential lender. (Notice that I choose the "weak" premiss of a known "possible" circumstance and intent, rather than the stronger one that they are known to be actual.)

(4) These known possibilities make the "as though" natural law of the universalized maxim relevant to a lender's state of mind. That is, the fully informed lender knows that if these possibilities are realized, then, being wholly rational, he or she will use the "as though" natural law to conclude that the promise is a false one.

(5) Any lender entertaining the possibility that he or she won't be repaid and the possibility that the promise is false will have a state of mind that renders M_2 false; that is, M_2, the borrower's belief that by firmly promising to repay he will unfailingly induce a lender's belief in repayment, is no longer true. A borrower's M_2 belief cannot survive under the condition that his universalized maxim is a known "natural law." Promising, like lying, is a social phenomenon; the success of promising depends upon inducing belief in others; when we nullify the conditions necessary to induce the appropriate beliefs, we make successful promising impossible. (On Kant's awareness of these conditions—per locutionary force—see his remark on "the force of evidence," *Practical Reason* [Beck], p. 45.)

(6) Negating M_2 in our "as though" natural law negates one of the antecedent causal conditions necessary for its (act) effect—promising to repay—to occur. Hence, there could be no such promising.

(7) Further, the known possibility that the promiser intends not to repay (R_3) nullifies R_4, which is everyone's intent not to produce a lack of confidence in potential lenders, because lenders will lack confidence in borrowers.

(8) Negating R_4 negates one of the necessary conditions for the effect—promising to repay—to occur. So again, as in (6), there could be no such universal promising.

(9) Hence, by (6) and (8), we have shown that universalizing about promising under these conditions results, when everyone is fully informed and wholly rational, in contradicting at least two necessary antecedent conditions (M_2 and R_4) of our "as though" natural

law.   In short, under universalization of our maxim, we generate   **367**
an internal inconsistency.

(10) Therefore, since according to the Categorical Imperative it is impossible to make the maxim in its "universal law" form true, we ought not to promise to repay under the stated conditions. This conclusion, (10), uses the Correspondence Principle to state a relation between a truth modality and a deontic modality.

Now let's look at the second application of the Categorial Imperative, which is to maxims of ends.

Kant states the Categorical Imperative for maxims of ends in this fashion: "The first principle of the doctrine of virtue is: act according to a maxim of *ends* which it can be a universal law for everyone to have" (*Virtue*, p. 55).

For an example of a maxim of ends in which we search for external inconsistency, I choose a maxim about beneficence (active kindness).   When we act with genuine beneficence toward someone, it is because we have adopted that person's happiness as our end.   The end maxim that Kant wants to test is *not* to be beneficent.   It can be stated briefly thus: (Out of self-love) I resolve not to help others achieve happiness when they are in need.   He will have found an external inconsistency when this maxim is universalized as a natural law, if he finds that it contradicts a true natural law; in this event, it will be unwillable.   It is impossible to will an end that contradicts a natural law.   An end that is impossibly willable by us leads, by the Correspondence Principle, to the impermissibility of willing that end.   Hence, if we find that it is impossible to will our own happiness exclusively, then we ought not to do so.   In short, we ought not to will egoism.

Here is Kant's argument for obligatory beneficence, which I will "reconstruct" and elaborate.

> It is every man's duty to be beneficent—that is, to promote, according to his means, the happiness of others who are in need, and this without hope of gaining anything by it.
>
> For every man who finds himself in need wishes to be helped by other men.   But if he lets his maxim of not willing to help others in turn when they are in need become public, i.e. makes this a universal permissive law, then everyone would likewise deny him assistance when he needs it, or at least would be entitled to.   Hence, the maxim of self-interest contradicts itself when it is made universal law—that is, it is contrary to duty.   Consequently the maxim of common interest—of beneficence toward the needy—is a universal duty of men . . . . (*Virtue*, pp. 120–21)

Maxims of ends consist of the End, Circumstances, Means, Results, and Act Elements of a complete maxim.   The argument that it is a duty to make the happiness of others our end does not require that we specify knowledge of particular means, nor that we specify a particular act in our end maxim,

368   because this is a "wide" duty; a wide duty requires only that we choose some act or acts from the set of possible acts that we believe will trigger the means to secure others' happiness. In these two respects, the search for external inconsistency in maxims of ends differs from the search for internal inconsistency in maxims of acts. Here are the elements we need for this end maxim.

> *Representation of an End,* E_1 I will make only my own happiness my end (self-love); that is, I will not make others' happiness my end.
>
> *Belief in Circumstances,* C_1: I believe another person is in need of help.
>
> *Belief in Means,* M_x: I believe there is some means, *x,* however minimal, available to me that would make it possible to help another who is in need.
>
> *Intended Results,* R_1: I intend, by not helping others in need, to increase my own happiness (so that self-love is fulfilled).
>
> *Resolved Act,* not B: I will refrain from helping others (an act of omission).

In the following argument I will show that universalizing this end maxim will produce an external inconsistency with what Kant believes is a true natural law. I emphasize that the argument doesn't show an internal inconsistency—it doesn't show the inconceivability of the act; rather, it shows the unwillability of the self-love end under universalization. Kant explicitly distinguishes unwillability from inconceivability when he discusses another end maxim, namely, neglecting to develop my talents. To neglect developing my talents will violate the obligatory end of perfecting myself; however, it is quite conceivable that I can adopt this end. Whether Kant's naive anthropological belief about the idleness of South Sea Islanders is true or false doesn't rule out his distinction.

> Now, however, let him ask whether his maxim of neglecting his gifts, besides agreeing with his propensity to idle amusement, agrees also with what is called duty. He sees [conceives] that a system of nature could indeed exist in accordance with such a law, even though man (like the inhabitants of the South Sea Islands) should let his talents rust and resolve to devote his life merely to idleness, indulgence, and propagation—in a word, to pleasure. (*Foundations,* p. 315)

Here now is the argument showing external inconsistency.

(1) We suppose that the person proposing the maxim of self-love knows the "as though" natural law that, when the antecedent elements are as stated, no one will help anyone else. The law is public, not secret.

(2) This known law is in the mind of the person who resolves not to help others, even in circumstances when they are in need of help.

(3) Our agent wills this known law: Given the antecedent elements as stated, everyone will refrain from helping others.

(4) We suppose that everyone knows the true natural law that everyone

wills their own happiness. ("Every man [by virtue of his *natural* **369** impulses] has *his own happiness* as his end" [*Virtue,* p. 44].)

(5) We all know that if we genuinely will an end, we must also will the means to achieve that end.

(6) In accord with our knowledge of (5), in willing our own happiness, which we all do by (4), we must also will the means to achieve that end. This includes willing that others help us when we are in need.

(7) But a consequence of universally willing our end maxim that we not help others (when they are in need), is that we will that they not help us (when we are in need).

(8) We notice that (6) and (7) are inconsistent. (6) says that, because of a natural law, we "inevitably" will that others help us; (7) says that, because of our universalized maxim, we will that others *not* help us.

(9) This inconsistency results from my willing a universalized maxim that contradicts a natural law.

(10) Our moral actions have to be performed in the natural, sensible world: we cannot will a law that is incompatible with a natural law. To do so is externally inconsistent. Willing the universalization of my maxim amounts to this: I will that I not will what is necessary to my happiness. This isn't possible because, by a natural law, I always will what is necessary to my happiness.

(11) Therefore, I will what is impossible.

(12) According to the Correspondence Principle, willing what is impossible is willing what is impermissible. Willing not to help others is not permissible; therefore, it is obligatory to help others and to adopt their happiness as our end.

Appendix Reflections

1 Kant gives an example of a maxim of omission that he thinks fails the universalization test. A person is in possession of a deposit given him by someone who has died; there is no record of it. The man is contemplating a maxim whose act element is omitting to tell that one has such a deposit.

> Now I want to know whether this maxim can hold as a universal law. I apply it, therefore, to the present case and ask if it could take the form of a law, and consequently whether I could, by the maxim, make the law that every man is allowed to deny that a deposit has been made when no one can prove the contrary. I immediately realize that taking

such a principle as a law would annihilate itself, because its result would be that no one would make a deposit. *(Practical Reason* [Beck], p. 27)

    (a) Identify and write out the elements of the complete act maxim that you think adequately and reasonably complete Kant's short maxim. Use as your model the act maxim of falsely promising to repay developed in this appendix.

    (b) Determine if you can or cannot support Kant's claim that this maxim is internally inconsistent. Is the act "inconceivable"? (Hint: Would tellers accept deposits if they weren't sure the money belonged to the depositors?)

2 Kant thinks that we have the wide duty of adopting as our end the development of our talents. A person

> finds in himself a talent which could, by means of some cultivation, make him in many respects a useful man. But he finds himself in comfortable circumstances and prefers indulgence in pleasure to troubling himself with broadening and improving his fortunate natural gifts. Now, however, let him ask whether his maxim of neglecting his gifts, besides agreeing with his propensity to idle amusement, agrees also with what is called duty. He sees that a system of nature could indeed exist in accordance with such a law, even though man (like the inhabitants of the South Sea Islands) should let his talents rust and resolve to devote his life merely to idleness, indulgence, and propagation—in a word, to pleasure. But he cannot possibly will that this should become a universal law of nature or that it should be implanted in us by a natural instinct. For, as a rational being, he necessarily wills that all his faculties should be developed, inasmuch as they are given to him for all sorts of possible purposes. *(Foundations,* pp. 314–15)

    (a) Identify and write out the elements of the complete end maxim that you think adequately and reasonably complete Kant's short maxim. Use as your model the end maxim of helping those in need developed in this appendix.

    (b) Determine if you can or cannot support Kant's claim that this maxim is externally inconsistent. Is the end "unwillable"? Remember that the development of talents provides us with the means of attaining our ends. According to Kant, one end we have by a natural law is our own happiness and one obligatory end is the happiness of others.

3 Many philosophers have been critical of Kant's Categorical Imperative test for moral laws. A familiar criticism has been to say that either (a) there are some acts we believe immoral that Kant's test shows are moral, or (b) there are some acts we believe moral that Kant's test shows are immoral. Since Kant's results don't correspond to our common-sense judgment, the Categorical Imperative test has either to be given up or modified.

Fred Feldman gives what he believes is an example of a maxim that passes Kant's test, but which "most of us would say . . . is morally wrong."[22] Out of laziness, Miss Perkins buys a term paper for her ethics course; she is assured of a good grade on it and there is no chance her deception will be discovered. Feldman puts Perkins's maxim this way:

> When I need a term paper for a course and don't feel like writing one, I shall buy a term paper and submit it as my own work.

Feldman universalizes this maxim as follows:

> When anyone needs a term paper for a course and doesn't feel like writing one, she will buy one and submit it as her own work

Feldman thinks that Perkins can't consistently will that her universalized maxim be a natural law; hence, by Kant's criterion, her act is forbidden.

> The essentials of this example are simple. Miss Perkins wills that the system remain as it is—thus providing her with the opportunity to take advantage of her instructor and her fellow students. She recognizes that if everyone were to submit a store-bought term paper, the system would be changed. Hence, she cannot consistently will that everyone should submit a store-bought term paper. (p. 115)

Feldman then maintains that Kant's test can be short-circuited by a trivial change in Perkins's maxim, which will yield a maxim that can consistently be willed but is morally wrong. The "new" maxim reads:

> When I need a term paper for a course and don't feel like writing one, and no change in the system will occur if I submit a store-bought one, then I shall buy a term paper and submit it as my own work.

If this "new" maxim were a law of nature, then the system would not be changed because of the addition of "and no change in the system will occur if I submit a store-bought one." "Apparently, then," says Feldman, "Miss Perkins can consistently will that [this "new" maxim] be a law of nature." Yet we would all think that what she proposes in her maxim is morally unacceptable.

Here are two defenses of Kant's theory. Do you think either shows that Kant can answer Feldman's criticism?

(a) Feldman's maxim is incomplete. He does not set out all the elements of an act maxim that are called for by Kant's theory. In particular, a reasonably complete maxim should make explicit the beliefs about the means that Perkins has, if she is honest and thoughtful about the nature of her act. One of the beliefs about means that such a maxim will contain—one that is relevant to "getting away" with the deception—is her belief that professors know a probability curve about

372 students' performances; she believes that professors think it highly unlikely that every student in a class will submit an "A" paper. If everyone submits an "A" paper, this will arouse the professor's suspicions. This in turn will lead the professor to make inquiries, which may very well lead to discovery of the deception. The professor's belief will be an element in the complete maxim of a fully informed and wholly rational person. Feldman's introduction of the "trivial" phrase "no change in the system" is actually *false* in relation to the more complete maxim. There will be a "change in the system" if everyone turns in an "A" paper. Therefore, his "trivial" change isn't a possible one and so can't be used to refute Kant's theory. We can't will that professors' beliefs about students' performance remain unchanged; that is, we can't will that there be "no change in the system."

(b) Here now is the second defense of Kant against Feldman. It is necessary to distinguish between act and end maxims. According to Kant's theory, forbidden acts are inconceivable and impermissible ends are unwillable. Feldman thinks that his incomplete maxim is an act maxim only; actually, if he had been more complete in his statement of the maxim, he would have found it to be an end maxim. Kant showed that it is obligatory to adopt as an end the development of our talents. This is obligatory because the development of our talents is acquiring the means to carry out ends that we elect; as rational creatures we are bound to have ends; we can't consistently will to achieve our ends and not will to develop our "means" talents; resolving to neglect our talents is thus unwillable, although conceivable. (See Reflection 2, p. 370.) The "new" maxim proposed by Feldman violates the obligatory end of developing our talents because Perkins, by having someone else write her ethics paper, fails to develop her own talents. Thus what our "common sense" finds to be immoral about Perkins's "new" maxim is that it proposes that she violate a duty she has to herself: to realize her capacities. This "immorality" of the maxim is, of course, over and above the immorality of giving herself a non-universalizable and hence unfair advantage over other students as argued in (a) above.

4 Following are some examples of maxims. Take one or more of them and develop a hypothetical complete act or end maxim out of it, then test it by Kant's procedure to determine the deontic status of its universalization. If you have some moral concern of your own that you wish to substitute for one of these examples, give its complete maxim and determine its deontic status instead.

(A) In order to be safe and to keep my family safe, I will give in to Hitler and his Nazi supporters' political aims and wishes.

(B) In order to buy a Jewish-owned store at a low price, I will give in to Hitler and his supporters' political aims and wishes.

(C) When there is an initiative on the ballot that will lower my taxes but will not serve the public (or some part of the public) good, I will vote against it.

(D) Two men love me and I love both of them; they both want to marry me. One is needy, the other kind. I will marry the needy one because the kind one will more easily find happiness with someone else.

(E) An editorial in a San Francisco newspaper commented on a New York Court's decision. Section 4801.5 of the California Civil Code holds

> that an ex-wife or ex-husband receiving "spousal support," a euphemism for alimony, must bear the burden of proof as to why that should not be decreased "if the supported spouse is cohabiting with a person of the opposite sex." A New York State Court of Appeals held that "a man must continue paying alimony even if his former wife is living openly with another man, as long as she is not representing herself as the wife of her current roommate." The majority decision—5 to 2—drew the acrid dissent that it "leaves the courts powerless to relieve the former husband of the obligation of subsidizing his former wife's affairs no matter how unfair this may be under the circumstances." In these less than Victorian times, when persons of whatever sexual persuasion decide to cohabit without benefit of clergy, such a ruling by the court's majority defies reason.[23]

(F) There is a tribe called the Onges that lives on the small Andaman Island in the Indian Ocean. They have declined in population (now to about one hundred) because, an Indian research team discovered, the potato-like tuber that is part of their staple diet contains dioscorea, a chemical used in the manufacture of contraceptives. Says a news article of one of their maxims:

> It is ironic that the tribe should eat itself into near extinction because the tribe has harsh tradition regarding unattached women. It is a sin to be a widow and when a husband dies, elder members of the tribe drown her in the sea.[24]

(G) Richard Bennett, an executive with the National Humanities Center, maintains the following:

> I believe that homosexuals who are overt and self-declared about their homosexuality, who have an interest in arguing for homosexuality as a lifestyle, and who make efforts to change student values about homosexuality in ways fundamentally inconsistent with values that the school and community affirm, should not be teaching in public schools.[25]

Bennett goes on to argue that schools have special purposes; not everything can be taught in them. What should be taught is to be decided by the local community and its representatives. Further, such restrictions do not violate free speech because (a) the right to free speech is not the same as the right to teach, and (b) the student is not "a visitor at a town forum or a campus lecture; he is a captive audience."

374   What if a majority of the public decide that homosexual persons may teach and advocate their sexual values in the classroom?

In the 1978 California election, the so-called "Briggs" initiative appeared on the ballot, providing for the dismissal of any teacher who was homosexual and of anyone who defended someone who was. The initiative was defeated. A news story about a "gay" teacher who worked against the Briggs initiative reported:

> Like many other gays, he is caught in a political Catch-22: He can remain silent and feel he has betrayed himself if the initiative passes, or he can fight the initiative and risk losing his job if his efforts don't pay off.
>
> A religious Republican man in his early 40s, his teaching is highly respected at his San Mateo county junior high school, but he worries that good teaching evaluations will be meaningless if the initiative passes and parents pressure the school board to fire him.
>
> Driven by a controlled anger at the Briggs measure and by memories of his own miserable days, as a lonely gay student in a Midwest high school, he has decided to accept the risks of campaigning.
>
> "Not doing anything would be a sin of omission," he said. "There comes a point in everyone's life when you just can't take things any more that are unfair to you as a person and to others."[26]

(H) Helen B. Andelin wrote a book in response to the women's movement, called *Fascinating Womanhood.*

> Mrs. Andelin's "angelic and human do's and dont's" for women include: "Be a domestic goddess; earn a place on a pedestal by building a noble character; revere your husband and honor his right to rule you and his children; learn to express yourself when your husband mistreats you by child-like sauciness; be changeful, unpredictable. Don't have a lot of preconceived ideas of what you want out of life; don't be efficient in men's affairs, such as leadership, making major decisions, providing a living; don't try to excel him in anything which requires masculine ability."[27]

The article quotes two biblical "maxims" on this theme.

> Let the woman learn in silence with all subjection. But I suffer not a woman to teach, nor to usurp authority over the man but to be in silence. For Adam was first formed, then Eve. *1 Timothy* 2: 11–13

> Wives, submit yourselves unto your own husband, as unto the Lord. For the husband is the head of the wife, even as Christ is the head of the church; and he is the saviour of the body. *Ephesians* 5: 22–23

(I) Look again at Reflection 2 (D) on p. 319, where a judge held that a cousin had no legal duty to provide marrow for a needed bone transplant. Kant distinguished between the legality and the morality of an act. While it was held that the cousin, McFall, had no legal duty, do you think he had a moral duty to provide his cousin with marrow? You might start by considering this as a maxim for McFall: Whenever a person is in need of a marrow transplant and my marrow is suitable, I will not provide my marrow.

(J) Here is a news story that introduces a maxim about trying to influence people without their knowledge or consent.

> Shoppers cruising the aisles of a store are being showered with softly spoken recorded messages encouraging them not to steal. "I am honest," "I will not steal," "I am not a thief," "Shoplifting is wrong." The messages come in rapid fire sequence, sometimes overlapping. The recorded messages are so soft and so well masked by the store's background music that most of the customers are not consciously aware of them. However, the messages register with at least some people in the store, more than one of whom otherwise might have slipped some small items into his or her pocket.
>
> If Hall Becker is to be believed, that scene with its Orwellian Big Brother overtones is not from 1984, or even further in the future, but is being acted out right now in six branches of a department store in a "large Eastern city." . . .
>
> The ethics of trying to influence people without their knowledge or consent is being questioned by Rep. Albert Gore, Jr., D. Tenn., and by Muzak Corp., whose affiliates provide background music for many stores. . . .
>
> In promoting his system, Becker has revived a controversy that surfaced in the late 1950s when it was reported that a movie theater in Fort Lee, N.J., was inserting into its feature film split-second messages urging patrons to buy popcorn and soft drinks in the lobby.
>
> Part of the debate focused on whether it is acceptable to try to influence people's behavior without their consent or knowledge. The American Psychological Association (APA), for example, responded to the movie-message incident by including in its codes of ethics a statement that such actions were unethical without the consent of those involved. . . .
>
> Becker is a proponent of what has been termed "situation ethics," meaning that something may be ethical in one context but not in another.
>
> "So long as we use subliminal techniques only to deter behavior universally considered illegal or criminal, or to promote behavior universally considered to be good, and appropriate, we consider we are on safe grounds from the point of ethical or moral grounds," he explained.[28]

(On situation ethics, see pp. 29–30.)

5 *The dilemma of a theoretical decision procedure for morals.* The technique of critizing Kant's theory by showing a disparity between the results of his Categorical Imperative test and what "we all know by common sense" to be moral or immoral, was exhibited in Appendix Reflection 3.

376   I gave defenses of Kant that turned on the assertion that the critics had an inadequate conception of Kant's theory; if properly understood, I said, that theory could not lead to the claimed results. This critical technique can be applied to any moral theory, not just Kant's, and presumably can be used to decide which of two or more theories is the "correct" one. This "decision" procedure would work this way.

Suppose we are contemplating some act such as buying a term paper instead of writing it. The common-sense judgment is that this act is wrong. Next, suppose we have three theories: Kant's, the egoists' and a rule version of utilitarianism. In Appendix Reflection 3, Feldman claimed that Kant's theory fails because it doesn't show the act is wrong. An egoism theorist, supposing that the term paper buyer won't be detected, would justify buying the paper and say it is right; hence, an egoistic theory fails to square itself with our common-sense judgment. A rule version of utilitarianism might find that the rule "I will cheat on my professor and fellow students by buying a term paper when I can get away with it" tends to produce a balance of unhappiness over happiness; thus the rule lacks social utility and so is wrong. This decision accords with our common-sense judgment; therefore, utilitarianism is verified as the "correct" theory.

While this decision procedure for finding which moral theory is correct may initially look plausible, particularly because it is modeled on the procedure for determining which of two or more scientific theories is correct (the one that accords with the "facts"), we can formulate the following dilemma, whose solution I suggest you try to reach.

If the above decision procedure is acceptable, then our common-sense moral judgment has priority over our theoretical judgment. That is, we can know what is right and wrong independently of our theory; therefore, moral theory is unnecessary.

On the other hand, we often find that people's common-sense moral judgments contradict one another; for example, some think abortion morally wrong and others think it morally right. Both cannot be correct; therefore, common-sense judgment is not always correct. To decide whose judgment is correct, we have to ask each judgment's defenders to provide reasons why they think abortion right or wrong. To give reasons is to appeal to moral principles, and to do this is to appeal to self-correcting standards proposed by moral theory. Because the conflict in common-sense judgment cannot be resolved without appeal to moral theory, we find that moral theory is necessary.

Now moral theory can't be both necessary and unnecessary; therefore, either we will have to give up the decision procedure based on common sense, or we will have to give up the notion that we can find theoretical solutions for conflicts in common-sense moral judgments.

Giving up a procedure for testing moral theories is to allow that our adoption of a moral theory is an arbitrary affair, and that there is no way of determining the correctness of moral theory. This is undesirable because it thwarts any rational attempt to create a social totality.   But giving up moral theory as a rational way of settling moral disputes makes moral judgments arbitrary; this too is undesirable because it thwarts any rational attempts to create a social totality.

It seems clear that we have to give up one or the other; but since both lead to undesirable arbitrariness, we necessarily are left with an undesirable result.

11
Human Goods
and the Basic
Moral Concept

11.1 Two Questions About Goods

Our exploration of Kant's ethics has shown that he emphasized the concept of obligation and moral laws. His test for moral laws is internal and external consistency of proposed maxims of actions and ends when we universalize the maxims and treat them as if they are natural laws. From this we can determine if a contemplated act is obligatory, forbidden, or morally indifferent. Moral psychologists do not use consistency and inconsistency as a test of obligation; they think that we should look to the consequences of our proposed act. If the consequences are on balance more good than bad, then the act is right; if on balance they are more bad than good, then the act is wrong. This "consequence" theory of obligation will be discussed and stated more precisely in section 11.8.

Because the consequence-test for the morality of actions depends on the goodness and the badness of consequences, a basic task for moral psychologists is to find out what things are good. This task precedes finding out what acts are right. This chapter will investigate some theories about good. It is organized around two questions:

(1) How many *kinds* of goods are there?
(2) Is there an *order* among goods such that some are higher than others, and is one of them the *highest*?

To grasp question (1) clearly, we should note that "kinds" has different levels of generality. Consider an apple; it belongs to several kinds in an ascending order of generality. It may be a Winesap apple, belong to the Winesap-kind; it also belongs to the more general apple-kind; and it also belongs to the still more general fruit-kind. We can diagram this in a simple tree structure.

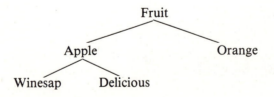

In asking (1), "How many kinds of goods are there?", I am asking how many *most general* kinds of goods there are.

Most moral psychologists hold that there is *one* most general kind. Aristotle is an exception, as we'll see. Kant thought there were *two* most general kinds, moral and non-moral goods. Of course, most moral psychologists don't deny that there is a distinction between moral and non-moral goods; there is a difference, but not at the most general level. It's as if **381** one acknowledges a difference between Winesap and Delicious apples but points out that, after all, they are both apples. But this is what Kant denies; moral and non-moral goods are radically different according to him; they are not sub-kinds of a more general kind. We'll see why he thinks this in the course of this chapter.

How can we tell if something belongs to one kind rather than another? One way is by noting its differing properties. When you go the grocery you can tell—or at least the grocer can—a Winesap from a Delicious by noting the different color, size, and shape these apples have. Or by cutting them and noticing a different firmness and texture. These are the *marks* of these different kinds.

Do we also look for these observable marks to determine if something is good? We can divide the world into two different value kinds—the goods and the ills. How do we tell what goes into the good kind and what into the bad kind? For example, is there some observable mark on a Winesap apple that reveals it is a good Winesap? Or a bad Winesap? Judges at county fairs certainly look the apples over in grading them and awarding prizes. They have quite strict criteria for a good Winesap; for instance, it must be very firm and quite tart. These are observable properties, so they must be the marks of a good Winesap.

What makes these properties the marks of a good Winesap, you may ask. According to moral psychologists, properties of a kind of object become marks of goodness either because we respond favorably to them when experienced or because they are useful in obtaining favorable future responses. Goodness is conferred on properties by favorable responses. Moral psychologists are "naturalists" about good because for them ultimately what is good is some naturally occurring psychological-physiological response, such as pleasure, wanting, satisfying a desire, liking, or being an object of interest, and so forth. Thus, eating a Winesap with its sharp, tart flavor may cause in me a pleasure. Or using it to make apple pies may show its properties useful because, for instance, firmness makes the slices hold up better when baked. Whether it gives immediate pleasure or is useful for providing future pleasure, an object is put in the good kind because of a human response.

Things are good because they are *good for* humans; they aren't good in themselves. What makes them good for humans is that they are the cause of good experiences, such as pleasure, satisfaction of a desire, or quelling of a need. This includes things said to be morally good. As you will learn in Chapter 12, Hume thinks that it is human traits—generosity, kindness, fairness—that are morally good; they are morally good either because they are immediately "agreeable" upon observation or are "useful" and lead to future "agreeable" responses. How he distinguishes between the two sub-kinds of moral and non-moral agreeableness is the subject of section 12.4c.

If one asks why human responses such as satisfaction of a desire or pleasure are a good, why they belong to the kind of good things, one can only answer "because they are good in themselves."

382   We can put moral psychologists' views about kinds of good in the following tree structure, with the most general kind being naturalistic goods.

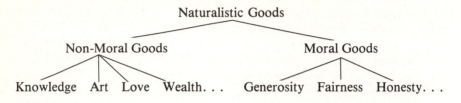

Kant disagrees with this monistic theory of good; instead, he is a dualist, as you might expect from someone who holds that there are two worlds, the sensible and supersensible worlds. Each kind of world has its own kind of good that is distinct from the other. In agreement with moral psychologists, Kant thinks that the sensible world contains naturalistic goods. These are the goods of our sensible part; they are the pleasures, satisfactions, and objects of interest that, when we fully possess them, amount to happiness.

We easily recognize that naturalistic and moral goods are different, because no one confuses happiness with worthiness. But according to Kant, they are radically different. We cannot have the following:

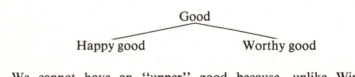

We cannot have an "upper" good because, unlike Winesap and Delicious apples, the two "lower" goods have nothing in common. Worthiness is a product of our will, happiness is not. Our will is free and is a faculty in the non-natural supersensible world; but happiness is an outcome of the natural world in which we are determined and unfree. Recall that Kant has a dualistic theory of the *summum bonum* because he thinks it is made up of both worthiness and happiness.

Turning now to the second question about an "order" among goods, you can see that if all goods are sub-kinds of a more general kind as moral psychologists claim, it is plausible to look for an ordering by rank among them and to suppose that one of the goods is at the "highest" end of the scale. But if Kant is correct in saying there are two wholly different kinds of good, then their sub-kinds can't be ranked on a comparative basis, although Kant does find another way of giving worthiness first place.

Kant points out that "highest" is an ambiguous term that has two meanings:

> The concept of the "highest" contains an ambiguity which, if not attended to, can occasion unnecessary disputes. The "highest" can mean the "supreme" or the "perfect." The former is the unconditional condition, i.e., the condition which is subordinate to no other; the latter is that whole which is no part of a yet larger whole of the same kind. . . . Virtue (as the

worthiness to be happy) is the supreme condition of whatever appears to us
to be desirable and thus of all our pursuit of happiness, and, consequently,
. . . it is the supreme good.[1]

The two different meanings of "highest," unconditional condition versus the whole that is not a part, can no more be compared than can a river
"bank" and a savings "bank." However, one good, virtue, can be made a
"condition" of the other; hence, it has first place and is "supreme." Kant
then goes on to point out that "first place" virtue isn't the "perfect" good,
for it is not the whole of the *summum bonum;* that whole also requires happiness.

11.2 Competing Naturalistic Conceptions of Good

In the previous section we found that for moral psychologists the most
general kind of good is naturalistic good.   Objects belong to this kind because
they have properties to which we respond favorably or because they have properties that are useful in providing future favorable responses.   In this section
I want to draw your attention to the fact that different kinds of responses
have been picked as the response that confers value.   Moral psychologists
have disagreed about which naturalistic response is the one that brings moral
and non-moral values into the world.   We do, as complex beings, have different kinds of responses.   Here are some different possible naturalistic
claims about good.

> X is a good   because X causes pleasure.
> because X is liked.
> because X satisfies a need (or drive).
> because X is approved.
> because X promotes survival (of an individual or a
> species).

I will speak of these as different "concepts" of good, because they may be
used singly or in combination as a criterion for deciding whether or not
something is a good.   I remind you that we distinguished between "good"
and "a good," the concept of good and goods, in 3.7 and 3.8.

The late eighteenth-century English philosopher and political activist
Jeremy Bentham, who co-founded with James Mill the Utilitarian movement,
was a hedonist.

> 1. Nature has placed mankind under the governance of two sovereign
> masters, *pain* and *pleasure*. It is for them alone to point out what we
> ought to do, as well as to determine what we shall do. On the one hand
> the standard of right and wrong, on the other the chain of causes and ef-

fects, are fastened to their throne. They govern us in all we do, in all we say, in all we think: every effort we can make to throw off our subjection will serve but to demonstrate and confirm it.[2]

Bentham answers my first question on p. 380—How many *kinds* of goods are there?—by saying there is but one kind, and anything that affords pleasure (or doesn't cause pain) belongs to this kind. Pleasure (or the absence of pain) is our standard for saying something is a good because only pleasure and the absence of pain are good in themselves; they are the natural, human responses that confer goodness on anything. The production of pleasure and pain by our acts is the way to assess the utility and morality of them. (There is a fuller discussion of Utilitarianism in 11.8.)

In a section entitled "Value of a Lot of Pleasure or Pain, How To Be Measured," Bentham addresses himself to my second question, about the order of goods. Since all pleasures for him have the same "quality," there being no "higher order" or "aristocratic" pleasures, his ordering relies on other features of pleasure. When an *individual's* pleasures are being ordered, a person should take into account their (1) intensity, (2) duration, (3) certainty or uncertainty, and (4) nearness or remoteness. When a *number* of persons' pleasures are being ordered, in addition to the above four features of pleasure, we should also take into account their (5) fecundity (the number of other pleasures produced by the first pleasure), (6) purity (whether or not pains follow the first pleasure), and (7) extent (how many persons will have the pleasures).

You recognize that one man's pleasure may be another man's poison, as they say. In ordering, we are to add pleasures and to subtract pains. The highest good for Bentham is the greatest sum of pleasure of everyone affected after subtracting the pains of everyone affected. Bentham's ordering theory is called the "hedonic calculus." Hedonism is the view that only pleasure (or the absence of pain) is a good, and that only pain is not a good.

Since every human has pleasures and pains—desires and wants, likes and dislikes, approvals and disapprovals, and so forth—you may wonder how naturalists decide which feature of human nature to use for the concept of good. It needs but little reflection to realize that these different features could lead to a conflict of what are thought to be goods and ills: for the masochist, pain is good if our concept of good is what is desired, which contradicts a hedonist like Bentham, whose concept of good is based on pleasure or the absence of pain.

Suppose you try to make a list of goods. How will you know what should be on the list and what not? Should fame be there? Power? Alcohol? Ambition? Heroin? Rolls Royces? Tobacco? Atomic energy plants? Fear? Wilderness areas? Taxes? Pride and humility? Great wealth? Religion? If someone challenged an item on your list of goods, how would you defend its being there? If you are a naturalist, you can use one of the above concepts of the good to cull or sort the goods from the nongoods. Or perhaps you have a naturalistic concept not listed here. (On an earlier discussion of a list of goods and the need for a concept of the good, see pp. 88–90.)

Some people, for instance, think great wealth is a good and others think **385** it is not. Those who think it is a good could defend their claim by appealing to the concept of good where "X is good" means "X is desired by most people." Opponents could claim it is not a good by appealing to a hedonistic, majoritarian concept: "X is good" means "X causes pleasure in most people." Since, due to a shortage of the world's goods, great wealth has to be confined to the few, great wealth isn't a good. The next phase of the dispute about great wealth must then shift to a defense of which naturalistic concept of the good is the correct one, or the best one, or the most defensible one, or the one favored by most people, or the one found to be scientifically verifiable.

11.3 Choosing a Naturalistic Concept of Good

You can see that a very interesting and difficult problem faces naturalistic moral theorists. I will outline two ways of trying to deal with it; the first is that of Ralph Barton Perry, an American philosopher, and the second is Aristotle's.

11.3a R. B. PERRY. Perry's solution for choosing the "correct" naturalistic concept of good is to use the more general term "interest," under which fall various of the other naturalistic concepts of the good such as liking, desiring, seeking, and so forth.

> It is characteristic of living mind to be *for* some things and *against* others. This polarity is not reducible to that between "yes" and "no" in the logical or in the purely cognitive [intellectual] sense, because one can say "yes" with reluctance or be glad to say "no." To be "for" or "against" is to view with favor or disfavor; it is a bias of the subject toward or away from. It implies, as we shall see more clearly in the sequel, a tendency to create or conserve, or an opposite tendency to prevent or destroy. This duality appears in many forms, such as liking and disliking, desire and aversion, will and refusal, or seeking and avoiding. It is to this all-pervasive characteristic of the motor-affective life, this *state, act, attitude or disposition of favor or disfavor,* to which we propose to give the name of *"interest."*
> This, then, we take to be the original source and constant feature of all value. That which is an object of interest is . . . invested with value. Any object, whatever it be, acquires value when any interest, whatever it be, is taken in it; just as anything whatsoever becomes a target when anyone whatsoever aims at it. . . . [The seventeenth-century Dutch philosopher] Spinoza was fundamentally correct when he said that "in no case do we strive for, wish for, long for, or desire anything, because we deem it to be good, but on the other hand we deem a thing to be good, because we strive for it, wish for it, long for it, or desire it." (*Ethics,* Part III, Prop. IX, Note)[3]

386   Perry's solution to the problem of determing which naturalistic concept of good should be used is to refuse to make a choice between them. Each of them confers value, and does so because each exhibits a human interest taken in an object, an interest of either favor or disfavor. It's analogous to our apple example.

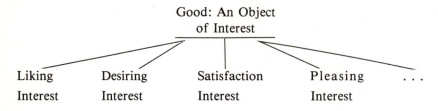

Good: An Object
of Interest

Liking   Desiring   Satisfaction   Pleasing   . . .

Interest   Interest   Interest   Interest

The criterion of belonging to the most general kind is being an object of interest; the sub-kinds are formed by different kinds of interest.

Notice two other things about Perry's view. First, as a moral psychologist he traces value to a naturalistic feature of humans, an aspect of our human nature, namely, our "motor-affective life." "Motor" is a psychological term for saying that we are active creatures; "affective," a term for saying that we are affected by our experience. Perry's theory is a variant of moral psychology. Recall the claim of Wilson, the sociobiologist, that our brains' hypothalamic-limbic systems "flood our consciousness with all the emotions. . . that are consulted by ethical philosophers who wish to intuit the standards of good and evil." (See Reflection 19, p. 23.) That Perry's view is a variation of moral psychology is confirmed further by his following remarks:

> The view here proposed may properly be termed a bio-centric or psycho-centric theory of value, in the sense that values are held to be functions of certain acts of living mind to which we have given the name of interest. (p. 139)

> Indeed it would not be too much to say that it is the central task of a scientific psychology to close the gap between man and nature, a gap created by man's pride in himself and widened by the misguided indulgence of metaphysics and religion. (p. 183)

The second thing to notice is Perry's approval of Spinoza's view. Good or value is dependent upon, or a product of, our wishes, desires, and longing, rather than the other way around. Kant agrees with this theory about our natural, sensible part and our natural, sensible values. But Perry's theory goes quite counter to Kant's view that our reason, not our motor-affective life, is the sole source of non-natural, *moral* value.

11.3b ARISTOTLE. Unlike Perry, Bentham, and Plato, Aristotle says that there are many kinds of good. Near the beginning of his *Nicomachean Ethics,* Aristotle argues against Plato's view that we have a single concept of

good. He first distinguishes between the concept of something good in itself **387**
and the concept of something good because it is useful for the sake of obtaining something else.   Then he goes on to maintain that even various things
good in themselves are comprehended by different concepts of good.

> But of honor, wisdom, and pleasure, just in respect of their goodness, the
> accounts are distinct and diverse. The good, therefore, is not some com-
> mon element answering to one Idea.
>   But what then do we mean by the good? It is surely not like the
> things that only chance to have the same name [like river "bank" and sav-
> ings "bank"].⁴

Aristotle then goes on to consider some possibilities for explaining a nonac-
cidental relation between the various concepts of good, but settles on nothing
definite, leaving us up in the air.

     In the first sentence of the *Nicomachean Ethics* Aristotle does, however,
give us a clue for relating the various concepts of good—that at which all
things aim: "Every art and every inquiry, and similarly, every action and pursuit, is thought to aim at some good; and for this reason the good has rightly
been declared to be that at which all things aim" (1094a, 1-3). Strictly speaking, this is not a criterion of good. We aim at many things, but not
everything we aim at is good. If our criterion of good were what "we aim
at," then everything we aim at would have to be good; but it isn't, therefore
we can't use this concept of good in this fashion. Aristotle recognizes that it
is tempting to think that a definition of "good"—"one good which is universally predicable of goods"—would be worthwhile, because "having this as a
sort of pattern we shall know better the goods that are good for us, and if we
know them shall attain them" (1096b, 33; 1097a, 1-2). However, he doubts
that such a pattern would be useful in everyday life.

> It is hard, too, to see how a weaver or a carpenter will be benefited in
> regard to his own craft by knowing this "good itself," or how the man
> who has viewed the Idea [of good] itself will be a better doctor or general
> thereby. For a doctor seems not even to study health in this way, but the
> health of man, or perhaps the health of a particular man; it is individuals
> he is healing. But enough of these topics. (1097a, 8-14)

     The fact that we aim at many goods that fall under different concepts of
good, doesn't prevent Aristotle from plausibly suggesting that we can rank the
goods and can learn what the highest one is.   He thinks the highest is
eudaimonia, which has been translated as both "happiness" and "well-
being." "Well-being" is perhaps the better translation because *eudaimonia* is
an activity, and not a state of being as "happiness" suggests. Specifically, well-
being—or perhaps "well-doing"—is an activity in accord with the excellence of
the kind of thing acting; humans' excellence is rationality, so we have well-
being when our reason controls the desires that motivate us to act. Aristotle
calls this "moral virtue."

388   Let's look now at the reasoning that leads Aristotle to conclude that happiness or well-being is the highest good. His first step distinguishes between means and ends and their respective good; then he proceeds to identify which end is the highest in the order of ends, which is well-being.

Aristotle thinks of an end as something to be achieved by some means or other. For him, ends and means are as intimately related as hills and valleys; one cannot exist without the other. In modern terminology, an end is said to have "intrinsic" value and a means an "extrinsic" value. Something has extrinsic value because it is good *for* something else rather than being good in itself; thus means have extrinsic value because they are good for achieving what has intrinsic value, or what is valuable in itself. Most people do not think work has intrinsic value—it isn't a good in itself; it is a good only because it is a means to an end that has intrinsic value (although "workaholics" may think there is intrinsic value in work itself).

"Wish," says Aristotle, "relates rather to the end, choice to the means; for instance, we wish to be healthy, but we choose the acts which will make us healthy, and we wish to be happy and say we do, but we cannot well say we choose to be so; for, in general choice seems to relate to the things that are in our power" (1111b, 26–29). With his use of "wish," Aristotle puts himself in the camp of value naturalism and moral psychology. (Also, note his use of "desirable" in the next quotes below.)

Among our ends, the things we wish for, Aristotle thinks that some are subordinate to others. If this is so, then we can order or rank our ends. Aristotle argues that well-being is a highest end. This gives us: End_1, End_2 . . . End_n, where End_n is well-being. Each of the subordinate ends can be considered a means in relation to a higher end. Thus, for an end, you may have learning to read and write, which are means to another end of getting an education, which is a means to getting a job, which is a means to getting the wherewithal to live, all of which are means to your well-being. Aristotle argues that well-being is the highest intrinsic good or end because it has the two features of finality and self-sufficiency.

Finality of well-being. Given a ranking among intrinsic goods, the highest must only be a good in-itself and not also a good for something else; if it were a good for something else, then it would be a means to, and consequently subordinate to, that other end. Finality, then, requires of an end that it not be a means for something else, and that all other ends be means to it.

> Now we call that which is in itself worthy of pursuit more final than that which is worthy of pursuit for the sake of something else, and that which is never desirable for the sake of something else more final than the things that are desirable both in themselves and for the sake of that other thing, and therefore we call final without qualification that which is always desirable in itself and never for the sake of something else.
>
> Now such a thing happiness [well-being], above all else, is held to be; for this we choose always for itself and never for the sake of something else, but honor, pleasure, reason, and every virtue we choose indeed for themselves . . . but we choose them also for the sake of happiness, judging that by means of them we shall be happy. (1097a, 28–1097b, 8)

The list of goods will include those things that are means to happiness, to well-being.   **389**

Self-sufficiency of well-being. Aristotle's definition of this feature is clear enough.

> The self-sufficient we now define as that which when isolated makes life desirable and lacking in nothing; and such we think happiness to be; and further we think it most desirable of all things, without being counted as one good thing among others—if it were so counted it would clearly be made more desirable by the addition of even the least of goods [and so would not be self-sufficient], and of goods the greater is always more desirable. Happiness, then, is something final and self-sufficient, and is the end of action. (1097b, 13–21)

By identifying the highest value with the help of such properties as finality and self-sufficiency, Aristotle establishes that at least one good should be on everybody's list and, furthermore, should top the list. Moreover, anything that is a means to it should be on the list of goods.

Aristotle says that well-being is "activity in accord with virtue" (1177a, 12). (Some translators use "excellence" rather than "virtue.") Virtue or excellence is of two kinds, moral and intellectual. Moral virtue is a state of character with the disposition to choose the mean between the extremes of too much and too little; reason restrains the extremism of our desires (1106b, 35). This choice of the mean is a matter of judgment; no formula can be given for deciding what the mean is. (For a wrestler four pounds of meat daily may be the mean, while for a secretary a half pound may be the mean and four pounds an excess.) Intellectual virtue is divided into the contemplative and the calculative; the object of the contemplative is what never varies and the object of the calculative, what does. Aristotle ranks the contemplative the higher of the two; it is the divine in humans.

> If happiness is activity in accordance with virtue, it is reasonable that it should be in accordance with the highest virtue; and this will be the best thing in us. Whether it be reason or something else that is this element which is thought to be our natural ruler and guide and to take thought of things noble and divine, whether it be itself also divine or only the most divine element in us, the activity of this in accordance with its proper virtue will be perfect happiness. That this activity is contemplative we have already said. (1117a, 12–18)

> But in a secondary degree the life in accordance with the other virtue [moral] is happy; for the activities in accordance with this befit our human estate. Just and brave acts, and other virtuous acts, we do in relation to each other, observing our respective duties with regard to contracts and services and all manner of actions and with regard to passions; and all of these seem to be typically human. (1178a, 8–14)

Perry, too, thinks that happiness is the highest good, but notes that what this consists of is a matter of dispute. He thinks, however, that he can resolve this "dilemma."

Sages have been divided on two questions: Does the supreme good consist in utility and pleasure, or in some deeper well-being, such as virtue, self-perfection or saintliness? Does the supreme good appertain to the human individual, or to some greater social or cosmic whole? These dilemmas disappear, and the demands which underlie them are met, if the supreme good is conceived as the object which satisfies all individuals, when individuals are both personally integrated and harmoniously associated; and if this object is interpreted to mean the joint and inclusive satisfaction of all individuals. In the conception of a happiness of all which is the condition of the happiness of each, there is standing-ground alike for Stoics and Epicureans, for Kantians and Utilitarians, for Christians and Pagans. The highest good is not sheer satisfaction of maximum intensity, but, as Plato taught, an *order* of satisfaction, whose form is prescribed by reason. The highest happiness is not that which is most comfortable and easy of attainment, but, as Christianity has taught, that tragic happiness which is at once the privilege and the penalty of love. (pp. 686–87)

Perry discusses what he means by the "*order* of satisfaction" in a chapter entitled, "The Commensurability of Values." He has four measures of interest: correctness, intensity, preference, and inclusiveness. The last three "define quantities of interest" and differ from the measure of correctness. Correctness applies to "interest-judgments" upon which judgments of value depend. If an interest-judgment is incorrect, the value disappears. Perry gives this example: "Thus a man who courts a woman whom he supposes to be an heiress [an interest-judgment], and becomes indifferent to her when he learns that she has been disinherited, reveals by his loss of interest the fact that this interest was founded on an erroneous judgment" (p. 613).

Those who subscribe to a naturalistic concept of good need some kind of ranking among goods in order to give a basis for rational choice among items that fall under the concept of the good. This is true whether that concept is "X is desired," "X is a cause of pleasure," "X promotes survival," or "X is the object of any interest," and true as well if, as with Aristotle, there are many concepts of good. A naturalistic theory of good can approximate the distinction between the moral and the non-moral good with the use of a ranking theory. However, Kant would not agree that the dualism of higher/lower corresponds to the dualism of moral/non-moral. A very good apple can never be a good orange.

11.4 Kant on Naturalistic Good

Because naturalists have a single source of value—our natural, sensible self—they have to derive moral value from it; they have no other possible source. But Kant thinks *it is impossible to derive moral good from natural good*. For him, these two goods are heterogeneous, that is, of two wholly different kinds; they are as heterogeneous as the sensible and supersensible aspects of humans. (*Hetero* is a Greek term for "different," as in "heterosexual.") To think natural and moral good are similar in kind is to confuse prudence, which is exercised to attain happiness, with morality, which is exercised to attain worthiness, although both happiness and worthiness (virtue) belong to the *summum bonum*.

> Now it is clear . . . that the maxims of virtue and those of private happiness are quite heterogeneous as to their supreme practical principle, and, although they belong to one *summum bonum* which together they make possible, yet they are so far from coinciding that they restrict and check one another very much in the same subject [person]. Thus the question: "*How is the summum bonum* practically possible?" still remains an unsolved problem, notwithstanding all the *attempts at coalition* that have hitherto been made.[5]

They "check one another" because sometimes we have a duty to do something that produces unhappiness; also, acts that produce happiness need not contribute to our moral worthiness. They check one another because they either conflict or vary independently. This view is popularly expressed by saying that "the rain falls on the just and the unjust alike." Thrasymachus indeed argued that the unjust are happier. Since there is this disparity between virtue and happiness, they cannot be identical goods.

Kant on happiness. Let us recall a few points briefly. (1) Kant agrees with Aristotle and Perry that the highest sensible, natural good is happiness. He thinks of it, however, not as one highest good in a list of goods but as a second-order good, which is a general name for the harmonious satisfaction of all of our wants and inclinations throughout our life (p. 281).

(2) Despite all the naturalists' attempts at ranking goods so we can make rational choices, Kant thinks our concept of happiness is so indefinite, and our knowledge and power so limited, that we can't make reliable, rational, prudential choices for obtaining happiness (p. 258).

(3) Kant does think that the satisfaction of our inclinations is good. This is not a source of evil; only a "perverse" will is a source of evil (p. 281).

(4) The variability of what is needed for happiness, both between ourselves and others and within ourselves at different times, makes happiness an unsatisfactory basis for objective, necessary moral laws. No naturalistic concept of the moral good escapes this variability; consequently, no naturalistic concept of good can be identified with the moral good (p. 254).

11.5 Kant on Moral Good and Dignity

Stated simply, Kant thinks that humans and other rational beings have moral value. The two kinds of moral good that humans have are moral *worthiness* and moral *dignity*. We have the first kind of moral value when we have a *good* will, that is, when we choose (by *Willkür*) to act from moral feeling, out of respect for the moral law. We have the second kind of moral

392 value because we have freedom through the possession of practical reason (*Wille* and *Willkür*). In this section I shall concentrate on the dignity value of humans.[6]

First, we need to distinguish two sets of moral terms: *deontic terms* and *moral value terms.* Deontic terms include "ought," "duty," "obligation," "forbidden," "permissible," "right," and "wrong"; they apply to acts and ends. Value terms include "worthy," "good" and "dignity"; they apply to humans. In this section, our interest is primarily in moral value terms.

Next, we need to remind ourselves that we have distinguished two different meanings of "moral" in English. One use occurs when we talk about "moral capacity"; here we have the moral/non-moral distinction. The other use occurs when we talk about "moral realization"; here we have the moral/immoral distinction. (See p. 243.)

The two different meanings of "moral" require us to distinguish two kinds of moral value terms. Good will and worthiness are one kind; they are moral realization terms. This is the kind Kant speaks of when he says that "nothing in the world—indeed nothing even beyond the world—can possibly be conceived which could be called good without qualification except a *good will.*"[7] Remember that we have a good will, that is, we are morally worthy, when our *Willkür* selects moral rather than pathological feeling as the cause of our action. Here "good" is being used in the moral/immoral sense.

Kant on dignity. Dignity is the other kind of moral value, which no other sensible creatures than humans have because only we have moral capacity. This moral capacity is our freedom—positive and negative. Thus when in his *Teleological Judgement* Kant says that freedom is "the supreme good in the world" (p. 99), we have to understand that "good" is here being used in the moral/non-moral sense. I will use "good" as the moral value term associated with the moral/immoral use (realization), and "dignity" as the moral value term associated with the moral/non-moral use (capacity). Not all persons are morally good, but all have dignity. This will prevent confusion of the two kinds of moral value.

For Kant, then, worthiness and dignity with its freedom are each the highest of the two kinds of moral values; both are distinct from happiness, and of course are connected to each other in the way that capacity and realization (potentiality and actualization) are connected to each other. (However, Kant sometimes uses "worth" as synonymous with "dignity." This use of "worth" should not be confused with being "worthy" or with "worthiness." "Worth" contrasts with "price," while "worthy" and "worthiness" contrast with "immoral.")[8]

Kant's distinctions are structured as follows:

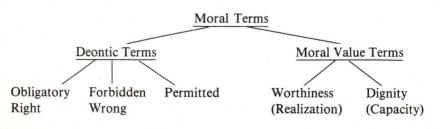

Dignity and Kant's Categorical Imperative. The fact that everyone has **393** dignity means that we have to respect every human. Since the source of our dignity is our free capacity for setting our own acts and ends, to respect others means we must not interfere with their freedom. So when we ask how we can utilize our capacity for setting our own acts and ends, we answer that minimally we can do so only if no one hinders anyone in the exercise of their autonomy. To achieve this freedom in actuality, we ourselves have to create cultural conditions in which our freedom is protected. Kant calls this cultural condition a "civil community," which is what I earlier called a "social totality."

> The formal condition under which nature can alone attain this its real end [human freedom] is the existence of a [political] constitution so regulating the mutual relations of men that the abuse of freedom by individuals striving one against another is opposed by a lawful authority centered in a whole, called a *civil community.* (*Teleological Judgement,* p. 96)

The chief and final touchstone for regulating the mutual relations between humans while preserving their freedom is the Categorical Imperative. Kant states three versions of it, which he thinks are equivalent to one another, but each of which emphasizes different aspects of the supreme law. The first version (the one to which he most often turns) he states as follows: "Act only according to that maxim [personal policy] by which you can at the same time will that it should become a universal law" (*Foundations,* p. 313).

The "formal condition" Kant is thinking of in the quotation cited above is the second version of his Categorical Imperative, which reflects the dignity humans have and the respect they deserve: "Act so that you treat humanity, whether in your own person or in that of another, always as an end and never as a means only" (*Foundations,* p. 319). If we treat others as a means, we subordinate them to something else; to do this is to degrade them from a final, intrinsic worth to an extrinsic price. For example, to kill a person so you will inherit the victim's insurance money is using another as a means to your own advantage; you put a price on the person.

> Reason, therefore, relates every maxim of the will as giving universal laws to every other will and also to every action toward itself; it does so not for the sake of any other practical motive or future advantage but rather from the idea of the dignity of a rational being, which obeys no law except that which he himself also gives.
>
> In the realm of ends, everything has either a *price* or a *dignity.* Whatever has a price can be replaced by something else as its equivalent; on the other hand, whatever is above all price, and therefore admits of no equivalent, has a dignity. . . .
>
> Now morality is the condition under which alone a rational being can be an end in itself, because only through it is it possible to be a [free] legislative member in the realm of ends [social totality]. (*Foundations,* p. 322)

Only humans, of all existing earthly beings, are ends in themselves and

"I just wanted to say, sir, that I couldn't agree more with what you said in there about me being a sycophant."

have intrinsic moral worth, that is, dignity; and among humans, those who have more worthiness are those who exercise their freedom more. Humans and freedom are what Kant keeps constantly before him in his moral reflections; therefore, these are what you must keep before you in order to understand Kant. Further, according to Kant, these are what you must keep before if you are to be morally worthy. (The third version of the Categorical Imperative deals with humans in a "realm of ends"; see p. 349.)

11.6 The Basic Moral Concept

As we saw earlier in section 9.1, p. 302, moral psychologists think good is the basic moral concept while Kant, like other deontologists, thought that right or obligation is the basic one. In sections 11.7–11.9, I explore this contrast between the two ethical schools more fully and draw out some further implications of this contrast.

This contrast, put simply, is a difference between those who emphasize the good life versus those who emphasize the moral life. What counts most for the first is the concept of naturalistic good; for the second, the deontic concept of obligation.

Taking "good" as applying to ends and "obligation" to acts, in asking which concept has priority over the other, I am asking about the relation between good ends and obligatory acts. Before proceeding further, we should decide just what is intended by "good ends." We saw how "obligation" is related to other deontic terms in 9.1.

11.7 Good as the Chief Moral Concept

First of all, note that the concept of good at stake here is not the concept of a good means but of a good end; hence, the "good" value being considered here is an intrinsic value rather than an extrinsic one. Anything intrinsically good is good in itself. The late English philosopher G. E. Moore uses "in itself" to mean "quite alone" and defines "intrinsically" good, bad, and indifferent in the following way.

> By saying that a thing is intrinsically good, it means it would be a good thing that the thing in question should exist, even if it existed quite alone, without any further accompaniments or effects whatever. By saying that it is intrinsically bad, it means that it would be a bad thing or an evil that should exist, even if it existed quite alone, without any further accompaniments or effects whatever. And by saying that it is intrinsically indifferent, it means that, if it existed *quite alone,* its existence would be neither a good nor an evil in any degree whatever.[9]

Moore expresses his notion of "intrinsically better" as follows:

> To assert of any one thing, A, that it is *intrinsically* better than another, B, is to assert that if A existed *quite alone,* without any accompaniments or effects whatever—if, in short, A constituted the whole Universe, it would be better that such a Universe should exist, than that a Universe which consisted solely of B should exist instead. (p. 37)

The second thing to understand about "good ends" is the kind of things that as ends can be intrinsically good. Candidates for such ends are persons, objects, and experiences. By "good ends," moral psychologists usually mean ends that will be either experiences themselves or some whole of which experiences can be a part. If there were no sentient creatures—that is, no creatures that had a motor-affective life, no creatures with feelings, desires, needs, or drives—there would be no value in the world. Moore says: "I think it is true that no whole can be intrinsically good, unless it *contains* some feeling towards *something* as a part of itself; and true also that, in a very important sense of the word 'good' (though not in the sense to which I have given the name 'intrinsically good'), many things which *are* good would not be good unless somebody had some feeling towards them" (pp.103–04).

Moral psychologists, having a monistic, naturalistic concept of good, generally hold that experience is the only kind of thing that may be intrinsically good or that can confer value. Moore illustrates this with the experience of pleasure; he says a hedonistic theory, which he himself rejects as wrong (see Reflection 16, p. 411), "holds, therefore, not only that any one effect or set of effects, which contains more pleasure, is always intrinsically better than one which contains less, but also that no effect or set of effects can be intrinsically better than another *unless* it contains more pleasure" (p. 38).

396   Objects, pretty clearly, aren't intrinsically good. I want food not for itself but for the pleasure I get because food puts an end to hunger and its tension. Wealth, cars, and possessions appear to be extrinsically good because they are means to producing desirable experience effects. Even unspent, hoarded money is only extrinsically good; it provides the experience of feeling secure. So objects, having extrinsic value only, do not confer value; rather, they have value conferred on them.

11.8 The Utility of Acts: Utilitarianism

We can now say what the moral psychologist thinks is the relation between good ends and right acts: it is a utility relation. Again, I will use Moore's formulation because he is clear and careful.* He distinguishes, as Plato did, between the concept of good and goods. The identification of intrinsic goods is all that the moral psychologist needs in order to have a *criterion* for the deontic properties of acts. Thus the concept of good might not be definable by a naturalistic concept such as pleasure, but it might be that the rightness of an act can be determined by considering the intrinsic goodness of the pleasure that it causes; it is the latter question I am addressing here.

Moore says that pleasure (or some other thing that is intrinsically good) is related to right and wrong acts in the following ways:

> This first principle is a very simple one; for it merely asserts: That a voluntary action is right, whenever and only when the agent could *not,* even if he had chosen, have done any other action instead, which would have caused more pleasure than the one he did do; and that a voluntary action is wrong, whenever and only when the agent *could,* if he had chosen, have done some other action instead, which would have caused more pleasure than the one he did do. (p. 19)

The deontic properties of right and wrong, when they apply to an act, do so because of the amount of "pleasure" effects it has. Moore here states the principle for determining whether or not an act is right in terms of the amount of pleasure caused. This is because in the first two chapters of *Ethics* he is examining a theory of hedonistic utilitarianism—which depends on the view that pleasure is the only thing intrinsically good. Moore explicitly rejects hedonism in the latter part of his book. The principle stated here can be easily modified to give a non-hedonistic utilitarianism; we need only add to "pleasure" the phrase "or some other thing that is intrinsically good."

---

* We should note at the outset, however, that in an earlier book, *Principia Ethica,* Moore argues against the possibility of a naturalistic definition of "good" (see Reflection 17, p. 411ff). Moore does say in that book, though, that we can "define" or identify things that are good, that we can say what thing, such as pleasure, is *the* good.

"Utility" is the term commonly used to refer to the effects of an act insofar as it is related directly or indirectly to intrinsic goods produced by it. Thus an act is said to have "positive utility" if it produces more intrinsic goods than ills for some specified person or persons affected, and is said to have "negative utility" if the ills outweigh the goods produced for some specified person or persons. Bentham was a "universal" utilitarian because he believed all affected persons had to have their goods and ills (pleasures and pains) counted equally in determining an act's utility.

Acts may have different degrees of utility and may be compared with one another; thus one act may have *more* positive utility than another. Moral psychologists commonly think an act's utility to be the criterion of right and wrong.

Moore warns that right and wrong do not depend upon what a person could have chosen, but only on *voluntary* actions that could have been chosen. We may very well choose to do something that we can't do such as lift a Rolls Royce off a person pinned under it; if we can't, then "right" or "wrong" don't apply.

Notice that Moore talks about "more" pleasure. This implies that acts may produce different amounts of intrinsic goodness and so have different deontic properties. This is what makes the idea of "intrinsically better," which he defined in an earlier quote (p. 395), relevant to a distinction he makes between the deontic term "right" and the deontic terms "ought" and "duty." "Ought" and "duty" are stronger terms than "right."

A voluntary act is our duty, says Moore, one we are obligated to perform, if and only if it produces effects that are intrinsically *better* than any other voluntary act we could have chosen (more utility)—that is, if and only if it produces *more* pleasure. It is perfectly possible that two voluntary acts could be chosen producing *equal* amounts of intrinsically good effects. In this case, neither is better than the other; hence, I don't have a duty to do one rather than the other (*Ethics*, pp. 22, 23). Thus every act that is a duty is right, but not every act that is right is a duty. Moore concludes that the hedonistic, utilitarian theory "does then . . . profess to give us an absolutely universal *criterion* of right and wrong; and similarly also an absolutely universal criterion of what ought or ought not to be done" (p. 29). He adds: "It goes on to assert that it is *because* they produce these results [a maximum of pleasure] that voluntary actions are right when they are right, and wrong when they are wrong" (p. 31).

Although using a pleasure concept of good as a criterion of right is not the same as defining the concept of right by the concept of good, it does give the concept of good priority over the concept of right. We first determine what and how much good, if any, is produced by a voluntary act, and then determine that it is right or wrong or a duty. Let's call this a "utilitarian" or "teleological" view of the relation between "good" and deontic terms. Moral psychologists are teleologists.

Before leaving utilitarianism, consider briefly two points. I emphasize first, that utilitarians do not have to confine themselves to pleasure as the only

398 intrinsic good. The utilitarian theory can be formulated by using intrinsic good, leaving it open as to just what things are intrinsically good. An act's rightness and obligatoriness is then measurable in terms of the balance of goods over ills that it produces for some or all persons, and in terms of how one act's balance compares to another's. Of course the theory can't be *applied* without specifying what things are intrinsically good.

The second point is that my formulation of utilitarianism has focused exclusively on the effects of a particular *act*; I have formulated only "act utilitarianism." There is also "rule utilitarianism," which measures the effects of persons following a moral rule. For instance, the rule "No one will ever lie," if followed, has effects different from "No one will ever lie except to save an innocent life." The effects of following the second rule may be better than those of following the first, even though some particular act of the first kind might have better effects than some particular act of the second kind. Richard Brandt criticizes act utilitarianism because he thinks it justifies acts that are clearly immoral; if it does that, it can't be the correct moral standard. That standard

> implies that if you have employed a boy to mow your lawn and he has finished the job and asks for his pay, you should pay him what you promised only if you cannot find a better use for your money. It implies that when you bring home your monthly pay-check, you should use it to support your family and yourself only if it cannot be used more effectively to supply the needs of others. It implies that if your father is ill and has no prospect of good in his life, and maintaining him is a drain on the energy and enjoyment of others, then, if you can end his life without provoking any public scandal or setting a bad example, it is your positive duty to take matters into your own hands and bring his life to a close.[10]

11.9 Obligation as the Chief Moral Concept

Kant disagrees with utilitarianism and Moore's view: "In all moral judgments the idea we frame is this, 'What is the character of the action taken by itself.'"[11] The action "taken by itself" excludes the effects or consequences of the action. A morality that puts duty before good "says I should not lie even though it would not cause me the least injury" (*Foundations*, p. 326). Rational will ethicists such as Kant are deontologists: they give first place to deontic terms. This won't surprise those who have noticed that a naturalistic occurrence such as pleasure is simply a factor in happiness, which is not a moral good, according to Kant. A non-moral intrinsic good, such as pleasure, cannot be a criterion of a moral, deontic property of an act.

Thus the moral worth of an action does not lie in the effect which is expected from it or in any principle of action which has to borrow its motive from this expected effect. For all these effects (agreeableness of [our own] condition, indeed even the promotion of the happiness of others) could be brought about through other causes and would not require the will of a rational being. (*Foundations,* p. 300)

That Kant distinguishes two kinds of good, moral and non-moral, is significant here. Just as you can't get "blood out of a turnip," so you can't get moral deontic properties out of non-moral value.

Another argument against ethical utilitarianism is made by W. D. Ross:

If, so far as I can see, I could bring equal amounts of good into being by fulfilling my promise and by helping someone to whom I had made no promise, I should not hesitate to regard the former as my duty. Yet on the view that what is right is right because it is productive of the most good, I should not so regard it. [12]

Keeping our promises is a duty. Despite the equally good consequences of two acts, we think it our duty to do the one that fulfills a promise. This contradicts the utilitarians' view that we don't have a duty when neither act produces intrinsically better results than the other. Hence, good results aren't an adequate basis for determining what our duty is.

The independence of an act's rightness from the goodness of the consequences became clear after the fact to Charles Colson, one of the Watergate conspirators. The following is from an interview with Colson reported by Seymour Hersh.

Q. Do you have any qualms about the morality, your morality, or the absence of morality in the White House?
A. Yes.
Q. In what sense?
A. Time and time again I can recall saying to myself, "Well, I'm not sure this is the right thing to do but we got to do it because this, you know, we'll get the election behind us." You lose sight of that; . . . there were a lot of times when I should have stepped up and said, "Well, we're not going to do this, this just isn't the right thing to do." . . . You tend to become ethically insensitive when your goal, I don't want to use the old cliché that the ends justify the means, but when a goal becomes so important to you. [13]

Let's see why Kant thinks an act's rightness is independent of its consequences, which should explain Colson's "qualms."

Let's put the priority of duty over moral good this way: moral worthiness is a morally good end that is possible only by doing our duty out of respect for the moral law; the dignity of others is preserved only because by acting in conformity to moral law we preserve the freedom of others. In both

400   cases we must know what our duty is *before* we can achieve the two morally
good ends; therefore, our duty must be independent of our ends, as Colson
realized.   Further, acting from a moral motive is possible only *after* we have
determined what our moral duty is.   "*Pathological* feeling precedes the
thought of the law; *moral* feeling can only follow from the thought of the law"
(*Virtue*, p. 59).   Notice the order of events: the thought of the law comes *before*
the moral feeling.   Colson realized he should have subordinated the goal of re-
electing Nixon to doing what is right.   Kant criticizes teleologists for failing to
make this distinction; the "eudaemonist" he refers to below is a person who
holds a teleological position, who says that good has priority over duty and also
holds that the chief good is happiness.   Aristotle was a "eudaemonist," as are
some other moral psychologists.

> Now the *eudaemonist* says: this delight or happiness is really his motive for
> acting virtuously.   The concept of duty does not determine his will *im-
> mediately;* he is moved to do his duty only *through the medium* of the hap-
> piness he foresees.   —But if he can expect this reward of virtue only from
> consciousness of having done his duty, then obviously, consciousness of
> having done his duty comes first.   In other words, he must find himself
> under obligation to do his duty before he thinks of the fact that happiness
> will result from doing it and without thinking of this.   (*Virtue*, p. 34)

This distinction in the temporal order of feeling, thought, and action
shows there are two orders; Kant calls one the "order of nature" and the
other the "moral order" (*Virtue*, p. 35).   We can achieve morally good ends
only by following the moral order, never by following the "happy" order of
nature.

			Being	
Moral Order:	Thought of →	Moral →	Act → Worthy →	Thought of
	Our Duty	Feeling		Happiness

			Being Un-or	
Natural Order:	Thought of →	Path- →	Act → Non- →	Thought of
	Happiness	ological	Worthy	Our Duty
		Feeling		

Occasionally, Kant's passions and humor poke up as in this pun on
Greek words:

> If we fail to observe this distinction [between the two kinds of order], and
> take as our basic principle *eudaemonism* (the happiness principle) instead
> of *eleutheronomy* (the freedom principle of inner legislation [of our duty]),
> we effect the *euthanasia* (painless death) of all morals.   (*Virtue*, p. 35)

To summarize: in this chapter I have pointed out that moral psychologists hold a monistic theory of value, holding that there is but one

kind of most general good. This good is naturalistic, although moral **401** psychologists differ about which of our natural responses is intrinsically good. Kant, by contrast, is a dualist: he thinks there are two kinds of good, moral and non-moral good. Further, there are two kinds of moral good: a good will (moral realization) and dignity (moral capacity as free, autonomous creatures). Moral psychologists give priority to the concept of good because they believe we use it as a criterion of deontic properties of acts (or rules). Kant gives priority to deontic properties because they lay down the prior requirements for having a good will and for preserving the dignity of others.

STUDY QUESTIONS

1 Explain what a concept of "naturalistic" good is, and why Kant thinks that naturalistic and moral concepts of good are heterogeneous (wholly different).

2 How many kinds of moral good does Kant think there are and how does he distinguish between them?

3 Explain the relation between a naturalistic good and the rightness and wrongness of acts, and the obligatoriness of acts. Explain also why the intrinsic/extrinsic distinction of value is important to a utilitarian theory in determining the deontic properties of acts.

4 How does Aristotle claim to prove that well-being (happiness) is the highest human good? Why does Kant's interpretation of "highest" lead him to a conclusion different from Aristotle's? Relate this to Kant's analysis of the *summum bonum*.

5 Why does Kant think that duty or obligation is a more basic moral concept than a moral good?

Reflections on Applications ◈

1 Here is an excerpt from an advertisement for an X-rated movie, "The Joys of a Woman."

> Nothing is wrong if it feels good. I'm Emmanuelle. In my new movie
> I will show you how to enjoy the new morality. If everybody else is
> taking part in today's new sensual freedom, why should you be left out?
> You have every right to pleasure. This is my life style. Make it yours.

Is this view closer to the moral psychologists' theory or to Kant's? Explain why.

Do you think that a moral psychologist has to agree with Emmanuelle's view? Would G. E. Moore have to do so?

2 Would you distinguish Emmanuelle's view from the one that a man seems to attribute to his daughter, the bride in the following news story? If you would, does it hinge on your concept of love? Love seems to be a naturalistic occurrence for humans. Is it a good-in-itself? Is it connected with right and wrong in some way? Which way?

> Because their daughter Ruth did not "honor thy father and mother," Mr. and Mrs. Lawrence Weilert have sued her for $10,000 and asked to have their names taken off her wedding invitations.
>
> "My wife and I haven't consented to the marriage and didn't really know about it until last week," Weilert said. . . . But if they had gone about it the right way, I told them I would pay $1,000 toward the marriage, send them to college, pay all their expenses on a house and groceries and buy them a car. . . . I wanted to teach them a lesson. Right is right, wrong is wrong, and love comes third, if that is what it really is. My family lives by the Ten Commandments," Weilert said. "I've asked Ruth not to forget the fifth: 'Honor thy father and thy mother.' "[14]

3 The Question Man once asked,[15] "Are you leading a full life?" Jill Jackson said:

> These last four years have been great, living up on the Stanislaus River. The trouble with living up in the mountains, you don't have any responsibilities. We need to apply ourselves to something. We need to direct our energies. We can't seem to make a decision as to what we should do with our lives. We are totally free but you have to have a few responsibilities and deadlines to completely enjoy life. We both agree we'll be happier when we have goals and responsibilities.

Do you think this is a criticism of the moral psychologists' theory? Can their theory supply a justification for having responsibilities? Does their theory necessarily imply that we have responsibilities? That we ought to have responsibilities? Is there any way that Ms. Jackson's remarks provide evidence for Kant's moral theory?

4 Does the following news story bear out what Ms. Jackson said, and do you think it is a good example of what she was proposing as a way of life? Can you relate it to Kant's idea about the *summum bonum*?

The story is about Father Alfred Boeddeker, who was being honored on his fiftieth anniversary of being ordained a priest in the Order of Friars Minor. In 1950 he founded St. Anthony's Dining Hall in San Francisco. St. Anthony's serves meals without charge to persons who haven't the money to buy food; it serves about 1200 to 1500 meals daily, more than 12 million since it opened.

Several years ago, the priest said that after a quarter century of working with the downtrodden he did not "despair for the human race. . . . I doubt if today's struggles are too different from those past.". . . Today, in spite of his insistence that "I never took a pessimistic or negative view of life," his musings have a troubled ring.

"There is such a confusion as to what is even good," he says, shaking his head sadly. "Everything is subjective; nothing is right or wrong. There must be some objective norms. If the only thing that keeps you from doing wrong is the policeman—oh, that can't be. I really worry when the greatest thing people can obtain is sexual pleasure," he continues. "This doesn't enrich the mind or the heart. All it does is give the feeling of flesh. Isn't there anything more in life?"

As always, it is the loss of human dignity that Father Boeddeker laments.[16]

5 How would you relate the explanations expressed in the following to the contrasting views on the highest human goods? And to the basic moral concept? Is the "American dream" un-Kantian?

Why are an increasing number of youths committing brutal, violent and often senseless crimes?. . .

"The American dream is, in part, responsible for a great deal of crime and violence," said Dr. David Abrahamsen, psychoanalyst specializing in behavioral disorders. "People feel that America owes them not only a living but a good living, and they take short cuts to get what they feel is owing to them . . . frustration is the wet nurse to violence.". . .

"An increasing number of parents have resigned their responsibility for the character of their child," said Amitai Etzioni, professor of sociology at Columbia University. "It's as elementary as that —where is a child supposed to get the distinction between right and wrong? From the home and school. The schools focus ever more on cognitive skills and less on character building."

Etzioni also attributed the increasing number of children "who don't know right from wrong" to broken homes, rotating "partners."

Abrahamsen is said to specialize in "behavioral disorders." This phrase is often used by people who think psychology, sociology, criminology, and related fields are "sciences." These "disorders" have to be "treated" just as tuberculosis, strep throat, or diarrhea are treated, by finding some means of attacking and removing their cause or causes.

Do you think that Etzioni's "explanation" is a "scientific" or a "moral" one, or a combination? Consider the two following ways of rewriting the question at the beginning of the above quotation; these two versions reflect two different ways of interpreting "why."
(1) What are the causes for an increasing number of youths committing . . .

(2) What are the reasons for an increasing number of youths choosing to commit . . .

6 I have said that most naturalists think that the only thing intrinsically good is experiences; the experience of pleasure or the absence of pain has been a popular candidate for intrinsic good. Typical naturalists also think that we are obligated to do that act or follow that rule which produces more intrinsic good than any other act or rule we could have chosen.

Consider the application of these theories—act and rule utilitarianism—to the following case and decide if Mrs. Berg is obligated, not just permitted, to commit suicide. The absence of pain as an intrinsic good is central to this case.

Mrs. Marjorie Berg had terminal cancer; she had an "understanding" husband and 9-year-old son. She once tried to die by taking 22 Seconal capsules but was "rescued" by a passerby.

> She says she remembers how close she came to a quiet death and asks, "Why are there human beings who like to play God?"
> Since then, she says, the months have been an endless ordeal of pain from the cancer that has crept through her body. . . . Mrs. Berg says, "If someone were to ask me what cancer is like, I'd say take the worst form of flu and multiply its effects ten times, plus having somebody stabbing you in different parts of the body. It's you and the pain. There's nothing else, just you and the pain."
> Mrs. Berg says that the Declaration of Independence procaims the right to the pursuit of happiness and "my pursuit of happiness would also include my ability to put an end to my suffering. I've never been afraid of death."[17]

7 Let's consider the application of the moral psychologists' theory further. The following news story suggests that we might be obligated to urge others to end their life. Assume that Mrs. Mott has no intrinsic good in her life, or that the amount of intrinsic good experienced and anticipated is heavily outweighed by the amount of intrinsic bad.

> Through the eye of a concealed police camera, millions of British televiewers Wednesday night peered into the bedroom of a nursing home and watched a 60-year-old woman urge her mother, 87, to commit suicide.
> "It isn't cowardly, Mum, for goodness sake," viewers heard Volande McShane say in the crisp accents of the well-to-do. "If you had a dog in this state you would take it to the vet, wouldn't you?"
> "A dog hasn't got a soul," replied her mother, Mrs. Ethel Mott, huddled in a chair. "I'm so afraid of being punished after."
> "Oh, Mummy, for this? You wouldn't be punished for this. Don't be having any doubts. Don't bungle it, Mummy, don't make a mess of it."

In the comfort of their homes or pubs, viewers then saw Mrs. McShane slip her mother a lethal dose of 15 barbiturate tablets, urge her to take them with a "big drink of whisky" and walk out. . . .

This was the start of a journey that ended in a Cheshire prison, where Mrs. McShane is serving two years for aiding and abetting an attempted suicide.[18]

If a person is obligated to help someone commit suicide, even if the person to commit suicide doesn't recognize or acknowledge his or her own obligation to do so, then Mrs. McShane ought not to have been put in prison but rewarded instead. Do you think that act utilitarianism would produce a different judgment about the rightness or wrongness of Mrs. McShane's act than rule utilitarianism?

If Mrs. McShane's act seems monstrous to you, even though justified by moral psychology's ethical theory, then this theory ought to be rejected by you as justifying immoral practices. Recall the claim I made at the beginning of this book, that moral theory makes a difference in moral practice.

8 Later in the news story, we learn that "the prosecution at her trial alleged that money was her motive for urging suicide. She was to inherit $70,000 on her mother's death." Suppose the allegation were true. Place the events of this story in Kant's "natural order" (p. 400).

If money was her motive, then Kant would think that Mrs. McShane was morally unworthy: she was motivated by a desire for happiness rather than by a respect for moral law, and furthermore interfered with the freedom and diminished the dignity of her mother. She was treating her mother as a means to her happiness rather than as an end in herself. This is a different conclusion than moral psychologists could come to, should Mrs. McShane's use of the $70,000 produce on balance a greater amount of intrinsic good than Mrs. Mott's continued possession of it, assuming, as before, that Mrs. Mott's experiences had no intrinsic good or a much lesser amount of good than of intrinsic bad.

With whom do you agree—Kant or the moral psychologists?

Additionally, there was a great outcry against a television showing of this scene secretly filmed by the police. Do you think it was wrong to show it on television? Did it degrade Mrs. McShane or her mother?

9 Václav Havel is a Czech dramatist. Kenneth Tynan quotes from a play of his, *The Increased Difficulty of Concentration*. In the play the social scientist Dr. Huml dictates to his secretary, Blanka, "a bumbling lecture on moral values which goes against the intellectual grain of his society."

HUML: Where did we stop?

BLANKA: (*reads*): "Various people have at various times and in various circumstances various needs—"

HUML: Ah yes! (*Begins to pace thoughtfully to and fro while dictating to Blanka, who takes it down in shorthand*)—and thus attach to various things various values—full stop. Therefore, it would be mistaken to set up a fixed scale of values—valid for all people in all circumstances and at all times—full stop. This does not mean, however, that in all of history there exist no values common to the whole of mankind—full stop. If those values did not exist, mankind would not form a unified whole—full stop. . . . Would you mind reading me the last sentence? . . . There exist situations—for example, in some advanced Western countries—in which all the basic human needs have been satisfied, and still people are not happy. They experience feelings of depression, boredom, frustration, etc. —full stop. In these situations man begins to desire that which in fact he perhaps does not need at all—he simply persuades himself he has certain needs which he does not have—or he vaguely desires something which he cannot specify and thus cannot strive for—full stop. Hence, as soon as man has satisfied one need—i.e., achieved happiness—another so far unsatisfied need is born in him, so that every happiness is always, simultaneously, a negation of happiness.[19]

Do you think Huml's ideas refute Aristotle's claim that happiness is a final end value? Or that it does so only if a person has a misconceived notion of happiness itself? Does it refute a eudaemonistic ethical theory (see p. 400)? And would Kant approve of Huml's views?

10 Does Havel's Dr. Huml show the falseness of the case that William Simon makes for what he calls our "capitalistic" system?

Individual liberty includes the individual's economic feedom, and the Founding Fathers knew it. When men are left free by the state to engage in productive action, guided by self-interest above all, they do create the most efficient and powerful production system that is possible to their society.

The enormously complex and productive system known as a free market operates without conscious supervision and direction. It works as follows: Day in and day out, people engage in economic activities called business—small individual ones and gigantic ones held together by a tissue of voluntary individual contracts. . . .

And what is the end result of these billions of individual decisions? It is the torrential outpouring of man-made wealth that characterizes the history of American capitalism in which 28 percent of the total production of the human race is created by only five percent of the world's population. . . .

These figures illustrate the "success of the free enterprise system": 96 percent of all American homes have a telephone; 50 percent of all Americans own at least one automobile; 96 percent of all American homes have at least one television set; after American farmers finish feeding the United States, they export 60 percent of their wheat and rice, 50 percent of their soybeans, one quarter of their grain sorghum and one fifth of their corn. . . .

Ironically, this connection between political and economic freedom is perfectly understood by totalitarians. . . . The Communist theoretician knows precisely how to destroy individual freedom; he destroys economic freedom, and the job is done.[20]

11 Read the following while imagining that General Goodpaster has hired you to design the ethics courses he plans to introduce at West Point.

A struggle to eliminate what many senior officers believe to be a moral rot that has infected the Army since the Vietnam war is to begin here in the classrooms of the U.S. Military Academy.

Lieutenant General Andrew J. Goodpaster, the superintendent, has included morals and ethics courses in the academy's new four-year curriculum. . . . And if the traditional honor code of the Army is to be restored, Goodpaster believes, four years of courses in morals and ethics at West Point are necessary. . . .

The general concedes that imposing stricter discipline will not be easy. The plebes who march through the sally port each year, he said, are the products of a permissive society in which a "you scratch my back, I'll scratch yours" approach is accepted.

The most difficult point to instill, Goodpaster said, is that a cadet must not tolerate lying or cheating in another cadet. It has to be impressed upon them, he said, that to tolerate such things damages the moral fiber not only of the man who lies or cheats but also of the man who tolerates it and in time the moral quality of the entire army.

"We put these problems on the tables in the course," the general said. "The cadets get a chance to talk them through and to come to grips with the consequences of cheating or lying or plagiarism."[21]

As a designer of the ethics courses for the cadets, would you recommend that a rational will ethics or a moral psychology theory be emphasized? Connect your recommendation to what Goodpaster wants to achieve. Is it clear whether Goodpaster thinks obligation or good is the chief moral concept?

Reflections on Theory

12 *Plato and Aristotle against hedonism.* G. E. Moore pointed out that hedonists think that pleasure itself is intrinsically good and is always a part of any whole that is intrinsically good, whether that whole is a single effect of an act, a set of effects, or a "whole universe" (*Ethics,* p. 43). Bentham thought pleasure (or absence of pain) the *only* thing intrinsically good, a view with which Moore disagrees (see Reflection

16).   Hedonism has been an attractive view through the centuries, beginning with the ancient Greek philosopher Epicurus, who gave it a clear, strong statement.   The next five reflections deal with some well-known objections to hedonism.

Neither Plato nor Aristotle thought that hedonism was an adequate theory of goods; nor did they think "good" could be defined in terms of pleasure.   In the *Nicomachean Ethics* Aristotle approvingly cites one of Plato's arguments against hedonism.

> He [Plato] argues that the pleasant life is more desirable with wisdom
> than without, and that if the mixture is better, pleasure is not the good;
> for the good cannot become more desirable by the addition of anything
> to it.   Now it is clear that nothing else, any more than pleasure, can be
> the good if it is made more desirable by the addition of any of the
> things that are good in themselves.   (1172b, 29–33)

Relate Plato's argument to Aristotle's argument that happiness is the highest value.   Does Plato appeal to the final or the self-sufficiency criteria? Relate it also to Moore's definition of "intrinsically" good.

13 *The privacy of pleasure and the hedonic calculus.*   Bentham (pp. 383–84) claimed that he could determine the amount of utility of a contemplated act by means of his hedonic calculus, which would measure the amount of pleasure to be produced by the act.   One of the factors in his calculus was the intensity of the pleasure.   Do you think the following argument shows that we can't measure the utility of an act with his calculus?

The pleasure that is felt is private to each sentient creature, man or animal; I cannot have your pleasure nor you mine.   Consequently, we cannot compare the intensity of my pleasure to yours, nor compare the intensity of our pains.   This comparison is required in order to use the hedonic calculus.   Since it can't be used, the hedonic calculus fails as a measure of the utility of contemplated acts.

Can you think of other arguments against the hedonic calculus that apply to other features of pleasure? How much weight would you give to each factor relative to the others?

14 *Pro and con the notion of "higher" and "lower" pleasures.*   Bentham did not distinguish between higher and lower kinds of pleasure; all pleasures are on the same footing.   John Stuart Mill was a follower of Bentham and his father, James Mill, both of whom were founders and advocates of Utilitarianism.   John Stuart Mill, however, thought that there were higher and lower pleasures.   Would you agree with what he says below? What consequences does this have for an hedonic calculus?

> The creed which accepts as the foundation of morals "utility" or the
> "greatest happiness principle" holds that actions are right in proportion
> as they tend to promote happiness, wrong as they tend to produce the
> reverse of happiness.   By happiness is intended pleasure, and the

absence of pain; by unhappiness, pain, and the privation of pleasure. To give a clear idea of the moral standard set up by the theory, much more requires to be said; in particular, what things it includes in the ideas of pain and pleasure. . . .

Now such a theory of life excites in many minds, and among them in some of the most estimable in feeling and purpose, inveterate [deep-rooted] dislike. To suppose that life has (as they express it) no higher end than pleasure—no better and nobler object of desire and pursuit—they designate as utterly mean and groveling; as a doctrine worthy only of swine, to whom the followers of Epicurus were, at a very early period, contemptuously likened. . . .

. . . If the sources of pleasure were precisely the same to human beings and to swine, the rule of life which is good enough for the one would be good enough for the other. The comparison of the Epicurean life to that of beasts is felt as degrading, precisely because a beast's pleasures do not satisfy a human being's conceptions of happiness. Human beings have faculties more elevated than the animal appetites. . . . But there is no known Epicurean theory of life which does not assign to the pleasures of the intellect, of the feelings and imagination, and of the moral sentiments, a much higher value as pleasures than to those of mere sensation. . . .

It is quite compatible with the principle of utility to recognize the fact that some kinds of pleasure are more desirable and more valuable than others. It would be absurd that, while, in estimating all other things, quality is considered as well as quantity, the estimation of pleasures should be supposed to depend on quantity alone.

If I am asked what I mean by difference in quality in pleasures, or what makes one pleasure more valuable than another, merely as a pleasure, except its being greater in amount, there is but one possible answer. Of two pleasures, if there be one to which all or almost all who have experience of both give a decided preference, irrespective of a feeling of a moral obligation to prefer it, that is the more desirable pleasure. . . .

It is better to be a human being dissatisfied than a pig satisfied; better to be Socrates dissatisfied than a fool satisfied. And if the fool, or the pig, are of a different opinion, it is because they only know their own side of the question.[22]

Do you think the following argument refutes Mill's version of hedonism?

(1) If one kind of pleasure is more valuable than another, it must be so because one pleasure contains more good than another.

(2) "More good" doesn't mean only "more pleasure," because that would contradict Mill's claim that some pleasures are *qualitatively,* not quantitatively, more valuable.

(3) Therefore, there has to be a test for this value quality other than pleasure itself.

(4) But if this test is something other than pleasure, then Mill is no longer holding a purely hedonistic theory of intrinsic value.

(5) Thus Mill's introduction of "quality" leads necessarily to abandoning the hedonism he professes.

(6) In fact, Mill himself tells us (in the fifth paragraph above) that there is another naturalistic test of value, namely, desirability, which we can identify on the basis of "preference."

(7) If one pleasure is more desirable than another, then it is more valuable; by (1) above, if it is more valuable, then it is intrinsically better (it contains more good).

(8) Hence, intrinsic value is not confined to pleasure alone but is also created by desirability, which is not a hedonistic theory.

15 *Bad pleasures and the refutation of hedonism.* Socrates is talking with Callicles, who is maintaining that the good life is one that is filled with pleasure, and that pleasure requires that we have appetites we can satisfy. In his last remark in the following quotation, Socrates raises a question about the logical relation or definitional relation between "good" and "pleasure."

> Socrates: . . . First of all then, tell me whether one who suffers from the itch and longs to scratch himself, if he can scratch himself to his heart's content and continue scratching all his life, can be said to live happily.
>
> Callicles: How absurd you are, Socrates, a regular mob orator!
>
> Socrates: That, Callicles, is why I frightened Polus and Gorgias and put them to shame, but you surely will not be dismayed or abashed, for you have courage. Only give me the answer.
>
> Callicles: Well then, I say that even one who scratches himself would live pleasantly.
>
> Socrates: And if pleasantly, happily?
>
> Callicles: Certainly.
>
> Socrates: If it was only his head that he wanted to scratch—or can I push the question further? . . .
>
> Callicles: Are you not ashamed, Socrates, to drag our discussion into such topics?
>
> Socrates: Is it I who do this, my noble friend, or the man who says so unequivocally that pleasure, whatever its nature, is the key to happiness, and does not distinguish between pleasures good and evil? But enlighten me further as to whether you say that the pleasant and the good are identical, or that there are some pleasures which are not good.
>
> Callicles: To avoid [the] inconsistency [that follows] if I say they are different, I assert they are the same.[23]

Socrates appears to be asking a simple question in his last statement above; in reality, it invites an argument that we find in Plato's *Republic*. There Socrates says: "What of those who define the Good as pleasure? Are they any less confused in their thoughts? They are obliged to admit that there are bad pleasures; from which it follows that the same things are both good and bad."[24]

The premiss that there are bad pleasures yields another argument **411** that challenges hedonists: If good and pleasure were identical, then it would be logically false to claim that there were bad pleasures, which is the same as saying there are bad goods. It is not logically false to say there are bad pleasures; therefore, good and pleasure are not identical.

16 *Elitism and qualitatively better pleasures.* G. E. Moore, who claimed that good is a criterion of right and obligatory acts, and who also claimed that pleasure is one of the things intrinsically good, agrees with Mill that intrinsic good can't be measured by the quantity of pleasure alone; quality of pleasure is a necessary factor in judging whether or not something is intrinsically better than something else. Below are some remarks of his. Do you think that Socrates' argument in Reflection 15 applies to Moore's remarks just as validly as to Mill's? Do you find in Moore's remarks considerations similar to those that Aristotle attributes to Plato (Reflection 12)?

> Is it true that one whole will be intrinsically better than another,
> whenever and only when it contains more pleasure, no matter what the
> two may be like in other respects? It seems to me almost impossible that
> any one, who fully realizes the consequences of such a view, can
> possibly hold that it *is* true. It involves our saying, for instance, that a
> world in which absolutely nothing except pleasure existed—no
> knowledge, no love, no enjoyment of beauty, no moral qualities—must
> yet be intrinsically better—better worth creating—provided only the total
> quantity of pleasure in it were the least bit greater, than one in which all
> these things existed *as well as* pleasure. . . . It involves our saying that,
> for instance, the state of mind of a drunkard, when he is intensely
> pleased with breaking crockery, is just as valuable, in itself—just as well
> worth having, as that of a man who is fully realizing all that is exquisite
> in the tragedy of King Lear, provided only the mere quantity of pleasure
> in both cases is the same. . . . And if anybody, after clearly considering
> the issue, does come to the conclusion that no one kind of enjoyment is
> ever intrinsically better than another, . . . there is no way of proving
> that he is wrong. But it seems to me almost impossible that anybody,
> who does really get the question clear, should take such a view; and, if
> anybody were to, I think it is self-evident that he would be wrong.
> (*Ethics,* pp. 146–47)

Do you detect a bit of elitism—the favoring of a special group or elite—in Mill and Moore? How would Socrates' "scratcher," for years with an itch, react to their lower estimate of his or her pleasure and relief in scratching, as compared with the rapture of an English literature student at a magnificent production of *King Lear*? Does Moore load the case by selecting a drunkard's pleasure to compare with that of a Shakespeare buff? If it were in your power to give either one person relief from an itch or another person the rapture of *Lear,* which would you give?

17 *Moore's "Naturalistic Fallacy" and the "Open Question Argument."* I

have tried to make sure that we don't confuse what things are good with the concept of good by repeating the distinction between "goods" and the "concept" of good. Kant thought it important that we not confuse non-moral goods with moral goods—that we not confuse happiness with worthiness and dignity. This is part of his anti-naturalistic ethical position. Further, Kant thought that happiness, a non-moral good, could never be a criterion of either right acts or duties. This is another part of his anti-naturalistic position. Only the Categorical Imperative could be such a criterion. There are, then, two distinct parts to Kant's anti-naturalistic theory: naturalistic goods are non-moral and they are not a criterion of duty.

In modern times the most discussed anti-naturalist was, perhaps to your surprise, G. E. Moore. But there is an important difference between Kant and Moore's anti-naturalism that we must understand; although both were critical of moral psychology, they were critical for different reasons.

Moore's stance toward naturalism can be divided into two parts. One part deals with goods, or what Moore often refers to as "*the* good," and the other part with the concept of good. Moore, unlike Kant, thought the utility of an act's producing non-moral goods was a *criterion* of an act's rightness. Pleasure, with its varying quality, is one such criterion. In this respect Moore was a naturalist.

But Moore was an anti-naturalist when it came to the *concept* of good; he did not think that "good" could be defined in terms of any natural, human factor. In his book *Evidence and Meaning,* Robert Fogelin divides Moore's anti-naturalist argument into two parts.[25] One part deals with the "naturalistic fallacy" and the other with the "Open Question Argument."

The naturalistic fallacy. This fallacy confuses goods with the concept of good. It is a fallacy in which a person infers from a property or properties possessed by everything that is good to a conclusion about the concept of good. Thus, starting from the statement *X is [a] good if, and only if, x is pleasant (or wanted or satisfying or . . .),* one might infer to the statement *Good, therefore, is identical with pleasant.* Fogelin puts it in this symbolically general way: the fallacy occurs when one infers from "'X is [a] good if, and only if, xϕ' to 'Therefore, good and ϕ are identical'" (p. 124). Here ϕ might be "pleasant" or "wanted" or "satisfying." Experiences, for example, might be a good if, and only if, they are pleasant. That this is a fallacy can be seen from the following analogy: suppose that in some world everything was square if, and only if, it was red; it wouldn't follow that the concept of square is identical with the concept of red.

The Open Question Argument. Fogelin then quotes from Moore's *Principia Ethica.* In the quote, Moore intends to show that no concept of a natural occurrence could ever be identical with the concept of good. The argument in this quotation assumes that, if two words name an identical thing, then wherever one name occurs the other can be substituted for it without any change in truth value. If "pleasure" and "good" are two names for the same thing, then we can substitute one for the other.

> Whoever will attentively consider with himself what is actually before his mind when he asks the [open] question "Is pleasure (or whatever it may be) after all good?" he can easily satisfy himself that he is not merely wondering whether pleasure is pleasant [the substitution]. And if he will try this experiment with each suggested definition in succession, he may become expert enough to recognize that in every case he has before his mind a unique object, about which a distinct question may be asked. Every one does in fact understand the question "Is this good?" When he thinks of it, his state of mind is different from what it would be, were he asked "Is this pleasant, or desired, or approved."
> (Moore, pp. 16–17)

Fogelin comments on this quotation to clarify Moore's Open Question Argument:

> Exactly what is the point of posing such a question? The underpinning of the argument seems to be this: if "pleasant" and "good" were simply alternative names for the same thing, then anyone who knew the meaning of these two terms would thereby recognize that the question "Is pleasure after all good?" is as empty as the question "Is pleasure after all pleasant?" Moore claims that the first question is not like the second in this respect, and even beyond this he suggests that, by trying this experiment on a sequence of definitions, we can become expert enough to see that no factual predicate [e.g., . . . is pleasant] will trivialize the question in the required way. Pleasure isn't simply the wrong thing to identify with goodness, it is the wrong kind of thing.
> (Fogelin, pp. 127–28)

Is the Open Question Argument an out-and-out refutation of naturalism, which says that all concepts of value and morality are ultimately concepts used in a natural science description of human nature? Forget for the moment whatever positive account you would give for these value and moral concepts; you need not produce a true theory in order to reject a false one.

Suppose the naturalist replies as follows to someone advancing the Open Question Argument: According to you, "Is pleasure good?" and "Is what we desire good?" are open questions that make sense, whereas "Is pleasure pleasant?" and "Is what we desire desired?" are trivial questions that don't make the same sense. But the reason you think they don't make the same sense is that you don't understand the meaning of "good." If you did, you'd see that they do make the same sense. Further, anyone who thinks they don't make the same sense is as ignorant of the meaning of "good" as you are.

414   Does this argument refute the anti-naturalist? How would you determine what the "true" or "real" meaning of a word is?

Alternatively, a naturalist might argue: "Personally, what I mean by 'good' is 'pleasant,' and I don't care what others mean by it. So 'Is pleasure good?' is for me just as trivial as 'Is pleasure pleasant?'"

Can we make a "moral" word mean anything we want? And can we then still carry on a meaningful conversation about morals?

12
Hume
and the Moral
Thermometer

12.1 Hume and the "Science of Man"

This chapter will focus on Hume's proposal that the study of morality, when properly understood, is a "science of Man." I will argue that, in Hume's scientific view of humans and moral phenomena, we bear some analogy to a thermometer and its readings; we can be seen as "moral thermometers."

Our interest in this chapter is not purely historical. We are not dealing with Hume merely to learn what an important philosopher had to say. He is still important today because he is the best and most original thinker who is responsible for how educated people are likely to think of themselves. If you think of yourself as a subject of psychological, sociological, and economic study, and if you think of psychology, sociology, and economics as sciences, then you think of yourself as a natural entity about whom knowledge may be gained by the methods of natural science. Although you may be more complex than other natural entities—monkeys, earthworms, bees, dolphins, flounder, wildflowers—you are of the same general *kind,* a natural kind. Nothing special about you makes you unfathomable by scientific methods; in the end you are no mystery, nor is anything about you a mystery. In principle, competent scientists can learn everything about you and then, using a complete set of natural laws, can wholly predict every thought, feeling, and action you will ever have or do. As an object of study you are on a par with thermometers.

This view that you are wholly natural is opposed to a more traditional, common-sense view that you may also hold, which is that we aren't wholly natural. For support of the common-sense view one may appeal, as Kant did, to freedom of the will—to a moral will power that is under our control and not subject to nature and nature's laws. In this view, to think that there is even a remote analogy between humans and thermometers is to entertain an absurdity.

Before stating and explaining the analogy, it will be useful to put scientific endeavor in a historical light, because this will help you grasp the notion of humans as moral thermometers—an analogy that can be made plausible and that is not intended as a lampoon of Hume's view. For us, science is so closely related to the technological benefits and wonders of modern industrial culture that it is easy to forget its powerful humanistic contribution. The word "science" once comprehended the whole of knowledge; its meaning today is more narrow. The university structure in the United States, for example, distinguishes science departments from the philosophy departments whereas in continental Europe the university structure still reflects the wider notion of "science"; there the Philosophy Faculty includes philosophy along with sciences such as physics, chemistry, and mathematics. In the following remarks, I will be using "science" and "scientific" in their newer, more restricted sense. Hume, who admired the success of the great Isaac Newton in physics, was thinking of this more restricted sense when he proposed that moral theory should be scientific or, in his term, "experimental."

The dominant theme in modern Western intellectual history was spelled out by the seventeenth-century French philosopher and mathematician René Descartes. He advocated the study of nature by a scientific method and the systematic organization of our scientific knowledge into a mathematical form. Today our attitude toward the world is shaped by the scientific temper; we take the scientific attitude for granted. But it was not always so. Hume did not take it for granted; he believed he was doing something new and supremely important in proposing that we adopt the scientific attitude toward human nature and "morals." To appreciate that the shift to a scientific temper was radical, you must know something of how it contrasted with the religious temper that it came to replace. Even though you may consider yourself a religious person, you look at the world differently from those who had a religious outlook untouched by the rise of science. Here are several considerations to remind you of how "modern" you are—unless, of course, you embrace mystery, swallow astrology, or believe fortunetellers.

First, for the scientific temper there are, in principle, no mysteries; human intelligence has the capacity to understand anything and everything. This gives humans a self-confidence that retires Christian humility to second place. The story of Faust, originally told from a Christian viewpoint, dramatizes how fearful some religious persons were of the powerful hold exercised by the new, scientific promise of unlimited knowledge. They represented Faust as willing to sell his soul to the Devil, as willing to trade his eternal salvation for universal knowledge, which for a Christian of that time was an absurd and disastrous trade-off. The scientific spirit that tempted Faust denies in principle that there are any mysteries, because everything has a natural explanation; the existence of mysteries depends on a belief that some things at least have a supernatural explanation beyond our mind's reach. The supernatural, in the Western tradition, has usually been some kind of a Deity—and sometimes a Devil as well. This Deity has attributes and powers that far exceed ours; we poor, finite beings must assume a humble stance in the presence of a perfect, infinite being. What, how, and why the Deity does and causes what It does is not understandable to our limited intelligence; God moves in mysterious ways. And this is precisely what Faust challenged.

Perhaps the only item that is still widely thought to be a mystery is the beginning of the universe. Religious tracts regularly cite the proclamation of this mystery by eminent scientists. Why should there be something rather than nothing? And if something, why does it have the nature that it does?

The reduction of the number of mysteries, including the limiting case where all are eliminated, has been a constant aim of most philosophers from the beginning of philosophy. Knowledge of some things is not a trivial possession, unlike knowing who had the top ten baseball batting averages in 1929. The status and value of some knowledge can be appreciated by con-

418 trasting it with ignorance. The ignorant are prey to superstition and to those who control the superstitions; they are under the control of others. Even kings and tyrants trembled at the words of their seers. The Caesars of ancient Rome waited in anguish for the interpretation of what a chicken's innards might reveal about their fortunes. Fear of what palmists might "reveal" makes their clients palpitate and sweat; the emotions of the ignorant rise and fall with astrological readings. But the influence of tea-readers, palmists, and astrologists is minor compared to what it was in earlier times. When we grasp the anxiety and the forfeiture of self-control that ignorance produces and remember how ignorance was once peddled to and bought by all alike—both the high and the low—then we can begin to understand why philosophers should have thought knowledge to be the prize that it is. With knowledge comes liberation—liberation from ungrounded, superstitious fears and from the manipulative control of the guardians of the mysteries.

Further, if the scientific method of gaining knowledge is available to everyone, then all of us can engineer our own liberation. We all are equal. Each individual can be as good as any other; caste is eliminated. We enter a democracy of minds and worth. Although no one can acquire all knowledge, by dividing our intellectual labor we can respect each for her or his special knowledge and welcome all as equal, contributing coworkers. The advantages of birth vanish before the equality of intelligence, ability, and knowledge.

Three things, then—self-confidence in our ability to understand all that exists, freedom from fear and manipulation, and equality—are underwritten by the scientific temper.

The veil of appearances is parted by scientific investigation. For example, our eyes tell us that animals inherit the attributes of the parents, that humans are more like humans than like other kinds, and that family members bear a mutual resemblance. The realities behind these appearances are genes that guide the production and repair of body cells; these genes are protein molecules, and behind these molecules are atoms. Similarly, table surfaces look smooth, but microscopic inspection reveals a multitude of fine scratches, and we know that these ultimately are arrangements of atoms. Galileo looked through the telescope and saw more than appeared to the naked eye. Newton discovered precise mathematical formulas for the gravitational forces that explain the regular movement of celestial bodies charted long ago from the observations of Greek mariners.

The knower increases the knowledge of the universe and its parts. But what about our knowledge of the knower? Is the knower too a subject of scientific method? What about the knower's conduct, including moral conduct? Can we part the veil of appearances here, too, and find the origin and explanation of human conduct? Or must "humanity" remain one of the mysteries?

Descartes did not claim that all existence lies within the realm of science. For him there were two kinds of existence, wholly different—mind and matter; science's realm extends to the border of matter and no farther.

Spinoza was bolder, believing that the human mind also would yield to ra-   **419**
tional investigation.   Stuart Hampshire remarks:

> The philosophy of ethics in modern times begins with some account of the
> relation between the scientific point of view and the moral point of view
> towards conduct and character. . . . When I first read Spinoza's *Ethics,* I
> was overwhelmed, as many others have been, by the fact that he was at
> once a moralist, writing from the moral point of view, and that he was also
> writing from the point of view of an imagined psychological and physical
> theory, deduced, as he thought, from first principles. . . . He made the
> assumption that no limit can be set to the development of systematic
> natural knowledge, and that a valid moral ideal must be compatible with
> the imagined future development of natural knowledge: more than com-
> patible: that the enjoyment of such knowledge, and the desire to have the
> understanding that it brings, is a principal part of a reasonable man's am-
> bition, and therefore of the moral ideal. . . . Therefore moral enlighten-
> ment, and the improvement of men and of society, have to be the effects of
> understood and controlled causes in the natural order of things.[1]

> Spinoza in the *Ethics* claims to be showing the path to a necessary moral
> conversion which philosophical and moral theory introduce. As physical
> theory reveals a new world of particles in motion behind the ordinarily
> perceived world of medium-sized objects [like hats and canes], so
> psychology and the philosophy of mind reveal a new psychic reality behind
> the ordinarily perceived passions and behind our ordinary purposes.
> (pp. 1–2)

The decline of the Rationalist school of thought to which Spinoza
belonged denied him the influence in philosophy and human affairs achieved
by Hume, whose Empiricist brilliance helped cause that decline of Ra-
tionalism; yet both believed that "science" could claim dominion over all
human conduct, including what we ordinarily think of as "moral" conduct.
Hume lived when Isaac Newton's achievements in physics impressed his contemporaries even more than Einstein's impress us today.

Hume, like many philosophers before him, saw the scientific temper as a
liberating factor. (See his *Treatise,* pp. 271–74, where he writes of his intellectual agony and "the origin of my philosophy.")[2] He lived in a Scotland
dominated by the severe Calvinism of the Presbyterian church. Conventional
moral wisdom was backed by theology, and what Hume called "vulgar
systems of morality" made much of religion as the foundation of morality.
Hume thought that just as physical science freed us from metaphysical
superstitions, so a "science of Man"—a psychology of human nature—might
free us from the moral superstitions fostered by religion:

> In every system of morality, which I have hitherto met with, I have always
> remark'd, that the author proceeds for some time in the ordinary way of
> reasoning, and establishes the being of a God, or makes observations con-
> cerning human affairs; when of a sudden I am surpriz'd to find, that in-

420   stead of the usual [verb] copulations of propositions *is,* and *is not,* I meet
with no proposition that is not connected with an *ought,* or an *ought not.*
(Treatise, p. 469)

Hume doubts that it is correct to pass from propositions such as "God
is" and "Man *is* a creature of God" to "Therefore, man *ought* to do what
God commands." In short, we cannot legitimately derive knowledge of virtue or vice, of good or evil, or of our duties from any theological or religious
statements. This view about the relation of "is" and "ought" is one for
which Hume is famous; it is discussed further on pp. 426–28 and p. 440.

From where, then, can we get knowledge of virtue and vice? To put it
another way, how can we *explain and justify* the moral conduct, moral
judgments, and assessments of character with which we are acquainted
daily? Hume tried to part the veil of appearance and to show scientifically
which of those causes of human conduct were moral ones. Following what he
believed to be Newton's approach, he proposed to use the "experimental"
method:

> There is no question of importance, whose decision is not compriz'd [in-
> cluded] in the science of man; and there is none, which can be decided with
> any certainty, before we become acquainted with that science. . . .
> And as the science of man is the only solid foundation for the other
> sciences, so the only solid foundation we can give to this science itself
> must be laid on experience and observation. . . . And tho' we must
> endeavour to render all our principles as universal as possible, by tracing
> up our experiments to the utmost, and explaining all effects from the
> simplest and fewest causes, 'tis still certain we cannot go beyond ex-
> perience; and any hypothesis, that pretends to discover the ultimate
> original qualities of human nature, ought at first to be rejected as presump-
> tuous and chimerical [wildly fanciful]. *(Treatise,* pp. xx and xxi, intro-
> duction)

Because theology is not experimental, it cannot discover the causes of
moral phenomena. The most it can do is try to justify religion's ways to
man. For Hume, nothing anywhere, including moral phenomena, may be
known without empirical observation, except "relations between ideas," of
which mathematics is an example. There is one method only for gaining
knowledge about the world. Hitherto, humans and their conduct had
perhaps been exempted from this one experimental method, but Hume proclaimed the end of this exemption. Henceforth, morals were not to be independent; they were to be part of the same cloth as physical phenomena.

In the contrasts between moral psychology and rational will ethics
discussed earlier, I gave Kant the first word; in this chapter, I will give it to
Hume. I have said that Hume is the preeminent spokesman for moral
psychology. Although there are variant theories within that school of
thought, Hume was the first to fully comprehend the whole program, take the
challenging steps that gave it its rationale, and boldly carry through the consequences of making "moral man" a scientific subject. Hume's clearly

delineated program put traditional philosophies and moral theories on the **421** defensive. Coming later, Kant saw this. Although he and Hume shared the view that morals are independent of religion, and although both wanted to liberate humans from the oppressive hand of the theologians, Kant wanted to defend a rational basis for morality and to preserve its autonomy—its independence—from science as much as from religion.

I stress the point that Hume believed there was but one kind of empirical knowledge, that our knowledge of all observable subject matters formed a unity. This was his bold claim:

> When we consider how aptly *natural* and *moral* evidence link together, and form only one chain of argument, we shall make no scruple to allow [shall have no doubt] that they are of the same nature, and derived from the same principles.[3]

Hume made these remarks in the course of arguing that our actions are as much caused as any physical events, and that "liberty" or free will does not cause any action.

And now for a word of caution: as you read my account of Hume's ethics, you may be struck by the fact that he, unlike Kant, gives no precise rules for determining what we ought and ought not do. He doesn't elaborate a decision procedure that compares to Kant's use of the Categorical Imperative. You shouldn't use this as a reason to reject Hume's position, however, because he does have something in his ethics that has received elaborate development and has been presented as the supreme test for obligation. This is the concept of the "useful," and the development was utilitarianism. A character trait is virtuous for Hume if it is either in itself agreeable to us or if it is *useful* to us. Utilitarianism has already been discussed (chiefly in 11.8, where I followed G. E. Moore's formulation of it).

12.2 Contrasting the Physical and the Moral Sciences

Hume aspired to be the "Newton of the Moral Sciences." By his own confession, he was ambitious for literary fame and money. But he delighted in baiting the writers who defended the conventional wisdom of his day. Advanced religious thinkers had found Newton's science no threat to established religion, and Newton himself prized his religious writings as much as or more than his physics. But Hume, by proposing that the "Moral Sciences" be brought under scientific scrutiny, was decidedly a threat to established religion. The books and essays attacking and condemning him were legion.

"Moral Sciences" had a broader comprehension for Hume and his contemporaries than our modern use does. "Social sciences" comes close to his

422 use, although it too is narrower than his conception. For Hume, "Moral Sciences" include "Logic, Morals, [art and literary] Criticism, and Politics." These are the subjects into which he divides the study "of the human mind":

> The sole end of logic is to explain the principles and operations of our reasoning faculty, and the nature of our ideas: morals and criticism regard our tastes and sentiments: and politics consider men as united in society, and dependent on each other. (*Treatise*, p. xix)

Hume published the first two books of his *Treatise,* "Of the Understanding" (his "Logic") and "Of the Passions," in 1739. His proposal for a "science of Man" has been one of the most debated topics in Western intellectual history. The controversy about it runs deep and long, has continued into the present day, and will continue; with the study of this topic, you enter into reflections on one of the great divisions of our time. The flavor of this dispute can be gathered from the opening paragraph of a review by Quentin Skinner of Richard Bernstein's book *The Restructuring of Social and Political Theory:*

> Before the intellectual and political upheavals of the [Nineteen] Sixties, many practitioners of the social disciplines had begun to convince themselves that they were well on the way to establishing a genuinely "scientific" method for the study of social life. But since that time, as the English sociologist Anthony Giddens has remarked, it has come to be widely agreed that "those who still wait for the Newton" of the social sciences "are not only waiting for a train that won't arrive, they're in the wrong station altogether." The main aim of Professor Richard J. Bernstein's survey *The Restructuring of Social and Political Theory* is to chart the course of this progressive disenchantment, and to ask whether it ought to be characterized an intellectual advance or merely a failure of nerve.[4]

The theoretical process of naturalizing the moral sciences is accomplished by naturalizing the human mind, which in turn is done by naturalizing the mental activities of reasoning, believing, valuing, judging, and willing. How Hume went about this and how it contrasts with Kant's conception of the mind is the subject of this chapter.

The key to understanding Hume's account of these mental activities is to see each of them as a psychological effect of some cause, either internal, external, or both. To naturalize our mind, then, means to discover its cause-and-effect operations. Beyond such operations, there is nothing; to think there is something is to make a mystery where there is none. If Hume is right, Kant's *Wille* and *Willkür*—his practical reason—disappear, and with them morals based on reason; reason could neither determine moral values nor cause action. There could be no supersensible world, only the sensible one.

If the moral sciences are modeled on the physical sciences, and if the physical sciences give only causal explanations of physical events and phenomena, then it would seem that the moral sciences too must give only causal *explanations* of human events and phenomena—nothing more.

For anyone trying to naturalize human activity, the really interesting and difficult trick to pull off is to deal with the *normative* aspect of human mental activities. There is "valid" and "invalid" reasoning; "true" and "false" believing; "wise" and "foolish" valuing; "justified" and "unjustified" judging; "blameable" and "praiseworthy" willing. Human mental effects, unlike physical effects, come in value pairs. Except metaphorically, on the other hand, there is no valid or invalid, true or false, wise or foolish raining. Human effects come in value pairs because there are norms or standards—standards for validity, truth, wisdom, justification, and praise. When mental events conform to the norms, they are valid, true, and so forth; when they don't, they are invalid, false, and so forth. There are rules for adding numbers; when you violate them, your total is wrong; when you don't, the total is correct.

Further, we need these norms not only to account for the difference between human mental effects and physical effects, but also to account for the difference between such value pairs as valid and invalid reasoning, true and false believing. Because both members of the value pairs are caused, and consequently in this respect are alike, it could be argued that something over and above causal explanation is required to explain why one caused belief is true and another is false. Both correct and incorrect additions of numbers are caused by occurrences in our brains; in that respect they are alike. But they are unlike when one is correct and the other not. The existence of rules not violated in correct addition and violated in incorrect addition explains the difference.

So far, our reasoning has shown that the moral sciences have more of a job to do than the physical sciences because the moral sciences have to account for standards and value pairs, whereas the physical sciences don't. Kant thought it necessary to go outside the sensible, natural cause-and-effect series in order to find the grounds for distinguishing between the value pairs of right and wrong, which for him are the foundations of morality. He thought morals *transcend* nature because they come from a domain *outside* it. (See the double links diagram of Kant's ethics on p. 353.) Hume, on the other hand, believed that morals are *immanent* because they come from *inside* nature; we can give a natural explanation not only for the occurrence of human mental events, but also for the norms we use in our mental operations and for the value pairs that result from their use.

The words "transcendent" and "immanent" have taken their main philosophic significance from their use in expressing the relation between God and the rest of existence. Most simply, they mean "beyond" or "outside" and "within" or "inside," respectively. The standard Christian view is that God is outside, beyond, transcendent to the universe. First comes God, then the world which is His/Her creation. Like the sculptor, God stands outside the clay. What takes place within the world, however, is immanent. The sun melting the snow is one natural object causing a change in another; both are inside nature. God may intervene occasionally in the immanent course of events, which is what people ordinarily call a miracle. Lazarus is dead, his heart is stopped; yet he rises because Jesus performed a miracle. The natural

424 course of events was altered by God's transcendent force reaching into nature to start Lazarus's heart. It can be pictured thus:

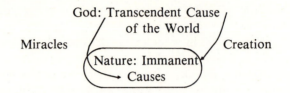

The difference between Hume and Kant can be expressed as the difference between a person who thinks there are only immanent causes and one who thinks there are both immanent *and* transcendent causes. What Kant thinks is transcendent is the rational will; it has a power, reaching from the supersensible realm, to alter the immanent course of nature. For Kant this transcendence of human will makes morality possible. Hume thinks morality is possible even though all causes are immanent, wholly natural.

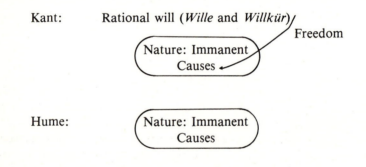

12.3 The Factual Base for Moral Standards: Going from *Is* to *Ought*

At first flush, Hume's confidence that he can find in nature the basis for norms and standards seems misplaced, as if he's "in the wrong station altogether." There appears to be an unbridgeable gap between the physical and the moral sciences; the former *de*scribe (Jack is hungry) and the latter *pre*scribe (Jack ought to be kind). In describing, we say what *is* the case; in prescribing, we say what *ought to be* the case. But what ought to be the case often *is not* the case; if Jack were always kind, there would be no point in saying that he ought to be. Descriptions are true because they state facts that now exist or did exist, whereas the facts mentioned in a prescription do not now exist but are potential only, awaiting a future existence.

This prompts a question: since often we are committed to prescriptions even though no existing facts validate them, and since scientific statements are validated only by facts, is it possible to provide a "scientific" account of prescriptive norms and their validity? Physicists don't talk of "moral" and "immoral" gravity, nor chemists of "justified" and "unjustified" acids, nor botanists of "blameable" and "praiseworthy" plants. But no investigator of "Logic, Morals, Criticism, and Politics" can ignore the fact that values and prescriptions are part and parcel of these topics. To ignore valuing and prescribing in such activities would be to miss an essential element of human activity.

In evaluating human activity, we do of course use facts. One of the premisses in Aristotle's practical syllogism is factual. Kant includes beliefs about circumstances in his maxims. A heated controversy arose when the Federal Trade Commission held hearings on TV commercials for children: should the Commission regulate ads aimed at children? Both sides to the controversy—advertisers and their opponents—had child and development psychologists testify about children's capacities to understand, evaluate, and resist advertising. In her column "Your Money," Sylvia Porter remarked:

> And a final provocative part of this controversy is that so much of this reflects a confrontation between two opposing interest groups, both arguing opinion, not facts. Millions of dollars being spent on the hearings—administrative expenses, legal, public relations fees, etc.—could achieve so much more if spent on research that would permit the issues to be settled on the basis of knowledge, not emotion.[5]

But while facts are relevant, they are not sufficient to settle the issues, Ms. Porter notwithstanding. Aristotle knew what Porter apparently doesn't; his practical syllogism also contains a *value* premiss (p. 20). Gathering all accurate facts and nothing else won't tell you whether the commission should regulate TV ads, unless you also have a way of determining whether or not the facts are "good" or "bad." Columnist George Will understands this:

> I am staring, raptly, at a headline: "TV Ads Are Said to Benefit Child by Developing Skepticism." An advertising executive says children "must learn the market-place." And: "Even if a child is deceived by an ad at age four, what harm is done? He is in the process of learning to make his own decisions."
>
> The theory that being deceived improves children is alarming. The problem with routine public deceit is not just that children are indeed harmed, but that the culture is, too. The "skepticism" instilled is really cynicism that seeps like a stain across society.
>
> Recently, an Army doctor claimed that his enlistment contract was void because the Army had used misleading advertising to recruit doctors. An Army lawyer responded that the advertisement's promises of modern equipment and other benefits were acceptable "puffery." But casualness about deceit in commerce leads to casually deceitful government.[6]

Will does not confine his argument to factual premisses. Notice the words "benefit," "harm," "deceit," "alarming," and "cynicism" in this extract. He knows these are value terms used to evaluate the facts and to criticize.

Porter says the issues should be "settled on the basis of knowledge, not emotion." Hume believes just the opposite. Emotion—or as he puts it "passion," "feeling," or "sentiment"—is the basis for settling the issues. Emotions are the source of values; reason's facts are not: "'Tis not contrary to reason to prefer the destruction of the whole world to the scratching of my finger" (*Treatise,* p. 416). Then he adds a remark that shows he thinks reason's facts are relevant but not the whole story:

> In short, a passion must be accompany'd with some false judgment, in order to its being unreasonable; and even then 'tis not the passion, properly speaking, which is unreasonable, but the judgment. (*Treatise,* p. 416)

Normally, the truth of factual statements can be verified: a description of the eating habits of a psychologist's child is verified by observing how much sugar-coated cereal the child eats. But what, if any, are the facts that validate the standards the psychologist will use to decide if such advertising should be banned? Hume thinks standards of evaluation can be validated by the facts about feeling responses. In a nutshell, his theory is as follows.

Cheerfulness is a virtue, sullenness a vice.

Why?

Because cheerfulness causes an agreeable response in us and sullenness a disagreeable one. (See *Enquiry,* pp. 250–51.) And agreeable and disagreeable responses are the standard for merit and demerit.

Why? How can we know that these standards are valid?

Because, Hume thinks, these *in fact* are universal responses, which universality is a mark of a valid standard. Any supposed variations from universality, he thinks, can be "corrected," as we will see in 12.6.

From here, one could go in either of two directions. The first is a relativistic way, denying that any standard or norm has more validity than another. The second or nonrelativistic way is to affirm that there are valid standards.

Hume did not take the relativist way of naturalizing the mind. He believed that there are valid universal standards of morals, taste, reasoning, and politics. That he thought there were such valid standards is evident: "The intercourse of sentiments, therefore, in society and conversation, makes us form some general inalterable standard, by which we may approve or disapprove of characters and manners" (*Treatise,* p. 603). In the later *Enquiry,* he repeats this sentence almost exactly (*Enquiry,* p. 229). But how can we go validly from the facts about feelings, from what *is,* from description, to standards, to what *ought to be,* to prescription? Hume knew this was the difficult—and interesting—question.

How to go and not go from *Is* to *Ought* is one of the two most discussed and famous contributions Hume made to philosophy. (The other one is his analysis of the causal relation.)

Hume announces the *Is* to *Ought* issue in the quotation on pages 419–20. I interpreted that passage as a criticism of religious thinkers (among others) who wanted to go by logical deduction from the *is* of God's existence **427** and His/Her creation of us to the *ought* of moral commands.[7] The following lines, immediately following the earlier quotation, show that Hume thought we had to go from *Is* to *Ought* by a route other than deduction:

> This change [from *is* to *ought* in "vulgar systems of morality"] is imperceptible; but is, however, of the last [most important] consequence. For as this *ought,* or *ought not,* expresses some new relation or affirmation, 'tis necessary that it shou'd be observ'd and explain'd; and at the same that a reason should be given, for what seems altogether inconceivable, how this new relation can be a deduction from others, which are entirely different from it. [*Ought* is "entirely different from" *is.*] But as authors do not commonly use this precaution, I shall presume to recommend it to the readers; and am persuaded, that this small attention wou'd subvert all the vulgar systems of morality, and let us see, that the distinction of vice and virtue is not founded merely on the relations of objects, nor is perceived by reason. (*Treatise,* pp. 469–70)

Here Hume is denying that we may by our reason logically *deduce* a sentence with "ought" in it from sentences that do not have an "ought" in them. The "ought" or "ought not" conclusion "expresses some new relation or affirmation" that is not in the premises; no conclusion can be validly drawn if it contains a term such as "ought" that isn't in the premises. Hence, we cannot by reasoning alone start from facts and arrive at moral standards. This criticism doesn't mean, however, that morals have no base; Hume says that "the distinction of vice and virtue is not founded *merely* [my emphasis] on the relation of objects, nor is perceived by reason." Not "merely." This leaves it open that there is another way of going from *Is* to *Ought.*

> To have a sense of virtue, is nothing but to *feel* a satisfaction of a particular kind from the contemplation of a character. The very *feeling* constitutes our praise or admiration. We go no farther; nor do we enquire into the cause of the satisfaction. We *do not infer* [my emphasis] a character to be virtuous, because it pleases: But in feeling that it pleases after such a particular manner, we in effect feel that it is virtuous. The case is the same as in our judgments concerning all kinds of beauty, and tastes, and sensations. Our approbation is imply'd in the immediate pleasure they convey to us. (*Treatise,* p. 471)

The first point to notice about this quotation is that our approbation *is* our feeling; our sentences are not our approbation. Moral approbation can do without language, "reporting" or otherwise. Parenthetically, Hume is stating here how we can go from *Is* to *Ought,* namely, by going from the contemplation of a character trait to feeling "a satisfaction of a particular kind." Here we see an important—perhaps the most important—step in

428   Hume's naturalization of morals.   We do not and cannot move from *Is* to *Ought* by inferring or by a "deduction" of reason, as "vulgar" moralists would have it (*Treatise,* p. 469).   Rather, it is a movement that occurs *causally* because of the nature of our mental operations.

Hume tells us that this feeling arises from four "different sources."

> Every quality of the mind is denominated virtuous, which gives pleasure by the mere survey; as every quality, which produces pain, is call'd vicious. This pleasure and this pain may arise from four different sources. For we reap pleasure from the view of a character, which is naturally fitted to be useful to others, or to the person himself, or which is agreeable to others, or to the person himself. (*Treatise,* p. 591)

> It appears, that there never was any quality recommended by any one, as a virtue or moral excellence, but on account of its being *useful,* or *agreeable* to a man *himself,* or to *others.* For what other reason can ever be assigned for praise or approbation [approval]?[8]

Approval and disapproval place items in value pairs. This is based on either of two grounds: if they are ends, then it is their agreeableness or disagreeableness, either to ourselves or others; if they are means, then it is their usefulness or uselessness, either to ourselves or others.   I will generally use the term "agreeableness" rather than "pleasure" to designate our positive response to things taken as ends; it is a wider term and expresses better what Hume wants to convey about the nature of our response.

Hume makes it clear that usefulness is secondary to agreeableness.   At bottom, it is our responses—of agreeableness or disagreeableness—that provide the source of "good" and "bad" pairing:

> Utility is only a tendency to a certain end; and were the end totally indifferent to us, we should feel the same indifference toward the means.   It is requisite that a *sentiment* should here display itself, in order to give a preference to the useful above the pernicious [harmful] tendencies.   This sentiment can be no other than a feeling for the happiness of mankind, and a resentment of their misery; since these are the different ends which virtue and vice have a tendency to promote. (*Enquiry,* p. 286; see also pp. 293, 214)

Usefulness (Uselessness) —— Tendency ⟶ *Agreeableness (Disagreeableness)*

to Ourselves   to Others   to Ourselves   to Others

In these remarks, we see Hume giving his explanation for value pairing, for which the moral sciences, unlike the physical, must account.   Ultimately, value pairing occurs because some end is agreeable (disagreeable) to ourselves or others.

How do we explain these responses?   Why should some things be agreeable and others disagreeable?   It is due to the human nature that we have:

The most probable hypothesis, which has been advanc'd to explain the distinction betwixt vice and virtue, and the origin of moral rights and obligations, is, that from a primary constitution of nature certain characters and passions, by the very view and contemplation, produce a pain, and others in like manner excite a pleasure. (*Treatise,* p. 296)

Why do we have the human nature or "primary constitution" that we have? Can this be explained? No. For Hume the experimental method is confined to establishing the presence of stable correlations between events; these correlations are learned by us because of a "Principle" of "Custom or Habit." Our mind establishes a habit of conjoining the ideas of two things after we have observed their conjunction repeatedly. I eat bread several times and notice that after eating I feel full and satisfied. Having observed this on several occasions, my mind forms the habit or custom of linking them, so that when I think of eating bread my mind carries me over to the thought of feeling fuller and to the satisfaction of my hunger: "Custom, then, is the great guide of human life" (*Enquiry,* p. 44). Our human frame is such that when I observe some personal quality in another, say generosity, it is followed by an agreeable feeling; the observation of meanness is followed by a disagreeable feeling. These conjunctions become habitually correlated in our mind, and we establish that these observed qualities cause "a pleasure or uneasiness of a particular kind." This occurs because there is some "principle" governing the occurrence of our feelings and passions. But there can be no further explanation of these principles of the mind, no explanation of why we have the human nature that we do:

But as to the causes of these general causes, we should in vain attempt their discovery. . . . These ultimate springs and principles are totally shut up from human curiosity and enquiry. (*Enquiry,* p. 30)

In this section, I have given a sketch of Hume's naturalization of morals. To see how he goes about this, we needed a bare-bones idea of his notion of morals. Fundamentally, he says, moral activity rests not on reason but on approving and disapproving, which are based on tendencies to usefulness and feelings of agreeableness. That approving and disapproving rest on these factors is simply a fact about our human nature and its principles of operation.

We have yet to see in a more careful way how Hume proposes to find a naturalistic account of valid standards, how he goes from *Is* to valid *Oughts.* Let us now consider his major ethical views; they will help us understand more fully what "standards" he purports to explain.

12.4 Some of Hume's Major Ethical Tenets

I have said in a general way what Hume claims about standards and have observed that it involves going from *Is* to *Ought.* Let's make it more

430   concrete by considering what kinds of things have moral worth—are virtuous or vicious—in accord with standards.

12.4a PERSONS ARE THE OBJECTS OF MORAL JUDGMENTS.

The anchoring idea in Hume's ethics is that the object of moral approval and disapproval is always persons, their qualities of mind and character. Actions do not in themselves have moral value or disvalue; they are pertinent to moral evaluation because they are clues to character and qualities. Thus when Hume talks about "utility," he is using it differently from later utilitarians, who thought actions themselves had moral properties on account of their good or bad consequences. For Hume, basically, "utility" attaches to human qualities and traits of character that are the cause or motive of acts whose results are found agreeable or disagreeable (although he does sometimes talk about the utility of acts, particularly in his discussion of justice).

When Hume begins "to discover the true origin of morals," he says:

> In order to attain this purpose, we shall endeavour to follow a very simple method: we shall analyse that complication of mental qualities, which form what, in common life, we call Personal Merit: we shall consider every attribute of the mind, which renders a man an object either of esteem and affection, or of hatred and contempt; every habit or sentiment or faculty, which, if ascribed to any person, implies either praise or blame, and may enter into any panegyric [glowing approval] or satire of his character and manners. (*Enquiry,* pp. 173–74)

There is a nice catalogue of these mental qualities in the "Conclusion" of the *Enquiry:*

> The preceding delineation or definition of Personal Merit must still retain its evidence and authority: it must still be allowed that every quality of the mind, which is *useful* or *agreeable* to the *person himself* or to *others,* communicates a pleasure to the spectator, engages his esteem, and is admitted under the honourable denomination of virtue or merit. Are not justice, fidelity, honour, veracity, allegiance, chastity, esteemed solely on account of their tendency to promote the good of society? Is not that tendency inseparable from humanity, benevolence, lenity [mercy], generosity, gratitude, moderation, tenderness, friendship and all other social virtues? Can it possibly be doubted that industry, discretion, frugality, secrecy, order, perseverance, forethought, judgment, and this whole class of virtues and accomplishments, of which many pages would not contain the whole catalogue; can it be doubted, I say, that the tendency of these qualities to promote the interest and happiness of their possessor, is the sole foundation of their merit? Who can dispute that a mind, which supports a perpetual serenity and cheerfulness, a noble dignity and undaunted spirit, a tender affection and good-will to all around; as it has more enjoyment within itself, is also a more animating and rejoicing spectacle, than if dejected with melancholy, tormented with anxiety, irritated with rage, or

sunk into the most abject baseness and degeneracy? And as to the qualities, immediately *agreeable to others,* they speak sufficiently for themselves; and he must be unhappy, indeed, either in his own temper, or in his situation and company, who has never perceived the charms of a facetious wit or flowing affability, of a delicate modesty or decent genteelness of address and manner. (pp. 277-78)

Included in this catalogue are the qualities of persons that are "useful" to ourselves and others. These quality names are the nouns that the adjective "useful" qualifies, when "useful" is used with its "moral" meaning. Actions are not themselves *morally* useful; they are clues or signs of "motives" and so of moral "character." Thus our moral evaluations proceed as follows:

acts → motives → character → person

'Tis evident, that when we praise any actions, we regard only the motives that produced them, and consider the actions as signs of indications of certain principles in the mind and temper. The external performance has not merit. We must look within to find the moral quality. This we cannot do directly; and therefore fix our attention on actions, as external signs. But these actions are still considered as signs; and the ultimate object of our praise and approbation is the motive, that produced them. (*Treatise,* p. 477)

If an *action* be either virtuous or vicious, 'tis only as a sign of some quality or character. It must depend upon durable principles of the mind, which extend over the whole conduct, and enter into the personal character. . . . We are never to consider any single action in our enquiries concerning the origin of morals; but only the quality or character from which the action proceeded. These alone are durable enough to affect our sentiments concerning the person. (*Treatise,* p. 575)

Hume stresses the durability of character. When we praise or blame someone for something, we hold them responsible; we couldn't do this if the act wasn't caused by a "durable or constant" quality of the person. If there were no durable continuity between Everett today and Everett yesterday, we couldn't hold today's Everett responsible for the acts of yesterday's Everett.

Actions are by their very nature temporary and perishing; and where they proceed not from some cause in the characters and disposition of the person, who perform'd them, they infix (attach) not themselves upon him, and can neither redound to his honour, if good, nor infamy, if evil. The action itself may be blameable; it may be contrary to all the rules of morality and religion: But the person is not responsible for it [if there is no steady cause of it in his character]; and as it proceeded from nothing in him, that is durable or constant, and leaves nothing of its nature behind, 'tis impossible he can, upon its account, become the object of punishment or vengeance. (*Treatise,* p. 411)

432   The utility of a person's character is judged by the end it has a tendency to promote. Hume says "tendency" because tenderness, for example, doesn't always effect a good end; an erring child sometimes needs firm rather than tender treatment. But this occasional failure of tenderness doesn't negate its usual effect and value.

Further, character has merit because of its tendency to promote *good* ends. The utility value of a good character derives from the value of the end it tends to produce. While the discernment of this utility is a function of reason, ultimately it is "sentiment" that endows a meritorious character's utility with value, because the sentiment of agreeableness gives value to the ends promoted by utility. Moral utility is finally traced, then, to the agreeableness of happiness and the disagreeableness of misery that humane persons experience:

> Utility is only a tendency to a certain end; and were the end totally indifferent to us, we should feel the same indifference towards the means. (*Enquiry,* p. 286)

Although Hume tells us above that utility's value depends on the agreeableness of the end it has a tendency to promote, he also says that utility *itself* is agreeable: "Usefulness is agreeable, and engages our approbation. This is a matter of fact, confirmed by daily observation" (*Enquiry,* p. 218).

While Hume seems of two minds about where utility's value comes from, he is clear that, although objects too may have utility, they do not have "moral" utility because they arouse sentiments different from those of human character. Humans do, and objects do not, excite the passions of love, hate, pride, and humility:

> We ought not to imagine, because an inanimate object may be useful as well as a man, that therefore it ought also, according to this system, to merit the appellation of *virtuous.* The sentiments, excited by utility, are, in the two cases, very different; and the one is mixed with affection, esteem, approbation, &c, and not the other. In like manner, an inanimate object may have good colour and proportions as well as a human figure. But can we ever be in love with the former? (*Enquiry,* n., p. 213)

Hume's standards for moral judgments apply, then, to persons' qualities, motives, and character. They are virtuous if they are immediately agreeable or disagreeable to (1) ourselves and (2) others, or tend to be useful to (3) ourselves and (4) others. Upon these four grounds Hume rests his theory of virtue and vice.

12.4b JUSTICE AND OBLIGATION. Hume begins his *Treatise* on morals with two observations: first, teaching morals is an attempt to influence people's actions, and so it is a part of practical rather than speculative philosophy; second, since passions alone can move us to action, morals can have an influence only if they are based on passions. If morals, then, are to **433** influence us to do our duty or fulfill our obligations, we have to tie our obligations to our passions, sentiments, or feeling. (*Treatise,* p. 457)

Hume's approach to obligation is to ask if there are motives that would induce us to do our duty, and to ask how these motives are related to those qualities of mind and character that are virtuous—that is, to those qualities of mind and character that are immediately agreeable and useful to ourselves and others:

> Having explained the moral *approbation* attending merit or virtue, there remains nothing but briefly to consider our interested *obligation* to it, and to inquire whether every man who has any regard to his own happiness and welfare, will not best find his account in the practice of every moral duty. (*Enquiry,* p. 278)

Hume does think that there are motives possessed by all that make it easy to do our duty; our very nature is suited to cultivating those qualities of mind and character that make us virtuous. (Hume himself was an agreeable, cheerful person who found it easy to be moral and companionable.) He divides our motives to duty into two kinds: natural and artificial.

The *natural* motive to do one's duty is one's "regard to his own happiness and welfare." Here we have something agreeable and useful to ourselves, easy to attain, and not at all forbidding:

> But what philosophical truths can be more advantageous to society, than those here delivered, which represent virtue in all her genuine and most engaging charms, and makes us approach her with ease, familiarity, and affection? The dismal dress falls off, with which many divines, and some philosophers, have covered her; and nothing appears but gentleness, humanity, beneficience, affability; nay, even at proper intervals, play, frolic, and gaiety. She talks not of useless austerities and rigours, suffering and self-denial. She declares that her sole purpose is to make her votaries and all mankind, during every instant of their existence, if possible, cheerful and happy; nor does she ever willingly part with any pleasure but in hopes of ample compensation in some other period of their lives. The sole trouble which she demands, is that of just calculation, and a steady preference of the greater happiness. (*Enquiry,* p. 279)

There are obligations that Hume calls *"artificial,"* although this doesn't mean "arbitrary." The "artificial" terminology is introduced in the section of the *Treatise* where he discusses whether justice is artificial or natural (Book III, Part II, Section I). He is careful to guard us from the impression that virtue and justice aren't natural:

> When I deny justice to be a natural virtue, I make use of the word *natural,* only as oppos'd to *artificial.* In another sense of the word; as no principle of the human mind is more natural than a sense of virtue; so no virtue is more natural than justice. (*Treatise,* p. 484)

434   Hume can maintain this apparently inconsistent position about both the naturalness and artificiality of justice by showing (1) that justice and its motive are "artificial" because they have their origin in human conventions and (2) that these conventions in turn are the result of natural conditions in humans. He does make both of these claims.

As to (2), Hume cites two natural conditions that lead us to fashion the "artificial" conventions of justice: the selfishness of humans and the uncertainty and scarcity of goods in the world:

> I have already observ'd, that justice takes its rise from human conventions; and that these are intended as a remedy to some inconveniences, which proceed from the concurrence of certain *qualities* of the human mind with the *situation* of external objects. The qualities of the mind are *selfishness* and *limited generosity:* And the situation of external objects is their *easy change,* join'd to their *scarcity* in comparison of the wants and desires of men. . . . Here then is a proposition, which, I think, may be regarded as certain, *that 'tis only from the selfishness and confin'd generosity of men, along with the scanty provision nature has made for his wants, that justice derives its origin.* (*Treatise,* pp. 494–95)

In the *Enquiry* he also says that justice takes its value from utility:

> Thus, the rules of equity or justice depend entirely on the particular state and condition in which men are placed, and owe their origin and existence to that utility, which result to the public from their strict and regular observance. . . . By rendering justice totally *useless,* you thereby totally destroy its essence, and suspend its obligation upon mankind. (p. 188)

Now let's consider (1): that justice and its motive have their origins in conventions. In the last quotation, Hume explicitly links the usefulness of justice to our obligation to follow the rules of justice. If justice is artificial because its rules are a set of conventions, then the motive to act justly is also an "artificial" one. The artificial motive comes into being only because the artificial rules of justice are useful in counteracting our natural selfishness and in providing an increase and equitable distribution of the scant resources that nature, unaided by human intervention, supplies. It is the usefulness of the artifice of justice that brings the motive of justice into existence; the motive doesn't exist naturally, that is, without the artifice. Something of what Hume has in mind by "conventions" is indicated in the following remarks, which show that by this term he means more than mere "rules" of justice:

> The common situation of society is a medium amidst all these extremes [of "extreme abundance or extreme want"]. We are naturally partial to ourselves, and to our friends; but are capable of learning the advantage resulting from a more equitable conduct. Few enjoyments are given us from the open and liberal hand of nature; but by art, labour, and industry, we can extract them in great abundance. Hence the ideas of property become necessary in all civil society: Hence justice derives its usefulness to the public: And hence alone arises its merit and moral obligation. (*Enquiry,* p. 188)

Notice Hume's reference to "art, labour, and industry," which are all **435** bound up with artifacts such as plows, tractors, tools, plastics, cultivation, and all the social conventions that enable us collectively to make and use them. Notice also Hume's use of "property," which he, unlike some socialists, thinks necessary in civil society. Property is obviously a convention, not a natural thing. Hume believes that property depends on justice. One can argue that because property is artificial, the condition on which it depends must be artificial, too; hence, justice is artificial. Hume makes the same dependency claim about "obligation"; hence, obligation must have an "artificial" motive, which must be due to the usefulness or utility possessed by artifacts:

> Our property is nothing but those goods, whose constant possession is establish'd by the laws of society; that is, by the laws of justice. Those, therefore, who make use of the words *property,* or *right,* or *obligation,* before they have explain'd the origin of justice, or even make use of them in that explication, are guilty of a very gross fallacy, and can never reason upon any solid foundation. A man's property is some object related to him. This relation is not natural, but moral, and founded on justice. . . . The origin of justice explains that of property. The same artifice gives rise to both. (*Treatise,* p. 491)

Hume has a "performatory" theory of promises and, consequently, of contracts needed for the institution of property. The transfer of property and the obligatoriness of promises in contracts depends upon the *performance* of a linguistic act, such as saying "I promise . . ." or signing your name to a document. Such acts are both linguistic and promising. "The will or consent . . . must be expressed by words or signs, in order to impose a tie on any man" (*Enquiry,* n., pp. 199–200; see also *Treatise,* pp. 516–25).

This linguistic "performatory" theory of property and contract, involving property transfer and promises, clearly puts property in the "conventional" or "artificial" category because language is a conventional construct, an artifact of humans. It is precisely this conventional, linguistic basis of property and promises that Hume thinks introduces artificial motives—"artificial" because they would not exist without the artifact of language:

> A resolution [such as privately intending to pay a sum of money] is the natural act of the mind, which promises express: But were there no more than a [mental] resolution in the case, promises wou'd only declare our former motives, wou'd not create any new motive or obligation. They are the conventions of men, which create a new motive, when experience has taught us, that human affairs wou'd be conducted much more for mutual advantage, were there certain *symbols* or *signs* instituted, by which we might give each other security of our conduct in any particular incident. (*Treatise,* p. 522)

So far, we have seen Hume's account of the origins of justice and obligation, their conventionality, and how these explain the creation of "artificial" motives. But we do not know as yet why justice is a *moral* virtue. He

436   has explained it as useful for our own self-interest, and traced its origin in part to the "selfish" nature of humans. Hume knows that by itself this does not explain why justice is a "moral" virtue. Let's see what Hume means by "moral" and how he shows justice is a "moral" virtue.

12.4c DISTINGUISHING MORAL FROM NON-MORAL RESPONSES.

Earlier I said that universality of response is one element required to establish moral standards. Besides universality, Hume uses two other essential features—sympathy and impartiality—to distinguish between moral and non-moral responses. We do after all have feelings aroused by many things, but which of these are moral ones?[9] Not all of them. For instance, the pleasures of a good ale are not. Of the first feature, Hume says: "Sympathy is the chief source of moral distinctions. . . . Justice is certainly approv'd of for no other reason, than because it has a tendency to the public good: And the public good is indifferent to us, except so far as sympathy interests us in it" (*Treatise,* p. 618). Sympathy makes *others'* good a concern of *ours.* We would not be concerned at the injustice of jailing an innocent person if we didn't have a way of sympathizing with the victim.

The other main "moral" feature is impartiality, which is opposed to self-interest or self-love: "'Tis only when a character is considered in general, without reference to our particular interest, that it causes such a feeling or sentiment as denominates it morally good or evil" (*Treatise,* p. 472). A good feeling toward an uncle would not be a moral one, of course, if it were aroused when we learned he had put us in his will. Impartiality needs no explanation, but Hume's notion of sympathy does. Notice first that Hume includes in the sources of morals the immediate agreeableness or usefulness of a character trait *to others.* An honest character is not useful just to us but to others as well, and so it is with all the other virtuous traits of character. Hume, unlike Hobbes, does not found morals on egoistic interests.

The second point to notice is a negative one. We often use "sympathy" to denote a particular feeling. We say, for example, "I sympathize with you, Mrs. Assaud, on the death of your beloved husband," indicating that we have a feeling. This is not what Hume has in mind. Hume's "sympathy" is a mental operation for transmitting others' feeling to us, not the feeling itself. Third, this principle or operation of the way the human mind works is a principle that makes possible the *communication* to us of what others are feeling. Sympathy is an "operation" of the mind that makes what is "agreeable and useful to others" available as a source of morality to everyone.

Since Hume founds morals on sentiments and feelings, and since others' feelings are their own, not ours, how can their feelings be a source of morals for us? If each of us can have only our own feelings, it would appear that in founding morals on feelings Hume would have to subscribe to egoism. He would, were it not for the mental operation of sympathy. Let's see how it works.

Hume distinguishes between "impressions" and "ideas." Impressions are what is mentally present to us when our senses are stimulated: light strikes our eyeball, setting off a reaction in the nervous system that ends up as a visual impression; similarly with our other sense organs. Although these impressions come and go, I can retain an idea of them; I have a present memory of the past visual impression of my grandfather's face. Impressions and ideas are alike, says Hume, except that impressions are more vivid. Similarly with the passions, feelings, or sentiments: when immediately apprehended, they are vividly present to us; after they have ceased, I retain an idea of them. Although we can never possess the feelings of others, Hume thinks that by analogy we can have an idea of them. Right now, for example, you can have an idea of my love for my daughter and son.

Sympathy is "the conversion of an idea [of others' feelings] into an impression" of ours; it is "that propensity [disposition] we have to sympathize with others, and to receive by communication their inclinations and sentiments, however different from, or even contrary to our own" feelings. (*Treatise*, pp. 595, 320, 316). So when others are responding with a feeling of agreeableness or its opposite upon contemplating a character trait or its utility, our *idea* of the response of others is transformed by the operation of sympathy into the "very *impressions*" that others have:

> 'Tis indeed evident, that when we sympathize with the passions and sentiments of others, these movements appear at first in *our* mind as mere ideas, and are conceiv'd to belong to another person, as we conceive any other matter of fact. 'Tis also evident that the ideas of the affections of others are converted into the very impressions they represent, and that the passions arise in conformity to the images we form of them. (*Treatise*, p. 319; on our response to utility, see *Enquiry*, p. 231)

If Francis Bacon feels Shakespeare's wit agreeable, and if I have an idea of Bacon's feeling, the operation of sympathy transforms my *idea* of Bacon's feeling into a *feeling* of agreeableness in me. The operation of sympathy makes it possible for the sentiments of others to be communicated to us; in fact, our ideas "are converted into *the very impressions* they represent."

Hume thinks that the operation of sympathy is one possessed by all persons; it is universally distributed (*Treatise,* p. 575). If so, it is a remarkably powerful social capacity. What it does, as Hume explains it, is to erase the boundaries that separate us. Egoism, as a moral doctrine, depends upon the claim that there is a plurality of individuals, each with his or her own private feelings, interests, and sentiments. For the egoist, this individualism and privacy cannot be breached. The boundaries marking the limits of each individual seal us off from one another, so that the pains and pleasures, triumphs and disappointments, anxieties and joys of others need not and cannot be a concern of ours. Believing, however, that we all have the capacity of sympathy, Hume thinks that we destroy these ego boundaries. The feelings of others literally become ours; morally, we many are made *one* by the operation of sympathy. This gives our sentiments their public, moral dimension.

438   Hume's insistence that feelings are moral only if they are disinterested or impartial, as opposed to self-interested, and his theory of sympathy as an operation that makes others' feelings our own, lead to the conclusion that a character trait is virtuous if (1) it is useful to ourselves *and* to others, or if (2) it is agreeable to ourselves *and* to others.

I emphasize the *and*. Both conditions in (1) or (2) must be satisfied; if something were useful or agreeable only to ourselves, we would simply have self-interested feelings, which according to Hume are not moral feelings. If something is agreeable to others but not to ourselves, then it isn't moral either because it is confined to *their* feelings, which makes it to *their* self-interest. The feeling would then lack the requisite universality that Hume demands of moral feelings as moral standards. Sympathy is the mental operation that makes universality of feelings possible.

Let us add *and* to the figure on page 428:

Usefulness —— Tendency ——→ Agreeableness

to Ourselves *and* to Others   or   to Ourselves *and* to Others

Now we are ready to understand Hume's answer to his question, "Why we annex the idea of virtue to justice, and of vice to injustice." The origin of justice was traced to overcoming our selfish nature and the scarcity of goods; Hume doesn't think our selfish interest makes justice a virtue. It can be a virtue only if it is useful also to others, and only if its being useful to others matters to us. Sympathy is what makes its utility to others matter to us. And it makes it matter to us *even when no* self-interest of ours is involved:

> Nay when the injustice is so distant from us, as no way to affect our interest, it still displeases us; because we consider it as prejudicial to human society, and pernicious to every one that approaches the person guilty of it. We partake of their uneasiness by *sympathy;* and as every thing, which gives uneasiness in human actions, upon the general survey, is call'd Vice, and whatever produces satisfaction, in the same manner, is denominated [called] Virtue; this is the reason why the sense of moral good and evil follows upon justice and injustice. . . . *Thus self-interest is the original motive to the* establishment *of justice; but a* sympathy *with public interest is the source of the* moral approbation, *which attends that virtue.* (*Treatise*, pp. 499–500)

To summarize 12.4: for Hume the standards of morality are the agreeableness or usefulness of human traits to ourselves and others. Morality rests on our and others' sentiments; it can rest on others' sentiments for us because of the principle of sympathy. Moral sentiments are distinguished from non-moral sentiments because they are (1) universal responses (2) to persons rather than objects, and also (3) responses, via sympathy, to other persons' responses ("public good"), and (4) impartial responses that are independent of our self-interest.

12.5 Moral Standards 439
and the Human Thermometer

We have now come to the really interesting philosophical question: how does Hume's theoretical "science of Man" show we can have valid practical standards? That is, how can reports on what "is" or 'is not" lead to valid standards for what "ought" or "ought not" to be?

Because Hume's philosophy naturalizes humans, it must provide "natural" explanations of everything human. This includes explaining how there can be valid moral standards, explaining our belief that such standards exist, and explaining our behavior in justifying such a belief. In addition, Hume must explain why we act in accord with what we believe are valid standards of what ought to be and of what ought to be done.

In giving a "natural" explanation of human behavior, we should not use any kind of explanation that we do not use to explain non-human events, though of course since humans are very complex, the explanation of their behavior has to be more complex than that of simpler things. Hume thinks that a natural explanation is an explanation principally by means of the relation of cause and effect. Consequently, I have chosen a thermometer as a non-human entity whose behavior can be explained causally; using it as an analogue for humans, it will illustrate—not prove—how Hume tries to naturalize moral and aesthetic standards.

A thermometer is placed in a liquid. If the mercury in the thermometer expands, moves upward in the glass column, and gives a high reading, then it "pronounces" that the water is warm; but, if the mercury contracts, moves downward, and gives a low reading, then it "pronounces" that the water is cool. Similarly for all such thermometers.

Place a human in the "liquid" of a character trait. If he "expands" with an agreeable feeling, then he pronounces that the character trait is virtuous; but if he "contracts" with an uneasy feeling, then he pronounces that the trait is vicious. Similarly for all humans.

The thermometer does not "infer" that the water is warm or cold; the height of the mercury in the column *is* the temperature. What is in the water is not the temperature (78 degrees), but rather molecular activity. The temperature response is a function of the activity in the liquid (molecule movement) and the nature of mercury; when these things function together, the mercury is made to expand, contract, or do neither.

Analogously, "The very *feeling* constitutes [is] our praise or admiration. . . . We do not infer a character to be virtuous" (*Treatise,* p. 471). The feeling response is a function of the character trait's nature or usefulness and the nature of our mind; functioning together, they cause our feelings to be agreeable, uneasy, or neither. Just as the height of the mercury in the column is the standard of temperature, so agreeableness and uneasiness are the standards of virtue and vice.

"Closing averages on the human scene were mixed today. Brotherly love was down two points, while enlightened self-interest gained a half. Vanity showed no movement, and guarded optimism slipped a point in sluggish trading. Over all, the status quo remained unchanged."

Drawing by Dana Fradon; © 1976, The New Yorker Magazine, Inc.

We can understand the movement from *Is* to *Ought,* from fact to standards, this way. The *Is* is the character-trait "liquid" that we "contemplate" and are immersed in, and our mind, like mercury, has a nature; these together cause the feelings, move us to the feelings that are the standards of *Ought.* There is nothing to the *Ought,* to virtue and vice, *except* the feeling, says Hume.

Now, let's consider two perspectives. One—the practical perspective—is that we are moral thermometers. We contemplate Brutus and respond with a feeling of agreeableness or uneasiness; we may put our approbation or disapprobation into words: Brutus is (is not) an honorable man. The other perspective—the theoretical one—is that of moral scientists. Morality is their subject matter. They observe that people say of character traits that these are virtuous, those vicious. They note the presence of agreeable feelings when traits are said to be virtuous, and of uneasiness when they are said to be vicious. The scientists believe they have found invariant correlations between the feelings and the traits, which leads them to conclude that there is a natural, causal relation here. They *report* on the correlation and the causal discovery. They believe that they have discovered a law governing our responses in their "science of Man." Further, they note and report that these feelings are correlated with actions of characteristic kinds. So they conclude that feelings or sentiments cause actions: agreeable feelings cause one set of actions, uneasy feelings another set of actions. Additionally, they observe that moral judgments evoke feelings in others and so cause actions in others.

But is this true? Well, it all depends on the observed facts and the natural theories. Scientists observe mercury thermometers giving similar readings when immersed in the same liquid. This observed correlation is analogous to their observed correlations about humans. Suppose (to move the thermometer analogy closer to humans) that thermometers and engines were made into a "thermoengine" unit. Scientists then observe that engines start up when the mercury expands and stop when the mercury contracts, and this correlation leads them to infer that there is a causal relation between the temperature readings and the engine's actions.

But is it true that, to explain the existence of human standards of morality, we need do nothing different in kind (allowing for greater complexity) than in explaining thermometer readings of temperature? Yes, providing that the features of thermometers used to explain why thermometers are standards of temperature are the same features that Hume uses to explain why humans are standards of morality. And a case can indeed be made that Hume's theory of human nature uses the same features that scientists use to explain why thermometers give us reliable standards of temperature. These features are the five identified in the sketch in 5.2 of simple moral psychology's theory of human nature: uniformity, fixity, comprehensiveness, naturalness, and causal power.

The form of this argument is simple. The presence of these features in thermometers gives us confidence that we can use this or that thermometer's response as a *standard* measure of temperature. If Hume's theory attributes these same features to human nature and the operations of the mind, then we will have learned why he believes he can explain *in wholly natural terms* how the feeling responses of humans are *standard* measures of morality. I say "in wholly natural terms" because no one doubts that behavior and readings of thermometers are wholly natural phenomena; if the features of thermometers that make them standards of temperature are shared by humans, and if these same features account for moral standards, then humans are wholly natural beings just as thermometers are. Let's see briefly why thermometers can be said to have these five features, then note those of Hume's remarks that show he thinks human nature has these same five features.

Uniformity. Every parcel of mercury contracts and expands at the same rate. This provides similar readings and makes any and every mercury thermometer an equally valid standard of temperature.

Fixity. The nature of mercury does not alter; because it doesn't, we can rely on it as a standard measure tomorrow as well as today and yesterday.

Comprehensiveness. Mercury expands and contracts in response to the influence of every external heat source within its causally effective distance.

Naturalness. Mercury is a natural phenomenon, not an artifact. Although humans may extract mercury from cinnabar ore, humans do not give mercury its properties; its *discovered* properties make it useful for temperature measurement.

Causal power. With proper connections to, say, an electrical switch, rising mercury can cause an engine to start and falling mercury can cause it to stop.

The features of uniformity, fixity, and comprehensiveness make mercury a suitable entity for a standard measure of temperature. Its naturalness justifies our saying that the "standard" behavior of mercury can be understood solely by reference to other natural phenomena and to the causal

442 relations between them, so that we have no need for "occult" explanations of this standard behavior. The causal power feature will provide an analogue to the causal power that sentiments have as motives for human action, starting and stopping the body.

If humans possess these same five features, then our understanding of how we can naturalize humans and still account for standards, of how we can go from *Is* to *Ought,* is similar to our understanding of mercury as a standard. The next step is to show that Hume believed these five features apply to humans.

Uniformity. "The minds of all men are similar in their feelings and operations" (*Treatise,* p. 575). The following remarks edge us right up to mercury and its uniform behavior and readings:

> The notion of morals implies some sentiment *common* to *all* mankind, which recommends the *same* object to *general* approbation, and makes *every* man, or *most* men, *agree* in the *same* opinion or decision concerning it. (*Enquiry,* p. 272) [My emphases.]

Again, Hume remarks: "The final sentence, it is probable, which pronounces characters and actions amiable or odious, praise-worthy or blameable, . . . depends on some internal sense or feeling, which nature has made universal in the whole species" (*Enquiry,* pp. 172–73). (Parenthetically, this last quotation states Hume's view that the universal, uniform moral sense is traced to "nature," showing that the standard of moral feeling has the feature of naturalness.)

Fixity. Our feelings or sentiments are the standard of virtue and vice, which we cannot change:

> All morality depends upon our sentiments; . . . But 'tis certain we can naturally no more change our own sentiments, than the motions of the heavens; nor by a single act of our will, that is, by a promise, render any action agreeable or disagreeable. (*Treatise,* p. 517)

This is strong language, leaving us in no doubt about Hume's view that the operation of our sentiments, our human nature, can't be altered. This fixity of our nature and sentiments goes over into a fixity of standards, which isn't surprising since sentiments are the standards:

> The intercourse of sentiments, therefore, in society and conversation, makes us form some general unalterable standard, by which we may approve or disapprove of characters and manners. (*Enquiry,* p. 229)

Comprehensiveness. Our moral sense responds to the causal influence of every person's character traits, and it comprehends all traits:

> But the sentiments, which arise from humanity, are not only the same in all human creatures, and produce the same approbation or censure; but they also comprehend all human creatures; nor is there any one whose conduct

or character is not, by their means, an object to every one of censure or approbation. (*Enquiry,* p. 273)

Comprehensiveness is a feature of sympathy as well:

In general, it is certain, that, wherever we go, whatever we reflect on or converse about, everything still presents us with a view of human happiness or misery, and excites in our breast a sympathetic movement of pleasure or uneasiness. (*Enquiry,* p. 221)

Naturalness. I have pointed out that Hume says "nature has made" our moral sense, which is our standard; he makes the same point when he argues that we couldn't be taught moral distinctions or the meanings of moral words by "education" alone. We don't "invent" moral distinctions; they are "made" by nature.

Had nature made no such distinction, founded on the original constitution of the mind, the words, *honourable* and *shameful, lovely* and *odious, noble* and *despicable,* had never had a place in any language; nor could politicians, had they invented these terms, ever have been able to render them intelligible, or make them convey any idea to the audience. . . . The social virtues must, therefore, be allowed to have a natural beauty.[10]

Hume concludes his *Enquiry* Appendix I with another strong claim for the naturalness and fixity of sentiment as the standard of morals: "The standard of the one [sentiment], being founded on the nature of things, is eternal and inflexible, even by the will of the Supreme Being" (*Enquiry,* p. 294).

Causal power. I illustrated mercury's causal feature by suggesting that its rise and fall could cause an engine to start and stop, if we connected the thermometer to an electric switch. Here we grasp a causal connection between events. Hume has a similar theory about the engine of our body. Our body starts and stops because of the "rise and fall" of our sentiments; our sentiments are the motives, the cause, and the body's motion is the effect:

Thus it appears, not only that the conjunction between motives and voluntary actions is as regular and uniform as that between the cause and effect in any part of nature; but also that this regular conjunction has been universally acknowledged among mankind. (*Enquiry,* p. 88)

Hume says this when he discusses whether our actions are free or caused. He thinks that all our actions are caused. In this he agrees with Kant, who also thinks all *sensible* actions are caused. The next question is: what is the cause?

Hume thought feeling alone is the cause, unlike Kant who thought our rational, supersensible self was the source of the moral feeling that could cause our action, if it was chosen by our *Willkür.* Since Kant thought the supersensible was outside the sensible, natural world, he did not naturalize human moral behavior. For him, negative freedom means that there may be a cause

444 of our actions other than natural inclinations and sentiments. Hume, however, thought reason had no causal influence:

> I shall endeavour to prove *first,* that reason alone can never be a motive to any action of the will; and *secondly,* that it can never oppose passion in the direction of the will. (*Treatise,* p. 413)

Here is the crux of the contrast between Hume's ethics and Kant's ethics. For Kant, reason is the source and motive for morals. Hume denies this because for him feelings or sentiments are the standard and motive:

> Thus the distinct boundaries and offices of *reason* and of *taste* are easily ascertained. The former conveys the knowledge of truth and falsehood: the latter gives the sentiment of beauty and deformity, vice and virtue. . . . Reason being cool and disengaged, is no motive to action, and directs only the impulse received from appetite and inclination, by showing us the [instrumental] means of attaining happiness or avoiding misery: Taste, as it gives pleasure or pain, and thereby constitutes happiness or misery, becomes a motive to action, and is the first spring or impulse to desire and volition. (*Enquiry,* Appendix I, p. 294)

Notice that Hume gives reason only an instrumental role in morals, not a morally determinative one as Kant does. It is at this point in Hume and Kant that "heart" and "mind" get their most explicit and opposing development. Hume opts unequivocally for happiness as the end for morality. For Kant, however, although it is the second component of the *summum bonum,* happiness is not a moral end; he thought the morally good end we are to aim at is a good will, or worthiness.

Let's briefly make sure we grasp how Hume thinks the five features of human nature and sentiments provide a standard for morals. Sentiments are the standards of vice and virtue; they are responses to character traits and as such are "subjective," meaning that vice and virtue are feelings in the subject, not properties in the object. But this subjectivity does not lead to relativity, if everyone's subjective response to the same trait is *uniform*. This uniformity of response assures agreement in our judgments of vice and virtue. When we have universal agreement, anyone and everyone's response is equally a standard; in this respect, we can say that Hume holds that our standards are "intersubjective."

Hume's ethics is intersubjective in another interesting sense because of the mental operation of sympathy: we get uniformly similar responses to others' responses. It is as if we were second-order thermometers, responding not only to heat but also to other thermometers' responses to heat.

Additionally, we can say that Hume thinks moral standards are "objective," although not in the sense that virtue and vice exist independently of human response, which Hume denies to be so. Hume's ethics is objective in the sense that our responses are facts in the world, subject to scientific investigation just like any other facts. And one fact he claims to have discovered is that our responses are uniform.

"Subjective," "intersubjective," and "objective" are words to be used with care. Their meanings are as variable as the surface of the ocean, and the meanings that different writers and speakers intend are not always the same, nor are the various meanings always clearly stated or distinguished. The most common use people make of these three terms is to designate different and opposed theories of moral judgment; this use requires that the meanings of the terms be incompatible. But they can have compatible meanings, too, as they do in Hume's moral theory.

Hume thinks it is also a fact that our responses to character traits are *fixed*. This means that the standards of the ancients are the same as ours, and those of future generations will also be the same.

The *comprehensiveness* of our responses means that no trait, act, or sentiment will elude a response; in short, because nothing escapes our sentiments, our responses are adequate as a standard. The following story of Hume's illustrates the facts of fixity and comprehensiveness. (Historical examples are typical of his "experimental method." If we respond in the same way to traits that temporally remote persons did, this is further evidence for uniformity, fixity, and comprehensiveness.)

> Once upon a time, a statesman, in the shock and contest of parties, prevailed so far as to procure, by his eloquence, the banishment of an able adversary; whom he secretly followed, offering him money for his support during his exile, and soothing him with topics of consolation in his misfortunes. *Alas!* cries the banished statesman, *with what regret must I leave my friends in this city, where even enemies are so generous!* Virtue, though in an enemy, here pleased him: And we also give it the just tribute of praise and approbation; nor do we retract these sentiments, when we hear, that the action passed at Athens, about two thousand years ago, and the persons names were Eschines and Demosthenes. (*Enquiry,* pp. 216–17)

We need say no more, I think, about the *causal power* of these standards, except to remark about the "internalist" position Hume adopts, meaning that the *standards* of morality and the *motives* of morality are one and the same, both being our sentiments. The standards of morality have the motive power to cause our body to start and stop its actions.

Hume's view on the *naturalness* of moral standards gives him the ability to counter a relativity attack. As we will see in the next section, our responses may be tampered with and our nature "distorted," but these distortions can be overcome and we can be restored to our natural state. Naturalness counters the claim that social conditioning and differing social and personal histories account for the different moral standards we hold. If these different conditions and histories were full explanations of why we hold the standard we do, then there would be no way of overcoming the claim that there are no universal standards; cultural and/or personal relativism would prevail. But Hume thinks moral standards are universal; he holds this as strongly as Kant does. They are universal because they are not the product of variant histories.

In this section I have argued that Hume attempts to naturalize moral standards. I have compared human responses as moral standards to a thermometer's mercury responses as temperature standards. No one can reasonably doubt that thermometers are wholly natural entities; if the features of thermometers that make them fit standards of temperature are shared by humans, then humans too are wholly natural entities that deliver moral standards. I have cited claims of Hume's showing his belief that thermometers and humans share the requisite five features.

12.6 Removing the Variance and Saving the Standards

Hume's course seems to run smoothly, but by this time you have probably anticipated trouble, particularly if you have reread or recall 5.4, the challenge to simple moral psychology. You have probably wondered whether Hume is factually correct about the uniformity of our moral sense, because you have often noticed disagreements in judgments about humans and their traits. If there is this variance, how can Hume say our sentiment responses are uniform and that each is a standard of judgment?

Further, can our standard of sentiment be as fixed, as inalterable, as Hume claims? After all, advances in psychology since Hume wrote have made it possible to manipulate people's responses. We can pre-condition and re-condition them. George Orwell's novel *1984* is not pure fantasy; Big Brother has a basis in scientific fact if we hearken to B. F. Skinner's *Walden II,* a tract arguing that behaviorist psychology can be used to create Utopian behavior. Positive and negative reinforcement can be used to alter human behavior just as well as to teach pigeons to play Ping-Pong. And who can discount Valium and the alteration of consciousness by other drugs, including marijuana, cocaine, amphetamines, LSD, and peyote? These challenges must be answered. If they aren't, Hume's program for naturalizing an ethics with "valid" standards fails. Remember how Kant warned against the variability, contingency, and shiftiness of feelings and inclinations? Unless they are correctible, they can't be a base for universal moral laws.

Being a first-class philosopher, Hume anticipated these difficulties and dealt with them. Although he didn't anticipate all these new drugs, Hume was aware of the frenzy into which persons are plunged by high fevers and pressing circumstances, not to mention insanity. Also, in his time alcohol was in great use, and we all know how it alters behavior; nor was Hume a teetotaler.

Hume's answer to these objections was to identify the conditions—"some *steady* and *general* points of view"—in which the spectator of human traits was to place himself or herself in order to get a standard response. This has been called an "ideal observer" theory of moral judgments. Whatever the causes—madness, drugs, drunkenness, self-interest, or a malconditioned upbringing—deviations from the ideal-observer standard can be accounted for. The solution is first to identify the causes, then either remove them or compensate for them. In this way the standard is saved from the ravages of whatever causes deviation. We could say that we "correct" deviations; Hume in fact uses this term (*Treatise,* p. 582).

Suppose Kant says that Brutus is vicious, but Hume says he is virtuous. Hume asks Kant why Kant thinks his own judgment is justified. Kant defends his judgment by saying Brutus is vicious because he made deceitful promises to Caesar and killed him; a deceitful and murderous character is vicious. "Why?" asks Hume. "Because," answers Kant, "Brutus chose to commit acts that are forbidden. The Categorical Imperative shows this to be so."

What would Hume reply to defend his judgment that Brutus is virtuous? "Why, Kant," he would say, "I contemplate the trait in Brutus that shows he loves his country above Caesar, who is harmful to it. This is a trait of patriotism, and upon this contemplation I respond with an agreeable feeling." "But," Kant asks, "do you have some standard to justify basing your judgment on your feeling?" "No," answers Hume, "the feeling *is* the standard. To go beyond this is to give reason credit for our judgments. 'Reason is, and ought only to be the slave of the passions'" (*Treatise,* p. 415). "How," asks Kant, "do you know this is the standard?" "Because," says Hume, "it is an observed fact that our responses are caused and our judgments are pronounced in accord with them. The move from the *is* of Brutus's traits to my judging him 'virtuous' is a movement of my sentiments. That's all there is to it."

But, you yourself now reply (getting into the argument with Hume), *I* have an *uneasy* sentiment upon the contemplation of Brutus; this too is caused by contemplating him and his deceitful traits, and there is no more arguing with my sentiment than with yours. So which is the "correct" sentiment?

Hume's move here has to be that the difference in responses is due to different causal conditions; the difference in conditions can be removed or compensated for, and agreement then restored. But, you ask, which causal conditions are to be removed or compensated for? How can we make a decision about this, if we don't know which causal conditions are "incorrect"? And how can we decide which are incorrect without standards? The "ideal" observer, alledgedly possessing standard sentiments, can't be identified without using a standard to assess the "correctness" of that observer's causes.

To help understand how Hume deals with this challenge, let's utilize our thermometer analogue. Two thermometers give a different reading. Which is the "correct" one? Clearly, there have to be different causal conditions that account for the different readings. Which are we to remove or compensate for? Scientists are well acquainted with variation in instrument readings; there is a field of study, called "error theory," to deal with this problem.

An obvious way out of this dilemma is to deal with thermometers the way we do with measuring rods. We simply pick a length and *make* it the

448 standard. This doesn't require assuming another standard because this *is* the standard—we've made it so. This is the "ultimate" step. But its abrupt appearance here may lead you to reject it because it seems so baldly arbitrary.

Such a selection of a standard will seem less arbitrary if we reflect on the fact that there is more than one way to measure distance—rods and timed light pulses, for instance. Similarly, thermocouples and mercury thermometers are two ways to measure heat. A thermocouple consists of two different metals fastened firmly together to make a band. Because the metals expand and contract at different rates, the two-metal band will bend; by fastening a pointer to one end of the band, you can get a reading on an attached scale.

Is there any reason, then, for selecting one *kind* of thermometer rather than the other as our standard thermometer, which doesn't involve us in any claims about which is the "correct" one? Yes: if thermocouples gave more uniform and more discriminatory readings, say in hundredths of degrees rather than tenths, we would select them—all the more so if the range of heat that thermocouples measure were greater than that of mercury thermometers. Thus, picking a standard need not be arbitrary, but the non-arbitrariness does not involve "correctness"; it involves the concept of a standard and its purposes, and the usefulness of an object for those purposes.

Suppose, then, that we have picked a standard kind of thermometer, and now we put two such thermometers in contact with a liquid. Lo, they give different readings. Which is the correct one? Now is the time to take again the ultimate step: *this* one. Still, we are interested in the causes of the different readings. We are interested because we can't carry this particular thermometer everywhere in the world to measure every instance of heat. We need more thermometers and want them to be accurate. We want to know what causes inaccuracy, so we can remove it or compensate for it.

Because of the nature of the case, there are two sources to which we can attribute the deviation from the standard's norm. A thermometer is one object; the liquid in which it is immersed is another; and the two are linked causally:

$$\text{Liquid} \quad \overbrace{\text{Causal Connection}} \quad \text{Thermometer} \rightarrow \text{Reading}$$

The deviation in readings can be caused by variation in the liquid, in the thermometers, or in both. Consider the liquid first: one thermometer rests in one place in the liquid, the second in another; the liquid in the two places may have different heats, causing different readings.

Different readings can also be caused by variations in the thermometers. Perhaps the mercury in one is "corrupted" by foreign materials that respond differently to heat than mercury. Perhaps the glass barrels don't have the same interior diameter or are placed differently on the scale, and so forth.

There are four possibilities:

┌── Causal Connection ──┐

1. Identical liquid heats   Similar thermometers   → Same readings
2. Non-identical liquid   Similar thermometers   → Different readings
   heats
3. Identical liquid heats   Dissimilar thermometers   → Different readings
4. Non-identical liquid   Dissimilar thermometers   → Same readings or
   heats   different readings

In the fourth case there are two possible outcomes: we could accidentally have the same readings because the variations in both the heat and the thermometers might cancel each other out.

Let's consider how we can deal with the variant reading possibilities by removing the causes or compensating for them. If we know, for example, that one thermometer's reading is consistently one degree higher than the standard one in identical liquid areas, we can *compensate* for this. We can "correct" the reading that is off simply by subtracting one degree. Or we can "correct" the thermometer by *removing* the cause for the deviation—say, by removing the impurities from the mercury, or by moving the scale markings downward by one degree, whichever is the cause.

We have now seen that we can interpret "corrected" as either "compensated for" or "removed." We have not gone outside the natural system of cause and effect. All it took was the selection of one thermometer as standard. The selection didn't appeal to some other source of standards such as a Temperature God, a Wise Man, a True Thermometer, or Reason. Everything was a natural occurrence.

To make them more analogous to humans, I complicated thermometers by connecting them to engines they can activate, giving us what we can call "thermoengines." We can further complicate them and make them still more analogous to humans by supposing they can communicate with one another, reflect on themselves and their states, and compensate for and/or remove the causes of their difference. We now have "Linguathermoengines." In short, they can take a theoretical stance toward themselves. Here is a brief conversation between two linguathermoengines, Hot and Cold.

> Hot: This liquid causes my mercury to expand and I notice that I read 98.6 degrees.
> Cold: This liquid causes my mercury to expand, too, and I notice that I read 98 degrees. It appears that we differ.
> Hot: Perhaps it's because we aren't immersed in the same liquid.
> Cold: Yes, come over here beside me. Snuggle up close so we're immersed in identical liquid heat. (*Hot and Cold snuggle.*)
> Hot: I read 98.6 degrees. And you still read 98 degrees.
> Cold: Then the difference in degrees must be due to a difference between us. Let's run a test on our mercury. Okay?
> Hot: Okay. (*They do; their mercury is equally pure.*)

450

Cold: Maybe the interior dimensions of our barrels are different. Let's check that. *(They do; they are different.)*

Hot: So it turns out that your dimensions are different from the standard thermometer's and that mine are the same. Then my reading is correct and yours is wrong. We can either compensate for that or you can have an operation, a dimensionobotomy to have your dimensions changed.

Cold: Operation? I don't want an operation!

Hot: Okay, cool it. We'll compensate for you—take your deviations into account. "Cold is a little off," we'll say, "just a bit eccentric."

Cold: Who's to say which of us thermometers is the standard? Who says I'm "eccentric"? *I'm* the standard! I've read Nietzsche and *One Flew over the Cuckoo's Nest.* I know I don't have to be part of the "herd."

Hot: Look, Cold, the important thing is agreement. You're too self-involved, too ego-oriented. When it comes to responses to heat in the world, we all have a stake in it; by standardizing and correlating our responses, we can build a common base for judgments and decisions. We build for peace and cooperation.

By this time, you will probably have discerned the analogue between variant thermometer readings and variant human moral "readings." Human moral readings are our feeling responses to character traits and their usefulness. Here also we have a two-entity structure: the character trait (liquid) is connected causally to the response sentiment (contraction or expansion) and prompts a judgment of "virtuous" or "vicious" (temperature reading). And just like variations in temperature readings, so variations in moral readings can be attributed either to the non-identity of the trait contemplated or to a dissimilarity in the persons, or to both. To overcome moral disagreement, we either have to compensate for or remove the variant causal factors responsible for the variant readings. The structural similarity of the moral and thermometer situations generates the same four possibilities:

┌─── Causal Connection ───┐

1. Identical traits   Similar persons → Same sentiments (judgments)

2. Non-identical traits Similar persons → Different sentiments (judgments)

3. Identical traits   Dissimilar persons → Different sentiments (judgments)

4. Non-identical traits Dissimilar persons → Same sentiments (judgments) or Different sentiments (judgments)

The case Hume wants is the first one, for it yields universal agreement in judgments. Hume thinks we can get it (1) if we make sure two or more persons are contemplating the identically same character trait, and/or (2) if we compensate for or remove the factors in us that cause us to be dissimilar. Let's see how Hume advises us on (1) and (2), taking (1) first.

451

12.6a ESTABLISHING IDENTITY OF THE OBJECT CONTEMPLATED.

Humans have reason; this makes us potential theoretical creatures. We can think about and correct our grasp of the facts. Hume's theory of morals is that our judgments of virtue and vice are the caused responses of sentiment. He tells us what the conditions for getting non-accidental agreement in judgments are. We can use his theory to correct any conditions that cause varying judgments; his theory has a practical use.

One condition we can correct is a diversity of objects contemplated. This correction isn't always easy, of course. Since the "social liquid" is a more complicated element than water, establishing identity of the object contemplated—that is, of the character trait contemplated—is a more complicated matter. Hume thinks that, to get the same sentiment, we have to "pave the way" for it by establishing identity of objects:

> But in order to pave the way for such a sentiment, and give a proper discernment of its object, it is often necessary, we find, that much reasoning should precede, that nice distinctions be made, just conclusions drawn, distant comparisons formed, complicated relations examined, and general facts fixed and ascertained. (*Enquiry,* p. 173)

Take as our example the story Hume told about Demosthenes. You might proclaim Demosthenes vicious; I might call him virtuous. If you do so because you are thinking of his role in having Eschines banished from Athens, and if I do so because I am thinking of his secretly helping Eschines after Eschines' banishment, then we are not contemplating the same object. This diversity in objects explains why different sentiments are aroused in us and why we have different judgments. Being mindful of our theoretical nature and using it to trace the causes for the difference in our responses, we will converse and try to establish an identity of object. For this, we both need to be aware of the same facts, form similar comparisons, examine the same relations, and so forth:

> All the circumstances of the case are supposed to be laid before us, ere we can fix any sentence of blame or approbation. . . . But after every circumstance, every relation is known, the understanding has no further room to operate nor any object on which it could employ itself. The ap-

probation or blame which then ensues, cannot be the work of the judgment, but of the heart; and is not a speculative proposition or affirmation,
but an active feeling or sentiment. (*Enquiry,* p. 290)

12.6b COMPENSATING FOR OR REMOVING DISSIMILARITY OF HEARTS.

Now let's consider the second factor that contributes to a difference in moral "readings": a dissimilarity in persons. Hume allows that
there may be a "corrupted heart." Such a person will say that all
"*benevolence* is mere hypocrisy, friendship a cheat, public spirit a farce,
fidelity a snare to procure trust and confidence" (*Enquiry,* p. 295).

This corrupted response can be removed as a basis for moral standards
by using the distinction between self-love and benevolence. The proper or
moral "point of view" to take is that in which our self-interest is not involved:

> Nor is every sentiment of pleasure or pain, which arises from characters
> and actions, of that *peculiar* kind, which makes us praise or condemn.
> The good qualities of an enemy are hurtful to us; but may still command
> our esteem and respect. 'Tis only when a character is considered in
> general, without reference to our particular interest, that it causes such a
> feeling or sentiment, as denominates it morally good or evil. . . . But this
> hinders not, but that the sentiments are, in themselves, distinct; and a man
> of temper and judgment may preserve himself from these illusions.
> (*Treatise,* p. 472)

Suppose that a charming, witty, clever, upright district attorney
manages to get us convicted of some crime. Of course we know he is opposed
to our desire to be declared innocent. Yet as theoretical beings, using Hume's
theory, we separate our self-interested response from our response to the
district attorney's charm, wit, and uprightness, and find that we esteem and
respect his qualities. We "correct" our response by "removing" the influence of self-interest. The "moral point of view" is disinterested and cool.

Here we arrive at a crucial juncture in Hume's argument. We arrive at
the same point that Cold did when he said to Hot, "Who's to say which of
us thermometers is the standard? Who says I'm 'eccentric'? *I'm* the
standard!" Indeed, who's to say that the moral point of view excludes my
self-interested response? Certainly an egoist would not.

Hume answers this challenge by pointing not to some person "who's to
say," but rather to the concept or notion of morals:

> Avarice, ambition, vanity, and all passions vulgarly, though improperly,
> comprised under the denomination of *self-love,* are here excluded from our
> theory concerning the origin of morals, not because they are too weak, but
> because they have not a proper direction for that purpose. The notion of
> morals implies some sentiment common to all mankind which recommends
> the same object to general approbation, and makes every man, or most
> men, agree in the same opinion or decision concerning it. (*Enquiry,* pp.
> 271–72)

Hume completes his argument that a "disinterested, cool" point of view **453** is the "proper" moral one by pointing out that self-love sentiments can never give us the requisite universality. Only "humanity" has the requisite uniformity for morals.

> One man's ambition is not another's ambition, nor will the same event or object satisfy both; but the humanity of one man is the humanity of every one, and the same object touches this passion in all human creatures.
> . . . On the contrary, those other passions, commonly denominated selfish, both produce different sentiments in each individual, according to his particular station; and also contemplate the greater part of mankind with the utmost indifference and unconcern.[11]

Using the distinction between the sentiments of self-love and humanity, Hume has told us what to use for a moral standard—the sentiment of humanity—and how to use it to reach agreement in moral judgments. This is "removal" advice: *in judging character traits, remove the self-love sentiments.* One way of doing so, in case you and another disagree about a mutual acquaintance's virtue, is to contemplate a like case far removed temporally or spatially, so that neither of your self-interests is engaged.

As Humean theoretical creatures, we can also learn to compensate for and so correct the variability that Hume concedes to exist even in our common sentiment of humanity, so central in his system. Distance from an object contemplated can affect our responses, but we learn to compensate for and correct the effects of different distances; we learn how to remain in the proper point of view:

> In general, all sentiments of blame or praise are variable, according to our situation of nearness or remoteness, with regard to the person blam'd or prais'd, and according to the present disposition of our mind. But these variations we regard not in our general decisions, but still apply the terms expressive of our liking or dislike, in the same manner, as if we remain'd in one point of view. Experience soon teaches us this method of correcting our sentiments, or at least, of correcting our language, where the sentiments are more stubborn or inalterable. Our servant, if diligent and faithful, may excite stronger sentiments of love and kindness than *Marcus Brutus* [who helped kill Caesar] as represented in history; but we say not upon that account, that the former character is more laudable than the latter. We know, that were we to approach equally near to that renow'd patriot [Brutus], he wou'd command a much higher degree of affection and admiration [than Hume's servant]. Such corrections are common with regard to all the senses; and indeed 'twere impossible we cou'd ever make use of language, or communicate our sentiments to one another, did we not correct the momentary appearances of things, and overlook our present situation. (*Treatise,* p. 582)

Both Brutus and Hume's servant have agreeable qualities, but the nearness of his servant produces stronger agreeable sentiments in him. Yet even though

454   Brutus causes weaker sentiments, Brutus is a greater man.   Hume thinks we can correct this imbalance by compensating; we can compensate because we know or can learn what degree of remoteness will produce what degree of sentiment, just as we can compensate for the distance of a thermometer from a heat source by correlating the decrease in its readings with the distance from that heat source.   Similarly, the moon looks smaller than my hand, but I can correct this impression.   (See the *Treatise,* p. 584.)

With this I conclude Hume's defense of his claim that there are universal standards in morals (and art) despite the variance in responses and judgments.   This variance is due either to non-identity in what is contemplated or to dissimilarity in the observers; ways can be discovered to either compensate for or remove its causes.   The validity of these ways can be ascertained, Hume thinks, by wholly natural considerations.   We can use these considerations as correctives because we are reflexive, self-correcting beings; Hume's theory is practical because we can use it to alter and correct our practical moral pronouncements.

12.7 Hume's Links Schema

Hume's links schema is one possible schema within the general links schema of moral psychology.   The diagram that follows is an expansion of moral psychology's links diagram, p. 139, and of the "Sensible Self" part of Kant's schema in 10.7, p. 354.

Moral psychology's links diagram was:

	Natural Link		Endowment Link		Selector Link		Purposive Link
Human Nature	→	Wants	→	Goods	→	Ends	→	Acts

Hume's expansion of this simple links diagram comes mainly in the endowment link where we have self-love and benevolent sentiments, which are non-moral and moral sentiments respectively; this distinction introduces pairs of endowment, selector, and purposive links; hence, the pairs of arrows:

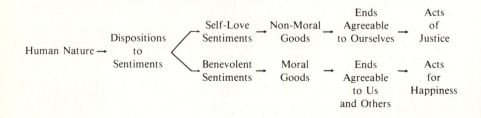

Further, to reflect his standards for goods, we have to add, in the fuller **455** diagram that follows, traits "useful or agreeable to ourselves and others," which expands on the selector link. Also, to the fuller diagram, I have added the "instrumental" and "correcting" role of reason to bring out the contrast between Hume and Kant's theories about reason's function in morals. See figure on p. 456.

First, moving from left to right, we have the natural, psychological sentiments that endow the good with which we select our ends; these ends produce the motive energy to cause the act that we find obligatory because it has utility. The motive power of our sentiments drives through to the acts.

Moving from right to left, we would never get the "obligatory" acts without the ends selected; nor the ends selected without the good endowed by our sentiments, which are the motives of our given human nature. Hence, motives have priority and are "internal" to our moral judgments. So the ultimate reason why we should be moral rests finally on our sentiments [wants]; we have these sentiments because we are the kind of beings we are, and this nature of ours, according to sociobiologists, results from natural selection in the evolutionary process.

Here now is a verbal summary of Hume's theory of morals.

Generosity is a virtue.

Why?

Because I and everyone else respond with an agreeable feeling to generosity (subjective), or because I respond by sympathy to others' responses to generosity (intersubjective).

What has an agreeable response to do with virtue?

Virtue has some source or other. There are two possibilities: (1) reason or (2) feeling. Reason has two functions: (a) to learn the relations between ideas as in mathematics and (b) to learn the relations between matters of fact as in natural science.

Reason, (1) (a), can't be the source. Consider a geometrician determining all the relations between the points, lines, planes, and angles of the Parthenon: nothing of this leads us to say the Parthenon is beautiful; we say so only because of our feeling response to it. (See *Enquiry,* p. 288ff.)

Reason, (1) (b), can't be the source either. Once we've determined all the facts, there is nothing left for reason to do; Demosthenes is judged virtuous or vicious only after our feeling has responded to all the facts about him. (See the *Enquiry* quotation on p. 451.)

Therefore, since we have eliminated reason as the source of virtue and vice, feeling must be the source.

How do you establish this by positive evidence, rather than by the process of elimination just used?

By observing a matter of fact. It is a matter of fact that an agreeable feeling is correlated with the observation of generosity. (*Enquiry,* p. 289) (Objective, contingent.)

The validity of these feeling standards is assured by a matter-of-fact truth about this observed correlation. The truth about moral standards rests

HUME'S LINKS SCHEMA

Natural Link	Endowment Link	Selector Link	Purposive Link

Human Nature → [Wants] Dispositions to Sentiments

Self-Love Sentiments ──┐
Benevolent Sentiments (Humanity) ──┘

Non-Moral Goods: Good for Self = Traits (i) Useful or (ii) Agreeable to Ourselves → Ends Agreeable to Ourselves → Acts of Justice (Artificial, Conventional)

Sympathy Makes Justice a Moral Value

Artificial Motives   Natural

Moral Goods: Good for Others and Ourselves = Traits (iii) Useful or (iv) Agreeable to Ourselves and* to Others → Ends Agreeable to Ourselves and* to Others → Acts Producing Happiness and Avoiding Misery

Instrumental Reason Determines Utility of Acts

Instrumental Reason

(a) ... (b)

Reason "corrects"
(a) by identifying traits and
(b) by removing dissimilarity in observers
to make sentiments universal (and standard)

* See the discussion of sympathy on pp. 436-37.

on the same factual foundation as any scientific statement, which explains why **457** we believe such standards exist, and explains Hume's way of justifying them. This is what is meant by a "science of Man." Any variations in correlations can be corrected, either by removing or by compensating for the causes of the variant feeling responses.

STUDY QUESTIONS

1 Why did the scientific temper represent a humanistic liberation? How does this make Hume's view that humans too may be fully comprehended by a scientific method attractive? Work with an example such as the difference between a Freudian and a Judeo-Christian view of the relations between parents and children.

2 What does Hume have to do to completely "naturalize" the human mind? Why is this important for his science of Man and for moral psychology?

3 What phenomenon does the explanation of human events have to deal with that the explanation of physical events does not? Relate this phenomenon to the differences between description and prescription and to norms and standards.

4 How does Hume's science of Man explain the existence of norms or standards, which is different from the validity of norms? How does he propose that the *Ought* in standards be legitimately traced to the *Is* of facts? And why does he use facts about objects and feelings as the factual basis for standards? Why must they be facts both for ourselves and for others, in order to be a factual basis for *moral* standards?

5 Why does Hume think that the ultimate object of moral approval and disapproval is a person rather than a person's acts?

6 Why isn't Hume contradicting himself when he says that justice is both artificial and natural? Your answer should connect the artificial with the conventional. Justice would not be a virtue, according to Hume, unless two "natural" conditions obtained, one of which is a condition of human nature and the other a condition of our environment. What are these two conditions, and why do they permit Hume to say justice is a natural virtue?

7 Why does Hume think that the idea of property and obligation depend on the idea of justice?

8 What are the four factors that Hume thinks distinguish moral from nonmoral responses of sentiment?

9 Explain how the analogy between humans and thermometers helps us to understand why Hume thinks he can show that there are factually based, valid moral judgments. Include a discussion of the five features shared by humans and thermometers that are relevant to standards of heat and morals.

10 How does Hume think it possible to defend the belief that there are valid, universal moral standards, even though different persons' responses to character traits and actions vary? In other words, how does he think he can meet a relativist's challenge?

11 Describe Hume's "operation of sympathy," and state why it is important to his ethical theory.

 **Reflections on Applications**

1 The following news story will provide you with some moral data. Your response to it is the kind of data that is central to Hume's ethics, and he has explained why this is so. Part of your assessment of Hume's philosophy will depend on your acceptance or rejection of this explanation.

> For most Americans the "energy crisis" is just an annoyance. But Clara Bowers of Lancaster, Pa., felt its full force on a recent cold Sunday.
>
> That day, the 62-year-old, partially blind widow ran out of kerosene for her space heater. Money to buy more had run out earlier. Mrs. Bowers needed about $60 a month for fuel and, what with the cost of rent, food and other necessities, she couldn't scrape it up from her $267 in monthly disability and pension payments. She was forced to leave her home of 42 years and live with her daughter.
>
> Thanks to an emergency fuel shipment arranged through Lancaster County's Office of Aging, Mrs. Bowers is back in her home. But she is worried about the future. "I don't want to leave my home, but it's hard to keep going," she says. "I'm only human and I have to stay warm."
>
> For millions of low-income Americans, it is a struggle just to heat and light their homes. . . .
>
> The reason for this is simple arithmetic. Energy costs are rising faster than poor people's ability to pay for them. There are roughly 25 million Americans who live below the federal poverty level—$3,140 a year for a single person living in a city ($64 less than Mrs. Bower's annual income). Among these people it now is common in many parts of the country during the winter to spend 20% to 30% of monthly income on heating and utility bills.
>
> In thousands of cases, that figure approaches 50%. A study by a federally funded antipoverty agency in Milwaukee last winter found that 800 particularly hard-hit households were paying an average of 45% of their monthly income on heat and utilities. When rent or mortgage

payments were counted, these people paid an average of 93% of their income on shelter costs. In one case, the study said, a couple living on $348 a month had $10 left for food and other essentials. . . .

But the poor never had much of a cushion, and now whatever cushion there was is, in many cases, completely gone. Some poor people are forced to take drastic measures.

Take 59-year-old Rudolph Alexander of Elmira, N.Y., a widower who lives with his ailing mother. With gas and electric bills taking about half his $206-a-month income, Mr. Alexander has cut back to one meal a day to make sure his mother has food. He also never burns more than one light at a time. . . .

More people have started tampering with their electric and gas meters to avoid being charged. Consumer groups tell of women stealing food and clothing for their children because they can't afford to buy them after paying for heat and light. One elderly woman reportedly tried stealing $200 from a bank to pay for her utilities. . . .

. . . Many older people are susceptible to "accidental hypothermia," a rapid drop in body temperature that can be fatal. While firm statistics don't exist, there are estimates that thousands die each year from this condition.[12]

What are your responses to this story? How many responses do you have and to what parts of the story? As we have seen, Hume classifies the data pertinent to virtue into four classes: traits agreeable (1) to ourselves and (2) to others, or useful (3) to ourselves and (4) to others. Vice would be disagreeable or disserviceable to ourselves and others—it would be characterized by disutility or negative usefulness (not uselessness). Put your responses under Hume's classifications. They are your "readings" as a moral thermometer.

2 Hume says that the ultimate subjects of moral judgment are persons; their traits are either virtuous or vicious. Upon reading the *Wall Street Journal* story, did you make a judgment about the traits of the persons responsible for the plight of the poor who cannot pay their rising utility bills? Did you think the persons responsible were or were not virtuous? Don't read on until you've answered this question.

Now relate your feeling responses to your moral judgment of the persons responsible. Here's an example. Suppose Jones responded to the poor people's plight with a feeling of unease and displeasure—a feeling that is disagreeable; and suppose further that Jones judged that the persons responsible for the increased costs were not vicious. According to Hume's theory, Jones has made the wrong judgment: if the persons responsible for the plight of the poor have traits that are harmful or disserviceable to others—in this case, to the poor—then those persons are vicious, not virtuous. Certainly the poor have unpleasant experiences. If, by the operation of sympathy, Jones turned his *idea* of their experiences into a *feeling* of disagreeableness that he felt, then, by Hume's theory of virtue and vice, Jones should have declared the persons responsible to be vicious. Any trait that is disagreeable upon contemplation, or that is disserviceable to ourselves and others, is vicious.

With this in mind, go over the moral data of your responses and your moral judgment, and determine if you are in accord with Hume's theory of virtue and vice.

3 Let's suppose that Jones thought the persons responsible for the price hikes to be the managers of a utility company, and suppose further that Jones owned stock in it. This could have influenced his judgment of the managers—perhaps even caused it to deviate from Hume's moral standard and so require correction. If Jones took his cue from 12.6b, how would he go about correcting his deviation? Or do you think Hume's theory of virtue and vice, rather than Jones's judgment is wrong? Or is the situation more complex than I make it out to be?

4 Hume thinks that we must prepare ourselves for a moral "reading." We must be certain we know all the facts and have got their relations straight; we have to make sure that we've identified the object of our response correctly. In complex situations like those involving petroleum prices, this may not be easy. You might say that the utility managers aren't vicious; they didn't raise prices deliberately to hurt and disadvantage the poor. They did so because their job is to make money for the company they work for, because stockholders depend on them to make a return on their investment. Perhaps even some of the poor hold a few shares in the utility company. So the managers are primarily responsible to people who have entrusted them with their savings and capital.

Further, the utility managers made money for their stockholders when petroleum was cheaper. They had to raise prices not to make a bigger profit, but because the oil companies from whom they purchased the petroleum raised their prices. So far, the utility managers' traits are virtuous: they are fulfilling their duties to the stockholders, and they had the higher prices forced on them.

Who, then, is the person responsible whose traits we are to judge? Not the utility managers, but the oil company executives? But the executives will say in turn that the oil producers forced them to raise their prices by selling crude oil at a higher price. They may tell us that if we want to find who is responsible, we should look at Saudi Arabia, Kuwait, Iraq, and other oil-producing countries who started the whole series of price increases. They may say that these countries' oil prices are determined by their heads of government, who then become the people whose traits we are to judge as virtuous or vicious.

So are the oil-producing countries' government officials virtuous or vicious? They are doing something that makes the poor in our country live a difficult and miserable life, which is disserviceable to others and so, according to Hume's theory, indicates vicious traits. Consequently, the government heads of oil-producing states are vicious.

But hold on, cry these men, you've made the matter much too simple. Proportionally, we have many more poor people in our country than you do in the United States, and our poor are much poorer than yours. Oil is a natural resource that will eventually be depleted; we have to make our country economically sufficient independent of our oil supply. Besides, you have exploited us for many years and have become rich while we stayed the same or got poorer; everything we bought from you has been expensive. Our first responsibility is to our own citizens and subjects. In general, you can afford higher fuel costs better than we can afford lower ones. Hence, we are to be judged virtuous rather than vicious. Ultimately, the responsibility for higher prices should rest on you, not on us. If you want to keep our poor poor, then *you* are the vicious ones. You want too good a life!

So we have come full circle: the responsibility is ours. Everyone shifts the responsibility to someone else, but it doesn't come to rest on anyone finally; it just keeps circulating.

How then can we determine who is responsible, so we can find the persons to be judged virtuous or vicious? Perhaps it's not any particular person or persons. Perhaps what is to be judged is the "system" that requires profit making, and the division of the world's people into self-seeking nations. Or is there some individual or some class of persons (the bourgeoisie?) who are responsible for maintaining a profit-making system?

Hume tells us to determine the facts and the relations and then let sentiment respond. But how can we satisfy his requirement? Is it possible or not? How will you connect your concern for the plight of the poor and elderly to the character traits of certain persons, if you can't find who are the responsible persons?

5 Hume knew a great deal of the seventeenth-century French mathematician and philosopher, Blaise Pascal and his opinions. He uses Pascal's traits in the conclusion of "A Dialogue" and compares them to the ancient philosopher Diogenes (who carried a lamp about, looking for but never finding an honest man). In "A Dialogue" Hume sets forth the arguments his opponents might make against him; being a great philosopher, he usually states the opponents' arguments better than they could themselves. Remember that Hume thinks universal standards of morals are possible, because it is a fact that humans share a human nature and respond similarly. Hume has Palamedes, the spokesman for his opponents, compare Diogenes and Pascal, pointing out that they are almost wholly dissimilar. If they are so dissimilar, how can their judgments provide a standard, and why should both be admired by their contemporaries? The conclusion toward which Palamedes pushes is that there must be no fixed standards by which to judge others. Palamedes states the differences between Diogenes and Pascal as follows:

> Let us compare him [Diogenes] to Pascal, a man of parts and genius as well as Diogenes himself; and perhaps too, a man of virtue, had he allowed his virtuous inclinations to have exerted and displayed themselves.

462

> The foundation of Diogenes's conduct was an endeavour to
> render himself an independent being as much as possible, and to confine
> all his wants and desires and pleasures within himself and his own mind:
> The aim of Pascal was to keep a perpetual sense of his dependence
> before his eyes, and never to forget his numberless wants and infir-
> mities. The ancient [Diogenes] supported himself by magnanimity,
> ostentation, pride, and the idea of his own superiority above his fellow-
> creatures. The modern [Pascal] made constant profession of humility
> and abasement, of the contempt and hatred of himself. . . .
> The great object of Diogenes's wit was every kind of superstition, that is
> every kind of religion known in his time. The mortality of the soul was
> his standard principle; and even his sentiments of a divine providence
> seem to have been licentious. The most ridiculous superstitions directed
> Pascal's faith and practice; and an extreme contempt of this life, in
> comparison of the future [in heaven], was the chief foundation of his
> conduct. (*Enquiry*, pp. 342–43)

This is a strongly worded objection that Hume makes to his own
theory. He concludes "A Dialogue" with a reply, part of which is
quoted below. Do you think Hume adequately answers himself?

> An experiment, said I, which succeeds in the air, will not always succeed
> in a vacuum. When men depart from the maxims of common reason,
> and affect these *artificial* lives, as you call them, no one can answer for
> what will please or displease them. They [Diogenes and Pascal] are in a
> different element from the rest of mankind; and the natural principles
> of their mind play not with the same regularity, as if left to themselves,
> free from the illusions of religious superstition or philosophical en-
> thusiasm. (*Enquiry*, p. 343)

In terms of the thermometer analogy, Hume seems to be saying that
"religious superstition or philosophical enthusiasm" are causes of deviation from the standard in humans. Because these gripped Pascal and
Diogenes, respectively, these men are a bit weird; they are exceptions
that don't disprove his theory. Thus, superstition and enthusiasm must
be "corrected." Do you agree that excesses of religion and philosophy
distort our nature and make us "artificial"?

6 To test your understanding of the analogy between thermometers and
humans, try to replace the thermometer terms with human terms in the
dialogue between the Hot and Cold on pp. 449–50.

7 Hume was a man of the world and saw a great variety of persons in a
great variety of circumstances—probably a greater variety of both than
you or I. He held high political posts, traveled extensively, and was acquainted with many persons of influence and power. He was
knowledgeable about the political wheeling and dealing of ambitious
men and women, the clash of parties, and the prejudice of people in
power. In a letter to an acquaintance he says, "Some hate me because

I am not a Tory, some because I am not a Whig, some because I am not a Christian, and all because I am a Scotsman.'' To appreciate these remarks, you should realize that his age was more passionately partisan than our own. A Tory and a Whig were as far apart psychically as a conservative Republican and a radical Marxist today. Not to be a Christian then was like a bishop's denouncing the Pope. And to be a Scotsman desiring to gain fame in England was like an alcoholic running for president of the Temperance Union.

Despite all this, Hume's basic ethical orientation was optimistic; he thought that almost everyone could take an impartial look at others and their acts, that the operation of sympathy could function effectively, and that our benevolent nature would move everyone often enough to make life comfortable for us all. But take a look at the following remarks of a young private eye, Sandra Sutherland, who specializes in disguises and ruses. As the journalist Carol Pogash says of her, she "possesses the best qualities of a chameleon and her own special sense of ethics":

> "The world is not composed of truthful people. They are devious," says Sutherland, as thin and taut as a piano wire. "You just have to be able to transcend that."
>
> "Justice or truth or someone else's life is way down (on some people's) list of priorities," she says. "So I think, well, too bad. Although I still feel bad about (deceiving them) afterwards. That's the least I can do." . . .
>
> It's "a sewer-eye view," Sutherland admits, but, like other private investigators, she wouldn't pass it up.[13]

Sutherland is much less optimistic about other people's moral priorities than Hume. Do you think that her special position as a private detective gives her a better vantage point for assessing human nature than Hume had, even though he was a man of the world? Or does her position make her an unreliable judge because she is embroiled only in troublesome situations? Does she need to remove or compensate for the causes that lead her to deviate from a "normal" judgment of human nature?

8 Hume's ethics gives a central place to the operation of sympathy which binds us together. Of course obstacles may at times prevent sympathy from functioning; the facts or a person's "corrupted heart" may need correction, so as to clear the way for it. How would you go about helping the mother in the following news story to clear away the obstacles that prevent her sympathy from operating?

> The mother of a kidnapped woman [in Milan, Italy] said yesterday that she does not love her daughter very much and is not going to pay ransom. . . .
>
> "I wouldn't pay one lira ransom," the widowed Mrs. Cattaneo

said. "I wouldn't dream of it. We have no money. We have just enough for our own living and that's all. And then, I am not interested in my daughter. Our relations are so strained and so bad that I am not interested in my children. They can keep her three or four months as far as I am concerned."

Mrs. Cattaneo did not say what her differences with her daughter were. [She finally relented and paid ransom.][14]

9 Hume found a great similarity between humans and animals, so great that he concluded that animals share with humans the passions of "pride and humility." (See the *Treatise*, pp. 324–28.)

'Tis plain, that almost in every species of creatures, but especially of the nobler kind, there are many evident marks of pride and humility. The very port and gait of a swan, or turkey, or peacock show the high idea he has entertain'd of himself, and his contempt of all others. . . .

The *causes* of these passions are likewise much the same in beasts as in us, making a just allowance for our superior knowledge and understanding. Thus animals have little or no sense of virtue or vice; they quickly lose sight of the relations of blood; and are incapable of that of right and property; For which reason the causes of their pride and humility must lie solely in the body, and never be plac'd either in the mind or external objects. (*Treatise*, p. 326)

Why would the absence of the ability to reflect and self-correct in animals show that they aren't capable of arriving at universal, valid moral standards, even though we may allow that their nature is rich enough to generate value pairs?

10 Hume thought that reason's function is to identify the facts and relations in a situation, and that feeling's function is to deliver approval or blame. It is to this that he attributes the "great difference between a mistake of *fact* and one of *right;* and hence the reason why the one [the latter] is commonly criminal and not the other" (*Enquiry,* p. 290). He contrasts the acts of the Greek tragic hero Oedipus and the Roman emperor Nero to show that his distinction is correct. Oedipus made a mistake of fact and Nero a mistake of right. Explain why Hume could think his contrast shows this.

When Oedipus killed Laius, he was ignorant of the relation [Laius was his father], and from circumstances, innocent and involuntary, formed erroneous opinions concerning the action which he committed. But when Nero killed [his mother] Agrippina, all the relations between himself and the person, and all the circumstances of the fact, were previously known to him; but the motive of revenge, or fear, or interest, prevailed in his savage heart over the sentiments of duty and humanity. And when we express that detestation against him to which he himself, in a little time, became insensible, it is not that we see any relations, of which he was ignorant; but that, for the rectitude of our disposition, we feel sentiments against which he was hardened from flattery and a long perseverance in the most enormous crimes. (*Enquiry,* pp. 290–91)

Nero grew "insensible," says Hume, because his feeling failed to deliver the appropriate detestation. Hence, Nero's killing his mother, whom he knew to be his mother, was a mistake of right, and, so, was criminal. But how could Hume show that Nero's insensibility was a mistake of right? After all, the bare fact is that Nero did not respond with the same sentiments that Hume did. Why should Hume's sensitivity prevail over Nero's insensitivity?

11 Do you think the following remarks of Stan, a veteran thief, show he has grown to have a savage heart like Nero? Or is his attitude justified by the facts he sets forth? If he's right about the facts, would you make a different judgment about his character traits than if he were wrong about them? If he is just factually wrong, Hume apparently thinks his acts are not "commonly criminal." Do you agree?

> Does Stan feel any guilt for his years of crime? "Not me," he
> sneered. "I'll get moral when I'm convinced that the people telling me
> to get moral are moral. There's an old saying: if there weren't any
> receivers, there wouldn't be any thieves. That's bull. There always
> have been thieves, always will. I'm just a businessman making a buck
> where I can, and when people buy from me they don't feel cheated.
> Every night, I lie down in my bed, think of the deals I've made that
> day, think of the deals I'm going to make tomorrow, then I sleep like a
> baby."[15]

Reflections on Theory

12 *Privacy of feeling and valid standards.* Hume's theory of valid standards requires that, with correction, we respond in the same way to the same things, just as "corrected" thermometers do. How does Hume know that we have the same feeling responses? Our feelings are private (I can't have your experiences nor can you have mine); hence, we can't compare them. Lacking knowledge of the feelings of others, we could conclude that Hume can't prove his theory is true or applicable. Is the following reply to this criticism sound?

We have the operation of sympathy. It turns my idea of another's feeling into the *same* impression or feeling in me. Thus we can have the same feeling.

Before giving your final answer, consider this counter to the reply just made: But how do we know that sympathy works successfully? I don't know that it does, unless I can verify its operation; but since I can't feel your feeling, I can't verify that sympathy works as claimed. So Hume's theory moves in a circle it can't get out of. Besides, the operation of sympathy doesn't work until I have an "idea" of your feeling. But how can I get that? Your telling me about your feeling won't do the job, because I have no way of verifying that your words, such as "pleasant," refer to the same kind of feeling I have when I say, "I'm having a pleasant feeling."

13 *Irreducible conflict and justice.* Hume thinks that we set up conventions of justice when we realize that there isn't enough of the world's goods to go around and that humans are selfish; these conventions are accepted by us because they are useful and because, by establishing property, they help us increase through cooperation and art what nature has failed to provide. (See the quotation from Hume, p. 434.)

But, a critic of Hume's view could ask, what if in some circumstances the conventions of justice are not useful to all? In that case, the convention is both useful and not useful and, by Hume's theory, both virtuous and not virtuous. This being so, another theory such as Kant's is surely more correct than Hume's. Kant has a test for proposed rules that is independent of usefulness: the rightness of a rule of justice has to be known *before* we determine its usefulness. Here is an example of what seems to be a rule of property concerning sunlight that necessarily leads to a conflict about its usefulness. Does it show Hume's theory is wrong?

> Solar energy development has created a monumental legal problem over how to provide "right to light" guarantees for those who install solar collectors. To be practical, solar collectors must receive not only direct sunlight from overhead but also the sun's rays across neighboring property during the hours of 9 A.M. to 3 P.M. . . .
>
> William Thomas, co-author of an American Bar Foundation study on the problem, said New Mexico enacted a law last year that says no one can cast a shadow over a neighbor's solar energy collector. But the statute seems unconstitutional, Thomas said, and may be repealed before it goes into effect July 1. . . .
>
> The New Mexico law, however well intentioned, runs contrary to a 13th-century legal doctrine holding that property lines extend "upward to the heavens." "Because a rule providing absolute ownership to the heavens was obviously incompatible with aviation, in the first half of this century the maxim was gradually weakened by the courts and by Congress," the Bar Foundation study said.
>
> It is well established in U.S. law today, the study went on, "that the surface owner has a right to receive light from that area of the sky directly above the property but not to receive it across neighboring land."[16]

14 *Kant doubts that moral feelings are standards.* Consider these statements: (1) Avarice causes an uneasy feeling in me and is not useful to others. (2) Avarice is a vicious trait. The first is an *Is* statement and the second an *Ought* (value) statement. Hume thinks there is a legitimate way to go from (1) to (2). What is it and how would Hume answer the following remarks of Kant?

The appeal to it [moral feeling] is superficial, since those who cannot think expect help from feeling, even with respect to that which concerns universal laws; they do so even though feelings naturally differ so infinitely in degree that they are incapable of furnishing a uniform standard of good and bad, also in spite of the fact that one cannot validly judge for others by means of his own feeling.[17]

15 *Is Hume's ethics inconsistent?*   Hume has a "concentric" theory about human responses and duties.   We love our own children more than our nephews, our nephews more than our cousins, and our cousins more than strangers, all else being equal.   "Hence arise our common measures of duty, in preferring the one to the other.   Our sense of duty always follows the common and natural course of our passions" (*Treatise,* p. 484).

Hume thinks this natural fact about degree of response being proportionate to the "distance" of others from us is "wisely ordained by nature . . . otherwise our affections and actions would be dissipated and lost, for want of a proper limited object" (*Enquiry,* n., p. 229).   We are limited in what we can do and in the favors we can dispense.   If we cared equally for everyone and tried to help all, our efforts would be so divided that we would accomplish so little for each of the others that it would virtually come to nothing.   The target of our duties will get more benefits if we limit our help to the smaller circle of those close to us.

Hume tells us that "a small benefit done to ourselves, or our near friends, excites more lively sentiments of love and approbation than a great benefit done to a distant commonwealth" (*Enquiry,* n., p. 229). Yet this disproportionate love and approval can be corrected, and we can "retain a general standard of vice and virtue, founded chiefly on general usefulness."   Consider the following claim that Hume's theory has a built-in difficulty: the operation of sympathy and his theory of correctible concentric responses are in conflict with each other.

The United States dropped two atomic bombs on Japan during World War II.   One justification used by President Harry Truman was that he did it to save American soldiers' lives by shortening the war; once Japan saw that it couldn't win the war, it would surrender, making an invasion of Japan unnecessary.   This justification seems to presuppose that Truman was prepared to drop more atomic bombs if the first ones didn't bring Japan to the peace table.   Here we see Truman arguing in accord with Hume's view that our duties to those closest to us are our first duties; we can't have duties to all, including the Japanese.   But it doesn't seem implausible that the harm to the Japanese far outweighed the benefit to the United States.   Consequently, if we stand back and eliminate our overrriding interest in those American soldiers who were "closer" to Truman than the Japanese were, we can "correct" the effect this proximity has on our "general standard of vice and virtue," and so allow our sympathy to operate.   This should give us an "uneasy" feeling about someone like Truman who decided to drop the atomic bombs and cause such widespread and long-term misery and death. Each year we read of the deaths from cancer of those who survived the blasts.

This presents a defender of Hume's ethics with the problem of reconciling (1) Truman's justification for dropping the bombs so as to save those closer to him, and (2) the preservation of valid, general standards by removing or compensating for his partiality toward American soldiers so that his sympathy and our own can operate without the distortion of the concentric effect.

Can Hume save his theory from this alleged difficulty? And the difficulty may not be just Hume's. It may be any moral psychologist's. That we do favor those closer to us seems factually correct. That valid, universal moral standards can be defended from the charge of relativism does seem to require discounting the proximity factor. Despite Hume's obvious, clever, and resourceful efforts not to lapse into relativism, this may be the bitter fate of moral psychology. Hume's "operation of sympathy" and his proposals about how to "correct" for deviations, which save him from relativism, may force him into an incoherent theory. In thinking about this issue, you should first arrive at a judgment about Truman's decision.

13
Moral Validity,
Free Will,
and Punishment

13.1 A Review of Contrasts

We've come a long way from the beginning of this book—when I first posed the contrast between heart and mind, feeling and thought, between the affective side of human nature and our reason—to the several contrasts between the moral theories of two philosophic giants, Hume and Kant. Let's briefly review some of the contrasts between a rational will ethics like Kant's and the ethics of moral psychologists like Hume and others.

NATURE OF HUMANS. Kant thinks that humans have a dual nature. As natural creatures we occupy the sensible world; as beings with a rational will, or practical reason, we are also members of the supersensible world. Hume and other moral psychologists think there is only the one natural world and that we, because we live only in this world, are wholly natural. Hume thought that our whole mental life—reasoning, believing, valuing, judging, willing—fits into the natural order of cause and effect. Humans in all their variety and competencies are as subject to scientific investigation as other natural phenomena are.

SOURCE OF MORALS. Kant thought that the source of our morals lies in our reason. The Categorical Imperative is a standard against which we measure our proposed policies for action. This standard requires that we search for logical consistency and inconsistency, which are reason's, not feelings', province. Such moral psychologists as sociobiologists think the source of our morals lies in our emotional responses, which are programmed by our genes; our genes, in turn, are the products of biological natural selection under the pressure of individual and species survival. Hume explained the source of our morals in our agreeable and disagreeable responses to observed character traits and in their usefulness and uselessness to ourselves and others. Our sentiment of humanity and the operation of sympathy make possible universally similar moral standards. We go from the *Is* of facts to the *Ought* of morality by the response of our sentiments to what is.

HUMAN GOODS. Kant thought that there are two distinct, heterogeneous kinds of human goods, non-moral and moral goods. The non-moral highest good is happiness; it is the harmonious, total, and continuous attainment of the wants of our sensible self. For him, there are two moral goods, the dignity we have because of our capacity for freedom, and the worthiness we acquire when we realize our free capacity by achieving a good will—always acting out of respect for the moral law. Perfect happiness and **471** worthiness make up the *summum bonum*. For moral psychologists, there are not two wholly different kinds of human goods; non-moral and moral goods are sub-kinds of the most general kind of good. This most general kind is identified by means of a naturalistic concept of good, several of which have been proposed—objects of want, desire, interest, or experiences of pleasure or satisfaction. Most generally for moral psychologists happiness has been the highest object of good; our end in life is to achieve happiness.

BASIC MORAL CONCEPT. Kant thought that the basic moral concept is obligation or duty; this is a deontological view and fits with his claim that the chief human good is worthiness. Moral psychologists have made good the basic moral concept; this is a teleological view; it fits with their claim that happiness is the highest human end or purpose.

GROUNDS OF DUTY. Deontologists such as Kant and others think that the ground of duty lies in the nature of the act itself. Kant asks whether a proposed maxim, if followed universally, is consistent with itself or with natural laws. Teleologists, which moral psychologists are, look to the consequences of the act rather than the act itself for the grounds of duty. Utilitarianism is such a view; it looks to the utility of the act in producing good and bad consequences for the measure of its rightness and wrongness.

NATURE OF REASON. Kant thought that reason is both causally efficient and determines values. It is causally efficient because it has the power to arouse moral feeling in us, which, when selected by our *Willkür,* has the motive power to cause us to act. It determines values because by the application of the Categorical Imperative it discovers the moral laws that express our moral duties. Hume, on the other hand, found that reason can't move us to act; only our passions and sentiments can do that. And he thought that our reason doesn't determine values; only our sentiments do that as well. Our reason cares no more for the destruction of the world than for the scratching of our little finger.

In this chapter, I will conclude the contrasts between rational will ethics and moral psychology. Section 13.2 deals with contrasting views about the kind of validity moral laws have. Kant thinks they have an unconditional, categorical validity, Hume that they have only conditional validity. Section 13.3 explains why Kant thinks we have free will and why Hume thinks we don't. In section 13.4 I outline how Kant defended himself against the charge that we cannot act both freely in accord with our self-given moral laws and unfreely in accord with the given laws of nature. Finally, in section 13.5 I will explore the different theories of punishment advocated by the competing schools of ethics.

13.2 Facts and the Validity of Moral Laws

The main question of this and the next section will be whether or not morality's flower depends on the roots of empirical conditions and facts. Hume, who expended his whole effort on the "science of Man," thought it is dependent; Kant firmly thought it is not.

There are two topics in morality about which we can ask this question. This section asks if the *validity* or truth of moral laws and standards depends on empirical factual conditions. The next section asks if the *motivation* for doing our duty in accord with moral laws depends on such conditions. Kant thought that in both cases morals are unconditioned by factual matters. Hume thought the opposite; for him, both are conditioned.

Kant's discussion of these topics and his answers to these questions are central to ethical literature. To connect my discussion here with Kant's and other writers' discussion of the topic, you have to know his terminology. Here then is the terminology that Kant uses to discuss the validity question.

A sentence with an "ought" in it is an *imperative* sentence. Kant thinks there are two kinds of imperatives: categorical imperatives and hypothetical imperatives. Moral laws and standards are categorical imperatives. They prescribe an *act* we ought to perform or refrain from, or an *end* we ought to adopt or reject. (Note: there is only *one* Categorical Imperative, which I always capitalize. It is the standard for moral laws, which Kant thinks express categorical imperatives, of which there are *many,* such as the ones that we ought not to murder, we ought to keep our promises, we ought to repay our debts.)

Categorical Imperatives	*Hypothetical Imperatives*
are *unconditioned,* that is, valid independent of empirical conditions;	are *conditioned,* that is, valid because of empirical conditions;
are *a priori,* that is, known to be valid *prior* to experience of any feeling responses and *prior* to empirical knowledge of the advantages or disadvantages of acting in accord with them.	are *a posteriori,* that is, known to be valid *after* our experience of feeling responses and/or *after* we have empirical knowledge of the advantages or disadvantages of acting in accord with them.

Kant thought that the validity of hypothetical imperatives is grounded in happiness. Suppose—or, in philosophical terms, hypothesize (hence the term "hypothetical")—that you want happiness. If you believe that getting married, having children and getting a good paying job are means to happiness, then you *ought* to get married, have children, and get such a job. These are counsels of *prudence;* they are hypothetical imperatives but not moral laws, according to Kant. These counsels are valid *providing* it is an empirical fact **473** that you want happiness, and *providing* it is an empirical fact that marrying, having children, and being well paid for your work are means to being happy. The validity of these counsels depend upon the truth of claims about empirical conditions; hence, these counsels are hypothetical, empirically conditioned imperatives only. Not being categorical, they aren't moral laws stating that you ought to get married, have children, and take only well-paying jobs.

The terms "categorical" and "hypothetical," then, contrast two different ways of grounding or validating imperatives. Hume grounded imperatives in our natural, empirical standards of agreeable and/or useful. Suppose I say to you, who are pinching me very hard on the nose, "You shouldn't do that." You ask, "Why shouldn't I?" You are asking me to ground or validate my imperative. Were I to give you a Humean answer, I would simply say, "Because it hurts." That's all that can or need be said, supposing that pain is a disagreeable or uneasy feeling. Disagreeableness is a standard. That it is such a standard is a matter of empirical fact about our human nature and our responses. This "ought not" ("shouldn't") isn't derived by reason; that something is "felt" constitutes our moral approval or disapproval.

You might think the Humean answer a good one. If the world were different and it didn't hurt when you pinched my nose, then it wouldn't be any more wrong to pinch my nose than a robot's; when the world's empirical conditions change, so should our imperatives. That does seem reasonable, but consider a different example and see if you continue to agree.

Trevor X is totally bored with life, sees no point in living, finds the prospect of waking up one more morning so utterly horrifying that he breaks into a sweat and gets the shakes. Some gamblers know this. They propose to him that he become their betting instrument to attract big international money. Trevor X is to play Russian roulette, while the gamblers bet on how many spins of the revolver's chamber it will take before he triggers the bullet that kills him. Trevor X agrees to the gamblers' proposal.

The empirical, matter-of-fact condition is that Trevor X doesn't care to live; the world's normal condition has changed for him. Would you agree that the imperative expressing our and the gamblers' duty to his life should change also? Do you think the gamblers need observe no imperative about Trevor X's certain death just because Trevor X no longer cares to live and agrees to play Russian roulette for their benefit?

It is a fact that I find a certain moist consistency in my omelettes agreeable. This validates the imperatives, "I ought to beat my eggs thoroughly and I ought not to cook them too long." Were I no longer to care whether or not my omelettes have a certain moist consistency, the imperatives would no longer be valid for me. Change the facts about my feeling responses, and my imperatives change. The omelette imperatives are hypothetical. But to compare abondoning the omelette imperative to the gamblers' abandoning their duty to preserve Trevor X's life would seem

474   monstrous to Kant: "In the doctrine of happiness empirical principles constitute the entire foundation, but in the doctrine of morality they do not form even the smallest part of it."[1]

The usually restrained, gentlemanly Kant lets his feelings show regarding anyone who accepts this "hypothetical" character for moral law. He scorns those who ground morality in a "moral feeling," who think that our "oughts" are based on the "agreeableness that a thing affords, either directly [immediately] agreeable and without a view to future advantage or with a view to [usefulness]."[2]   Of those who hold this view, he writes:

> The appeal to it is superficial, since those who cannot think expect help from feeling, even with respect to that which concerns universal laws; they do so even though feelings naturally differ so infinitely in degree that they are incapable of furnishing a uniform standard of the good and bad, and also that in spite of the fact that one cannot validly judge for others by means of his own feelings. (*Foundations,* p. 327)

For Kant, this lack of uniformity in feelings defeats an ethical theory such as Hume's which claims that our moral judgments are based on feeling; Kant believes that moral laws have the features of universality and necessity (see 8.4).

Although Hume did not discuss "moral laws" as Kant did, he claimed that moral theory is practical philosophy because it influences us to do our "duties." He also asked where we got imperatives—sentences containing "ought." Remember that Hume opposed the "vulgar moralists" and denied that we can derive imperative sentences from sentences containing only "is" or "is not." Although Hume concentrated most of his attention on learning what *motive* we have for doing our duty, he did insist that there are valid moral standards; he concluded that the standards of agreeable ends and useful means with regard to ourselves and others are valid, because it is an empirical fact that we use them as standards of moral approval and disapproval. (See 13.3, pp. 486–87, and 12.4b, p. 433, for Hume on the motive for doing our duty; and see pp. 426–27 and 420 for Hume on the source of the moral "ought.")

Kant thought that because hypothetical, factually validated imperatives fall short of being categorical, they cannot be moral laws; they have *neither the universality nor the necessity* required. In Kant's view, Hume didn't have a theory of morality but only a theory of prudence, a theory of how to take due care in seeing to our own and others' "happiness and welfare." Kant stressed that we should never confuse virtue with happiness.

Kant insists on a "pure moral philosophy," one that isn't based on variable feeling responses and the empirical conditions in which we happen to find ourselves. Only a "pure" moral philosophy can provide for the necessity and universality required of moral "oughts." This purity can be found only in *a priori* reason, where the *a priori* is that which is independent of any empirical matters of fact. Here is his argument:

I narrow the proposed question to this: Is it not of the utmost necessity to construct a pure moral philosophy which is completely freed from everything which may be only empirical and thus belong to anthropology? That there must be such a philosophy is self-evident from the common idea of duty and moral laws. Everyone must admit that a law, if it is to hold morally, i.e., as a ground of obligation, must imply absolute necessity; he must admit that the command, "Thou shalt not lie," does not apply to men only, as if other rational beings had no need to observe it. The same is true for all other moral laws properly so called. He must concede that the *ground of obligation* [my emphasis] here must not be sought in the nature of man or in the circumstances in which he is placed but sought a priori solely in the concepts of pure reason. (*Foundations,* p. 293)

Although the categorical/hypothetical distinction might seem to be so purely theoretical and remote as not to merit a controversy, a very practical long-term, pressing difference between Senator Edward Kennedy and President Jimmy Carter turns on just this distinction. Kennedy criticized Carter's stand on national health-care insurance. His criticism was that Carter believed that the imperative, "The United States ought to have national health care," is hypothetical only, whereas he, Kennedy, believes it is categorical. Here is part of the news story on Kennedy's criticism of Carter.

Senator Edward Kennedy took another slap at President Carter yesterday, declaring that tying national health care to economic indicators is a denial of human rights. The Massachusetts Democrat said health care is a "basic human right" and that "a conditional right is basically not a right." . . .

"It is wrong to tie the pledge and commitment of a right to the American people on some predictions that may or may not happen," he said. "We don't condition Social Security on the rate of inflation or the size of unemployment or the size of the deficit. We don't condition public education of the young people in our states on the size of the deficit or the size of unemployment."

When Carter outlined his ideas, he said any national health care plan should be phased in gradually, with the introduction of each new phase dependent on the general economic climate. He did not specify the indicators to be used.[3]

Kennedy's views on rights agree with Kant's. (See 9.2 for Kant on the relation between rights and obligations.) Rights are categorical; they are not subject to changeable, empirical conditions. And he agrees with Kant by a similar reasoning: "A conditional right is basically not a right." A conditional, hypothetical right is a contradiction in terms. Kennedy thinks it is logically absurd to say, "Yes, you have a right to health, *providing* the conditions are suitable." Conditions may or may not happen; they are contingent. If they don't happen, then according to the hypothetical theory of rights, there is no longer a right. So it turns out that you don't have a right under some conditions; this, in effect, is a denial of a right. But, as Kant maintained, one should not confuse a right with our ability to fulfill it. A person

476 lost in the frozen tundra has a right to health care, even if the conditions for its provision can't be met: "Laws must completely determine the will as will, even before I ask whether I am capable of achieving a desired effect or what should be done to realize it" (*Practical Reason* [Beck], p. 18).

Furthermore, life depends upon good health; therefore, if the right to health is contingent, it also follows that you don't have a right to life under some circumstances— even though you might be the most worthy of persons. Perhaps you believe that someone who criminally takes another's life forfeits his or her own right to life; but being unhealthy isn't such a forfeiture. You can see that the categorical/hypothetical distinction cuts pretty deep; it cuts right into the grave.

Kant's criticism of the moral psychologists' empirical theory of validation, which includes Hume's version of it, focuses on what he claims are two of its failings. First, it doesn't yield the *universality* that Hume and other moral psychologists agree moral laws or standards must have. Second, it doesn't give grounds for the *necessity* that he thinks moral laws must have.

Hume agrees with Kant that moral standards validated by empirical facts (matters of fact in the science of Man) are only contingent and do not have necessity. Hume argues that there is no necessity for any matter of fact. The sun may have risen every day, but it isn't contradictory to suppose that it won't rise tomorrow. The sun's rising tomorrow is contingent only, not necessary. Similarly, it may be a fact that we respond with an agreeable feeling to generosity, that all of us do and always have; but there is nothing contradictory in supposing that tomorrow all of us will respond with an uneasy feeling. Since this isn't contradictory, isn't "contrary to reason," it isn't necessary. So the facts about our moral responses, and consequently about our moral standards, are contingent only. It is a matter of fact, given the kind of human nature that we have, that the agreeable and the useful are our standards. Nature might have arranged otherwise; it may do so tomorrow. For now, however, this is just "the way things are."

The contingency of moral standards follows from Hume's theories about the factual source of the standards and about the contingency of facts. But if a moral standard or moral law must have necessity, then, by admitting only contingency for his standards, Hume would have to admit that his theory is incorrect. To defend his theory, Hume has to deny that necessity must be a feature of moral laws.

Having discussed Kant's ideas of why moral laws must have the deontic property of necessity in 8.4, 9.1, and 11.9 (pp. 399–400), there is no need to go into that extensively here; two reminders suffice. First, Kant thinks that our concept of a right, such as a right to life, the "sacredness" of human life, is something that a person can claim *regardless* of contingent circumstances; any theory that puts conditions on it, that makes the right to life or any other right merely hypothetical, fails to account for a central datum of morality. (Think of Trevor X.) Second, anyone who takes the universality requirement seriously, as Kant does in the Categorical Imperative, has to explain why it is a valid *constraint* on our actions and ends. Kant thinks the only valid ground for this constraint is one showing that an act or end proposed in a maxim **477** would be *impossible* to perform or to adopt universally. This impossibility is shown if the universalized maxim contradicts itself; contradiction is not an *a posteriori,* empirical, contingent factor, but an *a priori,* necessary one. Anyone wanting universality of maxims, as Hume does, must also accept necessity. Universality and necessity are locked together.

Now let's summarize why Kant thinks an empirical theory like Hume's or any moral psychologist's fails to provide universality. (Kant's arguments are taken from Remark I and Remark II of Theorem IV in *Practical Reason.*)

Kant thinks that our sensible self's nature is egoistic:

> All the material [in contrast to the form] of practical rules [maxims] rests only on subjective conditions, which can afford the rules no universality for rational beings. . . . Without exception, they all revolve about the principle of one's own happiness. (*Practical Reason* [Beck], p. 34)

If the spring of action for the sensible, empirical self is our own happiness, then, because my life circumstances differ from yours, we can expect that different conditions will be needed to secure our happiness; the non-uniformity of these conditions destroys a universal base for the validity of our moral judgments.

Hume thought that only disinterested, impartial sentiments—those not based on self-love—were "moral" ones; he also thought that the sentiments of others become morally relevant for us because of the operation of sympathy, and that we can correct variations in our feeling responses. So Kant's first argument doesn't refute Hume. To my knowledge, Kant doesn't directly address himself to Hume's *operation* of sympathy; the closest he comes is when he talks about a "sympathetic disposition," by which he means a nature that possesses the kind of want that is satisfied by the welfare of others. Kant says flat out, without supporting argument, that "this want, however, I cannot presuppose in every rational being, certainly not in God" (*Practical Reason* [Beck], p. 35).

Two other arguments that Kant uses against the moral psychologists' empirical theory of moral validation rely upon what we are capable of knowing and doing. We simply cannot know enough to determine what we ought to do to secure happiness; nor do we always have the power to actually attain the object of our happiness. It is otherwise with duties; they can be known and performed:

> What duty is, is plain of itself to everyone, but what is to bring true, lasting advantage to our whole existence is veiled in impenetrable obscurity. . . .
>
> It is always in everyone's power to satisfy the commands of the categorical command of morality; this is but seldom possible with respect to the empirically conditioned precept of happiness, and it is far from being possible, even in respect to a single purpose, for everyone. . . . It is also a question of capacity and physical ability to realize a desired object. (*Practical Reason* [Beck], p. 38)

478 These two arguments do not strictly refute Hume or any moral psychologist. The most they can do, if sound, is to show that it is easier to be morally successful with Kant's ethics than with Hume's.

Kant has another argument against moral psychology based on his view of punishment; it will be taken up in the final contrast in 13.5.

It isn't as easy to refute Hume's theory on the ground that his ethics doesn't provide universality as Kant seems to think it is. Clearly, Kant's most potent argument is that Hume's theory doesn't provide necessity for standards; but this refutation depends on the truth of the claim that moral standards and laws must have necessity. The crucial issue on which our choice between Hume and Kant turns is Kant's argument that the constraint of universality is logically tied to the impossibility of "everyone doing that," or equivalently, to the necessity of "everyone not doing that."

13.3 Humans' Relation to Nature (Free Will)

Suppose that moral laws and standards are categorical, *a priori,* and empirically unconditioned, as Kant claimed, and that Hume's theory that their validity rests on contingent matters of fact about our sentiments is wrong. This isn't enough to give us a fully unconditioned morality. To have that, we would also need to establish that our *motive* for acting in accord with valid moral laws is unconditioned. If this motive isn't free of sensible, empirical conditons, then in Kant's terminology we aren't "autonomous" but merely "heteronomous" beings.

"Autonomous" is roughly equivalent to "self-causing" and "heteronomous" to "other-causing." To act heteronomously is to be caused to act by our inclinations; inclinations are heteronomous causes because they are *nature's* causes, which are causes other than our own. We are autonomous when *our* respect for *our* moral laws causes us to act; here the motive of respect and the laws are our own and not nature's or another's.

The following news story illustrates what appears to be a man's shift from an autonomous, moral motive to a heteronomous, prudential motive:

> The finder of $415,000 in cash says he isn't sure honesty is the best policy. "If I had to do it over again, I'd probably keep the money," said an angry Donald Louk after he was given a $1000 reward Thursday [and a job offer] for returning two bags full of small, unmarked bills he found on a street two days before.
>
> Louk said he turned in the money because "my parents raised me to be honest."
>
> "I am very, very upset," he said. "My family and I don't even think it was worth the gas it took to drive 25 miles down to Trenton to pick up the reward. To me, it's like finding $1 million and being given a dollar for it," he added. . . . "I didn't want a fortune," Louk said, "maybe $3000 or $4000 to pay off all my bills. [Louk's only source of income is $138 a week in disability benefits.][4]

Louk's autonomous motive is turning in the money because his parents **479** raised him "to be honest." He evidently turned in the money out of respect for honesty as a moral policy. But his disappointment at the size of his reward shows that there may have been a heteronomous motive operating in him as well; turning in the money in order to get a reward is not acting out of respect for the law, although some degree of such respect seems to have been present, since Louk could have kept all of it and had a greater "reward."

The issue we wrestle with in this section is whether we do or don't have autonomous moral motives. Kant thinks that we have such a motive, that it is caused by our practical reason, and that this motive is "respect for the moral law as such." Only by acting from this motive do persons make themselves morally worthy. Hume thinks there is no such motive; reason is the slave of the passions.

Kant's later view was that morality is "a vain delusion and chimerical notion" if rational beings, including humans, aren't unconditioned in both the categorical and autonomy senses. Being able to give ourselves moral laws *a priori* (through *Wille*), and being able to move ourselves from respect for the moral law (through *Willkür*), are the two functions that our practical reason performs.

Interestingly, in his earlier *Lectures* Kant says we have "the instinct of benevolence"—a sensible, natural motive that we possess in addition to our self-interest in our own happiness. But later Kant advises sticking with unconditioned moral motives. Since this benevolent impulse is a contingent matter of fact about our nature, there is no guarantee that it will unfailingly motivate us to act morally. This is particularly true because it isn't the *sole* motive; having to compete for dominance in us with self-love, benevolence may well lose the struggle.

> Providence has implanted in our bosoms the instinct of benevolence to be the source of actions by which we restore what we have unrighteously procured. . . . This impulse makes a man merciful and charitable to his neighbour. . . . [But] if charity were the mainspring and sole motive of our conduct, there would be no such thing as "mine" and "thine"; the world would be the theatre, not of reason, but of inclination, and men would not trouble to earn but would rely on the charity of their fellows. But just as children share their sweets only so long as they have enough and to spare, so could this arrangement work only if there was in the world a superfluity [excess] of wealth. . . . Teachers and moralists must, therefore, concentrate as far as possible upon showing that charity is a duty which we owe to mankind and that in the last analysis it is a question of right.[5]

A few pages earlier, Kant talks about love:

> Love is good-will from inclination; but there can also be good-will on principle. It follows that the pleasure we find in doing good to others may be either direct or indirect. The direct pleasure comes from doing good from obligation, when we enjoy the consciousness of having done our duty.

480

> Doing good from love springs from the heart; doing good from obligation springs rather from principles of the understanding. Thus a man may act kindly towards his wife from love, but if his inclination has evaporated he ought to do so from obligation. (*Lectures,* p. 192)

Kant puts his finger here on what is wrong with every ethic, including Christian ethics, that bases our morality on love. One can't count on love's continuing existence; it is a matter of fact that I love someone today, but it is entirely possible that in the future I will not. Yet this doesn't relieve us of our obligation to act morally toward someone we no longer love. Consequently, our obligation must be based on something other than love or a feeling of benevolence.

The question about the existence of autonomous motives has traditionally been associated with the question about whether we do or don't have free will. The free will question, in turn, is related to our conception of nature. If nothing in nature is *auto*nomous, then everything in it is caused by something else (it is other-caused, or *hetero*nomous); and if humans are wholly natural and immanent in nature, as Hume believed we are, then humans have no autonomy. Kant saw the logic of this argument as clearly as anyone. He accepted the view that everything in nature is caused by something else; therefore, if humans are autonomous—that is, if they can cause their own actions—then they must not be wholly natural, but at least in part must be *above* rather than *in* nature. Kant did indeed claim this: our rational aspect is supersensible, transcendent, outside sensible nature.

It has often been argued that human autonomy—frequently tied to "free will"—is essential to morality because moral worthiness can't be attributed to someone unless that someone is responsible for what has happened, nor is that someone responsible unless he or she has caused what happened. Consider Highman and Lowman: Highman watches Lowman bump against Trevor X, who falls in front of an automobile and is killed. Certainly Highman, a mere observer, can't be held responsible, for Highman didn't cause what happened.

Consider next that Lowman bumped against Trevor X because Lowman was pushed by Snellcrook; consequently, Lowman can't be held responsible for Trevor X's death. By going backward in the chain of causes, we find who is responsible for Trevor X's death; responsibility travels on the back of the cause.

Now we focus on Snellcrook. Is he responsible? According to the prior steps, we would say so, because he was the cause of the chain of events that resulted in Trevor X's death. Did anyone push Snellcrook? No. Therefore, because he was the "first" cause, he is responsible and ought to be indicted for murder or manslaughter. Ordinarily, this is the way we locate responsibility.

But someone could challenge this attribution of responsibility to Snellcrook, saying that we haven't carried our causal theory of responsibility through to its proper conclusion. Look, they say, Snellcrook didn't cause himself. He was caused to exist by his parents; his human nature is a causal

effect of his genes; his genes were inherited from his ancestors, who were pro-   **481**
ducts of natural selection; his character and personality were caused by his upbringing, the circumstances of his life, the culture in which he lived, and his
friends and schoolmates—all of which causes together explain why Snellcrook
had the character with the motive that caused him to push Lowman, who
knocked Trevor X into the path of the auto that killed him. Now all these
causes, or the causes of these causes, precede Snellcrook, and because they
precede him, he had no power over them. Further, these causal relations
govern events with an "iron necessity"; Snellcrook can't change them. Consequently, because Snellcrook didn't cause himself or what he is, and because
he can't cause himself to be different now, he is not responsible for Trevor
X's death—no more so than Lowman was. Responsibility travels on the back
of the cause; because neither Snellcrook's existence nor his character are self-
caused—that is, because Snellcrook isn't autonomous—we can't put responsibility for what Snellcrook does on his back. In Kant and Hume's word,
Snellcrook was "predetermined."[6]

The great criminal lawyer Clarence Darrow argued in just this way, per-
suaded many juries, and had a profound effect on the law. In a debate with
Professor George Foster on the topic "Do Human Beings Have Free Will?"
Darrow said:

> Now, I am firmly convinced that a man has no more to do with his own
> conduct than a wooden Indian. A wooden Indian has a little advantage
> for he does not even think he is free. Everybody's life and position are cut
> out for them. . . . The great events of life are absolutely beyond his con-
> trol. He has not even much to say about getting married. . . . All this is
> cut out for you. It is cut out with no chance or power to change
> it. . . .Man is made up of only two things, heredity and environment.
> And all he is and all he has is the product of these two.[7]

Kant too believes that humans in their *sensible* existence are not
autonomous; from a psychological and physiological perspective, their acts
are wholly determined by causes, not by a free, autonomous will:

> all the actions of men in the [field of] appearance are determined in con-
> formity with the order of nature, by their empirical character and by the
> other causes which cooperate with that character.[8]

But, you might protest, we can hold Snellcrook responsible because
there is a difference between being caused to act by something outside
ourselves and by something inside ourselves. We don't hold Lowman responsible because the cause of his knocking Trevor X into the auto's path came
from outside himself—from Snellcrook; but we do hold Snellcrook legally
responsible because the cause was internal to him: no one pushed Snellcrook,
he caused himself to move.

This internal/external causation distinction does have a bearing on the
issue of responsibility. It is one way we distinguish between voluntary and in-

482 voluntary acts. Except for charges of negligence, we aren't responsible for involuntary acts. Although Hume thinks we do not have "liberty"—that is, free will—he does think we perform voluntary acts when we are "not a prisoner and in chains" (*Enquiry,* p. 94). Involuntary acts, Hume thinks, are "constrained." Lowman's knocking Trevor X was involuntary, being constrained by an outside force. The force of Snellcrook's shove constrained Lowman's "freedom of action"; Lowman had not the power to overcome the momentum that the shove gave him.

But the voluntary/involuntary distinction is not the same as the free/unfree, autonomous/heteronomous distinction. Kant thinks that the attempt to prove we are free by showing we are voluntary, and that the attempt to show we are voluntary by pointing out that sometimes we are moved to action by internal causes, "is a wretched subterfuge" (*Practical Reason* [Beck], p. 99). In that sense of free and involuntary, the motion of a clock's hands are free; they are moved by machinery internal to the clock. But this is an absurd notion of freedom for morals. Even though we said that humans are moved by internal *ideas* rather than by internal, material, cog-and-gear clockwork mechanisms, we still wouldn't have saved human freedom if we granted that there are psychological laws governing the occurrence of these ideas. A law specifying that a present idea is caused by a preceding one, and that by another, eventually gets us to a point in the causal chain lying in the past over which we have no power. These remote causes are no longer internal to us; they are someone else's ideas, so that the responsibility can't be put on our back. (See *Practical Reason* [Beck], pp. 99–101.) The "internal cause" concept of freedom, Kant says, would "be no better than the freedom of a turnspit, which when once wound up also carries out its motions of itself."

Let's turn to Hume's view of the matter. Here we are dealing with Hume's naturalization of willing, another part of his naturalization of humans that makes us a subject of the "science of Man." That we aren't free, that we don't have "liberty," means for Hume that our actions are "necessary," meaning that every act is caused. Hume thinks every act is caused by a motive; for example, the motive of hate causes vengeful acts. Hume's evidence that we aren't free is that we observe a constant conjunction between humans' motives and their acts; we find this constancy because human nature is uniform and fixed. We don't have the power to change these causal relationships; hence, the causes of our acts are heteronomous, are beyond our power:

> It is universally ackowledged that there is a great uniformity among the actions of men, in all nations and ages, and that human nature remains the same, in its principles and operations. The same motives always produce the same actions: The same events follow from the same causes. (*Enquiry,* p. 83)

Hume thinks that the relation of cause and effect is the same in matter as it is in humans, and that its presence is just as certain: "For is it more certain, that two flat pieces of marble will unite together, than that two young savages of different sexes will copulate?"[9] In the *Treatise,* as later in the *Enquiry,* he **483** concludes that natural and moral phenomena are similar in kind, which completes his naturalization of humans:

> And indeed, when we consider how aptly *natural* and *moral* evidence cement together, and form only one chain of argument betwixt them, we shall make no scruple to allow [we shall have no doubt] that they are of the same nature, and deriv'd from the same principles. A prisoner, who has neither money nor interest [influence], discovers the impossibility of his escape, as well from the obstinacy of the gaoler, as from the walls and bars with which he is surrounded. . . . The same prisoner, when conducted to the scaffold, foresees his death as certainly from the constancy and fidelity of his guards as from the operation of the ax or wheel. His mind runs along a certain train of ideas: The refusal of the soldiers to consent to his escape, the action of the executioner; the separation of the head and body; bleeding, convulsive motions, and death. (*Treatise,* p. 406; *Enquiry,* p. 90)

But, you may say, Hume's evidence that we aren't free isn't as good as he thinks. His evidence is the uniformity or constancy of motives and acts, but they aren't constant—hate doesn't always cause a vengeful act; therefore, he doesn't have the evidence he needs to show that we aren't free. Hume anticipates this objection and thinks he can answer it. We have to make an "allowance for the diversity of characters, prejudices, and opinions" of men (*Enquiry,* p. 85). This diversity leads us to recognize that we have to form a "greater variety of maxims [motivational laws], which still suppose a degree of uniformity and regularity." An observation of variety in behavior stimulates us to search for a variety of laws; but each of these laws, when and if discovered, is a law about constant conjunction:

> It is at least possible the contrariety [conflicting variety] of events [effects] may not proceed from any contingency in the cause, but from the secret operation of contrary causes. . . . They [philosophers] know that a human body is a mighty complicated machine: That many secrets lurk in it, which are altogether beyond our comprehension. . . .
> The philosopher, if he be consistent, must apply the same reasoning to the actions and volitions of intelligent agents. The most irregular and unexpected resolutions of men may frequently be accounted for by those who know every particular circumstance of their character and situation. A person of an obliging disposition gives a peevish answer: But he has the toothache, or has not dined. A stupid fellow discovers [shows] an uncommon alacrity [briskness] in his carriage [bearing]: But he has met with a sudden good piece of fortune. (*Enquiry,* p. 88)

But, you might reply, I know someone and his circumstances thoroughly—a person I've lived with in close friendship and who's honest and has plenty of money—yet this supposed constancy may not hold; my friend

484 may suddenly stab me and steal my money because a sudden frenzy overcomes him. Hume replies, "So may a sudden earthquake arise, and shake and tumble my house about my ears" (*Enquiry,* p. 91). In the face of unexpected natural events, we don't give up a belief in their causation; so we shouldn't give up the same belief about human events that surprise us. An earthquake is nature's frenzy.

As noted before, with respect to our natural, sensible existence, Kant agrees with Hume that all our actions are caused and that we do not have "liberty." For Hume, however, autonomy—freedom from natural causation—is equivalent to "chance," and since chance has "no existence," neither does liberty. Will is not a power but a "feeling" that we have when we act voluntarily (*Treatise,* p. 399). Kant, however, does not think freedom is non-existent. For him, freedom exists because our practical reason, which transcends the natural, sensible world, can be a cause of our acts. Just how our supersensible reason can cause a sensible moral feeling cannot be explained, Kant says (*Lectures,* p. 45). We all affirm that our reason can move us to act because we blame people, holding them responsible for something they did, even though all the evidence points to a host of natural causes of their act. Kant thinks we could not blame them if their reason couldn't fly in the face of all the empirically conditioned preceding events and cause an action. Responsibility, remember, rides on the back of the cause, over which we have control. If we are to be responsible, then *we,* exercising *our* reason, must be the cause, not some remote event long ago and far away. We affirm autonomy when we blame; if our reason couldn't cause events, we couldn't be blamed.

Kant gives us a case that puts our autonomous powers to the severest test. This case is an illustration, not a proof. Kant's "proof" for freedom, you should recall, is that we recognize the "fact of reason" that we "ought"; *Ought* implies *Can;* therefore, we "can" (autonomously). (A succinct statement of this argument is in *Religion,* p. 45, note. [See 7.4.])

Were we not autonomous—that is, were we not the cause of our own actions—we could not hold persons responsible for their actions; worthiness would be an empty concept, having no instances, and morality would be "a vain delusion." For Kant, the existence of morality hangs by this thread:

> Let us take a voluntary action, for example, a malicious lie by which a certain confusion has been caused in society [for instance, ex-President Nixon "stonewalling" Watergate]. First of all, we endeavour to discover the motives to which it has been due, and then, secondly, in the light of these, we proceed to determine how far the action and its consequences can be imputed to the offender. As regards the first question, we trace the empirical character of the action to its sources, finding these in defective education, bad company, in part also in the viciousness of a natural disposition insensitive to shame, in levity and thoughtlessness, not neglecting to take into account also the occasional causes that may have intervened. We proceed in this enquiry just as we should in ascertaining for a given natural effect the series of its determining causes. But although we believe that the action is thus determined, we *none the less blame the agent,*

not indeed on account of his previous way of life; for we presuppose that *we can leave out of consideration* what this way of life may have been, that we can regard the past series of conditions as not having occurred and the act as being *completely unconditioned* by any preceding state, just as if the agent in and by himself began in this action an entirely new series of consequences. *Our blame is based on a law of reason whereby we regard reason as a cause* that irrespective of all the above-mentioned empirical conditions could have determined, and ought to have determined, the agent to act otherwise. This causality of reason we do not regard as only a co-operating agency, but as complete in itself, even when the sensuous impulses do not favour but are directly opposed to it; the action is ascribed to the agent's intelligible [supersensible] character; in the moment when he utters the lie, the guilt is entirely his. (*Pure Reason* [Smith], p. 477; all emphases mine)

I have quoted Kant at such length because nowhere in moral literature is the fate of morality made to depend more explicitly on the autonomy of our moral motives. He squarely faces off against appeals that have been made a million times over. These appeals ask wives, husbands, parents, children, friends, juries, and judges to excuse, forgive, ameliorate, exonerate, and declare innocent, to give probation rather than imprisonment, to overlook, and to extend clemency. Television, movies, and novels good, bad, and indifferent make a stock in trade of heteronomy: all actions are caused; the causes are beyond the control of the person who committed the act; therefore, the actor should not be held responsible. For instance:

"He lived in a poor neighborhood; his father, in a drunken stupor, regularly beat his equally drunken mother into insensibility."

"This girl lived on the streets. She had to—there simply was no employment for either of the parents. And with seven brothers and sisters, welfare payments were inadequate."

"This boy suffered an early neurosis because he was seduced by his mother at the age of thirteen. The family was wealthy and socially involved, and traveled extensively, yet the boy never got the love, attention, and care that is normal. The only attention his mother gave him was when she seduced him. He never got over it."

"This woman went to ghetto schools. Her early promise was stunted; she was forced into the company of youths who dealt in drugs. There was no other way for her to acquire the affluence that the TV showed every day was the highest aspiration of an American. In the face of this, what use were Shakespeare, mathematics, history, Kant, or Hume to her? If you condemn this woman, you condemn yourself who are responsible for the conditions that caused her to do what she did. God forgive us."

You could write these scripts in your sleep. Perhaps you already have, in term papers. Kant recognizes the power of the forces cited in such appeals, but he is unimpressed. Anytime you choose, he says, you can do what you

486   recognize you ought to do. Every act is the dawn of moral creation. Do it! Don't whine. Don't give excuses. Don't hide behind your disadvantages. Don't throw yourself on the mercy of others and demean youself. Rule yourself with your practical reason, which means you should do three things: by means of *Wille,* (1) use the Categorical Imperative to test your maxims and give yourself moral laws and (2) think about the moral law, which will cause a moral feeling in you, a respect for the moral law; (3) develop your character so that by means of *Willkür* you have the strength and virtue to pick the moral feeling as your motive rather than a sensible feeling of inclination.

It is essential to Kant's ethics that we be autonomous, that our moral motive be *external* to our feelings of inclination. Kant is an externalist in his answer to the question, "Why should I be moral?"

As you probably noticed, the question "Why should I be moral?" can be interpreted in two ways. The "Why" has two possible meanings: (1) what *reason* is there for my being moral? and (2) what *motive* do I have for being moral? The question may mean (1) "Why should I return this $415,000 of unmarked bills that I found?" or (2) "What incentive (reward?) will cause me to do what I ought to do?"

Kant's answer to question (1) is that it is your duty and being moral is the only way you have of being worthy, of realizing your moral personality, as distinguished from merely being happy. In relation to question (2), Kant is an *externalist:* the motive for being moral is the moral feeling, the respect you feel when you think about your duty in the circumstances for which you have proposed a maxim of action; therefore, return the money to the owner. The moral feeling is external first of all to our natural, sensible self; this is what makes it unconditioned and autonomous. And it is external as well to the *reason* one should be moral, which is why the moral-feeling motive comes *after* the recognition of what we ought to do.

The autonomy of human moral motivation is essential to Kant's ethics because this autonomy, and it alone, is what makes worthiness an attainable end. If we acted from inclination only, then all our motives would be aimed at happiness; worthiness, the other half of the *summum bonum,* would be forever out of our reach. In Kant's opinion, a positive answer to "Do we have free will?" is necessary, if we are to be moral as well as prudent beings. If reason does not have motive power, we lapse back into purely natural beings—a numerous, dominant herd of two-footed animals roaming and occupying the world in search of satisfaction and survival alone, just like the other animal species.

Hume's ethics, on the other hand, does not require free will, because Hume has not separated the conditions of moral worthiness from sentiments of our inclinations. According to Hume, it's possible to have our acts caused by our moral inclinations and sentiments, and on that account to be virtuous. In his answer to "What motive do I have for being moral?" he is an *internalist.* Our sentiments are the *standard* of moral judgments of virtue and vice, and *those same sentiments* are also the *motives* for being virtuous and vicious. Hume is an internalist about our motives in opposition to the two ways in which Kant is an externalist. First, our motives are internal to **487** our natural, sensible self; they are conditioned and heteronomous. Second, our motives are not external to our reasons for acting, because they are identical to the reasons; this is why the very citation of a reason for being moral also provides us with a motive. Let's apply Hume's internalist theory to Donald Louk's reflections about returning the $415,000 of unmarked bills that he found.

Reason. Should I return this $415,000 of unmarked bills? Yes. Why? Because this action will be an indication of your "internal character, passions, and affections" (*Enquiry,* p. 99). So? So it would indicate you have the virtuous trait of honesty, a trait that is virtuous because it is either immediately agreeable or useful to yourself and others, which is the reason for returning the money.

Motive. Ah, but what motive do I have for returning the $415,000 and for being virtuous? The act of returning the money is useful; it produces happiness and welfare for the owner who lost it. Yes, but what is the owner's happiness to me? You have an idea of his or her happiness; the operation of sympathy transforms this idea into an impression of yours; so you will feel happy when the owner feels happy; this feeling of yours is a motive for you—the motive for being virtuous. Yes, but I can't help thinking I'd be happier if I kept all the money rather than returning it; the sympathetic happiness obtainable by returning the money seems less than my self-love happiness if I kept it; consequently, you haven't given me a motive for returning the money. Yes, I have. I don't doubt that you have a self-love motive; nor do I doubt that it may be stronger than your sympathetic motive, and I also grant that its being stronger may motivate you to keep the money rather than return it. But that doesn't prove my internal theory wrong. All my theory had to do was show that there is a motive, and that the reason why something is virtuous and the motive for being virtuous are one and the same; this I have done. I have supplied a motive for returning the money; I didn't have to show that it would be the strongest. I recognize as well as you do that people aren't always virtuous. (See *Enquiry,* pp. 282–83.) Any theory that showed people always act virtuously would be wrong. Further, I have shown you that you have a *moral* motive. Remember that a sentiment or feeling response is a moral one only if it is disinterested or impartial—that is, if it is not a self-love motive. I've done this, too.(For the discussion of the theoretical points in Hume's ethics applied here, see 12.4c, pp. 436–38.)

One of the points made by Hume and others who claim that we have no free will, no motive autonomy, is that free will would be *destructive* of morality. In the light of Kant's argument to the contrary, this may surprise you. I will summarize two of Hume's arguments to support his view. Be careful to note, as Hume does (*Enquiry,* p. 96), that the arguments for or against free will's destructiveness to morals do not prove that we do or do not have free will. If we do have free will, so much the worse for Hume's ethics and his fears for morality. If we don't have it, so much the worse for Kant's ethics and *his* fears for morality.

488   Hume uncompromisingly states his view that necessity rather than free will supports morality:

> Nay I shall go farther, and assert, that this kind of necessity is so essential to religion and morality, that without it there must ensue an absolute subversion of both, and that every other supposition is entirely destructive to all laws both *divine* and *human.* (*Treatise,* p. 410)

The plausibility of both his arguments in support of this position depends on his view that liberty is "chance" and that chance doesn't exist; thus, free acts would come out of nothing. Being without causation, they would have no tie to any prior existence; they would be wholly capricious.

Hume's first argument supposes that rewards and punishments are an essential feature of moral and legal systems because they provide a motive for being moral and lawful. For example, legislation makes theft a felony and prescribes a penalty for anyone convicted of it. Rewards and punishments "have a regular and uniform influence on the mind, and both produce and prevent evil actions" (*Enquiry,* p. 98). Now if our acts were produced by free will rather than being caused, then rewards and punishments would be useless means of influencing behavior. However, they do influence behavior; the threat of going to jail deters some people from stealing. Consequently, the supposition that our acts are caused instead of occurring by "chance" supports morality. The judicious use of rewards and punishments enables us to motivate people to perform right acts and refrain from wrong ones. If acts were uncaused, free, we couldn't do this.

The second argument points out that we can't hold people responsible for their acts, if they don't have a "durable" nature that persists through time. The Snellcrook of today must be identical to the Snellcrook of yesterday and tomorrow. If Snellcrook doesn't persist through time, then the person who did Act_1 at $Time_1$ is not the same person who did Act_2 at $Time_2$; we would have two Snellcrooks, $Snellcrook_1$ and $Snellcrook_2$. In fact, if nothing of Snellcrook persists through time, there would be as many Snellcrooks as there are distinguishable times. Who then could be held responsible for an act? $Snellcrook_2$, if not identical to the earlier $Snellcrook_1$, shouldn't be held responsible for the latter's acts. Hume, however, believes that persons have a persisting, "durable" nature because causality binds an earlier ($Time_1$) "cause" aspect of a person to a later ($Time_2$) "effect" aspect. Persistence through time is supplied by the glue of causality. He remarks that

> 'tis impossible, without the necessary connexion of cause and effect in human actions, that punishments cou'd be inflicted compatible with justice and moral equity. . . . The action itself may be blameable; it may be contrary to all the rules of morality and religion: But the person is not responsible for it; and as it proceeded from nothing in him, that is durable or constant, and leaves nothing of that nature behind it, 'tis impossible he can, upon its account, become the object of punishment or vengeance. According to the hypothesis of liberty, therefore, a man is as pure and un-

tainted, after having committed the most horrid crimes, as at the first moment of his birth, nor is his character any way concern'd in his actions. (*Treatise,* p. 411; *Enquiry,* p. 98)

If we have free will, each action is wholly unconnected with anything durable; it is radically discontinuous with earlier and later acts. Thus Hume concludes that responsibility, instead of depending upon freedom, requires just its opposite—causal necessity.

We have now explored humans' relation to nature. Kant maintained that we are and must be autonomous—independent of natural conditions—if we are to be held responsible for our acts and attain worthiness. Our autonomy is possible because the cause of our moral-feeling motive for acting is external to sensible nature; practical reason lies outside nature; our moral motives are unconditioned by nature and are produced by our practical reason. Kant thought, as do others, that responsibility for an act lies with the cause of the act. If *we* don't *cause* acts, *we* aren't responsible; and *we* wouldn't cause acts, if we were caused to act by causes remote enough to be beyond our power. Hume maintained that we are heteronomous and must be, if we are to be held responsible for our acts. Our heteronomy lies in the fact that our motives for acting are internal to sensible nature: we are part of nature; our motives are feelings produced in us by the effects that natural events have on our nature. This makes it possible to influence persons by rewards and punishments.

13.4 The Relation Between Reason's and Nature's Laws: Toys in the Attic

This topic is one of the most difficult in all philosophical literature. The contrasting views of moral psychology and rational will ethics on this issue are probably more hotly contested than any others in the list of contrasts. The arguments on either side reach for premisses as wide-ranging as any in philosophy. Here we are dealing with metaphysical issues because we are dealing with metaphysical freedom, not political or personal freedom. The arguments reach into the depths of religion as well, although I will not go into that here.

Although the topic is difficult, it is also heady and exhilarating. The self-image you embrace is at stake. A scientific world view that pictures the whole of existence as a causally determined, interwoven web of strings of events seems to some to crunch humans between the jaws of a demeaning vise, pressing them ever tighter and squeezing the glory out of them. To those on the other side, the notion that humans should be free exceptions in such a universe is a softheaded, ridiculously fantasized holdover from primitive religion and myth—a view held seriously only by the abysmally ignorant;

490 human freedom would destroy this cherished scientific world view. Which is your self-image?

Should you become lost in the welter of metaphysics, consider the image (coming up on page 492) of Jenny and Jerry tugging on the teddy bear in the attic. You'll see what I mean.

We can be very brief in stating Hume's view on this topic because, by naturalizing humans, he commits himself to the view that all our behavior, including our moral behavior, takes place in accord with the natural law relation of cause and effect. There are not two distinct kinds of laws; hence, there is no problem about the relations between them.

Kant, on the other hand, thinks there are two distinct kinds of laws—moral and natural; so he has to tell us how they are related. Like Hume, Kant thinks that all our actions are caused. He too is opposed to the conception of free will as caprice; "chance" is "nothing." But Kant, unlike Hume, sees will as a causality—and a causality under law. Yet if will is causality in accord with laws, it is "the property of the will to be a law to itself. . . . Therefore a free will and a will under moral laws are identical" (*Foundations,* p. 329). Will (*Wille*) is a "law to itself" because (1) it can give itself moral laws and (2) it can cause a moral feeling in our sensible nature that can be the cause of an action. Natural laws, on the other hand, are not laws that we give to ourselves; they are given to us. None of us legislated the law of gravity.

As we have seen, Kant says we think of ourselves in a twofold manner, as a sensible object in nature and as a supersensible, intelligible being:

> That it [this double-natured being] must think of itself in this twofold manner rests, with regard to the first, on the consiousness of itself as an object affected through the senses, and, with regard to what is required by the second, on the consciousness of itself as intelligence, i.e., as independent from sensuous impressions in the use of reason and thus as belonging to the intelligible world. (*Foundations,* p. 336)

As sensible beings, we are subject to a series of cause-and-effect relations and are not free. But as intelligible beings, we have the "power of originating a series of events" and are "positively" free (*Pure Reason* [Smith], p. 476).

Let's return to Donald Louk's circumstances. His discovery of $415,000 in unmarked bills takes place in the sensible world. The sensible world's events and the sensible person's actions are strung out in a series of cause-and-effect relations, among which are causes that influence him to keep the money. If, then, we had sufficient knowledge of natural laws, we could predict that he will keep it. This act would be in accord with natural laws. Despite this, Kant claims that this person, recognizing a moral law, could return the money because his will produces respect for that moral law; this respect has causality. Let's call this a law of moral causality. So we have two actions—returning and not returning the money—that conflict; so also must the respective moral and natural laws of causality conflict. The two actions cannot be performed simultaneously by the same person; obviously,

then, both causes will not have produced their effects in accord with their 491
respective laws. One law or the other must be violated.

In spite of his whole previous course of life, the agent could have returned the money. Even though, in the world of sensible appearances, the
necessary and sufficient conditions that would cause the agent to keep the
money are present, reason's causality may cause him to return it. But if an
action that supposedly is necessitated by the prior events in a natural, causal
chain can be blocked by a cause of reason, then the natural causal series does
not necessitate the act of keeping the money, which contradicts the prior claim
that a natural causal series always *does* necessitate an act. This reasoning
leads us to a logical absurdity.

Kant appears to have a problem that needs solving, and he admits it:
"Our problem was this only: whether freedom and natural necessity can exist
without conflict in one and the same action" (*Pure Reason* [Smith], p. 478).
But he thinks he has a solution, thinks he can show that nature's and reason's
laws are *logically* compatible. The natural causal series is in time; causes
come *before* their effects. Reason, being supersensible, is not in time;
therefore, reason's causal influence isn't conditioned by any *prior* event in the
natural world. Consequently, it is free to start a *new* causal series. There
can be no conflict of a causality in time with one out of time; hence, the laws
of reason's freedom do not conflict with the laws of nature's necessity:

> Reason is present in all the actions of men at all times and under all cir-
> cumstances, and is always the same but it is not itself in time, and does not
> fall into any new state in which it was not before. (*Pure Reason* [Smith],
> p. 478)

Reason's effect, however—our moral feeling of respect for the moral
law—is indeed in time, and that is why it can be a cause of action in the natural
world. Reason causes a moral feeling in us; this feeling can be a cause of an
action, just as a feeling of sensible inclination can. Thus a person who contemplates keeping found money has two feeling incentives operating on him.
The two kinds of cause, reason and inclination, and the two kinds of law, rational and natural, produce two feelings. Kant thinks he has eliminated the
logical conflict between the two kinds of causes of feeling because one, inclination, is in time and the other, reason, is not. There is nothing *logically*
impossible about two kinds of causes of feeling; since they operate under different circumstances, they are compatible. But because the two kinds of
causes produce two different feelings, the conflict now shifts from the logical
relation between rational and natural laws—that is, between freedom and
necessity—to the relation between these two kinds of feelings.

What is the relation between these two feelings? They may conflict, but
not logically. Therefore, there can't be anything *logically* absurd in supposing we have supersensible freedom and sensible necessity.

The conflict relation between these two feelings is one of *opposition*.
We are familiar with this relation in ordinary life. Two children are fighting
over a toy in an attic; one pulls in one direction, the other in the opposite

492   direction. They are in conflict; but it isn't a logical conflict; it is an opposition of forces, both of which are real. When we have a logical relation of contradiction, we have two propositions, not both of which can be true; if they can't both be true, then the facts that the propositions represent can't both be real. Suppose I say, "The tower is round," and you say, "The tower is not round." Not both of these propositions may be true, nor can the tower in reality be both round and not round. But the two opposing forces may be as real as the two children.

Jerry is pulling the teddy bear one way; Jenny is pulling it in the opposite direction. They may pull with equal force. If Jerry is pulling with force A and Jenny with force B, and $A = B$, then $A - B = 0$; that is, subtracting one force from another equal force results in no movement of the teddy bear. But if one force is greater than the other, movement results:

> The principle that realities . . . never logically conflict with each other is an entirely true proposition . . . but has not the least meaning in regard either to nature or to anything in itself. For real conflict certainly does take place; there are cases where $A - B = 0$, that is, where two realities combined in one subject cancel one another's effects. This is brought before our eyes incessantly by all the hindering and counteracting processes in nature, which, as depending on forces, must be called *realitates phaenomena* [real phenomena]. (*Pure Reason* [Smith], p. 284)

How does this point about "real conflict" and its difference from "logical conflict" apply to Kant's effort to reconcile natural and rational laws?

First, the statement that there is a law of natural, necessary causality and also a law of reason's free causality is not logically incoherent, because natural causality is in time and reason's causality is not. If God existed before the world did, and so existed outside of world time, the world couldn't inhibit God's creation choices.

Second, nature and reason's causality each produce their feeling effects. Reason's causality produces moral feeling, and natural causality produces "pathological" feeling. Both of these feelings are real forces in the sensible world; sometimes they pull us in opposite directions, sometimes not. These feelings, in short, may be in opposition; when they are, we typically say that we are in a "quandary" or that we are "tempted."

When opposing forces meet in the teddy bear, they may "cancel one another's effects." The event resulting from the operation of opposing forces on teddy bears and other things depends on the relative strengths of the forces; if Jenny is stronger than Jerry, the bear moves in her direction. Does Kant think it's this way in man's soul, too? Do moral and pathological feelings struggle for supremacy as Jenny and Jerry do?

Kant thinks that we have a radically free power, *Willkür,* by which we *choose* between these two feeling forces. *We* choose to "subordinate" one to the other; they don't fight it out. This is the other part of Kant's theory of will and freedom.

Kant thinks there is no person so evil that he or she will wholly repudiate

the moral law. Because no one does, each of us has a moral feeling of respect   **493**
when we recognize that a universalized maxim is a moral law. And because
the occasion for thinking up a maxim occurs only when there is some end that
we want, we also have a pathological feeling of desire for what we want. A
good person will subordinate the pathological to the moral feeling when they
are in opposition, whereas an evil person will subordinate the moral to the
pathological feeling (*Religion,* p. 31). Choosing the pathological over the opposing moral incentive is a deviation from the moral law; that is when we are
evil.

How are we to understand this power of choice between feelings, this
Willkür? It is "inscrutable," Kant tells us on several occasions. Furthermore, it is *necessarily* inscrutable; if it were scrutable—that is,
knowable—then it would be a capacity in the sensible, natural world open to
scientific investigation. But it cannot be a natural capacity, for nothing in
nature is free in this radical sense; therefore, we cannot know it. Since Kant
locates our radical freedom in this capacity of choice, freedom is not
something that can be intellectually comprehended by us.

Kant views responsibility as something belonging to a person; the
essence of our moral personhood is our *Willkür* capacity, our free choice
capacity; that *is* us. If we lacked this capacity, we wouldn't be persons, only
animals. This is the bottom line for Kant:

> Man *himself* must make or have made himself into whatever in a moral
> sense, whether good or evil, he is or is to become. Either condition must
> be an effect of his free choice[w][*Willkür*]; for otherwise he could not be held
> responsible for it and could therefore be *morally* neither good nor evil.
> (*Religion,* p. 40)

To summarize: Hume does not have to say what the relations between
natural and rational laws are, because all laws are natural laws. Kant thinks
there are two kinds of law—natural laws of causality and reason's law of
causality; they are logically compatible with each other. But each kind of
causality produces its own kind of feeling—pathological and moral feeling,
respectively—and these can be opposed. When they are, our inscrutable
Willkür capacity freely chooses between them. It is logically absurd to think
we can explain this free choice because, if we could, there would be natural
causes of this choice, in which case the choice wouldn't be free. (See
Religion, n., pp. 17–18.)

13.5 Punishment

Everyone seems to agree that in punishing we inflict pain on someone or
deprive them of their liberty or life; at least, that is the intent of those who
punish, although an abnormal or perverse personality may take pleasure in experiencing pain, in being imprisoned, or even in being executed.

494   Although punishment involves harming another, harming another in itself is not punishment; therefore, the two can't be equated. A person innocent of wrongdoing may be caused pain or killed, but since he or she didn't merit either, the person is not being punished. Harm to a person has to be linked to wrongdoing if it is to be correctly described as punishment.

Setting masochists aside, we can say that to inflict pain or to kill is to diminish someone's happiness. Normally, to do this is wrong by any theory of ethics, whether advanced by moral psychologists or rational will moralists. So what makes harming another for punishment right? What justifies diminishing the happiness of someone who has commited a crime? What gives public officials the right to curtail the liberty of criminals by imprisoning them?

One reason given is that punishment of persons who have committed a crime *deters* those who might otherwise do the same. Another reason is that imprisoning or executing a criminal *protects* others from further crimes the person might commit. So the question shifts to this: what right does the state have to punish criminals in order to deter others or protect them? One answer might be that the state has a right, even a duty, to do whatever will increase the happiness of the citizens. Deterring crimes against citizens and protecting them from criminals is a means of increasing the citizens' happiness; this happiness outweighs the criminals' unhappiness caused by their punishment. Thus the state has a right to punish because the act is right; it is right because it promotes the greater happiness.

You can see that this is a utilitarian justification, because a utilitarian theory of right acts says that an act is *right* if, on balance, it produces *as much* good as any other possible act, which would include the omissive act of not punishing criminals. Such theory also says that an act is our *duty* if, on balance, it produces *more* good than any other act open to the agent.

This utilitarian justification has been challenged. Kant challenges it because he thinks that the utilitarian ground for punishment ignores its central feature, which is that the criminal deserves it; punishing a person who deserves it insures that justice is done: "In every punishment as such there must first be justice, and this constitutes the essence of the concept" (*Practical Reason* [Beck], p. 39).

Punishing an *innocent* person could deter others and so have a utilitarian justification. But justice would not have been done; the state would have violated the second form of the Categorical Imperative, which says that we should never treat another as a means only, but always as an end; to treat the innocent as a means only to others' good reduces persons to the status of objects and thereby robs them of their dignity:

> Judicial punishment can never be used as a means to promote some other good for the criminal himself or for civil society, but instead it must in all cases be imposed on him only on the ground that he has committed a crime; for a human being can never be manipulated merely as a means to the purposes of someone else and can never be confused with the objects of the Law of things. . . . He must first be found to be deserving of punish-

ment before any consideration is given to the utility of this punishment for himself or for his fellow citizens. The law concerning punishment is a categorical imperative, and woe to him who rummages around in the winding paths of a theory of happiness looking for some advantage to be gained by releasing the criminal from punishment or by reducing the amount of it.[10]

A second argument against the utilitarian justification of punishment—or, as it has at times been called (somewhat inaccurately), the "deterrence" theory—is given by Kant at the end of the preceding quotation. A utilitarian might find that more good could be produced by not punishing the criminal; this too would thwart justice, because the criminal would not get the punishment deserved. Kant gives an example. Suppose that a criminal condemned to death consented to have dangerous and painful medical experiments performed on him, which if successful would produce knowledge of enormous benefit to others; and suppose that the court induced the criminal to undergo the experiments by agreeing to give him his freedom, should he survive. If he does survive and goes unpunished, justice will have been thwarted: "Any court of justice would repudiate such a proposal with scorn if it were suggested by a medical college, for justice ceases to be justice if it can be bought for a price" (*Justice*, p. 101).

A third argument against the utilitarian justification of punishment was made by Karl Marx. He thinks this justification is wrong because punishment doesn't accomplish its end of deterring or protecting citizens; consequently, they don't receive benefits from it. In the following passage Marx makes this argument and at the same time states what he thinks is the proper ground for justifying punishment:

Punishment in general has been defended as a means either of ameliorating or of intimidating. Now what right have you to punish me for the amelioration or intimidation of others? And besides there is history—there is such a thing as statistics—which prove with the most complete evidence that since Cain the world has been neither intimidated nor ameliorated by punishment. Quite the contrary. From the point of view of abstract right, there is only one theory of punishment which recognizes human dignity in the abstract, and that is the theory of Kant, especially in the more rigid formula given to it by Hegel. Hegel says: "Punishment is the *right* of the criminal. It is an act of his own will. The violation of right has been proclaimed by the criminal as his own right. His crime is the negation of right. Punishment is the negation of this negation, and consequently an affirmation of right, solicited and forced upon the criminal by himself."[11]

Hegel has almost captured Kant's justification for the use of force by the state, which would include using force on criminals to punish them. Hegel's central statement is, "Punishment is the negation of this negation." This requires explanation.

Kant says that freedom is the only "innate" right that humans have.

496 He connects this claim to his Categorical Imperative, which limits right acts to those that can be universally performed without inhibiting the freedom of others:

> Freedom (independence from the constraint of another's will), insofar as it is compatible with the freedom of everyone else in accordance with a universal law, is the one sole and original right that belongs to every human being by virtue of his humanity. (*Justice,* pp. 43–44)

A person who commits a crime constrains the freedom of another. This is wrong. If the threat of punishment deters, or imprisonment prevents, the constraint of another's freedom, then this is a constraint on a constraint or, to put it in Hegel's own words, a negation of a negation. A crime negates someone's freedom, and punishment negates the criminal negation of freedom. Two negatives make a positive; therefore, the negation of a negation of a right is right. That is, the punishment of crime is right.

The Kantian (and Hegelian) justification of punishment is based on human rights. Punishment is right, not because it deters crime and thus prevents the reduction of happiness, but because it deters crime and thus protects people's rights, including, according to Hegel, the criminal's rights. According to Kant, the state may coerce by punishment because this hinders a criminal's constraint of other persons' freedom. (You can see why I said that the utilitarian justification of justice is somewhat inaccurately called a deterrent theory. A "rights" justification of punishment also recognizes that punishment is a deterrent—it deters the violation of people's rights; consequently, "deterrent" isn't a useful term for distinguishing between a utilitarian and a rights justification of punishment.)

This orientation toward the protection of rights shows why it is unjust to "punish" innocent persons, even though doing so might result in greater happiness than not punishing them would: the innocent's right to freedom would be violated.

J. P. Day, a contemporary philosopher, provides another argument for a rights theory of justice, which he attributes to Hegel. If the state doesn't punish an offender—say, someone who steals another's car—then the state hasn't annulled the crime but in effect has condoned it. This is unjust to the person who was robbed, because the state has now treated this victim as if he or she had no more right to the car than the robber, even though the owner acquired it by honest toil and the robber didn't. If two persons are morally unalike, then they shouldn't be treated alike; to treat them alike is unjust.[12]

Here now is a glaring example of injustice done by unequally punishing people who are equally guilty. According to the article, the execution of Private Eddie Slovik was "to serve as an example." This was a utilitarian ground for executing him; presumably, it would encourage deserters to return to the army.

> Antoinette Slovik has emphysema, breast cancer, heart trouble, vitamin deficiencies and limbs that are withering from inactivity. But she has no

desire to quit in her quest for the Army insurance benefits denied to her as the widow of Private Eddie Slovik, the only American serviceman executed for desertion since the Civil War. . . .

Slovik was shot by a firing squad in France in 1945 to serve as an example for the 21,049 GIs listed as deserters during the war. But after he was killed, the Army decided to keep it secret. Mrs. Slovik did not learn of her husband's fate until eight years later.

A long campaign to clear his name and collect on his GI insurance led to a book and a television movie on Slovik, but his widow earned no royalties.*[13]

Day cites another rights justification for punishment, this one provided by W. D. Ross. Retributive punishment may involve redress: the thief may be forced to return what he has stolen (restitution) or to give something of equal value to the person robbed (compensation). The state has a tacit agreement with its citizens to enforce redress when they are wronged. A state's failure to punish by not forcing redress violates its agreement with its citizens, and this wrongs the victim. The only way the state can protect the promised right of redress is to force offenders to redress their wrong, which is to punish the offender.

So far in this discussion, I have concentrated on two theories about the justification of punishment, the utilitarian and the rights theories. The utilitarian theory is consistent with moral psychology, which makes good the chief moral concept and derives rights and duties of acts from their utility for producing goods. The rights theory is consistent with a rational will ethics such as Kant's, which makes right and duty the chief moral concepts. (See section 11.9.)

Assuming that punishment has one justification or another, what is the proper punishment for an offense? Here we reach the concept of retribution, which is popularly expressed as "an eye for an eye and a tooth for a tooth"—and a life for a life. People sometimes use "retribution" to signify a motive akin to vengeance or retaliation. "Retribution," however, is not properly the name for a theory to justify punishment, but rather the name for a theory of how much and what kind of punishment should be meted out. Kant holds a retributive theory of amount and kind of punishment that I will simply call a "retributive" theory; bear in mind that this is not the name for his justification theory.

> What kind and what degree of punishment does public legal justice adopt as its principle and standard? None other than the principle of equality (illustrated by the pointer on the scales of justice), that is, the principle of not treating one side more favorably than the other. . . .Only the Law of retribution (*jus talionis*) can determine exactly the kind and degree of punishment; it must be well understood, however, that this determination must be made in the chambers of a court of justice (and not in your private judgment). (*Justice,* p. 101)

---

* Mrs. Slovik died in September 1979, her campaign still unsuccessful.

498
    According to the "Law of retribution," a murderer must die: "there is no substitute that will satisfy the requirements of legal justice" (*Justice,* p. 102). This is harsh. Day remarks that the "stock objection to it [retributive theory] is that it cannot be morally justified, because two evils do not make a good" (p. 502). Day's definition of retribution shows that this objection, as he says, is simplistic.

    Day points out that the definition of retribution is a different issue from its justification. I use Day's definition of "retribution" here, altering only the terms he uses to identify the parties referred to in it. Day points out that "to retribute" means "to give back":

> So the basic formula is "B gives back an X to A in return for the X which A gave to B." Retribution is therefore a reciprocal interpersonal transaction. (Day, p. 500)

A person could "give back" either the same thing ("restitution") or something equivalent ("compensation"). Retribution and compensation are types of the more general relation of reciprocation. If I gave you a precious gem, you would make restitution if you gave me back the same gem; or compensation if you gave me money equal to the value of the gem; in private relations compensation is gratitude, and in commercial relations it is exchange. Here we have reciprocation where each gives something to someone else, either the same or an equivalent thing.

    When we are dealing with an offense, however, we have an instance when somebody *took* something from someone else. Here the basic idea is that someone should give back something. Further, the giving back may have to be imposed by an authority. The judge orders the car thief to give back the car; when this happens, the ordered and enforced giving back is retributive punishment. When the judge orders a person to give $100,000 to someone whose sight he has destroyed, the judge is ordering compensatory punishment.

    Day points out the difference between retaliation on one hand and restitution and recompense on the other. To retaliate, we return evil for evil, as to take an eye for an eye. To restore and recompense, we return good for good. These two together constitute the definition of "retributive punishment":

(1) The state makes the offender *give back a good,* the same or equivalent, to the victim, in return for the good which the offender intentionally made the victim (perhaps at gunpoint) give to the offender.
(2) The state thereby *gives back an evil* to the offender (the deprivation of what was taken) in return for the evil (the deprivation of a possession) which the offender intentionally imposed on the victim.

In short, the state imposes two returns in retributive punishment: (1) it makes the offender return good for good taken, and (2) it returns evil to the offender for the evil visited on the victim.

The "stock objection" against retributive judgment is simplistic, says Day, because it identifies retribution with only the second part of the definition, returning evil for evil; if we also include returning good for good, the "vengeance" odor that clings to retributive punishment vanishes. This vengeance charge looks like a plausible condemnation of retribution, because it ignores the good restored to the victim and concentrates on the evil imposed on the offender.

The proper kind and degree of retribution, Kant says, is based on the equality of the punishment and the crime. While he points out that it isn't always obvious what constitutes equality, he raises an even more interesting question about the equality of punishment and then recommends some rather harsh treatment:

> But how can this principle [of the equality of crime and its punishment] be applied to punishments that do not allow reciprocation because they are either impossible in themselves or would themselves be punishable crimes against humanity in general? Rape, pederasty [homosexuality, especially with young boys], and bestiality [intercourse with animals] are examples of the latter. For rape and pederasty, [the punishment is] castration (after the manner of either a white or a black eunuch in the sultan's seraglio [harem]), and for bestiality the punishment is expulsion forever from civil society since the criminal guilty of bestiality is unworthy of remaining in human society. (*Justice*, p. 132)

Let's shift our attention from the victim and from "honest" citizens to the offender—one guilty of either a civil or a criminal offense, either case being covered by the discussion that follows. It has often been objected that punishing the offender may be cruel because the conditions of his or her life have been so miserable that the moral personality has been destroyed. What such a person needs is not punishment but therapy; instead of being put in prison, the offender should be placed in a mental health institution for rehabilitation and reform. Further, the person needs education and training to acquire the self-respect of gainful employment. Kant, however, allows no excuses; he thinks that this isn't the way an offender should be treated, because a person is always free to refrain from crime despite the most horrible prior life. Yet even he recognizes that humans do not always do what is right because they are weak, unable to overcome immense and unfair disadvantages. Isn't there some limit, then, beyond which we cannot ask for or expect a firm resolve to refrain from a crime?

500   Jeffrie Murphy, from whose article Marx's quotation on punishment was taken, agrees that a rights justification of punishment is the correct theory; but he argues that this theory of punishment is inapplicable, because present human circumstances in a capitalist or class society make the "rational," free, individual will choices required by Kant practically impossible. The concluding part of Murphy's quotation from Marx expresses this view:

> Is it not a delusion to substitute for the individual with his real motives, with multifarious [many and varied] social circumstances pressing upon him, the abstraction of "free will"—one among the many qualities of man for man himself? . . . Is there not a necessity for deeply reflecting upon an alteration of the system that breeds these crimes, instead of glorifying the hangman who executes a lot of criminals to make room only for the supply of new ones? (Murphy, p. 218)

Murphy gives a contemporary example of the "multifarious social circumstances" pressing upon an offender or potential offender:

> Consider one example: a man has been convicted of armed robbery. On investigation, we learn that he is an impoverished black whose whole life has been one of frustrating alienation from the prevailing socio-economic structure—no job, no transportation if he could get a job, substandard education for his children, terrible housing and inadequate health care for his whole family, condescending-tardy-inadequate welfare payments, harassment by the police but no real protection by them against the dangers in his community, and near total exclusion from the political process. Learning all this, would we still want to talk—as many do—of his suffering punishment under the rubric of "paying a debt to society"? Surely not. Debt for what? I do not, of course, pretend that all criminals can be so described. But I do think that this is a closer picture of the typical criminal than the picture presupposed in the retributive theory—i.e., the picture of an evil person who, of his own free will, intentionally acts against those just rules of society which he knows, as a rational man, benefit everyone including himself. (Murphy, p. 242)

Concern for the offender is felt and advocated as proper because it is more "humane" than retributive punishment. This concern can be taken in at least two directions. One way is to alter the social relations; another is to provide therapy that will change the offender's personality and/or character so as to produce an "honest, law abiding citizen." But evil may lurk in this "humane" approach.

In Anthony Burgess's novel *A Clockwork Orange,* the hero-antihero Alex and his pals or "droogies" like to beat up drunken old men, torture and rape women, steal and kill. Yet for all this, Alex enjoys some of the finer things such as the music of Beethoven, Handel and Mozart. Alex is caught and put in prison, where he gets into still more trouble. He becomes the subject of a new government policy that deals with criminals by re-conditioning them; as a government official says, "Common criminals like this unsavoury crowd . . . can best be dealt with on a purely curative basis. Kill the criminal reflex, that's all. Full implementation in a year's time."[14]

Alex is tied into a bed, his eyes are fastened open, and he lies facing a screen on which movies of violence are shown: old women having their legs broken, Nazis shooting helpless people, Japanese soldiers laughing while they set fire to captured men. Alex has been given a drug injection that makes him vomit and get painfully sick while he's watching the films. He comes to associate violence with discomfort; this will make him ill when he thinks of or starts doing violence, causing him to avoid it. This aversive conditioning is to cure him of his "criminal reflex."

A hitch develops. Some of the films have music sound tracks by his favorite composers; naturally, because of his re-conditioning, hearing them again later makes him ill. Likewise with sex—even the thought of it makes him ill. The doctor allows that "delimitation" of the re-conditioning process is "always difficult." Alex's re-conditioning, while it has cured him of his criminal tendencies, has also robbed him of some normal, worthwhile goods.

It could be argued that aversive conditioning which destroys or drastically alters a personality is crueler than imprisonment. Although Alex consented to the re-conditioning, he didn't know what the side effects would be. It would be even crueler, were such "curative" re-conditioning given by a court order and contrary to or regardless of the offender's wishes. Who can forget what electric shock treatment did to Murphy in Ken Kesey's novel *One Flew over the Cuckoo's Nest*—shock treatment administered in the name of therapeutic control?

After going through a lot of re-conditioning, Alex begins to experience all the marginal effects. He begs them to stop the process, insisting that he's cured: "But, sir, sirs, I *see* that it's wrong . . . it's wrong because every veck on earth has the right to live and be happy without being beaten and tol-chocked and knifed." But Dr. Brodsky isn't impressed. This is too Kantian an appeal for him:

> "The heresy of an age of reason," or some such slovos [words]. "I see what is right and approve, but I do what is wrong. No, no, my boy, you must leave it all to us. But be cheerful about it. It will soon be all over. In less than a fortnight now you'll be a free man." Then he patted me on the pletcho [shoulder]. (*Clockwork,* p. 116)

Brodsky puts it to Alex as Alex saw it at first: by being decriminalized, he can get out of jail and be "a free man." However, in acquiring an altered personality, he may have become unfree in another sense of "free": he may have lost his freedom of choice to be evil. The price of being free of prison may be an imprisoned choice.

After Alex is let out of prison, he is beaten by his "droogies"—former pals in crime who are now policemen. He drags himself to a house for help. It happens that the house is owned by the man whose wife was killed there in one of Alex's earlier criminal escapades; the man, F. Alexander, is the author of *A Clockwork Orange*. Not recognizing Alex at first, he comforts him and

502 plans to use him as an example of the government's cruel re-conditioning policy. Summoning politicians who are rivals of the government in power, he tells them about Alex and how they can use him for their political purposes. F. Alexander also talks to Alex:

> "You've sinned, I suppose, but your punishment has been out of all proportion. They have turned you into something other than a human being. You have no power of choice any longer. You are committed to socially acceptable acts, a little machine capable only of good. And I see that clearly—that business about the marginal conditionings. Music and the sexual act, literature and art, all must be a source now not of pleasure but of pain."
>
> "That's right, sir," I said, smoking one of this kind man's cork-tipped cancers.
>
> "They always bite off too much," he said, drying a plate like absent-mindedly. "But the essential intention is the real sin. A man who cannot choose ceases to be a man." (p. 156)

F. Alexander believes that a government which replaces imprisonment with aversive conditioning may free people from prison punishment, but at the price of erasing their freedom of choice about at least some matters. The loss of freedom of choice is a harm far greater than the harm caused by the crime and thus violates the principle of retribution. In fact, may not the "cure" *be* punishment? F. Alexander thinks the re-conditioning has taken Alex's humanity from him; this may be a form of execution.

Further, imagine a case where the offender doesn't think that what she did was wrong or believe that her act is a manifestation of mental disease, and because of this rejects therapy. Even if she thinks she is unjustly deprived of her liberty when sent to jail, she may prefer that to mind-altering drugs or re-conditioning. Can't we choose to be what we want, even if we choose to be evil?[15]

Jeffrie Murphy points out that

> the therapeutic state, where prisons are called hospitals and jailers are called psychiatrists, simply raises again all the old problems about the justification of coercion and its reconciliation with autonomy that we faced in worrying about punishment. (Murphy, p. 243)

He suggests a second, better way of showing concern for the offender—not by providing therapy for the individual, but by altering the social relations that alienated the offender in the first place. Therapy simply helps the offender adapt to a given society. If that society itself is unjust, therapy doesn't seem morally justifiable. The only long-term moral way of dealing with offenders—who may be all of us—is by changing the society.

However, you might argue, the "revolution" may be a long way off; while you agree that true moral concern for us offenders calls for altering society, we have to deal with the "meantime." We have to punish in order to protect the rights of the "innocent." While retributive punishment may in- **503** volve some injustice to the offender in a class society, failure of the state to coerce retribution to the victim would be even more unjust; therefore, we have to continue punishing, and for the proper reason, which is to protect others' rights.

I have now distinguished two theories for justifying punishment: the utilitarian theory of moral psychology, the rights theory of rational will ethics. Both recognize the deterrence and protection that punishment provides. Objections can be raised to the utilitarian theory of justification: (1) it is wrong to punish the innocent even if it has utility; (2) a guilty person should be punished, even if not doing so has more utility; and (3) punishment fails to achieve the ends of deterrence and protection. One objection to the rights theory is that it ignores the overwhelming social odds against the offender's ability to will the moral act; another argument cuts against punishment itself, whether justified by utility or the protection of rights, by claiming that therapy and rehabilitation are the proper moral treatments and should replace punishment. The term "retribution" is properly applied to a theory of the appropriate nature and degree of punishment; Kant thought the standard should be equality.

STUDY QUESTIONS

1 What are imperatives? And what are the differences between categorical and hypothetical imperatives? Relate your answers to the difference between being prudent about your happiness and being morally worthy.

2 Why does Hume think imperatives, moral rules, and standards can be "grounded"—shown to be valid—by facts? Why does Kant think they can't be?

3 Explain the difference between autonomous and heteronomous creatures. Why does Kant, like many other thinkers, believe that there can be no moral responsibility if we aren't autonomous? Why does Hume think there is no moral responsibility if we aren't heteronomous? Remember Trevor X, Highman, Lowman, and Snellcrook.

4 Relate the autonomy/heteronomy contrast to Hume's naturalization of willing.

5 Because the word "why" in the question "Why should I be moral?" has two meanings, this sentence can be interpreted as asking two different things. What are they? Two different theories—externalism and internalism—deal with the relations between the foregoing two "why" questions and their answers. Explain externalism and internalism. Why does Kant hold the first and Hume the second?

6 Why does Kant think moral and natural laws are not logically incompatible?

7 Kant thinks moral and pathological motives (inclinations) may be opposed to each other. When they are, do they fight for supremacy like Jenny and Jerry do over the teddy bear in the attic? If not, how is the opposition—the opposing forces—resolved, according to Kant?

8 State the difference between a utilitarian and a rights justification of punishment. That is, what two kinds of reasons can be given to support the view that the state has a right to punish?

9 What are the differences between punishment as a deterrent, as a protection, and as a retribution? Why isn't retribution the same as retaliation?

10 Why could someone argue that therapy for the offender is punishment and may exceed the offense?

 ## Reflections on Applications

1 Convicted murderer John Louis Evans III was awaiting execution in Alabama's electric chair when he made the following remarks:

> "I was a rotten kid," said Evans. "It had nothing to do with my family. I would pull stuff just to see if I could get away with it. And then when I'd get away with it, I'd just feel so good for days. And then I'd just have to go out and do something a little bit bigger. . . . I knew where I was headed." . . .
>
> Evans said he has known love and has a woman friend who is "not discussable." But he said he rejected love because it would interfere with his criminal habits, just as he rejected his white, Roman Catholic, middle class home life.
>
> "I knew me too good," he said. "You hurt the people you love. When it comes down to it, I'm a pretty selfish person. . . ."
>
> "It's been a wasted life, sure," he said. "But I'm not down on myself, I'm just a realist. I was a rotten kid, I knew I was a rotten kid, I liked being a rotten kid. . . . I was going down society's wrong road and I didn't care."[16]

Do you think that Evans's remarks, if they accurately reflect his thoughts and feelings, refute central theses of both Hume and Kant? Hume claimed that the standards of morals are agreeableness or usefulness of character traits to ourselves and others. But Evans tells us that when he did something wrong and got away with it, he'd "just feel so good for days." He apparently found the character traits that made him "a rotten kid" agreeable or useful. Hume believed his standards are based on observed facts, but Evans seems to assert a fact that doesn't fit Hume's claims.

Kant claimed that everyone is conscious of the moral law and that our "boundless esteem for the pure moral law, removed from all advantage, as practical reason presents it to us for obedience," has a voice that "makes even the boldest sinner tremble and forces him to hide himself from it" (*Practical Reason* [Beck], p. 82). But Evans tells us that he knew he was a "rotten kid" and "liked being a rotten kid," evidently neither trembling nor hiding from the moral law.

Does either Hume or Kant have a reply that shows Evans's remarks don't refute their central theses?

2 People disagree about whether one should "legislate morality," which is to pass laws prohibiting conduct that some people think is wrong and that others think is their "own business" and not the government's. Prohibition against the sale of alcoholic beverages was tried in the United States and is now the law in India. Laws have been passed against prostitution, homosexuality, oral intercourse, and sodomy. Passing laws against such forms of behavior is legislating imperatives which say that legally you ought not to behave in those ways. Hume thought that imperatives can be grounded in facts about humans' responses. Consider the following statements by journalist Charles McCabe; then say if you think that they give Humean reasons why it is useless and invalid to "legislate morality":

> This thing of regulating people's conviviality by law has had a sorry history. There is nothing to indicate that India's essay into the noble experiment of prohibition will fare any better than ours did in the '20s. Of this Ring Lardner could write in 1925:
> ". . . the law went into effect about the 29 of Jan. 1920 and the night before everybody had a big binge. As these wds. is written the party is just beginning to get good."
> Laws against things that make people feel good are practically a contradiction in terms. They are written on water. Whether they are directed against whoring, or sodomy, or strong drink or what somebody or other decrees is bad taste, they have their failure written into them.[17]

3 Robin Smyth of the *London Observer* reported on a debate on French television by a politician, three prostitutes, a priest, and a policeman, the subject of which was the politician's proposed legislation to have France's brothels reopened. The politician was Joel Le Tac, a French Deputy from the Montmartre and Pigalle section of Paris, which contains a celebrated red-light district. Smyth pointed out that this is one of the world's oldest arguments about legislating morality:

> Should a man be free to pay for sex and a woman free to walk the streets offering it? Does society have a duty, or even a right, to clear its cities of the public spectacle of prostitution? Should a streetwalker be protected from the pimp who takes her money? Or should both be free from the harassment of the law that forbids him to live off her earnings? And is a prostitute ever free? or is she, as Père Talvas insisted, a victim of society, forced into a way of life where the chances of escape dwindle frighteningly as time goes by?

The question before the debaters was not whether there should be legal prostitution, but whether it ought to be confined to brothels and taken off the streets. Le Tac was supporting the German system, where prostitution is confined to "Eros Centers."

Kant thought there were categorical and hypothetical imperatives, but that only the former were moral imperatives, the latter being prudential counsels. Hume, on the other hand, thought all imperatives, including moral ones, were hypothetical. Do you think an imperative confining or not confining prostitution to brothels is hypothetical or categorical? Read the following arguments given by persons on both sides of the debate, before you make up your mind.

For

Le Tac did not think that brothels were oppressing prostitutes. In German Eros Centers the women rent a room as if it were a private apartment, have control of their own money, and are free to come and go as they please. One of the disciplines to which they are subjected is constant surveillance.

Doris, one of the prostitutes, had lived in an Eros Center. She said, "I was completely free. I could sleep late or work or not as I liked. There is a canteen and a kitchen on every floor. If you want drinks in your room you just lift the phone. You pay the rent of the room, bathroom and telephone included, each day. You have your own safe and can go to the bank when you like. There is no one to ask how much you earn and then demand their cut. . . . There are alarm bells everywhere around the room and if a client turns nasty he's seized before he can lay a finger on you."

Against

Clara, another prostitute said she had worked in a brothel. "It was impossible to choose one's clients. It was all too horrible. I am against that kind of slavery. . . . I work alone and for myself. I have won my liberty. We prostitutes don't have the right to a love life of our own, do we Monsieur le Commissaire [of the police]? We can't take a little fancy to a man without him being arrested. Are we animals, Monsieur le Commissaire?"

Manouchka, the third prostitute, agreed with Clara. "I won't tolerate that sort of life [in a brothel]. It's the street for me. Because there I can be free. I can do exactly as I like. . . . There's no question of compulsory housework or organized visits to the hairdresser."

The priest, Père Talvas, who runs a mission aiding streetwalkers, had this to say: "Have those who want these brothels asked themselves who is going to be put inside them? Are they objects or human beings? Where do these women come from? Most of them are people who have had no luck in their past lives. They have been victims of housing and work conditions. [To Le Tac] I don't think that it is your daughters, Monsieur, whom you propose to shut up in these houses? No, it is

young women who have had a bad start. . . . What you propose is contrary to human dignity and the rights of man. But we live in a world
of pornography where everything is for sale. Personal integrity doesn't
interest you, does it? Your viewpoint is exclusively commercial."[18]

4 The following two viewpoints differ about the imperatives, both
hypothetical and categorical, against taking a life. With which do you
agree?

George Will, the columnist, discussed the moral issue involved in
surgery separating Siamese twins. One had a complete heart; the other
did not. Surgery would involve the death of the twin with the incomplete heart. Should the operation be performed? Surgery was performed. One twin lived and the other died. The lawyers argued that
"no crime occurs if an act is done under a court order issued because
the good anticipated outweighs the bad."

> Now, what I am about to cite, from Dennis Bloodworth's *The China
> Looking Glass,* is ghastly, but germane:
> "Somerset Maugham tells us . . . . how he came upon a little
> tower on a Chinese hillside with a single small hole in its wall, from
> which came a nauseating odor. This was the baby tower, and it
> covered a deep charnel pit into which parents threw their unwanted
> children through the aperture. . . . "
> This passage refers to China during a period of hideous
> privation. The point is not that it is in "the nature" of any people to
> treat life casually. On the contrary, the point is that the value placed
> on life is to some extent contingent, socially rooted, changeable.[19]

The second viewpoint is that of Michael Prokes. Prokes had been
a spokesperson for the Reverend Jim Jones, the leader of the People's
Temple who induced 900 of his followers to commit suicide in
Jonestown, Guyana, in 1978. Prokes shot himself after holding a press
conference:

> [San Francisco] *Chronicle* columnist Herb Caen, after the Jonestown
> tragedy, recalled a discussion with Prokes that led him to believe that
> Prokes was "perfectly capable of killing himself for Jim Jones."
> Caen cited a letter from last summer in which Prokes wrote, "We
> have found something to die for, and it's called social justice. We at
> least will have had the satisfaction of living that principle, not because it
> promised success or reward, but simply because we felt it was the right
> thing to do."[20]

5 One of my ethics students, Paul Denegri, argued for the categorical
right to life as follows. Do you agree with him? If you don't, it is
either because you think there is a right to abortion, hypothetical or
categorical, or because you think the right to life is categorical for a
different reason. Which is it, in case you disagree?

Prudence is not synonymous with morality. The teleological approach ought not be utilized when a particular moral issue that is seen as a means to some *other* end is at stake; it is the universal implication of the act itself, and not some further goal, upon which the morality of an act hinges. . . . Consequently, any arguments which defend abortion by pointing to ends, however attractive, that are achieved by abortion, are inappropriate. This applies especially to the economic and social reasons often cited to justify abortion. The fact that legal abortions cut back on population growth, help the economy through reduced welfare payments, and cause fewer children to grow up "unwanted" and in adverse circumstances, cannot be used to defend the morality of abortion. . . . An analogy might make this point clearer. In a hideous way, the Nazi death camps also accomplished some of the above-mentioned goals. For example, they reduced the population of Europe, with all the benefits that (so sociologists tell us) reduced population brings.

The simple question upon which the morality of abortion hinges, and to which, until it is answered, no external teleological ends can be added for consideration, is whether or not the fetus is a human being. . . . Only when it has been decided that the fetus is not a human being, that it is a neutral hunk of matter, can teleological and prudential arguments be raised to discuss what advantages result from abortion. But if the fetus is a human being, then abortion is morally wrong.[21]

6 "The duty of business is to make a profit." Is this a categorical or hypothetical imperative? Give your reasons.

7 We learned from philosopher J. P. Day to distinguish between retaliation and retribution, because the latter involves returning both a good to the victim and an evil to the offender (pp. 498–99). According to him, those who think retributive punishment inhumane because it tries to make a right out of two wrongs are simplistic; retribution is not simply retaliation, the returning of evil for evil, but also the returning of good.

Do you agree or not, and for what reasons, with the following argument against capital punishment, based on Day's distinction between retaliation and retribution?

Offender murders Victim. Victim, being dead, cannot have a good returned to him or her. If Offender is executed for murdering Victim, then the state gives back an evil to Offender in return for the evil done to Victim. In this exchange, only evil is retuned; no good can be returned. This fits the definition of retaliation rather than retribution. Therefore capital punishment is retaliation, and as such is morally wrong.

8 Do you subscribe to the following counterargument against the argument in the previous reflection? Why or why not?

It's not true that there is no good to be returned to Victim. Victim isn't the only victim; the friends, relatives, family, and acquaintances of Victim are also victims. They will have no good returned to

them if Offender isn't put to death, because they think Offender
deserves death and this is the only punishment that will salve their
aching hearts. Giving Victim a mere five or ten years in prison will
make them bitter, contemptuous of the judicial system, and perhaps
even avengers of their loved one's death. Therefore capital punishment
is returning a good for a good taken, and as such is retributive rather
than retaliatory.

Do you think that people who are salved only by Offender's execution are vengeful and bloodthirsty, that their desires are evil, and
that the satisfaction of those desires is not a good?

9 We know it is aginst the law to steal something owned by someone
else. But suppose someone who owns radioactive material takes no
precautions for protecting persons who don't know of its presence or
harmful effects. You call the owner's attention to this negligence; the
owner does nothing about it. Maybe the owner is a nuclear power corporation. So, frustrated by the disregard the owner has for others'
safety and health, you steal the radioactive material and put it in a
place where it won't be harmful. The police catch you; the district attorney prosecutes you; the jury convicts you. The judge subscribes to a
retributive theory of punishment and accepts J. P. Day's definition of
retribution. Since you did good by stealing the material whereas the
owner had done evil, should he punish the owner and reward you?

10 The Chief Justice of the Supreme Court of the United States writes you
a letter asking you what the proper punishment for rape should be, supposing that the punishment should be equal to the offense. What
would you reply?

11 The scapegoat is a familiar figure in history and literature, one upon
whom the sins of others are visited. ''Scapegoating'' is normally condemned, although one of the most revered figures in human history or
imagination was a scapegoat. Jesus Christ ''died for the sins of all of
us'' and atoned for everyone, which is pretty straightforward
scapegoating; he was an innocent who suffered for our sins. For
believing Christians it was a good thing, because God the Father accepted the sacrifice of ''only begotten Son,'' and we are the
beneficiaries of God's Grace because of it. Christ's crucifixion was the
supreme sacrifice, which seems justified and even admirable because of
its utility to us. We are saved for heaven rather than condemned to
hell, and if this isn't useful to us, nothing can be.

Why, then, does the following description of scapegoating por-
trayed in a play reviewed by Walter Kerr seem so monstrous to us? Is it
because the utilitarian justification of punishment offends us as it did
Kant? The play is about the Donner party, a group of pioneers caught
in winter storms and freezing temperatures in the mountains of California in 1846–47; certain survivors were accused of cannibalism, even
of children. Kerr reviews a play, *Devour the Snow* by Abe Polsky, that
explores events that occurred afterward:

510

> He [Polsky] is examining the charges of a game-legged German giant of a survivor. The German, one Lewis Keseberg, has felt himself ostracized, shunned by his fellows: three other members of the group have spread the word that he'd robbed graves for money and deliberately killed friends (for meat) during the ordeal. And so he has brought suit for slander in the dirt-floored common room of Sutter's fort in [Sacramento] California.
>
> The rugged force of this work-in-progress comes neither from an orderly suspense nor from the recital of past horrors. It comes from what men are now—now that some have survived, now that the worst is presumably over, now that a healing bond ought to unite men and women who have shared a terrifying experience. When one of the defendants cries out, "Whatever did we let ourselves become?" he means just that. Not what were they in the mountains when they were eating their own dead children. What are they now that the crisis is past.
>
> They have become emotional savages, filled not with relief, but with new furies. They have emerged from the long struggle filled with hatred. Essentially, inevitably, it is a hatred for themselves, for the choices they did make, for the acts they forced themselves to perform. And there is only one possible release from this self-loathing. If any one man among them can be shown to be worse than the others, if he can be made to embody and symbolize the "crimes" that were committed, if he can—in short—be turned into ogre and scapegoat, then his companions may feel themselves justified, cleansed.[22]

12 As we know from our discussion of Kant's theory of the relation between the causation involved in natural and moral laws, Kant sees moral and pathological feelings as sometimes being in opposition, so that the goodness or badness of a will depends on its choice of one or the other of these opposing forces. If someone breaks a law, they deserve punishment, providing they had the capacity to exercise their will. The law distinguishes between first-and second-degree murder and voluntary and involuntary manslaughter, each of which carries a different punishment; this is because different conditions for willing or causing an act (per Kant and Hume respectively) apply to each.

The conditions for murder in the first degree are: (1) unlawful killing of a human being committed (2) with malice aforethought, when (3) it is willful, deliberate, and premeditated. Malice aforethought involves four factors: a person (a) must intend to kill someone, (b) must act for basic anti-social reasons, (c) must have a capacity to know there is a duty not to act, and (d) must keep the idea of a duty not to act in mind during the action.

One strategy often used by defense lawyers to lessen the sentence of someone sure to be convicted is to claim that the capacity of the defendant was non-existent or diminished. Conditions (c) and (d) for malice aforethought are favorites of defense lawyers, who pay for expert psychiatric testimony to show that the mental condition of the defendant was diminished, thus reducing the degree of responsibility and the severity of sentencing. Evidence of brain damage would be relevant to (c), the capacity to know there is a duty not to act. Severe depression or psychosis would be relevant to (d), the ability to keep the idea of duty not to act in mind during the action.

Do you think that Kant could accept the conditions for murder in the first degree and malice aforethought as outlined above? Could Hume? Do you think Hume would allow some evidence to show diminished capacity that Kant would not? If so, what kind would this be?

To loosen up your imagination, consider the following news story in which the facts appear to lend plausibility to the claim that the menstrual period should be considered when dealing with criminal culpability and its degree. Do you think Kant or Hume would advocate taking such evidence into consideration in a trial? Are premenstrual inclinations too much for *Willkür* to overcome?

> Female crime, often involving violence, may tend to increase during the premenstrual period, according to an article in the September issue of *Science Digest*. The article, written by retired Fairfield, Ohio, Police Chief Thomas O. Marsh, says there is mounting evidence that premenstrual tension could be an underlying factor in various types of crimes. . . .
>
> "Studies show," Marsh writes, "that about half of female crime (49 percent), mental hospital admissions (46 percent), and suicide attempts (53 percent) occur in the week before menstruation. And that four out of five of all crimes committed by women occur either during menstruation or in the week before.". . .
>
> The article also reports that French courts have ruled that premenstrual tension is a valid defense in crimes of violence.[23]

13 Kant thought punishment should be equal to the degree of offense. Do you agree that the offense involved in killing another human being has degrees, and that for each there is an appropriate degree of equal punishment? Or do you think there is no "degree" involved when someone kills another human being? One possible consequence of the view that there are no degrees, all being equal, is that *every* killer must be killed.

Philip Nobile reports on a conversation with Walter Berns, a resident scholar at the American Enterprise Institute in Washington, D.C., that gives you some material to use in thinking about your answer to this question. Berns advocates capital punishment and further claims that it is "a moral necessity":

> I refer you to Karl Menninger's book—*The Crime of Punishment*— which argues that the only criminals are law-abiding people who want to put "criminals" in jail. . . .

Retribution means to punish according to the offense. It implies that different criminals deserve different treatment. But if everyone possesses human dignity, as Justice Brennan insists, and human dignity is the standard of punishment, then nobody deserves to be treated differently. This reasoning blurs the distinction between law-abiding citizens and criminals.

Human dignity means moral responsibility. As Aristotle said, in politics men can act so as to resemble the gods or to become the fiercest of beasts. If everyone is dignified, then human dignity means nothing. [Does Berns ignore Kant's distinction between dignity and worthiness?]

Q. But how does it follow that capital punishment is dignified?

A. Assuming a fair trial and a capital crime, to execute a person is to acknowledge indeed the importance that the law places on human life. The murderer has used his human freedom to become worse than the beasts. Therefore, capital punishment does not deny human dignity, but recognizes it by holding us to the highest standards of human dignity.

Q. You also say that justice not only permits capital punishment but requires it. Why?

A. . . . A light sentence for heinous murder—most first-degree killers serve about ten years—is not a proper recognition of the enormity of the crime and fails to satisfy the anger that people should properly experience. The assassin of Martin Luther King, for example, should have been executed. . . .

Q. Since you say that capital punishment is a moral necessity, I wonder if you believe mercy is immoral?

A. Though its unjust to show mercy in certain cases, I don't think mercy is immoral. Since juries can make mistakes, I believe that governors should have the power of commutation.[24]

14 Sydney J. Harris addresses himself to the deterrence and justice arguments about capital punishment. Do you think he or Berns holds the correct moral position on capital punishment?

The main reason capital punishment doesn't work, and never has, is that deterrence works only when people are rational about something. People aren't rational about seat-belts in their cars, so the "restraint" system doesn't work; they're not rational about cigaret smoking, so the dire medical warnings on the packages don't work.

Nor are we rational about killing one another. We may know, abstractly, that the penalty for murder is likely to be our execution, but who thinks about that at a time of passion or crisis. . . .

What actually happens when you have capital punishment is not the reduction in the murder rate, but the execution of those killers who are poor, ignorant, friendless, and moneyless. Can anyone doubt Leopold and Loeb would have been sent to the electric chair if their families had not been able to afford the services of Clarence Darrow? . . .

What capital punishment does is provide a scapegoat for society. It allows society to relieve its anxiety and satisfy its appetite for "justice," while the most skillful, best connected and richest killers go scot-free.[25]

Who would be most likely to agree with Harris—Hume or Kant? **513**
Why?

15 India instituted measures to decrease the birth rate. People don't
always see the same urgency for cutting down the size of their families
as does the state, so legislation with punishment sanctions is often
passed. This happened in the state of Maharashtra, where in 1976
sterilization after two children was compulsory. The state of Punjab
dealt with the problem a little differently; there a fourth child may
result in a three-year prison sentence. Is this retribution? Is the punishment equal to the degree of offense?

Reflections on Theory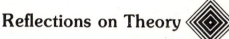

16 *Determinism of action and responsibility are compatible.* Hume
thought we have no "liberty," no free will, indeed no will at all.
Every act of ours is necessitated, is determined by motives that are the
causes of our acts. Hume did, however, distinguish between voluntary
and involuntary acts. Voluntary acts are those done without "constraint"—no gun to our head, no manacles on our legs, no sudden
mental or physical seizures, and so forth.

Some philosophers hold a "compatibilist" position on the relation
between the universal, uniform causation of action and the human
freedom needed for moral responsibility. Ferdinand Schoeman puts the
position this way: "The standard compatibilist argues that behavior can
be free, responsible, and still caused, provided that it is caused (in the
characteristic way) by internal states like desires, beliefs, values."[26]

An opponent of the compatibilist position, Schoeman writes, can
point out that other persons may induce desires, beliefs, and values in
us. This inducement, coming from outside, means we aren't acting
from our own internal states; hence, we aren't free. The induced factors are counterexamples to the compatiblist attempt to show that
freedom and universal causation can be reconciled. I may, for instance, induce a desire for heroin in you by giving you some, representing it as something else. I may induce a belief in you under hypnosis.
I induce values in you by giving you a taste for luxuries you didn't
know existed.

Schoeman tells us what he means by being free in the compatibilist
sense, which is sufficient to make us morally responsible for our actions: "So long as a person has the capacity to think and act on the
basis of relevant reasons, he is responsible for his subsequent behavior"
(p. 296).

He thinks compatibilists can maintain their position against
the opponents who claim that "manipulatively induced desires"
and, of course, manipulatively induced beliefs and values show the

falsity of the compatibilist position. It isn't the "induced" nature of the factors that gives the compatibilist trouble. After all, most of our desires, beliefs, and values come from outside; and as long as the induced ones aren't uncontrollable, they are simply factors we have to deal with just as we do with any others. If they aren't uncontrollable, we can put them into the ordinary rational process and so be responsible for acting or not acting on them. What makes us unfree is the *uncontrollability* of the induced desires, beliefs, and values that interfere with or short-circuit our rational processes. But this doesn't refute the compatibilists, for this is merely Hume's constraint, which makes some but not all of our acts involuntary. Further, uncontrollability is a problem even for persons such as Kant, who subscribe to the doctrine of a will. (These last two points are mine, not Schoeman's.)

Do you think Schoeman's position is one that Hume could consistently accept?

Let's push the position further and see if you think compatibilists can still defend themselves. Schoeman's defense depends upon the assumption that the rational process continues to function normally, enabling us to control induced desires, beliefs, and values. Let's suppose that the compatibilists share Hume's theory of naturalized reasoning about matters of fact: the associative principle in our mind leads us to relate matters of fact by the cause-and-effect relation. Hume observes that it is a matter of fact that an agreeable feeling occurs upon the contemplation of a character trait such as generosity; since our agreeable feeling *is* our approval, we come to believe, by the association principle of our mind, that generosity is good. Now suppose that by manipulation—for example, by clever surgery that "re-wires" our nerve circuits—the contemplation of generosity causes a disagreeable feeling in us. We then judge that this trait is not good and legislate that generous acts are misdemeanors so as to discourage such behavior. There is no "constraint" here, no added "uncontrollable" induced desire, belief, or value. Instead, there is an altered brain that, quite consistently with Hume's theory of value, simply reverses values without "inducement" by anyone else. The matter-of-fact grounded disapproval of generosity is now the valid norm. It's true that the re-wiring has made the disagreeable response uncontrollable, but so is our present agreeable response; since we were thought "free" with old wiring, we must be thought "free" now with the new. But isn't it absurd to suppose that we are free under these conditions? Regardless of our feeling response, isn't generosity good rather than bad? And if it is, then a theory consistent with its being bad and our being free to praise it must be wrong.

17 *Re-wiring Kant's Practical Reason.* A Humean might reply to the foregoing argument by pointing out that, if we are going to introduce surgical re-wiring to give Hume and other moral psychologists difficulty, the Humeans can do the same for Kant and other rational will moralists. Kant says that an act or end maxim that can't be consis-

tently universalized shows the act or end is prohibited. Now, says the Humean, let's re-wire Kant's brain so that what he thought consistent before he now thinks inconsistent, and what he thought inconsistent before he now thinks consistent. What was morally prohibited before no longer is. So Kant is subject to the same criticism as we Humeans are. This is a standoff and can't be used to reject our theory any more than his.

Do you think the following reply shows that re-wiring Kant's brain doesn't refute his theory, although re-wiring Hume's brain refutes Hume's theory?

Of course it is possible to re-wire Kant's brain so that he makes mistakes about consistency and inconsistency. But that doesn't make what is consistent inconsistent, or what is inconsistent consistent; it simply leads Kant to make mistakes. Even if Kant makes mistakes, it doesn't follow that generous acts ought to be prohibited, if their maxims can be consistently universalized. But since Hume's theory of value *identifies* his responses with the value, a change in *his* brain does change *his* values, according to his own theory. Kant's insistence on the transcendental nature of reason, which is not the same as our brain, allows him to escape the absurd consequences to which Hume's naturalization of reason—making it immanent in nature—leads him and those who follow him.

18 *Can our will be broken?* These last reflections will deal with our capacity to come out on the side of duty rather than inclination, when their forces are opposed.

As we saw in 7.4, p. 249, Kant thought that we learn we are free because we first recognize the obligatoriness of the moral laws. A person "judges, therefore, that he can do a certain thing because he is conscious that he ought, and he recognizes that he is free—a fact which but for the moral law he would never have known" (*Practical Reason,* p. 302). Kant here expresses the famous principle that *Ought* implies *Can,* which with the principle that *Can* implies freedom gives us the simple argument:

> Ought implies Can.
> Can implies Freedom.
> _____
> Therefore, Ought implies Freedom.

This freedom Kant calls a "transcendental" freedom, which we can also call a "supersensible" freedom. Kant says it "must be conceived as independence on everything empirical [sensible], and, consequently, on nature generally."[27]

The freedom that enables us to cause our sensible selves to act provides the occasions when the supersensible and the sensible worlds intersect. But may not things that occur in the sensible world, such as someone "breaking our will," influence the supersensible world? May not the intersection start either in the supersensible world or in the sensible world? Suppose, for example, that you have been a political ac-

516 tivist, doing what you believed you were morally obligated to do. The government is overthrown and a dictatorship is established. The dictators arrest you and invite you to endorse their cause, because your doing so will influence others not to resist them. You refuse, so they proceed to break your will by some means of torture or clever psychological manipulation, or by offering you a great reward such as not executing you.

Notice what kind of an argument we can now formulate, which is the reverse (contrapositive) of the above argument:

Broken Will implies Unfree.
Unfree implies Cannot.
Cannot implies No Obligation.
Therefore, Broken Will implies No Obligation.

Kant certainly seems to accept this because he says, "Without this (transcendental) freedom . . . no moral law and no moral imputation are possible" (*Practical Reason,* p. 332). [Note: Kant here refers both to positive freedom ("no moral law") and to negative freedom ("no moral imputation").] We get "no moral law" because if we are positively unfree we cannot give ourselves moral laws, and so cannot give ourselves obligations. We get "no moral imputation" because we can impute blame only if a person could have resisted his or her inclinations: with a broken will, a person cannot resist powerful inclinations.

These arguments, then, seem to show that (1) Cannot implies No Obligation and (2) blame cannot be imputed to us when we cannot. But this appears to contradict what Kant said earlier (7.2, p. 244), when quoted on the *"perversity* of the heart." To say we are "perverse" is surely to impute morally. Kant said such a heart "may coexist with a will which in general is good: it arises from the frailty of human nature, the lack of sufficient strength to follow out the principles it has chosen for itself" (*Religion,* p. 32).

If we are frail, the strength of our will is insufficient to hold out against our inclinations; in such a case, we cannot; therefore, Kant ought not to impute perversity to us; but he does, which contradicts what he should say. How, for example, if we have a frail will, can we keep someone from breaking it? Our frailty surely explains why we choose the cessation of pain from torture, or choose to preserve our life when it is threatened, rather than do our duty to oppose dictators.

Do you think the following response enables Kant to escape from this apparent contradiction?

Frailty indeed explains why we follow our inclinations instead of our duty; our will is sometimes weaker than our wants. But this does not show that we have lost our freedom. To say "our will was broken" is an excuse that we use to ward off blame, but there is no such thing as breaking our will. Whenever we ought, we always can. The mistake in the argument that accuses Kant of contradiction rests on moving from (1) frailty to (2) breaking the will and then to (3) perversity. If our will is broken, we cannot, and so should not, be charged with perversity. But if we recognize that breaking the will is a fiction, then we have removed reason (2) for thinking we cannot.

That there is no such thing as breaking the will can be seen by considering, first, our positive freedom to give ourselves laws and, second, our negative freedom to obey these laws.

First, suppose that we did succumb to our torturers' wishes and endorsed the dictatorship. If we did that, we would feel regret and perhaps even despise ourselves for it. This regret is possible only because we still recognize that we ought not to have endorsed the dictatorship; thus, we are still positively free to give ourselves moral laws and obligations—our positive will is not broken.

Second, no matter what the circumstances, we always know it is possible to follow our moral conscience rather than our inclinations; thus, our negative free will can't be broken. Kant offers the following two examples to show that our "experience confirms" our ever present negative freedom:

> Suppose some one asserts of his lustful appetite that, when the desired object and the opportunity are present, it is quite irresistible. [Ask him]—if a gallows were erected before the house where he finds his opportunity, in order that he should be hanged thereon after the gratification of his lust, whether he could not then control his passion; we need not be long in doubt what he would reply. (*Practical Reason,* p. 302)

> Ask him, however—if his sovereign ordered him, on pain of the same immediate execution, to bear false witness against an honorable man, whom the prince might wish to destroy under a plausible pretext, would he consider it possible in that case to overcome his love of life, however great it may be. He would perhaps not venture to affirm whether he would do so or not, but he must unhesitatingly admit that it is possible to do so. (p. 302)

19 *Will do versus could do.* But, it might be said, the very fact that Kant admits we are frail, that he knows our inclinations will sometimes overwhelm our will to perform our obligations, is enough to show that we cannot always do our duty. Therefore Kant shouldn't say that "it is possible" always to do it, nor should he call us perverse. The Scots philosopher John Laird thinks there are in fact occasions when we cannot—occasions when we aren't free:

> The fact remains that we are and must remain ignorant, in many respects, of our own capacities. We think we can do what in fact we can't; and we think we can't do what in fact we can. How is a recruit to know in advance what effect the terrors and the horrors of the battlefield will have upon his courage, or how far, if his courage ebbs, he will still be able to acquit himself in a soldierly fashion? How can a veteran know for certain that he will not flinch at the hundredth

518

danger, although he has successfully endured the previous ninety-nine? The imaginative soldier is likely to distrust himself more than he should and the unimaginative to trust himself far too easily.[28]

Laird's example seems as plausible as Kant's. But Laird may not be meeting Kant head-on, and so may not be refuting him. Do you think that the following reply to Laird would be an adequate defense of Kant?

In Kant's last example—where a prince orders someone to bear false witness on the pain of death—he acknowledges that a person "would perhaps not venture to affirm whether he would do so or not." Here he agrees with Laird that a person cannot predict whether or not he would face up to his duty. However, the person also knows that he could have done his duty, even if he didn't. Thus there are two kinds of knowledge: (1) knowledge of what in fact we will do and (2) knowledge of what we could do. Laird is referring to (1) while Kant is referring to (2); hence, Laird does not refute Kant. Further, unless we could, we have no basis for saying our will is weak; weakness presupposes possibility.

Would Hume have any reason to disagree with Laird? Would battle danger be a constraint for Hume?

20 *Weak wills can triumph indirectly.* Still, although you grant the distinction between predicting what you will do and what you could do if you willed it, you might be inclined to say that, given a frailty of will and strong desires, we couldn't have done otherwise; therefore, we ought not to be blamed for bearing false witness.

Here is the argument:

Frailty implies Cannot.
Cannot implies No Obligation.
Therefore, Frailty implies No Obligation.

However, suppose we can weaken, change, or eliminate our desires; in this case even a weak will can triumph. Since we can, it is invalid to infer no obligation, and so invalid to infer no blame.

Wright Neely, a contemporary philosopher, examines Bertrand Russell's caim that "we can do as we please, but we can't please as we please," which is a variation of Voltaire's statement, "When I can do what I want to do, there is my liberty for me, but I can't help wanting what I want." Neely disagrees with Russell and Voltaire. With whom do you agree?

A man may desire to kill his father but desire, with good reason, to be rid of that desire. . . . It *is* the case that our desires, like our beliefs, are not under our *immediate* voluntary control; one does not in general get rid of a desire or acquire a new one *simply* in virtue of desiring to do so. This does not, however, entail any special restriction on our freedom, for there are lots of things—indeed, almost everything of any importance—that we cannot *directly* do which we are, nevertheless, free to do. And we do have a measure of indirect control over our desires. . . . The degree to which we are free to alter our own desires, like the degree to which we are free to do anything else, depends on our knowledge, our circumstances, and our skills. . . . There are no more logical or metaphysical obstacles to success in making ourselves to be the kind of people we wish to be than there are to our success in making the world the kind of place in which we wish to live.[29]

Neely cites remarks of John Stuart Mill to the same effect. Mill, who held a moral psychological position, thought it a "grand error" to hold that a person's character is "formed *for* him, and not *by* him":

He has, to a certain extent, a power to alter his character. . . . His character is formed by his circumstances (including among these his particular organization); but his own desire to mould it in a particular way is one of those circumstances, and by no means one of the least influential. We cannot, indeed, directly will to be different from what we are. But . . . we . . . can place ourselves under the influence of other circumstances. We are exactly as capable of making our own character, *if we will,* as others are of making it for us.[30]

Neely and Mill agree that frailty of will in the face of strong desires is no excuse for avoiding blame, because we can indirectly alter our desires and our sensible character and all that flows from it. If what flows from it is wrong, then we are blameworthy for not having altered our character and desires in such a way as to avoid doing wrong.

21 *Reason and strength of will.* Neely and Mill advocate weakening or altering our desires. If we can indirectly do this as they say, then frailty of will need not be a hindrance to doing our duty; if it is no hindrance, then we can do our duty and are blameable if we don't.

Kant proceeds differently from Neely and Mill. Explain how his proposal to eliminate frailty as an excuse from blame differs from theirs:

Virtue signifies a moral strength of will. . . . Virtue is, therefore, the moral strength of a *man's* will in fulfilling his *duty,* a moral *necessitation* by his own legislative reason, in so far as reason constitutes itself a power *executing* the law.[31]

Inner freedom requires two things of the agent; to be *in control of* himself in any given case—that is, to *tame* his agitations—and to have *mastery* over himself—that is, to *govern* his obsessions. When these two conditions are fulfilled, the *character* is *noble;* otherwise it is *abject.* (*Virtue,* p. 69)

In so far as virtue is based on inner freedom it thus contains a positive command for man, over and above the prohibition against letting himself be ruled by his feelings and inclinations: the command, namely, to bring all his powers and inclinations under his (that is, reason's) control—hence the command of self-mastery. For unless reason holds the reins of government in its own hands, man's feelings and inclinations assume mastery over him. (p. 70)

Do you think that Neely's and Kant's proposals are compatible? Might we eliminate frailty of will as an excuse by both methods? Does Neely and Mill's method of forming one's own character presuppose Kant's method, because their method too requires putting "the reins of government" in reason's hands?

14
From Hume
and Kant
to Marx

The philosophers have only interpreted *the world differently; the point is, to* change *it.*

Karl Marx
XIth Thesis on Feuerbach

14.1 Marx's Dialectic

Up to this chapter, this book has presented the dialectical development of two opposing ethical views. Starting off with heart versus mind, we saw this opposition develop into one between moral psychology and rational will ethics, each represented in an elaborate, sophisticated way by Hume and Kant respectively. A dialectical process starts off with a simple opposition, a contradiction; each side then defends its position by altering and complicating the original claim, following which the new position of each is criticized in turn. This back-and-forth process produces complex theories that multiply into a set of oppositions—in the present case, into the several contrasts between moral psychology and rational will ethics.

The original, simple opposition could be expressed from Hume's side thus: morals have their source and verification in sentiment, in feeling, not in reason. And from Kant's side it could be expressed in this way: morals have their source and verification in reason, not in sentiment. Hume says in sentiment; Kant says not in sentiment. Kant says in reason; Hume says not in reason. Here the form of the opposition is *A* and *not A,* a contradiction.

But, you must be saying right about now, which of them represents the truth? How can we decide between these two theories, each of which has tried to make itself impregnable by increasing its distinctions and arguments as represented in the contrasts?

In this concluding chapter, I am going to present an interpretation of the nineteenth-century German social philosopher Kark Marx and his way of addressing himself to the questions you must be asking. I choose Marx for several reasons. First, his theory has had more practical moral and political impact on the world than any other modern philosopher's. Second, he had a notion of how to place philosophy, including moral philosophy, in a larger setting that gives quite a different perspective on our subject matter than any presented so far. Third, he had some definite views about Kant's place in history that he arrived at after being deeply influenced by Hegel, who in turn had been deeply influenced by Kant; also, Marx had some definite views about English philosophers such as Jeremy Bentham and Adam Smith, of **523** whom the latter, a friend of Hume's, was the economist who wrote *The Wealth of Nations* (1776). Smith and Bentham developed the utility side of Hume's theory ("useful to ourselves and others"). Fourth, Marx is becoming a respectable academic figure who, professors realize, had a brilliant theoretical power; he is becoming respectable now because the political climate enables intellectuals to write about Marx without being accused of "anti-American communism," although some professors continue to lose jobs and preferment if they become too ardent on the subject.

What follows is only a brief sketch of Marx's views, in contrast to the more detailed treatment of Hume and Kant earlier. As with all important, complex, and difficult thinkers, it should also be noted that Marxists and non-Marxists, followers and critics alike, are sharply divided about what Marx said and meant. The controversies over the correct interpretation of Marx are often passionate, which should be taken as a sign of life in the theory, and a warning not to accept any one interpretation, including the one that follows, uncritically.

In this section I will outline the views of the early-nineteenth-century German philosopher G. W. F. Hegel about the dialectical process and truth, and explain how Marx, while he adopted Hegel's dialectical method, also "turned it on its head."

One of Hegel's criticisms of Kant was that Kant presented the concepts of science and morals as too static, as if they were eternally given rather than being changing products of changing history. For Hegel, theories and concepts are products of a process of change. Hegel's grand scheme of change included all of history and the cosmos. Humans are alienated or estranged from the world of objects which is set over against us and opposes us; objects are "other" than us. The movement of history, according to Hegel, is one of de-alienation, which is the process whereby human subjects and objects become one, a unity; the otherness, the opposition of objects, will then vanish. The Real must become Rational. Thus the process of history is dialectical in that the contradictions or oppositions in it, such as that between subject and object, are overcome, transcended, superseded, so that the original opposition disappears into a new unity. Flour, milk, and eggs cease being exactly what they were when they become a cake, yet they are preserved in the new unity.

A and *not A* are not ultimately separate; each is a one-sided aspect of a larger unity. In his work *The Phenomenology of Mind,* Hegel traces the history of systems of philosophy, in the course of which each opposing pair (dogmatism vs. skepticism, individualism vs. collectivism, etc.) is transcended in a more comprehensive unity, which in turn is confronted by another opposed view, following which the new opposition is again transcended. The new, transcendental unity is an all-sided way of looking at what was looked at in a one-sided way by each of the opposing views before.

A and *not A* are not independent of each other, but live off each other. Neither is what it is without the other. Here follows a nice piece of ironic

524 dialectical criticism of one-sided views that shifts back and forth between good and bad—an alternation that, Hegel tells us, can cease only after a more comprehensive view is achieved. This example will show how the opposites of good and bad live off each other:

> In the age of OPEC [the alliance of oil-producing countries], Proposition 13 [a proposal to limit property taxes], the Carter administration, and the conservative revival, here is an objective report on the way things are:
>
> Bureaucrats are Bad, but Pentagon officials are Good, particularly when warning of the growing Soviet military advantage. Big government is Bad. But $30 billion for the MX missile is Good—until they want to build one of those 20-mile trenches through your backyard. That would be Bad. Inadequate public services like uncollected garbage are Bad. Lower taxes are Good. If you argue that this is inconsistent, you're a liberal. That's Bad. Candor in a politician is Good. But if he tells you that taxes have to go up to get the garbage collected, he is arrogant. That's Bad. . . .
>
> Talking about the causes of crime is Bad. But talking about getting tough on criminals makes you a Conservative and that's Good, unless getting tough on criminals requires public spending and higher taxes, which are Bad. Better advocate the death penalty, which is Good and costs little. . . .
>
> Inflation is Bad, but if you're a businessman, profits are Good; if you're a working man, higher wages are Good. If you're neither, cat food is Good because it beats starvation, which is Bad.
>
> Economic opportunity for every American is Good, but affirmative action for those who don't have economic opportunity is Bad. In fact, it's not affirmative action at all but reverse discrimination, which is worse because it means the reverse of what has traditionally been meant by economic opportunity for every American, which is Good.[1]

The preceding article lays bare some contradictions in people's thinking today. Hegel emphasizes that overcoming these contradictions is the result not simply of an individual's efforts, but of a historical process as we move toward the Absolute, which is the final, unitary result of the dialectical process. Truth isn't something clear, obvious, or easy:

> The truth is the whole. The whole, however, is merely the essential nature reaching its completeness through the process of its own [dialectical] development. Of the Absolute it must be said that it is essentially a result, that only at the end is it what it is in very truth; and just in that consists its nature, which is to be actual, subject, or self-becoming, self-development. . . .
>
> Truth and falsehood as commonly understood belong to those sharply defined ideas which claim a completely fixed nature of their own, one standing in solid isolation on this side, the other on that, without any community between them. [Think here of Hume and Kant's ideas.] Against that view [of separate, contradictory systems of ideas] it must be pointed out, that truth is not like stamped coin that is issued ready from

the mint and so can be taken up and used. Nor, again, *is* there something false, any more than there *is* something evil. . . . False and evil . . . have a nature of their own [only] with reference to one another. . . . Difference itself continues to be an immediate element within truth as such, in the form of the principle of negation.[2]

Truth and falsehood, good and evil—each has a nature that depends on the opposite's existence. *A* and *not A*, Hume and Kant, are not isolated, independent existences; each is essential to the dialectical, historical process whose end result is the unity overcoming the contradiction of these dualisms.

Marx sees something right and something wrong in Hegel's dialectic. One thing he considers right is Hegel's understanding that humans are self-creating through the dialectical process:

(XXIII) The outstanding achievement of Hegel's *Phenomenology*—the dialectic of negativity as the moving and creating principle—is, first, that Hegel grasps the self-creation of man as a process . . . and conceives objective man (true, because real man) as the result of his *own labor*.[3]

In that same manuscript Marx also says what he thinks is wrong about Hegel's theory: principally, that Hegel's dialectic deals only with thought instead of reality, that Hegel doesn't trace the contradictions to their source in the real world. Concerning the *Phenomenology,* which he calls the "birthplace" of Hegel's philosophy," Marx says:

When Hegel conceives wealth, the power of the state, etc. as entities alienated from the human being, he conceives them only in their thought form. They are entities of thought and thus simply an alienation of *pure* (i.e., abstract philosophical) thought. (p. 174)

He emphasizes the same point about Hegel more strongly in his later work, *Grundrisse (Foundations):*

Hegel fell into the illusion of conceiving the real as the product of thought concentrating itself, probing its own depths, and unfolding itself out of itself. . . . The totality as it appears in the head, as a totality of thoughts, is a product of a thinking head, which appropriates the world in the only way it can. . . . The real subject [the world, the real] retains its autonomous existence outside the head just as before; namely as long as the head's conduct is merely speculative, merely theoretical.[4]

Marx's rejection of this aspect of Hegel's dialectic points toward the positive use to which he thinks the dialectical method can be put, and which he himself employs in discovering the source of modern man's alienation—namely, that in capitalism the worker is alienated from his product because workers don't own their products and have no control over them. Capitalist economics, not some abstract thought process, is the source of the modern contradictions, which are to be overcome by changing the real world

526 and not merely by thinking a change in it. The head's conduct must be more than theoretical; it must be practical:

> In direct contrast to German philosophy which descends from heaven to earth, here we ascend from earth to heaven. That is to say, we do not set out from what men say, imagine, conceive, nor from men as narrated, thought of, imagined, conceived, in order to arrive at men in the flesh. We set out from real, active men, and on the basis of their real life-process we demonstrate the development of the ideological reflexes and echoes of this life-process. The phantoms formed in the human brain are also, necessarily, sublimates [mere shadows] of their material life-process, which is empirically verifiable and bound to material premises. Morality, religion, metaphysics, all the rest of ideology and their corresponding forms of consciousness, thus no longer retain the semblance of independence. . . . When reality is depicted, philosophy as an independent branch of activity loses its medium of existence.[5]

Marx starts with material life conditions—barren or fertile land, temperate or arctic climate, few or many natural resources, rudimentary or developed technology, etc.—and shows how these give rise to thought, ideology (including philosophy and religion), legal systems, political systems, and states; whereas Hegel and his followers start with thought. Marx finds that Hegel's dialectic is standing on its head; he sets it on its feet in the real world:

> My dialectic method is not only different from the Hegelian, but is its direct opposite. To Hegel, the life-process of the human brain, *i.e.,* the process of thinking, which, under the name of "the Idea," he even transforms into an independent subject, is the demiurgos [creative power] of the real world, and the real world is only the external, phenomenal form of "the Idea." With me, on the contrary, the ideal is nothing else than the material world reflected by the human mind, and translated into forms of thought. . . .
>
> The mystification which dialectic suffers in Hegel's hands, by no means prevents him from being the first to present its general form of working in a comprehensive and conscious manner. With him it is standing on its head. It must be turned right side up again, if you would discover the rational kernel within the mystical shell.[6]

14.2 Marx's Historical Materialism

Marx, as we have seen, accepted a dialectical method from Hegel, agreed that it works historically, but believed that its moving forces are the material life processes rather than the logical processes of mental life. Marx's theory about the human career on earth is called "historical materialism," the essence of which can be summarized as follows: human social life is produced by a historical process whose force comes from material life processes; history, then, is the key to understanding social life, and economics is the key to understanding history.

The perspective from which Marx tells us to view Hume and Kant is a historical one: we must see their philosophies as social products of a stage in the material life of humans. We are told to look at their philosophies as something that will be superseded, overcome, transcended, when the productive arrangements of humans as existing now under capitalism—with private ownership of the means of production, factories, raw materials, and tools—are replaced by new productive relations under communism, whereby the means of production will be socially rather than privately owned.

Marx thinks of the forces of production as the "base" of history—the "material" base upon which a "superstructure" is built. This superstructure includes the legal and political relations between persons in a society, and also the society's idea systems such as philosophy, religion, and art. Changes in the material base are followed by changes in the superstructure; these latter changes occur through revolution, which is an attempt to remake the superstructure so that it will fit its new material base better. For example, the overthrow of feudal monarchies and their titled allies, the nobility, whose power was based on control and income from the land, came through revolutions that replaced that political system with one more favorable to the growing new class whose power was based on control of commerce and manufacture. When the material base—the economic system—changes, it moves ahead and out from under the superstructure that once fit it. When this happens, the two are, in Marx's terminology, in "contradiction." This contradiction is overcome and superseded by a revolution which, while it preserves some of the old, also transforms it into something new. Not all the laws of a monarchy are thrown out, but they have to be altered to fit the new laws. For example, the people who till the land for landowners are no longer legally serfs but renters.

Let's look now in a little more detail at the concepts of materialism, history, classes, and capital, starting with materialism.

The essence of humans, according to Marx, is that they are producers, makers; they take matter and recombine and reshape it into human products: the wood of a tree is made into a chair. Humans differ from producers such as bees and spiders in that they can conceive what they will make before making it and they have a purpose in mind. Marx refers to this making or producing as the "material life process" that works on and alters the "material conditions"; the correct understanding of this process goes under the name of "historical materialism." The word "material" means something concrete to Marx: it is the tree's wood, ore, land, water, and the tools such as axes, picks, plows, and boats that we use to alter and recombine nature's matter.

There are four important aspects to this material life process that exist right from the beginning; these aspects remain as part of our social historical process, which we understand when we grasp the interconnected changes that occur among them over time.

First comes *the work to satisfy our basic needs:*

> But life involves before everything else eating and drinking, a habitation, clothing and many other things. The first historical act is thus the production of the means to satisfy these needs, the production of material life itself. (*German Ideology,* p. 16)

The initial efforts at keeping alive are simple and crude: hooks are made to catch fish; acorns are gathered on the ground; arrowheads are made of stone to kill animals whose hides become clothing; caves are converted into shelter. Compare such efforts with the sophisticated technology of today: large ships are equipped with sonar for locating and catching fish; massive machinery for agribusiness is used to till the land; artificial insemination, superfeeds, and mass processing of meat have replaced hunting; and we live and work in towering skyscrapers. Obviously, we have altered our ways of transforming nature's material into human products.

Second, in satisfying our basic needs we are led to *the creation of new needs.* Once you start using metal to make knives instead of chipping away at a piece of obsidian, you create needs for more and better metal, for better tools to extract ore, for better furnaces to recover the metal from the ore, and for more transportation to move all the material involved in satisfying these new needs—to say nothing of the newly created "need" to own a luxurious automobile, which wasn't even thinkable as a need until a host of new needs preceding it had been fulfilled, since wagons and carriages had satisfied earlier needs of transportation.

Third, from the beginning there is *a social relation* between persons, the first one being the family because humans "make other men"; people become parents and are responsible for their children's survival.

This first social relation gives rise to a fourth aspect of our life process—*cooperation:*

> By social we understand the co-operation of several individuals, no matter under what conditions, in what manner and to what end. It follows from this that a certain mode of production, or industrial stage, is always combined with a certain mode of co-operation, or social stage, and this mode of co-operation is itself a "productive force." (*German Ideology,* p. 18)

Given the relation between a mode of production or the material base and this social mode of cooperation or the social superstructure, it follows that when the mode of production becomes more complex, so then must the thought and the social life become correspondingly complex. The superstructure's complexity mirrors productions' complexity: Cro-Magnon man didn't produce Kant's *Critique of Practical Reason;* as production goes, so go the ideas. Capitalism is one production arrangement; with it goes one form of cooperation, social life, and ideology. Communism is a different production arrangement; with it will go a different form of cooperation, social life, and ideology—and different morals.

Now that we've seen what Marx and his collaborator Engels mean by the **529** "material" part of "historical materialism," let's see what they have to say about the "history" part:

> History is nothing but the succession of the separate generations, each of which exploits the materials, the forms of capital, the productive forces handed down to it by all preceding ones, and thus on the one hand continues the traditional activity in completely changed circumstances, and, on the other, modifies the old circumstances with a completely changed activity. (*German Ideology*, p. 38)

In the preceding paragraph, Marx and Engels give a place in history to the material, productive forces; this is the base. In the following paragraph, they give a place in history to ideas and the superstructure, which, they say, reflect the ideas of the class in power, which is the class that owns the means of production:

> The ideas of the ruling class are in every epoch the ruling ideas: i.e., the class, which is the ruling material force of society, is at the same time its ruling intellectual force. The class which has the means of material production at its disposal has control at the same time over the means of mental production, so that thereby, generally speaking, the ideas of those who lack the means of mental production are subject to it. The ruling ideas are nothing more than the ideal expression of the dominant material relationships, the dominant material relationships grasped as ideas. (*German Ideology*, p. 39)

Central to Marx's analysis of capitalist society is the existence of classes. The notion of a class should be distinguished from that of status; two people may belong to the same class but have different status; thus a worker on the assembly line generally is thought to have a lower status than an accountant in the counting room, although both belong to the same class. Here is what may well be Marx's most succinct, straightforward remark on classes:

> In so far as millions of families live under economic conditions of existence that separate their mode of life, their interests and their culture from those of the other classes, and put them in hostile opposition to the latter, they form a class. In so far as there is merely a local interconnection among these small-holding peasants, and the identity of their interests begets no community, no national bond, and no political organization among them, they do not form a class.[7]

In this quotation we see various defining elements of a class: (1) a similar economic condition; (2) a distinct mode of life, interests, and culture; (3) hostile opposition to another class; (4) not merely local but widespread consciousness of an identity of interests; and (5) a political organization among the members. Items (4) and (5) occur only when a class is ready for a revolution; when it isn't ready, it is identified by conditions (1) through (3).

Marx identifies two classes in the capitalist epoch of human history—the proletariat and the bourgeoisie. To understand them, let's apply defining elements (1), (2), and (3) to each. To do this, we need to have some idea of Marx's most important concept, the concept of capital. It is essential to grasp the crucial distinction between money and capital; they aren't the same, although all too often they are thought to be. Money is a medium of exchange; capital is not. The following relations exist for money: Commodity$_1$—Money—Commodity$_2$, which, as in Marx, can be abbreviated thus: C—M—C. Suppose you are a farmer and have corn. You sell your corn, Commodity$_1$, and get money for it. You want a pair of pants, Commodity$_2$, so you take your money and go to a clothing merchant who is willing to exchange your money for a pair of pants. Here money is a medium of exchange between the farmer and the merchant. At this point we don't have capital.

Capital is money that exists in a different relation: Money—Commodity—Money, or for short in Marx: M—C—M. Here money ceases to be a passive midpoint and becomes an active instrument of production; it has stepped outside the C—M—C exchange relation. In a capitalist system, M—C—M dominates C—M—C. The industrialist has money and buys raw material, say cotton; his workers transform the cotton into cloth that the industrialist then sells to obtain money. But Marx points out that something has happened in this M—C—M relation; the industrialist gets more money from the cloth than he paid for the cotton and labor; this is surplus value. The source of this surplus value comes from the fact that the workers have changed the cotton to cloth, have been paid for doing so—their labor power is a commodity, a C in M—C—M, that was bought—but they have been paid less for this labor power than it cost to produce and maintain it. This then is money out of the hide of the worker, as Marx sometimes puts it; the worker is "exploited" by the industrialist. In terms of the "capital" relation, we have M—C—M$'$, where M$'$ is the sum of money that the industrialist gets for the cloth—a sum larger than M, which is what he pays for the cotton and labor power.

In C—M—C, the commodities have "use-value." The farmer can use the pants; they have value for him because he wears them. Likewise, the merchant can use the corn by eating it. But in M—C—M, a commodity, say cotton, has only an "exchange value." The industrialist doesn't use it, but simply exchanges the cloth made from it for money. His interest is in increasing his money, which can be used again to make more money. Thus money becomes capital; it becomes active and increases itself:

> The circuit C—M—C starts with one commodity, and finishes with another, which falls out of circulation and into consumption. Consumption, the satisfaction of wants, in one word, use-value, is its end and aim. The circuit M—C—M, on the contrary, commences with money and ends with money. Its leading motive, and the goal that attracts it, is therefore more exchange value.[8]

Now let's see how this discussion of commodities, money, and capital helps us distinguish the proletariat from the bourgeoisie.

Economic condition. Those of us who do not command the M—C—M **531**
circuit belong to the proletariat as do members of the petty bourgeoisie, which
includes so-called middle-class persons such as merchants and shop owners.
The proletariat principally live as commodities in the circuit. Workers on
assembly lines, carpenters, accountants, salespersons, and teachers are caught
in the M—C—M circuit in a peculiar way. Unlike the farmer, they don't have
corn as a saleable commodity; all they have is their labor power. They sell this
labor power to their employer for as much as they can get; with the money they
receive, they buy other commodities such as food, clothing, shelter, insurance
policies, retirement plans, and transportation. As consumers of commodities,
they have quite a different relation to money than do the bourgeoisie. The
bourgeoisie have an economic condition that permits them to command the
M—C—M circuit. They use their money to make money and have no need to
sell their labor power to an employer.

Distinct mode of life, interests, and culture. In response to F. Scott
Fitzgerald's remark that the rich are "different from you and me," Ernest
Hemingway said yes, they are, they have more money. Marx, however,
would disapprove of this clever remark by Hemingway, which could be interpreted as saying that the rich differ in only one way from the rest of us, in
having more money. But their having more money is precisely what makes
for a larger, more profound difference: the proletariat and the bourgeoisie
have different interests. The proletariat sell their labor, skills, and
knowledge; the bourgeoisie buys it. The former want the best price they can
get for themselves, whereas the latter want to buy cheap so they can reap
greater surplus value. These interests are diametrically opposed. As to
culture, while you may sit near the rich at the opera, you don't have the same
influence over programs or conductors as those who contribute large sums to
make up the annual deficit.

Hostile opposition. We have just seen that the interests of the proletariat and bourgeoisie are opposed. If each tries to further its interests
through action, they will be overtly opposed. Working men forming a union
is one form of action that employers once fought bitterly; men and women
died in this struggle. Strikes are a form of action that unionized workers have
to take on occasion to wrest a higher price for their labor power from the
bourgeoisie. Eventually, says Marx, these actions will escalate into revolutionary actions.

Karl Vorländer, a twentieth-century philosopher who attempted to combine Kant and Marx, "recounts that it was said of Marx that he would burst
into laughter when anyone spoke to him of morality."[9] This laughter is
understandable from Marx's perspective if "morality" is taken to mean a set
of rules and standards expressive of the ruling class, for whom morality is
basically an intellectual expression of ways to protect their interests in the current social order. Moral dogmas for Marx and Engels are not "eternal, im-
mutable, or ultimate." Because previous societies were class societies,
morality—the "officially" approved morality—was always a class morality.
"A really human morality" becomes possible—not laughable—when society
reaches a stage in which class contradictions have been overcome and *for-
gotten.*

"The management has gone on strike demanding we take a 10 percent pay cut."

That Marx might have reason to laugh at the ruling class's morality can be easily gathered by reading *Capital,* where he cites appalling reports of living conditions in industrial England. The laughter presupposes a fiercely moral viewpoint in Marx. Here is a typical quotation from a medical report on living conditions:

> There are landlords who deem any [pig] sty good enough for their laborer and his family, and who yet do not disdain to drive with him the hardest bargain for rent. It may be but a ruinous one-bed-roomed hut, having no fire-grate, no privy, no opening window, no water supply but the ditch, no garden—but the laborer is helpless against the wrong. (*Capital,* p. 753)

Capital has long citations of other reports on working conditions: women milliners dying of overwork, sometimes having worked as much as thirty hours without ceasing, and sleeping in an unventilated, crowded room at the dressmakers; children trained to make lace and plait straw for strawhats at the age of four, often working in a space three feet square from six in the morning until eight at night, and then being given work to take home, which might be completed at midnight; children of five and six carrying clay from pits for making bricks, who generally died at twelve or fourteen. Small wonder that Marx laughed whenever anyone mentioned "morality." Such conditions of life are just as severe for millions of persons, including working children, in the world today. Poverty stalks unimpeded in underdeveloped countries; you need only look at the daily newspapers, where starving children with distended bellies and pencil-thin limbs stare out at us from photographs.

The following well-known passage from Marx's *A Contribution to the Critique of Political Economy* sums up the foregoing points:

In the social production of their existence, men inevitably enter into definite relations, which are independent of their will, namely relations of production appropriate to a given stage in the development of their material forces of production. The totality of these relations of production constitutes the economic structure of society, the real foundation, on which arises a legal and political superstructure and to which correspond definite forms of social consciousness. The mode of production of material life conditions the general process of social, political and intellectual life. It is not the consciousness of men that determines their existence, but their social existence that determines their consciousness. At a certain stage of development, the material productive forces of society come into conflict with the existing relations of production or—this merely expresses the same thing in legal terms—with the property relations within the framework of which they have operated hitherto. From forms of development of the productive forces these relations turn into their fetters. Then begins an era of social revolution. The changes in the economic foundation lead sooner or later to the transformation of the whole immense superstructure. . . . In broad outline, the Asiatic, ancient, feudal and modern bourgeois modes of production may be designated as epochs marking progress in the economic development of society. The bourgeois mode of production is the last antagonistic form of the social process of production . . . but the productive forces developing within bourgeois society create also the material conditions for a solution of this antagonism.[10]

The conclusion to which Marx points us, as we seek to overcome the contraditions between Hume and Kant, is that when history changes from capitalism to communism, then their philosophies too will be superseded. Both of them speak for the ruling class, the bourgeoisie. This class, because it owns the means of material production, also owns the means of mental production: Hume and Kant are employees of the bourgeoisie who produce our ethics. When communism succeeds capitalism and everyone owns the means of production, the new society will produce its own and different thoughts, including moralities different from Hume's and Kant's. The old ideas don't disappear wholly; when contradictions are superseded, the old is preserved but also transformed. We can illustrate this by considering the moral ideals of different economic epochs.

Here is a characterization of the knight, who was the moral ideal of the feudal epoch. It was written by the fourteenth-century French author Eustache Deschamps:

> You who would win the order of knighthood must lead a new life; devoutly you must watch in prayer, flee from sin, pride and baseness; you must defend the Church, and succor the widow and orphan; you must be bold and guard the people; loyal and valiant, taking nothing from others; thus should a knight conduct himself.
>
> He should have a humble heart, should always strive to follow deeds of chivalry; loyal in war, he should be a great traveler, should attend tournaments and joust for his fair lady; he must strive always for honor, so

that he may not be touched by blame nor be accused of cowardice; and among all men he should deem himself the least; thus should the knight conduct himself.[11]

To this statement Maria Ossowska, a professor of moral philosophy at the University of Warsaw, adds some interesting remarks:

> A knight was expected to test his valor constantly by glorious deeds. When Yvain [the hero of a romance by Chrétien de Troyes] marries the wife of the knight whom he has killed, his friend Gauvain urges him to leave his lady in order to seek opportunities for new battles. "Think first of all about your renown." . . . Like Homer's heroes the knight is absorbed by his "reflected ego," by what people think of him. "There is no use to behave well, if one does not wish to make it known."—this is the opinion of the knight Yvain. All medieval legends demonstrate this insatiable pride. (p. 133)

Although this picture of an ideal knight reflects the bygone feudal age, whose dominant ruling class was the nobility, elements in it are still preserved today. While men don't attend tournaments and joust, they do transform the ordinary street automobile into a low- or high-riding steed, cruise the streets on Saturday night, and strut and roar for their "fair lady." Strange, isn't it, how cultural forms persist?

What happens to the dominant ideal when the production relations change from feudalism to capitalism? That ideal must be replaced by a new one. The knight comes to seem ridiculous, pitiful, and useless when called upon to become the bourgeois ideal, a captain of industry. The bourgeois needed a new human ideal, an uplifting portrait to replace the ideal of the knight. Iris Murdoch, the English philosopher and novelist, supplies an interesting picture of the bourgeois ideal person. Although she attributes the genesis of this figure to "the advance in science"—unlike Marx, who attributes it to a change from the feudal to the capitalist mode of production, of which science and technology are a part—her picture is of interest:

> Kant abolished God and made man God in His stead. We are still living in the age of the Kantian man, or Kantian man-god. . . . How recognizable, how familiar to us, is the man so beautifully portrayed in the *Grundlegung* [*Foundations*], who confronted even with Christ turns away to consider the judgment of his own conscience and to hear the voice of his own reason . . . . This man is with us still, free, independent, lonely, powerful, rational, responsible, brave, the hero of so many novels and books of moral philosophy. The *raison d'être* [reason for being] of this attractive but misleading creature is not far to seek. He is the offspring of the age of science, confidently rational and yet increasingly aware of his alienation from the material universe which his discoveries reveal. . . . He is the ideal citizen of the liberal state, a warning held up to tyrants. He has the virtue which the age requires and admires, courage. It is not such a very long step from Kant to Nietzsche, and from Nietzsche to existentialism and

the Anglo-Saxon ethical doctrines which in some ways closely resemble it. **535**
In fact Kant's man had already received a glorious incarnation nearly a
century earlier in the work of Milton: his proper name is Lucifer [or Satan,
leader of the rebellious fallen angels].[12]

In the next section, in connection with Marx's views about how to
achieve human freedom, we will see his notion of the ideal person and his explanation of Kant's ideal man, which differs from Murdoch's.

It would be going past the evidence to say that there is *one* bourgeois
ideal that dominates our epoch. But here are some results from the research
firm of Yankelovich, Skelly and White, whose job it is to figure out the self-
image Americans have of themselves; their results are used by advertisers,
many of whom assume, probably correctly, that most United States citizens
aspire to move from the proletarian to the bourgeois class. Here is an outline
of the purported ideal up to the 1920s when, according to the researchers, the
concept of personal success prevailed and we had made a commitment
politically and socially to capitalism:

> An admirable person is self-sufficient, dependable, and trustworthy.
>
> A person can start with little or nothing and gain wealth, power, and
> status. This is desirable. Later we called it upward mobility.
>
> The way to achieve upward mobility is to embrace and practice the work
> ethic. This teaches that work is a virtue and idleness is (at worst) sinful or
> (at best) unacceptable.
>
> Material possessions are the outward symbols of success and happiness and
> the goal toward which reasonable people strive.
>
> Extensions of these ideas, and especially the work ethic, were
> myriad. Save money, spend wisely. Conform to what is expected by
> society. Use spare time to better yourself and your family.[13]

The story goes on to point out that there are two groups of holdovers
from this picture, the Traditionalists and the Retreaters, and that there are
newer groups that break away—though barely—which the researchers called
the Autonomous, the New Conformists, and the Forerunners. A typical
forerunner, for instance, is described as a Yale graduate son of a Yale
graduate lawyer who decides to work with his hands: "Creativity is more important . . . than upward mobility or work for its own sake. He likes being
his own boss, if possible, setting his own hours and creating something of
value with his own hands. He also wants to make his way in the world."
(McWhirter)

That the bourgeois ideal is not wholly admirable can be gathered by
simply recalling Marx's laughter about "morals." His scathing portrait of
Jeremy Bentham and what he says is Bentham's human ideal, the shopkeeper,
may amuse you. Marx describes Bentham as "that insipid, pedantic, leather-
tongued oracle of the ordinary bourgeois intelligence of the 19th century"
(*Capital,* p. 668):

Bentham is a purely English phenomenon. Not even excepting our [German] philosopher, Christian Wolf, in no time and in no country has the most homespun common-place ever strutted about in so self-satisfied a way. The principle of utility was no discovery of Bentham. He simply reproduced in his dull way what Helvetius and other Frenchmen had said with esprit [wit] in the 18th century. To know what is useful for a dog, one must study dog-nature. This nature itself is not to be deduced from the principle of utility. Applying this to man, he that would criticize all human acts, movements, relations, etc., by the principle of utility, must first deal with human nature as modified in each historical epoch. Bentham makes short work of it. With the dryest naiveté he takes the modern shopkeeper, especially the English shopkeeper, as the normal man. Whatever is useful to this queer normal man, and to his world, is absolutely useful. This yard-measure, then, he applies to past, present and future. . . . Had I the courage of my friend, Heinrich Heine [the great German poet], I should call Mr. Jeremy [Bentham] a genius in the way of bourgeois stupidity. (*Capital,* note, p. 668)

14.3 Hume and Kant
Criticized and Superseded

Marx considers both Hume and Kant as moments in the capitalist epoch. They both produced "liberal" ideologies which expressed bourgeois interests; consequently, they will both be superseded in the next epoch when communist relations of production replace capitalist relations, and when the antagonistic classes of the proletariat and the bourgeoisie disappear. Something of each will be preserved as well, although altered—principally, the humanist naturalism of Hume and Kant's passion for freedom.

I will pick out two of Hume's doctrines that Marx thinks mistaken: (1) Hume's ahistorical view that we have a fixed human nature and (2) his view about the usefulness and necessity of property. Similarly, I will select two views of Kant as targets of Marx's criticism: (1) Kant's reliance on the supersensible and (2) his excessive individualism.

14.3a CRITIQUE
Human nature. Hume thought that we have a human nature with its principles of operation given. Habit or custom is one such principle, by which we learn to associate events in the world as cause and effect. The sentiments of self-love and benevolence provide the source and verification of morality, while sympathy lets us convert our idea of the feelings of others into similar feelings of our own. Furthermore, says Hume, there is no hope of finding the causes of these principles of human nature. (See Chapter 12, p. 429.) Sociobiologists such as E. O. Wilson, however, disagree with Hume's

view that we can't explain the principles of mental and moral operation; **537**
Wilson explains them as adaptive mechanisms for individual and species survival.

Marx considers both Hume and thinkers like Wilson ahistorical; they
fail to understand that biological or psychological laws leave out of consideration the fact that human nature is changed by history, principally by changes
in the mode of producing the means for life. Human nature is not fixed, according to Marx, nor can its changes be explained without the history of
economic relations. Marx thinks Hume naive when Hume takes the appearance of humans as he experiences them for the reality; instead, one has to
dig beneath the surface to find why eighteenth-century humans, as Hume saw
them, had become the way they were:

> [Adam] Smith and [David] Ricardo [English economists and, like Hume,
> moral psychologists] still stand with both feet on the shoulders of the
> eighteenth-century prophets, in whose imaginations this eighteenth-century
> individual—the product on one side of the dissolution of the feudal forms
> of society, on the other side of the new forces of production developed
> since the sixteenth century—appears as an ideal, whose existence they pro-
> ject into the past. Not as a historic result but as history's point of depar-
> ture. As the Natural Individual appropriate to their notion of human
> nature, not arising historically, but posited by nature. This illusion has
> been common to each epoch to this day. (*Grundrisse,* p. 83)

As regards Marx's last comment, one might recall Plato.

In contrast to Hume and other human nature theorists, Marx thinks
humans make their own nature through their labor process. They cannot do
so freely and self-consciously until the laboring class is free from domination,
which will not occur until the communist epoch, nowhere as yet attained even
now:

> Labor is, in the first place, a process in which both man and Nature par-
> ticipate, and in which man of his own accord starts, regulates, and controls
> the material re-actions between himself and Nature. He opposes himself
> to Nature as one of her own forces, setting in motion arms and legs, head
> and hands, the natural forces of his body, in order to appropriate Nature's
> productions in a form adapted to his own wants. By thus acting on the ex-
> ternal world and changing it, he at the same time changes his own nature.
> He develops his slumbering powers and compels them to act in obedience
> to his sway. . . . We presuppose labor in a form that stamps it as ex-
> clusively human. A spider conducts operations that resemble those of a
> weaver, and a bee puts to shame many an architect in the construction of
> her cells. But what distinguishes the worst architect from the best of
> bees is this, that the architect raises his structure in imagination before he
> erects it in reality. . . . He also realizes a purpose of his own that gives the
> law to his modus operandi, and to which he must subordinate his will.
> (*Capital,* pp. 197–98)

538   Spiders and bees have a nature given by Nature, because they can neither plan what they will do nor conceive a purpose to which their activity is the means of achievement. They differ from humans, whose awakened powers of imagination, conception, and purpose free them from purely mechanical, natural laws. The discussion of Marx's conception of freedom in 14.3b will explain in more detail Marx's conception of labor as an "objectification" of ourselves, which makes it possible to conceive of ourselves and to set the stage for self-control and self-realization.

Property. Hume thought that the concepts of property, right, and obligation could not be understood unless one knew the origin of the concept of justice. (See 12.4b, p. 435.) Hume, remember, thinks that justice arises from conventions; these conventions are grounded in their usefulness for dealing with two conditions—the selfish principle in human nature and the scarcity of goods (p. 434). "The ideas of property," he said, "become necessary in all civil society."

Marx, on the contrary, thinks private property is not "necessary in all civil society." Social, cooperative production is necessary, but the private possession of the means of production—property—is not. In fact, property is what divides our society into antagonistic classes, distinguishing those who own the means of production, the bourgeois ruling class, from those who do not, the proletariat class who are ruled. Instead of being good because useful, property is the source of the greatest mischief. The person who controls capital dominates those who do not. This alienates the proletariat, making them strangers to their own products, their laboring activity, and others—even to their own essence. The essence of humans is to make things, material and intellectual. When you don't control the production and distribution of your products or their price—when you don't control your own work activity and are not equal in power to others—then your productive, cooperative life activity is torn from you, as is your human essence.

Hegel conceived of human history as a progressive reappropriation of objects—the Other—by subjects, due to a growing self-consciousness that the Other *is* the self. The separated object and subject progressively come to be seen as one, which constitutes a recovery of unity. Our alienation from the world will end when we see that the world is a product of our consciousness. Marx, as we have seen, also conceived of human history as a progressive reappropriation of objects, but he claimed to have turned the dialectic right side up, to have put it "on its feet," and conceived of human history as a progressive reappropriation of the products—the cars, chemicals, furniture, books, poems—of our labor. Our alienation in the world will end when we see our products reappropriated by the persons who actually make them, and not (as now) appropriated by those who own the capital and factories and buy the labor power of the workers. Where Hegel saw the cure for alienation in our ability to perceive the "Other" as the product of our *thought,* Marx saw the cure in our ability to perceive the "Other" as the product of our *labor,* of our active hands and brains.

Thus for Marx, unlike for Hume, property is not a necessity but a fetter.[14] To better understand what Marx meant by "alienation," we might consider the investigations of Dr. Gordon G. Gallup, Jr., a professor of psychology who found that adolescent chimpanzees begin to recognize themselves in a mirror after three or four days of looking; at the beginning, they think the mirror image is another chimpanzee. Similarly, children learn to recognize themselves after about two years of age. This inability to recognize yourself in a mirror is analogous to alienation from your own product of labor and has the same result—the loss of your species essence. You see objects made by you in pursuit of a hobby as yours and as part of you, unlike objects made by you for pay on the assembly line. Assembly line products are really commodities—not your products—because they are made for the owner who sells them and gives you money as your reward; consequently, these are alienated products. If you can't see yourself—can't recognize yourself—in your products, then you're like the chimpanzees who can't recognize themselves in the mirror. Capitalists, by appropriating workers' products, have taken away their mirror. As Gallup says, "If an organism is incapable of identifying itself in a mirror, how can it possibly identify itself as being a member of some particular species."[15] To get Marx's point about alienation, simply substitute "its product" for "a mirror" in Gallup's statement.

Supersensible. Kant divided the cosmos into two realms, the sensible, natural world and the supersensible, rational world. He did this in order to provide a residence for our free will. (See 7.4, 13.3, and 13.4.)

In this regard, Marx is on Hume's side: the natural world exists and nothing else. Whatever understanding we acquire of humans has to be confined to forces in the real, material world, and must not include some "fantastic" supersensible realm or supersensible powers. Humans in all their aspects are immanent, not transcendent; whatever new state they achieve transcending a former state is made from immanent material, by immanent material, and constitutes a new immanent state. Human freedom has to be characterized by reference to the powers we have through laws of nature, and not by reference to powers of will that Kant acknowledged to be "inscrutable."

Marx says that his method of approach to understanding "morality, religion, metaphysics, all the rest of ideology and their corresponding forms of consciousnes" is "not devoid of premises":

> It starts out from the real premises and does not abandon them for a moment. Its premises are men, not in any fantastic isolation or abstract definition, but in their actual, empirically perceptible process of development under definite conditions. As soon as this active life-process is described, history ceases to be a collection of dead facts as it is with the empiricists (themselves still abstract), or an imagined activity of imagined subjects, as with the idealists [who think all reality is a product of consciousness].
>
> Where speculation ends—in real life—there real, positive science begins: the representation of the practical activity, of the practical process of development of men. Empty talk about consciousness ceases, and real

knowledge has to take its place. When reality is depicted, philosophy as an independent branch of activity loses its medium of existence. (*German Ideology,* p. 15)

Reflecting on Kant's "good will" and the hope that our happiness will be proportional to our worthiness—a hope that the *summum bonum* will indeed be achieved—Marx notes that Kant has to project a "hereafter" in which this will occur. Unlike Murdoch, who explained Kant's ideal as a product of the rise of science, Marx explains it in terms of the political failures of the German bourgeoisie:

> The condition of Germany at the end of the last [eighteenth] century is completely reflected in Kant's *Critique of Practical Reason.* Whilst the French bourgeoisie raised themselves to supremacy and conquered the European continent by the most colossal revolution known to history, whilst the English bourgeoisie, already politically emancipated, revolutionized industry and subjugated India politically and all the rest of the world commercially, the impotent German bourgeois could get no further than "the good will." Kant contented himself with the mere "good will" even when it remained without any result, and placed the *realization* of this good will, the harmony between it and the needs and impulses of the individual, in the *Hereafter.* . . . Neither he nor the German bourgeois, whose euphemistic spokesman he was, noticed that the basis of these theoretical ideas of the bourgeoisie lay in material interests and in a *will* conditioned and determined by the material conditions of production: he therefore separated this theoretical expression from the interests it expresses.[16]

Lucien Goldmann, whose characterization of Kant's philosophy as a tragic vision is outlined in 7.8, accepts Marx's explanation of Kant's emphasis on a free will and Kant's retreat to the supersensible "hereafter." Instead of believing that virtue and happiness could be brought into greater harmony by a human, historical, and immanent effort, Kant thought it possible only if humans were immortal and could have an infinite amount of time in the heavenly "hereafter" to bring themselves to moral perfection, and only if a good God existed to ensure that our happiness would be as complete and perfect as our virtue.

Individualism. Goldmann argues that Kant's individualism kept him from believing that human effort would be sufficient to realize the *summum bonum* on earth rather than in heaven. Kant's moral subject is the self with its will, its practical reason, *Wille* and *Willkür.* The Categorical Imperative is a directive for generating *universal* laws to be carried out by an *individual* exercising his or her will; it is a command laid on each of us to have and act with a "good will." But it is this *universal* demand on merely *individual* wills that makes impossible the earthly attainment of the *summum bonum:*

> For the fundamental limitation of man in bourgeois individualist society is precisely that for him virtue and happiness are incompatible. So long as the *individual,* the *I,* is the subject of action, the search for happiness is not

universal but egoistic, and as such, contrary to virtue. The universal remains for him a duty which he can fulfill only in renouncing all content [of moral laws], his sensuous nature, his inclinations, that is to say, in renouncing his happiness. The union of these two heterogeneous elements of the highest good [*summum bonum*] thus presupposes [for Kant] a radical change in the community, a qualitatively different universe, the kingdom of God.[17]

Goldmann thinks Kant's pessimism about harmonizing the heterogeneous values of virtue and happiness here on earth is due to Kant's asking "What ought *I* to do?" rather than asking "What ought *we* to do?" Marx was optimistic about human progress. When we see how he supersedes Kant's concept of freedom in 14.3b, we will find that he projects the next historical stage as a communist society where humans think of themselves as *we* rather than as a collection of *I*'s—society where humans attain a communal rather than an individualistic identity.

Marx discusses individualism and its liberty when he reflects on the French Revolution in his essay "On the Jewish Question." There Marx distinguishes between "the state" and "civil society." The state is a political organization in which the role of each person is citizen. A civil society is an organization of our economics, of personal relations as in the family, of the kind of labor people perform, and so forth; the present form of civil society, ushered in by the French Revolution, is a bourgeois society. The state defines the "rights of the citizen" in its laws and divides them from "the rights of man"—liberty, equality, security, property—a division which Rousseau had earlier lamented. Thus the French Revolution divided humans and their rights into two parts; according to Marx, the rights of man, "are nothing else than the rights of the member of the bourgeois society." One of his main points is that the rights of man are individualistic rights, which constitute one of the pillar concepts of capitalistic, bourgeois ideology. These are rights "of the egoistic individual, of man separated from man and the community."[18]

Marx quotes from the French Constitution of 1793 to show the concept of liberty that predominated: "Liberty is the power which belongs to man to do everything which does not injure the rights of others." Notice that this contains something of Kant's idea of the Categorical Imperative, which requires that a maxim of action should be universalizable, should be possible for everyone to perform, and should not propose to treat others only as a means for our own ends, which would be an injury to others. Marx's comment on this concept of liberty ties it to individualism, which, he thinks, is one of the presuppositions behind Kant's conception of moral action:

> Freedom is therefore the right to do and perform that which injures none. The limits within which each may move without injuring others are fixed by the law, as the boundary between two fields is fixed by the fence. The freedom in question is the freedom of the individual as an isolated atom. . . . The right of man to freedom is not based upon the connection of man with man, but rather on the separation of man from man. It is the right to this separation, the right of the individual limited to himself. ("Jewish Question," p. 623)

542   Marx adds some thoughts to this in a challenge to Hume's account of the origin of justice, whereby human selfishness and the scarcity of goods force individuals to come together for mutual usefulness:

> None of the so-called rights of man, therefore, goes beyond the egoistic individual, beyond the individual as a member of bourgeois society, withdrawn into his private interests and separated from the community. Far from regarding the individual as a genetic being [connected to others of its kind], the generic life, Society itself, rather appears as an external frame for the individual, as a limitation of his original independence. The sole bond which connects him with his fellows is natural necessity, material needs and private interest, the preservation of his property and his egoistic person. ("Jewish Question," p. 624)

Thus the French Revolution destroyed the connections of the old civil society and dissolved the people into the unconnected, elemental parts of the new bourgeois society. Dissolution of the old connections, which had curbed egoistic interests, was replaced by no connections at all and was called "liberation." What it actually did was to give individuals unbridled freedom to pursue their private material and intellectual interests.

The following passage introduces us to Marx's theory of how the next or communist historical epoch will lead to the supersession, the simultaneous overcoming and preservation, of Hume and Kant's bourgeois ideology. Notice that in this statement Marx commits himself to freedom (emancipation) and self-realization, two of the themes in this book (pp. 42–43):

> Not until the real, individual man is identical with the citizen, and has become a generic being in his empirical life, in his individual work, in his individual relationships, not until man has recognized and organized his own capacities as social capacities, and consequently the social force is no longer divided by the political power, not until then will human emancipation be achieved. ("Jewish Question," p. 627)

Kant rightly demanded worthiness of us as both citizen and member of society, but the bourgeois split between the state and civil society—in Kant, the split between legality and morality, justice and virtue—has split persons as well. This split dooms full moral achievement; our individual wills aren't effective enough to overcome the individualist structure of our society. Kant's moral ideal casts us in the role of autonomous, spontaneous beings abstracted from the web of social relations; however, the tasks we must perform to man the economic, productive machinery are social; they require communal effort. Here we find the gap between *social* relations of production and *individualistic* relations of the superstructure—the contradiction that marks the ending of one epoch and the beginning of another. When the gap between an individualistic superstructure and social means of production becomes too great, a revolutionary class comes into existence that alters the superstructure and makes it conform to the material base of production; private property and its laws become social property.

14.3b SUPERSESSION. In this subsection I explain two parts of **543** Hume and Kant that Marx preserves, with transformations. He preserves Hume's naturalism, which makes humans immanent, but preserves it (as we saw) with a difference, because humans can make their own nature. This latter consideration also makes possible the retention, but transformation, of Kant's freedom and Kant's conditions for a moral totality, as set forth in the three formulations of the Categorical Imperative.

Naturalism. Humans need not and cannot depend upon some "transcendental" powers such as their own supersensible will or a god. They share the same kind of powers that other natural things do; in principle, nothing is a mystery to our understanding. However, our being wholly natural and immanent doesn't imply that we are locked into a human nature as Hume thought. Marx uses three key concepts to show how we can be both natural and capable of self-transformation: objectification, consciousness, and self-reference or feedback.

Objectification: The essence of humans is to produce things. We are *homo faber,* "Man the Maker." Kant put our essence in rationality, but Marx thinks this cuts us off from our practice of working on and transforming the material world in order to live. The division of labor—this one making shoes, that one farming, another managing workers, still another teaching philosophy—has a profound effect of making a major division between material and mental labor. Kant could think of the essence of humans as rationality because of this division of labor. But our mental and physical capacities ought not to be separated; this division invites the conclusion that in our material work we are natural beings and in our intellectual work transcendent beings. An empirical look at work, however, shows that people have to think: we plan, form purposes, discover means to accomplish those purposes, discuss them with one another, write about them, and so forth. This mental activity leads to actual operation on matter—on ore, soil, paper, animals, vegetables; these actual operations—work—change the original matter into a new, "human" object. This object is the "objectification" of our plans, purposes, talk, and thought. In effect, we are now "out there" in the objects we make. We project ourselves into our products.

Consciousness: Humans, remember, are unlike spiders and bees, because humans are conscious, have purposes, and can imagine the object to be made before it exists. These are natural powers that give us the ability to be *self*-conscious. Spiders and bees have a form of consciousness; spiders, for instance, see their webs and the objects to and between which they will stretch their threads. But because they don't have purposes or plans that precede their productions, says Marx, they can't see the objects they make as *their own*. Humans can see the objects *as their own* because the objects are the projection of *their* thinking, planning, imagining. Further, because the making of objects is a social activity involving the coordination of many people—think of all the persons involved in the manufacture of an automobile—the objects are the objectification of a social effort, a social person.

Self-reference: Humans are self-referring: you can refer to yourself,

544   think about yourself—"I don't fully understand Kant," you might say. This self-reference is achieved by feedback. Feedback is an ancient concept used in self-regulating machines; the Greeks had feedback mechanisms to regulate the pumping of water. A familiar modern example is the thermostat. You set it for 65 degrees. When the room gets below that temperature, the thermostat triggers an electric switch that starts the furnace, perhaps because a piece of metal has contracted and activated an electrical connection. When the temperature goes above 65 degrees, it switches the furnace off. The thermostat is "self"-regulating, we say, because we ourselves don't have to regulate the furnace fires; the temperature of the room is fed back to the thermostat as "information" that causes the appropriate reaction in the thermostat.

Similarly, a person or persons who have cooperated in the making of an object, because it projects and objectifies their thoughts, are able to see themselves in the object; the objectification is information fed back to the makers. These objects are now seen as the springboard to further plans, thoughts, purposes, which thereby makes us different after our work activity than we were before—in short, self-referring, conscious objectification is a process of *self*-transformation.

Carol Gould, a contemporary philosopher, gives the following illustration of this process:

> Consider the example of a person who wants to become a good cook. In order to realize this purpose, the person has to practice cooking, that is, has to engage in the activity of combining ingredients in accordance with a recipe and has to learn to use the appropriate utensils for specific tasks. It is thus by working on conditions in accordance with purposes that the agent acquires new or changed characteristics, in this case, a skill. It is also evident that this process of self-creation or self-change, as in the previous case of labor as the changing of things, requires the mediation of objective conditions. That is, according to Marx, it is necessary to transform one's objective circumstances in order to change oneself.[19]

Marx preserves Hume's naturalistic outlook while also explaining how we make our own selves and human nature. There is nothing "unnatural" about "objectifying" production, consciousness, and feedback. The relationships can be diagrammed as follows. Think your way through the diagram from (a) to (c).

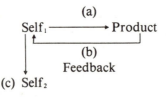

(a) Self₁ works on the external world and objectifies its purposes and plans in the product-object; unless alienated, it is conscious of its projection in the object and sees it as its own.

(b) This consciousness is fed back into Self₁ as additional information, **545** which gives Self₁ a new base from which to make new plans and purposes to be objectified through new work.

(c) Self₁ creates a new Self₂.

Freedom. Having learned from Hegel to despise the naive simplicity of British philosophers but admiring their direct attention to facts, Marx took Hegel's concepts of objectification, consciousness, and self-reference (as outlined above) and combined them with Kant's vision of a moral totality to forge a new and appealing concept of emancipation and freedom.

To put it simply, Marx's ideal human is free, self-conscious, and self-realizing. This ideal is attainable only if all persons have control over the conditions under which they objectify and create themselves. All production of objects is complex, cooperative, and social. If producers (workers) can't control the means of producing, as they cannot under capitalism, then they can't objective themselves and so can't create themselves; they will be formed by others instead. There will, then, be neither self-determination nor self-realization. The essence of humans is to produce and make things, including themselves; if they can't produce themselves, there is no self-realization and no self-determination, and they are reduced to the level of wage slaves. In short, in the light of the three theme questions posed at the beginning of Chapter 2, if workers can't control what they produce, they can't be free, morally self-determining, nor morally self-realizing.

Marx was as passionate a partisan of freedom, and was as interested in human attainment of the *summum bonum,* as was Kant. But unlike Kant, he refused to take refuge in some transcendental dream. Freedom and self-realization of our moral capacities should be within the reach of living men and women; they shouldn't have to wait for a "hereafter" or depend on the goodness of a transcendent god. The only way humans can attain freedom and their "real" self on earth is to "throw off the chains" of those who control them.

Marx's vision was of an association of workers who recover their Kantian dignity by treating one another as ends and equals, and who are not forced to sell their energies to others in order to live at a price extracted by those who control capital. With Kant, you gain worthiness by willingness to do your duty; even if you fail to accomplish your end, it does not detract from your worthiness. The "good" will and not the result is what makes one worthy. You have tried and are not found wanting. But this already is to accept an excuse for failure while glossing it over with personal heroism. Marx says we need not settle only for worthiness; we deserve happiness commensurate with our worthiness as well. The philosophical problem is to *change* the world so that it is no longer an obstacle to our happiness. This can be done only if humans achieve a totality where none are thrown into classes antagonistic to other classes, as is now the case when the proletariat and the bourgeoisie are pitted against each other for preservation of their interests.

Workers are alienated from their work and their products because, in Kantian terms, they are "treated not as ends, but merely as means" to the ad-

546   vancement of others. Kant's Categorical Imperative in its three formulations is mirrored in Marx: (1) will only those maxims everyone can will (no class has privileges over another class); (2) never treat another as a means only but always as an end (no one should buy the labor power of another for self-advancement); and (3) establish a "Kingdom of Ends" where everyone has equal legislative power over life's conditions and ends (the domination of one class by another is to cease). These are Kant's logical conditions for a moral totality, and they are also Marx's. But Marx says we can't depend upon the "good will" to bring these logical conditions into actuality; we have to alter the social, economic, and political relations between people in order for the "good will" to function as Kant envisioned it.

Negatively, Marx thinks that the conditions for achieving a moral totality are absent in a society organized as ours is. The result is that workers cannot realize themselves through self-determined, free work. They are estranged from themselves and their work because they do not partake of a moral totality. Their will is hopelessly unequal to the task of creating such a totality.

> Marx pointed to meaninglessness of work and a sense of powerlessness to affect the conditions of one's life, dissociation from the products of one's labor, the sense of playing a role in an impersonal system which one does not understand or control, the seeing of oneself and others within socially-imposed and artificial categories, the denial of human possibilities for a fully creative, spontaneous, egalitarian and reciprocal life. He attributed these, in particular, to the form taken by the division of labor under capitalism, and, more generally, to the fact of class society. . . .
>
> Alienation is found today in perhaps its most acute form among workers in assembly-line industries, such as the motor-car industry, where, as [sociologist Robert] Blauner writes in his sensitive study of workers' alienation . . . , "a depersonalized worker, estranged from himself and larger collectives, goes through the motions of work in the regimented milieu of the conveyor-belt for the sole purpose of earning his bread," "his work has become almost compartmentalized from other areas of his life, so that there is little meaning left in it beyond the instrumental purpose."[20]

But positively, Kant's call for a moral totality is one that Marx can second. Lucien Goldmann puts this well:

> Kant succeeds in concentrating into a few words the most radical condemnation of bourgeois society and in formulating the foundations for any future humanism: *"Act in such a way that you always treat humanity, whether in your own person or in the person of any other, never simply as a means, but always at the same time as an end."* [The second formulation of the Categorical Imperative.]
>
> Once we realize that this formula condemns any society based on production for the market, in which other men are treated as means with a view of creating profits, we see the extent to which Kant's ethic is an ethic

of content and constitutes a radical rejection of existing society. **547**
Moreover, and no less radically, it lays the foundations for any true
humanism in establishing the only supreme value upon which all our
judgments must be based. That supreme value is humanity in the person
of each individual man. . . . "Complete determination," the totality,
would be the realization of a "kingdom of ends" [Kant's third formulation
of the Categorical Imperative], that is to say, the very reverse of present-
day society where, with the exception of a few rare and partial com-
munities, man is never more than a means. (Goldmann, pp. 176–77)

While Kant projected an ideal totality as a "kingdom of ends," he did
not extend human freedom to the point of controlling and legislating moral
and legal laws in the economic sphere. Marx saw this extension to economics
as necessary, if we are to eliminate the greatest obstacle to the creation of a
moral totality. Humans are makers, taking nature and transforming it into a
human habitation filled with human objects; if they are not free in their making, but shackled by the rule of others, then they aren't free to make a moral
totality. This denies their moral personhood. Property and the freedom envisioned by Kant cannot both exist. If you value freedom, private property
must go. Marx's moral vision for a new society has a distinctly Kantian
flavor:

> Only in community with others has each individual the means of
> cultivating his gifts in all directions; only in the community, therefore, is
> personal freedom possible. In the previous substitutes for the community,
> in the State, etc., personal freedom has existed only for the individuals who
> developed within the relationships of the ruling class, and only in so far as
> they were individuals of this class. (*German Ideology,* p. 74)

Notice that Marx links freedom and personal self-realization, just as
Kant did. But for Marx this cannot be a freedom merely to will what is
moral; one must also achieve what one wills, and this can be done only if people will together under the right conditions. Marx won't settle for worthiness
as Kant did; he also wants results, consequences. In stating the conditions for
effective freedom, notice that he equates bourgeois freedom with chance,
which he contrasts with self-control:

> With the community of revolutionary proletarians on the other hand, who
> take their conditions of existence and those of all members of society under
> their control, it is just the reverse; it is as individuals that the individuals
> participate in it. It is just this combination of individuals (assuming the
> advanced stage of modern productive forces, of course) which puts the
> conditions of the free development and movement of individuals under
> their [own] control—conditions which were previously abandoned to
> chance. . . . This right to the undisturbed enjoyment, upon certain condi-
> tions, of fortuity and chance has up till now been called personal
> freedom. (*German Ideology,* p. 75)

548   By self-realization, Marx means the development of all our natural capacities.   The present division of labor prevents this because we are required to spend all our energies on one kind of work, so as to produce more at cheaper cost for the owners of capital.   Here is Marx's famous image of what humans could be in a moral economic totality:

> As soon as labor is distributed [division of labor], each man has a particular, exclusive sphere of activity, which is forced upon him and from which he cannot escape.   He is a hunter, a fisherman, a shepherd, or a critical critic, and must remain so if he does not want to lose his means of livelihood; while in communist society, where nobody has one exclusive sphere of activity but each can become accomplished in any branch he wishes, society regulates the general production and thus makes it possible for me to do one thing to-day and another to-morrow, to hunt in the morning, fish in the afternoon, rear cattle in the evening, criticize after dinner, just as I have a mind, without ever becoming hunter, fisherman, shepherd or critic.   (*German Ideology,* p. 22)

One could add, "What one becomes in a communist society is a man, in the generic sense."   Humans are the one generic being in the world, according to Marx, because we alone are conscious that we belong to a species and are members of it—something that lower creatures are incapable of understanding.   When we are most fully self-conscious—that is, when our powers are most developed—we truly become human.   In their different ways, Marx and Kant both see that what we ought to become is fully human.   Kant thinks we become so by the greatest development of our will into virtue, Marx by self-realization in the free objectification of ourselves in the products of our labor.

Marx criticizes Adam Smith's view that labor is necessarily a curse. Marx thinks it a means to fulfillment because work creates value, as when we weave a long twist of cotton into fabric.   This should be a source of wonder and congratulations, not a curse; that it becomes a curse is due to what happens to our products, not to the nature of work itself.

> In the sweat of thy brow shalt thou labor! was Jehovah's curse on Adam. And this is labor for Smith, a curse.   "Tranquillity" appears as the adequate state, as identical with "freedom" and "happiness."   It seems quite far from Smith's mind that the individual, "in his normal state of health, strength, activity, skill, facility," also needs a normal portion of work, and of the suspension of tranquillity.   Certainly, labor obtains its measure from the outside, through the aim to be attained and the obstacles to be overcome in attaining it.   But Smith has no inkling whatever that this overcoming of obstacles is in itself a liberating activity—and that, further, the external aims become stripped of the semblance of merely external natural urgencies, and become posited as aims which the individual himself posits—hence as self-realization, objectification of the subject, hence real freedom, whose action is, precisely, labor.   He [Smith] is right, of course,

that, in its historic forms as slave-labor, serf-labor, and wage-labor, labor always appears as repulsive, always as *external forced labor;* and not-labor, by contrast, as "freedom, and happiness." (*Grundrisse,* p. 611)

If you don't like to work, don't conclude too quickly that you're shiftless, lazy, and no good.   If you're forced to work at tasks that soon grow boring because that's all you do for hours on end during your most alert waking hours, you should blame the relations of production that put you into an unrewarding work situation.

While Marx thought there were "laws" of economic development, these were not "eternal natural laws independent of history" (*Grundrisse,* p. 87). The science of economics that he envisioned was not something produced by spectator scientists observing the "facts" and maintaining a "value" neutrality.   Our knowledge of the "facts" in the world can't be explained without including the role that our values play.   This is because knowledge is acquired when we act; we aren't disembodied spectators of the play and flash of events; we are involved in them and sometimes force the events.   Our involvement and action are undertaken because of our values; that's why value and knowledge aren't separate.   Sandra Bartky, a contemporary philosopher, illustrates this nicely with some remarks on feminism.   She thinks it important "to understand as concretely as possible how the contradictory factors we are able to identify are lived and suffered by particular people."   She makes a connection between the apprehension of what "ought to be" and the "facts":

Women have long lamented their condition, but a lament, pure and simple, need not be an expression of feminist consciousness.   As long as their situation is apprehended as natural, inevitable, and inescapable, women's consciousness of themselves, no matter how alive to insult and inferiority, is not yet feminist consciousness. . . .   Feminist consciousness *is* the apprehension of possibility.   The very *meaning* of what the feminist apprehends is illuminated by the light of what ought to be: the given situation is first understood in terms of a state of affairs not yet actual and in this sense a possibility, a state of affairs in which what is given would be negated and radically transformed.   To say that feminist consciousness is the experience in a certain way of certain specific contradictions in the social order is to say that the feminist apprehends certain features of social reality *as* intolerable, as to be rejected in behalf of a transforming project for the future.   "It is on the day that we can conceive of a different state of affairs that a new light falls on our troubles and we *decide* that these are unbearable." [Quoted from Jean-Paul Sartre.]   What Sartre would call her "transcendence," her project of negation and transformation, makes possible what are specifically feminist ways of apprehending contradictions in the social order. . . .   Feminist consciousness, it might be ventured, turns a "fact" into a "contradiction"; often, features of social reality are only apprehended *as* contradictory from the vantage point of a radical project of transformation.[21]

550   To summarize: one way of dealing with all the contrasts between the two moral theories advocated by Hume and Kant is not to think you must choose between them. Rather, you might deal with them as Marx did, viewing them as ideologies of a historical epoch that will pass. Marx sees intellectual structures, such as Hume and Kant's, as superstructure reflections of the economic base. When the present, capitalistic base changes to a communist economic base, Hume and Kant's ethics will be superseded, yet something of each will be preserved in a transformed way. That the economic base will change, Marx thinks, can be expected, because the growing social interdependency characteristic of the way our society produces goods will make the deprived proletariat realize that the individualistic capitalist social relations are in "contradiction" to the base. This will produce a revolutionary class demanding an economic order that gives them control over their own labor products. They will give up faith in a transcendent, supersensible realm as the place to achieve their happiness. Seeing that they can transform themselves and the conditions of life, they will move to do so and thereby transform themselves into free persons. Hume's naturalistic viewpoint will be preserved, as will Kant's commitment to the dignity and freedom of humans.

As a final point, you may ask if Marx isn't committed to a historical relativism. Does the shift of power from one class to another—from the feudal nobility to the bourgeoisie, then from the bourgeoisie to the proletariat—simply mean that the interests of one class prevail by power alone? Furthermore, you may ask, doesn't this carry us back to where we began with Thrasymachus' claim that justice is what is to the interest of the stronger (p. 71)?

Marx denies that he is a moral relativist, denies that he hands right over to might. This is because each succeeding revolutionary class has to satisfy interests wider than its own to succeed. As this process advances historically, the new, restructured societies will be designed to meet the needs of more and more people. The particular interests of classes will merge with the general, common interests of all. This final historical result is the disappearance of a class society and the realization of a classless, communist society.

> For each new class which puts itself in the place of one ruling before it, is compelled, merely in order to carry through its aim, to represent its interest as the common interest of all the members of society, put in an ideal form; it will give its ideas the form of universality, and represent them as the only rational, universally valid ones. The class making a revolution appears from the very start, merely because it is opposed to a *class,* not as a class but as the representative of the whole society; it appears as the whole mass of society confronting the one ruling class. . . . Every new class, therefore, achieves its hegemony [dominance] only on a broader basis than that of the class ruling previously. . . .
> This whole semblance, that the rule of a certain class is only the rule of certain ideas, comes to a natural end, of course, as soon as society ceases at last to be organized in the form of class-rule, that is to say as soon as it is no longer necessary to represent a particular interest as general or "the general interest" as ruling. (*German Ideology,* pp. 40–41)

STUDY QUESTIONS   551

1 How does Marx's conception of the dialectic resemble Hegel's, and how does it differ from Hegel's?

2 Explain how Marx's turning Hegel's dialectic "right side up" encourages us to look for contradictions in our economic life rather than in our head.

3 What, for Marx and Engels, is the relation between morality, philosophy, religion—all of the superstructure—and the mode of production? Why, in their view, does this imply that morality will change when the capitalist relations of production change to communist relations? And what does this imply about our deciding whether to side with moral psychologists or rational will moralists?

4 Explain Marx's critique of Hume's theory of human nature and his theory of property.

5 Explain Marx's critique of Kant's division of the world into the sensible and supersensible and of Kant's individualistic theory of moral worthiness.

6 What is "objectification," and why must one understand it in order to grasp Marx's concept of freedom and the ideal person?

Reflections on Applications

1 The newspaper columnist William Safire quotes some "old pro" middle-level people who work in the White House; they are loyal to President Carter but "let their hair down in separate not-for-attribution interviews." Safire asked what sort of an executive Carter is. Here is one answer:

> He has an algebraic mind, not a dialectical mind. The farthest thing from his mind is that there can be contradictions between good goals. So when it came time to make a decision between [Secretary of State Cyrus] Vance's soft line and [defense adviser Zbigniew] Brzezinski's hard line at Annapolis a few months ago, he took a little of one, added to some of the other, and wound up with nothing.[22]

This description of what Carter did makes it sound like he compromised. Compromise, according to this informant, isn't what a dialectical mind does. Review the idea of superseding or overcoming contradictions, which is central to Hegel's and Marx's concept of the dialectical process; then say what is missing from the way Carter supposedly deals with the contradictions facing him.

2 There may be contradictions between "good goals," as the above informant said. One person's goods may not be another's goods; this is

what puts them in "contradiction." Here is a chance for you to develop a dialectical mind and escape your "algebraic" limitations, by dealing with the pros and cons of an ordinance proposed for the city and county of San Francisco.

One supervisor had introduced an ordinance prohibiting taxicab companies and drivers from selling their permits. At the time it was introduced, taxi permits were selling for over $12,000. Additionally, the Yellow Cab Company had gone bankrupt, and a judge had ruled its permits to be assets; an investor then sought to buy the company and sell the permits to the New Yellow Cab Cooperative of taxi drivers. Here are some reasons put forth for and against the ordinance. Sort them out and put them into two groups: "for" and "against." Then, dialectically reason your way to a solution. Say too if the contradiction would disappear with the end of capitalism.

1 Taxi fares are high in San Francisco because the permits may be bought and sold on the open market.
2 Some people buy and sell permits without ever operating cabs.
3 To join the New Yellow Cab Cooperative would have cost drivers as much as $15,000.
4 Persons now operating cabs bought their permits for thousands of dollars; ending the sale of permits would cause them to lose their investment.
5 Some persons who had worked years for Yellow Cab would be unable to buy a permit because they don't have the necessary thousands of dollars.
6 The number of permits would be restricted by limiting the number now on the market.

To protect those now operating cabs, one supervisor wanted to amend the ordinance by allowing sale of a permit after it had been used to operate a cab for five years. Another supervisor proposed that there be two types of permits: those now held by the defunct Yellow Cab would be non-transferable, while others would continue to be transferable and salable. Can either of these be called dialectical solutions?

3 Here are two views about the relation between democracy and the role of government in economic matters—those of Milton Friedman, the Nobel Prize–winning conservative economist, and George Meany, former president of the AFL–CIO. Which view comes closer to agreeing with Marx? Explain. What is your view of the relation between democracy and government interventions in the economy, and what reasons do you give for it other than those expressed by Friedman or Meany? Here now is Friedman's view:

Last I come to the most fundamental factor of all—our basic values and beliefs. In this area, we have seen a shift in the climate of opinion from a belief in individual responsibility—from a belief in government as an umpire, government as a maker of laws and keeper of the peace, to a belief in government as Big Brother and as responsible for our welfare, a belief that if there is a problem the thing to do is to pass a law and throw money at it. Here, too, we have been following a suicidal course. . . .

Many of the same tendencies are present in institutions of higher learning. . . . No area of government policy seems to me a greater scandal than the government financing of higher schooling. When I want to state this demagogically, I say that we are following policies under which we are taxing the citizens of Watts to send the children from Beverly Hills to college. That is a literally exact statement of the effect of current state financing of higher education. Over 50 percent of the students at state-supported institutions of higher education come from the top 25 percent of the income bracket. Only 5 percent come from the bottom 25 percent of the income bracket. Yet people who do not go to college are forced to pay taxes to subsidize people who do go to college.[23]

Here now is a different view, from Meany:

On one side are some conservatives who argue that political democracy is the most important value and that the price Americans must be prepared to pay for it is a high level of economic inequality and social injustice. They argue that egalitarian social programs lead to the growth of state power, which in turn threatens liberty.

Another point of view, associated with many Third-World leaders, puts a premium on the alleviation of poverty through economic development and considers democracy an impediment to development, an unaffordable luxury.

The American labor movement subscribes to neither view.

We consider political democracy is sapped by, not rooted in, social inequality. Political democracy is not an impediment to economic development. It is the only assurance that it will proceed in a balanced and healthy way, not through the exploitation of workers.

Our whole experience at the collective bargaining table and in the legislative halls tells us that political and economic rights are not antagonistic but mutually reinforcing, mutually enriching, mutually indispensable.[24]

4 You have been going to school for most of your life and are now enrolled in higher education. You have had a great deal of experience with education, but Marx would insist that experience by itself without theory leaves us mystified and uninformed about what has happened to us. Does the following letter to the editor, in which Marx's notion of classes plays a critical role, give you a useful way of interpreting your educational experience or not? (Mortimer J. Adler is the co-author of *The Capitalist Manifesto* and a prominent philosopher.)

Mortimer J. Adler's article "Education in a Democracy" (Spring, 1979) raises a number of interesting points. Mr. Adler is correct when he asserts that American education has practically renounced the democratic ideal and that the educational community is by and large committed to utilitarianism in general and vocationalism in particular. This, it is necessary to remind Mr. Adler, is not a mere philosophic quirk, but rather an adjustment to the economic structure of Amerian society.

At times, moreover, Mr. Adler seems to avoid the intractable disparities of income and life-changes which this economic structure engenders. This avoidance is no more glaring than when he glibly talks about fostering an educational system which would promote equality in kind—a possibility which is clearly impossible under capitalism. From an abstract point of view, Mr. Adler's theoretics are highly plausible, and even commendable. However, he himself ultimately concedes that the ideals of liberal education are shortchanged whenever the demands of the capitalist labor market become preeminent. Even in the socialist countries, moreover, the gap separating manual from mental labor has not been completely bridged. Mr. Adler's discussion does not, in addition, seem to recognize how deeply embedded and resistant to change such class distinctions actually are. Consequently, he fails to contemplate the class divisions which will exist even during the early stages of a socialist society; and this leaves us with an impracticable ideal, rather than with a concrete philosophy and program for surmounting such thorns in the side of human equality and emancipation.[25]

5 One of my colleagues at San Francisco State University, Theodore Keller, led the chase that resulted in his capture of a man who had shot another colleague, Walter Hacker, after attempting to rob Hacker. Keller refused to testify against the suspect at the trial; for this refusal, the judge sentenced him to five days in jail and fined him $500 for each of his three refusals to testify. Interviewed in jail, Keller explained his refusal. He gave these reasons, which you should assess in the light of Goldmann's criticisms of the excessive reliance that Kant placed on the individual will (see pp. 258–59).

85 percent of that kind of crime [attempted robbery] is done by minorities from the ghetto. I'm in a cell now with three blacks and one Chicano. Either you have to say it's genetic or a product of the social system. I believe it's the latter. It's one thing to stop a man from doing something like that, and another thing to testify against him. We're all guilty. We have to change the social system. I'm not going to put the blame where it doesn't belong. We all share the guilt. . . . We are all going to have to share in the violence. We need a different social structure where everyone shares equally.[26]

6 Marx's vision for a classless future included everyone's having equal control over economic decisions. Private property and the private decisions over its use would disappear; instead, decisions would be made collectively. Certainly one economic factor is the birthrate; under some conditions it may be beneficial and under others harmful, depending upon the society's resources and its ability to provide amply for

children. China, having the world's largest population, has to deal seriously with population growth as an economic fact.

A delegation of people from the Planned Parenthood Federation of America visited China and observed how China was dealing with birth control. The delegation noted that China, both now and traditionally, is organized by units: many people live in the same area where they work, which facilitates communal decision-making. Some people consider that communal decisions "coerce" the individuals involved; others believe that, since everyone has a voice in matters such as the number of children permitted, individuals are emancipated by having some control over events that will affect their welfare. Examine this difference of opinion after thinking about the following report of an interview with Phyllis Vineyard, the leader of the Planned Parenthood delegation:

> Within each work unit, a health worker makes daily rounds to remind women to take their birth control pills. Even the decision to conceive a baby is made communally, rather than privately. . . . The permissible growth rate for each geographic area is prescribed by a provincial family planning committee, and then the allowable births for the following year are assigned to smaller units, such as factories and agricultural production teams.
>
> Despite the coercive nature of this approach, the Planned Parenthood delegates said they detected no signs of resistance from the general population. It may be well-accepted, they speculated, because the women members of each production team, rather than a remote factory manager, make the final decision about who is next in line to have a baby.
>
> "The women work it out among themselves so that their team won't be adversely affected by having too many out on maternity leave," Vineyard said.
>
> Another reason for the lack of objections is that, as Vineyard noted, "In China, you don't find the concern for privacy and confidentiality that exists in the United States. You can see the difference in Chinese houses, which are traditionally built in compounds around a common courtyard. The same ten families may have lived together around that courtyard for 3000 years." . . .
>
> If a mother with two children persists in her desire for a third, the standard procedure is for an older neighbor woman to be dispatched to her home for a heart-to-heart talk on the physical and economic strains caused by large families.[27]

7 What parts of Marx's theory do you think are reinforced by these remarks given in an interview by author Kay Boyle?

> Kay Boyle has been called the best American example of the writer *engagé*. . . . "It is more in the American tradition not to be involved," she replies, "but I can't think of anything good that ever came out of an ivory tower. All good writers are involved. Samuel Beckett is a

case in point. He is one of my oldest and dearest friends and people think of him as detached. But he was in the French Resistance [to the German occupation during World War II]. Joyce was political; Faulkner; Dante—was he political, wow."

"You can't find out who you are inside," she said, "except by the acts you do."[28]

 ## Reflections on Theory

8 *Forcing a second nature on us.* Marx rejected Hume's claim that human nature is fixed, asserting instead that it changes with history. Ideally, we should be able to change ourselves in a controlled way so that we become emancipated. There is another side to this changeability of human nature, however, that might not help our emancipation. Our nature might be changed under the control of others to conform to their model of what they want us to be. Herbert Marcuse thinks we have had an undesirable second human nature foisted on us. To put it in the terms I used in distinguishing between money and capital, we have a consumer second nature because we have been caught in the toils of M—C—M. Marcuse suggests that socially induced morality may sink to its original biological, instinctual level and become firmly established. Do you recognize yourself in the description that follows? How would you relate Marcuse's claim to the sociobiologists' claims about human nature (Chapter 5)—are they consistent or inconsistent? Is Marcuse's "second" nature just a biological survival adaptation to capitalist social conditions? Or is he warning against this way of viewing our life?

Once a specific morality is firmly established as a norm of social behavior, it is not only introjected—it also operates as a norm of "organic" behavior: the organism receives and reacts to certain stimuli and "ignores" and repels others in accord with the introjected morality, which is thus promoting or impeding the function of the organism as a living cell in the respective society. In this way, a society constantly re-creates, this side of consciousness and ideology, patterns of behavior and aspiration as part of the "nature" of its people, and unless the revolt reaches into this "second" nature, into these ingrown patterns, social change will remain "incomplete," even self-defeating.

The so-called consumer economy and the politics of corporate capitalism have created a second nature of man which ties him libidinally [sexually] and aggressively to the commodity form. The need for possessing, consuming, handling, and constantly renewing the gadgets, devices, instruments, engines, offered to and imposed upon the people,

for using these wares even at the danger of one's own destruction, has
become a "biological" need in the sense just defined. The second
nature of man thus militates against any change that would disrupt and
perhaps abolish this dependence of man on a market ever more densely
filled with merchandise—abolish his existence as a consumer consuming
himself in buying and selling.[29]

9 *The disappearance of egoism and achieving the* summmum bonum.
Kant's moral theory takes much of its character from his belief that our
natural, sensible motivation is an egoistic drive for happiness. The attainment of worthiness is sometimes difficult because we have to battle
this egoism. Kant, like Hume and some other moral psychologists,
thought that our sensible nature is fixed—a view that Marx rejected.
Marx took aim at and tried to shoot down the views of classical
economists, who assumed that humans were motivated by self-interest,
and who consequently thought that economic behavior is governed by
"eternal natural laws independent of history" (*Grundrisse,* p. 87).
These so-called natural laws of human behavior, Marx thought, were
bourgeois relations "quietly smuggled in as the inviolable natural laws
on which society in the abstract is founded."

Suppose, then, that human nature isn't fixed, but changes with
historical circumstances as Marx thought. Then new laws of human
behavior can come into existence and old laws perish, while at the same
time new social laws arise the old ones disappear. It is entirely possible, then, that egoistic human behavior as determined by our sensible
self's inclinations and drive toward happiness would no longer be a law
of nature. Egoism may be a "law of human nature" only when there
are antagonistic social classes, such as the proletariat and the
bourgeoisie; we are driven to egoism by the individualism advocated by
spokespersons of the bourgeoisie, of which Kant is one. Kant, one
might argue, didn't understand that he was reflecting only the aspirations of his own epoch. Once egoistic individualism is no longer a
needed ideal, humans will no longer find their personal drive toward
happiness a barrier to the creation of a "realm of ends" in which worthiness and happiness do not compete with each other for our loyalty.
Rather, these two ends will be seen as complementary and mutually
supporting, which will make the achievement of the *summum bonum*
possible on earth.

Do you believe this is a real possibility? Why or why not?

10 *The changing laws of nature and willing egoism.* Here is another consequence for Kant's ethics, if the above is possible. Kant argued that
refusing to help another in need is unwillable as a universal law; this is
because we ourselves may sometime be in need, and if we universalized
our maxim not to help others, we would be willing that others not help
us. Because we are egoistic, it is a law of nature that we want others
to help us when we are in need. We can't will a maxim to be a law if

558   it contradicts a law of nature such as the law that we strive for our own happiness. But if, as Marx claimed, our nature and its laws can change, then there may be a time when egoism is no longer a law of our nature. In that case we can will *not* to help others. But this means we would be able to will egoism, which neither Kant nor Marx would endorse. What, if anything, has gone wrong with this reasoning?

11 *What next?* You have come to the end of your course in ethics, yet at the same time you must realize that not everything has been settled. You may have more questions and fewer answers than when you started. Don't deplore this, but take it as a sign of growth open to you that wasn't evident before. Given the clash of philosophies and the struggle of parties for your intellectual assent and your active, emotional commitment—particularly as heightened by this last chapter— you may be wondering about such things as the following, which are food for continuing thought.

(1) To what extent does true communism exist in Albania, Russia, China, Vietnam, or some other place? Is the imperfect shift there from capitalism to communism simply a temporary stage on a truly progressive march?

(2) Is Marx's theory outmoded because it was based on nineteenth-century industrialism in England, and so is now bypassed by recent developments in more advanced countries such as the United States, where the oppressive, selfish conditions imposed by the early capitalists no longer exist (supposing that the latter is true)? In that case, however, maybe new capitalist conditions make his theory more pertinent. Here one might cite the growth of imperialism by military occupation, political control, or economic domination of underdeveloped countries by developed industrial nations that have made colonies of most of the world. Or one could cite the massive growth of monopolies, placing the control of capital in fewer hands than in Marx's time. Further, one might view with alarm the transformation of national monopolies into multi-national corporations that put profit before the interests of national peoples. Do these post-Marx developments show that we are heading toward an increasingly severe "contradiction" between the proletariat of all countries and a more isolated but still accumulating bourgeoisie? Do the increasing number of liberation movements in former colonies announce the start of a growing consciousness and political organization of the proletariat that marks the final stage in the emergence of a world-wide revolutionary class?

(3) Where do you find yourself in this grand historical movement? You are getting a college or university education that will most likely enable you to escape a lower status in our society. Yet most of you will not be commanders of capital. You will probably serve in middle-management positions. Are you the middle class that is

living proof that capitalism need not divide society into two antagonistic classes? Or are you caught helplessly in the middle? Or
can you even so take an active stand? As a middle-class person you
may suffer an "identity crisis" as described by Hendrik Ruitenbeek,
a European sociologist and psychoanalyst:

The identity crisis is most visible in urban and suburban areas, nevertheless, and its consequences are most evident in the middle-class
family. The contemporary middle class, as John R. Seeley notes, is
identified with the role of management and particularly with what the
textbooks in business administration call *middle management*. This
group transmits decisions from the top, or decision-making level, to the
bottom or production level and reports results from the bottom level to
the top. Middle management is intensely competitive, for it wants to
rise to the decision-making level. It is intensely prudent, for exercise of
judgment may alienate someone just above who has power to evaluate
performance. It is occupied primarily with manipulating people; middle
management "gets things done" through influencing people, not
through mastery of engineering or other physical techniques. . . .

Middle-class life is concerned with *action, organization,* and *control.* Spontaneity would be destructive to its aspirations. Contemplation might cause wonder about the validity of what a man was doing or
how he was living. And, like Tennyson's Light Brigadier, his is "not to
reason why."[30]

Which brings us back to the beginning of our moral reflections—to
Tolstoy's Ivan Ilyich. What additional theory will you master to see
your way through life and morals?

Endnotes

Chapter 1

[1] John Gardner, *Grendel* (New York: Ballantine Books, 1971), p. 138.

[2] G. W. F. Hegel, *Encyclopaedia of the Philosophical Sciences* (London: Oxford Univ. Press, 1931), pp. 10–11.

[3] G. W. F. Hegel, *The Logic of Hegel,* trans. W. Wallace (London: Oxford Univ. Press, 1931), pp. 258–59.

[4] Plato, *The Republic,* trans. Benjamin Jowett, 3rd ed. (New York: Random House, 1937), Vol. 1, Stephanus 439.

[5] Edward Westermarck, *The Origin and Development of the Moral Ideas* (New York: Macmillan, 1906), p. 4.

[6] W. D. Ross, *The Right and the Good* (London: Oxford Univ. Press, 1930), pp. 29–30.

[7] Ross, p. 17.

[8] John Dewey, *The Public and Its Problems* (New York: Holt, 1927), p. 8.

[9] John Dewey, *Human Nature and Conduct* (New York: Modern Library-Random House, 1930), p. 75.

[10] *Human Nature and Conduct,* p. 75.

[11] *Human Nature and Conduct,* p. 58.

[12] Fustel de Coulanges, *The Ancient City* (Garden City, N.Y.: Anchor-Doubleday, 1960), p. 12.

[13] Philip McCombs, *San Francisco Chronicle,* 15 Jan. 1975.

[14] Letter to Helen and Sue Bottel, *Sacramento Bee,* 25 Jan. 1973.

[15] *San Francisco Chronicle,* 20 Jan. 1975, reprint of *New York Times* story by Audrey Topping.

[16] *San Francisco Chronicle,* 3 Jan. 1975, a Reuters dispatch by Sochrjono.

[17] Aristotle, *Nicomachean Ethics,* trans. W. D. Ross, in *The Basic Works of Aristotle,* ed. Richard McKeon (New York: Random House, 1941), 1141b, 22.

[18] *Nicomachean Ethics,* 1140b, 20–21.

[19] *Nicomachean Ethics,* 1094b, 3–28.

[20] *Nicomachean Ethics,* 1112a, 17.

[21] *Nicomachean Ethics,* 1112b, 12–16.

[22] *Nicomachean Ethics,* 1139a, 31–32 and 1139b, 3–4.

[23] *Nicomachean Ethics,* 1139a, 35–36; see also Aristotle's "On the Soul," 433a, 20–30.

[24] See *Religion and the Rise of Capitalism* by R. H. Tawney for the history of how the rise of capitalism forced Christian theologians to retreat from their earlier prohibition against usury.

[25] George D. Kelsey, *Racism and the Christian Understanding of Man* (New York: Scribners, 1965).

[26] Jean-Paul Sartre, "Existentialism," trans. Bernard Frechtman (New York: Philosophical Library, 1947).

[27] Plato, *Euthyphro,* trans. Lane Cooper, in *Collected Dialogues of Plato,* ed. Edith Hamilton and Huntington Cairns (Princeton, N. J.: Princeton Univ. Press, 1973), Bollingen Series, Steph. 6.

[28] Joseph Fletcher, *Situation Ethics* (Philadelphia: Westminster Press, 1966).

[29] Fletcher, p. 151.

[30] Fletcher, p. 152.

[31] Fletcher, p. 153.

[32] Fletcher, p. 155.

[33] Fletcher, p. 157.

[34] Fletcher, p. 158.

[35] Fletcher, p. 162.

[36] Karl Jaspers, *Reason and Existenz,* trans. William Earle (New York: Noonday Press, 1955), p. 26.

[37] *Sacramento Bee,* story by Don Thorton, 14 Jan. 1975.

[38] For further examples of such paradoxical problematic situations see P. Watzlawick, J. H. Beavin, and D. D. Jackson, *Pragmatics of Human Communication* (New York: Norton, 1967), Ch. 6.

[39] *San Francisco Examiner,* 9 Feb. 1975, Associated Press story by Peter Arnett.

[40] In an interview with Oriana Fallaci; *San Francisco Examiner,* 16 Feb. 1975, story by Jessica Mitford.

[41] *San Francisco Chronicle,* 11 Aug. 1974, story by John P. Hoover.

[42] *Sacramento Bee,* 8 Jan. 1975.

[43] William A. Sadler, *Existence and Love* (New York: Scribners, 1969), pp. 356–57.

Chapter 2

[1] Drake Koka, *Northern California Labor* (1978).

[2] Leo Tolstoy, "The Death of Ivan Ilyich," in *The Cossacks and Other Stories,* trans. Rosemary Edmonds (Harmondsworth, Eng.: Penguin Books, 1974).

[3] Robert Coles, "Profiles: Walker Percy, Part II," *The New Yorker,* Oct. 9, 1978, p. 106.

[4] *Collected Papers of Clarence Irving Lewis,* ed. John Goheen and John Mothershead, Jr. (Stanford: Stanford Univ. Press, 1970), p. 220.

[5] T. H. Green, *Prolegomena to Ethics* (London: Oxford Univ. Press, 1906), p. 430.

[6] Jean-Paul Sartre, "Existentialism," trans. Bernard Frechtman (New York: Philosophical Library, 1947).

[7] Wright Morris, *The Field of Vision* (New York: Signet, 1957).

[8] Friedrich Nietzsche, *Beyond Good and Evil,* trans. Marianne Cowan (Chicago: Henry Regnery, 1955), Section 268.

[9] Nietzsche, Sec. 268.

[10] Nietzsche, Sec. 201.

[11] Nietzsche, Sec. 260.

[12] Nietzsche, Sec. 260.

[13] Nietzsche, Sec. 260.

[14] Nietzsche, Sec. 203.

[15] Nietzsche, Sec. 203.

[16] Nietzsche, Sec. 46.

[17] Nietzsche, Sec. 265.

[18] Nietzsche, Sec. 260.

[19] Nietzsche, Sec. 287.

[20] Nietzsche, Sec. 261.

[21] Philip Blair Rice, *On the Knowledge of Good and Evil* (New York: Random House, 1955), p. 289.

[22] *San Francisco Chronicle,* 3 Jan. 1975.

[23] Peter Marin, "The New Narcissism," *Harper's,* October, 1975, p. 45.

[24] Marin, pp. 47–48.

[25] Marin, p. 48.

[26] Advertisement in *Seventeen,* April, 1975.

[27] *San Francisco Chronicle,* 24 Dec. 1974.

[28] *San Francisco Chronicle,* "Question Man," 2 Sept. 1974.

[29] Nelson Rockefeller, quoted in Charles McCabe's column, "Himself," *San Francisco Chronicle,* 1975.

[30] Plato, *The Republic,* trans. G. M. A. Grube (Indianapolis: Hackett Publishing Co., 1974), Stephanus 618, 620.

[31] *Mao Tse-tung's Thought Is the Invincible Weapon* (Peking: Foreign Language Press, 1968).

[32] Wright Morris, p. 16.

[33] Morris, p. 186.

[34] Morris, p. 16.

[35] *San Francisco Examiner,* 18 Aug. 1974.

[36] Thomas Carlyle, *Sartor Resartus* (London: J. M. Dent-Everyman's Library, n.d.), pp. 158–59.

[37] *San Francisco Chronicle,* 19 Apr. 1975, story by Charles Petit.

[38] The *Stanford Observer,* Feb., 1975.

[39] *San Francisco Examiner,* 23 Feb. 1975, story by Stephen Cook.

[40] Brassaï (Gyula Halasz), *The Secret Paris of the 30's,* trans. Richard Miller (New York: Pantheon Books, 1976).

Chapter 3

[1] Plato, *The Republic,* trans. G. M. A. Grube (Indianapolis: Hackett Publishing Co., 1974), Steph. 338.

[2] *The Republic,* Steph. 360.

[3] *The Republic,* Steph. 360.

[4] Garret Hardin, "The Tragedy of the Commons," *Science,* 162, Dec. 13, 1968.

[5] *San Francisco Chronicle,* 25 Apr. 1975.

[6] Susan Brownmiller, *Against Our Will: Men, Women, and Rape* (New York: Simon and Schuster, 1975), as reviewed by Christopher Lehmann, *San Francisco Chronicle,* 2 Nov. 1975.

[7] Cited by Tom O'Connor, San Francisco City attorney; quoted by Dick Nolan, *San Francisco Examiner,* 20 July 1975.

[8] St. Paul, *Letter to the Romans,* Revised Berkeley Trans. (Gideon International, 1973), VII, 14–20.

[9] *The Upanishadic Lore in the Light of the Teachings of Bhagavan Sri Ramana* (*The Sage*), Sri Ramansramam, Tiruvannamali, South India (p. 149).

[10] Joseph Campbell, ed., *Philosophies of India* (Princeton, N. J.: Princeton Univ. Press, 1951), Bollingen Series XXVI, p. 535.

[11] Campbell, p. 540.

[12] Campbell, pp. 535–36.

[13] Plato, *Protagoras,* in *The Dialogues of Plato,* trans. Benjamin Jowett, 3rd ed. (New York: Random House, 1937), Steph. 358.

[14] *Protagoras,* Steph. 345

[15] *San Francisco Chronicle,* 20 Nov. 1975.

[16] Plato, *Gorgias,* in *The Dialogues of Plato,* trans. Benjamin Jowett, 3rd ed. (New York: Random House, 1937), Steph. 467–79.

[17] *Gorgias,* Steph. 468.

[18] *San Francisco Chronicle,* 19 Nov. 1975.

[19] John Dewey, *Human Nature and Conduct* (New York: Modern Library-Random House, 1930), pp. 152–53.

[20] *San Francisco Chronicle,* 1 Dec. 1975.

[21] "Question Man Column," *San Francisco Chronicle,* 27 Aug. 1977.

[22] Merla Zellerbach, "My Fair City," *San Francisco Chronicle,* 31 Jan. 1979.

[23] *San Francisco Examiner,* 5 Jan. 1975.

[24] *San Francisco Examiner,* 5 Jan. 1975.

[25] San Francisco State University *Info,* 175, Oct. 27, 1975.

[26] Kurt Baier, *The Moral Point of View* (Ithaca, N. Y.: Cornell Univ. Press, 1958), p. iii.

[27] Max Weber, *The Sociology of Religion,* trans. Ephraim Fischoff (Boston: Beacon Press, 1963), p. 106.

[28] Epictetus, *Discourses,* trans. George Long (Chicago: Encyclopaedia Britannica, 1952), Great Books Series, Bk III, Ch. 26.

[29] Robert Olson, *The Morality of Self-Interest* (New York: Harcourt, 1965), pp. 11–12.

Chapter 4

[1] Plato, *The Republic,* trans. G. M. A. Grube (Indianapolis: Hackett Publishing Co., 1974), Steph. 439–41.

[2] Steph. 443, Grube trans.

[3] Steph. 444, Grube trans.

[4] Steph. 588–92, Grube trans.

[5] Steph. 505, Grube trans.

[6] Steph. 519, Grube trans.

[7] *Philosophical Rudiments Concerning Government and Society,* footnote 3, quoted in *An Introduction to Ethics,* ed. Robert Dewey and Robert Hurlbutt III (New York: Macmillan, 1977), p. 37.

[8] Dewey and Hurlbutt, p. 38.

[9] Dewey and Hurlbutt, p. 37.

[10] Dewey and Hurlbutt, p. 38.

[11] Thomas Hobbes, *Leviathan* (London: Oxford Univ. Press, 1909), Ch. XIII.

[12] *Leviathan,* Ch. XIV.

[13] *Leviathan,* Ch. XV.

[14] *Leviathan,* Ch. XIV.

[15] Plato, *Crito,* in *The Diaglogues of Plato,* trans. Benjamin Jowett (New York: Random House, 1937), Steph. 48.

[16] *Crito,* Steph. 54.

[17] David Hume, *A Treatise on Human Nature,* ed. L. A. Selby-Bigge (London: Oxford Univ. Press, 1888), p. 457.

[18] *Treatise,* p. 415.

[19] *Treatise,* p. 416.

[20] *Treatise,* p. 416.

[21] Jean-Jacques Rousseau, *The Origin of Inequality* (Chicago: Encyclopaedia Britannica, 1952), Great Books Series, pp. 344–45; hereafter referred to as *Inequality.*

[22] *Inequality,* p. 363.

[23] *Inequality,* p. 346.

[24] *Inequality,* pp. 343–44.

[25] David Hume, *Enquiries Concerning the Human Understanding and Concerning the Principles of Morals,* ed. L. A. Selby-Bigge, 2nd ed. (London: Oxford Univ. Press, 1902), p. 231; hereafter referred to as *Enquiry.*

[26] *Enquiry,* pp. 214–15, "Concerning Morals," Sec. V, Pt. I.

[27] *Enquiry,* pp. 218, 219, Sec. V, Pts. I and II.

[28] *Enquiry,* p. 272; see also p. 273.

[29] *Enquiry,* p. 273, Sec. IX, Pt. I.

[30] *Enquiry,* p. 229, Sec. V, Pt. II.

[31] *Enquiry,* Appendix II, "Of Self-Love," p. 302.

[32] *San Francisco Chronicle,* 22 Feb. 1975.

[33] Quoted in F. C. Sharp, *Ethics* (New York: Century Company, 1928), p. 75.

[34] *San Francisco Examiner,* 27 Apr. 1975.

[35] *Exxon USA,* Third Quarter, 1975.

[36] *San Francisco Chronicle,* 1 Aug. 1975.

[37] John Dewey, *Human Nature and Conduct* (New York: Modern Library-Random House, 1930), pp. 254–58.

[38] *The Republic,* Steph. 436.

[39] Quoted by Charles McCabe, "Himself," *San Francisco Chronicle,* 21 Apr. 1976.

[40] *Times Literary Supplement,* 26 Sept. 1975.

[41] *Enquiry,* p. 214, Sec. V, Pt. L.

Chapter 5

[1] B. F. Skinner, *Beyond Freedom and Dignity,* excerpts reprinted in *Psychology Today,* 5, No. 3, Aug. 1971, p. 37.

[2] *The New Yorker,* Nov. 20, 1978, from a review by Liz Harris.

[3] Charles McCabe, "Himself," *San Francisco Chronicle,* 23 Feb. 1979.

[4] Edna Heidbreder, *Seven Psychologies* (New York: Appleton-Century, 1933), pp. 393–94.

[5] Heidbreder, p. 394.

[6] Charles Darwin, *The Origin of Species* (Chicago: Encyclopaedia Britannica, 1952), Great Books Series, p. 32.

[7] Darwin, p. 119.

[8] Darwin, p. 135.

[9] Charles Darwin, *The Descent of Man* (Chicago: Encyclopaedia Britannica, 1952), Great Books Series, p. 319.

[10] *San Francisco Chronicle,* 15 June 1977.

[11] *San Francisco Chronicle,* 15 June 1977.

566

[12] Michael J. Carella, "Instinct, Learning and the New Social Darwinism," *The Modern Schoolman,* LIV, 1977, p. 138.

[13] Konrad Lorenz, *On Aggression* (New York: Bantam Books, 1967), p. 230.

[14] Erich Fromm, *Escape from Freedom* (New York: Holt, Rinehart & Winston, 1941), p. 19.

[15] Fromm, p. 22.

[16] Erich Fromm, *The Sane Society* (London: Routledge & Kegan Paul, 1963), p. 19.

[17] Erich Fromm, *Man for Himself: An Inquiry into the Psychology of Ethics* (New York: Holt, Rinehart & Winston, 1947), p. 7.

[18] *San Francisco Examiner,* 7 July 1979.

[19] Skinner, p. 64.

[20] *San Francisco Chronicle,* 9 May 1979.

[21] Edward O. Wilson, *On Human Nature* (Cambridge, Mass.: Harvard Univ. Press, 1978), pp. 2–3.

[22] *San Francisco Chronicle,* 2 Aug. 1977.

[23] *San Francisco Chronicle,* 2 July 1977, Abrahamsen's article.

[24] *Sacramento Bee,* 14 Aug. 1977.

[25] Gabriel Garcia Marquez, *One Hundred Years of Solitude,* trans. Gregory Rabassa (New York: Avon Books, 1971), pp. 356–57.

[26] Louis-Ferdinand Céline, *Journey to the End of the Night,* trans. John H. P. Marks (New York: New Directions, 1960), pp. 109–10.

[27] Carella, p. 141. (Carella refers us to Ardrey's *African Genesis,* Chapter Six, and *The Social Contract,* pp. 93–101 for Ardrey's views on these matters.)

[28] *San Francisco Chronicle,* 15 June 1977, story by David Perlman.

[29] Ved Mehta, "Our Local Correspondents: Naturalization," *The New Yorker,* Aug. 29, 1977, p. 74.

[30] *San Francisco Chronicle,* 16 Aug. 1977.

[31] Skinner, p. 80.

[32] Richard Hofstadter, *Social Darwinism in American Thought,* rev. ed. (Boston: Beacon Press, 1955), pp. 68, 69.

[33] Hofstadter, p. 95.

[34] Aristotle, *Nicomachean Ethics,* trans. W. D. Ross, in *The Basic Works of Aristotle,* ed. Richard McKeon (New York: Random House, 1941), 1095a, 1095b.

[35] Erik Erikson, *Childhood and Society* (New York: Norton, 1950), p. 89.

[36] Erikson, p. 90.

Chapter 6

[1] *The New Yorker,* Sept. 26, 1977, p. 143, from John Updike's review of Reiner Kunze's *The Wonderful Years.*

[2] Immanuel Kant, *Religion Within the Limits of Reason Alone* (New York: Harper Torchbooks, 1960), Introduction, p. ix.

[3] Immanuel Kant, "An Answer to the Question: 'What is Enlightenment?'" in *Kant's Political Writings,* ed. Hans Reiss, trans. H. B. Nisbet (London: Cambridge Univ. Press, 1970), pp. 54–55.

[4] *The New Yorker,* Oct. 29, 1975, pp. 143–44.

[5] Jean-Jacques Rousseau, *Origin of Inequality* (Chicago: Univ. of Chicago Press, 1952), Great Books Series, p. 329; hereafter referred to as *Inequality.*

[6] Quoted from *The New Yorker,* Aug. 8, 1977, p. 17.

[7] *Mother Jones,* Feb.-Mar., 1979.

[8] *San Francisco Chronicle,* 23 May 1979.

[9] Hannah Arendt, *The Human Condition* (Garden City, N.Y.: Anchor-Doubleday, 1959), p. 36.

[10] *San Francisco Chronicle,* 2 Oct. 1977, review by Milton Moskowitz.

[11] *San Francisco Chronicle,* 24 Sept. 1977.

[12] Benedict Spinoza, *Ethic,* ed. John Wild, trans. W. H. White (New York: Scribners, 1930), Part III, Proposition XXIX, Scholium, p. 234.

[13] *San Francisco Chronicle,* 2 Oct. 1977, Sunday Punch.

[14] Martin Heidegger, *Being and Time,* trans. John Macquarrie and Edward Robinson (New York: Harper, 1962), p. 67; all my Heidegger page references are to this book.

[15] Quoted by Paul Nizan, *The Watchdogs: Philosophers and the Established Order,* trans. Paul Fittingoff (New York: Monthly Review Press, 1971), p. 168.

[16] Jean-Paul Sartre, *Being and Nothingness,* trans. Hazel Barnes (New York: Washington Square Press, 1966), pp. 76–77.

[17] Karl Jaspers, *Reason and Existenz,* trans. William Earle (New York: Noonday Press, 1955), p. 25.

[18] Michael Zimmerman, "A Comparison of Nietzsche's Overman and Heidegger's Authentic Self," *The Southern Journal of Philosophy,* XIV, No. 2 (Summer, 1976), p. 217.

[19] Jean-Paul Sartre, "Existentialism," trans. Bernard Frechtman (New York: Philosophical Library, 1947).

[20] Albert Camus, *The Myth of Sisyphus and Other Essays,* trans. Justin O'Brien (New York: Alfred A. Knopf, 1955).

[21] Edward O. Wilson, *On Human Nature* (Cambridge, Mass.: Harvard Univ. Press, 1978); my page references in this section are to this book.

[22] "Sociobiology—A New Biological Determinism" by the Sociobiology Study Group, Boston—Cambridge SESPA/Science for the People, mimeographed, n.d., p. 2; thirty-six persons were part of the Study Group at the time of writing.

[23] Clifford Geertz, "The Impact of the Concept of Culture on the Concept of Man," *Bulletin of Atomic Scientists,* April, 1966, pp. 2–8.

[24] Aram Yengoyan, "In Defense of Man: A Reply to Creeping Darwinism," *Rackham Reports,* University of Michigan, Ann Arbor, Vol. 4, No. 1, 1978.

[25] Michael J. Carella, "Instinct, Learning and the New Social Darwinism," *The Modern Schoolman,* LIV, 1977, p. 145.

[26] John Dewey, *Human Nature and Conduct* (New York: Modern Library-Random House, 1930), pp. 153–54.

[27] John Laird, *An Enquiry into Moral Notions* (London: George Allen & Unwin, 1935), pp. 47–48.

[28] Lawrence Kohlberg, "Education for Justice: A Modern Statement of the Platonic View," in *Moral Education: Five Lectures* (Cambridge, Mass.: Harvard Univ. Press, 1970), pp. 62–63.

[29] *San Francisco Examiner,* story by Don West, 18 Sept. 1977.

[30] *Sacramento Bee,* 13 Dec. 1977.

[31] *San Francisco Examiner,* 2 Oct. 1977, Sunday Punch.

[32] *San Francisco Chronicle,* 28 Oct. 1977.

[33] Fyodor Dostoevsky, *The Idiot,* trans. David Magarshack (Harmondsworth, England: Penguin, 1955), pp. 343–47.

[34] Gunther Anders, "The Phantom World of TV," trans. Norbert Guterman, *Dissent,* Vol. 3, 1956.

[35] Joel Greenberg in *San Francisco Chronicle,* "This World" section, 2 Oct. 1977.

[36] Edward O. Wilson, *Sociobiology: The New Synthesis* (Cambridge, Mass.: Harvard Univ. Press, 1975), p. 563.

[37] Ignace Lepp, *The Authentic Morality,* trans. Bernard Murchland, C. S. C. (New York: Macmillan, 1965).

[38] Jean-Jacques Rousseau, *The Social Contract,* trans. G. D. H. Cole (Chicago: Encyclopaedia Britannica, 1952), Great Books Series, Ch. 9, Sec. 8, "The Civil State," p. 393.

[39] A. Lubow, *San Francisco Examiner,* 30 Oct. 1977, Sunday Punch.

[40] J. L. Austin, *How to Do Things with Words* (London: Oxford Univ. Press, 1962), pp. 6, 14–18, 39–40.

[41] David Hume, *Enquiries Concerning the Human Understanding and Concerning the Principles of Morals,* ed. L. A. Selby-Bigge, 2nd ed. (London: Oxford Univ. Press, 1902), note 1, pp. 199–200.

[42] Kenneth Tynan, "Profiles: Tom Stoppard," *The New Yorker,* Dec. 19, 1977.

Chapter 7

[1] Immanuel Kant, *Critique of Judgement,* trans. James C. Meredith (London: Oxford Univ. Press, 1952), p. 14.

[2] Erwin Panofsky, *Meaning of the Visual Arts* (New York: Anchor-Doubleday, 1955), p. 1.

[3] Immanuel Kant, *Lectures on Ethics,* trans. Louis Infeld (New York: Harper Torchbooks, 1963), pp. 252 and 253, taken from Kant's students' notes; hereafter referred to as *Lectures.*

[4] Immanuel Kant, *Foundations of the Metaphysics of Morals,* trans. Lewis White Beck, in *Ethical Theories,* ed. A. I. Melden, 2nd ed. (Englewood Cliffs, N. J.: Prentice-Hall, 1955), p. 323; hereafter referred to as *Foundations.*

[5] Immanuel Kant, *Religion Within the Limits of Reason Alone,* trans. Theodore M. Greene and Hoyt H. Hudson (New York: Harper Torchbooks, 1960), p. 40; hereafter referred to as *Religion.*

[6] Romain Gary, "The Mystique of Moral Overkill," *Playboy,* June, 1966, pp. 115, 141, and 143.

[7] Immanuel Kant, *The Critique of Practical Reason,* trans. Thomas K. Abbott (Chicago: Encyclopaedia Britannica, 1952), Great Books Series, p. 303; hereafter referred to as *Practical Reason.*

[8] Immanuel Kant, *The Doctrine of Virtue. Part II. The Metaphysic of Morals,* trans. Mary J. Gregor (New York: Harper Torchbooks, 1964), note, p. 37; hereafter referred to as *Virtue.*

[9] *Practical Reason,* p. 302; see also p. 306.

[10] *Religion,* p. lxxxvii, Introduction, Part II.

[11] Erich Heller, *The Artist's Journey into the Interior* (New York: Random House, 1965), pp. 6–7.

[12] John Herman Randall, *The Career of Philosophy* (New York: Columbia Univ. Press, 1965), Vol. II, p. 392.

[13] Lucien Goldmann, *Immanuel Kant,* trans. Robert Black (London: NLB, 1971), pp. 170–72.

[14] Lucien Goldmann, *The Human Sciences and Philosophy,* trans. Hayden V. White and Robert Anchor (London: Jonathan Cape, 1969), p. 64.

[15] Marcus Aurelius, *Meditations* (Chicago: Encyclopaedia Britannica, 1952), Great Books Series, p. 264.

[16] "California Living," *San Francisco Chronicle,* 5 Feb. 1978.

[17] *San Francisco Chronicle,* 14 Feb. 1978.

[18] *San Francisco Examiner,* 11 Dec. 1977.

[19] *San Francisco Examiner,* 11 Dec. 1977.

[20] *San Francisco Chronicle,* 19 Nov. 1977.

[21] *San Francisco Chronicle,* 5 Oct. 1977.

[22] "Female Sexual Alienation," *Women: A Journal of Liberation,* Vol. 3, No. 1, October, 1972.

[23] *San Francisco Chronicle,* 15 May 1978.

[24] *San Francisco Chronicle,* 6 Nov. 1977.

[25] *The Emporia Gazette,* Emporia, Kansas, 17 May 1921.

[26] Art Rosenbaum, *San Francisco Chronicle,* 4 June 1978.

[27] Karl Marx and Friedrich Engels, *Manifesto of the Communist Party,* trans. Samuel Moore (Moscow: Progress Publishers).

[28] *San Francisco Chronicle,* 31 Oct. 1977; excerpted from Vance Packard's *The People Shapers* (Boston: Little, Brown, 1977).

[29] Robert Coles, *The New Yorker,* Mar. 13, 1978, p. 137.

[30] Michael Zimmerman, "A Comparison of Nietzsche's Overman and Heidegger's Authentic Self," *Southern Journal of Philosophy,* XIV, No. 2, 1976.

[31] R. N. Hare, *Freedom and Reason* (New York: Oxford Univ. Press, 1965), pp. 157–58.

[32] G. B. Kerferd and D. E. Walford, *Kant: Selected Pre-Critical Writings,* trans. G. B. Kerferd (Manchester, Eng.: Manchester Univ. Press, 1968), p. 54.

[33] F. H. Bradley, *Ethical Studies* (New York: Stechert, 1927), p. 206.

Chapter 8

[1] Immanuel Kant, *The Critique of Practical Reason,* trans. Thomas K. Abbott (Chicago: Encyclopaedia Britannica, 1952), Great Books Series, p. 332; hereafter referred to as *Practical Reason.*

[2] Immanuel Kant, *Foundations of the Metaphysics of Morals,* trans. Lewis White Beck, in *Ethical Theories,* ed. A. I. Melden, 2nd ed. (Englewood Cliffs, N. J.: Prentice-Hall, 1955), p. 338; hereafter referred to as *Foundations.*

[3] Immanuel Kant, *The Doctrine of Virtue. Part II. The Metaphysic of Morals,* trans. Mary J. Gregor (New York: Harper Torchbooks, 1964), p. 52; hereafter referred to as *Virtue.*

[4] Immanuel Kant, *Religion Within the Limits of Reason Alone,* trans. Theodore M. Greene and Hoyt H. Hudson (New York: Harper Torchbooks, 1960), pp. 31–32; hereafter referred to as *Religion.*

[5] R. M. Hare, *Freedom and Reason* (London: Oxford Univ. Press, 1963), pp. 90–91.

[6] Marcus Singer, *Generalization in Ethics* (London: Eyre & Spottiswoode, 1963), p. 31.

[7] Immanuel Kant, *Practical Reason,* trans. Lewis White Beck (New York: Library of Liberal Arts, 1956), p. 83; hereafter this translation will be cited as Beck.

[8] *San Francisco Chronicle,* 1 July 1978.

[9] Heinrich Böll, *The Clown,* trans. Leila Vennewitz (New York: Avon, 1975), p. 66.

570

¹⁰ Robert Coles, "Profiles: Walker Percy, II," *The New Yorker,* Oct. 9, 1978, p. 52.

¹¹ Sigrid Bathen, *Sacramento Bee,* 26 Jan. 1978.

¹² W. E. Barnes, *San Francisco Examiner,* 29 Jan. 1978.

¹³ Jim Lewis, *Sacramento Bee,* 26 Jan. 1978.

¹⁴ *San Francisco Chronicle,* 1 Dec. 1977.

¹⁵ George F. Will, *San Francisco Chronicle,* 27 June 1978.

¹⁶ Marcus Eliason, *San Francisco Chronicle,* 19 May 1977.

¹⁷ George Williamson, *San Francisco Chronicle,* 27 Oct. 1977.

¹⁸ "Dear Abby," *San Francisco Chronicle,* 7 June 1979.

¹⁹ *San Francisco Examiner,* 26 Mar. 1978.

²⁰ *San Francisco Examiner,* 16 Apr. 1978.

²¹ Amitai Etzioni, *San Francisco Chronicle,* 15 Oct. 1976.

²² *San Francisco Chronicle,* 1978.

²³ Wright Neely, "Freedom and Desire," *The Philosophical Review,* Vol. LXXXIII, No. 1, January, 1974.

Chapter 9

¹ Immanuel Kant, *Foundations of the Metaphysics of Morals,* trans. Lewis White Beck, in *Ethical Theories,* ed. A. I. Melden, 2nd ed. (Englewood Cliffs, N. J.: Prentice-Hall, 1955), p. 313; hereafter referred to as *Foundations.*

² Immanuel Kant, *The Doctrine of Virtue. Part II. The Metaphysic of Morals,* trans. Mary J. Gregor (New York: Harper Torchbooks, 1964), pp. 20–21; hereafter referred to as *Virtue.*

³ *The New Yorker,* June 12, 1978, p. 24.

⁴ *San Francisco Chronicle,* 11 July 1978.

⁵ Hans Reiss, ed., *Kant's Political Writings,* "On the Common Saying: 'This May Be True in Theory, but It Does Not Apply in Practice,'" trans. H. B. Nisbet (Cambridge, England: Cambridge Univ. Press, 1970), p. 77.

⁶ Immanuel Kant, *The Metaphysical Elements of Justice,* trans. John Ladd (Indianapolis: Bobbs-Merrill, 1965), pp. 33–35; hereafter referred to as *Justice.* Brackets are Ladd's.

⁷ *San Francisco Chronicle,* 23 Aug. 1978.

⁸ Robert Paul Wolff, *The Autonomy of Reason* (New York: Harper Torchbooks, 1973), p. 69.

⁹ Immanuel Kant, *Practical Reason,* trans. Lewis White Beck (New York: Library of Liberal Arts, 1956), p. 27, "Remark" on Theorem III, Part I, Book I, Ch. 1; hereafter this translation will be cited as Beck.

¹⁰ Onora Nell, *Acting on Principle: An Essay on Kantian Ethics* (New York: Columbia Univ. Press, 1975), p. 74.

¹¹ Immanuel Kant, *Religion Within the Limits of Reason Alone,* trans. Theodore M. Greene and Hoyt H. Hudson (New York: Harper Torchbooks, 1960), p. 19; hereafter referred to as *Religion.*

¹² Stuart Hampshire in *New York Review of Books,* Oct. 12, 1978, p. 66.

¹³ *San Francisco Chronicle,* 25 May 1978.

¹⁴ *San Francisco Chronicle,* 26 Sept. 1978.

¹⁵ *San Francisco Chronicle,* 27 July 1978. (McFall died soon afterward.)

¹⁶ Clarence J. Munford, "Africa and the Political Economy of Underdevelopment," *The Black Scholar,* September, 1978, p. 26.

¹⁷ *San Francisco Examiner,* 18 Nov. 1977.

[18] *San Francisco Chronicle,* 20 Mar. 1978.

[19] *San Francisco Chronicle,* 16 Sept. 1978.

[20] Donald Davidson, "Agency," in *Agent, Action, and Reason,* ed. Robert Binkley, Richard Bronaugh, and Ausonio Marras (Toronto: Univ. of Toronto Press, 1971), pp. 3-4, 6-7, 12.

[21] James Cornman, "Comments" (on Davidson), in *Agent, Action, and Reason,* p. 32.

Chapter 10

[1] Immanuel Kant, *The Doctrine of Virtue. Part II. The Metaphysic of Morals,* trans. Mary J. Gregor (New York: Harper Torchbooks, 1964), p. 48; hereafter referred to as *Virtue.*

[2] Immanuel Kant, *The Metaphysical Elements of Justice,* trans. John Ladd (Indianapolis: Bobbs-Merrill, 1965), p. 35.

[3] James Gould, "The Not-So-Golden Rule," *Southern Journal of Philosophy,* Fall, 1963, p. 10.

[4] Immanuel Kant, *Foundations of the Metaphysics of Morals,* trans. Lewis White Beck, in *Ethical Theories,* ed. A. I. Melden, 2nd ed. (Englewood Cliffs, N. J.: Prentice-Hall, 1955), p. 319; hereafter referred to as *Foundations.*

[5] Harold Gilliam, *San Francisco Chronicle,* 29 Mar. 1978.

[6] Amatai Etzioni, *San Francisco Chronicle,* 15 Oct. 1976.

[7] Henry Sidgwick, *The Methods of Ethics,* 6th ed. (London: Macmillan, 1901), p. 380.

[8] Marcus Singer, *Generalization in Ethics* (London: Eyre & Spottiswoode, 1963), p. 5; hereafter referred to as *Generalization.*

[9] J. M. Cameron in *New York Review of Books,* June 1, 1978, p. 9.

[10] Stan Roberts, "Do Doctors Know Best?" *People's Ideas,* 1978, p. 2.

[11] Immanuel Kant, *Practical Reason,* trans. Lewis White Beck (New York: Library of Liberal Arts, 1956), p. 39; hereafter this translation will be cited as Beck.

[12] *San Francisco Chronicle,* 20 May 1978.

[13] Kenneth Tynan, "Profiles: Tom Stoppard," *The New Yorker,* Dec. 19, 1977, p. 110.

[14] David Finn, "Human Values and Businessmen," *San Francisco Chronicle,* 7 July 1975; Finn is chairman of the board of Ruder & Finn, a public relations firm.

[15] Sylvia Rubin, "Employees Speak Up," *San Francisco Chronicle,* 14 Aug. 1978.

[16] Arthur C. Lathan, Affirmative Action Coordinator, *Phoenix,* 6 May 1976.

[17] Paulo Freire, *Pedagogy of the Oppressed* (New York: Herder and Herder, 1971), pp. 31–33.

[18] David Broder, *San Francisco Chronicle,* 30 May 1977.

[19] *San Francisco Chronicle,* 23 Sept. 1978.

[20] *San Francisco Chronicle,* 9 May 1979.

[21] Onora Nell, *Acting on Principle: An Essay on Kantian Ethics* (New York: Columbia Univ. Press, 1975), pp. 132–37.

[22] Fred Feldman, *Introductory Ethics* (Englewood Cliffs, N. J.: Prentice-Hall, 1978), pp. 114–16.

[23] Editorial, *San Francisco Chronicle,* 16 Feb. 1978.

[24] Prakash Chandra, *San Francisco Chronicle,* 21 July 1978.

[25] Richard Bennett, *American Educator,* October, 1978, p. 23.

[26] Katy Butler, *San Francisco Chronicle,* 26 Aug. 1978.

[27] *San Francisco Chronicle,* 16 Jan. 1975.

[28] Andrea Knox, Knight News Service, *San Francisco Exmainer,* 10 Dec. 1978.

Chapter 11

[1] Immanuel Kant, *Practical Reason,* trans. Lewis White Beck (New York: Library of Liberal Arts, 1956), p. 114.

[2] Jeremy Bentham, *An Introduction to the Principles of Morals and Legislation,* 1780, Section: "Of the Principle of Utility" (Atlantic Highlands, N. J.: Humanities Press, 1970).

[3] R. B. Perry, *General Theory of Value* (Cambridge, Mass.: Harvard Univ. Press, 1950), pp. 115–16.

[4] Aristotle, *Nicomachean Ethics,* trans. W. D. Ross, in *The Basic Works of Aristotle,* ed. Richard McKeon (New York: Random House, 1941), 1096b, 24–28.

[5] Immanuel Kant, *The Critique of Practical Reason,* trans. Thomas K. Abbott (Chicago: Encyclopaedia Britannica, 1952), Great Books Series, p. 339.

[6] Kant's thoughts about dignity are most fully developed in a later book, *The Critique of Teleological Judgement,* trans. James Creed Meredith (London: Oxford Univ. Press, 1952), which is Part II of *The Critique of Judgement;* hereafter referred to as *Teleological Judgement.*

[7] Immanuel Kant, *Foundations of the Metaphysics of Morals,* trans. Lewis White Beck, in *Ethical Theories,* ed. A. I. Melden, 2nd ed. (Englewood Cliffs, N. J.: Prentice-Hall, 1955), p. 295; hereafter referred to as *Foundations.*

[8] Foundations, p. 322. See also *The Doctrine of Virtue. Part II. The Metaphysic of Morals,* trans. Mary J. Gregor (New York: Harper Torchbooks, 1964), pp. 99–100; hereafter referred to as *Virtue.*

[9] G. E. Moore, *Ethics* (London: Oxford Univ. Press, 1947), p. 42.

[10] Richard Brandt, "Toward a Credible Form of Utilitarianism," in *Morality and the Language of Conduct,* ed. Hector-Neri Castaneda and George Nakhnikian (Detroit: Wayne State University, 1965), pp. 109–10.

[11] Immanuel Kant, *Lectures on Ethics,* trans. Louis Infeld (New York: Harper Torchbooks. 1963). p. 44.

[12] W. D. Ross, *The Right and the Good* (London: Oxford Univ. Press, 1930), p. 18.

[13] *San Francisco Chronicle,* 8 July 1974.

[14] *San Francisco Examiner,* 2 Sept. 1977.

[15] *San Francisco Chronicle,* 11 May 1975.

[16] Story by Blake Green, *San Francisco Chronicle,* 14 June 1977.

[17] *San Francisco Chronicle,* 3 Apr. 1975.

[18] *Sacramento Bee,* 26 Aug. 1977.

[19] Kenneth Tynan, "Profiles: Tom Stoppard," *The New Yorker,* Dec. 19, 1977, p. 71.

[20] Excerpts from *San Francisco Chronicle,* 2 Sept. 1978, excerpts from Simon's *A Time for Truth.*

[21] Drew Middleton, *San Francisco Chronicle,* 27 Aug. 1978, "This World" section.

[22] From J. S. Mill's *Utilitarianism,* ed. Ernest Rhys (London: Everyman's-J. M. Dent, 1944), pp. 6–9.

[23] Plato, *Gorgias,* trans. W. D. Woodhead, in *Collected Dialogues of Plato,* ed. Edith Hamilton and Huntington Cairns (Princeton, N. J.: Princeton Univ. Press, 1973), Bollingen Series, 494c–495a.

²⁴ Plato, *The Republic,* trans. Francis M. Cornford (New York: Oxford Univ. Press, 1955), Book VI, Steph. 504.

²⁵ Robert Fogelin, *Evidence and Meaning* (London: Routledge & Kegan Paul, 1967), pp. 122–29.

Chapter 12

¹ Stuart Hampshire, *Two Theories of Morality* (Oxford: Oxford Univ. Press for the British Academy, 1977), pp. 57–58. The two theories are Aristotle's and Spinoza's.

² David Hume, *A Treatise on Human Nature,* ed. L. A. Selby-Bigge (London: Oxford Univ. Press, 1888); hereafter referred to as *Treatise.*

³ David Hume, *Enquiries Concerning the Human Understanding and Concerning the Principles of Morals,* ed. L. A. Selby-Bigge, 2nd ed. (London: Oxford Univ. Press, 1902), p. 90; hereafter referred to as *Enquiry.*

⁴ Quentin Skinner in *The New York Review of Books,* June 15, 1978.

⁵ *San Francisco Chronicle,* 29 Jan. 1979.

⁶ *San Francicso Chronicle,* 29 Jan. 1979.

⁷ See Alasdair MacIntyre's essay, "Hume on 'Is' and 'Ought,'" in *Against the Self-Images of the Age* (Notre Dame, Ind.: Univ. of Notre Dame Press, 1978), especially pp. 120–22.

⁸ *Enquiry,* p. 336; from "A Dialogue," added to the second edition.

⁹ For instructive reading on this topic, see John B. Stewart, *The Moral and Political Philosophy of David Hume* (New York: Columbia Univ. Press, 1963), pp. 92–104.

¹⁰ *Enquiry,* p. 214; and *Enquiry,* pp. 292 ff.; see also *Treatise,* pp. 578 ff.

¹¹ *Enquiry,* p. 273; see also *Treatise,* p. 591.

¹² John R. Emshwiller, *The Wall Street Journal,* 21 Mar. 1979.

¹³ Carol Pogash, *San Francisco Examiner,* 20 May 1979.

¹⁴ *San Francisco Chronicle,* 7 Feb. 1979.

¹⁵ Robert Fenster, *San Francisco Sunday Examiner and Chronicle,* 4 Feb. 1979, "California Living" section.

¹⁶ Robert Lewis, Newhouse News Service, *San Francisco Examiner,* 30 Apr. 1978.

¹⁷ Immanuel Kant, *Foundations of the Metaphysics of Morals,* trans. Lewis White Beck, in *Ethical Theories,* ed. A. I. Melden, 2nd ed. (Englewood Cliffs, N. J.: Prentice-Hall, 1955), p. 327.

Chapter 13

¹ Immanuel Kant, *Practical Reason,* trans. Lewis White Beck (New York: Library of Liberal Arts, 1956), p. 95; hereafter this translation will be cited as Beck.

² Immanuel Kant, *Foundations of the Metaphysics of Morals,* trans. Lewis White Beck, in *Ethical Theories,* ed. A. I. Melden, 2nd ed. (Englewood Cliffs, N. J.: Prentice-Hall, 1955), note, p. 327; hereafter referred to as *Foundations.*

³ *San Francisco Chronicle,* 29 Aug. 1978.

⁴ *San Francisco Chronicle,* 10 Mar. 1979.

⁵ Immanuel Kant, *Lectures on Ethics,* trans. Louis Infeld (New York: Harper Torchbooks, 1963), p. 195; hereafter referred to as *Lectures.*

⁶ Immanuel Kant, *Religion Within the Limits of Reason Alone,* trans. Theodore M. Greene and Hoyt H. Hudson (New York: Harper Torchbooks, 1960), p. 45; hereafter referred to as *Religion.* Also, David Hume, *Enquiries Concerning the Human*

574 *Understanding and Concerning the Principles of Morals,* ed. L. A. Selby-Bigge, 2nd ed. (London: Oxford Univ. Press, 1902), p. 99; hereafter referred to as *Enquiry.*

[7] Little Blue Book No. 1286, ed. E. Haldeman-Julius (Girard, Kansas), pp. 20, 26, 27.

[8] Immanuel Kant, *Critique of Pure Reason,* trans. Norman K. Smith (New York: St. Martin's Press, 1965), p. 474; this translation hereafter cited as *Pure Reason* [Smith].

[9] David Hume, *A Treatise on Human Nature,* ed. L. A. Selby-Bigge (London: Oxford Univ. Press, 1952), p. 402; hereafter referred to as *Treatise.*

[10] Immanuel Kant, *The Metaphysical Elements of Justice,* Trans. John Ladd (Indianapolis: Bobbs-Merrill, 1965), p. 100; hereafter referred to as *Justice.*

[11] Quoted by Jeffrie G. Murphy in "Marxism and Retribution," *Philosophy and Public Affairs,* Spring, 1973, Vol. 2, No. 3, p. 217; Marx's remarks first appeared in his column in the *New York Daily Tribune,* 18 Feb. 1853.

[12] See p. 505 of Day's excellent article, from which I will draw an analysis of "retribution," "Retributive Punishment," *Mind,* October, 1978, Vol. LXXXVII, No. 348. All page references to Day are to this article.

[13] *San Francisco Chronicle,* 5 Mar. 1979.

[14] Anthony Burgess, *A Clockwork Orange* (New York: Norton, 1963), p. 92.

[15] See Herbert Morris, "Persons and Punishment," *The Monist,* October, 1968, Vol. 52, No. 4, for further development of the problems with the "therapeutic state," and on the right to be punished.

[16] Story by Kendal Weaver, *Sacramento Bee,* 25 Mar. 1979.

[17] Charles McCabe, "Himself," *San Francisco Chronicle,* 4 May 1979.

[18] *San Francisco Examiner,* 1 Apr. 1979.

[19] *San Francisco Chronicle,* 13 Apr. 1979.

[20] *San Francisco Chronicle,* 14 Mar. 1979.

[21] From a term paper, December 14, 1978, by permission.

[22] *San Francisco Chronicle,* 30 May 1979.

[23] *San Francisco Chronicle,* 24 Aug. 1978.

[24] *San Francisco Examiner,* 19 Aug. 1979, "This World" section.

[25] *San Francisco Examiner,* 18 May 1975.

[26] Ferdinand Schoeman, "Responsibility and the Problem of Induced Desires," *Philosophical Studies,* Vol. 34, 1978, p. 293.

[27] Immanuel Kant, *The Critique of Practical Reason,* trans. Thomas K. Abbott (Chicago: Encyclopaedia Britannica, 1952), Great Books Series, p. 332; hereafter referred to as *Practical Reason.*

[28] John Laird, *An Enquiry into Moral Notions* (London: George Allen & Unwin, 1935), pp. 120–21.

[29] Wright Neely, *Philosophical Review,* Vol. LXXXIII, Jan. 1974, pp. 51–53.

[30] From J. S. Mill's *System of Logic,* Book VI, Ch. ii, Sec. 3; page 52 in Neely's article.

[31] Immanuel Kant, *The Doctrine of Virtue. Part II. The Metaphysic of Morals,* trans. Mary J. Gregor (New York: Harper Torchbooks, 1964), p. 66; hereafter referred to as *Virtue.*

Chapter 14

[1] Tom Wicker's column, *Sunday Cape Cod Times,* 1 July 1979.

[2] G. W. F. Hegel, *The Phenomenology of Mind,* trans. J. B. Baillie (London: George Allen & Unwin, 1931), pp. 82, 98–99.

³ Karl Marx, *Economic and Philosophical Manuscripts,* "Critique of Hegel's Dialectic and General Philosophy," trans. T. B. Bottomore, in Marx's *Concept of Man,* ed. Erich Fromm (New York: Frederick Ungar, 1961), pp. 176–77.

⁴ Karl Marx, *Foundations of the Critique of Political Economy,* trans. Martin Nicolaus (Harmondsworth and London: Penguin Books and New Left Review, 1973), pp. 101–02; hereafter referred to as the *Grundrisse.* The *Grundrisse* is Marx's notes prior to writing *Das Kapital;* it was first published in Moscow in 1939 and 1941, and not fully translated into English until 1973.

⁵ Karl Marx and Frederick Engels, *The German Ideology,* ed. R. Pascal (New York: International Publishers, 1947), pp. 14, 15.

⁶ Karl Marx, *Capital,* trans. Samuel Moore and Edward Aveling (New York: Modern Library-Random House, 1936), Preface to the Second Edition, Vol. I, p. 25.

⁷ Karl Marx, *The Eighteenth Brumaire of Louis Bonaparte,* in *Selected Works* (London: Lawrence & Wishart, 1962), p. 334.

⁸ *Capital,* p. 167; see also *Grundrisse,* pp. 212–17.

⁹ Kai Nielsen, "Class Conflict, Marxism, and the Good-Reasons Approach," *Social Praxis,* Vol. 2, Nos. 1–2, 1974, p. 98.

¹⁰ Karl Marx, *A Contribution to the Critique of Political Economy,* trans. S. W. Ryazanskaya, ed. Maurice Dobb (Moscow: Progress Publishers, 1970), p. 21.

¹¹ Quoted from Maria Ossowska, *Social Determinants of Moral Ideas* (Philadelphia: Univ. of Pennsylvania Press, 1970), p. 132.

¹² Iris Murdoch, *The Sovereignty of Good* (New York: Shocken Books, 1971), p. 80, from her essay, "The Sovereignty of Good over Other Concepts."

¹³ Glenna McWhirter, Knight News Service, *San Francisco Sunday Examiner and Chronicle,* 16 Nov. 1975.

¹⁴ See Marx's "Alienated Labor," the first of the *Economic and Philosophical Manuscripts; Capital,* pp. 81–84, on "Fetishism," where labor products are seen as "commodities" for sale by the owner of capital; and *Grundrisse,* pp. 450–54.

¹⁵ Story on Gallup's article in the *American Scientist* by Walter Sullivan for the *New York Times,* reprinted in the *San Francisco Examiner,* 26 Aug. 1979.

¹⁶ Marx and Engels, *Selected Correspondence,* p. 531, quoted from Vernon Venable, *Human Nature: The Marxian View* (Cleveland: World Publishing Co., 1966), p. 206.

¹⁷ Lucien Goldmann, *Immanuel Kant,* trans. Robert Black (London: NLB, 1971), p. 198.

¹⁸ Karl Marx, "On the Jewish Question," in *Selected Essays,* trans. H. J. Stenning, reprinted in *The Philosophical Imagination,* ed. Raziel Ableson, Marie-Louise Friquegnon, and Michael Lockwood (New York: St. Martin's Press, 1977).

¹⁹ Carol Gould, *Marx's Social Ontology: Individuality and Community in Marx's Theory of Social Reality* (Cambridge, Mass.: MIT Press, 1978), pp. 84–85. This book is an excellent interpretation of, and makes explicit, the philosophical system lodged in Marx's *Grundrisse.*

²⁰ Steven Lukes, "Alienation and Anomie," *Philosophy, Politics and Society,* ed. Peter Laslett and W. G. Runciman (Oxford: Basil Blackwell, 1967), p. 151.

²¹ Sandra Lee Bartky, "Toward a Phenomenology of Feminist Consciousness," *Social Theory and Practice,* Vol. 3, No. 4, Fall, 1975, p. 428.

²² William Safire, "World of Politics," *San Francisco Chronicle,* 6 Sept. 1978.

²³ Milton Friedman, *The Stanford Magazine,* Fall/Winter, 1977.

²⁴ George Meany, 1979 Labor Day Message, *California AFL/CIO News,* 31 Aug. 1979, Vol. 22, No. 35.

²⁵ David Slive, Snyder, New York, in *American Educator,* a publication of the American Federation of Teachers, AFL–CIO, Fall, 1979, Vol. 3, No. 3.

576

[26] *San Francisco Examiner,* 26 Feb. 1975.

[27] Story by Linda Mathews in the *Los Angeles Times,* reprinted in the *San Francisco Chronicle,* 27 Sept. 1977.

[28] Blake Green, *San Francisco Chronicle,* 17 Feb. 1975.

[29] Herbert Marcuse, *An Essay on Liberation* (Boston: Beacon Press, 1962), p. 11.

[30] Hendrik Ruitenbeek, *The Individual and the Crowd: A Study of Identity in America* (New York: New American Library, 1964), p. 88.

Index

49; criticized, 208–21; and happiness, 274; links, *139;* and natural science, 240; on obligation, 380; theory of duty, 300; utilitarian theory of punishment, 137; as utilitarianism, 396. *See* Simple moral psychology
Moral psychosociobiologist, 152
Moral realization terms, 392
Moral sciences, 424–25; and physical sciences contrasted, Hume on, 421
Moral self-realization, 274–75, 350
Moral sentiment, 116; four features of, 438
Moral skepticism, 110; Christian, 27
Moral standards: contingency of, 476; factual base for, 424–29, 439–46; factual validation of, 439–46; naturalization of, 446; as universal, 445; validity of, 472–78. *See* Moral laws
Moral theory: and group practices, 23; impracticality of 8; practicality of, 24
Moral value terms, 392
Moral virtue, Aristotle on, 387
Moral worthiness: and happiness, 256; and motive, 312
Moralists' links diagram, *142*
Morality: of an act, 312–13; antinomian approach to, 29–30; approached legalistically, 29; based on feeling, 43; a delusion, 479, 484; and doctrine of virtue, 337; and legality, 542; master, 53; motives of, 445; rules of, not from reason, 114; situational approach to, 29–30; slave, 53; source or basis of, 26–30; standards of, 445; two ultimate bases for, 7; utility, 53
Morally indifferent, merely permissible, Kant's definition, 301
Morally perfect totality, 256–59
Morally perfect world, 352; nature of, 348–51
Morals, 444–45; practical, 432–33; relevance of human nature to, 137–38; source of (contrasts reviewed), 470–71; source in reason, 220–21
Mores, consciously approved practices called, 13
Morris, Wright, 50
Motion, contrasted to act, 287

Motions, their vagueness, 315
Motivation, God as source of, 27
Motive, appropriate. *See* Appropriate motive; distinguished from act, 187; and right, wrong acts, 189
Motive: artificial, 433–35; to duty and justice, 433–35; heteronomous, 479; and moral worthiness, 312; natural, 433–35; as unconditioned, 478, 485
Motive power, 19
Motives: autonomous moral, 479; for acting, 312–13; acts contrasted with, 333; of morality, 445; sentiments as, 488–89; as signs of character, 431
Motor-affective life, and naturalistic good, 386
Murdoch, Iris, 534; on bourgeois ideal, 540
Murdock, George, 213
Murphy, Jeffrie, 500
Myshkin, Prince Leo Nikolayevich, 192
Mystery, *Willkür* a, 279

Natural: humans as, 480; three meanings of, 194
Natural humans: existentialist's denial of, 200–02; humans not wholly, 240
Natural laws, 252, 282–84; conditional form of, 282; direction of, 283–84, 333–34; four features, 282; inconsistency of, 335–36; model for moral laws, 282; universality of, 282
Natural link, of moral psychology, *139*
Natural selection: applied to human nature, 43, 133, 153–57; of better, 157–60; diagram, *158;* and emotions, 470; explained, 151–53. *See* Darwin
Natural self, 190
Natural standard, contrasted with human standard, 150
Natural state: of men, Hobbes's definition, 110; Rousseau on, 115
Natural world, contrasted to supersensible, 204–41
Natural/artificial: contrasted, 180, 182–86; (contrasted) as origins of objects, 182; (contrasted) as real/unreal, 182, 183; (contrasted) in value,

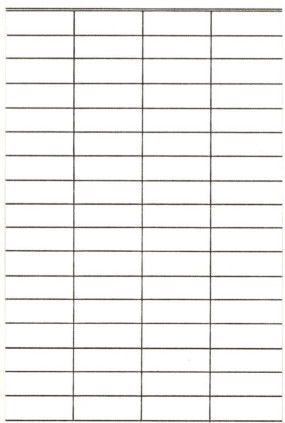

DATE DUE

A 0
B 1
C 2
D 3
E 4
F 5
G 6
H 7
I 8
J 9

PRINTED IN U.S.A.